7 5.00

Cruise Ship Tourism

Main photograph: Silversea Cruises' *Silver Shadow* is a superlative small cruise ship at 28,258 tons. In the Berlitz Guide to *Ocean Cruising & Cruise Ships 2005*, the author Douglas Ward placed the ship eighth best out of a comprehensive review of 256 ships. In addition Silversea Cruises was voted the *Best Small Cruise Ship Line in the World* in the 18th Annual Condé Nast Traveller Readers' Choice Awards in 2005. It was the ninth time Silversea has been voted number one in the prestigious readers' poll. My wife and I are privileged to work as onboard lecturers on the *Silver Shadow* and we agree that it is one of the finest cruise ships afloat. Source: Silversea Cruises.

Lower left photograph: Oceania Cruises' *Regatta*, 30,277 tons, in Santorini, Greece. Source: Oceania Cruises.

Lower centre photograph: Silversea Cruises' *Silver Cloud*, 16,927 tons, departing Picton, South Island, New Zealand, January 2005. Source: Gary Stocker.

Lower right photograph: Passengers on board the *Silver Shadow*, in Halong Bay, Vietnam, January 2004. Source: Ross Dowling.

Cruise Ship Tourism

Edited by

Ross K. Dowling

Edith Cowan University
Faculty of Business and Law
School of Marketing, Tourism and Leisure
Joondalup WA 6027
Australia

www.cabi.org

CABI is a trading name of CAB International

CABI Head Office
Nosworthy Way
Wallingford
Oxfordshire OX10 8DE
UK

Tel: +44 (0)1491 832111
Fax: +44 (0)1491 833508
E-mail: cabi@cabi.org
Website: www.cabi.org

CABI North American Office
875 Massachusetts Avenue
7th Floor
Cambridge, MA 02139
USA

Tel: +1 617 395 4056
Fax: +1 617 354 6875
E-mail: cabi-nao@cabi.org

A catalogue record for this book is available from the British Library, London,
UK.

Library of Congress Cataloging-in-Publication Data
Cruise tourism / edited by Ross K. Dowling.
    p. cm.
  Includes bibliographical references and index.
  ISBN-13: 978-1-84593-048-6 (alk. paper)
  ISBN-10: 1-84593-048-7 (alk. paper)
  1. Ocean travel. 2. Cruise lines. I. Dowling, Ross K. II. Title.

G550.C8327 2006
387.5′42--dc22
                                        2005018815

ISBN-10: 1-84593-048-7
ISBN-13: 978-1-84593-048-9

Typeset by SPi, Pondicherry, India.
Printed and bound in the UK by Biddles Ltd, King's Lynn.

This book is dedicated to

My wife Wendy who has accompanied me to the ends of the earth, I thank you for the way you share your life, love and spirit with me

My six children and their families who are now living in Australia, China, England and New Zealand

The memory of the late Professor William F. Grazer, esteemed Professor of Marketing at Towson University, Maryland, USA, one of this book's contributors who sadly passed away on 10 August 2005

Miss Pat Higgins, Formerly Manager of Enrichment Programs, Silversea Cruises, Fort Lauderdale, USA – the consummate cruise tourism professional and enthusiast

Silversea Cruises – undoubtedly the finest cruise line in the world today

Contents

_____

About the Editor

Dr Ross K. Dowling is Foundation Professor and Head of Tourism in the School of Marketing, Tourism and Leisure, Faculty of Business and Law, Edith Cowan University, Western Australia. He is an Executive Board Member of the Indian Ocean Tourism Organisation (IOTO) and a Board Member of Ecotourism Australia. In Western Australia he is Chairperson of The Forum Advocating Cultural and Eco Tourism (FACET), as well as a Council Member of the National Trust, the Royal Automobile Club and the Royal Agricultural Society. He was an inaugural Director of the State's Tourism Council.

Professor Dowling is an international speaker, author, researcher and consultant on tourism with over 200 publications. In recent years he has co-authored or co-edited six books on tourism. They are *Ecotourism Policy and Planning*, and *Tourism in Destination Communities* (both published by CABI); *Ecotourism*; *Natural Area Tourism: Ecology, Impacts & Management*; *Wildlife Tourism* and *Geotourism*. Professor Dowling has degrees in Geology, Geography and Environmental Science as well as diplomas in Educational Administration, Sport & Recreation, and Teaching. In 1993 he was awarded a PhD in Environmental Science from Murdoch University, for his ecotourism thesis 'An Environmentally Based Approach to Tourism Planning'. His model has since been applied in Australia, Canada, Indonesia, Malaysia and the USA.

The Editor is passionate about Cruise Ship Tourism and he has lectured on board Cunard's *Queen Elizabeth 2* in the Pacific as well as Silversea Cruises' *Silver Shadow* in South-east Asia and the Indian Ocean, and *Silver Cloud* around the east coast of Australia and New Zealand. In addition, he has led a tour with Quark Expeditions into the Antarctic on board the *Kapitan Dranitsyn*.

Contributors

Thomas Bauer, Hong Kong Polytechnic University, School of Hotel and Tourism Management, Hung Hom, Kowloon, PR China, e-mail: hmthomas@polyu.edu.hk

Arthur A. Berger, San Francisco State University, Broadcast and Electronic Communication Arts Department, San Francisco, CA 94132, USA, e-mail: arthurasaberger@gmail.com

Bradley M. Braun, University of Central Florida, College of Business Administration, Department of Economics, PO Box 161400, Orlando, FL 32816-1400, USA, e-mail: bbraun@bus.ucf.edu

Jacques J. Charlier, University of Paris-Sorbonne, Department of Geography, France 75005; University of Louvain-la-Neuve, Department of Geography, Belgium 1348, e-mail: charlier@geog.ucl.ac.be

Nancy Chesworth, Mount St Vincent University, Department of Business and Tourism, Halifax, Nova Scotia, Canada, B3M 2J6, e-mail: nancy.chesworth@msvu.ca

Suzanne Dobson, Simon Fraser University, Department of Geography, Burnaby, BC, Canada V5A 1S6, e-mail: sdobson@sfu.ca

Ngaire Douglas, Southern Cross University, School of Tourism and Hospitality Management, PO Box 157, Lismore, NSW 2480, Australia, e-mail: ngaire_d@hotmail.com

Norman Douglas, Pacific Profiles, PO Box 229, Alstonville, NSW 2477, Australia, e-mail: normandouglas@optusnet.com.au

Ross K. Dowling, Edith Cowan University, Faculty of Business and Law, School of Marketing, Tourism and Leisure, Joondalup, WA 6027, Australia, e-mail: r.dowling@ecu.edu.au

Claire Ellis, formerly University of Tasmania, School of Management, Tourism Programme, Hobart, Tasmania, Australia; currently Tourism Tasmania, GPO Box 399, Hobart, Tasmania 7001, Australia, e-mail claire.ellis@tourism.tas.gov.au

Chris Fanning, Flinders University, Cultural Tourism, School of Humanities, GPO Box 2100, Adelaide, SA 5001, Australia, e-mail: chris.fanning@flinders.edu.au

Alison Gill, Simon Fraser University, Department of Geography, Burnaby, BC, Canada, V5A 1S6, e-mail: agill@sfu.ca

Warren G. Gill, Simon Fraser University, Department of Geography, Burnaby, BC, Canada, V5A 1S6, e-mail: gill@sfu.ca

William F. Grazer, formerly of Towson University, Towson, Maryland, USA

Lindsey C. Holderfield, Upper James River Roundtable Highland County, Virginia, USA, e-mail: lindseycamille@hotmail.com

Jane James, Flinders University, Cultural Tourism, School of Humanities, GPO Box 2100, Adelaide, SA 5001, Australia, e-mail: jane.james@flinders.edu.au

Ross A. Klein, Memorial University of Newfoundland, School of Social Work, St John's, NL, Canada A1C 5S7, e-mail: ross@cruisejunkie.com

Lorne K. Kriwoken, University of Tasmania, School of Geography and Environmental Studies, Private Bag 78, Hobart, Tasmania 7001, Australia, e-mail: L.K.Kriwoken@utas.edu.au

Darren Lee-Ross, James Cook University, Faculty of Law, Business and Creative Arts, School of Business, PO Box 6811, Cairns, QLD 4870, Australia, e-mail: darren.leeross@jcu.edu.au

Jo-Anne Lester, University of Brighton, School of Service Management, Darley Road, Eastbourne, East Sussex BN20 7UR, UK, e-mail: J.Lester@brighton.ac.uk

Xiang (Robert) Li, University of South Carolina, College of Hospitality, Retail & Sport Management, School of Hotel, Restaurant & Tourism Management, Columbia, SC 29208, USA, e-mail: roblix@hotmail.com

Jan O. Lundgren, McGill University, Department of Geography, 805 Sherbrooke Street West, Montreal, Quebec, Canada H3A 2K6, e-mail: jan.lundgren@mcgill.ca

Robert J. McCalla, Saint Mary's University, Department of Geography, Halifax, Nova Scotia, Canada B3H 3C3, e-mail: robert.mccalla@smu.ca

Allan R. Miller, Towson University, Department of Marketing and e-Business, College of Business and Economics, Towson, MD 21252-0001, USA, e-mail: amiller@towson.edu

Gianna Moscardo, James Cook University, School of Business, Townsville, QLD 4811, Australia, e-mail: gianna.moscardo@jcu.edu.au

John M. Munro, Simon Fraser University, Department of Economics, Burnaby, BC, Canada V5A 1S6, e-mail: jmunro@sfu.ca

Andreas Papatheodorou, University of the Aegean, Department of Business Administration, 8 Michalon Street, Chios 82100, Greece, e-mail: academia@trioptron.org

Lori Pennington-Gray, University of Florida, Center for Tourism Research and Development, Department of Tourism, Recreation and Sport Management, PO Box 118209, Gainesville, FL 32611-8209, USA, e-mail: penngray@hhp.ufl.edu

James F. Petrick, Texas A&M University, Department of Recreation, Park and Tourism Sciences, 2261 TAMU, College Station, TX 77843-2261, USA, e-mail: jpetrick@tamu.edu

Bruce R. Prideaux, James Cook University, School of Business, PO Box 6811, Cairns Mail Centre, QLD 4879, Australia, e-mail: bruce.prideaux@jcu.edu.au

Lydia M. Pulsipher, University of Tennessee, Department of Geography, Knoxville, TN 37996-0925, USA, e-mail: lpulsiph@utk.edu

Sacha Reid, University of Technology, School of Leisure, Sport and Tourism, Sydney, PO Box 222, Lindfield, NSW 2070, Australia, e-mail: sacha.reid@uts.edu.au

Greg Ringer, University of Oregon, International Studies Program and Department of Planning, Public Policy and Management, Eugene, OR 97403-1209, USA, e-mail: gringer@uoregon.edu or drgreg@fulbrightweb.org

Derek Robbins, Bournemouth University, School of Services Management, Fern Barrow, Poole, Dorset BH12 5BB, UK, e-mail: drobbins@bournemouth.ac.uk

Lynnaire Sheridan, Edith Cowan University, Faculty of Business and Law, School of Marketing, Tourism and Leisure, Joondalup, WA 6027, Australia, e-mail: l.sheridan@ecu.edu.au

Ola Sletvold, Finnmark University College, Department of Tourism and Hotel Management Studies, Follums v 31, 9509 Alta, Norway, e-mail: ola.sletvold@hifm.no

Valene L. Smith, California State University Chico, Department of Anthropology, Chico, CA 95929-0400, USA, e-mail: vsmith@csuchico.edu

Helle Sorensen, Metropolitan State College, Department of Hospitality, Meeting, and Travel Administration, Campus Box 60, PO Box 173362, Denver, CO 80217, USA, e-mail: sorenseh @mscd.edu

Reg A. Swain, 1 Wild Rose Court, Guelph, Ontario, Canada, N1G 4X7, e-mail: ra4swain@ sympatico.ca

James E.N. Sweeting, Conservation International, The Center for Environmental Leadership in Business, Travel and Leisure, 1919 M Street, NW, Washington, DC, 20036, USA, e-mail: J.Sweeting@conservation.org

Gregory Teal, University of Western Sydney, School of Management, Campbelltown Campus, Locked Bag 1797, Penrith South, Sydney, NSW 1797, Australia, e-mail: greg.teal@uws.edu.au

Victor B. Teye, Arizona State University, School of Community Resources and Development, PO Box 874703, Tempe, AZ 85287-4703, USA, e-mail: teye@asu.edu

Dallen J. Timothy, Arizona State University, School of Community Resources and Development, PO Box 874703, Tempe, AZ 85287-4703, USA, e-mail: dtimothy@asu.edu

Fred Tramell, University of Central Florida, College of Business Administration, Institute for Economic Competitiveness, PO Box 161400, Orlando, FL 32816-1400, USA, e-mail: ftramell@bus.ucf.edu

Kaye Walker, James Cook University, Faculty of Law, Business and Creative Arts, School of Business, Tourism Program, Townsville, QLD 4811, Australia, e-mail: kaye.walker@jcu.edu.au

Scott L. Wayne, SW Associates, 2527 I Street, NW, Washington, DC, 20037, USA

Adam Weaver, Victoria University of Wellington, Victoria Management School, PO Box 600, Wellington, New Zealand, e-mail: adam.weaver@vuw.ac.nz

Clare Weeden, University of Brighton, School of Service Management, Darley Road, Eastbourne, East Sussex BN20 7UR, UK, e-mail: C.H.Weeden@brighton.ac.uk

Paul F. Wilkinson, York University, Faculty of Environmental Studies, 4700 Keele Street, Toronto, Ontario, Canada M3J 1P3, e-mail: eswilkin@yorku.ca

Robert E. Wood, Rutgers University, Department of Sociology, Camden, NJ 08102-1521, USA, e-mail: wood@camden.rutgers.edu

Preface

This book is an addition to CABI's excellent list of tourism books and it is the third that I have been involved in as editor, the first as sole editor. I have always been fascinated by the sea, perhaps a legacy of my early childhood spent collecting information about the cruise ships of the day (in the late 1950s and early 1960s), which I then kept and catalogued in scrap books. My interest was further enhanced in my teenage years when my father owned a gaff rigged schooner named *Kotiti* (Maori for wanderer). It was one of the larger yachts of its time on which we sailed and raced in the yachting *A Class* Division on Waitemata Harbour in Auckland, New Zealand. *Kotiti* also raced and cruised in the South Pacific, so my love of the sea, geography, harbours, ships and ports also expanded.

Years later when helping to establish a brand new university, the University of Notre Dame Australia, in the port city of Fremantle, Western Australia, I rekindled my love of cruise ships that I had previously engaged in, in childhood days. It began when Mr Noel Semmens, elder statesman of the tourism industry in Western Australia, invited me on board the *Queen Elizabeth 2*, when she was in port in February 1997. A chance meeting with one of Cunard's senior vice-presidents, led 2 years later to an assignment on the ship as a Special Interest Lecturer. My renewed interest was now pursued in earnest, leading to further assignments as Special Interest Lecturer, Destination Lecturer and Group Tour Guide on a variety of cruise ships to a range of destinations as varied as South-east Asia, the South Pacific and Antarctica. The one thing I noted, however, is that there appeared to be little in the way of cruise industry research, and so combining my professional involvement as an industry academic with my personal enthusiasm for cruise ships, I embarked on a voyage of discovery, if you will excuse the metaphor.

Earlier this decade the idea for this book was born after working on a state-of-the-art paper on cruising for the silver jubilee issues of *Tourism Recreation Research* (Dowling and Vasudavan, 2000). Three years later I approached a leading tourism academic and sought his nominations for possible contributors to a book on the subject. He gave me two names and suggested that there were not enough people researching the field to publish a book. But I like challenges, so in the latter part of 2003 when enjoying my first stint of Study Leave, at Murdoch University in Perth, I put forward a book proposal to CABI. My friend Rebecca Stubbs, the then Development Editor, was enthusiastic, as she always was, and the rest is history. Three years later this book is a reality.

The field of cruise tourism is a rapidly emerging one. It is enjoying huge growth and awareness, especially since 11 September 2001, as travel consumers look for perceived safer alternatives to their traditional holidays. At the same time the cost of cruises is now within reach of the baby boomers who have suddenly discovered the affordability of the larger liners with their family-oriented cruises. So the cruise industry is undergoing a major boom, as evidenced by the plethora of promotional broadcasts emanating from the Cruise Lines Industry Association (CLIA), based in the USA.

There already exist a number of reports and books on the subject. These include an industry overview (WTO, 2003) as well as books on cruise marketing (Dickinson and Vladimir, 1997), cruise issues (Klein, 2002), the cruise experience (Douglas and Douglas, 2004) and cruise culture (Berger, 2004). Of course the definitive industry and consumer guide is *Berlitz: Ocean Cruising and Cruise Ships*, now in its 16th year (Ward, 2006). Thus, much has already been written about the subject, but the focus of this book is aimed at lifting the level of awareness of the subject generally, as well as its theory, issues, impacts, marketing and management considerations. My belief is that the cruise industry can provide a number of benefits to governments, businesses, tourists and host communities. But this synergy will only be attained through increased knowledge, appropriate planning, sensitive development and active management. This is what this book is all about. The underpinning base of the approach to the subject is embedded firmly in my belief that cruise tourism is an exciting venture based on the twin goals of fostering client satisfaction alongside economic development. Of course the key question really is: economic development for whom? – the cruise companies or the multitude of stakeholders involved in this far-reaching industry.

This research book has been written for a broad audience including students pursuing university and training programmes, tourism industry professionals, planners and managers in the cruise industry, and finally government agency employees. As a general text, it should be useful to students in a range of disciplines including tourism, business development, geography, planning and regional studies. As a specific text, it provides an insightful overview of the industry covering a broad range of topics and issues. The book also has been written as a contribution to research and as such it brings together the essential elements of the cruise industry in addressing the provision of cruise ship tourism.

In this book, I have tried to present a 'snapshot' of what is happening in the world of cruise tourism at this time, in the early 21st century. It is not meant to provide a comprehensive overview as the subject is still in its infancy. The book has been enriched immeasurably by each of the contributions of the chapter authors who are an eclectic group comprising new and emerging researchers, world-renowned academics and industry professionals. The chapters represent a varied approach to cruise ship tourism with a range of shades of meaning ascribed to the subject and differing levels of understanding about it. Some of the chapters are well detailed and illustrated, others are more elementary. All are included because they represent the views of people passionate about the subject from a number of countries around the world. Whereas some chapters are little more than descriptive case studies, others illustrate cruise tourism in practice. Issues such as economic, social and environmental impacts are explored together with that of globalization. Case studies provide information on the phenomenal growth of the industry through real-world examples of markets, destinations and products. Through it all my hope is that further interest of this rapidly emerging subject has been generated, which will be the subject of considerably more analysis in future years.

The book is organized in five parts. Part I introduces the industry and some of its underpinning aspects, including examination of cruising from geographical, industrial and cultural perspectives. It is completed by an investigation of policy issues, based on the case of Bermuda. Part II focuses on the insatiable demand for cruising, including examination of passengers' perceptions of value, trends in the North American market, and passenger expectations and activities. Part III explores the supply side of cruising including cruise destinations and products with examples from around the world. Part IV explores the industry's interactions with the economic, social and natural environments. Part V, the final section, investigates a selection of a number of industry issues, before the book is brought to a close by a brief discussion of the future of the industry.

I request the reader to note that this book is neither a definitive text nor an encyclopedic overview of the subject. It has been compiled simply as an 'entrée' to the subject served with enthusiasm by the editor and contributors in order to communicate our love of the subject so that more will be done for it. We know that more detailed, scholarly research volumes will follow and this book is presented as a marker to stimulate further interest in, and research of, the subject.

I hope you enjoy it.

Ross K. Dowling
Western Australia
June 2006

References

Berger, A.A. (2004) *Ocean Travel and Cruising: A Cultural Analysis*. Haworth Press, New York.

Dickinson, B. and Vladimir, A. (1997) *Selling the Sea: An Inside Look at the Cruise Industry*. John Wiley & Sons, New York.

Douglas, N. and Douglas, N. (2004) *The Cruise Experience: Regional and Global Issues in Cruise Tourism*. Pearson Hospitality Press, Melbourne.

Dowling, R.K. and Vasudavan, T. (2000) Cruising in the new millennium. *Tourism Recreation Research* 25(3), 17–27.

Klein, R. (2002) *Cruise Ship Blues: The Underside of the Cruise Industry*. New Society Publishers, Gabriola Island, British Columbia, Canada.

Ward, D. (2006) *Berlitz: Ocean Cruising and Cruise Ships 2006*. Berlitz Publishing, London.

WTO (World Tourism Organization) (2003) *Worldwide Cruise Ship Activity*. World Tourism Organization, Madrid.

Acknowledgements

———————————

No book is written in isolation, in fact most require the efforts of a wide range of people including the support of family and friends, the contributions and encouragement of colleagues and of course the professional skills of those who are directly involved in its publication and subsequent promotion. This book is no exception and I wish to thank a number of people for their personal and/or professional support throughout the process.

First, I would like to thank the contributors, all 49 of them. Some I have known for many years and have worked with before, others were unknown to me before this project. Some are emerging new or younger researchers, whereas others are iconic academics and world-famous authors. All I have got to know better through the many iterations of the text during the evolution of the book and I salute each and every one of you for having the faith in this project and the fortitude to deal with my many demands over a long period of time. This book is yours and I know that it has been immeasurably enriched by your contributions.

Sadly, one of the book's contributors, Professor William F. Grazer, passed away on 10 August 2005 after a year-long battle with lung cancer. Professor Grazer was a highly esteemed professor of Marketing at Towson University, Maryland, USA, who published widely in the fields of Advertising and Marketing Research. He taught for over 25 years and was honoured with numerous teaching awards from students and institutions. This book is much the richer for his contribution.

Four researchers made contributions to this book. In the early stages, Joan Chan, one of my Edith Cowan University students on an international scholarship from Malaysia, assisted me with the editing of chapters. Another ECU student, Jeremy Dyer from New Zealand, interested in security issues, researched the safety and security of the cruise industry. He subsequently graduated and is working with the Royal Australian Airforce in logistics. Alvin Lee, ECU Marketing Lecturer, spent hours trawling websites for data on cruising and he managed to unearth a huge amount of information. Finally, Aldia Lai, an internationally recognized tourism industry event coordinator between assignments, worked on the research and editing in the final months of the book. I thank all of you for your contributions – it is much appreciated.

I also wish to acknowledge the enthusiasm and support of the publishers. CABI is an excellent company and I am very proud to be part of its stable of authors. Tim Hardwick as publisher is thanked for his acceptance of this project. The editors, formerly Rebecca Stubbs and now Claire Parfitt, are very dedicated and always inspirational to work with. Rebecca Stubbs, Development Editor, moved from professional adviser to close friend over the years I worked together with her. Rebecca, I thank you most sincerely for your professional advice, constant encouragement and continued belief in me. It was always uplifting and inspiring to work with you.

I also wish to thank Miss Jaya Bharathi, Project Manager, SPi, Pondicherry, India, for her contribution to this book. As proof editor she worked with me very closely for more than a year on a daily basis. Always organized, efficient and a person of much initiative, she spent a huge amount of time checking the proofs and entering the necessary corrections. She carried this out in a very professional manner and dealt with the many problems in a patient and understanding manner. I appreciated this very much and commend her contribution to this work.

A number of colleagues at ECU have encouraged me throughout my career and I would like to thank them for their ongoing professional support. My mentor is Professor John Wood (Deputy Vice-Chancellor), who is quite simply one of the most insightful and dynamic persons I have ever had the privilege to work with. He speaks into my life and guides me in my thinking and actions. To him I am extremely grateful for taking such an interest in my life. Among others at ECU, I wish to particularly thank Professor Robert Harvey (Executive Dean, Faculty of Business and Law), Professor Kandy James (Head, School of Marketing, Tourism and Leisure), Thandarayan Vasudavan, Lynnaire Sheridan and Shani Wood (Lecturers in Tourism). In addition, Julie Connolly and Anna Johansson (Administration Officers, School of Marketing, Tourism and Leisure) have also contributed to my work through their excellence as administrators and colleagues.

I also wish to thank my many Australian and international students from around the world, particularly Asia, Africa and Scandinavia, who have participated in my Cruise Ship Tourism classes. We have had a lot of fun and I have learned a lot about the industry from your research assignments and oral presentations.

One person in the cruise industry who has contributed to my enthusiasm for it is Pat Higgins, Manager of Enrichment Programs, Silversea Cruises, Fort Lauderdale, Miami, USA. I have worked with Pat since the days she was with Cunard, and over the many years since, I have built up enormous respect for her knowledge of, and enthusiasm for, the cruise industry. She is a real powerhouse of knowledge and is the most professional person I know in the industry. Thanks, Pat, for working with me and having faith in me as lecturer on board Silversea Cruises. I believe that it is the best cruise line in the world today.

I also wish to thank a number of close academic colleagues from around the world who have in some small way contributed to my own thoughts on cruising through discussion, debate and dialogue over time. They are Clare Weeden and Jo-Anne Lester (England), Lydia Pulsipher and Arthur Asa Berger (USA), Ngaire and Norman Douglas (Australia), Ross Klein (Canada) and Thomas Bauer (China). I also wish to thank Helle Sorensen (Canada) for her enthusiasm for this book and the e-mails of encouragement she sent. They always brightened my day and lifted my spirit. I look forward to continued collaboration of research with her in the future.

From Australia I wish to thank Steve Crawford (Tourism Western Australia) and Glenn Stephens (Fremantle Ports), both of whom are experts in Cruise Tourism and who promote the industry in our state. They are a continued source of knowledge about industry events. Thanks also to international cruise consultants Josephine Booth (Fiesta Holidays), Caroline Doeglas (Carnival Australia), Ann Hope (Classic International Cruises, Celebrity & RCL) and Peter French (Star Cruises and NCL) for sharing their knowledge both with me and my students. Your knowledge of, and enthusiasm for, the industry is outstanding. A thank you to John and Kerry Treacy, *World Wide Cruising News: Pictoral*, Brisbane, Australia, for your outstanding contribution to cruising and support of my work in this field. It is much appreciated. Also in Western Australia I thank my close friends Bret and Shellie Gaskin, Keith and Rhonda Amor, and Peter and Cathy Gleeson. You are always there to encourage and support me and my work and for this I am highly appreciative.

Finally I wish to thank my wife Wendy for her unfailing love and support through this my seventh book in the last five years. I could not have achieved this without her. I also wish to thank my children and grandchildren for the contributions they have made, and continue to make, to my life. They are Tobias Dowling (Shanghai, China), Aurora Dowling and daughter Helena (Christchurch, New Zealand), Frank and Jurga Dowling (Vilnius, Lithuania), Jayne Belstead, husband Trevor, and daughters Shenee and Paige (London, England), Simon MacLennan and wife Lynette McGrath (Perth, Australia) and Mark Dowling (Albany, Australia). This book is part of my legacy for you all.

Part I

Introduction

Part I introduces the cruise tourism industry and some of its underpinning aspects. It includes examination of cruising from geographical, industrial and cultural perspectives. This part is completed by an investigation of policy issues in Bermuda.

The traditional 'King Neptune Ceremony' held while crossing the equator on Silversea's *Silver Shadow*, February 2006. Source: Ross K. Dowling.

1 The Cruising Industry

Ross K. Dowling

Edith Cowan University, Faculty of Business and Law, School of Marketing, Tourism and Leisure, Joondalup, WA 6027, Australia

Introduction

A cruise is defined as 'to make a trip by sea in a liner for pleasure, usually calling at a number of ports' (*Collins English Dictionary*). It is characterized by the ship being similar to a mobile resort, which transports passengers (guests) from place to place. Today ships are not viewed as a means of transport but as floating hotels. Increasingly they are being viewed as floating resorts. According to the World Tourism Organization (WTO) (2003) the accommodation and related resort facilities comprise 75% of the ship with the remainder devoted to its operations. These floating resorts mimic their land-based counterparts with restaurants, bars, sports facilities, shopping centres, entertainment venues, communication centres, etc. Cabins are becoming larger and more luxurious. The trend is for more cabins to have windows and/or balconies.

Cruise companies are increasingly promoting and positioning their brand names to enable customers to identify the products as competition grows. Further, it enables customers to make fewer price comparisons and easier decision making. For instance, Carnival Cruises Lines associates the characteristics of 'fun ships' with its brand name, while the *Queen Elizabeth 2* suggests a more exclusive image and unique experience with its promotional theme, 'for once in your life, live'. Disney's Cruises create a distinct brand appeal for children. As the cruise market grows, the need for branding will become even more notable.

The growth of cruise tourism is phenomenal. The revival of cruising has taken place in the last four decades, and today it forms a small but growing part in the global tourism industry. Cruise tourism is a niche form or type of tourism. In regard to its size within the industry, cruise ships account for only 0.6% of the hotel beds offered worldwide (WTO, 2003).

The cruise industry has evolved markedly since the early days of the first passenger ships. This evolution has included excursion voyages, transatlantic travel, the post-war boom, the demise of passenger ships, and the advent of modern cruising (Dickinson and Vladimir, 1997). The industry is now growing rapidly and is one of the major areas of tourism growth at the start of the new millennium. Davidoff and Davidoff (1994) outlined five specific features of cruises that appeal to travellers:

1. Passengers have the opportunity to visit a variety of places in a short period of time without the problems of other modes of travel.
2. The ships are self-contained.
3. Cruise ships have a cruise director and staff whose sole function is to make sure passengers have an enjoyable time.
4. High-quality food is served in elegant style.
5. Everyone usually begins and ends their vacation on the same day.

Industry Growth

Key cruising areas are the Caribbean, Europe and Alaska. In North America the cruise industry is undergoing explosive growth according to the US-based Cruise Line Industry Association (CLIA). The Association comprises 19 leading cruise lines with more than 150 ships and 16,500 travel agencies. Founded in 1975, its aim is to provide a forum where companies engaged in the marketing of passenger cruises in the USA and Canada can meet and discuss matters of common interest and develop and agree on policies aimed at promoting the concept of cruise holidays.

In a series of press releases in the first half of 2005, the Association has illustrated the phenomenal growth of the industry. On 3 January 2005, it said that cruise vacations had reached a level of popularity that few observers believed was possible 30 years before, when the Association was founded. Research they had commissioned in 2004 showed that 30 million Americans had expressed an intent to cruise during the next 3 years (CLIA, 2005a).

On 19 January 2005 under the heading 'Industry predicts cruising will be the vacation of choice in 2005', it stated that during the last 15 years cruise ship passengers have increased by an average of 8% each year, and in recent years as much as 15%. They also indicated that the industry is worth US$23 billion a year (CLIA, 2005b). On 16 March 2005 under the heading 'Cruise Lines ride the wave of unprecedented growth', the Association indicated that its member lines had carried 10.5 million passengers in 2004, an 11% increase on the previous year (CLIA, 2005c). They add that this remarkable growth has been fuelled by the fact that their member lines' ships have sailed at 104% occupancy rate despite 62 new ships having been launched since 2000. In a further release in May 2005 entitled 'A future bright with promise', they noted that another 20 new ships would be added to their fleets by 2008 (CLIA, 2005d).

This rapid growth is illustrated by the large number of cruise ships, cruise lines and the advent of cruise corporations. Today the three major ones are Carnival, Royal Caribbean International and Star Cruise Corporation. The year 2004 saw the launch of the then world's largest cruise liner, *Queen Mary 2* (*QM2*), costing US$800 million and carrying around 3100 passengers and over 1000 crew (Fig. 1.1). The seriousness with which governments are taking this sector of the tourism industry is also shown by the increasing number of industry organizations as well as the number of national and regional cruise strategies.

Fig. 1.1.   Cunard Cruise Lines' *Queen Mary 2*, the second largest ship in the world. Source: Cunard Lines.

Due to this rapid increase in growth, and partly as a consequence of it, a number of key areas have been identified as requiring attention to meet the projected explosive growth. These include sustainability, safety and product development. Sustainability is a major issue for cruise ships and the cruise industry has been quick to adopt sustainable principles in its development and operations. According to Paige (1998) the cruise industry is dedicated to the five Rs – reduce, reuse, research, re-educate and recycle. However, a number of sustainable issues such as waste disposal, visits to sensitive areas and passenger–host relations in ports visited require still more attention.

Safety issues also require scrutiny, especially as the ships are becoming larger and are visiting relatively remote areas such as the Arctic and Antarctic. The sinking of the *Sun Vista* in the Strait of Malacca on 21 May 1999 highlighted once again the vulnerability of cruise ships. While no lives were lost during the event the fact that the ship caught fire and sank underlines the ever-present dangers of ocean travel (Dowling and Vasudavan, 2000).

This chapter outlines some of the present and future challenges facing the growth of the cruising industry. The last 5 years have ushered in new markets and products as well as larger ships. Consequently a number of new technologies, facilities and issues are facing the industry. Cruising's future will need to embrace these factors and be proactive in a range of others if it is to maintain the forward momentum that it has achieved in recent decades.

and for the world by Charlier and McCalla (Chapter 2, this volume), who place the overall number of cruisers as somewhat higher. It is estimated that there will be around 16 million cruisers in 2006 (Table 1.1).

There is currently a globalization of the North America cruise experience. Cruise passengers come from all segments of the population, and there is a high percentage of first-time cruises. Today's cruisers are younger than before and average approximately 45 years (Table 1.2), and their average income is high (US$50,000). Demand for cruising grew by 50% in the 7-year period 1989–1996 and again during 1996–2000 (WTO, 2003).

A recent analysis of the cruise market shows that today's cruise buyer is a married baby boomer who loves to travel and does so frequently (CLIA, 2004a). Baby boomers are the heart of the cruise market (Fig. 1.2). As many as 34% of cruisers are between the ages of 35 and 54. Three in four (76%) cruisers are married, and two in five (44%) are college graduates. Only one in four (25%) cruisers is retired. Families are an important segment of the cruise market. While a spouse is the most likely cruise companion, 16% of cruisers bring children under age 18 along on a cruise. Cruisers are frequent travellers. They average 3.8 vacation trips a year and 18.6 nights away from home. They also rely on travel agents with as many as nine out of ten (89%) cruisers who used a travel agent to book their last cruise. Cruises seek new experiences, search for undiscovered destinations and are quite comfortable in other cultures.

Demand

As can be seen from the above figures, there is continuing huge interest in cruise travel by potential passengers. According to the CLIA there were 13 million cruise passengers worldwide in 2004. However, these figures are not entirely accurate in that they only represent cruise passengers from their own members combined with those of the members of the European Cruise Association. These are then added to an estimate of cruisers for the rest of the world. Thus the overall numbers of cruisers have been challenged for the South Pacific by Douglas and Douglas (Chapter 17, this volume)

Table 1.1. Worldwide cruise demand.

Year	Number (millions)
1995	5.67
2000	9.61
2006	16.00 (est)

Table 1.2. Average age of cruisers.

Year	Age
1995	65
2000	55
2006	45

Fig. 1.2. Baby boomers cruising in Silversea Cruises' *Silver Shadow*, South China Sea, 2004. Photo: Ross K. Dowling.

Cruising will be the vacation of choice in 2005, according to industry experts, buoyed by strong customer demand, new ship introduction, more US homeport availability and renewed interest in exotic ports. CLIA says its member cruise ships are sailing at over 100% occupancy rate and a new online survey indicates that cruising will grow again in 2005. Among those responding to the poll, 85% said they will book another cruise in the coming year (www.travelersadvantage.com). The 'What I Like Best About Cruising' poll found that some 66% rated their most recent cruise vacation as excellent, while food service also scored high marks (61%). The favourite resort destinations, according to the survey, were Mexico (50%), Hawaii (25%) and Alaska (25%). Dream vacations for the future included cruises to the Caribbean (40%), Florida (17%) and Hawaii (11%). Favourite parts of the cruise included food (29%), spending time with family (20%), picture-perfect weather (18%), rest and relaxation (16%) and romance (12%). Caribbean cruises remain the most popular in the world.

Traditionally cruising has been the preserve of older people, mainly retirees. Today's retirees are more fit, more adventurous and have more time to spare than their predecessors. In their quest for ways to enrich their lives, members of this segment of society are discovering that cruises are ideally suited for this new phase of their lives (CLIA, 2004b). In addition to the value, cruise lines offer options for the health-conscious traveller with healthy dining modes and fitness programmes. On-board enrichment programmes allow them to expand their knowledge of such subjects as computers, art, music, politics, literature or take an in-depth look at the destinations they are visiting (Fig. 1.3). Cruise ships also offer soft adventure opportunities for the more active.

A major emerging market segment is the 'baby boomers' who were born, raised, grew up and developed their business careers and lifestyle yearnings, during the affluent post-Second World War boom (Table 1.3). In the USA alone about 4 million of them are turning 50 each year until 2014. They represent the largest, most affluent and most eager-to-travel generation of leisure enthusiasts in US history (Abels, 1998). This generation of baby boomers are seeking leisure travel experiences that are customized, easy, exotic, exclusive and which provide value and choice. They demand luxury and pleasure and seek activities that are healthy and fun. The cruise industry has recognized the potential of this sizeable market and also the increasing dominance of the leisure travel scene. As a result a whole new generation of cruise ships has been, and is being, built to their specifications. These are cruise ships that have a casual atmosphere and healthy food in a variety of dining modes.

Fig. 1.3. Enrichment lecture aboard Cunard Line's *Queen Elizabeth 2*, Tasman Sea, 1999.
Photo: Ross K. Dowling.

Supply

The cruise industry classifies ships according to size, number of passengers, and state rooms (Mancini, 2000). They range from very small or micro (under 10,000 t and 200 passengers) to the megaships (over 70,000 t and more than 2000 passengers; see Chapter 4, this volume). Another classification divides cruise ship categories into a range from Boutique to Megaliners (Ward, 2005). Cruising's capacity has increased markedly over the last decade and shows no abatement. Ships of all sizes are being built from small, luxury and/or expedition ships to large megaliners (Table 1.4). The small ships generally offer a higher degree of service and represent a more expensive market segment, and consequently their prices are usually correspondingly higher.

As well as an increase in the number of small ships, there is a huge growth in the number of large ships being built and the average size of each ship is growing. In the 1970s it was considered that a 25,000-t, 800-passenger vessel was the most cost-effective and profitable (Peisley, 1989). Cruise shipbuilders now believe that the economies of scale argument applies to much larger vessels, as new ships are being built between 100,000 and 150,000 t with capacities of over 3000 passengers. The trend towards larger ships and greater economies of scale mirrors that experience by the airline industry since the introduction of the wide-bodied aircraft in the 1970s. There are significant economies of scale in regard to investment costs in larger-sized cruise ships as evident from the many ships that are on order.

The larger ships offer a greater choice of facilities and activities. The changeover from

Table 1.3. Cruise market segments.

Type	%
New baby boomers	33
Regular baby boomers	20
Demanding buyers	16
Luxury lovers	14
Explorers	11
Ship enthusiasts	6
Total	100

Source: CLIA (2004a).

Table 1.4. Cruise ship categories.

Type	Gross registered tonnes ('000s)	Passengers
Boutique	1–5	<200
Small	5–25	200–500
Mid-size	25–50	500–1200
Large	50–100	1200–2400
Mega	100–150	2400–4000

Source: After Ward (2005).

cruise ships to floating resorts can only be completed when the ships are large enough to accommodate the kind of leisure and entertainment facilities that are available in lavish hotels ashore (Dowling and Vasudavan, 2000). The new cruise ships currently being built are designed for new generations of passengers with broader, more varied interests. In a bid to outdo each other cruise companies are investing in the 'biggest', 'grandest', 'first', such as the first wedding chapel, ice rink, in-line skating track or rock-climbing wall (Fig. 1.4). In addition, they have alternative dining, multi-venue events, entertainment, large rooms vs small rooms, cigar-smoking venues, improvements in stateroom amenities and passenger comfort. Today's cruise fleets run from under 100 passengers to superliners built to please more than 3500 pleasure-seeking passengers. Cruising is no longer a sedentary experience and cruise lines now compete with land-based vacation complexes. As shore-side lifestyles become more active, new liners are introducing a range of options that cover sports, recreation, entertainment and culture.

The new megaliners are giant floating resorts. They have large multilevel hotel-style atrium lobbies, glass elevators, impressive artworks, glitzy casinos, show lounges, shopping centres, health centres, computer and business centres, discos and observation lounges. Cabins with small portholes have been replaced by staterooms with large windows and private balconies. Ships are now destinations in themselves and ports of call, in many cases, have become almost secondary. Cruise ships are now being evaluated according to a number of differing classifications (Swain, Chapter 11, this volume). The most widely

Fig. 1.4. Royal Caribbean International Lines' Voyager Class ships have a rock-climbing wall up the funnel. These ships are 138,000 t and accommodate 3114 passengers. Source: Royal Caribbean International.

Table 1.5. Berlitz top ten ships 2005.

No.	Ship	Cruise line	Points (max 2000)
1	*Europa*	Hapag Lloyd Cruises	1858
2	*Sea Dream I*	Seadream Yacht Club	1790
3	*Sea Dream II*	Seadream Yacht Club	1790
4	*Seabourn Legend*	Seabourn Cruise Line	1786
5	*Seabourn Pride*	Seabourn Cruise Line	1785
6	*Seabourn Spirit*	Seabourn Cruise Line	1785
7	*Queen Mary 2*	Cunard Line	1764
8	*Silver Shadow*	Silversea Cruises	1757
9	*Silver Whisper*	Silversea Cruises	1757
10	*Hanseatic*	Hapag Lloyd Cruises	1740

Source: After Ward (2005).

used rating is that of Berlitz which evaluates ships according to facilities, accommodation, cuisine, service, entertainment and the cruise experience (Ward, 2005). Berlitz evaluates 256 ships in its 2005 book and rates the top cruise ship in the world as Hapag Lloyd Cruises' *Europa* (Table 1.5).

Today's cruise ships are much larger in size than previous ships. Cunard's *QM2* is the largest, longest, tallest, widest and, at US$800 million, the most expensive ocean liner ever built. It is 148,528 gross registered tonnage (GRT) and can carry 2620 passengers and 1253 crew. Its propulsion comprises four pods of 21.5 MW, two of which are fixed and two azimuthing. It was launched on 8 January 2004 by *Queen Elizabeth 2*. On board it has ten dining areas, three formal and seven informal. It also has five swimming pools, a basketball court, virtual golf, a learning centre, ballrooms, theatres, shops a winter garden and historic walks. In addition it has the first planetarium at sea.

However, in 2006 the *QM2* was surpassed in size by the new Royal Caribbean International (RCI) ship *Freedom of the Seas* (www.freedomof theseas.com; Fig. 1.5; Table 1.6). It is 158,000 t, 1112 ft (339 m) long, 184 ft (56 m) wide and 28 ft (8.5 m) draft. It cruises at 21.6 knot and has an occupancy of 4370 passengers. It now sails in the Caribbean on seven-night cruises.

Cruise lines

Over recent years one of the defining characteristics of the cruise industry has been the consolidation of the major players. Today it is dominated by three major companies: Carnival Corporation,

Royal Caribbean Cruises and Star Cruises Group (Table 1.7). Carnival Corporation is the largest company and it includes more than 60 ships and 13 brands. Started by Ted Arison, the company has grown from one ship in 1972 to a leading global tourism brand. Its parent company, Carnival Cruise Lines, has a fleet of 21 ships and is one of the world's youngest fleets. Carnival's success has been largely due to the introduction of its 'Fun Ships' marketing, which lifted the interest of potential cruisers in the 1980s and 1990s. In 1996 it introduced its 'Vacation Guarantee' aimed mainly at first-time passengers, which stated that if a passenger were not satisfied with their cruise experience, they could disembark at the first port of call and have their cruise payment fully refunded. It also introduced a number of other innovations into the industry including the *Paradise*, the first fully non-smoking ship.

Royal Caribbean Cruises is the second largest cruise group in the world. It comprises RCI and Celebrity Cruises and is strongly focused on the North American market. The third major corporation is the Star Cruises Group, founded by the Malaysian company Genting International Group in 1993. It rapidly rose in prominence and dominated the Asia-Pacific cruise region, and in 2000, it took over Norwegian Cruise Line and Orient Line. In 2004 it started NCL America based in Hawaii.

Cruise destinations

Climate is a major determining factor in ship destination deployment. This leads to the relocation of fleets from one destination to another.

Fig. 1.5.   Royal Caribbean 158,000-t megaliner *Freedom of the Seas* being floated out in Finland from Aber Finyards in mid-2005. When launched in April 2006 it was the largest cruise ship in the world. Source: Aber Finyards.

The main cruising grounds are North and Central America (57% market share), Europe (24%) and the rest of the world (16%), whilst 3% of ships are idle at any particular time (Charlier and McCalla, Chapter 2, this volume). The main cruising ground is the Caribbean based on its proximity to the North American market, followed by the Mediterranean, Alaska and the Pacific regions (Table 1.8).

North Americans are visiting the Mediterranean on cruise ships as the current strong euro makes land vacation options relatively more expensive. The number of cruises visiting European and Mediterranean ports has continued to rise over the last 2 years, and

North American cruisers have sought them due to the high cost of the euro against the US dollar (CLIA, 2005e). After a brief downturn in 2002 that paralleled a travel-industry-wide slump, more North Americans sailed to Europe and the Mediterranean in 2004 than at any other period in cruise history. In all, CLIA member lines will offer 2220 European sailings this year.

Cruise products

Whereas in the past a typical cruise lasted for a number of weeks, over recent years short

Table 1.6.   The world's largest cruise ships.

No.	Ship	Cruise line	Tonnage
1	*Freedom of the Seas*	Royal Caribbean International	158,000
2	*Queen Mary 2*	Cunard Line	148,528
3	*Explorer of the Seas*	Royal Caribbean International	137,308
4	*Voyager of the Seas*	Royal Caribbean International	137,280
5	*Adventure of the Seas*	Royal Caribbean Cruises	137,276
6	*Mariner of the Seas*	Royal Caribbean Cruises	137,276
7	*Navigator of the Seas*	Royal Caribbean Cruises	137,276
8	*Caribbean Princess*	Princess Cruises	116,000
9	*Diamond Princess*	Princess Cruises	113,000
10	*Sapphire Princess*	Princess Cruises	113,000

Table 1.7. Major cruise corporations.

Rank	Parent group	No. of ships	Cruise lines
1	Carnival Corporation	70	Carnival Cruise Lines Holland America Line Windstar Costa Crociere Cunard Seabourn Cruise Line P&O P&O (Australia) Princess Cruises Swan Hellenic Aida Cruises
2	Royal Caribbean Cruises	27	Royal Caribbean International Celebrity Cruises
3	Star Cruises Group	19	Star Cruises Norwegian Cruise Line NCL America Orient Lines

cruises have been introduced to meet the latent demand. Short cruises are relatively inexpensive and offer value for money, and provide the opportunity for first-time cruisers to try this style of holiday. In a 'time-strapped' world they are also more convenient for families and busy executives.

Theme cruises have existed since the earliest days of cruising, but cruise lines began marketing themed cruises in the early 1980s as a way to differentiate themselves to gain an edge. Popular theme cruises have included a focus on dance, music, food, wine, and health and well-being (Fig. 1.6). More specialized offerings have included nude cruises, gay and lesbian cruises and motorcycle cruises.

Today virtually all cruise lines offer themed cruises. For example, Crystal Cruises offer a Wine and Food Festival, Health and Fitness Cruises, Big Band and Jazz Cruises, and The Computer University @ Sea. Hebridean Island Cruises has castles, gardens, walking or cycling as their themes; Norwegian Coastal Voyage has its Northern Lights Voyages; Fred Olsen Cruise Lines offers its Art Clubs and Flagship Golf Programs; and Royal Olympia Cruises has recently adopted the strapline 'The Intelligent Way to See the World' to reflect its commitment to cultural cruising. Some of the innovative theme cruises offered in 2005 were:

1. Culinary Arts – Silversea Cruises and Relais and Chateaux – Relais Gourmands
2. A Cruise to Die For – Royal Caribbean and Whodunit Productions
3. Savour the Caribbean – Celebrity Cruises and Bon Appetit Magazine
4. Hot Ports, Cool Sounds – Costa Cruises and leading jazz musicians
5. This is Your Brain on Vacation – Crystal Cruises
6. Delta – Delta Steamboat Company

It is argued that the notion of themes on cruise ships or cruise lines has been taken to higher

Table 1.8. Major cruise destinations.

Rank	Destination	%
1	Caribbean	46
2	Mediterranean	11
3	Alaska	9
4	Northern Europe	8
5=	West Mexico	6
5=	Panama Canal	6
7=	South Pacific	2
7=	South America	2
9	Other	10
	Total	100

Fig. 1.6. Ships are now catering to the more active passenger. Walking track on Silversea Cruises' *Silver Shadow*, Kuching, Sarawak, Malaysian Borneo, 2004. Photo: Ross K. Dowling.

levels by the Carnival Cruise Line, with the promotion of its 'Fun Ships', as well as by the Disney Cruise Line, which extends the Disney Corporation into the marine environment (Weaver, Chapter 35, this volume). He argues that the relationship between pleasure and profit is created via themed environments, attractively presented merchandise and friendly customer service, all important to the operation of these seaborne 'money machines'.

The convention and incentives market industry is becoming an increasingly important segment of cruising. The luxurious nature of cruising is attractive to this segment (WTO, 2003, p. 48). Cunard estimates that 15% of its business is from the conference and incentives industry. RCI has approximately 20% of the US cruise market share of this segment and their *Voyager of the Seas* has the largest hall afloat capable of seating 1350 people (WTO, 2003). The Celebrity Cruises ship *Celebrity* has dedicated conference facilities installed by Sony. It has a conference hall that can accommodate 242 people and is equipped with the latest audiovisual systems, simultaneous language translation capability, the capacity for multimedia presenta-

tions, computer-generated graphics, videoconferences via ship to shore satellite, etc.

Star Cruises has been promoting its 'Meetings At Sea' programme to the Meetings, Incentives and Conferences Industry for several years, and in 2005 it staged the biggest offshore conference of its kind ever held in the South-east Asia region. Clipsal Australia chartered the *SuperStar Virgo* to celebrate its tenth anniversary and cruised with 1900 delegates on the 77,000-t ship. It was the first time the ship had visited Phuket, Thailand, since the Boxing Day 2004 tsunami devastated the region, forcing Star Cruises to alter itineraries for the Singapore-based ship. Post-tsunami rebuilding and a concerted effort by the Tourism Authority of Thailand (TAT) to alert the world that the popular resort was open again and 'better than ever' inspired Clipsal to include Phuket in its charter itinerary. The total cost of the charter was around AUS$7 million.

MSC Lirica is MSC Italian Cruises' first new build. Weighing 58,600 t the ship plies the Mediterranean (June–November) and the Caribbean (December–May). The ship places an emphasis on fun and employs a dedicated team of young social catalysts called 'The Animation Team', whose job it is to ensure everyone is socially engaged and enjoying the cruise (Petrie, 2004).

Recently Celebrity Cruises teamed up with Cirque du Soleil to offer passengers a unique on-board entertainment experience on its Millennium-class ships *Constellation* and *Summit*. The observation lounges on the ships were transformed into the Bar at the Edge of the Earth, where Cirque du Soleil characters took the stage for 2 hours each evening.

Just as the 'greening' of tourism has been a major advance in the last decade, the new millennium has introduced the concept of 'wellness' amongst tourists. The latest cruise liners have large health centres incorporating the latest in high-tech muscle exercising, aerobic and weight-training equipment. Spas are regularly voted by passengers as being far superior to land-based spas and all new cruise ships have large areas devoted to health and well-being, and spa treatments are one of the biggest on-board revenue generators. Spas are operated by concessionaires, the largest of which is Steiner, which also owns Mandara Spa, with its Balinese influence. Cunard's flagship *QM2* has a spectacular two-storey-high Canyon Ranch spa, which offers a thalssotherapy pool with underwater air bed recliner lounges, neck fountains, a deluge waterfall, air tub and body massage jet benches.

In response to the growth in popularity of low-carb diets, Carnival Cruise Lines has introduced specially designated low-carb dining selections on dinner menus throughout the fleet. Main dishes comprise vegetables, meat and fish, and for each item on the menu the number of carbohydrate grams is written alongside it. Both Princess and Royal Caribbean offer The Zone Diet, and many of the crew follow it too (Bryant, 2004). Cruise companies are also enhancing shore programmes by offering more in-depth experiences and providing more sports and adventuresome options for the active traveller.

Impacts

The tourism industry impacts both positively and negatively on the economic, sociocultural and natural environments. The cruise industry is no exception, and for such a small niche its impacts are disproportionate to its size. First, it has a considerable economic impact. For example, the US cruise industry generates more than 450,000 jobs accounting for US$15 billion in wages and billions of dollars in the purchase of goods and services. Second, the industry also impacts on local government revenues and expenditures. Revenues earned by local governments from the cruise industry may be made up from:

- sales taxes generated by local governments as a result of local spending by cruise ship passengers, crew and from cruise lines directly;
- transient room taxes paid by cruise passengers;
- revenues from fees paid by cruise lines and cruise passengers including docking fees, littering fees and other port charges;
- garbage disposal fees and charges for water sales;
- passenger fees including admissions and payments for medical services;
- tax payments made by businesses selling goods and services to cruise visitors or sales taxes paid by business;
- local purchases in support of their business operations;
- secondary or indirect tax revenues (such as sales and property tax payments) made by employees (and their dependants) of the cruise industry.

Revenue raising

In the past cruise ships were sold as 'all-inclusive vacations', i.e. once the fare was paid, there were few extras to pay for items other than those of a personal nature such as for shopping, alcoholic drinks and of course, end-of-cruise tips. Today that has all changed and the all-inclusive element has given way to a 'user-pays' situation. This includes on-board revenue centres that include optional 'extra-tariff' restaurants and food outlets, mini bars, recreational activities and same-day newspapers. Onshore revenue generators include land-based tours and shopping programmes.

The industry has also been successful in reducing costs with savings having been achieved through consolidation and mergers.

Cruise lines have also maintained their profitability by keeping labour costs low, by cutting unnecessary costs (such as use of bunker fuels rather than fuels that are more environmentally 'green') and by gaining concessions and incentives from ports (Klein, Chapter 24, this volume).

Social/cultural

Because passengers on-board cruise ships interact with local communities, there is much scope for both beneficial and adverse impacts. According to Sheridan and Teal (Chapter 29, this volume), cruise tourism is continuously portrayed as bringing prosperity and development for local communities but this does not correspond seamlessly with the local reality. They argue that in the case of Ensenada, Baja California, Mexico, cruise tourism thrives on constructed fantasies where the destination is really just an extension of the ship.

Across on the eastern side of Mexico, the island of Cozumel is a major cruise destination in the Caribbean. Here the challenges of a small island evolving from a little-used dive destination to a heavily used cruise destination are substantial, and it is suggested that Cozumel's rapidly growing cruise tourism industry does not benefit the island much (Sorenson, Chapter 32, this volume). This is also noted elsewhere in the Caribbean (Pulsipher and Holderfield, Chapter 28, this volume). They argue that the cruise tourism product provides tourists with an impoverished experience and leaves local communities disempowered and underpaid. Whereas in the past, tourists in the Caribbean would spend at least a few days and nights in an island hotel and have at least some encounters with island people and places, now most visitors are cruisers visiting individual islands for only a few hours at best, and often not even that as cruise companies discourage tourists from going ashore.

The social impacts of cruising are not confined to destination regions where ships visit. The International Transport Workers Federation (ITWF) claims that cruise crews have poor working conditions with little leisure time and are accommodated in unsatisfactory conditions. This occurs despite the protection afforded to workers by the International Labour Organization and International Maritime Organization. The ITWF allege that crew members are underpaid and have few rights – a situation it notes that has not changed for decades. Lee-Ross (Chapter 4, this volume) notes that this occurs because the industry's occupational community is an example of a unique culture in practice that fosters hegemony largely due to the top-down management approach and the heterogeneity of cruise ship workers.

Environmental issues

Environmental issues facing the cruise industry are many and complex. This is especially true given the frequency with which cruises now visit major conservation areas of the world.

The 'International Convention for the Prevention of Pollution from Ships 1973 and the Protocol of 1978', commonly referred to as MARPOL, specify ship waste disposal, record-keeping practices and pollution control equipment to be carried by all ships. These regulations have recently been amended in a new regulation that came into force in 1998. It specifies the use of three complementary techniques to manage garbage: source reduction, recycling and disposal. A cruise vessel can either process material and discharge it in concert with MARPOL requirements or store it for discharge at ports for landfill, incineration or recycling. Cruise lines are opting to invest in on-board waste-disposal technologies and have adopted environmentally sensitive practices.

Timothy (Chapter 37, this volume) notes that because cruise ships are typically registered in 'flags of convenience' countries and spend most of their time in international waters, they are relatively free from the laws of any particular nation and only slightly affected by international regulations. This then could allow them to pay scant attention to the environment and in some cases this has been the case (Klein, Chapter 34, this volume). However, advances have been made in recent times. Ward (2005, p. 21) states that 'cruise ships refuse oil, treat human waste, and incinerate garbage', but that is not enough today, as pressure continues to mount for clean oceans. He notes that 'the cruise industry is fast approaching "zero discharge", which means that nothing is discharged into the world's oceans at any time' (Ward, 2005, p. 25).

Overall the cruise industry is beginning to take its environmental responsibilities more seriously. In 2004 Royal Caribbean Cruises was honoured by the American Academy of Environmental Engineers for the development and implementation of the cruise industry's first comprehensive ISO 14001-certified environmental management system and environmental officer training programme (*Cruise News*, 2004). The line has introduced a sustainable environmental system that reduces shipboard waste and its impact on the environment. It includes the comprehensive monitoring of shipboard operation, technical advancements and fleet-wide changes to waste-management programmes.

Holland America Line's new 85,000-t 'Vista Class' ship *Oosterdam* also boasts environmental systems allowing it to operate in Alaskan waters. This includes a sophisticated waste plant, advanced recycling, as well as a water system that allows reuse of all on-board water for technical purposes rather than discharging it at sea. Sewage sludge can be used as additional fuel for various mechanical systems and recycled waste including plastic and aluminium is sold, with the proceeds going into a crew fund, thus creating an incentive for higher efficiency (Knego, 2004).

Safety and Security

The rise of global acts of terrorism combined with the growth of the cruise industry has inevitably led to a heightened interest in, and practice of, security and safety. The two main aspects of cruise safety are guarding against accidents (e.g. ship flooding or fire) and direct threats (e.g. hijacking or terrorism). Safety issues are generally addressed by the International Maritime Organizations' Maritime Safety Committee.

In the weeks following the 11 September 2001 terrorist attacks on the USA, eight lines went bankrupt (Ward, 2005). Many other lines had to redeploy their ships and others had a dramatic drop in passenger numbers. As a direct result of this incident, and subsequent war against Iraq in 2003, US citizens have travelled overseas less, preferring to travel within their own borders. In response to this the US cruise industry has established 'homeland' cruising

with ships now being homeported across the country in a range of new ports. This has lessened the need for Americans to fly to another city for embarkation on their cruise, and in addition, the ships have stayed close to US shores. According to Ward (2005) the effects of the increased attacks and wars during the last 5 years have translated in a lack of confidence in out-travel, and this is why homeland cruising has become increasingly popular. These issues will become a major focus of the cruise line associations around the world in future. Most are marketing and promotion and/or lobby organizations (Table 1.9) but their future will be predicated on the security and safety issues.

Conclusion

During the last decade the cruise industry has been the tourism niche that has experienced the most rapid growth of all. While the global demand for international trips grew at around 4.3%, the cruise market grew at 7.9% (WTO, 2003). However, this form of tourism is still in its infancy and has not been relatively well researched. This volume is one of the first to contribute to our knowledge on the subject and it brings together an eclectic mix of authors, topics and views. But weaving throughout the various themes and topics is a desire to understand cruise tourism more so that the industry can grow on more sure-footed foundation in future.

Structure of the Book

This book could have been presented in a variety of ways with a plethora of different subdivisions. Indeed it went through a number of iterations before resting in its current form. Overall the book is presented in five parts:

1. Introduction
2. Demand – Cruise Passengers and Marketing
3. Supply – Cruise Destinations and Products
4. Interactions – Economic, Social and Environmental Impacts
5. Industry Issues

Part I introduces the industry and some of its underpinning aspects in Chapters 2–5. It begins by examining the geographical overview

Table 1.9.   Cruise line associations.

Association	Abbreviation	Base	Activity
Cruise Line Industry Association	CLIA	New York	Represents North American cruise lines
International Council of Cruise Lines	ICCL	Washington, DC	US lobby group
Florida–Caribbean Cruise Association	FCCA	Miami	Promotes the relationships between the US Cruise Industry and the Caribbean Islands
Passenger Shipping Association	PSA	London	British Government and European Union lobby group
Croisimer		Paris	Promotes cruising and staff training
Verband der Faehrschiffahrt un Faetouristik e.V	VFF	Hamburg	Promotes cruising and staff training
International Cruise Council Australasia	ICCA	Sydney	Promotes the global cruise experience
Cruise Down Under	CDU	Sydney	Promotes cruising in Australasia
Japan Oceangoing Passenger Ship Association		Tokyo	Promotes cruising and ship safety and security

of the world cruise market, its seasonal comple-mentarities and the lack of comprehensive worldwide statistics on both the supply and demand for cruising. This is followed by an industrial perspective, which examines the nature of the cruise product, the dimensions of competition and the various barriers to market entry. Then a sociological perspective is presented to introduce a cultural framework for identifying and understanding the attitudes and behaviour of 'hospitality workers' on cruise ships. The part concludes with a description of the unique characteristics of Bermuda's cruise industry and an investigation of policy issues, based on the case of Bermuda.

Part II comprises Chapters 6–12 related to the insatiable demand for cruising. It includes examination of passenger' perceptions of value, trends in the North American market, and passenger expectations and activities. These contributions are supported by the importance of the visual image in destination marketing, the important role of interpretation by cruise guides and the need for a standardized ship-rating system. This part concludes with a cultural studies approach to understanding the ocean-cruising phenomenon.

Part III explores the supply side of cruising with examples from around the world. In Chapters 13–23 case studies are presented on a number of cruise destinations including the Baltic Sea, Alaska, Atlantic Canada, the Caribbean, the Pacific and the Antarctic. A number of cruise products are described and discussed including the round-the-world segment and the Norwegian Coastal Express. Finally the specific niches of coastal, adventure and expedition cruising are presented.

Part IV explores the industry's interactions with the economic, social and natural environments in Chapters 24–32. It begins with a discussion on economic elements in relation to a destination region, ports, and the day-cruise industry. Next it identifies the importance of on-board revenue centres, and the introduction and development of a range of new revenue sources. Sociocultural aspects are discussed in relation to local communities (host) and cruise tourist (guest) interactions in the Eastern Caribbean and Baja California, Mexico. The industry's environmental record is investigated and some suggestions are advocated in relation to industry self-regulation and voluntary guidelines vs command and control regulation. This part concludes with two reports on the impacts of cruise tourism in the state of Alaska, USA, and on the island of Cozumel, Mexico.

Part V investigates a selection of a number of industry issues across Chapters 33–38. It starts with an examination of the industry in relation to its economic contribution to ports, social issues and problems, and theme park reflection. This is followed by two contributions on the globalization and supranationalism of cruise tourism. Finally the book is brought to a close by a brief discussion on the future of the industry.

References

Abels, J.M. (1998) *Cruise Sellers are on a Roll.* Available at: http://www.traveltrade.com/editorial

Bryant, S. (2004) Pampering playgrounds. *Cruise Passenger* 17, 46–50.

CLIA (2004a) Married baby boomers heart of cruise market. *Cruise Lines International Association News Release*, 23 March. Available at: www.cruising.org

CLIA (2004b) Cruising suits lifestyle, demands of today's new generation of retirees, says CLIA. *Cruise Lines International Association NewsRrelease*, 2 August. Available at: www.cruising.org

CLIA (2005a) CLIA celebrates 30 years of excellence with ambitious growth and marketing agenda. *Cruise Lines International Association News Release*, 3 January. Available at: www.cruising.org

CLIA (2005b) Industry predicts cruising will be vacation of choice in 2005. *Cruise Lines International Association News Release*, 19 January. Available at: www.crusing.org

CLIA (2005c) CLIA Cruise Lines ride the wave of unprecedented growth. *Cruise Lines International Association News Release*, 16 March. Available at: www.cruising.org

CLIA (2005d) A future bright with promise. *Cruise Lines International Association News Release*, May 2005. Available at: www.cruising.org

CLIA (2005e) 2005 Europe cruises on all CLIA lines: demand is at all-time high so book now. *Cruise Lines International Association News Release*, 14 March. Available at: www.cruising.org

Cruise News (2004) Cruise news. *Cruise Travel* 26(1), 25.

Davidoff, P.G. and Davidoff, D.S. (1994) *Sales and Marketing For Travel & Tourism*, 2nd edn. Prentice-Hall, UK.

Dickinson, B. and Vladimir, A. (1997) *Selling the Sea: An Inside Look at the Cruise Industry.* John Wiley & Sons, New York.

Dowling, R.K. and Vasudavan, T. (2000) Cruising in the new millennium. *Tourism Recreation Research* 25(3), 17–27.

Knego, P. (2004) Ship of the month: *Oosterdam. Cruise Travel* 26(1), 30–35.

Mancini, M. (2000) *Cruising: A Guide to the Cruise Line Industry.* Delmar, Albany, New York.

Paige, M.M. (1998) Caribbean cruising towards the millennium. *World Travel & Tourism Development* 3, 77–80.

Peisley, T. (1989) New developments in world cruising. *EIU Travel and Tourism Analyst* 7, 5–19.

Petrie, G. (2004) Ship of the month: *MSC Lirica. Cruise Travel* 26(3), 30–35.

Ward, D. (2005) *Berlitz – Ocean Cruising and Cruise Ships 2005.* Berlitz Publishing, London.

WTO (World Tourism Organization) (2003) *Worldwide Cruise Ship Activity.* World Tourism Organization, Madrid.

2 A Geographical Overview of the World Cruise Market and its Seasonal Complementarities

Jacques J. Charlier[1,2] and Robert J. McCalla[3]

[1]University of Paris-sorbonne, Department of Geography, France 75005;
[2]University of Louvain-la-Neuve, Department of Geography, Belgium 1348;
[3]Saint Mary's University, Department of Geography, Halifax,
Nova Scotia, Canada B3H 3C3

Introduction

The world cruise industry is one of the most dynamic segments of the tourism industry with dramatic growth that has been widely acknowledged, albeit in a limited way in economics and geography textbooks about the tourism industry (Hall, 2004). A difficulty in knowing about and understanding the dynamics of the industry is the lack of comprehensive worldwide statistics on both the supply of and demand for cruising. Most of the published figures, including those in commercial publications (Peisley, 1997, 2004; Wild and Dearing, 1999, 2004), are based upon quarterly and yearly reports issued by the Cruise Lines International Association (CLIA), a US-based body whose geographical coverage is far from comprehensive. CLIA only focuses on cruises offered in North American waters or elsewhere in the world to North American consumers by its member lines or by their main competitors as identified by CLIA.

There are, however, many more cruises offered by other lines, as shown in popular consumer guides, the most comprehensive of which is the *Berlitz Guide to Ocean Cruising and Cruise Ships* (Ward, 2004). Consequently, any analysis based solely upon figures released by CLIA has a geographical bias to it (Charlier, 1996, 2000).

This chapter attempts to rectify that bias by drawing upon a more comprehensive source of cruise shipping operations, namely a yearly publication of the Swedish consultancy ShipPax (Brogen, 2004). As a result, we hope to offer a valuable contribution to the limited, but growing body of scientific literature about the geography of the cruise industry (Marti, 1990; Marti and Cartaya, 1996; McCalla, 1998; Ridolfi, 2000; Wild and Dearing, 2000; Charlier, 2004).

For 2004, CLIA's estimates of cruise supply amounted to 77.3 million bed-days aboard about 150 cruise ships (CLIA, 2004). Of this offer, 66.4% was in North and Central American waters, 22.3% in Europe and 11.2% in the rest of the world. As discussed above, this estimate is geographically biased to the North American cruise industry. The *Guide 2004: Ferry, Cruise and RO-RO Register Yearbook* (Brogen, 2004) is a more comprehensive and less geographically biased source of information featuring many more cruise ships to many more destinations than identified in CLIA documents. For this chapter, we have reworked the ShipPax database by excluding some vessels that should not be classified as pure cruise ships (North American one-day excursion ships, Baltic one-night cruise ferries and Norwegian *Hurtigruten* passenger ferries). As a result, we have created our own original and, we think, more comprehensive database of world cruise supply. This database shows a grand total of 105.7 million bed-days on offer in 2004 aboard about 250 ocean-going cruise ships. Compared to CLIA figures, the modified ShipPax database shows about 28 million more bed-days and includes 100 more cruise ships, most of which are small- or medium-sized vessels, and often older on average.

Before exploring the macro-geography of world cruise operations, we should make it clear that we approach the exercise from the *supply side*, not from the demand side. Consequently, we look at *where the cruises are taking place*, not from where the passengers originate. From our experience, there are no comprehensive reliable *worldwide* statistics on the total number of cruise passengers. There are only such figures for North American and European passengers, estimated at 8 million and 2.7 million in 2004, respectively, by CLIA and European Cruise Council (ECC), whereas there are simply educated guesses for the rest of the world. They range between 2 and 2.5 million cruise passengers, meaning that the world grand total was around 13 million in 2004 (Peisley, 2004).

If the average length of a cruise worldwide amounts to 7 days, as is the case for North American passengers, there were approximately 91 million bed-days of demand in 2004. If the figure we are quoting for the overall supply, i.e. 105.7 million bed-days, is correct, the average occupancy ratio (taking into account vessels temporarily idle) amounts to 86.1%. (Actually, it is much higher for some well-known American cruise lines, but it is significantly lower for many other operators.) This is a very high occupancy ratio when compared to those observed in the land-based tourist industry, except perhaps for a few major world cities. One of the reasons to account for the high occupancy is the fact that cruise ships, which are fundamentally mobile floating resorts, can be moved seasonally from one cruise area to another in order to maximize their occupancy ratio by always sailing in climatically attractive areas (Charlier and Arnold, 1997; Charlier, 1999). Therefore, the cruise industry is characterized by a unique feature: the seasonal interregional and intraregional migrations performed every year by many vessels. The most spectacular – but also the most marginal – of these migrations, namely round-

the-world cruises, are explored elsewhere in this book (McCalla and Charlier, Chapter 19, this volume).

The Three Main Macro-geographical Areas and their Seasonal Complementarities

As already mentioned, our grand total of supply (a theoretical capacity) during 2004 amounts to 105.7 million bed-days (Table 2.1), including 2.8 million bed-days made up by temporarily laid-up vessels (on a seasonal basis, between two charters, for major refurbishments or after a bankruptcy, but excluding very old laid-up ships with little, if any, prospects of seeing service again). The bed-days of laid-up vessels, accounting for 2.7% of the world grand total, have been kept in our database because their share features a highly seasonal dimension (ranging from 5.6% for the first quarter to just 0.5% for the third quarter). Because our analysis is done on a seasonal basis, their exclusion would have introduced a significant geo-seasonal bias, as most of them are sailing in the Mediterranean between March/April and October/November.

CLIA's above-mentioned 77.3 million bed-days should therefore be compared to our own 102.9 million (105.7 million – 2.8 million) bed-days for the effective cruise offer, i.e. 44.2% more than the offer accounted for by CLIA. In North and Central American waters, the difference is quite small relatively (60.4 million for our database against 51.4 million for CLIA for a shortfall of 14.9%), whereas it is quite high in Europe (25.5 million against 17.3 million, a 32.1% difference) and even more in the rest of the world (17 million vs 8.7 million, a 48.8% difference). Therefore, our own estimates for the actual shares of the three main cruise areas are quite different: 57.1% for North and Central America (against 66.4% for CLIA), 24.1% for Europe (against 22.4%) and 16.1% for the rest of the world (against 11.2%), plus another 2.7% for idle vessels (not accounted for by CLIA).

Moreover, our database has been computed on a monthly basis and we are thus able to show the monthly and quarterly fluctuations of the world offer for cruising (in graphical and tabular form, respectively). As Table 2.2 shows, the

Table 2.1. Quarterly capacity by regional cruise area, 2004 ('000 bed days, lower berths).

	First quarter	Second quarter	Third quarter	Fourth quarter	Whole year
North/Central America	**15,767**	**14,430**	**14,454**	**16,287**	**60,938**
Caribbean/Bahamas	13,582	8,888	7,155	12,974	42,599
Mexican Riviera/Panama	2,182	1,586	1,246	2,549	7,563
Alaska	0	3,190	4,091	12	7,293
North-east Atlantic	3	766	1,962	752	3,483
Europe	**1,433**	**8,395**	**10,644**	**5,012**	**25,484**
Mediterranean	1,419	5,847	6,579	5,012	18,857
North-west Europe/Transatlantic	14	2,548	4,065	0	6,627
Rest of the world	**6,251**	**3,183**	**2,425**	**5,112**	**16,971**
South-east Asia and Far-east	1,269	1,384	1,340	1,579	5,572
South Pacific and Hawaii	1,745	936	890	1,992	5,563
Other submarkets	3,237	863	195	1,541	5,836
Subtotal active fleet	**23,451**	**26,008**	**27,523**	**26,411**	**103,393**
Laid-up vessels (temporarily)	1,382	456	137	871	2,846
Grand total world cruise fleet	**24,833**	**26,464**	**27,660**	**27,282**	**106,239**

Source : Own database adapted from Brogen (2004).

seasonal factor is crucial in the geography of cruising, especially when comparing the first and third quarters (corresponding to the winter and summer seasons in the Northern hemisphere, and vice versa in the southern hemisphere).

In the first quarter, some 63.3% of the world offer is concentrated in North and Central American waters (actually only in the southern, warmest part), and another 25.3% in the rest of the world (excluding Europe) with, as shown in Table 2.2, about 20% in the southern hemisphere. At that time of the year, Europe as a whole accounted for just 5.8%, and 5.6% of the theoretical offer was not available (much of it accounted for by idle ships in the Mediterranean). Whereas for the third quarter, the picture was quite different with Europe accounting for 38.7% and just 0.5% of the theoretical capacity not being offered. At the same time, North America

still accounted for 52%, but the rest of the world was down to just 8.8% of the world offer, showing just how complex the situation is on a global, macro-geographical scale.

The differences in the European offerings between the first and third quarters can be explained by three factors: (i) idle vessels being locally put in service again after a winter lay-up; (ii) ships sailing back from the southern hemisphere, be they from the Pacific, the Indian Ocean or the South Atlantic; and (iii) ships crossing the North Atlantic. Capacity-wise, the latter West–East interregional migration from Caribbean waters to European ones is less important than the South–North repositionings undertaken by the vessels sailing in the southern hemisphere in the first quarter (the vast majority of which sails to Europe, with a few crossing the Pacific Ocean to cruise in Alaska in summer).

Table 2.2. The overall structure of the world cruise market in 2004 (in % of bed-days worldwide).

	First quarter	Second quarter	Third quarter	Fourth quarter	Whole year
North and Central America	63.30	54.31	52.03	59.51	57.15
Europe (incl. Transatlantic)	5.80	31.88	38.66	18.46	24.10
Rest of the world	25.30	12.08	8.81	18.83	16.05
Idle vessels	5.60	1.73	0.50	3.20	2.70
Grand total	**100.00**	**100.00**	**100.00**	**100.00**	**100.00**

Source : Own database adapted from Brogen (2004).

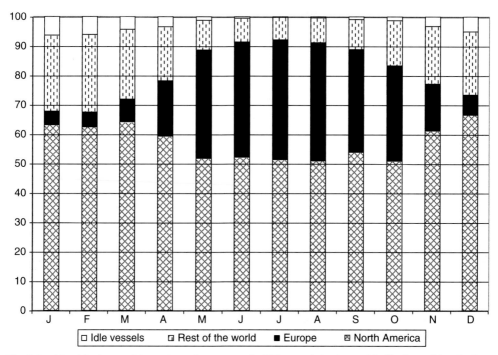

Fig. 2.1. Monthly shares of the main cruise areas and of idle vessels in the world offer for cruising (in % of bed-days).

As shown in Fig. 2.1, the seasonal geographical redistribution of the world offer for cruising takes some time to develop, be it during the second quarter, when Europe's share increases to an average of 31.9%, or during the fourth quarter, when Europe's share is already down to an average of 18.5%. This lengthy transition seen in the statistics reflects the poor cruising season in Europe that starts in November and declines rapidly in December as the Northern Hemisphere winter sets in. Technically, one should consider that there are two four-month-long peak seasons in the world cruise market, namely December–March and June–September, with two two-month-long shoulder seasons in between (April–May and October–November) during which many ship migrations take place from one major cruise area to another. Because we could not extend our database back to December 2003, we refer here to 2004, whereas the period from December 2003 to November 2004 would have been somewhat more appropriate.

With this general overview in mind, we now present a detailed analysis on a quarterly basis of the three main cruise areas (North and Central America, Europe and the rest of the world) on a subregional scale. Such an analysis not only reinforces the *interregional* migrations just discussed, but also shows *intraregional* repositionings that are equally important to understand the seasonal geographical patterns of the world cruise industry.

Intraregional Seasonal Complementarities in North and Central American Waters

In 2004, North and Central American waters accounted for 57.1% of the overall offer for cruising worldwide, with a high of 63.3% in winter and a low of 52% in summer. There are two series of submarkets in the North and Central American arena: there are areas in which cruises are offered year-round, but there are also areas where cruises operate on a seasonal basis. In the first category, there are on the Atlantic side, the Caribbean and the Bahamas, and on the Pacific side, the Mexican Riviera

Table 2.3. The overall structure of the North American cruise market in 2004 (in % of bed-days worldwide).

	First quarter	Second quarter	Third quarter	Fourth quarter	Whole year
Year-round markets	63.29	39.29	30.05	56.70	46.96
Seasonal markets	0.01	15.02	21.98	2.81	10.19
Subtotal	**63.30**	**54.31**	**52.03**	**59.51**	**57.15**

Source: Own database adapted from Brogen (2004).

sensu lato (between southern California and the Panama Canal). In this analysis, the latter area includes the Panama transcanal cruises (even though there are no summer cruises at all on the Panama Canal). In the second category featuring seasonal cruise offerings, there are the north-east Atlantic (including Bermuda, New England and Eastern Canada) and the north-west Pacific where Alaska accounts for the bulk of the offer.

As can be seen in Table 2.3 and Fig. 2.2, these two series of submarkets are characterized by opposite seasonal patterns; they are, therefore, highly complementary. On the one hand, the more or less year-round submarkets account for almost two-thirds of the world offer during the first quarter (63.3%), but they lose more than half of that market share in the third quar-

ter to just 30% of the world offer. This decline in importance is accounted for by more than half of the ships sailing in the year-round operating arena repositioning elsewhere in summertime, be it intercontinentally to Europe (for about one-third of the ships' migrations) or intracontinentally to more northern North American waters (for the other two-thirds).

Table 2.4 and Fig. 2.3 both show that the Caribbean and Bahamas market dominates year-round cruising in North and Central American waters. But the Mexican Riviera including the Panama Canal cruises follows the seasonal high and low pattern of the Caribbean and Bahamas, albeit at a much lower scale.

The same dissymmetry (but inverted) can be found in the seasonal cruise markets of the more northern waters (Table 2.5 and Fig. 2.4).

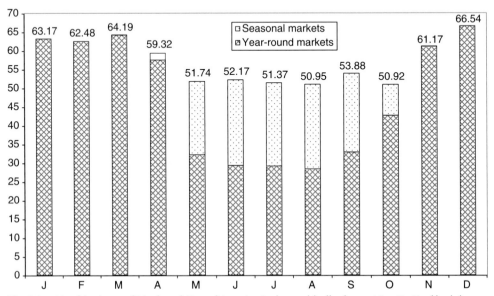

Fig. 2.2. Monthly shares of North and Central America in the world offer for cruising (in % of bed-days; year average: 57.15%).

Table 2.4. The internal structure of the North American year-round cruise markets in 2004 (in % of bed-days worldwide).

	First quarter	Second quarter	Third quarter	Fourth quarter	Whole year
Caribbean/Bahamas	54.46	33.27	25.52	47.31	39.81
Mexican Riviera/Panama	8.83	6.02	4.53	9.39	7.15
Subtotal	**63.29**	**39.29**	**30.05**	**56.70**	**46.96**

Source: Own database adapted from Brogen (2004).

The geographical pattern is also reversed with the *Atlantic* submarket accounting for much less of the offer (3.3% for the whole year and 7.1% in summer) than the *Pacific* submarket, centred around Alaska (6.9% and 15.0%, respectively). Besides their uneven weight, these two cruise areas feature another difference. For climatic reasons, the season is much shorter in Alaska than in the north-east Atlantic where the Bermuda cruise season is quite long because of the Gulf Stream. Moreover, the *Indian Summer* phenomenon and the *fall colours* are reasons why September and October are still highly popular for New England and Eastern Canada cruises. (At that time of the year, the additional capacity needed is provided by ships sailing back from northern Europe on their way, eventually,

to take up position in the Caribbean and Bahamas waters for the winter season.)

Cruising in Europe: A Tale of Two Seasonal Markets

At first glance Europe shows quite a simple seasonal pattern, with a peak of 38.7% of the world capacity in summer and a very limited offer in winter. In between, there are two transitional shoulder seasons. But, as is the case for North and Central America, there are two highly different submarkets within Europe, both in terms of bed-days offered and in their seasonality (Table 2.6 and Fig. 2.5). There is a year-round submarket, i.e. the Mediterranean (including

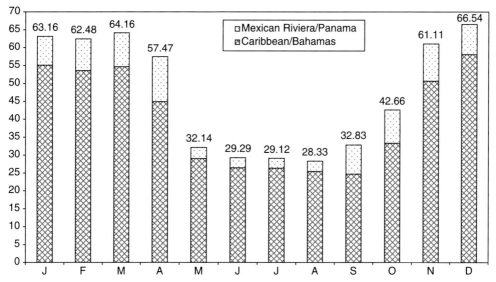

Fig. 2.3. Monthly shares of North and Central America's year-round markets in the world (in % of bed-days; year average: 46.96%).

Table 2.5. The internal structure of the North American seasonal cruise markets in 2004 (in % of bed-days worldwide).

	First quarter	Second quarter	Third quarter	Fourth quarter	Whole year
Alaska	0.00	12.11	14.85	0.04	6.90
North-east Atlantic	0.01	2.91	7.13	2.77	3.29
Subtotal	**0.01**	**15.02**	**21.98**	**2.81**	**10.19**

Source: Own database adapted from Brogen (2004).

the Black Sea), and a seasonal one of north-west Europe (north of Gibraltar including the Baltic Sea), whose respective world shares of yearly offer are highly unequal: 17.8% and 6.3%. For the Mediterranean there is a temporal bimodal submarket, with peaks in late spring and mid-fall, and a somewhat more limited offer in the summer months indicating a quite long cruise season (April to mid-November). In contrast, the winter months have a very limited, yet non-negligible offer. For northern Europe (as for Alaska), the cruise season is rather short with an early start in the spring (again thanks to the Gulf Stream) and a peak in mid-summer. This mid-summer peak in northern waters explains somewhat the bimodal pattern in the Mediterranean as ships move north with the finer weather. As was the case for cruising in North American

waters, there is no offer at all for cruising in northern Europe in winter (except for one- or two-night minicruises in the Baltic and the *Hurtigruten* ferries, both of which were excluded from the analysis, as these are not real cruise products in the general understanding of what are a cruise and a cruise ship).

The intracontinental repositionings from the Mediterranean to north-west Europe are undertaken twice a year: northbound by mid-spring and southbound after the summer season. This is the case for most ships, but the two flows are not symmetrical. After the summer season some vessels, instead of sailing back from north-west Europe to the Mediterranean, cross the Northern Atlantic to offer more lucrative New England and eastern Canada cruises. This unique migratory pattern, combining two

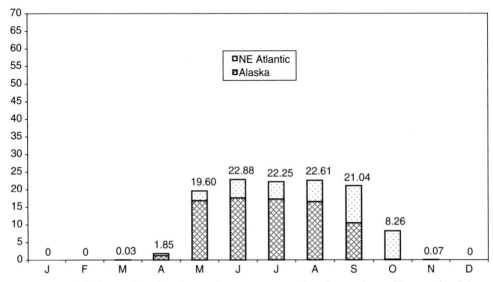

Fig. 2.4. Monthly shares of North and Central America's seasonal markets in the world (in % of bed-days; year average: 10.19%).

Table 2.6. The internal structure of the European cruise markets in 2004 (in % of bed-days worldwide).

	First quarter	Second quarter	Third quarter	Fourth quarter	Whole year
Mediterranean	5.74	22.20	23.90	18.46	17.83
North-west Europe	0.06	9.68	14.77	0.00	6.27
Subtotal	**5.80**	**31.88**	**38.67**	**18.46**	**24.10**

Source: Own database adapted from Brogen (2004).

interregional and two intraregional repositioning cruises, allows ships to cruise in *four* different submarkets in a year-long cycle. They sail first in the Caribbean in winter, in the Mediterranean in spring, in north-west Europe in summer, in New England and eastern Canada in autumn and again in the Caribbean in the next winter season. After the round-the-world cruises explored in much greater detail elsewhere in this book (McCalla and Charlier, Chapter 19, this volume), this is the second most complex ship-deployment pattern in the cruise industry. Interregionally, it implies two different transatlantic routes: a rather southern one eastbound, and a very northern one westbound, whereas the more numerous vessels combining the Caribbean in winter with the Mediterranean for the spring and fall seasons cross the Atlantic on southern routes both eastbound and westbound.

The Diversity of Cruising in the Rest of the World

Cruising in the rest of the world is often seen as marginal or 'niche-like', and it has been less documented in the literature before the publication of this book. It will be dealt with here more superficially than the North American or European cruising areas, even though its overall contribution to world cruising is far from negligible. In total, all submarkets in the rest of the world accounted, in 2004, for 16% of the world

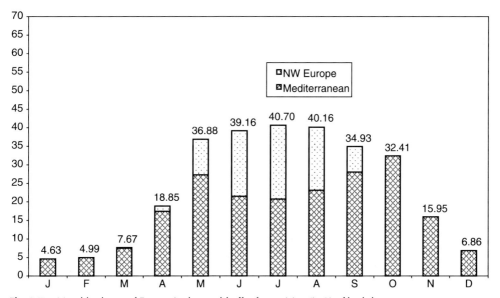

Fig. 2.5. Monthly shares of Europe in the world offer for cruising (in % of bed-days; year average: 24.10%).

Table 2.7. The internal structure of the cruise markets in the rest of the world in 2004 (in % of bed-days worldwide).

	First quarter	Second quarter	Third quarter	Fourth quarter	Whole year
South-east Asia and Far East	5.14	5.25	4.87	5.82	5.27
South Pacific and Hawaii	7.06	3.55	3.23	7.34	5.26
Other submarkets	13.10	3.28	0.71	5.67	5.52
Subtotal	**25.30**	**12.08**	**8.81**	**18.83**	**16.05**

Source: Own database adapted from Brogen (2004).

offer with a peak of 25.3% for the first quarter and a low of 8.8% for the third quarter (Table 2.7 and Fig. 2.6). The peak in the first quarter is largely accounted for by cruises in the waters of the southern hemisphere (its summer). The decline through the second quarter to the third and increase in the fourth are explained by interregional repositionings mostly from these southern waters to and from Europe, with a few ships crossing the Pacific Ocean to and from Alaska.

South-east Asia and the Far East accounted for 5.3% on a yearly basis. This is the only regional submarket where the offer for cruising is more or less equal all year long. The other two categories of submarkets (South Pacific (including Australia) and Hawaii, and

'other markets') also account each for slightly more than 5% of the world cruise offer on a yearly basis. The 'other markets' include South America and the Antarctica (2.6% overall), Africa and the Indian Ocean (1.7%) and the above-mentioned round-the-world cruises (1.2%). These cruising areas are combined here because their individual weights are quite small and because their seasonal patterns are rather identical (Arnold and Charlier, 1999; Charlier, 2000). However, the two submarkets are significantly different: on the one hand, the South Pacific and Hawaii submarket features some offer for cruising during the third quarter (3.3%), whereas there is very little offer left at that time in the smaller 'other markets' (0.7%). Also, the latter markets feature a peak at a

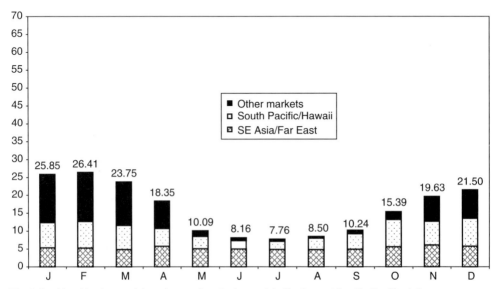

Fig. 2.6. Monthly shares of the other markets in the world offer for cruising (in % of bed-days; year average: 16.05%).

much higher level in the first quarter than is the case for the South Pacific and Hawaii area.

As can be seen, there is a wide spectrum of regional patterns outside North and Central America, Europe and Asia-Pacific, and more research (as offered in Chapter 19, this volume), is needed in order to understand how these smaller submarkets fit into the general pattern of world cruising.

Conclusion: An Industry Governed by Seasonality and Repositioning Strategies

In this chapter, we have raised a series of methodological issues and shown how complex the world cruise market is in its geographical dimensions. On the methodological front, as for other aspects of science in general and of geography in particular, the accuracy of the findings is conditioned by the accuracy of the data. In this respect, we feel that our own database featuring the regional and monthly deployment of the world cruise fleet in the year 2004 is the most comprehensive and the least geographically biased available among those referred to in the literature. It does not restrict itself to cruises sold to the North American public, as is the case for CLIA, but aims at a global coverage outside North and Central American waters, in Europe and in the rest of the world.

Methodologically, we have attempted a *dynamic* view of the industry through a consideration of its seasonality, which we view is key to understanding world cruising. Regular year-round cruising in a given area is more an exception than the rule in the industry. Even the Caribbean features a strong seasonal pattern in its monthly offer for cruising. This leaves only two truly year-round submarkets: South-east Asia and Hawaii. Everywhere else in the world, there are significant differences between the peak and low seasons, and in several cases, there is no cruise offer at all during a significant part of the year, as for Alaska, north-west Europe and some southern hemisphere submarkets.

The seasonal movement of very expensive assets like cruise ships from one cruise area to another is a key factor of financial success for cruise lines, making cruise shipping quite a unique branch of the tourism industry.

Table 2.8 summarizes the main patterns of vessels' deployment that we have identified on a quarterly basis in North and Central American waters, in Europe and in the rest of the world. As can be seen, in a minority of cases, the ships are able to sail year-round within the same cruising areas, either with or without intraregional movements. In several cases, highlighted in italics, ships are redeployed interregionally, with long oceanic-repositioning cruises in between. Except for a limited number of 'vagabonds of the seas' (usually luxury ships), the only cases of deployments featuring calls within each of the three major areas are world cruises, especially of the round-the-world variety.

As already highlighted, there are two different types of repositioning voyages undertaken by vessels shifting seasonally from one submarket to another. On the one hand, there are the (rather short) intraregional repositioning cruises arranged within the same macrogeographical area; on the other hand, there are (usually longer) interregional repositioning cruises between two of the said three major areas. A typology of these combinations is shown in Table 2.9, where they are arranged in a tabular way, from North and Central American waters to Europe and the rest of the world, with a breakdown between inter- and intraregional repositionings. In a limited number of cases, the two strategies can even be combined in order to seize an optimal number of opportunities.

Deploying cruise ships on a global basis is very much an art, rather than a science. Each cruise line undertakes this exercise by taking into consideration a series of parameters varying from one line to another. Until recently, the size of the vessels was not a major limiting factor (except for the former *Norway* of Norwegian Cruise Line, now idle after a major technical incident). But cruise shipping has entered into the post-Panamax era, with more than 20 ships in service or on order unable because of their hull dimensions (especially their beam, but also their length for the larger of them) to transit the Panama Canal (Charlier, 2004). As sailing around South America is not a commercially viable option under normal circumstances, these megavessels cannot be redeployed as easily as the Panamax-sized ships forming the bulk of the world cruise fleet. In particular, the seasonal

Table 2.8.   Main seasonal cruise patterns for the main cruise markets.

First quarter	Second quarter	Third quarter	Fourth quarter
North America			
Caribbean	Caribbean	Caribbean	Caribbean
Caribbean	Caribbean/Alaska	Alaska	Caribbean
Caribbean	Caribbean/NE Atlantic	NE Atlantic	NE Atlantic/Caribbean
Caribbean	*Caribbean/Mediterranean*	*Mediterranean*	*Mediterranean/ Caribbean*
Caribbean	*Caribbean/Mediterranean*	*NW Europe*	*Mediterranean/ Caribbean*
Caribbean	*Caribbean/Mediterranean*	*NW Europe*	*NE Atlantic/Caribbean*
Mexican Riviera	Mexican Riviera	Mexican Riviera	Mexican Rivera
Mexican Riviera	Mexican Riviera/Alaska	Alaska	Mexican Riviera
Panama Canal	Panama Canal/Alaska	Alaska	Panama Canal
Asia-Pacific	*Asia-Pacific/Alaska*	*Alaska*	*Alaska/Asia-Pacific*
Europe			
Caribbean	*Caribbean/Mediterranean*	*Mediterranean*	*Mediterranean/ Caribbean*
Caribbean	*Caribbean/Mediterranean*	*NW Europe*	*Mediterranean/ Caribbean*
Caribbean	*Caribbean/Mediterranean*	*NW Europe*	*NE Atlantic/Caribbean*
Idle	Mediterranean	Mediterranean	Mediterranean
Mediterranean	Mediterranean	Mediterranean	Mediterranean
Mediterranean	Mediterranean/NW Europe	NW Europe	Mediterranean
Asia-Pacific	*Asia/Mediterranean*	*Mediterranean*	*Mediterranean/Asia*
Africa	*Africa/Mediterranean*	*Mediterranean*	*Mediterranean/Africa*
Africa	*Africa/Mediterranean*	*NW Europe*	*Mediterranean/Africa*
S. America	*S. America/Mediterranean*	*Mediterranean*	*Mediterranean/ S. America*
S. America	*S. America/Mediterranean*	*NW Europe*	*Mediterranean/ S. America*
Rest of the world			
Asia-Pacific	Asia-Pacific	Asia-Pacific	Asia-Pacific
Asia-Pacific	*Pacific/Alaska*	*Alaska*	*Alaska/Pacific*
Asia-Pacific	*Asia/Mediterranean*	*Mediterranean*	*Mediterranean/Asia*
Africa	*Africa/Mediterranean*	*Mediterranean*	*Mediterranean/Africa*
Africa	*Africa/Mediterranean*	*NW Europe*	*Mediterranean/Africa*
S. America	*S. America/Mediterranean*	*Mediterranean*	*Mediterranean/ S. America*
S. America	*S. America/Mediterranean*	*NW Europe*	*Mediterranean/ S. America*
Special cases			
Round the world	Variable	Variable	Variable
Other world cruises	Variable	Variable	Variable

Lines shown in italics imply interregional repositionings and appear therefore twice, for two markets.
Caribbean includes Bahamas, NE Atlantic includes Bermuda, Asia-Pacific includes Hawaii, Africa includes the Indian Ocean and South America includes Antarctica.
Source: Derived from the analysis above and based upon the authors' understanding of the market.

Table 2.9. Main inter- and intraregional repositioning patterns for the cruise industry.

Interregional repositionings	Intraregional repositionings
From and to North and Central America	**Within North and Central America**
Caribbean–Mediterranean (WB and EB)	Caribbean–Alaska (NB and SB)
Caribbean–NW Europe (mostly EB)	Caribbean–NE Atlantic (NB and SB)
Asia-Pacific–Alaska (EB and WB)	Panama Canal–Alaska (NB and EB)
NW Europe–NE Atlantic (WB only)	Mexican Riviera–Alaska (NB and EB)
To and from Europe	**Within Europe**
Caribbean–Mediterranean (EB and WB)	Mediterranean–NW Europe (NB and SB)
Caribbean–NW Europe (mostly EB)	
NW Europe–NE Atlantic (WB only)	
Asia-Pacific–Mediterranean (NB and SB)	
Africa–Mediterranean (NB and SB)	
S. America–Mediterranean (NB and EB)	
To and from the rest of the world	**Within the rest of the world**
Asia-Pacific–Alaska (EB and WB)	Within the Asia-Pacific area (SB and NB)
Asia-Pacific–Mediterranean (NB and SB)	
Africa–Mediterranean (NB and SB)	
S. America–Mediterranean (NB and EB)	

Caribbean includes Bahamas, NE Atlantic includes Bermuda, Asia-Pacific includes Hawaii, Africa includes the Indian Ocean and South America includes Antarctica.
EB = eastbound; NB = northbound; SB = southbound; WB = westbound.
Source: Derived from the analysis above and based upon the authors' understanding of the market.

repositionings between the Caribbean and Alaska are not possible, and this is a somewhat limiting factor for their owners, as they lose in geographical flexibility. The current and future deployment strategy for these post-Panamax cruise ships is one of the many avenues left open for research in the promising field of the geography of cruise shipping.

References

Arnold, P. and Charlier, J. (1999) Panorama contemporain de l'offre mondiale de croisière. *Acta Geographica* 120, 3–16.

Brogen, K. (2004) *Guide (and Pocket Guide) 2004: Ferry, Cruise and Ro-Ro Register Yearbook.* ShipPax Information, Halmstad.

Charlier, J. (1996) New geographical trends in cruise shipping. In: Roehl, W. (ed.) *Proceedings of the Second Environments for Tourism Conference.* University of Nevada's Department of Tourism, Las Vegas, Nevada, pp. 51–60.

Charlier, J. (1999) The seasonal factor in the geography of cruise shipping. *The Dock and Harbour Authority* 79, 2214–2219.

Charlier, J. (2000) An introduction to the geography of cruise shipping. In: Casteljon, R. and Charlier, J. (eds) *El Renacer de los Cruceros: La Mundializacion de los Negocios Turisticos y Maritimos.* Fundacion Portuaria, Madrid, pp. 17–24.

Charlier, J. (2004) The cruise shipping industry in the corporate mergers and the overpanamax eras: a comparison with the container shipping industry. *Belgeo* 4, 433–460.

Charlier, J. and Arnold, P. (1997) Les complémentarités saisonnières du marché mondial des croisières. *Bulletin de la Société Belge d'Etudes Géographiques* 66, 181–198.

CLIA (2004) *The Cruise Industry: An Overview.* Cruise Lines International Association, New York.

Hall, D. (2004) Ocean cruising: market dynamics, product responses and onshore impacts. In: Pinder, D. and Slack, B. (eds) *Shipping and Ports in the 21st Century. Globalisation, Technological Change and the Environment.* Routledge, London, pp. 99–130.

Marti, B. (1990) Geography and the cruise ship port selection process. *Maritime Policy and Management* 17, 157–164.

Marti, B. and Cartaya, S. (1996) Caribbean cruising: an analysis of competition among US homeports. *Maritime Policy and Management* 23, 15–25.

McCalla, R. (1998) An investigation into site and situation: cruise ship ports. *Tijdschrift voor Economische en Sociale Geografie* 89, 44–55.

Peisley, T. (1997) *The World Cruise Ship Industry to 2000*. Travel and Tourism Intelligence, London.

Peisley, T. (2004) *Global Changes in the Cruise Industry 2003–2010*. Seatrade, Colchester.

Ridolfi, G. (2000) The new myth of Ulysses: marine cruising in the Mediterranean Sea. In: Casteljon, R. and Charlier, J. (eds) *El Renacer de los Cruceros: La Mundializacion de los Negocios Turisticos y Maritimos*. Fundacion Portuaria, Madrid, pp. 137–154.

Ward, D. (2004) *Ocean Cruising and Cruise Ships 2004*. Berlitz Publishing, London.

Wild, P. and Dearing, J. (1999) *Maritime Tourism to the Year 2004*. G.P. Wild International, Haywards Heath.

Wild, P. and Dearing, J. (2000) Development of, and prospects for cruising in Europe. *Maritime Policy and Management* 27, 315–333.

Wild, P. and Dearing, J. (2004) *Outlook and New Opportunities for the Cruise Industry to 2014*. G.P. Wild International, Haywards Heath.

3 The Cruise Industry: An Industrial Organization Perspective

Andreas Papatheodorou

University of the Aegean, Department of Business Administration,
8 Michalon Street, Chios 82100, Greece

Introduction

Most policymakers in the developed world today seek actively to establish conditions for effective competition among existing and potential market participants. Competition is highly desirable by economists as it is believed to facilitate productive, allocative and dynamic efficiency. Moreover, effective rivalry among firms may lower prices and increase product quality to the benefit of consumers and social welfare. For these reasons, industrial economics has emerged as a special area of microeconomics to deal with the organization of the various economic sectors, the associated corporate practices and their role in promoting or hindering competition. Market regulation, deregulation, liberalization and the related institutional and legal frameworks are set within the sphere of industrial economics.

As the word 'industrial' reveals, this area of economics was originally preoccupied with the analysis of the secondary sector of the economy. Over time, however, the tertiary or service sector managed to dominate the economies of the developed world; hence, this sector received increasing attention by industrial economists. Still, the tourism industry remains rather unexplored in this context. First, it is usually argued that tourism does not encompass a solid base as an industry and is characterized as a conundrum, at least from the supply side (Eadington and Redman, 1991). Second, the 'pleasure' nature of the sector and the existence of many small traditional firms make tourism unjustifiably 'less serious' and 'not crucial' for some policymakers who find an industrial organization analysis pointless. None the less, tourism is one of the largest industries in the world today with a notable market structure, dualism (Papatheodorou, 2004): in addition to the multitude of niche players there are a small number of powerful companies, often with global reach, that operate profitably in concentrated markets. In this context, the recent wave of mergers and acquisitions in the hotel industry and the travel distribution system alerted analysts and policymakers. In terms of transport for tourism the focus has primarily been on the airline industry; this is occasionally thought as completely separate from tourism, despite the derived character of its demand. It was not until the recent merger story between Carnival and P&O Princess Cruises (POPC) that industrial economics have started exploring the cruise industry in more detail. Admittedly, the significance of the cruise industry in the tourism economy is much smaller compared to other sectors. Still, the nature of the product is unique as it combines fruitfully elements of both transport and hospitality. Moreover, the highly concentrated market structure at a global level (as discussed later) proves that the economics of cruising can only be poorly analysed by the traditional microeconomic setting of perfect competition.

Having the above in mind, this chapter aims at contributing to the literature by analysing the cruise sector from an industrial organization perspective. The second section deals with the nature of cruise economics, focusing on issues of scale and scope. It provides a rationale for pursuing large company size in the industry. The third section explores the dimensions of competition in the cruise sector in terms of prices, service/product characteristics and capacity. These dimensions are structurally interrelated with the cruise liners' size and scale. The fourth section focuses on barriers to market entry; in conjunction with the previous sections, it can explain the observed concentration in the industry. The chapter subsequently discusses issues of major importance in competition analysis, assessing the impact of market dominance, mergers and acquisitions; in this context, it deals with definitions and boundaries of product and geographical cruise markets. This framework offers the necessary background for the brief case study on the recent merger between Carnival and POPC. The last section concludes by providing directions for further research.

Nature of Cruise Product Economics

The cruise industry is characterized by significant economies of scale, i.e. average (unit) costs decrease as the scale of production becomes larger. Hence, it makes good commercial sense to pursue company magnification if market conditions are satisfactory. Drawing similarities with the airline industry, we can identify two main categories of such savings: economies of density and economies of fleet size. Regarding the former, successful cruise economics dictate the construction of mega cruise ships, usually of post-Panamax size, with a large number of cabins and lower births. In this way, the substantial fixed costs can be spread over many passengers resulting in lower unit costs; the break-even point can be achieved then at lower prices, which facilitates the financing of a cruise and makes the product more appealing and affordable to wider parts of the population.

To achieve such economies, however, high utilization of the cruise ship is necessary. Large berth capacity per ship may facilitate unit cost reduction in principle; none the less, if the general market conditions are unfavourable and the particular cruise product characteristics unappealing, large capacity might become a problem as the liner will fail to fill the ship with passengers. The issue becomes more serious when we consider time scale. Similarly to the airline and hotel industries, an unsold berth is lost for ever. None the less, while an unsold aircraft seat remains unused for a few hours and an unsold hotel bed is lost for a day, an unfilled berth may remain empty for a period of 1 or 2 weeks depending on the duration of the cruise. Moreover, there are substantial consumption complementarities losses when berths remain unsold. An air passenger might buy some duty-free goods on board and/or some basic beverages and meals in the case of no-frill carriers, but on-board consumption overall is usually somewhat low in monetary terms. In-house bills of hotel guests can be substantially higher because of restaurants, bars and other facilities in a hotel; however, guests are usually not spatially constrained and may have a wide array of alternative choices in the vicinity of their hotel. On the other hand, passengers on a cruise ship do not have any alternatives *ex post*, i.e. after their embarkation. While the cruise product is usually characterized by an all-inclusive mentality, there are great opportunities for extra revenue generation, such as the sale of duty-free goods in the ship's shopping malls, the sale of alcoholic drinks, photos, satellite telephony and other services (Dickinson and Vladimir, 1997). In essence, the opportunity cost of a lost passenger can be quite substantial; therefore, the cruise liners have a strong incentive to achieve very high utilization ratios even by engaging into heavy discounting – an issue discussed later in the chapter.

Turning now to economies of fleet size, these are derived by spreading fixed costs over a large number of cruise ships. More specifically, research, design, construction and training on a ship require substantial financial resources; fleet homogenization and ordering of a large class of ships reduces, therefore, unit costs. Similar argument can be made for outlays related to sales, administration, marketing and advertising. In addition, a large fleet endows a cruise liner with important bargaining power over purchases of fuel, bunker and food. Cost savings can be achieved then that may be passed to the consumer and/or contribute positively to the liner's profitability. A large fleet may also facilitate company expansion in many different geographical and product markets and thus establish a network of operations. The importance of such a network can be substantial given the integrated nature of cruising. In contrast to the airline industry, the ship is an end in itself, as the associated product combines transportation, lodging and catering. Moreover, there are synergies in terms of holiday package formation. For example, most people who depart from Miami or Barcelona for a cruise in the Caribbean and the Mediterranean Sea respectively do not live in the area: fly–cruise packages, therefore, are very popular and the whole idea of product bundling plays a major role in shaping competition as discussed later in the chapter. In many cases, cruises also offer excursions and other services as part of the overall package to make the product even more appealing.

Dimensions of Competition in the Cruise Industry

As for most goods and services, prices play a dominant role in competition among cruise companies and their products. In this context, yield or revenue management becomes very important for a liner's profitability. Yield management may be defined as 'the method employed by a company in setting price points to attain maximum revenue while ensuring that the ship sails with 100% capacity' (Competition Commission, 2002, p. 147). Following the principles of this method, many liners change their prices according to the time of booking compared to the actual date of the cruise. In some cases, early bookers are charged less and late ones more: the former are given financial incentives as they provide the company with money early in the season and help reduce the overall uncertainty over reservations; conversely, the latter are penalized as the company takes advantage of the limited choice in the market close to the cruise date. On the other hand, because an unsold berth is lost for ever, some cruise liners might decide to offer very low prices to last-minute bookers to ensure that the ship is filled with passengers.

These deep discounting policies, however, may have a negative effect. First, they can cause dissatisfaction among customers who booked the same product at much higher prices. To avoid any damage in reputation, therefore, these passengers might be offered a free cabin upgrade, if possible. Second, despite the gradual 'democratization' of the cruise industry, its product is still associated with Veblen effects and conspicuous consumption (Bagwell and Bernheim, 1996): some people choose cruising just because it is expensive as a signal of status and prosperity. Such people would want to socialize only with their peers in the confined environment of a ship (Cartwright and Baird, 1999) and would abstain from booking with a cruise liner that offers such discounting. Third and perhaps more serious, the gradual emergence of sophisticated, yet price-conscious, travellers who have developed a last-minute-booking mentality, can create financial turbulence in the cruise industry, destroying inventory planning and obliging liners to enter overt or secret price wars to retain their market share. The resulting deviations from the prices quoted in brochures open the sacks of Aeolus to manipulations by travel agents and the loss of transparency in transactions. For all these reasons, cruise liners might prefer not to enter the dangerous route of discounting; instead, they might relax price competition overall by exploring other dimensions of competition.

In fact, cruising is characterized by substantial heterogeneity similarly to other tourism products (Papatheodorou, 2001). This offers the opportunity to differentiate both vertically (in terms of quality) and horizontally (in terms of variety and offerings). There are four main dimensions of competition in this context: the ship itself, the time of the cruise, the itinerary and the booking. With respect to the ship, what seem to matter are its age and size (tonnage), the nationality and number of the crew and their ratio to passengers, the size and number of decks and the number of lower beds as a percentage of all berths. Emphasis is also put on the number of passengers (too few might be uninspiring, too many might cause congestion and commoditization), the cabin (size, outdoor or interior view, accommodation of single-traveller needs, private balcony), the existence and size of fitness centres (sauna, steam and massage facilities), cinema, library, dining rooms with full service and/or on a 24-hour basis, casino (and gaming tables), number and size of swimming pools (indoor and outdoor) and whirlpools (Competition Commission, 2002).

Regarding time, the main differentiating element is the actual date of the cruise, i.e. whether it is in low or high season: institutional factors in the origin (e.g. school holidays) and climatic conditions in the destination (e.g. periods of monsoons, dryness or heat waves) can shape substantially the popularity of a cruise. In terms of itinerary, cruises might take place in cold or warm waters (oceanic or inland); they may have a specific destination, visit a group of ports or just cruise around; and they can be associated with specific activities both on board (e.g. black tie dinner with the captain) and outdoor (e.g. trekking on a Caribbean island). All the above create diverse holiday experiences and can successfully provide extensive variety to the cruise product. Differentiation can also occur through the method of booking. The latter can be made directly over the telephone or through the Internet, and indirectly with the intermediation of a travel agent or as part of a wider package organized by a tour operator.

Price, therefore, is not the sole dimension of competition among cruise liners, which can successfully pursue rivalry on the characteristics of the product as such. It would, however, be an omission not to address a more subtle aspect of potential competition – available capacity. This refers first of all to the overall number of ships and berths of a cruise liner. A large company can build and spread its reputation more easily, especially if it is acknowledged as one of the market leaders with effective lobbying power. Capacity also refers to changing configurations within ships; in some cases, a cruise liner might decide to refurbish an existing ship adding more capacity and facilities; this may be occasionally used as a public relations exercise to boost the image of the company with an air of fleet modernization. Finally, capacity might be used to deter market entry as discussed in the following section.

Barriers to Entry in the Cruise Industry

Exploring barriers to entry is of major importance in industrial organization analysis. If such barriers are low, the market is contestable inducing firms to behave competitively to the benefit of consumers. In fact, what matters in this case is potential rather than actual competition. The threat of a new market entrant poses a credible threat to existing competitors to avoid exploitation of their market power; they might charge lower prices or provide a better product quality just to pre-empt newcomers in the market (Baumol, 1982). On the other hand, if barriers are high, the market is prone to oligopolization by a small number of firms. These may behave competitively, entering occasional price wars; on the other hand, they may realize their interdependence and agree explicitly or tacitly to share the market, form a cartel and abuse collectively their market power. This section of the chapter, therefore, identifies potential barriers in the cruise industry – it is a matter of empirical analysis, though, to assess their importance in limiting competition.

The first issue to consider is brand awareness and the associated reputation effects (European Commission, 2002). These are of major importance in tourism, which is a risk-averse activity often related to high expenditure – customers are prone, therefore, to trust and purchase a product from an established and financially robust company, which is unlikely to go bankrupt and/or leave them stranded in unknown destinations. Moreover, if customers are satisfied with a specific cruise liner and its brand(s), they will probably remain loyal and avoid switching to other competitors unless their favourite liner starts underperforming systematically or charging unreasonably high prices. In other words, reputation and successful branding may endow a cruise liner with market power. Not surprisingly, the market leaders in the global cruise industry, i.e. Carnival, POPC, Royal Caribbean Cruise Lines (RCCL) and the Star Group, are established and successful companies. Admittedly, new entrants have recently joined the cruise market, such as TUI, First Choice and Disney. These firms, however, are not exactly newcomers: they actually engage in brand stretching exploiting their reputation in other sectors of the tourism and leisure industries. For example, the World of TUI and First Choice are robust conglomerate tour operators while Disney has a dominant position in leisure and theme parks. Similarly, easyCruise, which started operations in 2005, aims at capitalizing on the success of low-cost branding pursued by easyJet, the British air carrier. It is, therefore, a matter to see in the future whether smaller cruise liners will manage to grow or whether new entrants with no reputation in other business activities will be successful in entering the market.

Second, the role of the travel distribution system in manipulating competition should be explicitly addressed. Unlike the air transport or the hotel sector, disintermediation in the cruise industry has not yet advanced substantially (European Commission, 2002). This is related to the nature of the product, which is more complicated and expensive than a simple purchase of a seat or a bed, and the characteristics of its patrons, who are usually people aged over 50 years with perhaps limited exposure to DIY packaging and Internet sales. Consequently, cruise liners have still strong incentives to pamper the travel agents, who act not only as ticket issuers but also as effective travel consultants in the industry (Dickinson and Vladimir, 1997). Moreover, the liners can use a number of practices to restrict access of other companies to the travel distribution system. For example, they may offer commission overrides to travel agents in exchange for directional selling. In this case, the latter agree to promote aggressively the products of the paying liner or conversely disregard the products of its rivals. A cruise company can further capitalize on such practices by acquiring a shareholding in a travel agent demanding *in extremis* exclusive dealing of the latter with the particular liner. Such 'most favoured customer' practices can misguide consumers and become anti-competitive, especially in the case of multiples, i.e. travel agents with a wide network of high-street outlets. Milder practices inducing directional selling include familiarization cruises and benefits in kind for travel agents. Cruise liners might also ask travel agents to sell the customer database of their rivals to them but avoid converse disclosures.

Third, relations between liners and tour operators should also be considered. The larger firms among the latter engage in vertical integration practices creating conglomerates that control airlines, hotels, travel agents and providers of ancillary services. Consequently, an agreement between a liner and a tour operator endows the former with a wide range of complementary products such as seats on charter carriers as part of a fly–cruise product bundle and the offering of excursions, which render the overall cruise experience more appealing. Such integrated product services may benefit the customer and therefore do not harm competition per se. None the less, such agreements can be anti-competitive if they contain clauses that restrict access to services by rival cruise liners. In essence, therefore, effective manipulation of the relations between the liners and the travel agents or the tour operators may result in significant barriers to entry for newcomers with no exposure to the distribution system and limited financial means to offer high commissions or sign commercial agreements.

In addition to brand awareness and relations with the travel distribution system, access to the cruise ship market is also important to discuss. In general, a newcomer does not need to enter the market with new vessels as there is a good secondary market for cruise ships; sunk costs associated with such transactions are, therefore, relatively low (European Commission, 2002). None the less, the alternative functionality of a cruise ship (asset specificity) as such is very limited as its conversion into a standard passenger or cargo vessel might not make good commercial sense, especially for post-panamax cruise ships. Therefore, although barriers to entry might be low, barriers to exit may be higher, especially in periods of economic recession when the demand for cruise ships is low. Still, the cruise industry is highly dynamic and exhibits substantial growth patterns in the longer term; consequently, any cruise liner is almost guaranteed to sell its ships at some stage – economic depreciation is of course an issue to consider in this context. Access to the ship market is also inevitably related to developments in the shipbuilders industry. A new ship might take up to 3 years to deliver and some liners might try to take advantage of this time lag to the detriment of their rivals. Similarly to the travel distribution system, a liner can enter into an agreement with a shipbuilder to restrict access to new ships by its rivals – if the remaining shipbuilders have orders to operate at full capacity in the coming years; such an agreement can have a real, negative impact on the other liners.

The fourth category of potential barriers to entry is access to ports and their associated facilities (Competition Commission, 2002).

Cruise liners may experience difficulty in gaining access to some destinations or ports (e.g. in Bermuda or in the Glacier Bay in Alaska), while popular embarkation ports may face problems of capacity constraints. This situation resembles access to airport slots in the airline industry: these may constitute very real market barriers, effectively foreclosing access to new entrants with no slots. Several systems exist regarding slot allocation (e.g. administrative rationing, swap in a market environment, albeit under a 'grey' regime regarding ownership of slots) with various advantages and caveats (Papatheodorou, 2003). Building of extra capacity in airports and ports may offer a solution but this might have negative environmental impacts – alternative solutions, therefore, should also be sought. A port of call might also engage in a secret deal with a large cruise liner offering concessions to fees or even subsidies; this may happen if the port belongs to a regional or local authority, which may believe strongly that such an agreement would be beneficial for reasons of regional development. Such deals, however, might be anti-competitive if they effectively foreclose port access in equal terms to other cruise liners.

The final issue to consider under barriers to entry is effective manipulation of available capacity. In other words, an incumbent cruise liner may decide to overinvest in the number of available ships and berths on offer to pre-empt credibly any potential market entry: any attempt by a newcomer will trigger a flood of extra capacity in the market by the incumbent, which will then result in low, unsustainable prices. Consequently, the newcomer will be made to exit; inductively, they will probably decide not to enter the market in the first place. Such strategies, however, are costly (Federal Trade Commission, 2002a). In fact, building a new ship or even buying a vessel from the secondary market can be expensive, and it might not make commercial sense to have it inactive and use it purely for reasons of entry deterrence: a cruise ship can only make money if it travels. Moreover, redeployment of ships to other markets where newcomers appear is not cheap either. First, these markets may be smaller and the inevitable reduction in prices and/or occupancy ratios will result in high opportunity costs, if the ships are redeployed from a large

and profitable market. Second, these markets may be characterized by a different style of cruising. Switching the nationality mix of passengers can be difficult because of variations in national tastes and preferences: e.g. the required ship configuration (hardware) and the service quality (software) expected by Americans are different from those expected by British or Germans (Competition Commission, 2002). Such required changes, therefore, can consume substantial monetary and time resources. Third, successful redeployment of a cruise ship may need re-branding, re-marketing and effective advertising; such sunk costs are not trivial and may discourage a cruise liner from engaging in strategic manipulation of capacity altogether.

Competition Analysis – Dominance and Mergers

Competition analysis can be greatly facilitated by the use of industrial and other benchmarks. In this context, it is important to define the market under examination. The term 'market' has been heuristically used in economics but essentially refers to 'a group of products that are reasonable substitutes for at least one good in the group and have limited interaction with the rest of the economy' (Yarrow, 2001). A realistic market definition should consider both demand- and supply-side substitution. It should study issues of horizontal and vertical differentiation and therefore step beyond the physical characteristics of the products involved (NERA, 2001).

In the cruise industry, we may identify two major markets: the product and the geography. Regarding the former, the essential question to ask is whether the appropriate definition should include the wider holiday market or focus solely on cruises; the latter may be further segmented into standard, premium and luxury. While the cruise sector is part of the wider leisure industry, there are distinctive characteristics that render it a separate market for reasons of competition analysis (European Commission, 2002). From the demand side, customer demographics in the cruise industry are usually different from the other leisure products: on average, customers are older (over 55 years), wealthier, of higher social class and travel without their children. From the supply side, cruise liners perceive only their peers as serious rivals, as shown by their yield management strategies and their brochure competition. On the other hand, further segmentation within the cruise market may be unnecessary as threshold points are usually blurred. In any case, however, oceanic cruises are different from rival and coastal ferry ones (European Commission, 2002). As for geographic markets, the question is whether to consider the international level or focus on national or even regional markets. While there are well-known global brands, markets seem to be national for reasons of legislation (e.g. framework of bookings, rights of cruising in the seas including cabotage), marketing and pricing policies, which usually differ among countries to fit consumer preferences and available income.

Dominance is a structural characteristic of the market. It refers to a situation where the leading firm possesses a very high market share. In cases of overall high market concentration, we might also encounter collective dominance, where the few leading firms constitute an effective oligopoly (Court of First Instance, 2002). Dominance is not a problem per se; its existence, however, is consistent with the abuse of market power. From this perspective, competition analysis should examine whether dominant firms affect the competitiveness of the market adversely and have the power to take corporate decisions independently of their competitors. Given the focus of competition authorities on safeguarding the public interest, emphasis here is on market conduct that is harmful to competition and the consumers and not to other competitors per se. For example, a cruise liner may manage to dominate the market because of successful service delivery to its customers. If this service is of good quality and priced competitively (and consequently there are no complaints by potential and actual tourists) then the cruise liner should not be penalized for its dominance: this would discourage efforts to innovate and succeed. Still, it is important to ensure 'fair play': the company should not raise unnecessary market entry (or exit) barriers or use non-transparent restrictive practices in its contractual arrangements with suppliers and distributors. After all, market competitiveness should always be examined from a dynamic perspective. If a dominant firm, for example, engages in predatory pricing, it harms its

competitors but benefits the customer in the short run. None the less, if the other competitors are made to exit the market in the longer term, the dominant firm may decide to abuse its market power without fear to the permanent detriment of the consumer.

Similar spirit should prevail on merger appraisal. Mergers between firms within the same supply chain (vertical merger) and especially in directly competing activities (horizontal merger), are of primary importance to consider (NERA, 1999). These are in many cases associated with production advantages. In particular, efficiency gains may arise from savings on fixed/sunk cost duplication. From a Schumpeterian perspective, these gains can be used for research on product innovation – the merged firms generate resources that were previously lost in destructive competition and loss of scale and scope economies (Schumpeter, 1996). Moreover, there are cases where a firm will go bankrupt unless taken over by a more powerful one – the merger prevents potentially unnecessary scraping of capacity and the lay-off of valuable labour. Competition analysis should, therefore, effectively weight any potential production gains from a merger in relation to the creation of a dominant position and the potential abuse of market power. Again, it is important that the consumer actually benefits from the production gains either directly (e.g. price reduction, quality improvement) and/or indirectly (e.g. product innovation). This can only happen if the merging firms are prevented from restricting competition.

Having the above in mind, we may now assess briefly the recent merger between Carnival and POPC decided in 2002. As shown in Table 3.1, the global cruise market is dominated by four large groups: Carnival, RCCL, POPC and the Star Group; their joint market share in terms of passengers is over 70%. All groups operate in various geographical markets with one or more companies to account for different consumer segments. They have ambitious plans for expansion up to 2006 both in terms of ships and berths to accommodate the expected increase in demand. To take advantage of scale economies, they also raise the berth-per-ship ratio. Market concentration will rise further in the future, as the merger between Carnival and POPC has been approved by the British,

Table 3.1. The Global Cruise Industry in 2001 and 2006.

Company	S 01	S 06	D%	B 01	B 06	D%	Pax 01	Share	Pax 06	Share	D%	B/S 01	B/S 06
Carnival	**46**	**60**	**30.43**	**61,404**	**93,866**	**52.87**	**3,229,345**	**28.69**	**4,909,763**	**32.04**	**52.04**	**1,335**	**1,564**
C. Cruise Lines	16	21	31.25	32,906	46,028	39.88	2,055,300		2,711,400		31.92	2,057	2,192
Holland America	10	15	50.00	13,352	21,598	61.76	590,830		992,030		67.90	1,335	1,440
Costa Crosiere	8	12	50.00	10,262	19,296	88.03	412,215		913,833		121.69	1,283	1,608
Cunard-Seabourn	8	8	0.00	4,128	6,188	49.90	133,200		254,700		91.22	516	774
Windstar	4	4	0.00	756	756	0.00	37,800		37,800		0.00	189	189
RCCL	**23**	**30**	**30.43**	**46,904**	**63,942**	**36.33**	**2,615,600**	**23.24**	**3,271,900**	**21.35**	**25.09**	**2,039**	**2,131**
RCI	15	21	40.00	32,896	47,984	45.87	1,915,200		2,474,000		29.18	2,193	2,285
Celebrity	8	9	12.50	14,008	15,958	13.92	700,400		797,900		13.92	1,751	1,773
POPC	**17**	**24**	**41.18**	**27,153**	**42,617**	**56.95**	**1,093,999**	**9.72**	**1,938,635**	**12.65**	**77.21**	**1,597**	**1,776**
Princess	10	12	20.00	18,020	24,590	36.46	864,850		1,193,350		37.98	1,802	2,049
P&O Cruises	4	5	25.00	5,817	9,621	65.39	124,849		343,545		175.17	1,454	1,924
P&O Holidays	1	1	0.00	1,200	1,200	0.00	36,000		36,000		0.00	1,200	1,200
Aida Cruises	1	5	400.00	1,816	6,906	280.29	59,300		356,740		501.59	1,816	1,381
Swan Hellenic	1	1	0.00	300	300	0.00	9,000		9,000		0.00	300	300
Star Group	**14**	**16**	**14.29**	**20,848**	**24,828**	**19.09**	**1,354,970**	**12.04**	**1,399,480**	**9.13**	**3.28**	**1,489**	**1,552**
Star Cruises	5	5	0.00	6,330	6,460	2.05	723,420		641,680		−11.30	1,266	1,292
NCL	7	8	14.29	12,666	14,866	17.37	566,800		676,800		19.41	1,809	1,858
Orient Lines	2	3	50.00	1,852	3,502	89.09	64,750		81,000		25.10	926	1,167
4 liners	**100**	**130**	**30.00**	**156,309**	**225,253**	**44.11**	**8,293,914**	**73.70**	**11,519,778**	**75.18**	**38.89**	**1,563**	**1,733**
All liners							**11,254,052**	**100.00**	**15,322,432**	**100.00**	**36.15**		

Note: S = ship; B = berth; Pax = passengers; D = difference.
Figures for 2006 are based on existing orders, options and letters of intent.
Source: Based on data collected by the Cruise Industry News Annual 2001 that appears in Competition Commission (2002).

European Union and US competition authorities (TravelMole, 2003). Originally, RCCL was expected to merge with POPC but Carnival reacted aggressively and eventually won the battle to create the largest cruise company in the world. The competition authorities judged that the relevant market is the cruise sector with national geographical boundaries. They agreed that the already high market concentration globally raised issues of anti-competitiveness but they decided that the proposed transactions would not result in abuse of dominance either unilaterally (by the newly merged firm) or in coordination with the other big players. They concluded that the various barriers to entry are rather low and do not discourage new market entry; still, there were some objections about the RCCL shareholding in First Choice, the British tour operator (Competition Commission, 2002). Finally, the competition authorities expect that the alleged efficiencies from the merger will outweigh any potential harm to competition. It should be noted, however, that not everybody agreed with these decisions. In fact, two US Commissioners issued a dissenting statement expressing their concerns (Federal Trade Commission, 2002b). Although the author of this chapter respects the decision of the competition authorities, he believes that the two Commissioners make also valid points.

Conclusions

This chapter has discussed issues in the cruise sector from an industrial organization perspective. An introduction on the importance of this approach was followed by the examination of the nature of the cruise product, the dimensions of competition in the industry and the various barriers to market entry. Subsequently, the analysis focused on competition highlighting the importance of dominance and merger investigations; the latter were further explored in the context of a brief case study on Carnival and POPC. Although chapter size limitation did not allow a full exposition of the relevant industrial economics argumentation, it is believed that the present analysis offers a good benchmark for understanding the major relevant issues in the cruise industry. Future research in the area should emphasize further the importance of synergistic links between cruising and the other tourism products and assess the impact of economic geography and regional development policies in shaping corporate market strategies and relations between cruise liners and port authorities.

References

Bagwell, L.S. and Bernheim B.D. (1996) Veblen effects in a theory of conspicuous consumption. *American Economic Review* 86, 349–373.

Baumol, W.J. (1982) Contestable markets: an uprising in the theory of industry structure. *American Economic Review* 72, 1–15.

Cartwright, R. and Baird, C. (1999) *The Development and Growth of the Cruise Industry*. Butterworth-Heinemann, Oxford, UK.

Competition Commission (2002) *P&O Princess Cruises Plc and Royal Caribbean Cruises Ltd: A Report on the Proposed Merger*. Competition Commission, London.

Court of First Instance (2002) *Annulment of Commission's Decision C (1999) 3022*. European Communities, Luxembourg.

Dickinson, B. and Vladimir, A. (1997) *Selling the Sea: An Inside Look at the Cruise Industry*. John Wiley & Sons, Chichester, UK.

Eadington, W.R. and Redman, M. (1991) Economics and tourism. *Annals of Tourism Research* 18(1), 41–56.

European Commission (2002) *Case No COMP/M.2706 – Carnival Corporation/P&O Princess. Regulation (EEC) No 4064/89 Merger Procedure*. European Commission, Brussels, 24 July.

Federal Trade Commission (2002a) *Statement of the Federal Trade Commission concerning Royal Caribbean Cruises Ltd/P&O Princess Cruises plc and Carnival Corporation/P&O Princess Cruises plc, FTC File No. 021 0041*. Federal Trade Commission, Washington, 4 October.

Federal Trade Commission (2002b) *Dissenting Statement of Commissioners Sheila F. Anthony and Mozelle W. Thompson regarding Royal Caribbean/Princess and Carnival/Princess, FTC File No. 021 0041*. Federal Trade Commission, Washington, 4 October.

National Economic Research Associates (1999) *Merger Appraisal in Oligopolistic Markets, Research Paper 19*, Office of Fair Trading, London.

National Economic Research Associates (2001) *The Role of Market Definition in Monopoly and Dominance Inquiries, Economic Discussion Paper 2*, Office of Fair Trading, London.

Papatheodorou, A. (2001) Why people travel to different places? *Annals of Tourism Research* 28(1), 164–179.

Papatheodorou, A. (2003) Do we need airport regulation? *Utilities Journal* 6(10), 35–37.

Papatheodorou, A. (2004) Exploring the evolution of tourism resorts. *Annals of Tourism Research* 31(1), 219–237.

Schumpeter, J.A. (1996) *Capitalism, Socialism and Democracy*. Routledge, London.

TravelMole (2003) *Princess Deal is Sealed*, 22 April. Available at: www.travelmole.com

Yarrow, G. (2001) *Economics of Market Definition*. Presentation in the Regulatory Policy Institute, Oxford.

4 Cruise Tourism and Organizational Culture: The Case for Occupational Communities

Darren Lee-Ross

*James Cook University, Faculty of Law, Business and Creative Arts,
School of Business, PO Box 6811, Cairns, QLD 4870, Australia*

Introduction

During the last 30 years, management researchers have focused their efforts on organizational culture in an attempt to understand behaviour in the workplace; this has not been the case in the cruise tourism sector (see Foster, 1986). The position remains little changed currently and Wood (2000, p. 347) comments that 'studies of cruise tourism remain practically non-existent'. The sector remains relatively free from substantial academic inquiry, particularly from a human resource perspective. In part, this is because the area is novel. From a management perspective, topics having an implicit impact on the single bottom line such as human resource management and sociological phenomena appear less popular than inquiries from an economic perspective (see Dwyer and Forsyth, 1998 and Zlotkowski, 2004 for a review of the economic impacts of cruise tourism). At best most related extant material is descriptive and only outlines the roles and duties of crew, with scant attention to on-board working conditions for hotel operations staff (e.g. see Cartwright and Baird, 1999; Mancini, 2000; Douglas and Douglas, 2004). This is surprising because anecdotal evidence suggests that working conditions on cruise ships are impoverished. Furthermore, these allegations are supported in a recent report from the International Transport Workers' Federation (ITWF) that claims that many cruise ship workers suffer sweatshop working practices, poor living conditions and intimidation from superiors (Wazir and Mathiason, 2002).

Academically, cruise tourism is yet to undergo significant study in the field of organizational behaviour and its related human resource management area. Therefore, this situation and sector present an almost unique opportunity for future research and a greater understanding of cruise ship workers.

Using a sociological perspective, this chapter aims to introduce a cultural framework for identifying and understanding the attitudes and behaviour of 'hospitality workers' on cruise ships. It tacitly advocates that an understanding of the phenomenon is the most effective way to comprehend and thus manage employees. Akin to Foster's notion of 'short-lived shipboard society . . . likely to form quickly because of the limiting effects of [cruise ships'] preexisting routines and past experience' (1986, p. 218), the overall proposition is that cruise hospitality workers may form themselves into an 'Occupational Community' (OC). This cultural grouping is a managerial challenge as it is a distinct organizational occurrence often running counter to official or 'espoused' cultures assumed to be present by managers and supervisors. An OC forms for a variety of work and organization-based reasons.

Notably, these groupings have been identified in the hospitality industry whose operations, working conditions and staff profiles are similar to those employed as hospitality workers on cruise ships.

The remainder of this chapter outlines some basic cultural constructs by way of introducing OCs, which themselves are understood as a specific type of organizational culture. The chapter proceeds by defining OCs and identifying organizational characteristics responsible for establishing and maintaining them. A case is then made for the likely existence of OCs on cruise ships by evaluating the heterogeneity of cruise ship workers. It continues by reviewing the organizational structure and characteristics of cruise ships, and identifying parallels between (hotel operations) working conditions on cruise ships and onshore hotels.

Towards an Understanding of Organizational Culture

Whilst there is debate about the exact nature of culture, most authors concur that it comprises a few key elements. Mullins (1996, p. 18) provides an adequate summary definition:

> [Culture is] a distinctive pattern of values and beliefs which are characteristic of a particular society or sub-group within that society . . . [with] values and beliefs . . . transmitted by previous generations through socialization.

Consistent with this generic definition, Robbins' idea of organization culture is also useful. He (2001, p. 510) considers it to be '[a] common perception held by the organization's members; a system of shared meaning'. Other definitions do not differ significantly from Robbins and this common perception of organizational culture usually underpins culture-oriented research.

In an attempt to establish a framework for understanding organizational cultures, some researchers have used a broad template to identify, map and apply features of society to structural elements of firms. This approach assumes that organizations are a reflection of society at large. Hofstede (1980) pioneered this method and identifies five macro-cultural dimensions as a basis for understanding organizational culture. His typology remains popular and is used

in many related studies (e.g. see Harvey, 1997; Rodrigues, 1997). Others such as Harrison (1972) and Handy (1978) have also made contributions to the area. Using the work of these two authors, Trompenaars (1993) categorizes organizational culture according to equity hierarchy and person–task orientation. These classifications are entitled 'Family' (power), 'Eiffel Tower' (role), 'Guided missile' (task-oriented), and 'Incubator' (fulfilment). Similar to Hofstede, Trompenaars suggests that when these metaphorical cultural classifications are identifiable in society at large, they are also characteristic of organizations.

Whilst the above constructs are useful as points of reference, they do little to explain other influences on the formation of organizational cultures. Robbins' perspective (2001) is helpful here because he identifies a number of important developmental elements including:

- history and location;
- environment and size;
- primary function and goals;
- management and staffing.

The above are summarized and reclassified according to Fig. 4.1.

Philosophy of founders concerns early culture formation when the organization is first established (cruise examples). Usually because the firm is so small, the vision of the owner is easily communicated to members. Selection criteria, reward systems, training development and so on are often formed around the founder's image. Top managers act in support of the founder's philosophy using symbols and techniques to reinforce key values, norms and goals of the firm. Socialization is again linked to the founder and typically manifests as self-sustaining myths and legends about how the firm began. Use is also made of specific company language, acronyms and rituals. In the case of the cruise tourism industry, white crew uniforms for summer and navy blue for winter and the 'captain's table', are examples of these artefacts (although the latter is becoming less important).

Whilst Fig. 4.1 allows an understanding of the process of culture formation in organizations it does not show the complexities and almost endless iterations of the procedure. Furthermore, it fails to acknowledge the perceptual and value differences between

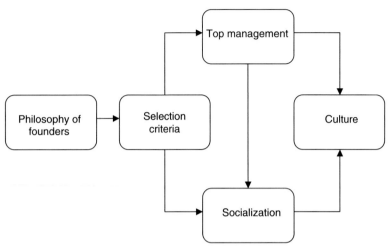

Fig. 4.1. Key elements affecting the formation of organizational culture. Source: Adapted from Robbins (2001, p. 523).

organizational members, particularly those of workers and managers or owners.

Schein's work (1985) on organizational culture acknowledges the subtlety of values, norms and perceptions and his model divides these variables into three areas. The first and lowest (the unconscious) of these is the 'basic assumptions' level, which determines how members perceive, think and feel. If managers are to inculcate a strong culture, this is the level at which they should focus because successful 'programming' allows subtle control measures to enter the employees' unconsciousness. Ethically, these training programmes are questionable but many companies use them including Disney and McDonalds.

Schein's second or 'values' category helps explain individual and group behaviour. Predetermined by what happens at the basic assumptions level, here shared norms and values may be observed. Those that dominate firms are known as 'core'. How significant these are amongst workers determines whether the overall organizational culture is said to be 'strong' or 'weak'. The final or 'artefacts' level, is characterized by visible clues of signs such as dress codes, physical design, adherence to rules and so on.

Schein's contribution (1985) to the literature is helpful because first, it can be used by management as a tool for establishing and

maintaining a specific organizational culture (at least notionally). Second and more important for this chapter is that members can now be understood as thinking feeling individuals with the choice to embrace (or not) company values. However, Schein (1985) discusses neither this nor the corollary of establishing 'alternative' cultures to any great extent. On the other hand, Legge (1995) considers this a vital issue and summarizes the lengthy related debate, and concludes that organizations are likely to have two cultures existing simultaneously. The first, the 'espoused' one, is that of management and relates to rules, regulations and other official protocols. The second is known as 'culture in practice' and is a summative outcome of social interaction in the workplace.

There is some debate as to which one is most important in forming and maintaining cultures in organizations. If culture is objective and formed on the basis of the founder's and top management's philosophy, values, rituals and so on, it becomes manageable. Alternatively, if it is something that just simply 'is' as a result of interaction in the workplace, it can at best only be described and interpreted (Lashley and Lee-Ross, 2003).

Despite the contributions made to organizational research by the above constructs, none goes uncriticized for alleged anomalies, errors and omissions. The one most pertinent for this chapter is the apparent failure of models to ascribe sufficient importance to the roles, duties and responsibilities of job incumbents. Consistent with this view, Gomez-Mejia (1984) considers that much culturally oriented research fails to consider the potential impact of the job itself or 'occupation' upon organizational culture. Some evidence suggests that certain jobs or occupations play a significant role in affecting organizational culture independent of broader societal characteristics. This is particularly likely where job holders perceive themselves to be different or in isolation from mainstream society, or where their job is considered unique or unusual in some way. This 'occupational' view of work is related to the 'social processing of information model' that focuses on the socializing effect of an individual's occupation or type of work (Gomez-Mejia, 1984). In other words, individuals in a particular occupation or work group are said to share more values in common than those in different occupations. This is chiefly because of the amount of similarity in work and social settings.

The occupational view of work is likely to be more common than might be first imagined, chiefly because it is an under-researched phenomenon. Nevertheless, OCs have been identified in a broad range of industries including fishermen (Weaver, 1977), forensic accountants (Lawrence, 1998) and engineers (Bechky, 2003), with similar observations in emergency services and some other professions. OCs have also been found in the hospitality industry with work-based cultures defined by strong worker group cohesion, for example, by Chivers (1971), Shamir (1975), Mars and Nicod (1984), Leinster (1985), Cameron (2001), Wood (1992) and Lee-Ross (1996).

Consistent with the view of Gomez-Mejia (1984), J. Pryce (2004, unpublished data) contends that the 'hospitality OC' extends beyond individual organizations to become a generalized overall industry sense of occupational identity. In a sense this pan-organizational or 'cosmopolitan' (Salaman, 1974) occupational culture is similar to Waters' notion (1995) of 'social' globalization where organizational culture becomes increasingly less constrained by geography or nationality. Wood (2000) comments that a central feature of globalization is the disembedding of social relations from their local context. Earlier, Sorkin (1992) and Zukin (1992) explained the process as one where 'place' becomes increasingly separated from historically rooted space. Similarly, a recent study of international hospitality workers (D. Lee-Ross, 2005) confirms that organizational culture driven by the occupational view of work pervades firms irrespective of nationality or geographical location. This is crucial because the social globalizing effect or cosmopolitan occupational view of work will almost certainly moderate relationships between organizational variables; in particular, questioning the a priori links between *antecedents* and organizational outcomes such as job satisfaction, commitment, productivity, labour turnover, absenteeism and so on. The following section defines and introduces some key characteristics of OCs.

Occupational communities

Salaman (1974, p. 19) defines OCs thus:

> People who are members of the same occupation, or who work together, have some sort of common life together and are to some extent separate from the rest of society.

Van Maanen and Barley's notion (1992, p. 281) is more comprehensive but basically replicates the above when they consider this phenomenon as:

> A group of people who consider themselves to be engaged in the same sort of work, whose identity is drawn from the work, who share with one another a set of values, norms and perspectives that apply to but extend beyond work-related matters and whose social relationships meld work and leisure.

Unlike the organizational or managerial perspective, the occupational approach ascribes the meaning of work to the person doing it. An OC is therefore a group of individuals who see themselves as members of the same occupation rather than people who are simply working together in the same organization (Berger, 1964). OCs have a number of defining characteristics, which are summarized in Table 4.1.

Table 4.1. Some defining characteristics of occupational communities.

Characteristic	Explanation
Jobs	Pervasive and set norms for activities outside workplace
Tasks	Set limits over non-work activities influencing friendship patterns, non-work norms and values
Non-job activities	Organization directly controls activities outside work like sleeping, eating and recreation
Job duration	Jobs of short duration may cause cultural norms and values to be constructed outside the workplace to be 'imported'
Skills – procedural and cognition – maintain the 'mystery' of certain jobs	It is one thing to know what to do (knowledge, facts and descriptions) but another knowing how to do it ('know-how')
Self-control	Reliance on ill-defined procedures and techniques to maintain 'mystery' and thus the community's self-control: once tasks are understood and codified, self-control of the group is reduced
Work-based friends, interests and hobbies	Members discuss work outside the organization, read work-related literature, have work-related hobbies, join work-related clubs, and their friends are also members of the Occupational Community

Source: Adapted from Goffman (1961), Salaman (1974), Kanter (1979), Child and Fulk (1982) and Van Maanen and Barley (1992).

Hirschmann (1970) and Pfeffer (1983) claim that 'self-control' is a key feature of OCs. The more self-control it enjoys, the more distinct is its culture. For OCs to develop and thrive, self-control must be maintained.

Additionally, certain conditions must be present or must 'surround' a job before OCs can exist. One important feature is that the organization is pervasive and sets norms or controls activities outside work such as sleeping, eating and recreation. The job therefore sets limits over non-work activities influencing friendship patterns, non-work norms and values. Factors that lessen the potential of occupational culture in practice include the imposition of organizational rules and regulations, high levels of pay, lengthy job tenure and jobs where skills can be codified or simplified thereby reducing any job-related mystique.

In short, OCs are social frameworks that create and sustain unique perspectives of work. They have identifiable characteristics that include task rituals, standards for acceptable behaviour, work codes surrounding routine practices, rituals, standards, codes and occupational self-control.

Structure and Working Conditions

Size and operations

The direct and indirect economic contribution of global cruise tourism is substantial and is currently the fastest growing sector of the tourism industry (Wood, 2000). Moreover, despite fluctuations in demand due to recent international military conflicts, Peisley (2002) forecasts that the worldwide capacity and passenger growth for cruise tourism by 2009 will increase by 66% and 58%, respectively. Regionally, cruise tourism also makes a sizeable contribution to wealth generation and job creation. For example, in Cairns Australia, recent plans to increase existing visits by P&O Cruises in 2005 by a factor of 16 are estimated to inject AUS$8 million into the region or AUS$500,000 per visit (Zlotkowski, 2004). The most popular cruise destination remains the Caribbean, which accounts for almost half of all passenger capacity. The South Pacific region, including Australian and New Zealand, attracts a smaller but still lucrative 1.3% of worldwide passenger capacity (Douglas and Douglas, 2004).

The cruise industry measures and classifies the size of its ships in three ways: (i) by gross registered tonnage (GRT); (ii) by number of state rooms; and (iii) by the number of passengers. Using both GRT and passenger capacity, cruisers can be classified as:

- Very small – under 10,000 GRT and under 200 passengers;
- Small – 10,000–20,000 GRT and 200–500 passengers;
- Medium – 20,000–50,000 GRT and 500–1200 passengers;
- Large – 50,000–70,000 GRT and 1200–2000 passengers;
- Megaship – 70,000 GRT or more and 2000 passengers or more (Mancini, 2000, p. 26).

This chapter contends that OCs are likely to form even in the 'small' and 'very small' categories because the marketed 'luxury' of many cruise ships means they employ many staff. Even a staff of 20 or so individuals is sufficient for an OC to become established. Typically, there is one employee for every two to three passengers (Wood, 2000).

Essentially, cruise ships comprise two areas: (i) the technical operations and navigation of the ship; and (ii) the hotel operations, which is larger. Broadly the workforce is represented by three categories: officers, staff and crew. The captain is at the top of the hierarchy and has a duty of care for all. He is assisted by the staff captain, chief engineer, hotel manager or chief purser and cruise director (Douglas and Douglas, 2004).

On-board hotel operations are similar to those in land-based firms. The organization of roles and jobs is 'traditional' and grouped by function and department with several levels of vertical hierarchy present. This apparent formality is mirrored in the overall governance of the cruise ship and the use of unequivocal cultural artefacts such as uniforms and strict disciplinary protocols. Dickinson and Vladimir (1997, pp. 72–73) go further and consider cruise ships as having a paramilitary structure. Figure 4.2 shows the typical structure of hotel operations on cruise ships.

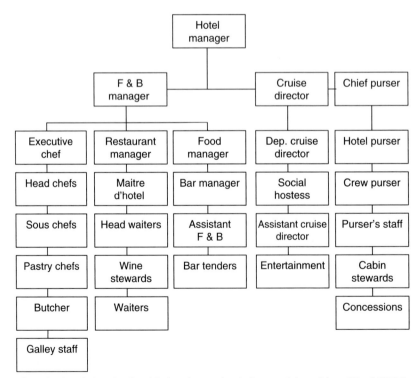

Fig. 4.2. Organizational chart (cruise ship hotel operations). Source: Adapted from Ward (1994).

Figure 4.2 shows the clear similarities between land- and cruise-based hotel operations. Indeed, with only a few obvious exceptions, departments and job classifications are the same. Therefore in the main, these roles are outlined below by exception.

The hotel manager, hotel director or chief purser has duties similar to a land-based hotel manager but with specialized understanding of cruise experience. Areas of responsibility include guest satisfaction, human resources, security, expenditures and revenues (Mancini, 2000). Typically, the hotel manager commands more employees than anyone else on board. These duties are onerous and may sometimes be divided into those for a chief purser (banker, information officer and complaint handler) and hotel manager (food and beverage management, hotel operations, entertainment, passenger services including retail outlets aboard and the casino). Specific departmental managers also look after these areas of distinct responsibility (Douglas and Douglas, 2004).

The job of the purser is similar to that of a front-desk manager or assistant manager. Duties include administration of everyday matters such as passenger accounts, mail, messages, printing, storage of valuables, immigration and customs requirements. Larger vessels have two of these: one looks after the crew and the other, the passengers. Usually the cruise director coordinates all entertainments and social events between crew and passengers (Mancini, 2000).

Workforce and Conditions

There is much evidence to suggest that the ethnicity of the cruise ship workforce is mixed. Some companies recruit from only one or two European countries, whereas others draw from a larger pan-Asian labour force from 40 or more countries. Douglas and Douglas (2004) note that most managerial and 'front-line' positions are held by Americans, Australians, Britons and various other European nationalities but concede that the ethnic mix of staff is becoming more diverse. Wood (2000) also points out that many more Europeans and North Americans tend to be employed in the luxury sector, particularly in 'front-line' service jobs. However,

increasingly the trend appears to be towards employing individuals from diverse national and cultural backgrounds. Despite some apparently prevalent ethnic demarcation, it would therefore seem reasonable to conclude that most hotel jobs are undertaken by a diverse group of employees. Wood's further comments (2000, p. 359) are useful in this context when he notes that on one particular cruise ship the diverse ethnicity of employees is marketed as part of the overall experience, with the cruise director referring to his workers as 'one big happy family'. He continues by concluding that

> . . . crews are probably the most globally diverse yet physically compact labour forces anywhere. They constitute a virtual laboratory for studying what a truly globalized labour force might look like and how global companies are responding to the challenge of recruiting and managing such diverse aggregations of workers.

> (Wood, 2000, p. 365)

Interestingly, this summary quote has another purpose in that the word 'challenge' suggests that managing a diverse workforce successfully may present some difficulties. Indeed, evidence implies that managers are not dealing with these challenges satisfactorily. It is this very combination of management styles, organizational structure and working conditions that enables and sustains OCs on cruise ships.

Figure 4.2 shows the structure of hotel operations to be formal, complex and hierarchical. According to Shamir (1975), Mullins (1996), Robbins (2001) and others, where these designs persist, so too does reliance upon the 'grapevine' or informal communication system for employees. Evidence from the hotel industry suggests that informal communication systems established as an alternative to official procedures are often symptomatic of OC presence (Lee-Ross, 1996).

Like the tall structural hierarchy on cruise ships, a heterogeneous workforce may also contribute to the existence of OCs because communication is likely to be impoverished between workers. The sheer diversity of workers and their backgrounds will also give rise to individuals with widely differing work attitudes. In these situations, managers often lead workers dispassionately and autocratically with a 'product' (rather than 'worker') focus in order to optimize a veneer of 'efficiency'. It is therefore likely that a strong OC will be established counter to employees embracing one overarching managerial vision. Invariably, this management style gives rise to poor working conditions and has also been identified by many researchers as a characteristic of the hospitality industry (see below). Poor working conditions are yet more enablers of OCs and some are discussed below.

Working conditions for hospitality staff onboard cruise ships are poor and pay is low. Moreover, many cruise ships from developed nations (notably North America) fly flags of convenience to deliberately circumvent their own labour laws. This means that employees invariably have few, if any, employment rights because cruise companies register in countries with impoverished labour protection laws (Wood, 2000; Douglas and Douglas, 2004). Moreover, according to Wazir and Mathiason (2002), an ITWF report accuses the cruise ship industry of exploiting almost all of its workers.

Despite the protection afforded workers by the International Labour Organization and International Maritime Organization, the federation claims that in practice employees have poor working conditions with little leisure time and are accommodated in unsatisfactory conditions. For example, employees often work 14–16-hour shifts, 7 days a week. The report also accuses many cruise ships of keeping a portion of employees' wages to ensure they do not abscond. Inspectors also found only two showers and one working toilet for 100 male and female employees with six staff expected to sleep in one

cabin. Moreover, the ITWF inspectorate also accuse management of bullying and imposing unrealistic codes of conduct, which, if transgressed, results in immediate dismissal (Douglas and Douglas, 2004). The ITWF summarized the situation by reporting that working conditions have not changed in decades. They allege that people are still underpaid, have few rights and many are reluctant to complain. A summary comparison of the main findings of the ITWF report is given in Table 4.2 and compared with characteristics of the hospitality industry.

Another key characteristic shared by both cruise ships and hotels is the provision of staff accommodation. This facility plays a crucial role in the formation of OCs. Wood (1992) identifies a linked issue and contends that the availability of accommodation attracts individuals with a similar 'orientation to work'. Furthermore, these employees are often marginalized by the rest of society because of their atypical backgrounds and the 'unusual' working conditions their occupations bestow. Therefore, there is a strong possibility that workers may 'turn inwards' and form informal self-supporting groups of their own. Cruise ships provide a situation where these relationships can be easily formed.

Whilst individually the above conditions may be unremarkable (in an OC sense), together they present a serious challenge for managers because incumbents' work attitudes and behaviour become difficult to predict. Furthermore, in tandem with other characteristics such as a tall organization hierarchy with formal and

Table 4.2. A summary comparison of working conditions between cruise ships and the hotel industry.

Cruise ships	Hotels
Insecure, short-term contracts	Job tenure – mainly seasonal, part-time and of short duration with an over-reliance on 'tipping', unofficial remuneration and other non-pecuniary benefits
Low wages with a reliance on 'tipping'	Low pay and inadequate training opportunities
Long intense working hours	Working long and 'unsocial' hours
Poor management practices, including bullying, favouritism and racial and gender discrimination	Despotic and non-supportive management styles
High labour turnover, inadequate training	High levels of labour turnover
Union-hostile employers resistant to collective bargaining	Virtual absence of trade unions

Source: Adapted from Douglas and Douglas (2004, p. 36).

specialized roles, a counter-culture (in practice) is likely to develop. Additionally, an ethnically diverse pool of employees and the actual nature of the work itself (consistent with the characteristics shown in Table 4.1) will almost certainly conspire to enable an OC amongst hotel workers on cruise ships.

Summary and Conclusions

Using an overarching organizational behaviour standpoint, this chapter has advanced the notion that hotel workers on cruise ships may be best understood in terms of a culture in practice. This was discussed first within the context of broader cultural constructs and eventually culminated in a notion of occupational communities. Examples of organizations where this type of cultural grouping exists were also presented with an emphasis on land-based hotels. An OC was defined and inherent characteristics were identified.

Based on these criteria, the likelihood of on-board OCs was advocated in terms of design characteristics of hotel operations and the typical nature of worker cohorts. Additionally, parallels were drawn between the working conditions of hotel workers on cruise ships and their land-based counterparts.

Cruise tourism has consistently outstripped other sectors of the industry in real terms during recent times. The field is new and so has understandably attracted less research interest than other more substantial areas. Most of the existing cruise-related investigations have economics as the underpinning discipline. However, because of the vast number of workers it employs absolutely and as a proportion of all individuals on-board ships, cruise tourism represents an important new area for sociological and management-based study.

In essence, the 'artificiality' of cruise ships, the short duration of trips and the operational consistency with land-based hotels presents a challenge for human resource managers. Inherent structural design characteristics of tall and formal hierarchies in the hotel area of cruise ships cause employees to behave in a certain but distinct manner. Furthermore, diverse ethnicity amongst staff and the nature of the jobs themselves also contribute to a spe-

cific cultural phenomenon known as an OC. This informal 'grouping' of workers is an example of a culture in practice that thrives when certain conditions prevail and often runs counter to the espoused culture thought to exist by management.

Some key enablers of OCs include provision of accommodation, pervasive jobs that impinge on 'off-duty' activities such as sleeping, eating and recreational activities, and short-term, temporary employment. Furthermore, impoverished working conditions and poor official communication channels also contribute to the formation of this culture in practice.

Recent evidence suggests that the effective management of hotel workers on cruise ships is at best mediocre. Clearly, improvements in working conditions would improve this situation. However, some characteristics of the work may be more difficult to change and so OCs remain likely. Therefore, the present notion of OCs could provide valuable insight into understanding more about hotel workers on cruise ships. Moreover, a better comprehension of apparently complex attitudes and behaviours should result in improved management policies and procedures. Also, the seemingly equivocal relationship between employees' attitudes, behaviour and outcomes such as job satisfaction, reduced labour turnover, high productivity and so on would become more predictable.

References

Bechky, B.A. (2003) Sharing meaning across occupational communities: the transformation of understanding on a production floor. *Organization Science* 14(3), 312–326.

Berger, P.L. (1964) *The Human Shape of Work*. Gateway, South Bend, Indiana.

Cameron, D. (2001) Chefs and occupational culture in a hotel chain: a grid group analysis. *Tourism and Hospitality Research* 3(2), 103–114.

Cartwright, R. and Baird, C. (1999) *The Development and Growth of the Cruise Industry*. Butterworth-Heinemann, Melbourne, Australia.

Child, J. and Fulk, J. (1982) Maintenance and occupational control: the case of professions. *Work and Occupations* 9, 155–192.

Chivers, T.S. (1971) Chefs and cooks. PhD thesis, University of London.

Dickinson, B. and Vladimir, A. (1997) *Selling the Sea: An Inside Look at the Cruise Industry*. John Wiley & Sons, New York.

Douglas, N. and Douglas, N. (2004) *The Cruise Experience*. Pearson Hospitality Press, New South Wales.

Dwyer, L. and Forsyth, P. (1998) Economic significance of cruise tourism. *Annals of Tourism Research* 25(2), 393–415.

Foster, G.M. (1986) South seas cruise: a case study of a short-lived society. *Annals of Tourism Research* 13, 215–238.

Goffman, E. (1961) *Encounters*. Bobbs-Merrill, Indianapolis, Indiana.

Gomez-Mejia, L.R. (1984) Effect of occupation on task related, contextual and job involvement orientation: a cross-cultural perspective. *Academy of Management Journal* 27(4), 706–720.

Handy, C.B. (1978) *The Gods of Management*. Penguin, London.

Harrison, R. (1972) How to describe your organization. *Harvard Business Review*, May/June, 119–128.

Harvey, F. (1997) National cultural differences in theory and practice: evaluating Hofstede's national cultural framework. *Information Technology and People* 10(2), 132–146.

Hirschmann, A.O. (1970) Exit, voice and loyalty: responses to decline in firms. *Organizations and States*. Harvard University Press, Cambridge, Massachusetts.

Hofstede, G. (1980) *Culture's Consequences: International Differences in Work-Related Values*. Sage, Beverly Hills, California.

Kanter, R.M. (1979) *Men and Women of the Corporation*. Basic Books, New York.

Lashley, C. and Lee-Ross, D. (2003) *Organization Behaviour for Leisure Services*. Butterworth-Heinemann, London.

Lawrence, T.B. (1998) Examining resources in an occupational community: reputation in Canadian forensic accounting. *Human Relations* 51(9), 1103–1132.

Lee-Ross, D. (1996) A study of attitudes and work motivation amongst seasonal hotel workers. Doctoral thesis, Anglia Polytechnic University, Cambridge.

Lee-Ross, D. (2005) Perceived job characteristics and internal work motivation: an exploratory cross-cultural analysis of the motivational antecedents of hotel workers in Mauritius and Australia. *Journal of Management Development* 24(3), 253–266.

Legge, K. (1996) *Human Resource Management: Rhetorics and Realities*. Macmillan Business, Basingstoke, Hampshire.

Leinster, C. (1985) Playing the tipping game. *Fortune Magazine* 112(11), 139–140.

Mancini, M. (2000) *Cruising: A Guide to the Cruise Line Industry*. Delmar, Albany, New York.

Mars, G. and Nicod, M. (1984) *The World of Waiters*. Allen & Unwin, London.

Mullins, L.J. (1996) *Management and Organisational Behaviour*, 4th edn. Pitman, London.

Peisley, T. (2002) The world cruise market update. *Travel and Tourism Analyst*, Mintel.

Pfeffer, J. (1983) Organizational demography. In: Cummings, L.L. and Staw, B.M. (eds) *Research in Organizational Behaviour*, Vol. 5. JAI press, Greenwich, Connecticut.

Robbins, S.F. (2001) *Organizational Behaviour*, 9th edn. Prentice-Hall, Upper Saddle River, New Jersey.

Rodrigues, C.A. (1997) Developing expatriates' cross-cultural sensitivity: cultures where 'your culture's OK' is really not OK. *Journal of Management Development* 16(9), 690–702.

Salaman, G. (1974) *Community and Occupation*. Cambridge University Press, Cambridge.

Schein, E.H. (1985) *Organizational Culture and Leadership*. Jossey-Bass, San Francisco, California.

Shamir, B. (1975) A study of working environments and attitudes to work of employees in a number of British hotels. PhD thesis, London School of Economics.

Sorkin, M. (1992) *Variations on a Theme Park: The New American City and The End of Public Space*. Hill & Wang, New York.

Trompenaars, F. (1993) *Riding the Waves of Culture*. Irwin, Chicago.

Van Maanen, J. and Barley, S.R. (1992) Occupational communities: culture and control in organizations. *Research in Organizational Behaviour* 6, 287–365.

Ward, D. (1994) *Berlitz Complete Guide to Cruising and Cruise Ships*. Berlitz publishing, New York.

Waters, M. (1995) *Globalization*. Routledge, London.

Wazir, B. and Mathiason, N. (2002) Cruise liner crews slave below decks. *Sunday Observer*, September 8. Available at: http://observer.guardian.co.uk/uk

Weaver, C.N. (1977) Occupational prestige as a factor in the net relationship between occupation and job satisfaction. *Personnel Psychology* 30(4), 607–623.

Wood, R.C. (1992) Deviants and misfits: hotel and catering labour and the marginal worker thesis. *International Journal of Hospitality Management* 11(3), 179–182.

Wood, R.E. (2000) Caribbean cruise tourism: globalization at sea. *Annals of Tourism Research* 27(2), 345–370.

Zlotkowski, M. (2004) Cruise boom. *The Cairns Post*, February 23, pp. 1–2.

Zukin, S. (1992) Postmodern urban landscapes: mapping culture and power. In: Lash, S. and Friedman, J. (eds) *Modernity and Identity*. Blackwell, Cambridge, pp. 221–247.

5 Cruise Sector Policy in a Tourism-dependent Island Destination: The Case of Bermuda

Victor B. Teye

Arizona State University, School of Community Resources and Development, PO Box 874703, Tempe, AZ 85287-4703, USA

Introduction

Relying on its favourable climate, natural beauty and post-Second World War period of relative political stability, as well as its proximity to the USA and Canada, Bermuda may be described as an upmarket microstate resort destination catering to high-income visitors. The destination (staying) visitor market segment that arrives by air is supplemented by a significant cruise visitor subsector. The purpose of this chapter is to describe the unique characteristics of Bermuda's cruise line industry and cruise sector policy, examine how this policy has evolved, discuss some of the factors that have driven, and continue to drive, this policy. The chapter concludes with a discussion of the implications for Bermuda as the North American cruise line industry continues to expand.

Salient Characteristics of Bermuda

Bermuda consists of about 150 small islands located in the Atlantic Ocean less than 1000 km east of the northeastern seaboard of the USA. Of the 20 islands that are inhabited, the seven largest that form a narrow chain connected by a land transportation system of bridges and causeways are collectively known as the Island of Bermuda. The total land area is about 55 km^2

with an estimated population of about 64,000 in 2002, giving a high population density of approximately 1127 persons per square kilometre. This figure compares with about 326 in Japan, 26 in the USA and 17 in the Bahamas. As a state with less than one million people, Bermuda is classified as a microstate (Wilkinson, 1989; Teye, 1992). This island nation is, however, not located in the Caribbean where there are 12 other island microstates. Instead, it is an isolated island destination in the North Atlantic Ocean. The significance of this location is that Bermuda, unlike most Caribbean islands to the south, is a single rather than a multiple cruise destination. Despite its small land mass and limited natural resource base, Bermuda has one of the highest per capita incomes in the world, estimated in 2000 at US$55,000 per capita gross domestic product (GDP) (Bermuda Government, 2003). This economic prosperity derives from the two sectors comprising international businesses and international tourism, the latter being the major source of income, public sector revenue, export revenue and employment.

Historical Context of the Role of Tourism in Bermuda's Economy

Tourism has been a source of economic activity in Bermuda since at least the early 1920s. The mainstay of the island economy was, however, agriculture. The expansion of the tourism sector was paralleled with corresponding decline in the importance of the agricultural economy, particularly onion export. For example, onion export decreased from 153,000 crates in 1914 to a mere 21,570 crates in 1925 – a steep decline in about 10 years. The situation with potato cultivation and its export further illustrates the rapid decline in the agriculture sector. Bermuda exported 91,777 barrels of potatoes in 1919 but in 6 short years, it exported only 23,448 barrels (Conlin, 1993). The contribution of agriculture to the domestic economy in 2001 was estimated at only US$5.6 million (Bermuda Government, 2003).

The growth of tourism and its expanding role in Bermuda's economy in the 1920s up to the end of the Second World War was enhanced and sustained by water transportation, specifically, passenger steamships. These forerunners to today's cruise ships carried wealthy American visitors from the north-eastern coastal cities of the USA including New York and Boston. Bermuda's mild winter climate and relative proximity to the USA encouraged and sustained the growth of tourism even during the Second World War (Conlin, 1993).

With the advent of air travel in the 1930s, islands to the south of Bermuda became accessible and, more importantly, increasingly popular with Americans and Canadians due to their guaranteed sunshine (Burkart and Medlik, 1981). This resulted in Bermuda shifting its emphasis to the summer months, which was more in line with the travel habits of middle- and upper-income Americans, the market segment that today still constitutes about 85% of all arrivals.

Between 1945 and around 1990 military considerations played a significant role in Bermuda's economy as well as the tourism industry. Experiences of the USA in the Pacific and Atlantic Oceans during the Second World War as well as the emerging needs of the new North Atlantic Treaty Organization (NATO) alliance were pivotal in these considerations. Bermuda was a colony of Great Britain and its ally, the US government, recognized the strategic importance of Bermuda's location in the Atlantic Ocean close to US mainland. It negotiated with Britain to build two naval bases on the island. Soon after, Canada also built a military base on the western end of the island near Somerset. On one of the US naval bases near St George, a runway was built that was capable of handling large commercial aircraft. It was later expanded to accommodate even larger aircraft such as the Boeing 747. These military activities injected significant capital into the island economy through large military infrastructure projects, military personnel payroll, hiring of Bermudian civilian workers and payments to the Bermuda government that brought in foreign investment. It also provided political stability, especially during the cold war. These activities also further consolidated Bermuda's present tourism industry. Indeed, until the US bases were closed and the land returned to Bermuda in the early 1990s, the only international airport was located technically on US property and as such was operated by the USA. Resulting from the closer relationships with the two North American countries, the island became even more attracted to American and Canadian visitors, to the extent that in the last 20 years the two markets have a combined average of 88% of total arrivals (Europe accounts for about 10%, of which arrivals from the UK represent about 9%). Arrivals by both cruise and air increased from 170,622 to 549,368 between 1961 and 1989. Tourist expenditure also increased from US$30.6 million to US$437.8 million during the same period (Archer, 1989a,b, 1999; Department of Tourism, 1990).

By the late 1980s, the leading role of tourism as the principal contributor to the Bermudian economy was being threatened by the International Business sector, which consists mostly of insurance businesses. For example, in 1976, the contribution of international businesses to the economy was only about US$80 million compared with about US$180 by the tourism sector. By 1998, the two sectors had reversed their roles: international business contributed US$758 million to the economy, compared with the US$472 million by tourism (Treaster, 1999). Tourism, however, continues to be the leading employer creating about 5800 direct employments in 2001 (Bermuda Government, 2003).

Evolution of Bermuda's Cruise Line Industry

Prior to the 1890s, visitors to Bermuda had been limited to a few adventurous types, the most famous of them being Mark Twain. It is to him that is attributed the infamous quotation: 'Bermuda is Paradise, but you have to go through Hell to get to it' (Zuill, 1973). He was referring to the fact that travelling to Bermuda entailed a generally uncomfortable sea voyage across the Gulf Stream in winter on relatively slow steamships. During this period, decades before the invention of the aircraft, visitor arrivals by steamships helped to lay the foundation of what was to become a vibrant economic sector and the backbone of Bermuda's economy well into the twenty-first century. The 'formal' origins of modern tourism in Bermuda are traced to the opening of Princess Hotel in Hamilton in 1885. The hotel, named after Britain's Princess Louise, is even today considered to be the grand dame of all Bermuda hotels. Recently renovated, it is presently classified as 'Bermuda's only urban luxury resort'. It marked the first significant investment in hospitality facilities to serve the strong and unmet needs of visitors arriving by sea. Accommodation requirements for these early tourists were in short supply to the extent that an old passenger vessel, SS *Trinidad*, was moored in Hamilton Harbor in 1905 for 6 weeks as a temporary 'floating' hotel, much to the chagrin of its 'guests' (Zuill, 1946).

As tourism increased before the First World War, the industry expanded to meet demand by an increasing number of visitors from the USA and Canada. The growth in Bermuda was closely linked to the early period of cruise ship travel in the Caribbean (Lawton and Butler, 1987). The critical link was provided by the Quebec Steamship Line, which not only held virtual monopoly on steamer service to Bermuda but was pioneering cruise travel to several Caribbean islands further to the south of Bermuda. Ober (1908, p. 453) provides some details about the services provided by the Quebec Steamship Line:

> The Quebec Line, which has given much attention to the development of tourist travel hither, and has provided as regular a service as the travel and traffic would warrant. Many have taken advantage of their excursion tickets, in the few past years, to visit these islands, and all speak with delight of the trip afforded by voyaging on such steamers as the 'Caribbee' which makes leisurely tour of the chain, stopping a few days at the principal ports, giving ample time to excursions into the country, providing a comfortable home for its passengers, to which they can retreat as occasion demands.

The Quebec Steamship Line's monopoly of routes to Bermuda came to an end by the onset of the First World War. The Royal Mail Packet Company and the Bermuda Atlantic Steamship Company both began to offer regular service out of New York and forced ticket prices to decline sharply. For instance, in 1910, the Bermuda Atlantic Steamship Company offered round trips to Bermuda for as little as US$10 (Zuill, 1946). This made cruise travel to Bermuda even more popular and accessible to a broader market segment. The fierce competition also led to the demise of the Quebec Steamship Company. Following the company's liquidation in 1919, its assets, including three ships (all named after fortifications in Bermuda: *Fort Hamilton*, *Fort St George*, and *Fort Victoria*), were acquired by the English Shipping entity, the Furness, Withy & Company.

Following the First World War, tourism grew dramatically in Bermuda. In 1920, 13,327 people visited the island. By 1930, visitors coming to stay in Bermuda's hotels had more than doubled to 46,463, in addition to the 7668 visitors who arrived as part of a sea voyage holiday. By 1937, regular visitors totalled 58,646 and a further 24,169 visitors came on cruises (Zuill, 1973). One of the principal forces driving tourism in Bermuda was the Furness, Withy & Company, which had made significant investments in land-based tourism infrastructure. In 1920, the company opened Bermudiana Hotel in Hamilton and several years later, Castle Harbor Hotel and Mid-Ocean Club, both in the Tucker's Town area in St George's parish. These hotels formed part of the company's integrated tourism plan in which it owned and operated both the means of transportation to Bermuda and the accommodations and amenities for visitors at the destination. It was during this period that Bermuda consolidated its position and reputation as an upscale destination by catering to 'well-to-do American[s]' (Zuill, 1973).

It is important to understand some of the forces at work during this period and not only how they establish Bermuda as a popular destination to the extent that it became necessary to adopt policies for the cruise sector. Passage of the Volstead Act in 1919 ushered in the prohibition era until the ban was repealed in 1934. The Act prohibited the sale of alcohol in the USA but also facilitated what has come to be known as the era

of 'booze cruises' that 'proved to be highly profitable to steamship companies and their clientele' (Lawton and Butler, 1987, p. 331) because
as McAllester (1932) pointed out:

> The presence of a legitimate bar on board ship,
> with the opportunity of enjoying healthful
> refreshment with congenial and decent company,
> adds something to life and takes away the
> restraint and snoppers [sic] and all that goes
> along with prohibition.

Bermuda's proximity to the USA provided
advantages over Caribbean destinations to the
south. For example, the Furness Line was able
to offer express ship service from New York to
Bermuda in less than 36 hours (Owen, 1979).
Lawton and Butler (1987, p. 334) also concluded:

> From its inception until the early 1930s the
> cruise-ship industry had therefore been an
> overwhelmingly North American phenomenon.
> Its major impact in the Caribbean before 1943
> was restricted to the more northerly ports of
> Nassau, Havana, Hamilton and St George,
> Bermuda.

The Second World War and the rapid growth of
the aviation industry had further tremendous
impact on Bermuda's tourism industry as well
as the steam and passenger ship transportation
systems. In 1938, Pan American Airways
teamed up with Imperial Airways (a predecessor
of BOAC) to offer flying boat air service to the
island. Between 1949 and 1979, tourist arrivals
in Bermuda grew from 54,899 to 599,145.
During this period, three trends were evident:
the percentage of air arrivals increased, the percentage of cruise ship arrivals increased dramatically and traditional arrivals by ship
decreased significantly. For example, in 1949 air
accounted for 51% of total arrivals, whereas
conventional ship arrivals were 42% of the
total. In that year, cruise arrivals were just 7% of
the total. Until 1956, conventional ship arrivals
continued to be greater than cruise arrivals,
while air arrivals continued to grow. In 1956,
air accounted for 69% and conventional ship
arrivals accounted for 18% with cruise accounting for 13% of the 109,131 visitors that year
(Conlin, 1993).

After 1956, the trend towards air and cruise
arrivals continued, but were accompanied by

a continuing decrease in conventional ship
arrivals. By 1979, air accounted for 75%, cruise
24%, with only 686 people arriving by ship out
of the total of 599,145 visitors. Table 5.1 shows
the growth in tourism and historical trend in visitor arrivals to Bermuda for air, ship and cruise
ships between 1949 and 1979.

Bermuda's Cruise Line Policies

It can be concluded from the previous section
that the steamship industry, followed later by the
cruise line industry, played significant roles in
the development of Bermuda's tourism industry.
While Table 5.1 shows the growth in both cruise
ship and air arrivals during the period
1949–1979, Tables 5.2 and 5.3 show the comparative situations for arrivals by the two modes
of transportation during the more recent period
1989–2003.

Bermuda's contemporary cruise line industry can be described as unique compared with
other island cruise destinations, particularly in
the Caribbean:

• It is a single destination, rather than the multiple destinations that involve several ports of
  call in regions such as the Caribbean, Hawaii,
  the Mediterranean or Northern Europe/
  Scandinavia.
• The cruise ships dock in Bermuda for 3–4
  days on their 7-day itinerary from the north-
  eastern US ports of New York, Boston and
  Baltimore. In essence, they serve as floating
  hotels, supplementing the accommodation
  or lodging inventory of the island. This also
  means that passengers are tourists, not
  excursionists, since they spend more than
  24 hours in the country. Deriving from this
  fact, their impacts (economic, social and
  environmental) tend to be substantial on
  this island microstate.
• The cruise season is short, from April to
  October. While the annual total air arrivals
  are distributed throughout the year, total
  cruise arrivals are concentrated in 7 months'
  time, as clearly indicated in Table 5.4.
• Bermuda has three ports: St George (the
  former capital city); Hamilton, which is the
  commercial and administrative capital; and

Table 5.1.   Tourist arrivals in Bermuda between 1949 and 1979.

Year	Air	Ship	Cruise	Total
1949	28,258	23,231	3,410	54,899
1950	37,609	26,558	3,649	67,816
1951	57,185	23,745	11,136	92,066
1952	57,394	25,089	10,583	93,066
1953	65,591	24,096	13,814	103,501
1954	68,408	23,360	15,036	106,804
1955	74,802	21,128	14,721	110,651
1956	75,211	19,809	14,111	109,131
1957	86,313	16,256	18,415	120,984
1958	92,479	15,960	22,382	130,821
1959	96,682	12,833	32,815	142,330
1960	99,295	11,992	40,119	151,406
1961	113,280	10,371	46,971	170,622
1962	124,098	9,173	59,531	192,802
1963	132,689	8,954	62,538	204,181
1964	137,985	7,122	43,885	188,992
1965	180,752	6,513	50,517	237,782
1966	205,534	5,064	46,174	256,772
1967	235,392	1,771	44,004	281,167
1968	265,378	2,064	63,937	331,379
1969	279,262	1,725	89,933	370,920
1970	301,604	1,172	86,138	388,914
1971	318,371	939	93,637	412,947
1972	338,574	1,208	81,168	420,950
1973	384,474	767	82,015	467,256
1974	420,089	1,132	110,347	531,568
1975	411,783	739	99,602	512,124
1976	449,359	678	108,837	558,874
1977	439,454	1,571	131,830	572,855
1978	419,028	756	131,682	551,466
1979	458,095	686	140,364	599,145

Source: A Statistical Review 1980–1989; cited in Conlin (1993).

the Dockyards at the west end of the island. These three ports allow ships to rotate while in the country, thereby spatially spreading visitor numbers across the east, west and central portions of the island.

- The cruise itinerary and market segments have remained nearly the same for more than a century. The ships depart from the north-eastern ports of the USA and passengers are predominantly from the USA as indicated by the breakdown of origin in Table 5.5.

Bermuda's cruise sector policy has evolved since the early 1980s. The policy derived from the small spatial size of the island (55 km²); small population (64,000); very high resident population density (1127 persons per square kilometre); a rapidly growing tourist industry with increasing arrivals by both air and cruise ships; a fairly distinct seasonality with peak concentration of tourists during the summer months when visitor/resident ratios are very high. For example, during June and July, total visitor numbers sometimes exceeded the total number of residents. This situation added significantly to the already high population density noted above:

When tourist arrivals reached the highest ever-recorded figure of 609,556 in 1980, Bermuda realized the urgent need for a tourism policy that also includes specific policy measures for the cruise sector. The policy that

Table 5.2. Tourist arrivals in Bermuda between 1989 and 1999.

Mode	1989	1990	1991	1992	1993	1994	1995	1996	1997	1998	1999
Air	418,352	434,909	386,178	375,231	413,134	416,990	387,556	391,450	380,795	369,530	355,260
Cruise	131,322	112,551	128,151	131,006	153,944	172,865	169,712	180,226	181,885	188,331	195,586
Total	549,674	547,460	514,329	506,237	567,078	589,855	557,268	571,676	562,680	557,861	550,846

Source: Bermuda Government (2003).

Table 5.3. Tourist arrivals in Bermuda between 2000 and 2003.

Mode	2000	2001	2002	2003
Air	332,191	278,153	284,024	256,579
Cruise	207,881	179,960	200,065	226,097
Total	540,072	458,113	484,089	482,676

Source: Bermuda Government (2004).

evolved essentially stated that: The number of cruise passengers to be restricted to 2500 on ships alongside Hamilton at any one time and, in any event, the number of vessels to be limited to two at any one time. One ship at anchor in the Great Sound at any one time and an additional vessel at the West End when it is completed. Two ships berthed alongside in St George at any one time and one anchored elsewhere.

(Bermuda Department of Tourism, 1989)

The overall effect was to limit the number of cruise ships in Bermuda's ports at any one time to a total of seven. The key elements of the cruise sector policy were:

- Total cruise arrivals would be limited to 120,000 visitors during the May to October period with four regularly scheduled vessels and a maximum of 12 occasional cruise ship dockings.
- There would be no weekend cruise calls from Friday afternoon until Monday morning.
- Occasional cruise ship calls will be encouraged to visit Bermuda during the off season from November to April.
- Scheduled service would also be explored, if possible, during the November to April off-season period.

The policy was expected to:

- reduce the demand on the infrastructure, particularly in the capital city of Hamilton;
- retain the quality of life as a result of the above and by allowing for a common period of rest for Bermudians on the weekend, with a slower pace of life and a relatively quieter environment;
- spread cruise arrivals throughout the year, particularly in the off season;
- maintain Bermuda's image as a quality destination.

Community Contribution to Cruise Policy Debate

The cruise sector policy described above was derived from community participation in extensive discussions, especially in the media. The tourism community consisting of residents, tourism stakeholders such as the hotel association, tourism merchants, travel agents, as well as those in the cruise ship industry played a significant role in the debate that contributed to government policy. The opening of the third port at the West End Dockyards was supposed to spread cruise passengers across the island. Weekend cruise ship dockings were also aimed at accomplishing the objective of spreading visitor numbers over a 7-day period. Spreading out of arrivals failed to accomplish the intended outcome, since both cruise and air visitors still converged in the commercial center of Hamilton. Cruise ship dockings on weekends, as well as the convergence of residents and tourists on the island's Central Business District (CDB), were at the centre of the debate due to their implications for the overall quality of life. The city of Hamilton dominates every aspect of Bermuda's socio-economic life, and therefore factors into every major decision. Today the city of Hamilton houses only 3% of the island's population; however, it accounts for 85% of Bermuda's retail floor space and 95% of office floor space. In addition, Hamilton is the seat of government, location of administrative offices and major port for cruise lines, as well as the main cargo port for the island's vital external trade. Finally, the city of Hamilton is the prime centre for entertainment on the island, and houses terminals for public buses, ferries and taxis. All these functions combine into a strong pull factor drawing vehicular and pedestrian traffic into Hamilton.

Bermuda also has a no-car-rental policy and allows only one car per family. As a result, the majority of air and cruise visitors rent mopeds, while families that require additional transportation also utilize mopeds and motorcycles. Traffic problems, therefore, were central to the discussions in the cruise sector policy. The traffic issues centred on three factors: residents commuting to and from work, particularly in Hamilton; tourists travelling around the island, especially on their cycles; and the movement of freight, especially containers from the three

Table 5.4. Cruise ship arrivals by month from 1991 to 2001.

Year	Total	Jan	Feb	Mar	Apr	May	June	July	Aug	Sept	Oct	Nov	Dec
1991	128,151	–	–	899	6,844	18,675	19,381	24,733	22,574	19,540	14,666	839	–
1992	131,006	–	–	1,858	10,342	17,566	20,722	20,926	24,139	19,861	14,267	1,312	13
1993	153,944	–	–	–	9,876	24,603	25,060	22,820	30,316	20,284	19,176	1,809	–
1994	172,865	–	–	–	10,476	28,870	24,583	26,596	37,239	22,391	22,710	–	–
1995	169,712	–	–	–	7,410	34,123	23,393	31,203	28,305	21,423	22,188	1,667	–
1996	180,226	–	–	112	15,107	25,998	26,651	34,824	28,215	24,860	24,459	–	–
1997	181,855	–	–	–	16,176	24,930	30,317	33,538	29,623	29,098	16,544	1,659	–
1998	188,331	–	–	451	12,857	26,029	33,390	29,092	34,730	27,899	17,326	5,522	1,035
1999	195,586	–	–	917	14,688	30,234	31,593	32,267	41,819	21,296	22,433	339	–
2000	209,727	–	668	–	10,751	35,778	31,431	35,645	37,174	27,569	30,711	–	–
2001	179,435	–	411	717	8,598	30,097	23,374	34,997	29,430	25,918	25,893	–	–

Source: Bermuda Government (2003).

Table 5.5. Cruise ship arrivals by origin from 1991 to 2001.

Year	Total	Country of embarkation				
		USA	Canada	UK	Other Europe	Other
1991	128,151	120,643	2,816	1,990	2,115	587
1992	131,006	121,947	3,272	2,461	2,139	1,187
1993	153,944	143,981	3,703	2,099	2,283	1,878
1994	172,865	161,410	4,049	3,345	1,857	2,204
1995	169,712	156,977	3,029	3,755	3,268	2,683
1996	180,226	164,641	4,437	5,343	3,527	2,278
1997	181,885	168,219	3,794	5,662	2,405	1,805
1998	188,331	177,420	2,479	4,111	3,102	1,219
1999	195,586	184,533	2,926	3,232	2,749	2,146
2000	209,726	195,526	4,024	5,279	2,177	2,720
2001	179,435	168,222	3,136	4,555	1,951	1,571

Source: Bermuda Government (2003).

ports (Teye, 1992). Since the transportation problems are accentuated during the main tourist season from May to October, traffic management measures affect the tourist industry, including the cruise sector.

Cruise ships can overwhelm island destinations because of the large number of visitors that disembark. Cruise ships calling at Bermuda ports normally operate 7-day runs from the north-east coast of the USA. The industry is unique in Bermuda because, as discussed earlier, the ships dock for about 3–4 days instead of morning arrival and same-day evening departure, as is the normal practice on most Caribbean islands. Hence, the cruise ships in Bermuda literally become docked resorts, supplementing the fixed land tourist accommodation stock.

Against this background, a watershed year was 1987 when cruise arrivals during the period July to August exceeded 80,000 (Riley, 1997). On any given day there were as many as 4500 cruise passengers on the island in addition to the 15,000 air tourists. Community reaction to the situation was intense. A popular forum is the 'Letters to the Editor' column of the local daily newspaper, *Royal Gazette*. Residents as well as visitors used this medium to vent their concerns about the large number of tourists converging on the island. One such letter from a resident echoed the sentiment of many: 'I detest the cruise boat syndrome slowly driving our regular visitors to other destinations' (*Royal Gazette*, 1987, p. 4a). A prominent businessman accused the government of misleading the public with the 'numbers game'

and complained that there were too many cruise ship visitors for the island to service (*Royal Gazette*, 1987, p. 1d). A visiting travel agent made use of the column to add his voice: 'Can Bermuda adequately support the increasing numbers of tourists, especially the ones that come on cruise ships? After talking to several locals, I'm not sure that bigger is better' (*Royal Gazette*, 1987, p. 4c).

The severest criticism, however, came from the island's hoteliers. In a letter to the Tourism Minister, they stated that too many cruise ship visitors endangered the island's advertised image as a quality destination. They further stated that 'the infrastructure, whether it be restaurants, transportation or shopping and other businesses have great difficulty in offering efficient and hospitable services during peak demand' (*Royal Gazette*, 1987, p. 1d). They also expressed the view that cruise ships were in direct competition with hotels.

Absent from the debate was the perceptions of cruise ship visitors. The government therefore commissioned a study among visitors in July and August of 1987. It found that 'Bermuda is perceived very positively by most visitors with overcrowding being only a very minor concern' (FCB/Leber Katz Partners, 1988, unpublished data).

The cruise policy was finally announced in early 1989. Since then, cruise ship arrivals have declined from 131,322 in 1989 to 112,551 in 1990 (see Table 5.2). It gradually started increasing from 153,994 in 1993 to the estimated 226,097 arrivals in 2003 (see Table 5.3).

Conclusion

The cruise line industry laid the foundation for Bermuda's tourism industry from its early days. Its origins were also linked to the Caribbean cruise line industry, which today represents half of the global cruise ship activity. Despite the intense competition with the well-established destinations as well as the new emerging ports of call in the Caribbean, Bermuda's cruise line industry has maintained most of its unique historical attributes. It is a single destination; the most important market segment is from north-eastern USA; the ships dock for 3–4 days, and act as docked resorts supplementing the fixed land hotel inventory. The cruise sector policy that emerged is a testimony to the importance of community participation in tourism development, sustainable development, enhancement of quality of life and the leading role of the government. The challenge for Bermuda is to maintain these policy measures in the face of declining air arrivals, the tendency towards mega cruise ships, competition from established destinations in the Caribbean, as well as emerging ports of call not only in that region but in Central and South America.

References

Archer, B. (1989a) *The Bermudian Economy: An Impact Study*. Report of an independent study carried out for the Ministry of Finance, Government of Bermuda, Hamilton.

Archer, B. (1989b) *The Contribution of Tourism to the Economy of Bermuda, 1988* (Ministry of Finance). Government of Bermuda, Pembroke, Bermuda.

Archer, B. (1999) *The Contribution of Tourism to the Economy of Bermuda, 1998* (Ministry of Finance). Government of Bermuda, Pembroke, Bermuda.

Bermuda Department of Tourism (1989) *Staff Handbook*. Hamilton, Bermuda.

Bermuda Government (2003) *Facts & Figures 2002*. Department of Statistics, Cabinet Office, Bermuda.

Bermuda Government (2004) *Bermuda 2003 Economic Annual Review*. Ministry of Finance, Pembrooke, Bermuda.

Burkart, A.J. and Medlick, S. (1981) *Tourism: Past, Present and Future*. Heinemann-Butterworth, London.

Conlin, M.V. (1993) Bermuda tourism: a case study in single segmentation. *Journal of Travel & Tourism Marketing* 1(4), 99–112.

Department of Tourism (1990) Statistical Department, Government of Bermuda, Bermuda.

Lawton, L.J. and Butler, R.W. (1987) Cruise ship industry-patterns in the Caribbean 1880–1986. *Tourism Management* 8, 329–343.

McAllester, E.A. (1932) Cogent reasons: laws, unions and prohibition blamed for decline of our shipping. *New York Times*, 8 January, p. 20.

Ober, F.A. (1908) *A Guide to West Indies and Bermudas*. Dodd, Mead & Co., New York, p. 38.

Owen, C. (1979) *The Grand Days of Travel*. Webb and Bower, Exeter, UK.

Riley, C.W. (1997) Missing the mark. *The Bermuda Magazine* Fall, 57–60.

Teye, V.B. (1992) Land transportation and tourism in Bermuda. *Tourism Management* 12, 395–405.

Royal Gazette (1987) Letters to the editor. 9 May, 29 June, 3 July, 8 July, 21 July, 7 August.

Treaster, J.B. (1999) Bermuda takes the risk from tourist paradise to heaven for insurance business. *New York Times*, 28 April, pp. C1–C6.

Wilkinson, P.F. (1989) Strategies for tourism in island microstates. *Annals of Tourism Research* 16, 153–177.

Zuill, W.S. (1946) *Bermuda Journey*. The University Press, Glasgow, Scotland.

Zuill, W.S. (1973) *The Story of Bermuda and Her People*. Macmillan, London.

Part II

Demand: Cruise Passengers and Marketing

Introduction

Part II comprises seven chapters related to the insatiable demand for cruising. It includes examination of passenger perceptions of value, trends in the North American market, and passenger expectations and activities. These contributions are supported by the importance of the visual image in destination marketing, the important role of interpretation by cruise guides and the need for a standardized ship-rating system. This part is completed by a cultural studies approach to understanding the ocean cruising phenomenon.

In Chapter 6, Jim Petrick and Xiang (Robert) Li (USA) examine issues relating to cruise passenger perceptions of value and offer new insight into the ramifications of using price discounts to attract cruise passengers. They suggest that a thorough understanding of customers' perceptions of value is one of the keys to cruise management success.

In Chapter 7, Allan Miller and William Grazer (USA) outline the trends of the cruise tourism segment in the North American market and suggest that growth will come from both repeat and new cruisers. They also suggest that it is up to the cruise lines to maintain an excellent level of service and deliver an outstanding experience for all passengers.

In Chapter 8, Chris Fanning and Jane James (Australia) present a case study investigating passenger expectations, activities, spending and satisfaction levels whilst in a port that is a relatively new cruise destination.

In Chapter 9, Clare Weeden and Jo-Anne Lester (England) explain why it is important to examine the increasing importance of the visual image in society and marketing for tourism, before looking at the portrayal of the Caribbean as a holiday destination. They go on to discuss the promotion of cruise tourism in the region with specific reference to the UK market and the impact that image and expectations may have on tourist behaviour and experiences.

In Chapter 10, Kaye Walker and Gianna Moscardo (Australia) analyse the provision of quality interpretation and the role it can play in enhancing the experience and conservation awareness and support of passengers on expedition cruises.

In Chapter 11, Reg Swain (Canada) explores ways in which a standardized rating system that would apply to all cruise ships would give cruise ship guide authors more authority for the information they provide to any potential cruise vacationer.

Chapter 12, the final one in this part, is a refreshingly different and entertaining article by Arthur Asa Berger (USA). Here the author takes a cultural studies approach to understanding the ocean cruising phenomenon and investigates the different methodologies for understanding the economic, semiotics and psychoanalytical theory of cruising.

This part sets the scene for Part III, which explores the supply side of cruising through a number of examples from around the world.

My wife Wendy enjoying a trans Tasman Sea crossing from Auckland, New Zealand to Sydney, Australia on *Queen Elizabeth 2* in February 1999. Source: Ross K. Dowling.

6 What Drives Cruise Passengers' Perceptions of Value?

James F. Petrick[1] and Xiang[2] Li (Robert)

[1]Texas A&M University, Department of Recreation, Park and Tourism Sciences, 2261 TAMU, College Station, TX 77843-2261, USA; [2]University of South Carolina, College of Hospitality, Retail & Sport Management, School of Hotel, Restaurant & Tourism Management Columbia, SC 29208, USA

Introduction

Over the past two decades, cruise travel has been one of the fastest-growing sectors in the tourism industry. Since 1980, the cruise industry has seen an annual growth rate of almost 8%, which is two times faster than the overall tourism industry (Wood, 2000). It is estimated that at least 17 million passengers will take cruise holidays by the year 2006 (Lois *et al.*, 2004).

However, further investigation suggests that problems may lie ahead. According to Lois *et al.* (2004), the cruise industry is characterized by an oligopolic structure, where the majority of cruise capacity development (shipbuilding) comes from four major cruise lines. To continue the current market balance and deter potential competitors from market entry, these cruise lines have been investing heavily on increasing fleet sizes and increasing cruise capacity by building new, larger ships. It has been suggested that this building boom caused a saturation in the market, which resulted in 2001 being the first year that the cruise industry saw a decline in the total number of passengers (ShipPax, 2002). Since the vast majority of cruise bookings for a year are completed prior to August, this change probably had little to do with the events of 9/11. It has further been suggested that this decline has caused a vast reduction in the markets for smaller cruise operators, and a shift to the larger ones (ShipPax, 2002).

Amplifying the potential danger of this highly competitive industry is a current change in the demographic profile of passengers. Data from Cruise Lines International Association (2003) suggest that cruise passengers are younger (average age 52 years) and less wealthy (median income $57,000) than they have been in the past. These changing demographics of cruisers imply that 'high-end' cruise lines will be losing a share of the market, and value-oriented cruise lines may be gaining a competitive edge.

Since the cruise industry has been shown to be increasingly competitive, it is crucial for cruise line management and tour operators to examine the variables that influence cruise ship passengers to purchase and/or repurchase a cruise vacation. The construct of perceived value has been identified as one of the most important measures for gaining competitive edge (Parasuraman, 1997), and has been argued to be the most important indicator of repurchase intentions (Parasuraman and Grewal, 2000). Yet, in regard to services, repurchase intentions and consumer loyalty are often predicted solely by measures of consumer satisfaction and/or service quality (Petrick, 1999).

Looking at how cruise lines evaluate their success, it thus could be argued that they are measuring the wrong variable. Most cruise lines utilize a post-cruise questionnaire to gather data, to determine how successful they have been. The typical survey asks questions related to guests' satisfaction with their experiences, but neglects to ask questions related to guests' perceptions of value. According to Woodruff (1997, p. 139): 'If consumer satisfaction measurement is not backed up with in-depth learning about customer value and related problems that underlie their evaluations, it may not provide enough of the customer's voice to guide managers where to respond.' Further, just because passengers are 'satisfied' with their cruise, does not necessarily mean they perceived the purchase as having good value. It is quite possible a cruise passenger who is very satisfied with a cruise may consider it a poor value if the costs for obtaining it are perceived to be too high. On the contrary, a moderately satisfied cruiser may find a cruise to have good value if he or she believes they received good utility for the price paid. This phenomenon might explain why some high-end cruise lines with extremely high satisfaction ratings (i.e. Royal Viking Line) have failed to be successful. It is thus believed that the key to competitive survival in the cruise marketplace today is through providing value to the customer. Therefore, the purpose of this chapter is to highlight the relevance of the concept of 'perceived value' for the cruise industry. Specifically, the authors give an overview on the concept and structure of perceived value, discuss perceived value's role in cruisers' repurchase decisions, and examine differences in the role of perceived value for different markets (e.g. first-timers vs repeaters; low, moderate, and high price-sensitive groups). To establish a holistic understanding of cruiser' perceived value, results from a series of recent studies conducted by the first author on cruisers' perceived value will be reviewed, discussed and integrated.

The Concept of Perceived Value

Perceived value has been defined as 'the consumer's overall assessment of the utility of a product based on perceptions of what is received and what is given' (Zeithaml, 1988, p. 14). Within this definition, Zeithaml (1988) identified four diverse meanings of value: (i) value is low price; (ii) value is whatever one wants in a product; (iii) value is the quality that the consumer receives for the price paid; and (iv) value

is what the consumer gets for what they give. The vast majority of perceived value research has focused on the fourth definition.

Zeithaml (1988) is often credited with formulating the fundamental base for the conceptualization of the perceived value of a service. Results of her study showed that perceived quality leads to perceived value, which leads to purchase intentions. Both intrinsic (i.e. how the purchase makes you feel) and extrinsic (i.e. reputation of the product or service) attributes, as well as price, were found to be positively related to perceived quality. Moderating variables of perceived value included perceived sacrifice (non-monetary price), extrinsic attributes and intrinsic attributes. Overall, Zeithaml (1988) reported that quality, price (monetary and non-monetary), reputation and how the product or service makes one feel (emotional response) were dimensions related to perceived value. Her full conceptual model can be seen in Fig. 6.1.

Similarly, the Profit of Impact Marketing Strategies (PIMS) study conceptualized value as the relationship between quality and price (Buzzell and Gale, 1987). They ascertained that competitive success is obtained through 'perceived relative value' of the total package of products and services that influence customer behaviour. Relative value is the value received from one product or service, in comparison to similar offerings. According to Bojanic (1996, p. 10): '[T]he notion of relative perceived value results in three possible value positions: (1) offering comparable quality at a comparable price, (2) offering superior quality at a premium price, or (3) offering inferior quality at a discounted price.' Therefore a cruise line's perceived value can be altered if cruise management changes what they are doing, competitors change what they are doing, or if consumers' desires or needs change.

More recently, Parasuraman and Grewal (2000) conceptualized perceived value as a dynamic construct consisting of four value types: acquisition value, transaction value, in-use value and redemption value. They define acquisition value as the benefits received for the monetary price given, and transaction value as the pleasure the consumer receives for getting a good deal. In-use value is the utility derived from utilization of the product or service, while redemption value is the residual benefit received

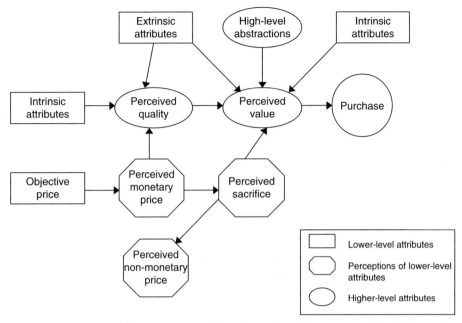

Fig. 6.1. A means–end model relating price, quality, value and purchase. Source: Adapted from Zeithaml (1988, p. 4).

at the time of trade-in or end of life (products) or termination (for services). Utilizing these definitions, the relevance of each of the four dimensions is different during varying times of the product or service's life (i.e. acquisition and transaction value are most salient during purchase, while in-use value and redemption value are more pertinent after purchase). Thus, cruise management needs to be cognizant that passengers' perceptions of value might be very different before, during and after a cruise.

Measuring Dimensions of Cruisers' Perceived Value

Historically, it has been argued that perceptions of value are hard to quantify (Semon, 1998). Perceived value has often been analysed with a self-reported, unidimensional measure (Gale, 1994). The problem with a single-item measure is that it assumes that consumers have a shared meaning of value. According to Zeithaml (1988, p. 471): '[Q]uality and value are not well differentiated from each other and from similar constructs such as perceived worth and utility'.

Thus, it has been argued that single-item measures of perceived value lack validity (Woodruff and Gardial, 1996). Another inherent problem is that unidimensional measures result in the knowledge of how well one is rated for value, but give no specific direction on how to improve value. Thus, multidimensional scales for measuring perceived value are necessary.

While multiple scales have been generated for measuring the perceived value of tangible products, only recently have scales been created for measuring the perceived value of less tangible products (services). A scale that has been developed specifically for measuring cruise passengers' perceptions of value is the SERV-PERVAL scale (Petrick, 2002).

In developing the SERV-PERVAL scale, the dimensions of perceived value were identified based on the notion of comparing what a cruise passenger 'receives', with what the cruiser 'gives' for the attainment of a cruising experience (Zeithaml, 1988; Jayanti and Ghosh, 1996; Grewal *et al.*, 1998; Parasuraman and Grewal, 2000). Petrick (2002) identified two dimensions related with what a cruiser 'gives' to obtain a cruise. The first dimension was termed 'perceived price'. This dimension explores how cruise passengers encode the monetary price that they paid for the cruise (i.e. was it expensive or inexpensive).

The other 'give' dimension identified by Petrick (2002) is related to the evaluation of non-monetary costs associated with the purchase of a cruise. Non-monetary costs include such factors as time, search costs, brand image and convenience. It is therefore a combination of both perceived monetary and non-monetary costs that equate to consumers' overall perceived sacrifice, which, in turn, affects their perception of a cruise's value. For the purpose of developing the scale, the definition utilized for monetary price was the price of a service as encoded by the cruiser (Jacoby and Olson, 1977), while behavioural price was defined as the price (non-monetary) of obtaining a service (i.e. a cruise vacation) that included the time and effort used to search for the service (Zeithaml, 1988).

With regard to what a cruise passenger 'receives', three dimensions of perceived value were revealed from the literature review and focus groups. The first dimension identified was emotional response, or the joy received from experiencing a cruise. For the development of the SERV-PERVAL scale, emotional response was defined as a descriptive judgement regarding the pleasure that a cruise gives the purchaser (Sweeney et al., 1998).

The second dimension identified was quality. Quality was defined as a cruiser's judgement about the cruise service's overall excellence or superiority (Zeithaml, 1988). The third dimension identified was reputation. Reputation was defined as the prestige or status of a cruise, as perceived by the purchaser, based on the image of the cruise line (Dodds et al., 1991). Thus it could be argued that the value dimensions of what a consumer receives from the purchase of a service include the emotional response to the service, quality received from the service and the reputation of the service rendered.

With the use of the definitions of the five dimensions identified, Petrick (2002) generated an initial pool of items from a review of the literature. A panel of expert judges was then selected to refine and edit the items for content validity. The resultant scale consisted of 25 items. Of these items, four were assigned to the

dimension of 'quality', six to 'perceived monetary price' and five each to 'emotional response', 'behavioural price' and 'reputation'. A pretest on 344 undergraduate students supported the reliability and internal validity of the instrument. Finally, the scale was administrated to samples on two different 7-day Caribbean cruises, on board the same vessel. Combined, the five-dimension, 25-item scale has been found to be both reliable and valid, with all items significantly ($P < 0.05$) assisting in the prediction of their assigned factor, and each of the factors of perceived value reliably measuring their respective construct (Petrick, 2002, 2004a,b).

First-timers' vs Repeaters' Perceptions of Value

By measuring the aforementioned dimensions of perceived value, and understanding how each of the dimensions are related, cruise management should be better prepared to serve their clientele. As indicated previously, the fundamental base for the conceptualization of perceived value was developed by Zeithaml (1988). She found that perceived quality leads to perceived value, which leads to purchase intentions. Both intrinsic (i.e. how the product or service makes you feel) and extrinsic (i.e. the reputation of the product or service) attributes were found to be positively related to perceived quality, while perceived monetary price was found to be negatively related to perceived quality. Moderating variables of perceived value included perceived sacrifice, extrinsic and intrinsic attributes and high-level abstractions (see Fig. 6.1). In order to obtain a better understanding of how the dimensions of perceived value were related to each other within a cruise setting, Petrick (2004a) analysed the interrelationships of the five dimensions inherent in the SERV-PERVAL scale using cruise passengers as subjects. Another purpose of this study was to examine if quality has both a moderating and a direct effect on cruise passengers' repurchase intentions. While the Zeithaml model (1988) (Fig. 6.1) suggests only a moderating effect, research in the field of marketing has suggested that it may also have a direct effect on repurchase (Cronin et al., 2000). A final goal of the study was to identify differences between first-timers' and repeat cruisers' perceptions of quality. This was done as it was believed that these markets were quite different, and should be studied separately. Thus, the purpose of the Petrick study (2004a) was to examine how well the theoretical framework proposed by Zeithaml (1988) explains the perceived value of both first-time visitors and repeat visitors.

Results of data collected on two separate cruises suggested that cruise passengers' perceptions of value might be different than those in other settings, and that differences exist between first-timers and repeaters. Thus, revised conceptual frameworks for understanding the determinants of perceived value were developed for both first-timers (Fig. 6.2) and repeaters (Fig. 6.3). While a majority of the Zeithaml model (1988) was confirmed, it was found that for both first-timers and repeaters the extrinsic attribute of reputation is a very good predictor of quality, but a poor predictor of perceived value. Additionally, for repeat visitors, it was found that behavioural price is not a good predictor of perceived value. It was further found that quality has both a moderating (through perceived value) and a direct effect on repurchase intentions for both first-timers and repeaters.

Results of the Petrick study (2004a) offered insight into direction for cruise management. For example, results suggested that cruise management should understand the causes of their clientele's perceptions of quality, reputation, monetary price, behavioural price and emotional responses in order to understand their perceptions of value and repurchase intentions. By understanding the determinants of these perceptions, cruise management should be better prepared to alter their offerings in order to improve their visitors' perceptions of value and intentions to repurchase.

More specifically, Petrick (2004a) found that reputation, emotional response and monetary price were all related to first-timers' and repeaters' perceptions of quality. Thus, cruise passengers' perceptions of quality are influenced by their perceptions of how fair the price was, the reputation of the cruise line and how good the experience made them feel.

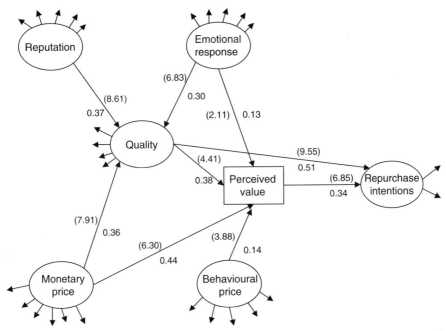

Fig. 6.2. Final model relating price, quality, value and revisit intentions for first-timers. Source: Petrick (2004a, p. 36).

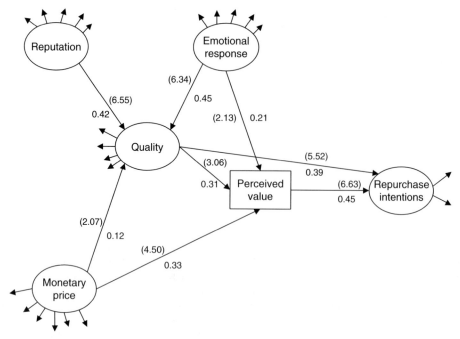

Fig. 6.3. Final model relating price, quality, value and repurchase intentions for repeat visitors. Source: Petrick (2004a, p. 36).

Petrick (2004a) also revealed that in comparison to first-timers' response, visitors' emotional response is a much stronger predictor and monetary price is a much weaker predictor of perceptions of quality. Therefore, repeaters are more likely to base their perceptions of quality on how a cruise makes them feel, while first-timers are more likely to base their perceptions on price. This makes sense, as repeaters are more likely to have more salient perceptions of how the cruise makes them feel, while first-timers must make their perceptions of quality on the information that they know (i.e. the price they paid for the cruise). Of all the variables, reputation was found to be the best predictor of quality, which suggests that cruise management wishing to position themselves with the use of quality should pay considerable attention to their reputation.

Moreover, Petrick (2004a) also found that quality, emotional response and monetary price were antecedents of both first-timers' and repeaters' perceived value, while behavioural price was an antecedent of first-timers' perceived value, but not that of repeaters. Reputation was found not to be related to either

segments' perceived value. As most studies have revealed, monetary price and quality had the most influence on both first-timers' and repeaters' perceived value. This implies the importance of offering cruise experiences with good quality at a good price that make people feel good in order to promote perceptions of value in visitors.

It was further revealed that behavioural price is more important for first-timers than repeaters. This difference probably occurred because repeaters are more experienced at purchasing cruises, and are thus less likely to consider the effort it takes to purchase a cruise as a burden to the overall perceptions of their experience. Thus, cruise line managers should place more emphasis on easing the effort it takes to purchase a cruise for first-timers than they do for repeaters.

Of all the antecedents, monetary price was found to be the best predictor of perceived value. This finding differs from the majority of past research, which has found that quality is the best predictor of perceived value for services. From a cruise management perspective, this finding suggests that monetary price may be more important than previously reported. This finding may help to explain why some of the more prestigious cruise lines (lines providing high quality) are losing market share to cruise lines with better perceived price.

It is also noteworthy that reputation was not found to be related to perceptions of value for either first-timers or repeaters, even though it was the best predictor of quality. This finding implies that cruise management utilizing value as a framework for making decisions should be less concerned with marketing their reputation than for those who use quality as a framework for making decisions.

Similar to Cronin et al. (2000), Petrick (2004a) discovered that perceived value and quality were directly related to both first-timers' and repeaters' repurchase intentions. This finding amplifies how important it is for cruise management to understand the antecedents of both perceived value and quality. It was further revealed that quality was a better predictor than perceived value for first-timers, while perceived value was a better predictor than quality for repeaters. This finding reveals that cruise management wishing to retain first-timers should concentrate on providing quality experiences, while cruise management concentrating on visitor retention should make cruise passengers' perceptions of value a priority. Thus, marketing efforts focusing on first-timers should be based more on the antecedents of first-timers' quality (reputation, emotional response and monetary price), while marketing towards repeaters should focus on the antecedents of repeaters' perceived value (price, quality and emotional response).

By understanding the Petrick models (2004a) (Figs 6.2 and 6.3), cruise management should be better prepared to understand the derivatives of potential repurchase behaviour for both first-timers and repeaters. This knowledge could be useful in determining how to alter visitors' experiences, in order to maximize the utilization of resources to both retain and attract clientele.

Role of Perceived Value in Repurchase and Word of Mouth

Most cruise managers would acknowledge that they strive to provide quality, satisfying and valuable experiences to their passengers in the hope that they will return for another cruise. Past research has suggested that each of these constructs (value, satisfaction and quality) should be measured to understand more thoroughly why tourists decide to return and/or provide positive word-of-mouth publicity regarding their experiences (Baker and Crompton, 2000; Petrick et al., 2001; Petrick and Backman, 2002a). Yet, these conceptually different constructs are often used interchangeably. It can be argued that this is the reason why most cruise lines make the error of only using one measure (usually quality via an exit survey) to examine the antecedents of repurchase. By understanding the relationships among the antecedents of repurchase and their determinants, cruise managers should be better equipped to manage their resources to maximize the likelihood of passengers repurchasing their product.

Perceived value (Petrick and Backman, 2002b), satisfaction (Spreng et al., 1996) and quality (Baker and Crompton, 2000) have all been shown to be good predictors of repurchase intentions. Research has also shown that these concepts are quite distinct (Caruana et al., 2000). According to Cronin and Taylor (1994, p. 127):

> Service quality perceptions reflect a consumer's evaluative perception of a service encounter at a specific point in time. In contrast, consumer satisfaction judgments are experiential in nature, involving both an end state and a process, and reflecting both emotional and cognitive elements.

In contrast, value has been argued to be more individualistic than satisfaction and quality (Oh, 2000), and involves the benefits received for the price paid (Zeithaml, 1988). Furthermore, quality and perceived value are cognitive responses to a service experience, while satisfaction is an affective response (Baker and Crompton, 2000; Cronin et al., 2000).

Rust and Oliver (1994, p. 14) suggested the importance of empirically assessing the 'antecedent, mediating and consequent relationships' among satisfaction, perceived value and quality. Since their assertion, many studies have attempted to model these relationships (e.g. Zeithaml et al., 1996; Baker and Crompton, 2000; Cronin et al., 2000; Petrick and Backman, 2002a). While consensus seems to exist that all three variables are related to behavioural intentions, conflicting arguments have been made related to: (i) which variables are most important to measure; (ii) which variables are moderating and which have direct effects on behavioural intentions; and (iii) the causal order of these relationships.

In order to examine these relationships for cruise management, Petrick (2004b) examined the interrelationships of these constructs using data obtained from cruise passengers. Results revealed a model with an excellent fit to the data, which revealed that cruise passengers' behavioural intentions are related to their overall satisfaction, perceived value and perceived quality (Fig. 6.4). It was further revealed that both perceived value and quality are antecedents of cruise passengers' satisfaction in the prediction of behavioural intentions. Thus, cruise passengers' perceptions of quality and value lead to satisfaction, which inevitably leads to their intent to repurchase.

According to Petrick (2004b), quality was found to be a better predictor of cruise passengers' intentions to repurchase than both perceived value and satisfaction. This finding suggests that if managers are only able to use one variable for predicting intentions to repurchase, quality may be the preferred variable. However, since satisfaction and perceived value were also found to be good predictors, it is suggested that managers should use all three if possible.

Petrick (2004b) also revealed that cruise passengers with higher intentions to repurchase are more likely to discuss their experiences positively with others (word of mouth) than those with lower intentions to repurchase. This finding shows that loyal customers are more likely to create word-of-mouth publicity at no extra cost to the service provider. Thus, providing a quality

experience that is perceived to have value and to be satisfying not only leads to repeat clientele but also elicits free publicity for the business.

While Petrick's model (2004b) offers more theoretical implications than managerial implications, it does provide a framework for assisting management in making decisions. By understanding the antecedents of perceived value, quality and satisfaction, management could be given specific direction on how to alter tourists' experiences in order to retain clientele, and to receive word-of-mouth publicity. Thus, if cruise management determines which attributes (i.e. food service or entertainment) are best at predicting quality, they would be best served by moving resources to these areas. Furthermore, if attributes are poor predictors of the antecedents (satisfaction, quality and value) of behavioural intentions, management might be able to reduce the resources allocated to these areas. Thus, as suggested by Petrick (2004b), future research should determine the antecedents of satisfaction, quality and value.

Role of Price Sensitivity in Cruisers' Perceptions of Value

As indicated previously, it has become increasingly difficult for cruise lines to gain market share in recent years. Because of this, many cruise lines have started value pricing. This change in pricing has made it possible for the total collection of fares on a full ship not to exceed the costs associated with operating the ship (Klein, 2002). Therefore, cruise management must generate additional revenues from passengers while they are on board (through the

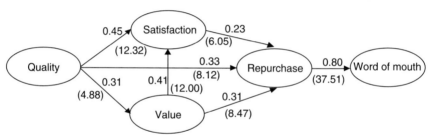

Fig. 6.4. Final model of the variables related to behavioural intentions. Source: Adapted from Petrick (2004b, p. 404).

sale of beverages, tours, gambling, etc.) in order to break even or generate a profit.

According to Dickenson and Vladimir (1997), discounting cruise fares is now more the norm than the exception. Research has shown that discounts from published fares (in cruise brochures) of over 25% are easily obtained throughout the various cruise markets (Cartwright and Baird, 1999). These 'value fares' have had an impact on the quality that cruise lines can provide, and may be the driving force behind the demographic changes in the current cruising clientele. It has been suggested that discounted cruises have degraded the industry's standards (Ward, 1994), and that value-oriented cruise lines are gaining a competitive advantage over 'high-end' cruises (Cruise Information Service, 2003). Combined, these market changes have made it necessary for the cruise industry to examine the ramifications of offering discounts, and whether or not 'price-watching' passengers are desirable.

Petrick (2005) examined the effects of price discounts by segmenting passengers based on their price sensitivity, and by comparing the resultant segments with various variables. Price sensitivity describes how individuals respond to various prices (Goldsmith and Newell, 1997). Therefore, a price-sensitive passenger is one who is more likely to base the purchase decisions on price than a passenger who is less price-sensitive, and would more likely require discounted prices in order to purchase a cruise.

In order to segment cruise passengers based on their price sensitivity, Petrick (2005) utilized the price sensitivity scale provided by Lichtenstein et al. (1988). Their interpretation of price sensitivity is related to how conscious consumers are to price when making a purchase. Thus, their measures are related to how much consumers rely on price when making a purchase, and the importance of making a purchase when it is on sale. With the use of this scale, Petrick (2005) identified three distinctly different segments of cruisers, based on their price sensitivity: low sensitives, moderate sensitives and highly sensitives.

Results of comparisons between the three segments showed that passengers who are less price-sensitive have higher household incomes, spend more money per day on their cruise and are more likely to purchase a more expensive cabin than passengers who are more price-sensitive. This finding is congruent with past research (Kalyanaram and Little, 1994), which has found that consumers who are less price-sensitive are more apt to spend more. Thus, at face value, it appears that offering cruise discounts may attract less desirable markets, as respondents who are more price-sensitive (more apt to cruise if there are discounts) were found to spend less. Yet, it is unknown if ship capacity would be high enough without the use of price discounts. With the large amount of money spent per passenger per day, the loss of a substantial number of passengers who even spend less than the average could make it extremely difficult to be profitable.

Conversely, in comparison to 'less sensitives', the segments of 'moderates' and 'high sensitives' were found to be more attached, perceive the price more favourably, be more satisfied overall, rate the quality of services or activities higher, perceive the value to be higher and be more likely to repurchase in the future. These findings would suggest that offering discounts may attract cruise passengers who are more likely to appreciate the cruise line. These findings are relevant, as past research has consistently found that visitors who rate their experiences more positively are more likely to not only repurchase but also provide more positive word-of-mouth advertising after their experiences. As stated by Reid and Reid (1993, p. 3), the importance of generating positive evaluations from customers is that they represent more than just a stable source of revenues, but also act as 'information channels that informally link networks of friends, relatives and other potential travelers to a destination'.

Even though more price-sensitive markets have been found to rate a cruise line more positively, it does not mean that they are necessarily viable markets. As proposed by Kotler et al. (1998), market segments must be measurable, substantial, actionable and accessible, if they are to be successfully utilized by management. Since less price-sensitive markets were found to be more substantial (higher incomes and spend more), marketing to price-sensitive markets might not be desirable. More research is necessary in order to determine if price-sensitive markets are substantial enough to be viable cruise markets.

Theoretically, the findings from Petrick (2005) offer new insight into the ramifications of using price discounts to attract cruise passengers. Results propound that offering discounts to cruise passengers will attract passengers who will spend less, but appreciate the cruise line more. Thus, long-term success may be found by offering discounts, due to the retention of clientele (repurchase) caused by more positive evaluations of the cruise experience, and the generation of positive word-of-mouth advertising. Conversely, not offering discounts may result in attracting a more affluent clientele, which may not be substantial enough to sustain long-term profitability.

References

Baker, D.A. and Crompton, J.L. (2000) Quality, satisfaction and behavioral intentions. *Annals of Tourism Research* 27(3), 785–804.

Bojanic, D.C. (1996) Consumer perceptions of price, value and satisfaction in the hotel industry: an exploratory study. *Journal of Hospitality and Leisure Marketing* 4(1), 5–22.

Buzzell, R.D. and Gale, B.T. (1987) *The PIMS Principles: Linking Strategy to Performance.* Free Press, New York.

Cartwright, R. and Baird, C. (1999) *The Development and Growth of the Cruise Industry.* Butterworth-Heinemann, Oxford.

Caruana, A., Money, A.H. and Berthon, P.R. (2000) Service quality and satisfaction: the moderating role of value. *European Journal of Marketing* 34(11/12), 1338–1352.

Cronin, J.J. and Taylor, S.A. (1994) SERVPERF vs SERVQUAL: reconciling performance based and perceptions-minus-expectations measurement of service quality. *Journal of Marketing* 58, 125–131.

Cronin, J.J., Brady, M.K. and Hult, G.T.M. (2000) Assessing the effects of quality, value and customer satisfaction on consumer behavioral intentions in service environments. *Journal of Retailing* 76(2), 193–218.

Cruise Information Service (2003) Value cruising. Available at: http://www.cruiseinformationservice. co.uk/press/factsheetdetail.aspx?id = 45

Cruise Lines International Association (2003) Cruise industry overview-marketing edition 2003. Available at: http://www.cruising.org/press/overview/ind_overview.cfm# execsum

Dickenson, R. and Vladimir, A. (1997) *Selling the Sea.* John Wiley & Sons, New York.

Dodds, W.B., Monroe, K.B. and Grewal, D. (1991) The effects of price, brand and store information on buyers' product evaluations. *Journal of Marketing Research* 28(August), 307–319.

Gale, B.T. (1994) *Managing Customer Value: Creating Quality and Service That Customers Can See.* Free Press, New York.

Goldsmith, R.E. and Newell, S.J. (1997) Innovativeness and price sensitivity: managerial, theoretical and methodological issues. *Journal of Product and Brand Management* 9(3), 163–174.

Grewal, D., Monroe, K.B. and Krishnan, R. (1998) The effects of price-comparison advertising on buyers' perceptions of acquisition value, transaction value and behavioral intentions. *Journal of Marketing* 62(April), 46–59.

Jacoby, J. and Olson, J.C. (1977) Consumer response to price: an attitudinal, information processing perspective. In: Wind, Y. and Greenberg, P. (eds) *Moving Ahead with Attitude Research.* American Marketing Association, Chicago, pp. 73–86.

Jayanti, R.K. and Ghosh, A.K. (1996) Service value determination: an integrative perspective. *Journal of Hospitality and Leisure Marketing* 34(4), 5–25.

Kalyanaram, G. and Little, J.D.C. (1994) An empirical analysis of latitude of price acceptance in consumer package goods. *Journal of Consumer Research* 21(December), 408–418.

Klein, R.A. (2002) *Cruise Ship Blues: The Underside of the Cruise Industry.* New Society Publishers, Gabriola Island, British Columbia, Canada.

Kotler, P., Bowen, J. and Makens, J. (1998) *Marketing for Hospitality and Tourism*, 2nd edn. Prentice-Hall, Upper Saddle River, New Jersey.

Lichtenstein, D.R., Bloch, P.H. and Black, W.C. (1988) Correlates of price acceptability. *Journal of Consumer Research* 15(3), 243–252.

Lois, P., Wang, J., Wall, A. and Ruxton, T. (2004) Formal safety assessment of cruise ships. *Tourism Management* 25, 93–109.

Oh, H. (2000) Diners' perceptions of quality, value and satisfaction. *Cornell Hotel and Restaurant Administration Quarterly* 41(3), 58–66.

Parasuraman, A. (1997) Reflections on gaining competitive advantage through customer value. *Journal of the Academy of Marketing Science* 25(2), 154–161.

Parasuraman, A. and Grewal, D. (2000) The impact of technology on the quality-value-loyalty chain: a research agenda. *Journal of the Academy of Marketing Science* 28(1), 168–174.

Petrick, J.F. (1999) An examination of the relationship between golf travelers' satisfaction, perceived value and loyalty and their intentions to revisit. Doctoral dissertation, Clemson University, Clemson, South Carolina.

Petrick, J.F. (2002) Development of a multi-dimensional scale for measuring the perceived value of a service. *Journal of Leisure Research* 34(2), 119–134.

Petrick, J.F. (2004a) First timers' and repeaters' perceived value. *Journal of Travel Research* 43(1), 29–38.

Petrick, J.F. (2004b) The roles of quality, value and satisfaction in predicting cruise passengers' behavioral intentions. *Journal of Travel Research* 42(4), 397–407.

Petrick, J.F. (2005) Segmenting cruise passengers with price sensitivity. *Tourism Management* 26(5), 753–762.

Petrick, J.F. and Backman, S.J. (2002a) An examination of golf travelers' satisfaction, perceived value, loyalty and intentions to revisit. *Tourism Analysis* 6(3/4), 223–237.

Petrick, J.F. and Backman, S.J. (2002b) An examination of the construct of perceived value for the prediction of golf travelers' intentions to revisit. *Journal of Travel Research* 41(1), 38–45.

Petrick, J.F., Morais, D.D. and Norman, W.C. (2001) An examination of the determinants of entertainment vacationers' intentions to revisit. *Journal of Travel Research* 40(1), 41–48.

Reid, L.J. and Reid, S.D. (1993) Communicating tourism suppliers: services building repeat visitor relationships. *Journal of Travel and Tourism Marketing* 2(2/3), 3–20.

Rust, R.T. and Oliver, R.L. (1994) Service quality: insights and managerial implication from the frontier. In: Rust, R.T. and Oliver, R.L. (eds) *Service Quality: New Directions in Theory and Practice.* Sage, New York, pp. 1–19.

Semon, T.T. (1998) Existing measures make value hard to quantify. *Marketing News* 32(11). Available at: http://www.ama.org/pubs/article.asp?id= 1058

ShipPax (2002) Number of cruise passengers down in 2001. Available at: www.shippax.se/ In Tutto Crociere, www.Cybercruises.com/nucrpado01 may02.htm. pp. 1–2.

Spreng, R.A., Mackenzie, S.B. and Olshavsky, R.W. (1996) A reexamination of the determinants of consumer satisfaction. *Journal of Marketing* 60, 15–32.

Sweeney, J.C., Soutar, G.N. and Johnson, L.W. (1998) Consumer perceived value: development of a multiple item scale. *American Marketing Association Conference Proceedings* 9, 138. American Marketing Association, Chicago.

Ward, D. (1994) *Berlitz Guide to Cruising and Cruise Ships – 1994.* Berlitz, Princeton, New Jersey.

Wood, R.E. (2000) Caribbean cruise tourism: globalization at sea. *Annals of Tourism Research* 27, 345–370.

Woodruff, R.B. (1997) Customer value: the next source for competitive edge. *Journal of the Academy of Marketing Science* 25 (Summer), 139–153.

Woodruff, R.B. and Gardial, S.F. (1996) *Know Your Customer: New Approaches to Understanding Customer Value and Satisfaction.* Blackwell, Cambridge, Massachusetts.

Zeithaml, V.A. (1988) Consumer perceptions of price, quality and value: a means–end model and synthesis of evidence. *Journal of Marketing* 52(July), 2–22.

Zeithaml, V.A., Berry, L. and Parasuraman, A. (1996) The behavioral consequences of service quality. *Journal of Marketing* 60(April), 31–46.

7   Cruising and the North American Market

Allan R. Miller[1] and William F. Grazer[2]

[1]Towson University, Department of Marketing and e-Businesss, College of Business and Economics, Towson, Maryland, USA; [2]Formerly Towson University, Towson, Maryland, USA

Introduction

Cruising is the fastest-growing segment of the North American (Canada and the USA) tourism market, with an annual growth rate of 8% since 1980 when 1.4 million North Americans cruised. This number has grown to 8.1 million in 2003 (CLIA, 2004a). Of the North American passengers 71% began their cruise in a US port (*Travel Weekly*, 2003). However, only about 15% of the North American population has ever cruised (Covey, 2004; Dickinson and Vladimir, 2004). The North American cruise market will continue to grow, as stated in the Cruise Lines International Association (CLIA) survey, which indicates that 44 million individuals, 25 years or older, are interested in cruising in the next 3 years. Of these, 43.5 million indicated they will 'definitely' or 'probably' cruise in the next 5 years (CLIA, 2004a).

CLIA (2004a) also indicates that since 1980, almost 100 million passengers have taken a cruise of 2 or more days and that 37% of these passengers have cruised within the last 5 years. According to Bob Dickinson, President and CEO of Carnival Cruise Lines, the largest competition for cruise lines has not come from other cruise lines but rather from land resorts (B. Dickinson, 2004, personal communication). The North American cruise market attracted approximately 8 million tourists compared to the 68 million who visited Las Vegas and Orlando (Dickinson and Vladimir, 2004).

Cruise line operators have positioned their products as spectacular 'floating resorts' offering all the amenities and facilities of a land vacation, along with exciting ports of call and a relaxing, hassle-free experience that can't be beaten (B. Dickinson, 2004, personal communication; Worldwide Cruise Ship Activity, 2003). Cruise ships are positioned as floating hotels and not as a mere means of transportation (Fig. 7.1). This formula has been successfully adopted in Las Vegas. Many cruise ships have itineraries that include Las Vegas style reviews and the interior decorations of the ships are similar to Las Vegas hotels.

North American Cruise Market

Seventeen cruise lines are marketed primarily to the North American market. These companies, who are members of the CLIA, are shown in Table 7.1. These cruise lines have a total of 206,423 lower berths on 142 ships and have carried 8.2 million passengers in 2003 (CLIA, 2004a). The ships of these cruise lines are shown in Table 7.2 along with the year the ship was built, its tonnage, length, capacity and speed.

These lines contain as few as one ship (Orient Cruise Lines with 845 lower berths) and as many as 21 ships (Carnival with 40,984 lower berths). In addition, some cruise lines are owned by one corporation. Royal Caribbean owns Royal Caribbean and Celebrity. Carnival Corporation

Fig. 7.1. Carnival Cruise Lines' *Carnival Miracle,* at 85,920 tonnes a large resort ship.

owns Carnival, Costa, Cunard, Holland America, Princess, Seabourn and Windstar. Orient Lines and Norwegian are owned by Star Cruises, which is *not* a member of CLIA and does *not* market to North American passengers.

Since the events of 11 September 2001, many cruise lines have adjusted their itineraries by dropping European, Eastern Mediterranean and Holy Land cruises. These itineraries have been shifted to the Caribbean, Alaska, Canada and New England areas. Consequently, over-crowding in the Miami and Fort Lauderdale, Florida, ports has resulted, causing the development of cruise ports around the USA and Canada. Like a string of pearls, the cruise ships are homeporting in North America. Holland America has extended the traditional 'Fall Season' for Eastern Canada and New England cruises into the spring and summer seasons. Celebrity Cruise Lines is offering 10- and 11-

day Caribbean cruises from Baltimore, Maryland, between March and October. The 2004 summer brought additional ships to Alaska, which resulted in overcrowded ports. Canadian ports include Montreal and Vancouver while the USA homeports include Boston (Massachusetts); New York; Philadelphia (Pennsylvania); Baltimore (Maryland); Charleston (South Carolina); Jacksonville, Fort Lauderdale, Port Canaveral and Miami (Florida), Mobile (Alabama); New Orleans (Louisiana); Galveston and Houston (Texas); San Diego, Long Beach, Los Angles and San Francisco (California); Seattle (Washington); as well as Alaska, Hawaii and San Juan (Puerto Rico) (Carnival, 2004; Official Steamship Guide International, 2004). The major growth in cruise ports is taking place in the second-tier ports and not in the major ports (i.e. Miami and Fort Lauderdale, Florida; Tobin, 2004). Maurice Zarmati, Vice-President

Table 7.1. Cruise Line International Association (CLIA) members (cruise lines who market to North American passengers).

Carnival Cruise Lines	Holland America Cruise Lines	Radisson Seven Seas Lines
Celebrity Cruise Lines	MSC Italian Cruise Lines	Royal Caribbean International
Costa Cruise Lines	Norwegian Cruise Lines	Seabourn Cruise Lines
Crystal Cruise Lines	Oceania Cruise Lines	Silversea Cruise Lines
Cunard Cruise Lines	Orient Cruise Lines	Windstar Cruise Lines
Disney Cruise Lines	Princess Cruise Lines	

Source: CLIA (2004b).

Table 7.2. Cruise line ships and relevant data.

Cruise line	Ship name	Year built	Tonnage	Length (feet)	Capacity (lower berth)	Speed (knots)
Carnival	Carnival Conquest	2002	110,000	952	2,974	21.0
	Carnival Destiny	1999	101,353	893	2,642	21.0
	Carnival Glory	2003	110,000	952	2,974	21.0
	Carnival Legend	2002	86,000	963	2,124	22.0
	Carnival Miracle	2004	86,000	963	2,124	22.0
	Carnival Pride	2002	86,000	963	2,124	22.0
	Carnival Spirit	2001	86,000	963	2,124	22.0
	Carnival Triumph	1999	102,000	893	2,758	21.0
	Carnival Valor	2004	110,000	952	2,974	21.0
	Carnival Victory	2004	102,000	893	2,758	21.0
	Celebration	1987	47,262	727	1,486	21.0
	Ecstasy	1991	70,367	855	2,040	21.0
	Elation	1998	70,367	855	2,052	21.0
	Fantasy	1990	70,367	855	2,056	21.0
	Fascination	1994	70,367	855	2,052	21.0
	Holiday	1985	46,052	727	1,452	21.0
	Imagination	1995	70,367	855	2,052	21.0
	Inspiration	1996	70,367	855	2,040	21.0
	Jubilee	1996	47,262	727	1,486	21.0
	Paradise	1998	70,367	855	2,040	21.0
	Sensation	1993	70,367	855	2,052	21.0
Celebrity	Celebrity Expedition	2001	2,842	296	100	15.0
	Century	1995	70,606	815	1,750	21.5
	Constellation	2002	91,000	965	1,950	24.0
	Galaxy	1996	77,713	866	1,870	21.5
	Horizon	1990	46,811	682	1,354	21.4
	Infinity	2001	91,000	965	1,950	24.0
	Mercury	1997	77,713	965	1,950	24.0
	Millennium	2000	91,000	965	1,950	21.5
	Summit	2001	91,000	965	1,950	24.0
	Zenith	1992	47,255	682	1,374	21.4
Costa	Costa Allegra	1992	28,500	616	1,072	21.5
	Costa Atlantica	2000	86,000	960	2,680	24.0
	Costa Classica	1991	53,000	833	1,764	18.5
	Costa Europa	1986	58,872	798	1,494	20.5
	Costa Fortuna	2003	105,000	885	2,720	19.5
	Costa Magica	2004	105,000	885	2,720	19.5
	Costa Mediterranea	2003	86,000	960	2,114	24.0
	Costa Romantica	1993	53,000	722	1,779	18.5
	Costa Tropicale	1982	36,674	671	1,022	22.0
	Costa Victoria	1996	76,000	828	2,464	23.0
Crystal	Crystal Harmony	1995	49,400	790	940	22.0
	Crystal Serenity	2003	68,000	820	1,080	22.0
	Crystal Symphony	1990	51,044	781	940	22.0
Cunard	Caronia	1973	24,492	627	668	20.0
	Queen Elizabeth 2	1969	70,327	960	1,791	28.5
	Queen Mary 2	2004	150,000	1,132	2,620	30.0
Disney	Disney Magic	1998	88,000	964	1,750	21.5
	Disney Wonder	1999	88,000	964	1,750	21.5
Holland America	M/S Amsterdam	2003	61,000	780	1,380	25.0
	M/S Maasdam	1993	55,451	720	1,258	22.0
	M/S Noordam[a]	1984	33,930	704	1,214	21.0

Table 7.2. *Continued.*

Cruise line	Ship name	Year built	Tonnage	Length (feet)	Capacity (lower berth)	Speed (knots)
	M/S *Oosterdam*	2003	85,000	950	1,848	23.0
	M/S *Prinsendam*	1988	37,845	673	793	21.4
	M/S *Rotterdam*	1997	60,000	778	1,316	25.0
	M/S *Ryndam*	1994	55,451	720	1,258	22.0
	M/S *Statendam*	1993	55,451	720	1,258	22.0
	M/S *Veendam*	1996	55,451	720	1,258	22.0
	M/S *Volendam*	1990	63,000	780	1,440	23.0
	M/S *Westerdam*	2004	85,000	950	1,848	23.0
	M/S *Zaandam*	2000	63,000	780	1,440	23.0
	M/S *Zuiderdam*	2002	85,000	950	1,848	23.0
MSC Italian	*Lirica*	2003	58,600	824	1,590	21.0
	Melody	1982	36,500	671	1,076	21.0
	Monterey	1952	20,040	563	576	20.0
	Rhapsody	1977	16,852	541	768	19.0
	MSC Opera	2004	58,600	824	1,590	21.0
Norwegian	*Norwegian Crown*	1998	34,205	614	1,052	22.0
	Norwegian Dawn	2002	91,000	965	2,240	25.0
	Norwegian Dream	1992	46,000	754	1,748	21.0
	Norwegian Majesty	1992	38,000	680	1,460	21.0
	Norwegian Sea	1998	42,000	700	1,518	20.0
	Norwegian Spirit	1998	77,000	880	1,996	24.0
	Norwegian Star	2001	91,000	965	2,240	25.0
	Norwegian Sun	2001	77,104	853	2,012	23.0
	Norwegian Wind	1993	50,760	754	1,246	21.0
	Pride of Aloha	1999	77,104	853	2,002	23.0
	Pride of America	2004	81,000	922	2,156	22.0
Oceania	*Regatta*	1997	30,227	594	684	18.0
	Insignia	1997	30,227	594	684	18.0
Orient	*Marco Polo*	1966	22,080	578	800	19.5
Princess	*Caribbean Princess*	2004	116,000	951	3,110	22.0
	Coral Princess	2003	88,000	964	1,970	22.0
	Dawn Princess	1997	77,000	856	1,950	21.4
	Diamond Princess	2004	113,000	951	2,600	22.0
	Golden Princess	2001	110,000	951	2,600	22.0
	Grand Princess	1998	109,000	951	2,600	22.0
	Island Princess	2003	88,000	954	1,970	22.0
	Pacific Princess	1997	30,277	592	670	20.0
	Regal Princess	1991	70,000	811	1,590	22.5
	Royal Princess	1984	45,000	750	1,200	21.5
	Sapphire Princess	2004	113,000	964	2,600	22.0
	Star Princess	2002	110,000	951	2,600	22.0
	Sun Princess	1995	77,000	856	1,950	21.4
	Tahitian Princess	1997	30,277	592	670	20.0
Radisson	*Explorer II*	1996	12,500	436	394	16.0
Seven Seas	M/S *Paul Gaugin*	1998	18,800	513	320	18.0
	M/S *Seven Seas Mariner*	2001	50,000	709	700	20.0
	M/S *Seven Seas Navigator*	1999	50,000	560	490	20.0
	M/S *Seven Seas Voyager*	2003	33,000	670	700	20.0
	SSC *Radisson Diamond*	1992	20,295	420	350	20.0
Royal Caribbean	*Adventure of the Seas*	2001	142,000	1,020	3,114	23.7
	Brilliance of the Seas	2002	88,000	962	2,501	25.0
	Empress of the Seas	1990	48,563	692	2,020	19.5

Table 7.2. *Continued.*

Cruise line	Ship name	Year built	Tonnage (feet)	Length	Capacity (lower berth)	Speed (knots)
	Enchantment of the Seas	1997	74,140	916	2,446	22.0
	Explorer of the Seas	2000	142,000	1,020	3,114	23.7
	Grandeur of the Seas	1996	74,140	916	2,446	22.0
	Jewel of the Seas	2004	88,000	962	2,501	25.0
	Legend of the Seas	1995	69,130	867	2.076	24.0
	Majesty of the Seas	1992	73,941	880	2,744	19.0
	Mariner of the Seas	2003	142,000	1,020	3,114	22.0
	Monarch of the Seas	1991	73,941	880	2,744	19.0
	Navigator of the Seas	2003	142,000	1,020	3,114	23.7
	Radiance of the Seas	2001	88,000	962	2,501	25.0
	Rhapsody of the Seas	1997	78,491	915	2,435	22.0
	Serenade of the Seas	2003	88,000	962	2,501	25.0
	Sovereign of the Seas	1988	73,192	880	2,852	19.0
	Splendour of the Seas	1996	69,130	867	2,076	24.0
	Vision of the Seas	1998	78,491	915	2,435	22.0
	Voyager of the Seas	1999	142,000	1,020	3,114	23.7
Silversea	Silver Cloud	1994	16,800	514	296	20.5
	Silver Shadow	2000	25,000	597	388	21.0
	Silver Whisper	2001	25,000	597	388	21.0
	Silver Wind	1994	16,800	514	296	20.5
The Yachts	Seabourn Legend	1993	10,000	439	208	18.0
of Seabourn	Seabourn Pride	1989	10,000	439	208	18.0
	Seabourn Spirit	1988	10,000	439	208	18.0
Windstar	Wind Spirit	1988	5,350	360	148	14.0
	Wind Star	1986	5,350	360	148	14.0
	Wind Surf	1990	14,747	535	308	15.0

[a]Noordam scheduled to leave service in November, 2004.
Source: Compiled from Sandler (2004), Green (2004) and CLIA (2004c).

of Sales for Carnival Cruise Lines said: 'You can cruise from virtually any city that has a port facility. At Carnival, there are 20 homeports in [North America]' (M. Zarmati, 2004, personal communication).

Listed in Table 7.3 are some areas and ports of call for the major destinations of North American tourists. The most popular destination is the Caribbean for 7-plus days and the Bahamas for 3- and 4-day cruises.

As shown in Table 7.4, the largest cruise lines are Royal Caribbean with over 43,000 lower berths, followed by Carnival, Princess, Norwegian and Holland America.

The cruise lines will continue to build new ships in the next 5 years. Table 7.5 shows the new ships on order contracted for until 2006.

A total of seven ships (Norwegian has two ships) are on order that contain an additional 18,300 lower berths. Table 7.6 illustrates the berths on order for the major cruise lines.

Demographics

Demographics for 2003 cruisers are shown in Table 7.7. These data only cover cruisers who are 25 years or older with a minimum annual household income of US$20,000.

Segments

CLIA has determined that there are six segments in the cruise market. These segments and their major characteristics are shown in Table 7.8.

Table 7.9 shows who individuals are travelling with when vacationing on one of the

Table 7.3. Major cruise destinations for North Americans.

Area	Examples of ports of call
Caribbean	
Eastern	St Thomas; St Maarten; Antigua
Western	Cozumel; Grand Caymen; Jamaica
Southern	Barbados; Aruba; St Lucia
Bahamas	Nassau; Freeport; Private Island
Bermuda	St George; Hamilton
Alaska	Ketchikan; Juneau; Sitka
Canada/New England	Halifax; Prince Edward Island; Bar Harbour
Mexican Riviera	Cabo San Lucas; Acapulco; Mazatlan
Panama Canal	The Canal; Colombia; Mexico
Hawaii	Hilo; Kola; Honolulu

Source: CLIA (2004c).

major cruise lines, and Table 7.10 shows who is the primary decision maker when choosing a cruise vacation. It would appear that a cruise decision is primarily a joint decision. Over half of the decisions (52%) were jointly made while 45% (self and spouse) were made by only one spouse.

Passenger Characteristics

Recall that the North American cruise market has been growing at the rate of 8.1% a year, and approximately 8.2 million North American passengers sailed in 2003. Cruise lines can be segmented by type or style. CLIA (2004b) uses the following classification to distinguish amongst types of passengers: Niche/Specialty; Luxury; Premium Resort/Contemporary and Value. Table 7.11 demonstrates the cruise lines associated with each of the marketing segments.

Ward classifies ships and cruise lines based upon lifestyles. These styles are Luxury, Premium and Standard (Ward, 2004; CLIA, 2004c). The authors constructed Table 7.12 that classifies ships by lifestyles based on Ward and CLIA.

Activities and Relaxation

The major cruise lines are building these larger ships with more on-board amenities. Royal Caribbean's *Voyager* and *Explorer of the Seas* have rock-climbing walls and ice-skating rinks. Princess Cruise Lines has pioneered 24-hour alternative dining. Passengers have the choice, in addition to the main dining room, of dining in any of the three alternative restaurants.

Table 7.4. North American market share major cruise corporations, June 2004.

	Lower berths	Market share (%)	
Carnival	98,917	47.9	Total
Carnival	40,984	19.9	
Costa	15,567	7.5	
Cunard	5,079	2.5	
Holland America	16,319	8.0	
Princess	19,740	9.6	
Seabourn	624	0.3	
Windstar	604	0.2	
Royal Caribbean	59,488	28.8	Total
Celebrity	16,018	7.8	
Royal Caribbean	43,470	21.0	
Norwegian	18,803	9.1	Total
Norwegian	17,959	8.7	
Orient	845	0.4	

Source: CLIA (2004a).

Table 7.5. Selected cruise lines' new builds for the North American market, June 2004.

Cruise line	Ship name	Tonnage	Lower berths	Delivery date
Cunard	*Queen Victoria*	88,000	1,968	March 2005
Carnival	*Carnival Liberty*	110,000	2,974	Autumn 2005
Royal Caribbean	*N/A*	160,000	3,600	Autumn 2005
Norwegian	*Norwegian Jewel*	93,000	2,400	Autumn 2005
Holland America	*Noordam*[a]	85,000	1,858	January 2006
Norwegian	*Pride of Hawaii*	93,000	2,400	Spring 2006
Princess	*Caribbean Princess 2*	116,000	3,100	June 2006

[a]Will recycle the ship name: Noordam from older ship leaving service in 2004.
Source: Ward (2004) and Travel Trade (2004).

Moreover, Princess passengers can dine at fixed times and at the same table with the same staff. They can also dine within a 5-hour period of their choosing at a different table in the other main restaurants. Norwegian Cruise Lines has instituted 'free-style' cruising, which allows you to dine whenever you want (Miller and Grazer, 2002). With flexible dining, alternative dining, traditional dining and 24-hour room service, passengers can eat whenever and wherever they choose.

There is no better method to get relief from the everyday stresses of the world than to take a cruise vacation. If you shut off your mobile phone and refrain from utilizing the Internet café on the ship, you are on a stress-free vacation. A cruise is a floating city and resort where the passenger is catered to and treated like royalty. You can travel with your family, friends, organization and significant other or just by yourself. Dave Stockert, Director of Promotions for Holland America Lines, said: 'There is no better way to connect and have quality time with your family than on a cruise' (D. Stockert, 2004, personal communications).

The same is true of couples where they can relax and not be subject to the stresses of work and maintaining a household. Vicki Freed, CTC, Senior Vice-President of Sales and Marketing for Carnival Cruise Lines, indicates:

Table 7.7. Demographic characteristics of 2003 cruisers.

Demographics	Per cent of category
Marital status	
Married	78
Single	22
Gender	
Females	50
Males	50
Age	
25–29	4
30–39	16
40–49	18
50–59	21
60–74	26
75 and over	15
Mean age: 55	
Median age: 52	
Household income (US$ '000)	
20–39.9	18
40–59.9	26
60–79.9	21
80–99.9	14
100–149.9	10
150 and over	3
Refused to state	8
Mean income: 71	
Median income: 57	

Source: CLIA (2004a).

Table 7.6. Berths on order in major cruise lines.

Cruise line	New berths
Carnival	2,974
Cunard	1,968
Holland America	1,858
Norwegian	4,800
Princess	3,100
Royal Caribbean	3,600

Source: Ward (2004) and Travel Trade (2004).

Table 7.8. Cruise market segments.

No.	Segment	%	Characteristics
1.	Restless baby boomers	33	Cost may be an impediment to trying different vacations
2.	Enthusiastic baby boomers	20	Convinced and excited about cruising; live a stressful life; want escape and relax; look forward to vacations
3.	Luxury seeker boomers	14	Can afford and are willing to spend money for deluxe accommodations and pampering
4.	Consummate shoppers	16	Look for best value (not cheapest); committed cruisers
5.	Explorers	11	Well-educated; well-travelled; curious about different destinations; like to explore and learn
6.	Ship buffs	6	Most senior segment; cruise extensively

Source: Worldwide Cruise Ship Activity (2003).

[W]hile changing demographics and the introduction of new, state-of-the-art 'floating resorts' have certainly played a role in the growing popularity of cruising, perhaps the greatest contributor is the all-inclusive value of the experience. With meals and entertainment, along with fun-filled activities for adults and kids alike included in the cost, more consumers than ever are discovering that cruising is an inherently better value than land-based vacations.

(V. Freed, 2004, personal communication)

A cruise gives the traveller the advantage of visiting a multitude of destinations with only having to pack and unpack once. Some cruise ships are destinations in themselves besides their obvious purpose as a means of transportation. Included in the cruise fares are accommodations that include twice-daily cabin service, food, activities and entertainment to include Las Vegas Style Review Shows (on many ships). Items of a personal nature are not included except on some small, upscale cruise lines. These personal items may include, but are not limited to, alcoholic beverages, sodas, shopping, pictures, gambling and tips.

A cruise vacation allows you to relax and unwind in comfortable surroundings and to be catered to by a trained staff. You can dine in a gourmet restaurant each night, participate in a variety of activities and meet interesting fellow passengers. You have the ability to escape from reality and visit interesting ports of call. You can try foods that you normally do not eat and engage in activities that are different from your normal routine.

Table 7.9. Travel companions.[a]

Category	%
Spouse	77
Partner/companion	3
Children under 18	12
Adult children 18 and over	6
Other family members	20
No one else (alone)	1

[a]Categories are not mutually exclusive and therefore do no add up to 100%; 99% of cruise passengers do not travel alone.
Source: CLIA (2004a).

Table 7.10. Primary decision maker for cruise vacations.[a]

Category	%
Self and spouse	52
Self	34
Spouse	11
Friend	2
Partner/companion	2
Children under 18	2
Adult children 18 and over	2
Another family member	3

[a]Categories are not mutually exclusive and therefore do no add up to 100%.
Source: CLIA (2004b).

Table 7.11. Types of passengers.

Niche/specialty	Luxury	Premium	Resort/ Contemporary	Value
Costa	Crystal	Celebrity	Carnival	MSC Italian
MSC Italian	Cunard	Holland America	Costa	
Orient	Orient	Oceania	Disney	
Windstar	Radisson Seven Seas	Princess	Norwegian Royal Caribbean	
	Silver Seas			
	Seabourn			
	Windstar			

Source: CLIA (2004a).

Except for the casino, there is no reason to carry cash. Each passenger is given a shipboard card upon which to charge purchases to their account. On the newer ships, this card also serves as the cabin key. Most ships have cabin safes where you can store your identification, money and other valuables.

Cruise activities are often segmented by types of passengers. Cruise lines and passengers are often segmented by demographics. The cruise lines often attempt to match not only the food to the type of passenger but also the activities to the type of passenger mix (e.g. Royal Caribbean has the rock-climbing wall and ice-skating rink for its younger, more adventurous passengers). Royal Caribbean also has a 'Johnny Rockets' (retro hamburger restaurant) for its many teenagers. More salads and other nutritious foods are offered for the health-conscious passengers. The average age of cruisers has dropped from 50 to the early forties in the last 5 years (Sullivan,

2004). Cruise ships with older passengers still offer 'daily, high tea'.

The Caribbean Princess has introduced the activity of 'Movies Under the Stars'. Each evening, a feature film is shown at the poolside on a 300-ft^2 (27-m^2) LED screen that has 69,000 watts of sound (Princess Cruises, 2004). Passengers are invited to sit on lounge chairs or on floats in the pool during the movies. According to Jackie Simkins, District Sales Manager for Princess Lines, 'Music Videos' are shown on-screen during the daytime (J. Simkins, 2004, personal communication).

In an effort to appeal to its more upscale segment, Celebrity Cruises has performers from the Cirque du Soleil appear on its ships, *Constellation* and *Summit* (Tobin, 2004). These Cirque-created characters entertain each evening at one of the ships' bars. A 'Masquerade Ball' is held one evening during the cruise.

On the Queen Mary 2, sophisticated entertainment is used to match its clientele. There is also a four-person harmony group that performs limited shows (up to 15 minutes) at different venues throughout the evening. Often passengers follow the group around the ship. On the upscale ships it is not uncommon to see string quartets and trios playing old standards and classical music. An example of the type of activities is provided in Table 7.13.

Table 7.12. Classification of ships by lifestyles.

Luxury	Premium	Standard
Crystal	Celebrity	Carnival
Cunard	Holland America	Costa
Radisson Seven Seas	Oceania	Disney
Seabourn	Windstar	MSC Italian
Silversea		Norwegian
		Orient
		Princess
		Royal Caribbean

Food

One of the major attractions and activities for any cruise passenger is dining. Food is available

Table 7.13. Holland America activities.

Television	Movies in theatre
CNN; TNC; CNN Financial; Cartoon Network	Religious services Port lectures Art activities
Movies	**Beauty salon and**
Shore excursion talk	**massage shops**
Disembarkation talk	**Bars and lounges**
View from bridge	**Wine desk**
Cruise video	**Model shipbuilding**
Ship's location, weather	**sea trials** **Talk on drydock**
Gaming	**Service club**
Casino games and slots	**meetings** **Bridge tournament**
Snowball jackpot bingo	**Internet** **Library**
Blackjack tournament	**Sports equipment**
Showtime and more	**Crafts**
Seaquest game	**Ship's art tour**
Crew talent show	**Afternoon tea**
Guest oldies show	**Daily quiz**
Las Vegas style show	**Trivia contest**
Music and dancing	***New York Times***
Piano	**(ship edition)**
Trio	**Games**
Combo	
Classical music	
Light music	
Disco music	
Passport for fitness	
Walk a mile	
Yoga	
Healthier body seminar	
Hair care explained	
Hand and nail clinic	
Skin care clinic	
5-minute makeover	
Quoits	
Ping pong	
Fitness fashion show	
Volleyball	
Sit and be fit class	

Source: Daily Programs, M/S *Statendam*, 6–16 January 2004.

24 hours a day on all major cruise ships. While breakfast menus seldom change, lunch and dinner menus change daily. Two menus from a Holland American cruise are provided in Table 7.14. Dishes are not repeated on a cruise, which gives the passenger many choices that are normally not consumed outside of the cruise. The passenger can order as many items from each course as desired, as well as having second helpings. Passengers can also put in special requests as long as sufficient notice is given to the staff. The hallmark of any cruise is staff service.

On a 1-week Caribbean cruise from Baltimore, Maryland, the Carnival ship *Miracle* used 5000 lb (1865 kg) of chicken; 18,000 shrimp; 32,000 eggs; and 5220 heads of iceberg lettuce. In total US$300,000 worth of food is consumed by passengers and crew (McCausland, 2004).

Conclusion

The North American cruise market will continue to grow. As life becomes more stressful, a cruise becomes the ideal way to alleviate the problem. As indicated by a sociologist, a cruise is relaxing. You can spend a good deal of time eating, wandering, reading and engaging in activities that take you away from your daily routine. It is a kind of forced relaxation (Berger, 2004).

The hallmark of the cruise is service. On Holland America, for example, crew members are trained to greet each passenger with a smile and to remember passengers' names. If you return to a bar for a drink, the bartender should remember what you ordered on your previous visit (D. Stockert, 2004, personal communication). One of the authors recently visited a ship that had sailed a year earlier. As he inspected the ship, he was greeted by name by three different crew members from his previous voyage. It is this high level of service that most working people do not receive in everyday situations. This service helps to set cruise vacations apart from other forms of vacation. Celebrity Cruise Lines recently ran a series of advertisements with the theme: 'I was King, I was a Queen' (authors' observations of television commercials, July 17, 2004, Bravo Television Network).

Projections for growth in the North American market will come from both repeaters and new cruisers. Since 85% of North Americans have not cruised, a vast market potential exists. Carnival Cruise Lines was expected to carry 3 million passengers in 2004. This is almost double the number they carried 7 years ago (B. Dickinson, 2004, personal communication). George Williamson, Port

Table 7.14. Holland America dinner menus.

Day 3 of cruise	Day 4 of cruise
Appetizers	**Appetizers**
Mellon Pearls	Garden Symphony
Hors D'oeuvre Plate	Seafood Pate
Prawns	Seared Sliced Duck
Crab Cake	Breast
Fettucini	Fried Hazelnut Crusted
	Brie
	Linguini
Soups	**Soups**
Onion	Frijoles
Lobster Bisque	Tomato Florentine
Gazpacho	Chilled Strawberry
Salads	**Salads**
House	House
Caesar	Gourmet Mixed Greens
Entrées	**Entrées**
Supreme Salmon	Fillet of Grouper
Sea Scallops	King Crab Legs
Medallions	
Roast Turkey	Prime Rib of Beef
Double Rib Lamb	Prosciutto Wrapped
Chops	Chicken Breast
Sweet and Sour Tofu	Pork Chop
Chicken Breast	Vegetable Lasagna
Fillet of Halibut	Chicken Breast
	Fillet of Salmon
Desserts	**Desserts**
Baked Alaska	Chocolate Mousse
Assorted Cookies	Cake
Strawberry Sundae	Bourbon Pecan
Ice Cream	Nut Pie
Sorbet	Strawberry Sensation
Frozen Yogurt	Cake
Tiramisu	Chocolate Fudge
Kiwi Jello	Sunday
Fresh Fruit Plate	Peach Melba
Assorted Cheese	Ice Cream
Plate	Sorbet
	Frozen Yogurt
	Lemon Mousse Cake
	Cranberry Jello
	Assorted Cheese Plate
	Fresh Fruit Plate
	Dining venues
	Breakfast
	Continental
	Buffet
	Dining room (served)
	Lunch
	Buffet
	Pasta bar
	Deli bar
	Pizza, hamburgers and
	hotdogs

Table 7.14. *Continued.*

Day 3 of cruise	Day 4 of cruise
	Ice cream bar
	Salad bar
	Dining room (served)
	Dinner
	Casual buffet (some
	ships serve the
	meals)
	Alternative reservations-
	only restaurant
	(served)
	Dining room (served)
	Late night snack
	Themed extravaganza
	Ice cream bar
	Room service
	All day (24/7)

Source: Menus and Daily Activity Sheets, M/S *Volendam*, 7–8 January 2002.

Director in Tampa, Florida, stated that ports are branching out and seeing how they can better accommodate customers (Tobin, 2003). In other words, ports are starting to market directly to cruisers. The purpose of the marketing is to get the consumer to demand cruises from the local port. With the growth of second-tier ports, it will become easier to drive rather than to fly long distances to begin and end a vacation. This is important as the three major markets in the USA are New York, the South Atlantic and the Pacific Coast (Worldwide Cruise Ship Activity, 2003). It is up to the cruise lines to maintain an excellent level of service and deliver an outstanding experience for all passengers.

References

Berger, A.A. (2004) *Ocean Travel and Cruising: A Cultural Analysis.* Haworth Hospitality Press, Binghamton, New York.

Carnival (2004) *2004–2005 Cruise-At-A-Glance.* Carnival Cruise Lines. Miami, Florida.

CLIA (2004a) *The Overview*, Spring. Cruise Lines International Association, New York.

CLIA (2004b) Chiefs profit diet. *Travel Trade*, 21 June, p. 18.

CLIA (2004c) *2004 Cruise Manual.* Cruise Lines International Association, New York.

Covey, C. (2004) Homeport growth transforms cruise industry. *Travel Professional*, June/July, p. 66.

Dickinson, B. and Vladimir, A. (2004) *The Complete 21st Century Travel & Hospitality Marketing Handbook*. Pearson Custom Publishing, Upper Saddle River, New Jersey.

Green, M. (2004) Celebrity expedition: adventure with amenities. *Cruise Travel*, 7 June, pp. 4–14.

McCausland, C. (2004) Charting many courses. *Baltimore Sun*, 16 June, pp. F1 and F4.

Miller, A.R. and Grazer, W.F. (2002) The North American cruise market and Australian Tourism. *Journal of Vacation Marketing*, June, pp. 221–234.

Official Steamship Guide International (2004) Transportation Guides, Knoxville, Tennessee, Summer.

Princess Cruises (2004) Advertisements. *Travel Weekly*, 5 July, pp. 38–39.

Sandler, C. (2004) *Cruises 2004*. The Globe Pequot Press, Guilford, Connecticut.

Sullivan, M.C. (2004) It's all aboard the ship. *Washington Post*, 20 June, pp. F1 and F5.

Tobin, R. (2003) Small cruise-port cities become big players. *Travel Weekly*. Available at: www.travel weekly.com

Tobin, R. (2004) To bring actors on two ships. *Travel Weekly*. Available at: www.travelweekly.com

Trade Travel (2004) Cruise Trade: Annual 2004/2005 Cruise Guide, August 2005. Travel Trade Publications, New York.

Travel Weekly (2003) By the Numbers. *Travel Weekly*. Available at: www.travelweekly.com

Ward, D. (2004) *Ocean Cruising & Cruise Ships*. Berlitz Publishing, London, Great Britain.

Worldwide Cruise Ship Activity (2003) World Tourism Organization, Madrid, Spain.

8 When One Size Doesn't Fit All

Chris Fanning and Jane James
Flinders University, Cultural Tourism, School of Humanities,
GPO Box 2100, Adelaide, SA 5001, Australia

Introduction

Australia, particularly South Australia, is a relatively new cruise ship destination, and needs to ensure that it meets cruise market and passenger expectations both on board and on shore.

This chapter, which is based on a specific study conducted from December 2003 to March 2004 during the cruise ship season in Adelaide, investigates passenger expectations, activities, spending and satisfaction levels whilst in port. To provide context to the study, Australia and South Australia's cruise destination position on a global scale is also investigated.

Recent research with cruise ships that visit South Australia implies that not only are all passengers not the same in terms of cruise ship choice, expectations and desired cruise experience but also the product they are offered, both on board and on land, should not necessarily be a generic product aimed at meeting all needs.

This chapter considers the limited cruise passenger markets in South Australia and the needs and interests of the passengers. The case study provides the focus for analysing what passengers do whilst in port and their satisfaction levels with the experiences they have.

Finally the implications for the stakeholders (passengers, cruise companies, operators, government and host community) of not providing tourism products and services that meet expectations will be considered.

Background

There is very little previous research either from Australia (Douglas and Douglas, 2003) or internationally (Gabe *et al.*, 2003) available about how, what and why cruise passengers undertake various activities or purchase certain products whilst on a cruise, or as part of the land content of tours, port visits, etc. Information has tended to concentrate on the passenger's actual cruise experience rather than experiences whilst in port and their expectations and desires whilst there. Other research (Henthorne, 2000; Knowles, 2002, unpublished report) has focused primarily on economic impacts and purchases that are made whilst in port.

The Cruise Lines International Association (CLIA, 1996) suggests that many cruise passengers are repeat cruisers; however, there is much less known about their decision-making processes in regard to alternative vessels, destinations, ports or attractions. This chapter will consider tourism products in relation to cruise passengers from a particular region to see if all visitors look for similar tourism products and experiences.

Much has been written about the consistent increase in cruise tourism in the past and the likelihood of a positive future (Baratta, 1994; CLIA, 2002; Department of Infrastructure, 2002; Kaye, 2004). What is not clear is which geographical regions stand to prosper from the increase and how those destinations are attempting to meet the needs of the cruise passengers.

Context of the Case Study: Adelaide, South Australia

In the summer of 2003/04 (December 2003–March 2004), 11 visits were made to South Australia waters by international cruise ships, ranging in size from the *Europa* (with over 400 passengers and 217 crew) to the *Star Princess* with a passenger capacity of 2900 and 2000 crew. *Star Princess* visited Adelaide four times during the summer. In total almost 16,000 passengers and 8000 crew visited Adelaide during the season and a sample were surveyed regarding activities and spending patterns as part of a South Australian Tourism Commission (SATC) investigation aimed at analysing satisfaction levels amongst cruise ship passengers to South Australia.

Outer Harbour, the docking port of Adelaide, is located 21 km north-west from the city centre with access to the city centre by train. The port is also within easy reach of metropolitan beaches and a golf course.

The port of Adelaide is a multifunction port with a dedicated passenger terminal for cruise ships. A trading village was established at the passenger terminal, as a specific tourism initiative offering quality Australian-produced products, including clothing, opals, and food and wine from regions that were generally too distant for day-trip passengers to visit.

Passengers arriving during the 2003/04 season were from three main international origin regions: the USA, UK and Germany. Australians were also a visitor source as they travelled from elsewhere in Australia, with Adelaide used as an embarking or disembarking point for some local passengers. There was a clearly distinguishable difference between passengers from different countries and the ships they travelled on. Predominantly the US visitors arrived on the larger vessels that were on short-haul cruises, with most cruising for 10 days, travelling between Auckland and Sydney via various Australian ports or in the reverse order of ports. UK and German visitors tended to arrive on the smaller vessels that were on long-haul cruises (some up to 120 days), whilst the Australians were spread across all vessels.

Methodology

Face-to-face visitor surveys were conducted for the first time in Adelaide during the cruise ship season of December 2003 to March 2004. The surveys were conducted at Outer Harbour International Shipping Terminal to assess the experiences, satisfaction and expenditure of the passengers. Only limited surveys were obtained from crew so the research reflects primarily the passenger's results.

Debriefing discussions held with visitor surveyors, information officers and tour operators as the data was analysed provided further anecdotal information about passenger behaviour patterns, activities and satisfaction levels.

Australia as a Relatively New Cruise Destination

Australia's distance from the main North American and European cruise ship regions has limited the number of ships that visit Oceania each season. The location of Adelaide, on the southern coast of Australia, away from the eastern seaboard of Australia, is a primary contributor to the relatively small number of cruise ships that have visited the state so far. Adelaide, the capital of South Australia has a population of 1.1 million people and is within easy access of some iconic visitor experiences: wildlife on Kangaroo Island; wineries in Barossa Valley; cultural heritage on North Terrace Boulevard; the largest collection of Aboriginal artefacts in the southern hemisphere in South Australian Museum; and examples of early European free settlement in the Adelaide Hills at Hahndorf.

The North American market comprises 80% of the world cruise market (Frost, 2004), and the South Pacific region attracts only 2.2% of this (Douglas and Douglas, 1996). Australia as a target market for cruisers is also quite low as the Australian cruise passenger market has been consistently small and specific in its product requirement (Douglas and Douglas, 2003). Passengers in this study came from a range of countries (Table 8.1).

Table 8.1. Source region of cruise passengers to South Australia in case study.

	USA (%)	UK (%)	Germany (%)	Australia (%)
Source region	50	17	6	15

South Australia's tourism product is very similar to that identified by Victoria (Department of Infrastructure, 2002 unpublished report) and Tasmania (Knowles, 2002, unpublished report), which have both identified that personal safety, friendly people and a clean environment are key strengths. Victoria also identified ease of access to the city centre, wineries and natural and historic attractions – which can also be said of Adelaide. Tasmania had many similar comments made to those in the case study that reflect positively on the architecture, people and ambience of the city and state. Queensland, however, sees its climate, geographic location and major attractions (e.g. Great Barrier Reef) as its strengths in the cruise tourism market (Tourism Queensland, 2001).

Passengers from Limited Markets

Whilst the South Australian Tourism Plan 2003–2008 (SATC, 2002) does not specify cruise tourism in detail, there is a strategy within the plan that relates to this market. The demographics of South Australia's prime target markets are discerning and high-yielding visitors from Europe, UK and the Americas (SATC, 2002). These markets compare favourably to the case study demographics, which showed that most international visitors were from USA, UK and Germany. The repeat visitation by the *Star Princess*, which had primarily US passengers, indicated a strong interest in the Australian and New Zealand region by the North American market.

For the *Star Princess*, Adelaide was the biggest touring port in the region, indicating not just a strong interest in cruising in the region but also in taking part in onshore activities.

Passengers Have Different Needs and Interests

A major tourist market segmentation study undertaken by Lang in 1991 identified a number of specific market segmentation groups in the North American market, including 'Ocean Cruise Enthusiasts' (Lang Research, 1991, unpublished report). This group has different characteristics from segments such as 'scenic tour seekers' who were noted as having lower levels of education and household income and a greater number of mature mainstream singles, whilst 'exotic tour seekers' tended to have above-average education and household income but were less likely to travel beyond North America and the Caribbean.

Ocean cruise enthusiasts, however, were noted as having a high representation of 'affluent mature' and 'senior couples' with many respondents tending to have higher-than-average household incomes and being older than cruisers in other segments. They were more likely than other North American travellers to have visited other international vacation destinations, indicating a preference for international rather than domestic travel (Lang Research, 1991, unpublished report). From an Australian perspective this market segment was also more likely to take a trip during the northern hemisphere autumn, winter or spring (Lang Research, 1991, unpublished report). This coincides well with the Australian cruise season, which peaks during the North American winter months of December to March.

'The explorer' – a passenger segment identified by CLIA (1996, 2000) – is a category of visitor seen on Australian cruises and noted as being intellectually motivated, wanting to travel to 'remote places of scientific and historical interest', with an average age of 64 and annual income of US$81,000. These demographics are similar to the case study results where 67% had an average age over 60. In 1986 the average age of cruisers was 56 (CLIA), whilst in 2000 the CLIA Market Profile Study found the average age to be 50, with a median income of US$64,000. Jamaican research found that 80% of passengers were less than 50 (Henthorne, 2000), which is very different to the 'typical' or 'traditional' image of a cruise passenger. It should be noted, however, that the Jamaican research was primarily based on 2–3-day cruises, whilst the Australian case study had passengers primarily on 7–10-day itineraries.

The age and demographics of passengers have implications for tourism product and itineraries, which should not presume that all cruise passengers are 'senior couples'. Each destination needs to be aware of the demographics of passengers likely to tour in their region, so that onshore products and experiences can be matched accordingly.

There are a number of high-priority factors for North Americans whilst travelling, including safety, common language, friendliness and similarity of food (Tourism Queensland, 2001). Many of these were confirmed in the South Australian study where Australia was recognized as a safe destination. However, the Americans were also strongly motivated to visit Australia as it was on their priority list and most had never visited before. In contrast, the reasons the German market came to Australia were spread across several motivators, including 'having been here before' and Australia just happening to be 'on their itinerary'.

Maslow's theory of motivation (cited in Hudson, 1999) offers a hierarchy of needs ranging from basic physiological needs through to health and safety; from sense of belonging to ego and self-actualization. Whilst this theory may seem simplistic, the parameters are still provided for consideration.

It is almost an anomaly that many cruisers see themselves as curious and adventurous (CLIA, 1996). Initial observation of cruisers indicates that they are primarily motivated to be on a cruise because of a sense of belonging to a group, safety and satisfaction of physiological needs such as excellent meals, accommodation and services. These, however, are all low-level motivations according to Maslow (1943, cited in Hudson, 1999), distinct from curiosity and adventure, which tend to satisfy the highest motivation of self-actualization.

Many cruisers have a desire to travel to foreign places that they have not visited before (CLIA, 1996). Whilst in port they have the opportunity to see local sights or take a day tour and then reboard the ship without having to consider baggage, accommodation and meals (CLIA, 1996). This seems to satisfy the basic motivators of travellers whilst still allowing the cruisers to feel adventurous and daring in seeking out new destinations. Cruises allow passengers to experience soft adventure on shore whilst ensuring their basic physiological

needs, safety and 'sense of belonging' are met by the cruise liner.

There are also passenger segments that are either more interested in the cruise ship or the cruise experience than the itinerary ports of call (CLIA, 1996). Douglas and Douglas (2004) support this with evidence that shows many consumers prefer the shipboard experience, where they can receive the 'ultimate cruise experience' without the distraction of a port visit. It is also an economic advantage for cruise lines to have guests remain on board, as revenue is generally not generated for the cruise liner whilst the passengers are ashore (KZN's Cruise Tourism Industry, n.d.).

CLIA (1996) identified the following cruise passenger segments:

- The restless boomer – interested in different types of vacations; want a family, planned, fun-filled holiday.
- The enthusiastic boomer – motivated individuals; want a comfortable holiday away from their daily fast-paced lives.
- The consummate shopper – look for best cruise value; have taken an average of five cruises; know the cruise lines and ships; have an average age of 55 years.
- The luxury seeker – are sophisticated in world travel and experiences; want the most luxurious service and accommodation available.
- The explorer – intellectually motivated people; travel to remote places for scientific and historical interest; cost is not a factor, though they do not look for luxury.
- The ship buff – cruise more for the ship than for the itinerary; have cruised on average 6.3 times; have an average age of 68 years.

Research by Douglas and Douglas (1996) concluded that whilst there are similarities in behaviour, there is no substantial evidence to support the idea that cruise passengers act in a manner that can categorize their behaviour. Clearly there is an opportunity for further investigation in this area.

What Passengers Do and How the Activity or Experience Is Provided

CLIA (1996) recognized that there is a propensity for cruisers to do multiple trips, with about a third of their vacations during the past 6 years being a cruise. This was supported in the case study with strong anecdotal evidence indicating that many passengers were not on their first cruise. Tourism Australia (2004) recognizes that due to the increased time and effort needed to get to Australia, most visitors are not first-time travellers. Long-haul travellers have often previously taken smaller distance trips, each time extending their boundaries, until they feel prepared for long-haul destinations such as Australia.

The diversity of passenger origins (USA, UK, Germany, etc.) and the degree of sophistication of travellers (based on previous travel experience) would suggest that a corresponding degree of diversity of cruise passenger's expectations, and subsequently experiences, should be expected. It is unlikely that one size (tourism product, experience, etc.) would fit all. The South Australian case study showed US passengers were high users of organized tours into South Australia that had been pre-booked on board, compared to German travellers who were more likely to be free and independent travellers (FITS) with the highest use of public transport. What is not clear is how much information was given out on the different ships about the ports and whether the results are indicative of the general behaviours of the market. The results could also be influenced by those who had visited before, as with the German and UK passengers, or not, as with the US passengers.

The reasons why some passengers did not come ashore in Adelaide were outside the scope of this study. However, the reasons for staying on board are many and varied, and may include lack of interest towards onshore activities, health restrictions, previous visit to the port; lack of knowledge about what the port has to offer or more exciting activities to do on board whilst in port. Generally the percentage of passengers who did not venture ashore in the Adelaide case study was slightly higher for those ships on a long-haul itinerary, where it could be expected that passengers would be keen to venture on to land when the opportunity arises (Table 8.2).

Those who took organized tours (TOTS) relied heavily on the prepared itineraries to satisfy the experiences they were seeking, compared to FITS, who either sought public transport or arranged their own tours through private operators once they had arrived in port.

This places a large responsibility on the inbound tour operators to provide tours that meet, and indeed exceed, the needs and expectations of the visitors, given that for many US passengers, the distance and the passengers' age may restrict them returning to Australia in the future. However, US passengers were keen to note in the case study that they would still recommend Adelaide as a destination even though they did not feel they were in a position to return themselves.

The number of FITS was much greater for UK and German markets, which is reflected in the profile of these markets for the South Australian tourism industry in general (SATC, 2003b,c). Most visitors from these markets travel here independently, with a higher incidence of visiting friends and relatives (VFRs) for the UK market. Of the German visitors to Adelaide during the cruise ship season, 39% were repeat visitors to Adelaide, were high users of public transport and preferred making their own individual arrangements. The possible familiarity with the destination would allow the passenger to feel confident whilst in port, but would not diminish their expectation for top-quality tourism products and service.

Of those who came ashore whilst in Adelaide, the ships with the highest percentage of cruisers were also those that had the highest percentage of US travellers on board. As mentioned previously, the US cruisers were more likely to take part in an organized tour with many of these tours going to regional areas, including Barossa Valley, Adelaide Hills, Mt Lofty Summit and Hahndorf. These regions are recognized by the SATC (2003a) as the most visited by all US visitors to South Australia. A substantial number of US visitors also visited city attractions such as Haigh's chocolate factory and the National Wine Centre or undertook cultural activities and city shopping.

The trend of US passengers taking organized tours was confirmed in the spending patterns of the passengers within the case study, where the US visitors spent the most on tours, whilst Australians and Germans spent the most on public transport (Table 8.3).

One activity that appeared common to the US, UK, Australian and to a lesser extent German markets was that of shopping, with a preference for local or Australian-made products.

Table 8.2. Organization of onshore activities and method of transport in Australian case study.

	USA (%)	UK (%)	Germany (%)	Australia (%)
How day was arranged				
By myself	29	54	62	72
Cruise company	58	40	42	42
Transport used				
Private car	3	10	4	6
Walk	7	18	16	11
Taxi	7	8	4	6
Public transport	30	35	64	37
Coach/Minibus/Limo	66	38	32	46

Studies in Bar Harbor, Maine, USA, where most passengers are American, show a high percentage of purchases relate to local eateries (Gabe et al., 2003). The South Australian case study highlighted that many passengers ate on board and spent most of their money on either tours or purchases, which had a local flavour or content. These included local produce such as award-winning wines, chocolates and food products (e.g. dried fruits, nuts, gift baskets, fruit juices), which they took with them rather than consumed on site. Whether passengers ate on board because the meals had been prepaid or because they did not feel comfortable with the process ashore was not clear from the case study, but onshore dining does not appear to be a highly desired experience.

Several respondents from the UK stated that they had taken part, or intended to take part, in land content whilst in Australia, by disembarking at one point and reboarding at another. US passengers tended to spend more per day on gifts and souvenirs than other passengers, with a preference for Australian-made or -produced items. In some instances comparisons were made between ports, prior to purchase, to ascertain prices, as products such as opals were available in all Australian ports.

The land content involved either driving or train travel and is not reflected in their spending whilst in Adelaide. The land content also increases the opportunity for increased economic activity of cruise ship passengers in regional areas. Including land content into cruise experiences has been recognized as a growing trend, though not necessarily as independent travel. Cruise lines in Maine, USA, utilize tours that are sponsored by the parent company (Gabe et al., 2003). This initiative of the cruise lines gives them the opportunity to not only provide an all-inclusive onshore experience but to also increase their influence with passengers' onshore spending, where they go, what they see; consequently the cruise lines dictate the 'sense of place' experience – we hope accurately!

Table 8.3. Activities undertaken by cruise passengers in Australian case study.

	USA (%)	UK (%)	Germany (%)	Australia (%)
Shopping	34	44	20	36
City tour	33	28	47	22
City attractions	18	33	37	18
Visiting friends and relatives	2	12	4	21
Regional tour	26	14	3	13

What Passengers Think of Their Onshore Experiences

The very fact that many visitors to Australia, whether on a cruise or not, are experienced, sophisticated travellers will have an impact on the expectations they will have of their experiences, relating to both product delivery and product diversity. Given that most cruises include port calls, this expectation will apply to both cruise and land content.

All tours showed a high satisfaction rating; however, the privately organized tours received particularly positive comments, which were indicative of the individual nature of the tours, providing a more personalized experience that was designed for specific visitor interests, or providing a 'value-added' experience, apart from a more general tour.

Whilst similar stores and products can be found in each Australian port, each city is large enough to support local and regional product and produce of sufficient diversity to allow a genuine and unique shopping experience. National and multinational retail companies exist in each Australian city, which can be both a comfort and a curse as cruise passengers strike a balance between the familiar and the different. Research in the Caribbean has shown that many passengers find it difficult to find variety and diversity with limited locally owned stores (Klein, 2003). This is a valuable point for Australian retailers as visitors in the case study stated that they wished to buy good-quality, Australian-made products and not cheap imported products. This was also stated in the Maine Case Study (Gabe *et al.*, 2003), where locally made works without logos were a sought-after product. This type of purchase is not restricted to cruisers as travellers in general seek locally made, quality products (ICM Research, 2004).

South Australia's product strengths have been identified as an 'authentic' Australian lifestyle, food and wine, nature-based assets and a 'sense of difference' (SATC, 2002). Overwhelmingly, comments from the case study supported these strengths in relation to the friendliness of the people, food and wine, and quality nature-based experiences. The architecture and cleanliness of the city and regions were also mentioned often. Cultural based activities by cruise ship passengers involved indigenous,

heritage and arts-based activities. There were also many comments in the case study that acknowledged and appreciated Adelaide's accessibility, parks and gardens, lack of crowds and general positive ambience. Comments such as 'Nice city – well-planned city and public transport'; 'very friendly and helpful people'; 'very interesting and charming' were common.

German visitors in particular (72% in 2003; SATC, 2003b), are noted for visiting South Australia to experience nature, landscapes and wildlife – almost twice the number compared to the US and UK markets. UK visitors used South Australia as a gateway to rural areas or the outback (SATC, 2003c), which was also reflected in the case study by the UK cruise passengers, where some passengers indicated they were going to take part in independent land content prior to reboarding the cruise.

It has been recognized by Tourism Australia (2004) that Australia as a long-haul destination needs to attract repeat visitation by delivering quality, value, varied and enriching experiences. The Australian Tourism Commission (2003) identified that it is not only Australia's natural environment but also the distinctive quality of the Australian people and the free spirited lifestyle and culture that appeals to overseas visitors. The case study noted these three qualities as experiences that were enjoyed whilst ashore in Adelaide. Tourism Australia (2004) acknowledges that the first and final impressions of travellers as they arrive and leave are powerful. The use of volunteer 'Meeters and Greeters' provided the opportunity for both information to be distributed and friendliness to be extended to arriving and departing passengers. The 'Meet and Greet' programme provides a particularly inviting and welcoming atmosphere for visitors to Adelaide and was commended by cruise passengers in the case study as a positive reflection of the people, lifestyle and ambience of the port.

What became clear from the study is that visitors were looking not just for quantity and visiting as many sites as possible but rather to visit fewer sites and receive a quality experience that provided interpretation and education whilst there. The Victorian Tourism Operators Association tried to overcome this by providing 'smaller, flexible, personalized tours' in the summer of 2000/01 to cruise ship passengers (Frost, 2004). This allowed for better interpretation and education, and enhanced the visitors' experience and increased their satisfaction levels.

Another opportunity to enhance the visitor experience is to stop in towns or locations en route to the main site or attraction (Belize Cruise Tourism, n.d.). Visitors in the case study wanted not only to visit a major site but also to travel through or visit the Central Business District (CBD) en route, to gain a sense of having visited the port of a major city. Hence, if passengers were travelling from Outer Harbour (21 km from the CBD of Adelaide) to a regional area such as Barossa Valley (75 km from the CBD), they wanted to be diverted via the CBD of Adelaide to give them a sense of having been to the destination marked on the itinerary. Overall it would allow them to get an appreciation of the 'sense of place' that local residents have (Hall, 1991).

Implications for Cruise Ship Stakeholders

Implications exist for stakeholders to provide experiences that are perceived by cruise passengers as being of top quality and value for money. The case study highlighted that there were occasions when some passengers felt that the attraction they were visiting was overcrowded. This sense of overcrowding needs to be acknowledged and addressed by all onshore tour planners, as an example of exceeding the perceptual carrying capacity of the visitors (Hall *et al.*, 1997). Visitors need to feel that they are special and not just being herded through a site. This applies to sites where passengers are able to spend money, as well as to natural attractions, as passengers feel strongly that insufficient time in a location detracts from their overall experience (Henthorne, 2000).

The visitor experience in relation to regional areas often relates to day trips whilst the ship is in port and indeed for many passengers this will be their total experience of the country or region. However, the opportunity exists for countries such as Australia to explore not only day trips whilst in port but also to provide information to passengers to manipulate their time and take part in land-based content between ports. This is particularly so for passengers from long-haul markets such as the UK and Germany who have visited Australia before and

feel comfortable as independent travellers, despite being cocooned on a cruise.

Research into the Australian cruise industry has highlighted that new product development needs to include quality shore attractions and add-on tours, particularly with special interest tourism or product (Dwyer and Forsyth, 1996). This could include educative nature-based experiences that would fit well with South Australia's established tourism product and build on the attributes of the state that have been recognized by the SATC (2002) and documented in the State Tourism Plan.

Conclusion

A port's tour and attraction base is the asset that provides opportunities for cruise passengers to enrich their travel experience and learn about the community's history, culture and contemporary lifestyle (McDowell Group, 2003, unpublished report). For Adelaide these experiences are already recognized by our tourism marketers as assets. The planned city, free settlement history, lifestyle and climate all add to Adelaide's mix when establishing itself as a desirable location for cruise passengers and subsequently cruise liners.

All passengers are different in terms of cruise ship choice, expectations and desired cruise experiences, based not just on their demographics or geographic base but also on their personality traits and behavioural patterns. The case study provided insights into the US, UK and German markets but the desires and expectations from the currently lesser markets such as the Asian region or South America should not be underestimated. There is potential for Australia to increase its cruise passenger markets from these regions. At the same time it should not be presumed that the experiences and services that are desired by the North Americans and Europeans will flow on to passengers from other areas.

Cruise passengers to Australia are becoming increasingly sophisticated and need to be given the opportunity to experience quality tourism products and services, which are diverse and delivered with a degree of excellence. The implication for all stakeholders, whether they be government, tour operators or cruise lines, is that more passengers want experiences that provide a degree of interpretation and education and not to be rushed through their time on shore. Visiting less but spending more time is a concept that should be considered.

Opportunities for long-haul passengers to take part in extended land content whilst in Australia is another area that has the potential to grow. As cruise lines visit more Australian ports, information and perhaps tour products need to be available for those independent travellers who wish to disembark and reboard at an alternative location.

In summary, one size doesn't fit all! As in many other marketing structures, matching products and experiences to visitor needs will almost guarantee that their expectations are met, or exceeded, and provide benefits for both the cruise ship industry and the ports of call.

References

Australian Tourism Commission (2003) *ATC White Paper*. Commonwealth of Australia, Canberra.

Baratta, A. (1994) Interest in cruises soars, according to CLIA market study. *Travel Weekly* 53(55), 8.

CLIA (Cruise Lines International Association) (1996) *Market Profile, Cruise Dynamics and Segmentations Studies*, edited by Halterman, R. Available at: www.spaceconsult.biz/text.htm

CLIA (2000) *Market Profile*. Available at: www.cruising.org/press/press-kits/kits/pko-57.cfm

CLIA (2002) *The Cruise Industry: An Overview*. Marketing edition. Cruise Lines New York: International Association, Spring.

Department of Infrastructure (2002) *The Victorian Cruise Shipping Strategy*. Destination Victoria, Summary 2002–2005.

Douglas, N. and Douglas, N. (1996) P&O's Pacific. *Journal of Tourism Studies* 7(2).

Douglas, N. and Douglas, N. (2003) The cruise experience in Pacific Asia: is there a common cruise culture? *CAUTHE 2003 Conference Proceedings*.

Douglas, N. and Douglas, N. (2004) *The Cruise Experience*. Pearson Education, French's Forest, New South Wales, Australia.

Dwyer, L. and Forsyth, P. (1996) Economic impacts of cruise tourism in Australian. *Journal of Tourism Studies* 7(2).

Frost, W. (2004) *Travel and Tourism Management*. Pearson Education, French's Forest, New South Wales, Australia.

Gabe, T., Lynch, C., McConnon, J. and Allen, T. (2003) *Economic Impact of Cruise Ship Passengers in Bar Harbor*. Department of Resource Economics and Policy, University of Maine, Maine.

Hall, C.M. (1991) *Tourism in Australia: Impacts, Planning and Development*. Longman Cheshire, Melbourne.

Hall, C.M., Jenkins, J. and Kearsley, G. (1997) *Tourism Planning and Policy in Australia and New Zealand*. McGraw-Hill, Rose Hill, New South Wales, Australia.

Henthorne, T.L. (2000) An analysis by cruise ship passengers in Jamaica. *Journal of Travel Research* 38 (February), 246–250.

Hudson, S. (1999) Consumer behaviour related to tourism. In: Pijam, A. and Mansfield, Y. (eds) *Consumer Behaviour in Travel and Tourism*. Haworth Hospitality Press, New York.

ICM Research (2004) *Tasteful not Tat – Brits Go for Upmarket Souvenirs*. Lloyds TSB Travel Services, London.

Kaye, L. (2004) Book early cruise warning. *Travel Week*, 13 October.

Klein, R. (2003) Cruise ships: the industry's dark side. *Conscious Choice* 10(1), 24–25.

SATC (South Australian Tourism Commission) (2002) *South Australian Tourism Plan 2003–2008*. South Australian Tourism Commission, Adelaide.

SATC (2003a) *International Visitors to South Australia: North America*. South Australian Tourism Commission, Adelaide.

SATC (2003b) *International Visitors to South Australia: Germany*. South Australian Tourism Commission, Adelaide.

SATC (2003c) *International Visitors to South Australia: UK*. South Australian Tourism Commission, Adelaide.

Tourism Australia (2004) *Tourism Australia*. UK presentation, September.

Tourism Queensland (2001) *Queensland Cruise Shipping Plan 2001*. State Development, Queensland Government.

9 Ways of Seeing the Caribbean Cruise Product: A British Perspective

Clare Weeden and Jo-Anne Lester
University of Brighton, School of Service Management, Darley Road, Eastbourne, East Sussex BN20 7UR, UK

Introduction

The Caribbean for many is a dream destination and its popularity with holidaymakers is clear. As a region, it ranks sixth in the world for tourism receipts (Jayawardena, 2002), and millions of tourists every year travel to the Caribbean in order to experience first hand what could be termed as the 'Holy Grail' of mass tourism – sun, sea and sand (Duval, 2004). For the cruise market, the Caribbean is an essential part of the global product, presently claiming more than 45% of the world cruise market (CLIA, 2002), and indications are that the popularity of the region will continue to grow (Mintel, 2004).

Third-world destinations such as the Caribbean have long been and continue to be the subject of much discussion regarding the ways in which the region and its people have been represented and portrayed within tourism promotion (see Palmer, 1994; Morgan and Pritchard, 1998; Echtner and Prasad, 2003). The ubiquitous image most often associated with the Caribbean, a perceived commodity routinely packaged and marketed to tourists and cruise passengers, consists of a pristine and deserted beach of white sand, fronted by an azure sea and framed by the iconic palm tree. This common portrayal of the region as a hedonistic pleasure beach purely for visitors' delight is very often far removed from reality and, it could be argued,

merely a convenient image used for promotional purposes by commercial tourism organizations.

Such superficial and often cursory representations of the region as a holiday destination tend to gloss over the complex history of the Caribbean and ignore the region's inextricable links with slavery and colonial rule; and certainly the images used to promote cruise tourism do just that, with images of anonymous beaches, quaint harbours and ships being repeated endlessly in company literature for the region. This rather anodyne treatment does not just occur in cruise brochures and other promotional material but is also replicated on board the ship, as highlighted by Wood (2004, p. 160), when he asserts: 'Caribbean motifs, cruising and music – to say nothing of Caribbean history and society – are entirely absent from the cruise experience on most cruise ships in the region.'

These are the issues this chapter aims to address. First, it will examine the increasing importance of the visual image in society and marketing for tourism, before looking at the portrayal of the Caribbean as a holiday destination. The relationship between commercial representation of destinations and tourists' 'ways of seeing' will be explored. The chapter will then go on to discuss the promotion of cruise tourism in the region, with specific reference to the choice of images used by P&O in current cruise promotional literature for the UK market, and the impact that image and expectations may have on tourist behaviour and experiences.

Visual Culture and Tourism

It is contended that image performs an important role in the holiday decision-making process (Baloglu and McCleary, 1999) with the media, including literature, television, film and music, highlighted as increasingly playing an influential role in determining 'the impressions and images people have of landscapes and places' (Shaw *et al.*, 2000, p. 275). Certainly the increasing prominence and significance of the 'visual' in Western society and culture is emphasized by Sturken and Cartwright (2001), while Macnaghten and Urry (1998) argue that sight is one of the most important senses in terms of the knowledge we now have of the modern world. The importance of the visual in tourism is further exemplified by Jenkins (2003, p. 306):

> In the post-modern cultural studies framework, visual tourist destination images are a form of 'text' used to 'represent' the world. In this context the term 'text' is used broadly beyond the printed page, to include paintings, maps, photographs and even landscapes.

Despite the recognition of the importance of visual data in tourism, it is surprising that to date there is seemingly little attention given to the area of marketing and promotion of cruise tourism. One notable exception is the work of Douglas and Douglas (2004, p. 152) who acknowledge the significance and impact of the visual elements of cruise promotional material. In particular, the prominence of visual imagery in cruise brochures is highlighted, stating that very often the brochures 'contain from 50 to 100 pages consisting of dazzling images of vessels and their interiors and the most striking features of their destinations'.

Highlighting the importance of images within travel and tourism marketing and tourist behaviour, Jenkins (2003) refers to the 'circle of representation' making the link between the images used in marketing and tourist behaviour. In particular, Jenkins refers to Urry's work (1990) and the 'hermeneutic circle', whereby Urry draws on how photographs can create anticipation of places and subsequently high-

lights the relationship between imagined places, a desire to visit them and then to take home photographic images of the place and attraction visited, often perpetuating and disseminating the iconic imagery of destinations as first conceived through visual media.

Figure 9.1 adapts Jenkins' conceptualization (2003) of the 'circle of representation' (after Hall, 1997), which serves to highlight that the myriad of images infiltrating a particular society and culture often have strong historical connections. In the case of cruise tourism in the Caribbean, this is the impact and influence of colonialism. In addition, the model suggests a clear correlation between the visual data that is omnipresent in society and the subsequent iconic and stereotyped imagery identified in tourism marketing.

Figure 9.1 also suggests that promotional material can be a powerful medium in influencing people's 'ways of seeing' (Berger, 1972) and thus may to some extent control tourist travel behaviour as well as their experiences (see Urry, 1990, 2002; Dann, 1996; Wang, 2000). As the model indicates, there is clearly a relationship between the visual representation of places and people in tourism and visual consumption, even to the extent of the significance of visual reminders, such as photographs and mementoes collected by tourists. It is suggested that when these mementoes are brought back into the tourist's own cultural setting they serve to further reinforce and influence the ways in which places are imagined, and the circle of representation therefore continues.

Marketing of the Caribbean

Representation of the Caribbean in tourism and cruise promotion is not incidental, and it could be argued that much of the iconic imagery currently used can be traced back to the late fifteenth century with initial European consumption of the region and the 'discovery' of the land, animals, vegetation and people. These discoveries were to have a major impact on future European society and culture, and initiated a fertile period of scientific discovery, exploration and inevitably, colonization (see Sheller, 2003, pp. 13–35 for a detailed chronological

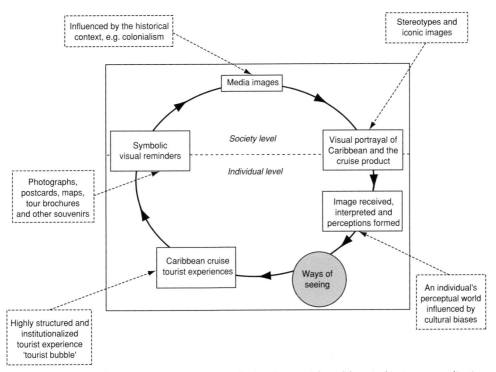

Fig. 9.1. The place of imagery in cruise tourism marketing. Source: Adapted from Jenkins' conceptualization (2003) of the 'circle of representation' (after Hall, 1997).

discussion of colonization and the contribution of the Caribbean to global development).

As a consequence, the region's significance to Europe increased, and travel between the continents grew rapidly from this time. Images of the region and its landscapes were brought back to Europe portraying the natural environment, in particular the abundance of tropical vegetation, exotic fruits and trees such as the palm. The sudden realization of the existence of a far-away wild and undiscovered land with its profusion of tropical and exotic 'Otherness' was presented to European imagination as a luxuriant utopian fantasy (Sheller, 2004). From this, Europe's fixation with the fantasy of 'Paradise' emerged, and thus began the consequent imagining of the Caribbean as a Garden of Eden (Sheller, 2003).

In addition, tropical islands themselves, seen as tropicalized and idealized landscapes, continue to hold great fascination for the European imagination. Indeed, Sheller (2004, p. 23) cites Grove (1995, p. 51), who states that

in discovering the tropical island, 'Paradise had become a realisable geographical reality'. From this it is clear how the Caribbean has fallen victim to a romanticized European notion of desire, an artificial representation, almost 'an invention of the idea of the Caribbean' (Sheller, 2003, p. 8).

Certainly, in terms of tourism, Wang (2000, p. 164) makes the connection between the images of tropical paradise in marketing and identifies the importance of the physical attributes of the Caribbean. He suggests that through promotion the region is symbolically transferred into a tourist's paradise with imagery of 'tropical, palm-fringed islands surrounded by golden sand and clear blue sea'. This stereotypical description of the Caribbean alludes to some of the physical attributes that serve as key pull factors for tourists in the choice of destination. The depiction of tropical abundance and promise of physical pleasure awaiting the (Western) tourist is further highlighted by Cohen (1995, p. 404) who addresses the use of images to promote tourism to the British Virgin Islands. Essentially, she argues that the islands have been eroticized and presented as 'untouched', a commodity packaged for Western consumption. Wang (2000, p. 165) calls this the feminized destination, which further promotes 'the erotic ambience and sexual lure of the destination'.

As indicated in Fig. 9.1, the use of images for creating identity is a key factor in shaping tourists' perceptions of holiday destinations. These identities can be manufactured or real, the difference being less than important for many tourist groups, and in this the Caribbean is no exception. For example, although each island has its own rich history, culture and government, the Caribbean is often referred to in promotional literature as a single entity, and represented by simple iconic images, such as the palm tree, for tourist consumption. These images are found not only in tourism marketing material produced by tour operators and cruise companies but also in regional and individual islands' marketing activities. Such emphasis on a unidimensional representation can only be negative and damaging in the long term to a complex region such as the Caribbean.

It is clear that for successful marketing, the individual identity of any tourism destination is crucial as the competitiveness of the industry demands that each location demonstrate differentiation. Indeed, for those destinations primarily attracting the mass market seeking a sun, sea and sand holiday, this quest for individuality and differentiation takes on an increased urgency (Morgan and Pritchard, 2000). However, rather than highlighting their identity, many destinations in the Caribbean choose to illustrate their advertising material with images of sandy beaches and ocean (with a fringing of palm trees). This continued emphasis on depicting the natural environment as the primary reason for visiting potentially dilutes their uniqueness and emphasizes the substitutability of some of the region's primary attractions.

In reality, of course, the Caribbean is not a single entity and this fact complicates an already complex situation, not helped by the region's high dependency upon tourism for income (Lester and Weeden, 2004). There is no doubt that cruise tourism is of huge economic value to the Caribbean, generating more than US$1 billion in cruise passenger expenditures alone during 2000 (Wood, 2004). Nevertheless, such economic dependency can result in the development of challenging and unequal power relations between cruise companies, regional marketing organizations and individual island governments. A now famous example of this is the dispute from the early 1990s when the Caribbean Community and Common Market (CARICOM) attempted to standardize head taxes in the region in order to distribute more fairly the economic value of cruise ships in the region (Pattullo, 1996). Ultimately, however, the islands could not maintain solidarity in their stand against the cruise companies and so their economic dominance over the development of cruise tourism in the region has continued.

Of course, image creation is not the sole responsibility of the Caribbean's regional marketing organizations; nor can cruise companies be blamed solely for the bland images often associated with the area. Indeed, as Smith and Duffy (2003, p. 125) assert, 'the private sector, governments and non-governmental organisations all assist in the creation and promotion of a specific image for consumption by tourists'.

This view is supported by Morgan and Pritchard (1998, p. 5) who point out:

> Although the dominant worldview is created within the centres of power by the enfranchised rather than by the disenfranchised on the margins of power, it is often a collaborative relationship, largely for economic reasons.

In part, of course, the images presented to tourists are a response to what the tourists want and expect from a destination, which in turn has been shaped by advertising, which in turn has created their expectations of the region. If the Caribbean is continually portrayed in all visual media as a tropical paradise, tourists will want to travel to experience such a paradise and, as Sheller (2004, p. 24) comments: 'Caribbean tourism is vested in the branding and marketing of Paradise.'

Promotional activities therefore become a vicious circle of expectation and desire, but one that is clearly driven by a need to satisfy the consumer, especially in countries that have a high reliance upon the revenue generated through tourism. Indeed, as Lanfant (1995, p. 32) noted: 'Tourism marketing shapes the image of a place, and then correlates the motivational systems of potential clients with the components of its identity'.

Ways of Seeing and Tourist Behaviour

As suggested earlier a variety of media perform a powerful role in the ways in which the world is visualized, and in the context of tourism the power of visual images to mediate tourist experiences is an important area of enquiry. It is clear that travel and tourism marketing in contemporary society relies heavily on the visual elements of promotion, such as that found in advertising, brochures, company websites and promotional videos. Arguably, these examples of promotional material perform a dual role. First, the primary function is its advertising and sales role; secondly, and perhaps more implicitly, the images and photographs used to represent places, people and tourist experiences become highly influential in controlling and directing the tourist gaze (Urry, 1990, 2002).

In the absence of formal training in how to sightsee, the power that the visual elements of advertising and promotion have on travel behaviour is further emphasized by Wang (2000, p. 161), who points out that the set of mental images held by tourists pertaining to a particular holiday experience or destination may result in the seeking out and gazing at particular sites and attractions during the holiday and at the same time being 'indifferent and blind to other sights that do not suit their stereotyped images'.

Certainly, omission of certain sights in advertising may contribute to the superficial consumption of places and destinations, a sentiment echoed by Bruner (1995, p. 233), who asserts that tourists' motivation for sightseeing is to visit places seen in the media rather than to experience the destination at a deeper level. Bruner explains:

> The touristic mode of experiencing is primarily visual, and to have been there, to have 'seen' it, only requires presence. The tourist 'sees' enough of the [local] ritual to confirm his prior images derived from the media, from brochures and from *National Geographic*.

Significantly, Wang (2000, p. 161) agrees, pointing out that not only do 'tourists roman-ticize sights that confirm the images presented by the mass media and advertising' but often tourists' travel experiences are thus confined to these must-see sights. This is a theme echoed by Dunn (2004) in his discussion of postcolonial travel to Africa, where he notes that tourists travel with their own prejudgement of a destination, one that has been configured through experience but also preconfigured through exposure to media representation.

In highlighting the temporary nature of the travel experience, Wang (2000) contends that tourist's sightseeing often takes place with little awareness or exposure to the local customs, norms and laws pertaining to a destination. Often the tourist map is predetermined, made up of sites and attractions that have been socially and culturally constructed as the important ones to be visited, and these are then gazed upon in isolation with little concern for the social context. In addition, the brief nature of a visit to a site or destination can result in a hurried and rather shallow impression, with the tourist often unaware of the culture and heritage of the destination, its attractions and its people.

As a stereotypical example of the focus of the tourist gaze, Fig. 9.2 serves to illustrate an image that has come to symbolize visual representation of the Caribbean. However, this particular photo serves as a pertinent reminder of the anonymity of certain landscapes, and a tourist may have to reach far into the recesses of memory to recall the exact location. As a popular view, it remains ubiquitous yet superficial, and thus the identity of the individual island is lost among the symbolic beach paradise fantasy echoed in much of the promotional material for the region.

These points of view hold particular significance for the Caribbean cruise product where the promotional material can be very selective regarding the images used to illustrate the holiday experience. This selectivity can be a powerful force in constructing, organizing and controlling tourists' 'ways of seeing', and although Caribbean cruise itineraries reflect an eclectic array of destinations and islands, the industry often presents an homogenous view of the region, one based on iconic images such as the palm tree and views of turquoise seas.

Fig. 9.2. Photograph taken on cruise excursion ashore in the Caribbean. Photo: Jo-Anne Lester.

Caribbean Cruise Tourism Imagery

In the case of cruise tourism generally, the traditional UK cruise experience has long been associated with echoes of Englishness and Empire, and of course colonialism. Images used to promote Cunard, for example, have exploited nostalgia for a golden era when 'Britannia' ruled the waves. Significantly, the importance of colonialism to the marketing of the UK cruise market is especially associated with P&O, whose traditional target market, seen as older and wealthier, values the 'Britishness' of the company. However, Cunard also connects 'Britishness' with ships such as the *Queen Elizabeth 2*, which was designed and operated to emphasize British ambience (Douglas and Douglas, 2004).

In their evaluation of the imagery most often associated with the cruise product, Douglas and Douglas discuss the prominent use made by the industry of universal themes such as romance, luxury, exotica and nostalgia (see Douglas and Douglas, 2004, pp. 151–174 for an extended discussion of

these themes). Taking the theme of romance, for example, they draw attention to the names of ships such as Carnival's *Fantasy* and *Ecstasy*, and highlight the role of the cruise ship in the heyday of the Hollywood movie, mentioning films such as *Romance on the High Seas* starring Doris Day and *An Affair to Remember* with Deborah Kerr. Nostalgia too is discussed with regard to its role in marketing for cruise companies, especially with reference to the UK market. With its references to Empire and hints of bygone eras, Douglas and Douglas (2004, p. 166) argue: 'Elements of nostalgia as a marketing tool are better seen in cruising than in any other form of travel'.

Wood (2004, p. 153) too addresses the aura and imagery that has developed around not only cruising but also the cruise ships themselves, and his work is specifically concerned with the relationship between cruise tourism and the Caribbean. He argues that the Great White Fleet (so-called because of the colour of the ships) of the United Fruit Company, the 'dominant cruise presence' in the area in the early part of the twentieth century, did much to perpetuate the neo-colonial associations already apparent in the region. In addition, the sheer physical appearance and presence of large modern cruise ships, some of which are now able to carry up to 5000 people on board, is clearly symbolic within such a historical context.

As highlighted earlier, the visual element is highly prominent in cruise brochures (Douglas and Douglas, 2004) with the importance of the brochures generally to the marketing functions of tour operators highlighted by Horner and Swarbrooke (2004). In order to illustrate the points highlighted in this chapter and to reflect on a current UK example of the visual portrayal of cruise holidays in the region, the following description provides an analysis of the dominant imagery contained within the brochure of P&O Cruises (2004/05).

Within the brochure there are 17 full-page images, which can be categorized into two themes: those of the destination and those that depict scenes on board the ship. A dominant theme of the destination imagery is that of the iconic palm tree. Significantly, the pristine, untouched paradise is emphasized within the first page of the brochure, with the stereotypical palm tree, deserted beach and pristine blue seas.

Another striking picture depicts an idealistic image of a tourist relaxing on a pristine beach amongst the palms and blues seas, almost as if to suggest 'this is paradise, you too can have some'.

Other images offer a sense of companionship by hinting at beach activity with some tourists, sun beds and umbrellas nestled within the palm-fringed beaches. These images could be perceived as offering a tranquil and secluded setting, at the same time avoiding the reality of the mass market. Interestingly, one picture that features the ship as part of the landscape depicts the stereotypical image of the palm tree, fringing the white sand with the blue sea stretching out in front of the cruise ship. This faultless representation of the ship amidst the idyllic setting again hints at perfect paradise, and the central position of the ship in the image denotes power, as if to signify 'all of the Caribbean is set out for tourists and cruisers' delight' (Fig. 9.3).

The most striking theme of the ship-based images, of which there are six, is that five of these depict the presence of heterosexual couples and in many cases the pose and positioning of the couples indicates happiness, intimacy and of course, romance. Other signifiers of these emotions such as cocktails, wine and champagne are common features. Interestingly, one of these images portrays an elegantly dressed single female passenger in her cabin on the balcony, whilst gazing out to sea. However, the presence of two glasses of wine would appear to indicate that she is not alone, and on closer inspection, the carefully framed photograph indicates the presence of a discarded suit jacket and tie to signify that she is part of a (heterosexual) couple, i.e. not a widow or a single lady.

From the above it would appear that the passengers feature significantly in the representation of life on board a ship. Interestingly, only one of the full-page images features ship personnel, this being a female entertainer. Local culture is not prominently displayed, with the only hint of the cultural environment being confined to one full-page image depicting the architectural features of what appears to be a traditional colonial residence. Ironically, this image is not of the Caribbean but taken in New Orleans, the base port for a particular cruise itinerary.

Fig. 9.3. Copy of image in brochure of P&O Cruises (2004).

Significantly, there is no palm tree in evidence but an abundance of vegetation and tropical plants is portrayed.

To some extent the dominant imagery displayed in P&O's brochure is a key indicator that the cruise industry does in fact rely heavily on the natural, pristine environment to market the cruise experience in the region. The type of iconic imagery associated with the destination is not uncommon to that already identified in travel marketing of the Caribbean in general, as explored earlier. However, in the case of cruise tourism, it could be argued that notions of 'paradise' and 'getting away from it all' are not entirely accurate portrayals of reality. One only has to imagine – mass ships, mass people, mass disembarkation into the destinations and embarkation into the environment, often with little time to witness or enjoy the pristine paradise emphasized by the imagery. By contrast, other imagery that suggests romance, glitz and glamour, fine wine and dining and the cruise ship taking centre stage are key features not uncommon to the cruising experience, certainly in the case of the traditional P&O product.

The influence that the strong imagery of the Caribbean and the cruise experience has on individuals' 'ways of seeing' and thus the extent to which imagery controls the tourist gaze, experiences and behaviour is empirically an underexplored area in tourism studies and would certainly be worthy of further enquiry. However, whilst reflecting on the nature of the cruise experience some interesting issues arise, particularly regarding tourists' sightseeing patterns and their consumption of the Caribbean.

Destination and Operational Control

It could be suggested that given the travel patterns of cruise tourists, these being of a tightly controlled nature, with limited time ashore and highly organized excursions operated by the cruise companies, those promoting cruise tourism in the Caribbean play a powerful role in directing the tourist gaze. Significantly, the cruise ship has already been, and continues to be, compared with both a tourist enclave (Wood, 2000; Lester and Weeden, 2004) and a tourist bubble, with the cruise ship being 'a controlled, safe, pleasurable environment with a wide range

of recreational facilities and activities' (Jaakson, 2004, p. 46). As Lester and Weeden (2004, p. 47) highlight:

> [C]ruise ships dock in a destination, the vessel is the accommodation, passengers need not venture ashore unless desired and often the time ashore is limited with brief excursions. Passenger activities are usually carefully coordinated and controlled within distinct spatial areas.

This raises the question of whether cruise passengers want to experience the port destinations, languages and people, as this is not what they have seen in the promotional literature. Indeed, as Henthorne (2000, p. 24) states, cruise 'lines seek to ensure that guests have only positive experiences in port' and as the average time passengers spend in port is less than 5 hours (Henthorne, 2000), the experience of life outside the bubble is likely to be superficial and unrepresentative. Indeed, in some islands, port visits can be as little as 90 minutes, with passengers seemingly wanting to walk less than 200 m from the beachfront disembarkation point (Jaakson, 2004). Of course, this may be exactly what tourists seek on their holiday, an issue discussed by Pattullo (1996, p. 172) when she talked of nervous package tourists 'being affronted by authentic Caribbean life' on the island of Bequia. The same may be said for cruise passengers because many of them prefer to remain on board rather than go ashore on a port visit (Dahl, 1995, as cited in Jaakson, 2004).

Significantly, this perceived reluctance to engage in the authentic experience of the Caribbean is echoed in the safe and sterile images used to promote the region. As a result the myth locks these destinations into 'a permanent pristine paradise' (Echtner and Prasad, 2003, p. 674), and they become objects of desire as seen mirrored in a key theme associated with the Caribbean, that of the Western playboy, with the islands functioning purely as a fantasy backdrop. In the context of cruise tourism, some may argue that the cruise ship is the pristine paradise and that the Caribbean is the insignificant backdrop. In fact, described as floating resorts (Wood, 2000), the ships are now so large that they almost become a backdrop for the Caribbean.

The comforting cocoon of the ship, detaching passengers from the world (Douglas and

Douglas, 2004), certainly helps the tourist to forget the harsh realities of life, both at home and in the Caribbean. Indeed it is easy to understand how uncomfortable the tourist might feel, lying by the swimming pool, topping up the tan, if what came to mind was how Caribbean history is 'built on plantations, slavery and brutality' (Morgan and Pritchard, 1998, p. 222). As Jaakson (2004) points out, the difference between the cocoon of a luxury cruise ship and the actuality of life in a poor Caribbean country can be shocking and extreme, and attempts to minimize the impact on the cruise passenger could clearly become a prime objective for cruise companies.

Another interesting dimension of the cruise experience and the tourist encounter with local cultures is the extent to which passengers come into contact with people from the different islands. Even the workforce on the ship rarely encompasses the local people of the islands being visited to any significant degree (Wood, 2000), and this reinforces the lack of connectivity with the history and cultural identity of the different destinations in the region.

Conclusion

The popularity of the Caribbean for tourism and as a key destination for the cruise industry is undeniable. To date much attention in tourism studies has focused on the ways in which the region is promoted for tourism in general, with the industry endlessly portraying a pristine, natural environment using the palm tree in its visual material as a common signifier of 'paradise'. It is argued, that to some extent, the origins of this popularized and somewhat superficial image of the Caribbean as a tropical and exotic holiday destination for Western consumption emerged during the region's colonial era.

A brief analysis of the ways in which cruise tourism in the region is visually promoted suggests that the cruise industry also relies extensively on visual markers such as the palm tree emphasizing the natural environment, imbued with white sandy beaches surrounded by crystal clear waters. While these idealized images remain significant promotional elements within cruise marketing material, images depicting the individual identities of the various islands do not take centre stage. Thus whether the cruising experience focuses on tourist experiences of different landscapes and cultural encounters or whether the ship is indeed the core destination is a concern for many islands that rely on the economic benefits of the industry. Certainly the full-page images used in the brochure of P&O Cruises (2004/05) reinforce the observations made by Douglas and Douglas (2004) that prominent features of cruise brochure imagery include the magnificence of the vessels emanating luxury and romance.

The extent to which the visual portrayal of the Caribbean and the cruise experience influences consumer perceptions, subsequent travel experiences and tourist behaviour would benefit from further enquiry. However, a cruise holiday is unique in that the itineraries are highly organized and controlled by those selling and operating the holidays, which inevitably commands the extent of the tourist's encounter with the various islands and their ports of call. Often onshore experiences, which are usually limited in time, are confined to the 'must see' sites depicted and reinforced in the promotional material as the important ones to experience. Therefore it could be suggested that not only does the cruise industry, in its marketing and operational aspects, play a major role in determining tourists' time ashore and the attractions visited but there is also the inevitable occurrence that tourists' appreciation and ways of seeing the unique identities of the various islands and ports of call become somewhat limited. Consequently, tourist experiences and visual reminders brought home from holiday, such as photographs, continue to play a role in the representation of the region, one that relies on notions of 'paradise' and the natural environment.

References

Baloglu, S. and McCleary, K.W. (1999) A model of destination image formation. *Annals of Tourism Research* 26(4), 868–897.

Berger, J. (1972) *Ways of Seeing*. Penguin Books, London.

Bruner, E.M. (1995) The ethnographer/tourist in Indonesia. In: Lanfant, M.-F., Allcock, J.B. and Bruner, E.M. (eds) *International Tourism: Identity and Change*. Sage, London, pp. 224–241.

Cohen, C.B. (1995) Marketing paradise, making nation. *Annals of Tourism Research* 22(2), 404–421.

CLIA (Cruise Lines International Association) (2002) Cruise industry rebounding at record pace in 2002. Press Release. 10 September. Available at: http://www.cruising.org/CruiseNews/news

Dahl, J. (1995) Why go ashore when the ship's so nice? *The Wall Street Journal* 11 August, B1 and B9.

Dann, G. (1996) *The Language of Tourism: A Sociolinguistic Perspective.* CAB International, Wallingford, UK.

Douglas, N. and Douglas, N. (2004) *The Cruise Experience: Global and Regional Issues in Cruising.* Pearson Education, Frenchs Forest, New South Wales, Australia.

Dunn, K.C. (2004) Fear of a black planet: anarchy, anxieties and post-colonial travel. *Third World Quarterly* 25(3), 483–499.

Duval, D.T. (ed.) (2004) *Tourism in the Caribbean: Trends, Development, Prospects.* Routledge, London.

Echtner, C.M. and Prasad, P. (2003) The context of third world tourism marketing. *Annals of Tourism Research* 30(3), 660–682.

Grove, R. (1995) *Green Imperialism: Colonial Expansion, Tropical Island Edens and the Origins of Environmentalism.* Cambridge University Press, Cambridge, pp. 1600–1860.

Hall, S. (1997) *Representation: Cultural Representations and Signifying Practices.* Sage, London.

Henthorne, T.L. (2000) An analysis of expenditures by cruise ship passengers in Jamaica. *Journal of Travel Research* 38, 246–250.

Horner, S. and Swarbrooke, J. (2004) *International Cases in Tourism Management.* Butterworth-Heinemann, Oxford.

Jaakson, R. (2004) Beyond the tourist bubble? Cruiseship passengers in port. *Annals of Tourism Research* 31(1), 44–60.

Jayawardena, C. (2002) Mastering Caribbean tourism. *International Journal of Contemporary Hospitality Management* 14(2), 88–93.

Jenkins, O.H. (2003) Photography and travel brochures: the circle of representation. *Tourism Geographies* 5(3), 305–328.

Lanfant, M.-F. (1995) International tourism, internationalization and the challenge to identity. In: Lanfant, M.-F., Allcock, J.B. and Bruner, E.M. (eds) *International Tourism: Identity and Change.* Sage, London, pp. 24–43.

Lester, J. and Weeden, C. (2004) Stakeholders, the natural environment and the future of Caribbean cruise tourism. *International Journal of Tourism Research* 6, 39–50.

Macnaghten, P. and Urry, J. (1998) *Contested Natures.* Sage, London.

Mintel (2004) Cruises – North America and the Caribbean. Travel and tourism analyst, June. Mintel International Group Limited, London.

Morgan, N. and Pritchard, A. (1998) *Tourism, Promotion and Power: Creating Images, Creating Identities.* John Wiley & Sons, Chichester, UK.

Morgan, N. and Pritchard, A. (2000) *Advertising in Tourism and Leisure.* Butterworth-Heinemann, Oxford.

Palmer, C. (1994) Tourism and colonialism: the experience of the Bahamas. *Annals of Tourism Research* 21(4), 792–811.

Pattullo, P. (1996) *Last Resorts: The Cost of Tourism in the Caribbean.* Cassell, London.

P&O Cruises (2004/05) *Caribbean,* 2nd edn. October 2004–April 2005. P&O Cruises, Southampton.

Shaw, G., Agarwal, S. and Bull, P. (2000) Tourism consumption and tourist behaviour: a British perspective. *Tourism Geographies* 2(3), 264–289.

Sheller, M. (2003) *Consuming the Caribbean: From Arawaks to Zombies.* Routledge, London.

Sheller, M. (2004) Natural hedonism: the invention of Caribbean islands as tropical playgrounds. In: Duval, D.T. (ed.) *Tourism in the Caribbean: Trends, Development, Prospects.* Routledge, London, pp. 23–38.

Smith, M. and Duffy, R. (2003) *The Ethics of Tourism Development.* Routledge, London.

Sturken, M. and Cartwright, L. (2001) *Practices of Looking: An Introduction to Visual Culture.* Oxford University Press, Oxford.

Urry, J. (1990) *The Tourist Gaze: Leisure and Travel in Contemporary Societies.* Sage, London.

Urry, J. (2002) *The Tourist Gaze: Leisure and Travel in Contemporary Societies,* 2nd edn. Sage, London.

Wang, N. (2000) *Tourism and Modernity: A Sociological Analysis.* Pergamon Press, Oxford.

Wood, R.E. (2000) Caribbean cruise tourism: globalization at sea. *Annals of Tourism Research* 27(2), 345–370.

Wood, R.E. (2004) Global currents: cruise ships in the Caribbean Sea. In: Duval, D.T. (ed.) *Tourism in the Caribbean: Trends, Development, Prospects.* Routledge, London, pp. 152–171.

10 The Impact of Interpretation on Passengers of Expedition Cruises

Kaye Walker[1] and Gianna Moscardo[2]

[1]James Cook University, Faculty of Law, Business and Creative Arts, School of Business, Tourism Program, Townsville, QLD 4811, Australia;
[2]James Cook University, School of Business, Townsville, QLD 4811, Australia

Introduction

Sustainability is arguably the most commonly cited theme related to tourism at the start of the twenty-first century and this is as true for cruises as for any other form of tourism. While the concept of sustainability is a complex and contested one there is general consensus that for tourism it involves at least three dimensions: the minimization or elimination of negative impacts; the provision of positive contributions to the destination and host community; and the provision of a quality experience for the participating tourists (Weaver, 2000; Ritchie *et al.*, 2001). One of the potential positive contributions that tourism can make is to foster the development of environmental and cultural awareness and pro-conservation attitudes in tourists. One of the tools that can be applied by tourism operators and managers to achieve this positive contribution is the provision of quality interpretation (Lane, 1991; Moscardo, 1998a; Weiler and Ham, 2001). This chapter will analyse this tool and the role it can play in enhancing the experience and conservation awareness and support of passengers on expedition cruises.

Interpretation and Sustainability

Moscardo (2000, p. 327) defines interpretation as 'any activity which seeks to explain to people the significance of an object, a culture or a place.

Its three core functions are to enhance visitor experiences, to improve visitor knowledge or understanding, and to assist in the protection or conservation of places or culture.' It is through these three core functions that interpretation can contribute to the sustainability of tourism operations. Improving knowledge and awareness provide the foundation for encouraging minimal impact behaviours. Visitors must have the relevant knowledge to be able to make better choices about where they go, what they do and how they do it. Knowledge by itself, however, is rarely sufficient to result in behavioural and attitudinal changes. In addition to providing knowledge, a quality interpretive experience should contribute to positive and rewarding experiences. This combination of rewarding experiences and knowledge can encourage the development of positive conservation attitudes and changes in values (Moscardo, 1998a,b; Newsome *et al.*, 2002). Newsome *et al.* (2002) also argue that effective interpretation can make tourists more aware of human impacts on the global environment and this further contributes to greater support for wider conservation efforts.

Expedition Cruises

As noted elsewhere in this book, within the traditional cruise ship industry, there are a number of alternative types of cruise. While these alternatives may make up only a small percentage of the total sector, they have experienced rapidly increasing growth rates in recent years (Cartwright and Baird, 1999). One of these alternatives is a form of ecotourism referred to as expedition cruises. There are many remote parts of the world that can only be visited by sea and access is provided to these areas by these smaller expeditionary cruise ships (Cartwright and Baird, 1999) carrying up to 120 passengers and offering an educational experience with teams of environmental and cultural guides on board (Douglas and Douglas, 2004). These expedition guides, as well as local guides and park rangers in certain situations, provide intensive interpretation through the conduct of a number of activities such as lectures, tours, guided walks, guided snorkelling and zodiac boat trips. Zodiacs are approximately 4-m-long rubber dinghies that take 12 passengers at a time and are stored on the ship for use at locations where the ship cannot dock at the shore or where there is no shore, e.g. at coral reef sites. Typically the expedition cruise staff are experienced and/or qualified in various aspects of the ecological and cultural setting of the destinations. Some guides also drive the zodiacs to provide passengers with access to land or wildlife and scenic viewing in many of the locations.

This intensive interpretation and the central role of guides in this interpretation are major features of expedition cruises. Both Hall (1993) and Smith (1993) suggested that the primary role of the tour guides on expedition cruises in Antarctic regions is to educate and control the behaviour of visitors. Ham and Weiler (2002) provide a more detailed analysis of the role of the guide with a focus on the attributes of guides most valued by passengers on expedition cruises in Alaska and the Galapagos Islands. In this research, passengers valued guides who were passionate, insightful, enjoyable, relevant and easy to follow, who had local experience, and time and group management skills. This study also highlights the important role that guides and interpretive activities play in this type of ecotourism. None of these studies, however, address the effectiveness of the guides and the interpretive activities in terms of contributing to passengers' knowledge and awareness of their impacts and conservation issues, or influencing their attitudes, values and behaviours. Ham and Weiler (2002) did conclude that the more detailed findings of their study were consistent with existing principles of interpretive practice, suggesting that guides who displayed the attributes noted as important by passengers could be effective interpreters with respect to ensuring that ecotourism does contribute to global conservation.

While Ham and Weiler (2002) note the existence of a set of basic principles of effective interpretation, there exists only minimal evidence of the success of interpretation in achieving the goals of encouraging change in tourists' conservation attitudes, values and behaviours (Medio et al., 1997). This lack of evidence may be partly due to a lack of actual research and partly due to the challenges of conducting this type of evaluation research. Loomis (2002) provides a review of some of the main barriers to conducting evaluations of interpretation, including the challenge of demonstrating a substantial and/or statistically significant change in any one case. A study by Beaumont (1998) provides an example where no differences were found in the environmental knowledge, attitudes and ratings of environmentalism of tourists who had taken a guided ecotour and those who had not. The researcher concluded that the findings may be due to a 'ceiling effect' in that most people had reasonably strong environmental attitudes prior to taking part in their ecotourism experience and such attitudes were not affected by a small increase in knowledge. Alternatively it was possible that a short ecotourism experience may be insufficient for changing or strengthening environmental attitudes and behaviours. This is a conclusion also offered by Lee and Moscardo (2006) in their study of visitors spending time at an ecolodge. These researchers also note the possibility of the impact of cumulative interpretation experiences. In their study, visitors who had a positive ecotourism experience, which included interpretive activities, were more likely to intend to participate in these activities in the future and appeared to be more open to changing attitudes and values.

Stewart et al. (1998) offer a third reason for the limited evidence to support the effectiveness of interpretation in influencing conservation attitudes and values, that of limitations in the methodologies typically used to study interpretation. In their study of visitors to Mount Cook National Park in New Zealand, Stewart et al. (1998) opted for a qualitative open-ended interview method and focused on the themes of appreciation of place in their content analyses. This critique consists of two parts: the need for greater use of qualitative methodologies and the need to broaden the range of concepts used as measures of interpretation effectiveness. Interpretation evaluation studies commonly use quantitative methodologies and explore changes in factual knowledge and/or awareness of impacts or conservation issues (see Roggenbuck, 1992 and Moscardo, 1998b for reviews of literature in this area). Some studies have explored attitudinal and behavioural changes, but few have attempted to examine more complex changes in people's understandings about conservation issues (Moscardo *et al.*, 1998). Armstrong and Weiler's approach (2002) is one of the few that combines a qualitative and quantitative evaluation in this area. Their investigation of the conservation 'messages' delivered and received in a number of tour operations in a protected area incorporated the qualitative method of participant observation. They stated that this method was able to get beyond the anecdotal and limited research evidence that has been used up to now to inform protected area management.

Passenger Perspectives on Expedition Cruise Interpretation

Expedition cruises offer a rare opportunity to explore a situation where tourists are exposed to multiple forms of intensive interpretation over an extended time period. This setting is also relevant to the question of the extent to which the interpretive elements of ecotourism experiences can contribute to the sustainability of tourism operations. The following section describes the main results of a study of passengers on three expedition cruises in Australia and Papua New Guinea. The three cruises were each about 12 days in duration: one focused on Tasmania and the south-eastern coast of Australia; one that moved along the eastern Australian coast with a focus on the Great Barrier Reef; and one that was concentrated on the far northern section of the Great Barrier Reef, Torres Strait and Papua New Guinea. One of the authors was a guide, lecturer and zodiac driver on board for all three trips. The cruises were conducted upon an expedition ship

belonging to the US-based company, Clipper Cruises. This company operates four small ships, two of which are dedicated to US waters, one to the Pacific region, and another to far northern and southern global locations. Cartwright and Baird (1999) would refer to these particular cruises as 'soft' expeditions, distinguishing them from 'hard' expeditions with respect to providing 'mainstream standards of accommodation, but on smaller vessels' as opposed to 'most basic conditions'. The study used a qualitative methodological style that sought to explore how passengers described in their own words their conservation awareness, attitudes and values in relation to the interpretive activities offered throughout the cruise. A total of 60 passengers completed a short, semi-structured survey centred on four open-ended questions, towards the end of their voyage. Observations and conversational interviews were also conducted to supplement the analysis of the responses given to the questions. The questions related to perceived learning and benefits gained, and the importance and evaluations of the interpretive experiences offered on the cruises. The responses to these questions were analysed using a laddering technique adapted from the means–end theory following from work by Klenosky *et al.* (1998). Klenosky *et al.* (1998) used this technique to explore the relationships between interpretive services and personal values for tourists interviewed in six South Carolina state parks.

Means–End Analysis and Interpretive Theory

Means–end theory comes from the area of consumer behaviour and was developed as a theoretical construct to explain and predict the choices and decisions that people make with respect to product and service purchases. In means–end theory three core elements combine to result in product or service choice: the attributes or features of the product or service; the benefits that consumers see as resulting from these attributes; and the values these benefits contribute to. Consumers buy products and services (the means) that reflect their values (the ends) (Gutman, 1997; Klenosky *et al.*, 1998; Mort and Rose, 2004). The three elements represent different levels of abstraction or types of knowledge starting with concrete product details (attributes), moving to the more general benefits that are seen as the consequences of these attributes (benefits), and finishing at the abstract level of personal values (Gutman, 1997; Mort and Rose, 2004). These elements and the links between them are referred to as attribute–benefit–value chains (ABVs) and these chains are summarized as graphic images called hierarchical value maps or HVMs (Klenosky *et al.*, 1998). These ABVs and HVMs are derived from an interviewing format known as laddering. In laddering, respondents are asked to offer attributes of products or services that are important to them and then state why that attribute is important. In turn they are asked why that feature or benefit is important and the questioning continues seeking the elements in the ladder of abstraction (Klenosky *et al.*, 1998).

This notion of differing levels of abstractness of knowledge is based on a common or core concept in psychology referred to as cognitive schemata (Orsingher and Marzocchi, 2003). A cognitive schema is a mental representation that organizes knowledge about topics in a person's memory. Orsingher and Marzocchi (2003, p. 203) define a cognitive schema as 'a hierarchical cognitive structure that contains individual knowledge about a domain, the attributes that pertain to that particular domain and the set of relationships among these attributes'. These schemata assist in the interpretation and processing of new information, the retrieval of memories and the direction of action, and they link what we know to what we feel and want (Moscardo, 1998b; Orsingher and Marzocchi, 2003). Changes in cognitive schemata are at the core of many theoretical perspectives on effective interpretation and persuasive communication, and in these interpretive theories it is assumed that effective interpretation is that which results in more extensive changes to the more abstract or deeper levels of cognitive schemata (Cialdini, 1996; Ham and Krumpe, 1996; Ballantyne, 1998; Moscardo, 1998b).

Given these shared assumptions, means–end theory would appear to offer an alternative approach to understanding the outcomes of interpretive experiences. In essence, this use looks at the ABVs in reverse and links perceived learning to more specific types of outcomes associated with certain interpretive elements. This process is presented in Fig. 10.1 and

is similar to approaches that have been taken in other areas (see Bagozzi and Dabholkar, 2000; Orsingher and Marzocchi, 2003 for examples).

Expedition Cruise Interpretation Attributes, Benefits and Resulting Values

The majority of passengers rated the inclusion of interpretation with the presence of expedition staff in their choice of cruise as either 'important' (19%) or 'very important' (66%). The present study of expedition cruise passengers explored responses to the following four questions:

- What do you consider was the best interpretive activity or activities on the expedition?
- Why was this activity or activities the best and what specific features contributed to this?
- What was the most important or significant thing you learnt or achieved from this activity or activities?
- What was the most important or significant thing you learnt from the trip overall?

The first stage of the analysis examined the responses to these in terms of the attributes of the cruise interpretation noted by passengers, the benefits they felt accrued from these attributes and the resulting values connected to these benefits. The passengers' stories about their interpretive experiences were examined for examples of attributes, benefits and values. These elements were defined as follows:

- Attributes were defined as features of interpretive activities or actual interpretive activities (e.g. staff knowledge or first-hand experience).
- Benefits were defined as the psychological, physical and/or social outcomes or consequences that were generated from the identified attributes (e.g. an enhanced or more rewarding experience, having fun or increased knowledge).
- Values were defined as abstract beliefs identified as having personal significance or importance to the passenger (e.g. developing a sense of place for the visited destination and having a greater level of environmental concern).

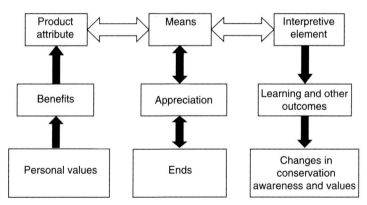

Fig. 10.1. Adapting means–end chains to assess interpretation.

The 60 passenger responses generated 172 means–end ladders. More than half of the passengers (57% of the sample) identified more than one and up to four interpretive activities within their responses to the questions about which interpretive activities were better than others. For many passengers choosing any one activity over another was often difficult and several suggested in their responses that it was a combination of activities that provided the 'best' results. Overall 27 passengers included snorkelling *with* expedition staff in their best interpretive experiences, 27 included walks and zodiac tours *with* expedition staff, 20 referred to land tours *with* local guides and 19 passengers included lectures/briefings/recapitulations in their answers. Also, 17 passengers answered these questions by talking about the features of this particular type of cruising in addition to specific interpretive components. Table 10.1 provides a summary of the attributes, benefits and values determined from the laddering analysis for these four types of interpretive activity and expedition cruising in general.

The three most common attributes overall were the experiential nature of the activities, staff expertise and staff dedication. The two staff-related categories referred to recognition of the staff's degree of knowledge and competence (expertise), and staff enthusiasm and dedication to their role in assisting passengers to participate, learn and understand from the interpretive activities. The experiential activity component referred to the identification of the importance of actually experiencing the environment or activities first hand. Examples of passenger responses within these categories are:

- 'Robert is very knowledgeable in his history field.' (Staff expertise.)
- 'Listening to caring and experienced expedition staff.' (Staff dedication.)
- 'I didn't even know about harvesting kelp and now I've *tasted* it at the plant. I did know a little about Australia's convict history, but now I've *stood* in a convict's stall in the chapel at Port Arthur and *felt* the isolation. And I've *wallowed* with seals.' (Experiential activities.)

A total of nine types of benefit were also identified for these interpretive and expedition cruise attributes. Environmental awareness was the most commonly reported benefit and was defined as the recognition and/or understanding of environmental and/or cultural issues, concerns, balances, connections or concepts. A sample response was 'a totally new understanding of who the Aboriginal peoples are, the land, sea life and spiritual meanings in their culture'. Learning was reported only slightly less often and was defined as the recognition of the importance of having learnt and/or increased knowledge. Enjoyment was used for responses that included words such as 'enjoy', 'fun', 'liked' and 'loved'. Staff interaction referred to the accessibility of the staff as a consequence of the way the activities were designed as distinct from the staff-related attributes. In this category passengers referred to the benefit of one-to-one interaction with respect to increasing their ability to

Table 10.1. Interpretation attributes, benefits and values.

Categories	Lectures/ briefings/ recaps	Local land tours	Walks/ zodiac tours	Snorkel tours	Expedition cruising in general	Total n	%
Attributes							
Experiential activities	1	12	10	15	11	49	82
Staff expertise	12	12	12	7	1	44	73
Staff dedication	6	3	4	7	6	26	43
Presence of staff	1	1	1	2	7	7	12
Facilitation	–	–	–	–	9	13	22
Interpretive signs	–	–	–	–	1	1	2
Local guides	–	–	–	–	–	1	2
Benefits							
Environmental awareness	14	13	8	14	2	51	85
Learning	15	17	6	6	5	49	82
Enjoyment	4	3	7	4	3	18	30
Experiential	11	3	1	1	1	16	27
Enhancement	2	4	4	5	–	18	30
Staff interaction	–	–	1	1	–	1	2
Connectedness	–	–	1	–	–	1	2
Exercise	–	–	–	–	–	1	2
Excitement	–	–	–	–	–	1	2
Passenger interaction	–	–	–	–	–	–	–
Values							
Appreciation	4	10	4	3	–	21	35
Global perspective	4	4	1	1	13	10	17
Self-appreciation	–	2	1	–	–	4	7
Sense of place	2	1	2	1	–	3	5
Environmental concern	–	1	–	–	–	2	3
Stories to tell	–	–	–	–	–	1	2
Appreciation for this type of cruising	–	–	–	–	–	13	22

Note: All figures, except for the last column, refer to the number of times the category is included in passenger responses. Figures in the last column indicate the per cent of the sample including this category in a response.

understand, learn and enjoy, e.g. 'The interest that staff show in the subjects and in finding the answers to questions and sharing that . . . brings together my understanding of what other forms (lectures, book, etc) give as cold facts'. Experiential enhancement was the fifth most common benefit and the last category used by more than a single passenger. It referred to the cumulative effect of the attributes in making an experience more rewarding, e.g. 'All these activities . . . helped "train" or prepare you for the subsequent activity. For example, visit to marine research centre made subsequent snorkelling much more informative and interesting.'

Finally, seven more abstract concepts or values were determined. Two of these, appreciation and a global perspective, dominated the responses in this section. Appreciation was used for passenger responses that demonstrated a development beyond mere enjoyment or understanding of a place to include the discussion of the significance of a place or culture in a personal context such as in the following example: 'A positive understanding of the many facets of Tasmania as compared to the world I had already known'. The category of a global perspective was typified by the following response: 'Better appreciation for preserving our environment throughout the world'. This response highlights a movement to concerns and awareness beyond the specific location visited.

It is interesting to note that those passengers who talked about expedition cruising as a particular type of tourist experience did not talk about a higher or more abstract level of knowledge. Rather it seemed that they focused on this particular form of cruising and noted the attributes, especially the presence of the expedition staff, which contributed to an appreciation of, and enthusiasm for, this form of ecotourism. This is consistent with Lee and Moscardo's finding (2005) that for first-time participants a rewarding ecotourism experience can encourage an intention to pursue more ecotourism options in the future. In turn, this is likely to expose these visitors to a wider range of conservation messages and offers the potential of contributing to conservation awareness over a more extended period of time.

Table 10.2 presents a summary of the benefits and values reported by passengers for the expedition cruise experience overall, and these are the outcomes of the combinations of the various interpretive elements included in the cruise programme. A very simple pattern emerges from these responses. The interpretive programme contributes to environmental awareness and in turn this appears to be linked to environmental concern and the building of bridges between the individual and the destination experienced (referred to as appreciation). Environmental concern was the category applied to passenger responses, which expressed a position or value of concern for the current status of, or future implications for, the place or culture experienced, e.g. 'It deserves to be protected as it currently is. It added to our understanding of the world. Ecologically delicate but currently well preserved. Hopefully this will continue. Beware of large tourist attraction.'

The Main Linkages Between Attributes, Benefits and Values

The second step in the analysis was to explore the linkages or co-occurrence of these attributes, benefits and values to build HVMs. Figure 10.2 presents a summary of the main linkages made across all four of the interpretive activities that were included in passenger responses. In this figure interpretive attributes are presented within rectangles, the benefits of these attributes within diamonds and the more abstract levels of knowledge or values within ellipses. In addition, the thickness of the con-

Table 10.2. Interpretation of benefits and values for the cruise overall.

Categories	Total	
	n	%
Benefits		
Environmental awareness	38	63
Enjoyment	1	2
Staff interaction	1	2
Values		
Appreciation	22	37
Environmental concern	10	17
Global perspective	3	5
Self-appreciation	2	3
Sense of place	2	3
Environmental responsibility	3	5

Note: All figures, except for the last column, refer to the number of times the category is included in passenger responses. Figures in the last column indicate the per cent of the sample including this category in a response.

necting arrows reflects the frequency with which the connection was made in the responses of the passengers.

In summary the map indicates that it is a combination of the expedition guides and the experiential, first-hand nature of the activities offered on expedition cruises that promotes learning and environmental awareness. In turn, environmental awareness is strongly and directly linked to an enhanced appreciation of the personal significance of the expedition experience and the knowledge gained.

Taking into consideration the passenger responses about what they had learnt from the overall cruise, it was found that environmental awareness was also linked to positive conservation attitudes by 10 of the 38 passengers who listed environmental awareness as a benefit of the cruise. This suggests that for the cumulative experience of the interpretive activities offered on these expedition cruises there is a core pathway that starts with the presence of the expedition guides (in particular their expertise and enthusiasm) and the intensive first-hand environmental experiences offered. This combination contributes to learning and environmental awareness via experiential enhancement, staff interaction and enjoyment. In turn, awareness

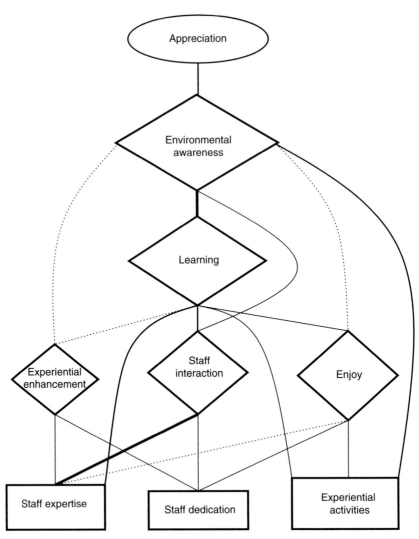

Fig. 10.2. Summary hierarchical value map for all interpretive activities.

of environmental issues and challenges encourage self-reflection on the part of some passengers, who not only developed a personal appreciation of their experience but were also able to place this appreciation into a global perspective with regard to environmental concern.

This pathway is consistent with several theories of persuasive communication and attitudinal change, and of effective interpretation. For example, the core pathway described above matches very closely the proposed process outlined in the Elaboration Likelihood Model of attitude change (Petty *et al.*, 1992). In addition,

the emphasis on first-hand experience is at the core of Tilden's classic set of interpretation principles (1977). Both the varied and multisensory nature of the first-hand experiences and the need for visitors to build a personal link to the material presented (as described in the appreciation value) are also core elements of Moscardo's Mindfulness approach (1998a,b) to interpretation.

In addition to confirming some of the existing interpretive theories and principles, these results also highlight two important features of the interpretation offered on expedition cruises. First, the results confirm the value of cumulative and varied interpretation experiences in enhancing environmental conservation awareness. This possibility has been suggested elsewhere (Beaumont, 1998; Lee and Moscardo, 2005) but little research has been done to investigate it. Secondly, the present study highlights the importance of the expedition guides for fostering the development of conservation attitudes. While Ham and Weiler's study (2002) found that passengers believe that enthusiastic and expert guides are important to their experience, they did not demonstrate a link between these qualities and increases in passenger knowledge and awareness or conservation support.

The Impact of Interpretation on Expedition Cruise Passengers

This study, conducted on expedition cruises in Australia and Papua New Guinea, demonstrated that it is possible that this form of ecotourism can make a positive contribution to the sustainability of this type of cruising. Specifically it found that the type of interpretation offered by these cruises can contribute to environmental awareness, a personal connection to the destinations visited and a broader or global sense of environmental concern, whilst enhancing the passenger experience. It is important to note some limitations to this conclusion. First these links between the interpretation and environmental concern were established only for a subsection of the passengers who participated in the study. Secondly, it is not possible to determine if these attitudes and concerns were lasting or if they were further developed into changed behaviour at home or in other locations. But the study does suggest that the cumulative and varied interpretive experience offered on expedition cruises can help develop and elicit conservation values amongst passengers. Passengers experienced many different interpretive activities a number of times throughout the cruise. They were therefore being exposed repeatedly to the same interpretive staffs' environmental messages throughout these interpretive activities. It would appear that this potential could also be reinforced by further expedition cruise experiences. The results demonstrated that the

cumulative impact of the interpretation mattered within a single cruise. It is possible that this could be strengthened by further expedition cruise experiences. Given that there was a group of passengers who were enthusiastic about repeating this type of cruising experience, it is possible that this type of interpretive experience could further contribute to the long-term impact of expedition cruises on tourists' environmental awareness.

Finally, the research highlighted the importance of knowledgeable and enthusiastic expedition guides. The staff dedication and expertise were a core component of the interpretive experiences described by the passengers. The results suggested it was the combination of these features with the experiential activities that had the greatest impact, and that there may be some core pathways to be further investigated with respect to this achievement. There is the potential that this type of interpretive configuration could be extended to other forms of tourism with respect to contributing to their sustainability.

> Although I prefer to live in cities, it is important to have beautiful places not touched much by humans so you can experience it and appreciate the natural beauty, culture, and wildlife of that area, so expand your horizons.

> (Passenger comment, Alaska, 2003)

References

Armstrong, E.K. and Weiler, B. (2002) Getting the message across: an analysis of messages delivered by tour operators in protected areas. *Journal of Ecotourism* 1, 104–121.

Bagozzi, R.P. and Dabholkar, P.A. (2000) Discursive psychology: an alternative conceptual foundation to means–end chain theory. *Psychology and Marketing* 17, 535–586.

Ballantyne, R. (1998) Interpreting 'visions': addressing environmental education goals through interpretation. In: Uzzell, D.L. and Ballantyne, R. (eds) *Contemporary Issues in Heritage and Environmental Interpretation*. Stationery Office, London, pp. 77–97.

Beaumont, N. (1998) Promoting pro-environmental attitudes and behaviours through ecotourism: that's the theory, but what happens in practice? In: McArthur, S. and Weiler, B. (eds) *Australia's Ecotourism Industry: A Snapshot in 1998*. Ecotourism Association of Australia, Brisbane, pp. 21–28.

Cartwright, R. and Baird, C. (1999) *The Development and Growth of the Cruise Industry*. Butterworth-Heinemann, Oxford.

Cialdini, R.B. (1996) Activating and aligning two kinds of norms in persuasive communication. *Journal of Interpretation Research* 1, 3–10.

Douglas, N. and Douglas, N. (2004) *The Cruise Experience: Global and Regional Issues in Cruising*. Pearson Hospitality Press, Frenchs Forest, New South Wales, Australia.

Gutman, J. (1997) Means–end chains as goal hierarchies. *Psychology and Marketing* 14, 545–560.

Hall, C.M. (1993) Ecotourism in the Australian and New Zealand sub-Antarctic islands. *Tourism Recreation Research* 18, 60–72.

Ham, S.H. and Krumpe, E.E. (1996) Identifying audiences and messages for nonformal environmental education: a theoretical framework for interpreters. *Journal of Interpretation Research* 1, 11–13.

Ham, S.H. and Weiler, B. (2002) Toward a theory of quality in cruise-based interpretive guiding. *Journal of Interpretation Research* 7, 29–49.

Klenosky, D.B., Frauman, E., Norman, W.C. and Gengler, C.E. (1998) Nature-based tourists' use of interpretive services: a means–end investigation. *Journal of Tourism Studies* 9, 26–36.

Lane, B. (1991) Sustainable tourism: a new concept for the interpreter. *Interpretation Journal* 49, 1–4.

Lee, W. and Moscardo, G. (2006) Understanding the impact of ecotourism resort experiences on tourists' environmental attitudes and behavioural intentions. *Journal of Sustainable Tourism* (in press).

Loomis, R.J. (2002) Visitor studies in a political world: challenges to evaluation research. *Journal of Interpretation Research* 7, 31–42.

Medio, D., Ormond, R.F.G. and Pearson, M. (1997) Effects of briefings on rates of damage to corals by SCUBA divers. *Biological Conservation* 79, 91–95.

Mort, G.S. and Rose, T. (2004) The effect of product type on value linkages in the means–end chain: implications for theory and method. *Journal of Consumer Behavior* 3, 221–234.

Moscardo, G. (1998a) Interpretation and sustainable tourism: functions, examples and principles. *Journal of Tourism Studies* 9, 2–13.

Moscardo, G. (1998b) *Making Visitors Mindful*. Sagamore, Champaign, Illinois.

Moscardo, G. (2000) Interpretation. In: Jafari, J. (ed.) *Encyclopedia of Tourism*. Routledge, London, pp. 327–328.

Moscardo, G., Verbeek, M. and Woods, B. (1998) Effective interpretation and sustainable tourism. In: *The Fourth Asia Pacific Tourism Association Conference Proceedings – The Role of Tourism: National and Regional Perspectives Series B*. Asia Pacific Tourism Association, Pusan, South Korea, pp. 148–155.

Newsome, D., Moore, S.A. and Dowling, R.K. (2002) *Natural Area Tourism: Ecology, Impacts and Management*. Channel View, Clevedon, UK.

Orsingher, C. and Marzocchi, G.L. (2003) Hierarchical representation of satisfactory consumer service experience. *International Journal of Service Industry Management* 14, 200–216.

Petty, R.E., McMichael, S. and Brannon, L. (1992) The elaboration likelihood model of persuasion. In: Manfredo, M.J. (ed.) *Influencing Human Behaviour*. Sagamore, Champaign, Illinois, pp. 77–102.

Ritchie, J.R.B., Crouch, G.I. and Hudson, S. (2001) Developing operational measures for the components of a destination competitiveness/sustainability model: consumer versus managerial perspectives. In: Mazanec, J.A., Crouch, G.I., Ritchie, J.R.B. and Woodside, A.G. (eds) *Consumer Psychology of Tourism Hospitality and Leisure*, Vol. 2. CAB International, Wallingford, UK, pp. 1–18.

Roggenbuck, J.W. (1992) Use of persuasion to reduce resource impacts and visitor conflicts. In: Manfredo, M.J. (ed.) *Influencing Human Behaviour*. Sagamore, Champaign, Illinois, pp. 149–208.

Smith, V.L. (1993) Safeguarding the Antarctic environment from tourism. *Tourism Recreation Research* 18, 51–54.

Stewart, E.J., Hayward, B.M., Devin, J.D. and Kirby, V.G. (1998) The 'place' of interpretation: a new approach to the evaluation of interpretation. *Tourism Management* 19, 257–266.

Tilden, F. (1977) *Interpreting our Heritage*, 3rd edn. University of North Carolina Press, Chapel Hill, North Carolina.

Weaver, D. (2000) Sustainable tourism: is it sustainable? In: Faulkner, B., Moscardo, G. and Laws, E. (eds) *Tourism in the Twenty-First Century: Lessons from Experience*. Continuum, London, pp. 300–311.

Weiler, B. and Ham, S.H. (2001) Tour guides and interpretation. In: Weaver, D.B. (ed.) *The Encyclopedia of Ecotourism*. CAB International, Wallingford, UK, pp. 549–563.

11 Cruise Guide Star-rating Systems: A Need for Standardization

Reg A. Swain
1 Wild Rose Court, Guelph, Ontario, Canada, N1G 4X7

Introduction

Potential cruise ship passengers need consistent standards to make informed decisions when planning their vacations. It is important to the tourism industry that accurate information about the quality of cruise ships is available. The cruise industry is a major economic portion of the world tourism business. According to the World Tourism Organization (WTO) report by Kester (2002) worldwide cruise demand had reached 9.6 million passengers in 2000. Cruise ship guidebooks publish information about most passenger ships around the world. When referring to multiple guidebooks, the prospective passenger will find contradictions and confusion when attempting to compare cruise ships by star ratings. This chapter will look at four cruise ship guidebooks and propose a simple, standardized system for ship selection that could be used by any potential cruise vacationer.

The Cruise Guidebooks

There is no consistent measurement for the quality of cruise ships. Each guidebook espouses its own system of star rating as the best one for the reader. For example, it is difficult to compare ships when one guidebook allocates five stars, another six (with pluses for each star) and another ten stars or ribbons. Each cruise guidebook author uses different criteria to qualify their star ratings. A standardized star-rating system for cruise ships would be of value to potential cruise passengers, cruise book authors and individual cruise lines for the marketing of their passenger ships as well as planning for future ships.

In this chapter, four popular 2004 cruise ship guidebooks will be looked at: *Berlitz*, *Econoguide*, *Stern's Guide* and *Unofficial Guide*. These guides are usually issued on a yearly basis and contain information on cruises and assessments of more than 400 passenger ships. They keep passengers up to date about a continually changing and growing cruise line industry. However, each rating system is different and does not conform to a standard system. The cruise ships themselves do not physically change from year to year unless they are renovated. On the other hand, the quality of food, services and maintenance may change from year to year.

Berlitz Ocean Cruising & Cruise Ships 2004

Douglas Ward, the author of the *Berlitz* book, is president of the Maritime Evaluations Group of England, an independent international agency that rates cruise ships worldwide. Ward has been involved in cruising since 1965, spending more than 5000 days at sea on more than 900 cruises. Ward splits his guide of 686 pages into two parts: the initial 125 pages contain information about what to expect when cruising, cabin layouts and ship talk; the remaining 561 pages describe more than 300 passenger cruise ships of all sizes, practical information on cruising as well as indices of major cruise lines – addresses and websites, ships rated by score and an alphabetical index. He profiles 256 ocean-going vessels and rates 244 of these ships. In addition to Ward's personal cruise experiences, he is supplied with regular reports from a small team of trained professional passengers.

His star-rating system is based on each ship accumulating points by completing a chart. The points are awarded in six principal areas, each of which Ward claims is almost as important as the next: 25% for the ship, 15% for accommodation, 15% for cuisine, 20% for service, 7.5% for entertainment and 17.5% for the cruise experience. For example, one area designated 'The Ship' takes into account the condition and maintenance of the hardware (railings, steel, painting, etc.), safety, outdoor facilities, interior facilities, space and flow, decor, furnishings, artwork, spa and fitness facilities. The total points per ship can range from 600 to 2000 and are converted into 1 to 6+ stars (highest).

In his comments about the quality of his assessments, Ward (2004, p. 128) makes the statement: 'The ratings are conducted with *total objectivity* from a set of predetermined criteria and a modus operandi designed to work *globally*, not just regionally, across the entire spectrum of ocean-going cruise ships today, in all segments of the marketplace. The ratings more reflect the *standards* of the cruise product delivered to the passengers (the software) and less the physical plant (the hardware)'. This latter viewpoint is based on subjective opinions of the person completing the chart and does not necessarily reflect the reactions of the passengers actually on that voyage.

Cruises 2004, Econoguide

Corey Sandler is a former newsman and editor who has compiled 400 pages for his cruise guide. Sandler begins with 172 pages of cruising information on almost every related experience that might be encountered on a cruise. He also provides examples through 12 diaries of actual cruises. In the next 150 pages, he lists

cruise lines alphabetically and provides insights into their ships. Listings of smaller ships used for adventure cruises, and sailing vessels, are followed by a history of cruising, a glossary, cruise line phone numbers and websites and five special indices: a quick-find index, cruise diaries, cruise lines, cruise ships and ports of call. He lists 180 ships in the guide, giving ratings for most of them.

Sandler's star-rating system is based on scoring each ship out of 100 points, equalling from 1 to 6 stars (highest). This guide also lists separate ratings for cruise lines, ship size, category (style) and price range (Sandler, 2004, p. 174). The category of cabins and their price range with the present market of discount fares would not appear to provide a useful aid to the reader.

The final result is classification information that would add more comparisons for the prospective passenger to consider, thus complicating the ship selection. If there was an industry-wide, single consolidated rating, it would be helpful.

Stern's Guide to the Cruise Vacation

Steven Stern has had 35 years of experience on cruise ships in preparing his cruise vacation guide. Stern's paperback guide contains 736 pages, with 214 pages of information on four case studies, getting ready, at sea, singles, children, excursions, sports, where to cruise and how long and the airlines. The cruise lines are listed alphabetically in 481 pages, with comments about their ships, pictures and even sample menus. At the back is an alphabetical index of the cruise ships with value categories and star ratings. There is also a rating by cruise line for dining rooms, service, cabin, public areas, special activities and good ships for single passengers. These are followed by indices of cruise lines, cruise ships and ports of call. Star ratings are given for 125 ships out of the 331 listed.

It is the opinion of Stern that there is a constant change in quality of food, service, entertainment and the general physical condition of ships. He states: 'It is risky to attempt to compare or rate cruise ships. Any such attempt must reflect a great deal of personal preference and may be somewhat undependable.' He admits he has succumbed to peer pressure to attempt to rate cruise ships as definitively as possible, and tells us: 'Again, I must emphasize that these are my personal, subjective opinions. An intelligent passenger should not take the ratings of any guide as gospel. Obviously, every reviewer has his personal preferences and prejudices that may or may not coincide with your own' (Stern, 2004, p. 698).

The 'peer pressure' appears to have led the author in a different direction. The six ratings are really 12 because each number may have a plus factor. These are from 1 to 6+ (highest), although there does not appear to be a 0+. In addition, there are four market categories according to the price per day of the cruise. Then the complications set in: 'A five-star award given a ship in Category A does not necessarily mean that the ship offers less overall than a six-star award given vessels in Categories B, C, or D. Be careful not to compare our ratings with those in other cruise guides' (Stern, 2004, p. 700).

Unofficial Guide to Cruises

This is one of the *Unofficial Guide* series of many cities and attractions in the world. The authors, Showker and Sehlinger, have put together a paperback of 659 pages. They open with 125 pages explaining, describing, selecting and preparing for a cruise vacation, along with 15 maps and illustrations. Each cruise line is listed alphabetically with a commentary on their ships. Of the 414 ships mentioned in their guide, they give ratings for 141. Alternative types of cruising are also listed: river, adventure, expedition and sailing ships. The book is completed with indices of the cruise ships, their itineraries, some destinations and a subject index.

Showker and Sehlinger explain their rating purpose: 'To differentiate ships by overall quality of the cruise experience and to allow a comparison of ships from different lines, we give ships a rating of 1 to 10, with 10 being the best'. Their numerical rating is based on a diversity of the ship's features and service. They contend that some colleagues have 'hopelessly muddled the more familiar star ratings'. They claim that ships traditionally have been rated 1 to 5 stars, which were 'easily understood by the cruising public and provided a quick way to compare critics' opinions'. Apparently, several years ago,

some authors changed to other scales precluding a meaningful comparison. 'We believe a standardized rating system helps consumers' (Showker and Sehlinger, 2004, p. 128).

Value ratings of ships are included in this guide: A (a real bargain) to F (significantly overpriced). In the latter case they state: 'Any discount you are able to obtain will improve the value rating for the ship in question' (Showker and Sehlinger, 2004, p. 129). The question then arises as to how can the better deal on quality be evaluated: is it a 50% discount on a 'B' value ship or a 25% discount on an 'E' value ship?

In a monograph on an empirical approach to developing classification and rating schemes, Barth and Walsh found that ratings are useful to consumers and travel agents who lack the knowledge, expertise or time to make their own comparisons. Ratings are often a source of pride and competition between top hotels and restaurants (Barth and Walsh, 1997). Marketeers can efficiently communicate the character of their products and services by rating systems. The hotel and restaurant five-star rating method is a standard of quality for food, service and amenities that has been accepted worldwide.

In summary, these four guides are examples of information that is available to the public. They differ in how they describe cruise lines and assign star ratings. The next section reviews some physical components that are not usually mentioned in the star-rating assessment of ships in these guides.

Components

Many components can be considered when assessing a cruise ship. Some components are intangible: ambience, friendliness of the crew, personal service, enjoyment, etc. Tangible factors are in the ship design: free space, ship size, physical activities and cabin size. Following are six physical factors that are not usually highlighted by cruise ship guides as a basis for star ratings.

Gross registered tonnage

The size of a ship is measured by gross registered tonnage (GRT). This refers to the enclosed interior space used to produce revenue on a vessel. It is a measure of volume rather than weight. One GRT represents 100 ft^3 (2.8 m^3) of enclosed revenue generating space, including cabins, dining areas, lounges, promenades, theatres and game rooms. This calculation originated in the earlier days of sailing ships, when a ship's size was measured by the number of casks of wine that a ship could hold. It became a standard for all merchant ships in those days as a means for taxing vessels. It is important as a factual comparison of size between ships.

Officers and number of crew

Expected service on a ship is based on the ratio of crew members to the number of passengers. The resulting ratio defines a presumable service comfort level for the passengers. The acceptable level is one crew member for every three passengers. Some ships have only one crew member for every two passengers (1:2). More crew per passenger usually results in a higher per diem that has to be paid by the passengers, but it ensures that they will receive a better level of service, which should make the voyage a more pleasant experience.

Number of passengers

Two different methods are used to report the number of passengers on board a ship. The most common calculation is by two passengers in each cabin and suite. It is not accurate because the family cabins and the large suites may contain several passengers. This measurement (two times the number of cabins) is used to calculate the space/passenger ratio (described later). The second method of reporting is a higher figure based on the maximum capacity of passengers if every berth on the ship is occupied. The potential ship passenger should consider this measurement and decide whether he or she wants a voyage with 400 or 3000 fellow passengers. The bonus is that the larger ship may have many more amenities, while the smaller ship will provide the opportunity for more socialization as a group.

Cabins: average square footage and verandas

Previously, passengers looked to ships simply as transportation to cross the oceans. They had to live in small cabins or even bunks in steerage on the lower deck. Nowadays, ships are designed more for tourism and pleasure cruises, with bigger cabins and large open areas for socializing. Older ships have fewer and smaller cabins and are not attractive to large cruise lines because of their higher operating costs and lower revenue. The square foot area per cabin has increased: when the *Queen Elizabeth 2* was launched in 1969, its smallest cabin was 107 ft^2; on the *Carnival Spirit*, launched in 2001, the smallest cabin was 185 ft^2.

On the other hand, newer ships in the last 10 years have a larger number of outside cabins with private verandas. Many passengers are willing to pay extra for the privacy, quietness and ocean view that a veranda provides as shown in Table 11.1. It shows a comparison of three ships built 30 years apart.

Space/passenger ratio

Space/passenger (S/P) ratio is calculated by dividing the GRT by the number of cabins, times two passengers each. The S/P ratio is a standard industry figure, which is readily available and printed in many brochures and cruise guidebooks. Larger S/P ratios appear to enhance the cruise experience and have increased steadily over the years. Ships built in the 1960s had an S/P ratio of 25:30, and in the 1980s, 30:35, while new ships have a S/P ratio of 45, with a few reaching 70.

The Year of Launch

Jim West writes that 'sometimes the size of the ship is less important than the age of the ship'. His reasoning is that newer ships offer the latest technology, with conference rooms, Internet computers, enormous children's playrooms and health facilities. He adds that 'the cabins are more attractive, . . . the public rooms provide more space, . . . and the ships boast more sophisticated safety systems' (West, 2003, pp. 35–36).

Table 11.1. Examples of per cent of verandas on outside cabins.

Launch year	Cruise line	Ship	GRT	Outside cabins	Verandas	Ratio (%)
1969	Cunard	*Queen Elizabeth 2*	70,327	659	32	5
1990	Princess Cruises	*Regal Princess*	69,845	624	184	29
1999	Royal Caribbean	*Voyager of the Seas*	137,280	939	757	81

Source: Primary data.

In 2002, 2003 and 2004, 39 new passenger cruise ships were launched. The rating of an individual ship does not necessarily reflect the overall standards of the cruise line. When individual ships are compared within the same cruise line, they may vary considerably in quality, but it increases with the year of launch. The average star rating of three Royal Caribbean Cruise Line ships from the four books is shown in Table 11.2.

These ships are from the same cruise line and are similar in size. Table 11.2 shows that the average of star ratings from the four guides has increased with the newer ship.

Several questions arise that need to be considered: Are there common, major components of ship assessment among the four guides? How do they compare with the same guidebooks published in the year 2000? Is there another rating method that would identify a simple standard that potential cruise passengers could use to quickly assess the approximate star value of a ship for comparison purposes?

Methodology

Primary data was collected on 377 ships recorded in the four guides. Of these, 288 ships were rated in at least one book. Removing smaller ships of less than 2000 GRT and those with less than 100 cabins reduced this listing. This provided a higher common standard without the potentially distorting factor of smaller vessels, many of which do not conduct more than 2-day cruises. The book authors did not usually rate these smaller passenger ships: tramp steamers, inland riverboats, sailing ships, expeditionary ships, day trippers and overnight ferries. The remaining 210 cruise ships are available to potential passengers around the world for cruises of more than 2 days, are of a size more than 2000 GRT and have at least 100 cabins.

The stars given for each ship were recorded as decimals, e.g. 5 stars as 5.0; 5+ stars as 5.5; 6 stars as 6.0; etc. As each book was tested separately, the relationship of the stars to each other

Table 11.2. Average star ratings by year of launch.

Ship	Launch year	2004 Average of five-star maximum[a]	GRT
Monarch of the Seas	1991	2.99	74,000
Legend of the Seas	1995	3.56	69,000
Vision of the Seas	1998	3.88	78,500

[a]This calculation is explained later in the Heuristic System section.
Source: Primary data.

was kept significant and not distorted because of the different calibrations.

Linear regression was selected as the best method to locate the components that made up the star rating in each cruise guide. It measures the strength of the relationship between the dependent variable (stars per ship in each book) and several independent variables (physical characteristics of the rated ships). The R-square result is the strength of the relationship between several independent variables and one dependent variable. It therefore identifies the proportion of variance in the dependent variable accounted for by the independent variables. In reality, this is a bivariate correlation and is an accurate value of the sample.

Eight physical factors and two ratios were cross-tested using linear regression: year of launch, GRT (size), ship length, number of crew required, number of cabins times two (passengers), number of verandas, total cabins, minimum square footage of cabins, crew/passenger ratio and space/passenger ratio. The intent is to identify the relationship of any major components to the stars attributed in each cruise book.

The dependent variable was the mean of the number of stars of each rated ship in each book. The predictor or independent variables were tested in combinations of two, with the four dependent variables (each book). The R-square was recorded for each book with respect to the predictor variables' influence on the dependent variable. In this manner, the difference of rated stars between books (5, 6+, 10 and 6) was not a factor to distort the R-square result. In order to maintain the minimization of any explanation due to linear dependencies alone, two independent variables are used in each test.

Results

Question 1. Are there common, major components of ship assessment among the four guides?

Utilizing Linear Regression analysis, the highest R-square results were in the combination of predictors: S/P ratio and launch year. Table 11.3 shows the 2004 star-rating results for each guide.

The R-square result when averaged over the four guidebooks shows that these two physical factors contribute to 60% of the components of the star rating for the number of ships reviewed in each cruise guide. That leaves only 40% for all of the remaining factors that the authors took into consideration for the rating of these ships. Table 11.4 gives the mathematical details of the 2004 regression.

Question 2. How do they compare with the same guidebooks published in the year 2000?

Swain and Barth found that the R-square regression results for each guide 4 years earlier evidenced the major components of S/P ratio and year of launch. Table 11.5 shows the 2000 star-rating results for each 2000 guide: Sandler (2000), Showber and Sehlinger (2000), Stern (2000) and Ward (2000).

Note that while the number of rated ships is greater in Table 11.3 than in Table 11.5, and the individual R-square percentages have changed among the cruise guides, the average results for 2004 are almost the same as for 2000.

The regression results and the guidebook authors appear to differ in the definition of the major components of the star ratings. Ward (2004, p. 128) in *Berlitz* states: 'The ratings more reflect the *standards* of the cruise product delivered to the passengers (the software) and less the

Table 11.3. Year 2004 linear regression of 544 star ratings (predictors: space/passenger ratio and launch year).

Cruise guide	Number of rated ships	R-square results (S/P ratio and launch year; %)	R-square results (S/P ratio and others; %)
Berlitz 2004	192	70.8	59.5
Econoguide 2004	133	52.9	58.4
Stern's Guide 2004	120	67.5	64.0
Unofficial Guide 2004	99	47.4	46.3
Average		**59.65**	**57.05**

Source: Primary data calculation.

Table 11.4. 2004 Frequency and linear regression results (these are the mathematical details of the 2004 regression).

	Berlitz	Econoguide	Stern's Guide	Unofficial Guide
N	192	133	120	99
Maximum stars	5.5	6.0	6.5	10.0
Mean	3.6823	3.88	5.1438	6.879
Standard deviation	0.78474	0.9538	0.87487	1.7159
R-square (Pearson)	0.708	0.529	0.675	0.474
Adjusted R-square	0.705	0.522	0.669	0.463
Standard error of estimation	0.42648	0.6597	0.50321	1.2573
ANOVA F	228.834	72.962	121.346	43.263
Significance (p)	0.000	0.000	0.000	0.000

Source: Primary data calculation.

physical plant (the hardware)'. 'Any such attempt [to compare or rate cruise ships] must reflect a great deal of personal preference and may be somewhat undependable' (Stern, 2004, p. 698). The *Unofficial Guide* reports: 'The numerical rating is based on the quality and diversity of the ship's features and service' (Showker and Sehlinger, 2004, p. 128).

A Simplified, Heuristic, Comparable Rating System

Question 3. Is there another rating method that would identify a simple standard that potential cruise passengers could use to quickly assess the approximate star value of a ship for comparison purposes?

Each guidebook and many cruise brochures show the S/P ratio of most ships. By

Table 11.5. Year 2000 linear regressions of 497 star ratings (predictors: space/passenger ratio and launch year).

Cruise guide	Number of rated ships	R-square results (%)
Berlitz 2000	195	60.7
Econoguide 2000	104	68.5
Stern's Guide 2000	109	56.4
Unofficial Guide 2000	91	53.7
Average		**59.83**

Source: Swain and Barth (2002, p. 56).

calculating 10% of the S/P ratio of any ship, it is possible to predict fairly closely the approximate star rating of any ship. The result is comparable to the average of the stars these four guidebooks will assign.

First, each ship's star rating was converted to decimals by prorating to a five-star maximum. For example: *Econoguide* 6 stars = 5.0, 3 stars = 2.5; *Stern's* 6+ stars = 5.0, 4 stars = 3.08; *Unofficial Guide* 10 stars = 5.0, and 5 stars = 2.5; *Stern's Guide* is on a five-star basis already. Each ship rating was then totalled and averaged for the four guides.

Table 11.6 is an example of this simplified, comparable rating system, based on the same three ships from Table 11.2, of the Royal Caribbean Line built in 1991, 1995 and 1998.

On these three ships, the difference is only 0.15 (4.3%). Using a base of 272 rated ships in the 2004 guidebooks, there were 60 ships where the difference was plus or minus 0.2, and on 150 ships the difference was within plus or minus 0.5 (or 2 of one star) of the average of a five-star rating. Thus, a potential passenger could establish within half of a star, the rating of 55% of the passenger-carrying ships weighing more than 2000 GRT and having 100 cabins.

Conclusions

In these four cruise ship guidebooks, prospective passengers have a variety of sources with which to research their cruise vacations and obtain comforting background information, especially

Table 11.6. Simplified rating system using 2004 cruise guides.

Ship name	Berlitz	Econoguide	Stern's Guide	Unofficial Guide	Average	10% of S/P ratio
Monarch of the Seas	3.5	2.5	3.5	2.5	2.99	3.14
Legend of the Seas	4.0	2.5	4.2	3.5	3.56	3.84
Vision of the Seas	4.0	3.3	4.2	4.0	3.88	3.92
Average					**3.48**	**3.63**

Source: Primary data calculation.

for the novice passenger. However, there is confusion when comparing two or more of these books searching for a quality assessment of ships. Mathematical regression identified S/P ratio and year of launch as consistent and major components of these four cruise guide-rating systems, similar to the result from the year 2000. Regardless of the authors' claims of objectivity and observation, there is the underlying relationship that 60% of their ratings are based on these two physical factors, leaving only 40% based on other tangible and intangible factors.

Information on cruise ships can be found on cruise line websites, in their brochures, in newspaper articles and cruise ship guidebooks. However, there is no standardized cruise ship rating system that is common to all. Existing guidebook star-rating systems are not uniform or consistent. Individual guidebooks may vary in their criteria for rating the same ship, as the author of each book may have difficulty trying to evaluate in person 300 ships each year, every year. If there was an industry-wide quality standard such as a five-star maximum, the public would have a consistent guide to understand, and the ability to compare, the quality of ships on an equal basis. This standard of five stars continues to work well in the hotel and dining industry.

A simple rating system with results comparable to existing star ratings can be based on 10% of the S/P ratio. In future, this system could rate a ship as soon as the final plans have been prepared for the construction. The exceptions would be the five-star, smaller ships.

There are opportunities for further research to explore the components in the remaining 40% of the cruise star ratings. It would be helpful to investigate the relationship between the satisfaction of a cruise experience

and the star ratings. An exploration of the meanings to the passengers regarding why they took a cruise vacation and why they participated in available activities or not, would be of interest to the tourism industry. If there were found to be a difference in perception and satisfaction of the cruise experience due to age, it would provide knowledge for marketing to the increasing senior population of potential passengers.

In conclusion, reliable and accurate information is essential for potential cruise passengers, ship owners and cruise book authors. As there is no standard established in the industry, cruise books have used different methods of quality assessment of a ship. This is confusing to the prospective passenger. A standardized rating system would give the cruise ship guide authors more authority for the information they provide. Cruise ship owners would have a common standard to evaluate their ships. International tourism would benefit greatly. There is a need for a standardized star-rating system that would apply to all cruise ships.

References

Barth, J.E. and Walsh, J. (1997) An empirical approach to developing classification and rating schemes. *Journal of Hospitality and Leisure Marketing*, 5(1), 16.

Kester, J.G.C. (2002) Cruise tourism. *Tourism Economics* 9(3), 337–350.

Sandler, C. (2000) *Cruises, Econoguide 2000–01.* Contemporary Books, Chicago, Illinois.

Sandler, C. (2004) *Cruises 2004, Econoguide.* The Globe Pequot Press, Guilford, Connecticut.

Showker, K. and Sehlinger, R. (2000) *Unofficial Guide to Cruises 2001.* IDG Books Worldwide, New York.

Showker, K. and Sehlinger, R. (2004) *Unofficial Guide to Cruises*, 8th edn. John Wiley & Sons, Hoboken, New Jersey.

Stern, S.B. (2000) *Stern's Guide to the Cruise Vacation*, 11th edn. Pelican Publishing, Gretna, Louisiana.

Stern, S.B. (2004) *Stern's Guide to the Cruise Vacation*, 14th edn. Pelican Publishing, Gretna, Louisiana.

Swain, R.A. and Barth, J.E. (2002) An analysis of cruise ship rating guides. *International Journal of Hospitality and Tourism Administration* 3(4), p. 56.

Ward, D. (2000) *Berlitz Complete Guide to Cruising & Cruise Ships 2001*. Berlitz Publishing, Princeton, New Jersey.

Ward, D. (2004) *Berlitz Ocean Cruising & Cruise Ships 2004*. Berlitz Publishing, London.

West, J. (2003) *The Essential Little Cruise Book: Secrets from a Cruise Director for a Perfect Vacation*, 3rd edn. The Globe Pequot Press, Guilford, Connecticut.

12 Sixteen Ways of Looking at an Ocean Cruise: A Cultural Studies Approach

Arthur A. Berger

San Francisco State University, Broadcast and Electronic Communication Arts Department, San Francisco, CA 94132, USA

Introduction

Cruise lines are selling you a dream. The power of your dream, your imagination, creates a challenge that the cruise industry is trying to meet. Television commercials and glossy colour brochures about cruises all promise the same thing – an unexcelled excursion into the glamorous life, with romantic evenings, a perfect tan, six or eight gourmet meals a day, and intermittent forays into picturesque and exotic ports of call where the sun always shines, the shopping is splendid and the natives are friendly and photogenic. Oddly enough, more often than not, it works out that way (Slater and Basch 1997, pp. 10–11).

Embarking

The development of cultural studies in recent years has brought a multi-disciplinary approach to the study of media, popular culture and other related concerns, and unrelated concerns as well. Everything, it seems, is now grist for the cultural studies mill whose advocates and practitioners, when faced with a topic of interest, say to themselves 'round up the usual suspects', by which they mean disciplines and approaches for analysing anything.

A Cultural Studies Approach

We now recognize that we can see life from more than one side and more than both sides, and that, in reality, just as there are many different ways to skin a cat, there are a number of different approaches that may be taken to analyse everything from comic strips to ocean cruises.

From my perspective, cultural studies is not a discipline, per se, but an approach to culture and society that uses various disciplines, in whatever combination seems most fruitful, to analyse and interpret whatever a person using that approach finds interesting and worth investigating. It is an approach that seeks to overcome the problem found in the poem 'The Blind Men and the Elephant' in which each blind man, grasping a particular part of an elephant, came to wildly different conclusions about what elephants are like. One blind man, touching the elephant's trunk, thought elephants were like snakes. Another, touching its ear, thought that elephants were like fans. The concluding verse of John Godfrey Saxe's poem makes my point. It reads:

> And so these men of Indostan
> Disputed loud and long.
> Each in his own opinion
> Exceeding stiff and strong.
> Though each was partly in the right,
> And all were in the wrong.

The solution that cultural studies brings to the problem of knowing reality is to use many different approaches, to simulate the experience of the various blind men, each of whom, for our purposes, represents a single discipline. Cultural studies advocates are foxes, who know a lot of 'little things' in contrast to those in single disciplines – hedgehogs – who know 'one big thing', so to speak. Some would say that knowing a little bit about a lot of things means you do not know very much about anything, but that criticism strikes me as simplistic and reductionistic. Cultural studies has its problems – it has to find ways of integrating its findings, but other approaches have their problems as well.

The Sociological Approach

During a cruise to Alaska on the *Regal Princess* in 2001, I first became interested in the cruising phenomenon. My wife and I had taken two short cruises before our trip to Alaska, and had taken a river cruise in China a number of years before that, but we were not serious cruise-takers. When Princess brought the *Regal Princess* to San Francisco for round-trip cruises to Alaska, which meant we would not have to do any air travel, we decided to book a cruise to Alaska. There was an advertisement in the *San Francisco Chronicle* for the round trip by Zoe's cruises, so I called up and booked the cruise with her agency. Zoe, I found, had booked 150 or so passengers on that voyage and plied her customers with flowers, sweatshirts, candy and special cocktail parties. Zoe, as you might well imagine, has a lot of clout with Princess.

During the cruise, as is the custom nowadays, for breakfasts and lunches we did not sit in a reserved table but instead with many different people. During conversations with various table mates I discovered that some of the passengers on the ship had been on 15 or 20 different cruises. I was simply astounded and the 'sociologist' in me started doing some thinking. 'What's going on here?' I asked. 'Who are these repeat cruise-takers? Are there any important sociological matters to be explored here, other than age?' – for it was obvious that a very large percentage of the passengers were senior citizens.

For the sociologist, a cruise is a fascinating problem, with all kinds of research possibilities. A cruise is not a 'total institution' but it is, in many respects, like one. You have a group of people who find themselves 'all on the same boat together' for a certain period of time. How do passenger lists break down in terms of age, gender, race, religion and socio-economic class? Were any groups over-represented? Were any under-represented? How do people use their time on the cruise? What are their interests? What do they talk about? Why did they choose the Princess line instead of another one?

We took our cruise in early June, when school was still in session, so there were hardly any children aboard. But once school lets out, as I understand things, there are many young children on cruises and cruise lines hire teachers and others with experience in dealing with children and adolescents to look after them. So, when you take a cruise, in addition to the nature or status of the cruise line you are on, makes a big difference. One thing I learned was that the fact that the *Regal Princess* was leaving from San Francisco, and returning there was a primary motivation for many of the passengers. In recent years, cruise lines have developed a number of different ports so people do not have to fly to take a cruise. This is a powerful selling point.

Another was the ambiance on the cruise – what I chose to call 'carnivalization', basing my notions on the work of the Russian literary critic, Mikhail Bakhtin. There was, unquestionably, a sense of joyousness and celebration that was found, Bakhtin explained, in medieval carnival periods. So that was an element of the appeal of ocean cruising. There is a kind of forced sociability as people find themselves sitting with different people at breakfast and lunch – if they dine in the dining room, that is.

A Psychoanalytic Interpretation

By looking around and observing the people on the cruise, I was able to answer a number of questions relating to sociological aspects of cruise taking. Then another question struck my attention – why do people cruise? What is it about cruising that makes it so appealing to people and how does one explain the matter of people taking so many cruises. One way I had to explain this was the idea that it has become a kind of compulsion – that cruise takers feel compelled to have pleasure. There is also the element of fantasy involved in cruising and, perhaps, a mythic element to it.

As I talked with passengers (and noticed their behaviour) I found that the quality of the food and the dining experience was an important part of cruising. It struck me (and the notion was confirmed by a psychoanalyst I know who was on the cruise) that being on cruises is, generally speaking, a regressive experience, a regression at the service of the ego. People on cruises have momentary regressions to their oral stages, where eating and ingesting become primary. There is nothing wrong with this. We often have moments of regression to help us deal with the anxieties and disappointments of everyday living. On ships we experience the same kind of unconditional love we experienced when we were children. The staff is trained to be friendly and accommodating and waiters and their assistants are happy to satisfy any needs we have in the dining halls.

It struck me that on cruises we are, psychologically, back in the Garden of Eden and that there is a paradisical element to cruising. We never touch money (filthy lucre) while on cruises, but pay for everything with plastic cards. Cruising enables passengers to escape, if only for a short time, from their everyday routines and condense a lot of living, gourmet dining, shows, dancing, lectures, into a short period of time.

The Economics of Cruising

Cruise lines compete for passengers with other kinds of vacations: packaged tours, independent travel, or some combination of the two. People who are considering taking a cruise have a number of choices to make, also. They have to decide where they want to cruise and which line to choose. In many cases, people considering cruises are helped by travel agents, who recommend certain lines and specific ships. There are numerous Internet cruise travel agencies, and people familiar with the Internet can find information on what cruises are available for specific time periods and find out how much it would

cost to book a cruise. Once they have decided where to go, they have to decide where they want to be on the ship and whether they want an inside stateroom or a suite, or something in between. So it is possible to book a cruise on the Internet or use the Internet to get information and then call one of the Internet cruise travel agencies and speak with an agent, to get information about matters of interest.

There is the question of whether the choice of lines and places to visit is a matter of individual decision making or is shaped by sociological forces. A social-anthropologist, Mary Douglas, has argued that consumer choices (and that would include cruise-taking decisions) are based more on cultural alignments than on psychological desires. She argues that there are four consumer cultures or lifestyles (individualists, egalitarians, hierarchical elitists and fatalists) and that we all belong to one of these lifestyles, which shape our decision making.

In their book *Selling the Sea*, Dickinson and Vladimir (1997) argue that taking a cruise is approximately as expensive as taking a land-based vacation, and this is often the case, especially if one stays in an inside stateroom and takes a cruise when the rates are low. Many cruises cost passengers around US$75 per night, which, when tips are added, comes to around US$100 per person per night. But I have seen cruises advertised for much less than that. So, from a cost-effective point of view, considering passengers on cruises get elaborate hotel-style meals, have free entertainment, and other benefits, it is reasonable to suggest that a cruise can cost around the same amount of money as a land-based vacation and, in some cases, less.

It is because cruises can be, relatively speaking, bargains, the cruise industry has had incredible growth over recent decades. Cruising is now a middle-class phenomenon. In 1970, some 500,000 people took cruises. By 2001, almost ten million people took cruises. So cruising has experienced phenomenal growth in recent decades. For the economist, there are many things to consider about cruising: the growth of the industry, the financial arrangements that are found in the cruise industry and the treatment of workers (some would say exploitation of workers) on cruise ships. There are almost 135,000 Americans who work in the cruise industry and another 450,000 or so who are indirectly involved with it. The industry itself has invested billions of dollars in cruise ships and new ones are coming into service every year. So there is a great deal for the economist to study.

The Semiotics of Ocean Cruising

Semiotics is the science that studies signs (the term 'semeion' means signs) and the way people find what things mean. For those who study semiotics, which is an imperialistic science, everything is a sign and every branch of knowledge is a subcategory of semiotics. A sign can be defined as anything that can stand for something else, which means signs can tell the truth but also lie. Think, for example, of our facial expressions. Many people, especially poker players, have trained themselves to give false signs or not to give any signs at all, to the extent that this is possible.

For the semiotician, for the analyst of signs and how they convey meaning to people, ocean cruise ships are full of interesting signs. Cruise ships are paradise for semioticians since they are, in effect, sign systems – full of signs designed to convey certain meanings and feelings to passengers. Consider, for example, the paintings that cruise ships hang on the walls you look at while walking up or down the stairs. Original paintings and other works of art are meant to suggest the cruise ship is, in part, a museum and that taking a cruise is a refined experience. This notion is reinforced by the presence of string trios and string quartets on cruise ships. We are, here, in the realm of elite culture and the paintings and classical music signify 'class', and an elite status. Think, also, of the dining experience. The dining rooms are generally understated, as far as colours are concerned. The tables have starched table clothes and napkins and elegant tableware. When you sit down, you see before you a beautiful display of silverware, wine goblets, folded napkins and plates, and if you are not quick enough, your waiter or assistant waiter will open your napkin and place it on your lap.

The menus are generally elegant and full of French terms and loaded with superlatives. You are offered, to start the meals, 'double Chicken consommé' and 'Sevruga Malassol Caviar on an

Ice Throne'. From there you might move on, after salad and pasta, to lobster tails or pheasant. All of these dishes suggest sophistication and an elite status. The number of plates used to serve a person during a meal is astronomical. All of these things, plus the way the waiters and assistants are trained, to be unobtrusive but always there, heightens a person's sense of well-being and, alas, enlarges a person's waistline. But people do not go on cruises to starve themselves, and they figure, or try to convince themselves, that once they are back home, they can diet and lose the 6 lb (or whatever) that cruise takers generally gain on a cruise. In fact, food is a primary consideration for cruises, as the quotation with which I opened this analysis makes clear.

Because ocean cruise liners are such complicated and complex vessels, they are full of signs of interest to semioticians. The teak decks found on many ships are also generally recognized signifiers of ocean cruise ships (what the French semiotician Roland Barthes would describe as 'cruise-shipness') and are often used in advertisements because of the strong association of teak decks with fine ocean cruise ships. The layout of the decks with their swimming pools and spas, the quality of the bathrobes that many cruise ships provide, the thickness of the towels and nature of shampoos and lotions found in cabins – all these things are designed to give people a sense of well-being and of an elite and privileged status, even if this only lasts during the cruise. Many people on cruises return to ordinary lives that are quite far removed from their experiences on the cruises they take. But that is perfectly fine to my way of thinking and may have a number of psychological benefits.

Debarking

This essay is meant to suggest some of the possibilities that ocean cruise ships and the cruising phenomenon offer to the cultural analyst. I deal, in greater detail, with these subject in my book *Ocean Travel and Cruising: A Cultural Analysis* (Berger, 2004a) and with tourism in my book *Deconstructing Travel* (Berger, 2004b). Let me say something about advertising and the ocean cruise industry and about the Internet and the industry. Many of our ideas about cruising come from the romantic television commercials we see and the cruise line brochures, featuring good-looking and classy women drinking champagne with handsome grey-haired, executive-type men and gazing out at some exotic port in the distance. So our heads are full of fantasies about what to expect on cruises and the ports the liners visit. The cruise industry is highly segmented and people are able to establish social distance by choosing lines that the kind of people they do not want to be with cannot afford.

There are hundreds of thousands of websites devoted to every aspect of cruising. For example, it is possible to read reviews, by professional writers and by cruise takers, of various ships. I have found that the Internet reviews by cruise takers of particular cruises they have taken fall into two camps: one group of people loved the cruise and was positive about the cruise and another group hated the cruise, did not like much about the cruise, decided never to cruise on that line again and so on. I would imagine that most people fall in between, and it is only those who were generally positive or generally negative who bothered to make their comments available to others. What is particularly interesting is when you read two or three people writing about the same cruise. For one person, the service was terrible, the stateroom ugly, the food barely edible and it was pure hell. For others it was a blissful and marvellous experience, the food was superb and the service extraordinary. So you learn to take the reviews with a grain of salt. Some of them are very revealing, suggesting that a study of Internet cruise reviews might lead to some important insights.

From what I have seen, as an observer, more precisely a participant-observer, of ocean cruising, most of the passengers seem to be enjoying themselves and having a good time, whether it is lying on a deckchair in the sun, reading a book, taking a dance lesson, going to a show or eating a six-course meal in the dining room. Some critics have scornfully described cruising as a spectacle of hedonistic excess in which people indulge themselves in every way,

and suggest it is a phenomenon with no redeeming social value. But psychologists now tell us that it is very important for people to take vacations and get away from their everyday routines, to recharge their batteries, so to speak.

I have not offered all 16 ways of looking at an ocean cruise in this brief essay. To do this, the social-scientist and cultural studies critic in me says 'more research is indicated'. Let me conclude by offering a list of some questions that anyone studying the ocean cruising phenomenon might find worth considering:

* Who is gazing at whom on cruise ships? Is there a female gaze?
* What significance does the language used in menus have?
* Do the names of cruise ships and cruise lines have any significance?
* What impact do cruise ships have on the ecologies of the places they visit?
* What is the economic impact of tourism on the ports visited?
* What are the effects of the consolidation going on in the cruise industry?
* What is the global impact of the cruising industry?
* What impact is the cruising industry having on tourism, in general?
* What psychological gratifications does cruising offer passengers?
* What do the workers on cruise ships really think about passengers?

References

Berger, A.A. (2004a) *Ocean Travel and Cruising: A Cultural Analysis.* Haworth Hospitality Press, Binghamton, New York.

Berger, A.A. (2004b) *Deconstructing Travel: Cultural Perspectives on Tourism.* AltaMira Press, Walnut Creek, California.

Dickinson, B. and Vladimir, A. (1997) *Selling the Sea: An Inside Look at the Cruise Industry.* Haworth Hospitality Press, Binghamton, New York.

Slater, S. and Basch, H. (1997) *Fielding's Alaska Cruises.* Fielding Worldwide, Redondo Beach, California.

Part III

Supply: Cruise Destinations and Products

_____

Introduction

Part II dealt with the demand for cruising. Part III explores the supply side of cruising with examples from around the world. Case studies are presented on a number of cruise destinations including the Baltic Sea, Alaska, Atlantic Canada, the Caribbean, the Pacific and the Antarctic. A number of cruise products are then described and discussed including the round-the-world segment and the Norwegian Coastal Express. Finally the specific niches of coastal, adventure and expedition cruising are presented.

In Chapter 13, the first of four Canadian contributions, Jan Lundgren (Quebec) discusses how the evolution of the Baltic Sea-based excursion and cruise phenomenon can best be appreciated when viewed within the framework of a 'phases process', where each phase can be defined and discussed and also the future of Baltic Sea cruising.

In Chapter 14, John Munro and Warren Gill (British Columbia) review the evolution of the Alaska cruise industry and the various roles played in the development of this market. This leads to a discussion of the economic impacts of the Alaska cruise industry on the various regions along its routes and concludes with the observations on the prospects for expanding the economic impact for this industry.

In Chapter 15, Nancy Chesworth (Nova Scotia) presents a case study of cruise tourism in Atlantic Canada. She reveals a brief history of the cruise industry in the four Atlantic Provinces, then poses a question for its future: can the Atlantic Canada Cruise Association develop the strength of purpose to stand together for the good of all and sustain the industry in the Atlantic region?

In Chapter 16, Paul Wilkinson (Ontario) examines the growth of the cruise tourism in the Caribbean. He analyses the geography of the cruise arrivals in terms of ports of origin and destination ports, and shows how the patterns have changed over time.

The next chapter is authored by Ngaire and Norman Douglas (Australia). Their contribution to the cruise tourism literature is large, culminating in their 2004 text *The Cruise Experience*. In Chapter 17, they explore the foundation of organized cruise tourism in the islands of Hawaii and the South Pacific and the imagery of Pacific cruising as a 'paradise'.

In Chapter 18, Thomas Bauer (China) and Ross Dowling outline the growth of cruise tourism in Antarctica.

In Chapter 19, Robert McCalla (Canada) and Jacques Charlier (Belgium) contribute their second chapter to this book. Here they describe the round-the-world segment of the cruise industry and seek to establish the descriptive characteristics that are largely determined by the world's geography.

In Chapter 20, Ola Sletvold (Norway) outlines the development of the Norwegian Coastal Express as a form of transport with some seasonal tourism to a full-blown coastal voyage. Sletvold investigates the direction towards cruise ship business and reveals that the product is a unique combination of qualities that reflect some central aspects of Norwegian national identity.

In Chapter 21, Sacha Reid and Bruce Prideaux (Australia) examine the structure, operation and future potential for coastal cruising activities. The authors draw on a number of Australian examples to illustrate aspects of the framework that has the capability of being applied in any coastal setting.

Chapter 22 is a contribution by the legendary Valene Smith (USA). The noted professor's 1977 book on *Hosts and Guests* is one of tourism's seminal texts. In her latter years, amongst a host of other activities, she has found a new life as a cruise ship lecturer, and in this chapter she analyses the adventure cruise niche in terms of four difference types. She explains how each cruise type involves distinct differences in itineraries and destinations, lifestyles and activities and marketing strategies differ due to considerable variation in cost. Smith reveals that adventure cruising is virtually unreported in the scholarly tourism literature and this chapter provides a baseline for further research.

In Chapter 23, the final one of Part III, Claire Ellis and Lorne Kriwoken (Australia) present a case study of planning and management of expedition cruise ships to the Tasmanian Wilderness World Heritage Area. They argue that scoped research on environmental impacts should play a pivotal role in determining whether expedition cruise ships should be granted permits to operate in these highly sensitive marine ecosystems.

This part leads to Part IV, which investigates the industry's interactions with the economic, social and natural environments.

Silversea Cruises' *Silver Cloud* in Sydney, Australia, January 2005.

13 Spatial and Evolutionary Characteristics of Baltic Sea Cruising: A Historic-geographical Overview

Jan O. Lundgren

McGill University, Department of Geography, 805 Sherbrooke Street West, Montreal, Quebec, Canada, H3A 2K6

Introduction

Contemporary cruises prefer balmy seas and climates although the first generation of steam engine paddle wheelers applied the sea tour concept to the rough seas off Scotland in the mid-1830s (*Berlitz Cruise Guide*, 1997). The peripheral Baltic Sea saw its 'maiden voyage' in 1834 when the S/S *Frithiof* sailed the Stockholm–Visby–Vastervik 'pleasure tour' (Jansson, 1996).

The evolution of the Baltic Sea-based excursion and cruise phenomenon can best be appreciated when viewed within the framework of a 'phases process', where each phase can be defined and discussed.

The phases identified

Baltic Sea tourism started some 160 years ago. Its *first phase* lasted to the mid-1860s, when more reliable passenger steamships expanded schedules and connected with an increasing number of ports. The early beginning of pleasure tours and mini cruises is one reason why this presentation has adopted a historic-geographical approach.

A *second phase* begins around 1860, again with more numerous regular sailing schedules such as those out of Visby towards the Swedish mainland (Jansson, 1996) – and better ships. Also, more dependable steamship lines are established, among them the Gotlandsbolaget (1865/66) and the Sveabolaget (1872). This phase includes the turn-of-the-century years as well as the years leading up to the summer of 1914, which saw noticeable expansion in trans-Baltic tourism travel (Worthington, 2003) and the establishment of a third 'historical' shipping line, the Finnish Bore Line in 1908.

The *third phase* covers the interwar years and sees major post-Second World War geopolitical changes along the south shore of the Baltic Sea region, which produces new development patterns. Positive market dynamics among Nordic countries and the newcomer states of Finland, Estonia, Latvia, Lithuania and Poland extend trans-Baltic tourism travel links, including the first era of modern-style cruises (Jansson, 1996; Worthington, 2003).

In 1950, the modern era of ferry and passenger ship services begins with a gradual adaptation to mass tourist travel. Overall, the second half of the century records a never-stopping growth continuum, while the *fourth phase* ends with the collapse of the Eastern Block in 1989/90. The phase incorporates the decades of West European reconstruction and economic development, followed by a restructuring of the shipping lines business, a transformation of the aged ferry and passenger fleets (Jansson, 1996;

Viking Line, 1989, pp. 10–17), the creation of Silja Line in 1957 and the new Aland-based Viking Line in 1959. The Baltic Sea-based tourist trade registers a remarkable passenger growth, best demonstrated by the Viking Line (1960: 174,000; 1965: 332,000; 1970: 866,000; and 1988: 3.8 millions) – all in spite of a non-participation stance by Eastern Block shoreline states.

The demise of the Eastern Block initiates the *fifth phase* and the consequences in terms of the geopolitical liberation of the Baltic Sea region, and international markets becoming involved. The liberated political and commercial system of the interwar era returns but with a politically reconstituted Russia actively engaging in Baltic tourism. Since then, ferry and cruise travel growth has often been dramatic as demonstrated by Stockholm cruise ship visitations that grew from 108 in 1990 to 175 in 2002 (Stockholm Port Statistics).

Today, the Baltic Sea serves as a 'public provider' of a marine transport space for shoreline stakeholders and cruise line users alike – a cooler, northern European, equivalent to Braudel's interpretation of the historical functioning of the Mediterranean Sea (Braudel, 1973).

Focus Upon Geographic Perspectives

Conceptualizations and spatial applications of tourist travel

The above discussion defines maritime tourism development in the Baltic Sea Basin by way of an approximate, historical phase process that reflects partly the importance of geopolitical changes, partly performance improvements in maritime transport, partly market demand forces. From these perspectives we can envisage spatial parameters important to tourism at large, but to tourism in a Baltic Sea context in particular.

By studying the master list of tourist models presented by Pearce (1987) we can conceptualize the fundamental, spatial factor in the tourism travel phenomenon, notably the touring component. Campbell's model (1967) in particular fortuitously defines contemporary tourist travel as a circuit or loop, both histori-

cally and in a modern context – the European Grand Tour on one hand (Burgess and Haskell, 1967) and today's less extravagant vacation tour on the other.

Modern tourism often functions as a circuit or loop – be it on the time/space/cost level of the family vacation or the cruise (Campbell, 1967; British Tourist Board, 1976; Pearce, 1987; Lundgren, 2001). This applies for the waterborne tour version – the cruise – as well as Campbell's land version – the trip.

Applications to the Baltic Sea situation

International Baltic Sea cruises originate in the North Sea rim and conduct extended circuits or loops with pre-selected port-of-call visits. This contrasts with today's regionally more confined Baltic Sea cruises, presently highly popular among the coastal travel markets – the shorter, triangular excursion voyages, such as the Stockholm–Helsinki–Riga–Stockholm loop, or the long-haul city-to-city sea voyages Stockholm–Gdansk or Helsinki–Lubeck/Travemunde.

The business economics of excursion trips depend upon the dual transport role of most Baltic Sea-based ferry and passenger companies, with ships featuring interport roll-on–roll-off truck/rail/car designs and regular passenger traffic generating the steady annual revenue compared to that of the strongly seasonal cruise traffic.

The geographical characteristics of loop travel are essential to our understanding of Baltic Sea cruises. Thus, the cruise phenomenon is spatial, with an extended trans-Baltic operational range (Fig. 13.1), place-focused destinations and local impacting.

Our interpretation is designed around different regional geographic aspects that allow for an account of the importance of physical and human geographic parameters both on regional and local levels: a set of coastal attractions await the cruise tourist and constitute his or her principal source of satisfaction. On-board distractions compare poorly with the passenger's inherent excitement over entering a foreign port – a locale visually radiating distinct geographical and cultural differences. Thus,

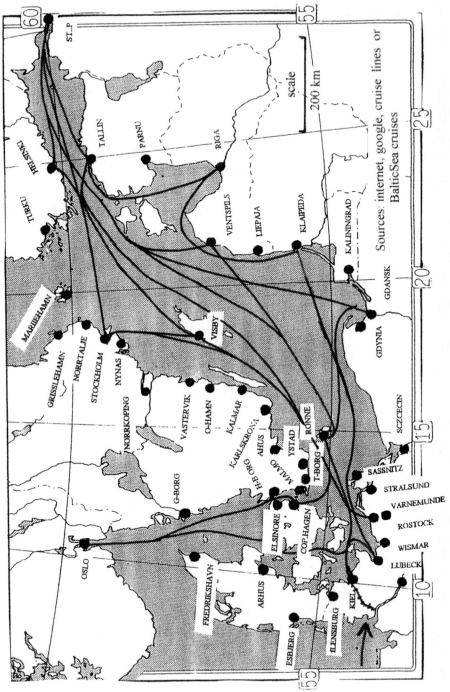

Fig. 13.1. Itinerary maps: sample of international cruise lines promotional (printed) material for northern Europe and the Baltic Sea region.

diverse 'land geography' encounters makes the cruise experience unique!

Component Themes

Our investigative methodology includes a set of broad themes, for which the defined phases previously discussed serve as a discreet framework.

Component 1: physical – geographic factors.
Component 2: resource bases – geographic resources and their tourist utility.
Component 3: the growth process – development of modern excursion and cruise services.
Component 4: cruise ship impacting – destination area consequences – 'the tourist in his tourist bubble?' (Jaakson, 2004).

Components Discussion

As a start for the components discussion, comparative data are given in Table 13.1.

Component 1

The Baltic Sea Basin ranks in the middle of the sea domains listed above. It is almost twice as large as the Adriatic but clearly dwarfed by the Caribbean Sea.

What makes the Baltic an interesting tourist attraction is its northward extension into a relatively unknown Nordic–Baltic world, effectively aided by two sea arms: one east-to-north towards the Aland archipelago and the other the 400-km-long eastward stretch of the Gulf of Finland.

In latitudinal terms, the Baltic Sea compares with the North Sea, with the former having certain advantages as a cruise tourism domain, such as the following:

1. A sheltered location: summer sailings usually experience fine weather due to the sheltered, inland sea location. Further, the average width of the Baltic is only half of that of the North Sea, which makes for a relatively tranquil sea, devoid of Atlantic-sized swells and lacking strong currents or tides. Vicious storms do occur; one sank the M/S *Estonia* in September 1994 (Langewiesche, 2004).
2. Easy navigation: Baltic Sea navigation is easy, and can be done with simple orienteering tools and methods. Also, the 300-km-width of the sea surface, at its widest, is halved by midway located, strategic islands: Bornholm, Gotland and the Stockholm–Aland–Finland archipelago to the north. Thus, early steamships made comforting midway island landfalls after the first half day of sailing out from the Swedish mainland. By this calculation, sufficient daylight hours remained for sailing the second leg the same afternoon, thus making their final landfall in the evening. Today the dimensions of the sea basin and the average speed of ferries and cruise ships facilitate crossings even more, except on a few deliberately set long-haul voyages, such as the Helsinki–Lubeck–Finnjet passenger and ferry service.
3. Time-saving sea voyages at improved speed: the dimensions of the sea basin and the speed of today's ferry and cruise ship sailings make crossings easy. However, speed improvements were slow in coming. From the 1840s well into the twentieth century, 10 knots was standard speed, although, in 1866, the Gotlandsbolaget proudly

Table 13.1. Comparative (inland) sea data. (From Encyclopedia Britannica Macropedia, 1981.)

	Maximum distance dimensions (km)	Surface (km²)	Crossing time at maximum 20 knots
Baltic Sea	1150 × 300 × width	420,000	8 hours 6 minutes
North Sea	930 × 700 × width	570,000	10 hours 12 minutes
Adriatic Sea	750 × 380 × width	285,000	10 hours 12 minutes
Aegeian Sea	611 × 299 × width	214,000	8 hours 6 minutes
Black Sea	1150 × 600 × width	660,000	14 hours 51 minutes
Caribbean Sea	2850 × 1400 × width	3,990,000	37 hours 48 minutes

announced its first 'fast' passenger ship on the Visby–Stockholm route, operating at a formidable 11 knots (Jansson, 1996). Only 45 years later, the Finnish Steamship Company introduced a faster ship at 14 knots – a record-breaking 'vitesse', to be broken only in the interwar years. Only in 1999 did the Gotlandsbolaget introduce modern high-speed ferry and passenger ships, with a cruising speed of 35 knots, on the Nynashamn–Visby route, effectively halving crossing time to 3 hours (Gotlandsbolaget Annual Report 2000, 2002–2003). This brought one Baltic Sea star tourist destination, the Viking Island of Gotland and medieval Visby, within comfortable day-excursion range for the Stockholm area travel market. Consequences? Most likely a shrinking in the tourist dollar amount spent on the island, only partially compensated by increases in day visitors traffic!

4. Land-based transport infrastructure improvements: a final aspect of accessing the Baltic Sea from population-rich extra-regional markets relates to EU's transport infrastructure policy, especially the long-term strategic freeway and bridge construction programme. Overland access to distant Baltic destinations has improved dramatically with the final development, in the Baltic Danish Straits, of the interisland bridge link becoming a reality in the year 2000. Afoot are plans for a final replacement of the inconvenient 45-minute Puttgarten–Rodbyhavn ferry service with a bridge, which would shorten driving times for car travellers between heavily populated metropolitan areas in northern Germany and the Baltic Straits conurbation of Copenhagen, Malmo, Sweden and other Scandinavian tourist destinations further north (Infrastructure, 1992).

Disadvantages for Baltic Sea cruising should also be recognized as they may inconvenience cruise tourists and consequently affect the competitiveness of Baltic cruises. Among them are the following:

- Long-approach voyages – Harwich, a major cruise embarkation point in the Thames estuary for Baltic Sea cruises, is faced with the disadvantage of being 350 nautical miles from the Baltic Sea via the North Sea Canal on the Elbe River estuary, and requires 15-hour sailing. Few route alternatives exist as the circumnavigation of the Jutland Peninsula to reach the Danish Baltic Straits, the only alternative Baltic Sea entry passage, is highly time-consuming at 35-hour sailing to Copenhagen direct; and it is costly! A relocation to embarkation points at the edge of the Baltic Sea Basin is an alternative; some cruises favour Copenhagen as an embarkation/disembarkation hub. Making North Sea ports of call before entering the Baltic can partially justify the longer alternative route arrangement, however, only with a reduction in Baltic Sea cruise content.

- To everything there is a season – the international (north European) cruise peak season starts in early May and ends in September, not so much due to the weather but rather the behaviour of the European (summer) vacation market. Similar factors are at play on the international travel markets. Off-season Baltic cruises exist – in fact, the lower prices and less-crowded ships make them popular for city-to-city weekend cruises. Fall weather conditions can deteriorate, and even normal winters produce sea ice conditions disruptive for sailings.

- The cul-de-sac question for today's cruise ship tonnage – as cruises enter the Baltic Sea from the west, no alternative exit route exists, especially for modern big-tonnage ships; they usually leave the inland sea the same route as they entered. The Baltic has always been a time-consuming cul-de-sac to sail, which is in sharp contrast to the historic sailings 'that once were'! The Vikings, with their deliberately small ship designs, happily exited both eastward and westward. For them it mattered little whether one did it via the East European river systems or westward through the Haithabu–Dannevirke–Treene River passage, north of today's North Sea Canal.

Component 2

The famous study 'The view from the road' by Appleyard *et al.* (1964) analyses the car driver's response to the surrounding landscape en route, and stresses the relationship between declining attentiveness (fatigue), landscape monotony and increased accident risk.

The cruise tourist on his 'sea road' faces a similar, but not as fatal, a risk: over time, the 'sameness' of the seascape scene becomes monotonous – even boring. His eye, and mind, might only react positively to land falls – approaching islands, distinct shorelines or ports. Gotland Island, the white cliffs of Rugen, the Stockholm archipelago passages, the spires of Maria Kirche in Lubeck are all visually interest-perking views! In fact, many Baltic Sea shore-lines offer just that – novel landscape scenes with different settings for curious minds!

1. Contrasting Baltic Sea coasts: the southern and south-eastern coastline – from west-side Lubeck to east-side Tallin – is a low lying, sandy, pine-forested shore, like Cape Cod. However, inland, the topography is undulating, rural and dotted with extensive interlocking lake systems, its geophysical features being a product of the most recent ice age. The characteristics are not visible from the cruise ship, but the lakes can be accessed via organized land excursions from certain cruise ports of call (Holland America Line 2002 Cruise Brochure).

The northern coastline (the Swedish east coast and Finland's south coast) is rocky and skerry-filled, and makes an enchanting archi-pelago zone, inside which are cities, towns and villages, many already on the cruise itinerary; Also, the varied and distinct human imprints in the rural landscape – historic towns, medieval fortifications, quaint villages – may all pique the cruise tourist's interest.

2. Cultural heritage resources: if the distinc-tiveness of the coastal landscapes of the Baltic Sea coast can be muted (they are not Norwegian fjords!!), the port towns and cities are powerful historic attractions with roots dat-ing back to the twelfth century or earlier (The Baltic, 1980; Ambrosiani and Clark, 1996). Settlements often began as hamlets, eventually survived the Viking era and, by luck, evolved into permanent centres. Thus, German Schleswig was a reconstitution of the plun-dered and famous Viking Haithabu trading post; Visby had also trading origins, but for a major sacking by the Danes in 1361, it func-tioned as a wealthy, and strategically positioned Hansa seaport (Encyclopedia Britannica Macropedia, 1981; Brockhaus, 1997); Danzig

(Gdansk) benefited from its location at the mouth of the Vistula River, a resource-rich hin-terland, but with a dangerous access to the open sea. Stockholm emerged through isostatic land rise, which in around 1250 blocked the direct sea passage with the Lake Malaren region, thus forcing the locals to establish a goods depot site, and eventually developed into a fortified settlement – the 'stockade holme', today's Old City island – thus becoming the con-troller of cargo trans-shipments to and from strategic hinterlands, one being the heartland of the Swedish nation state (Ambrosiani and Clark, 1996).

Towns were sometimes founded by state or royal edict, such as St Petersburg in the east and the naval city of Karlskrona in south-eastern Sweden, both products of geopolitics and 'proper' town planning. St Petersburg is the foremost Baltic Sea cruise destination with 212 cruise visitations and 143,000 cruise passen-gers (Cruise Europe Port Statistics, 2002), while Karlskrona's success has yet to come!

The coastal urban system includes some 70 ports, some of which were popular tourist desti-nations already in the interwar years. Among today's top 10–15, five are capitals: Copenhagen, Helsinki, Riga, Stockholm, Tallin; and three medieval: Lubeck, Visby and Gdansk. Others, such as Kalmar, Mariehamina, Elbing (Elblag) and Memel (Klaipeda) are just histori-cally interesting, but *all* are on the cruise circuit (Fig. 13.1).

Component 3

For the historical and spatial reconstruction of Baltic Sea tourism development, three studies from the mid-1990s provide interesting infor-mation: Jansson (1996), Olsson (1996) and Jarnhammar (1994). The third makes an inter-esting regional case on the Stockholm archipel-ago steamship development, the coastal steamship services and the Baltic Sea links. All three books are in Swedish. Some historical doc-umentation on the interwar decades has been extracted from two major dailies: *Svenska Dagbladet* (Stockholm) and *Hufvudstadsbladet* (Helsinki).

Direct contacts with Baltic Sea-based shipping lines have also yielded interesting results on individual shipping lines, but the databases are not longitudinal enough for comparative analysis. Port statistics on ship traffic for the recent development phase have been collected for select ports like Kiel, the North Sea Canal, Stockholm and Visby.

1. Innovating steps: the 1820s–1840s saw the establishment of many short-distance Sweden–northern Europe ferry and passenger services, thus breaking down the isolation of coastal Sweden: in 1824 Ystad–Germany; in 1836 Malmo–Copenhagen, Malmo–Lubeck, Stockholm–Turku and Stockholm–Helsinki.

Already in the early years, cruises were promoted as pleasure tours with steamships operating them for a few summer seasons (Jansson, 1996). Thus, the years 1837, 1838 and 1840 saw more cruises organized, but the (undeveloped?) Stockholm national market was unable to generate sufficient travel demand. It took decades for the travel market to correct itself and to start generating year-round traffic – a prerequisite for profitable services.

The entrepreneurial drive among shipping lines was strong, as demonstrated by the introduction of impressive long-distance routes: the Stockholm–Kalmar–Ystad–Rostock route (1838) or the the longest of them all, the St Petersburg–Lubeck service.

For some years, the entrepreneurial drive shifted from the Capital to the periphery with Visby-based shipping lines promoting Swedish mainland ports, mostly Stockholm (1840). One also linked up with existing long-haul services, such as the Stockholm–Lubeck service with Visby and Kalmar as ports of call in 1851.

Among the various steamship passenger services, the Stockholm–Visby connection seems to have been the most profitable route, and was also promoted as a pleasure tour. The extensive steamship service network out of Visby in 1862 may be an indicator of the successful generational development (see Fig. 13.2): four mainland ports with Stockholm in the north and Kalmar in the south; via Kalmar, another five ports, plus Lubeck and Stettin; via Stockholm, connections with northern mainland ports (Olsson, 1996), which more

effectively integrated Visby with the wider Swedish east coast market and the German north coast. The only gap in the network was eastward.

Still, the Visby merchants were not satisfied, hence the founding in 1865 of the Gotlandsbolaget – the Gotland Company – which in 1866 launched the modern S/S *Visby*, a substantial cargo/passenger ship, with a capacity of 300 passengers, but with a rather uninteresting speed. The first year's traffic results of 5000 passengers were positive as was the growth to 12,000 10 years later, in 1875. The 'take-off' stage in the passenger and tourist traffic for Gotland was a reality!

In the 1890s, the Gotlandbolaget served three principal mainland ports – Stockholm, Vastervik and Kalmar – all three having smooth links to the national railway system. Also, a first trans-Baltic connection with the Baltic coast via Libau (Liepaia) was operating – temporarily!

2. Fin-du-siècle and pre-1914 era of Baltic sea tourism: at the turn of the century, Baltic Sea tourism was a reality, partly as a result of the improved land-based railway access to strategic embarkation/disembarkation points around the Baltic coast, partly as an improved passenger and ferry ship service. Coastal railways linked 'mainland with sealand with mainland'. Thus, Gotland steamship services relocated from Stockholm to nearby Nynashamn, the latter with rail connection to Stockholm, which reduced the sea voyage to Visby to some 6–7 hours. Similar arrangements were put into effect with other mainland ports: Norrkoping, Kalmar and Karlskrona further south. A comparable rail infrastructure linked German Baltic Sea ports with a rapidly urbanizing, industrializing and travel-generating hinterland, which resulted in extensive seaside resort growth in the 1890s both in Germany and Estonia (Worthington, 2003). Also, east–west trans-Baltic services linked Stockholm with Baltic mainland ports, such as Riga. Result: an increasing flow of foreign tourists destined for Visby in the middle of the Baltic Sea, and Stockholm (Nord-Ostsee Kanal Passagierschiffspassagen, 2003).

Pleasure voyages became more popular, although they mostly operated as budget-priced excursions rather than expensive cruises. Consequently, passenger volumes grew throughout

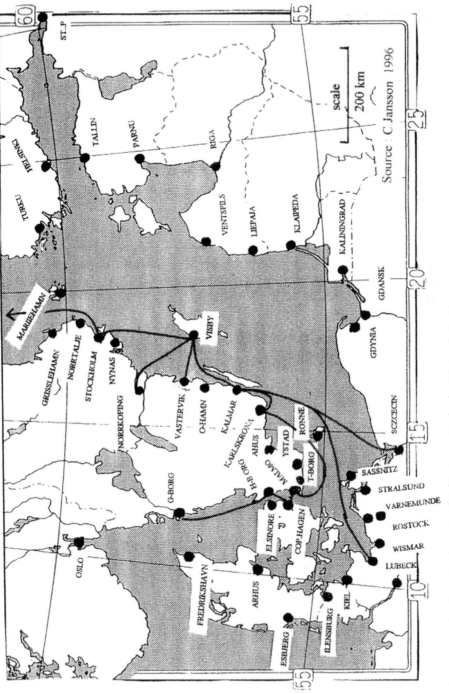

Fig. 13.2. Web information for regional Baltic Sea cruises by the Kristina Cruise Line.

the port system, with Gotland and medieval Visby recording over 10,000 summer tourists per annum. Discrete tourism impacting is being felt around the island as the first resort facilities open. Gotland's central location, paired with Visby's historic atmosphere, becomes a major draw with the reintroduction of a 'real' continental connection of Stockholm–Stettin; even the long-haul Finnish express service to Copenhagen, at 14 knots, schedules en route stops in Visby.

The opening of Germany's North Sea Canal in the mid-1890s brought consequences lasting to this day for international Baltic Sea cruising. **3.** The interwar period: the post-First World War geopolitical transformation changed the Baltic world of shipping. The creation of the Soviet Union reduced shipping operations at major transport hubs such as St Petersburg. Thus, the Baltic Sea travel market temporarily lost a touristic destination already then having a certain star quality.

Eventually, the geopolitical situation stabilized with the new states recording impressive economic growth, which in turn translated into substantial expansion of pan-Baltic and international shipping, and to a degree cruise tourism. Finland can serve as an example: 7 years after independence, the Finnish Steamship Lines operated trans-Baltic passenger and freight services to eight ports, from Tallin in the east to Lubeck in the south-west (Hufvudstadsbladet, 1926).

Typical cruise operations entered the Baltic in 1928 when the elegant M/S *Stella Polaris* made its first principal capitals tour, including a visit to the islands of Gotland and Visby. The end of the 1930s saw the Cunard cruises visiting Copenhagen, Stockholm, Visby, Helsinki and Danzig – a precursor to today's typical cruise itinerary – with the Norddeutscher Lloyd steamship lines tailing the Cunard circuit (Norddeutscher Lloyd, 1936). Still, cruises were relatively few, and tourism impact limited. **4.** The post-1945 era – new beginnings for cruises: the changed geopolitical situation in northern Europe should, in theory, have brought an end to cruise traffic. With the indefinitely set post-Second World War cold war boundaries, the free and open Baltic Sea cruise of the interwar era could not function. The long coastline held by Eastern Block countries made the outcome a given.

However, the pessimism did not hold – post-war Marshall aid, post-war reconstruction and the rebuilding of the West European economies produced in less than a decade a feeling of back-to-normal pre-war conditions for Baltic passenger and ferry services (Postan, 1967). The inter-Nordic maritime links reopened first – the excursion and cruise operations in the south-western part of the Baltic Sea as well as those between Stockholm and Finland. Still for 40 years, the Eastern Block coast contributed little to Baltic Sea trade.

Select ferry connections with Eastern Block countries were slowly resurrected, starting in 1965 with the Helsinki–Tallin fery shuttle (Worthington, 2003), followed by Poland and East Germany's gradual involvements. Nevertheless, one half of the Baltic Sea Basin was passive.

Port statistics for Visby demonstrate the successful cruise travel development in the past 25 years. Annual cruise ship ports of call doubled between 1978 and 1983 from 15 to 30, reaching 92 on the eve of the collapse of the Eastern Block and Soviet Union, and 106 visitations delivering 78,000 tourists in 2002. The Visby figures should have their corollaries in most major port destinations (Visby Port Cruise Statistics 1978–1992, 2001–2003; Baltic Tourism Cooperation, 1993).

The more peripheral location of the Baltic Sea region compared to other popular international cruise regions may have moderated the development tempo. However, with the final geopolitical transformation in 1990, the whole of the Baltic Sea, finally, was open for cruises. **5.** Contemporary cruise ship itineraries – the international traffic: today's planning of Baltic Sea-based cruise itineraries is an exercise in destination selection among some 40 suitable ports of call. Clearly, for the final selection, numerous factors have to be considered, among which are: (i) sailing time and distances from east to west; (ii) tourist appeal of ports; (iii) cruise ship size vs port dimensions.

Sailing the whole length of the Baltic Sea in one continuous long-haul voyage may be less preferable than a 'stepwise' approach with its numerous, enjoyable en route port-of-call visits.

An analysis of the spread of 57 cruise departures from the Kiel or North Sea Canal gateway eastward reveals, surprisingly, a strong appeal for long-haul voyages at the start up of the cruise. Thus, distant Stockholm and Visby attract 22 direct cruise arrivals from Kiel (38% of all Kiel-generated sailings) compared with only eight for nearby Ronne-on-Bornholm. Evidently, direct long-haul voyages sometimes make practical sense, especially viewed in the wider context of Baltic Sea cruise itinerary planning. Even remote Tallin on the Gulf of Finland receives direct sailings from Kiel (Kiel Hafenamt Kreutzfahrtshiffsliste 2004–2003–2002). However, Kiel's 'foreland spread' also includes numerous nearby port destinations: Copenhagen, Travemunde/Lubeck, Sassnitz–Mukran (with potential day visits to Berlin), historically reconstructed Gdansk, etc. Still, a first continuous long-haul sailing leg does produce subsequent itinerary advantages.

Typical international cruise itineraries can be gleaned from cruise travel brochures, with few surprises in store. Baltic Sea loops are advertised as a 'combined experience', or a 'Scandinavia–Russia and Baltic Heritage' tour (Cruise Line brochures 2002). The length of cruises varies from a minimum of 10 days to a maximum of 2 weeks, of which the latter seems to be preferable considering sailing distances, number of worthwhile port visits and amount of 'land time' for the tourist. Typically, cruises include five to seven ports, of which five have star capital city quality. Sometimes planners make the extra effort of identifying smaller, unique ports such as Gdansk, Kalmar, Riga or Turku.

Port capacities work against big-sized cruise ships, which often force passengers to disembark via time-consuming cumbersome tender shuttle services from the ship to port docksides. The procedure wastes passenger 'land time', which affects sightseeing. Off-centre satellite ports such as Nynashamn make land visits to Stockholm even more tiresome due to additional land transport travel, and the shortened overall land time allocation relative to the rich supply of local and regional tourist attractions. Tight sailing schedules add to the rush – the cruise cannot afford missing a reserved berthing place at the next port of call!

6. Contemporary cruise ship itineraries – the regional version: Baltic Sea-based cruises differ from the international version for a variety of reasons. First, the cruise lines are owned and operated by Baltic-based national or pan-Baltic corporations such as the EffJohn concern, holding company for eight separate shipping lines (Baltic Line/2/Kryss-93, 1993). Second, smaller cruise line planners design lower-priced, shorter cruises for the regional mainland markets. Third, the cruises focus upon a distinct part of the Baltic, which reduces open sea crossing times while increasing land time for the tourist (Fig. 13.3). Smaller cruise ships are used – often older renovated passenger ships, such as the M/S *Kristina*, 4500 (Baltic Line Kryss-93, 1993).

As the Baltic Sea in 1990 regained its pan-Baltic character as a Common, the re-established shoreline states rapidly engaged in trans-Baltic shipping, which initially involved city-to-city passenger and ferry services, e.g. between Stockholm and Riga, or Gdansk and Karlskrona.

Many national shipping lines also became involved in the popular city-to-city traffic, which in fact emerged as an alternative trans-Baltic cruise, typically found between Helsinki and St Petersburg, Karlskrona and Gdynia and Kiel and Stockholm, to mention a few (Baltic Line Kryss-93, 1993), or the longer St Petersburg–Tallin–Visby–Helsinki loop. Even shorter, triangular tour loops are offered by Sally Line with its popular Stockholm–Tallin–Visby–Stockholm tour. The potential loop diversity seems endless – but they sell well!

Component 4

1. Port destination impacting – big and small: Baltic ports are popular tourist destinations attracting massive tourist flows from the nearby Nordic markets, the European continent as well as international markets beyond. Still, cruise-related impacts are generally only a minor force on the local–regional destination level and cannot be compared with the huge and diverse impacts that have been measured for international island destinations in the Caribbean, Bahamas, Bermuda, San Juan, etc., which are all exposed to large-scale year-round international cruise traffic (Klein, 2002).

First, cruise traffic levels in Baltic Sea ports differ. The top six cruise destination ports – Copenhagen, St Petersburg, Stockholm, Tallin,

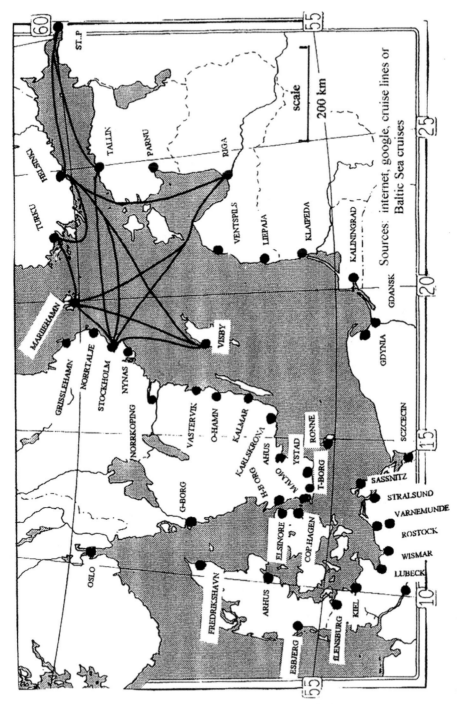

Fig. 13.3. Visby Port Cruise Statistics (2002), Jansson (1996).

Helsinki and Riga – all register a minimum of 100,000 cruise tourists annually. St Petersburg has also recorded the most impressive growth, from practically zero in 1990 to today's 212 cruise ship ports of call and 150,000 cruise tourists disembarking (Cruise Europe Port Statistics, 2002). Smaller, idyllic ports are (mini) impacted – Hamlet inspired Elsinore with three ships and 234 passengers, Swedish Karlskrona receiving two with 840 passengers (Cruise Europe Port Statistics, 2002).

The ratio of cruise tourists disembarking/ destination population size calibrates cruise-related impacting. Thus, Defert's statistical Tourism Function Index (Defert, 1967) for individual Baltic ports reveals the basic tourism impact situation, the index being highest for Visby (358.94) but insignificant for metropolitan St Petersburg (3.40). Between the extremes we find the low Copenhagen and Helsinki scores, 10.9 and 10.8, respectively, still three times higher than that of St Petersburg, which also manifests itself in the urban landscapes simply due to their smaller city sizes.

Second, local and regional scale dimensions must be accounted for as well as visitor land time, as both influence the spatial spread of the impact!

Third, economic impacting through direct cruise tourist consumer spending behaviour is spatially restricted due to tourist 'land time' allocation. Tourists exploring an unknown territory, a foreign environment, while negotiating a foreign language milieu, quickly run out of money, effort and land time.

2. The Stockholm and Visby impacting situations: in Stockholm and Visby cruise impacting is spatially concentrated due to the berthing site of cruise ships and the density of the urban landscape. In contrast to dockings of the popular and massive ferry and passenger ships in more off-centre port sections, cruise ships moor centrally and sometimes ride at buoys in the historic harbour basin from where the passengers invade a small city townscape – in Visby a 1.5 × 0.6-km medieval milieu (~100 ha). In Stockholm, the harbour basin serves as a central lookout point from the arriving ship, a 360-degree panorama of visible tourist attractions, a formidable Urry-styled tourist gaze (Urry, 1990) – all within a 1.6-km radius space, easily accessible via a short

taxi ride, a quick bus trip, a 10-minute subway journey or a half hour's walk! Proximity and access direct the impacting beautifully.

Proximity to first-class tourist attractions is common for Baltic Sea ports, and for many international cruise port destinations. In Helsinki, cruise and ferry ships dock at the northern end of the south harbour basin, at the local fresh-food market, thus embracing the historic downtown core; the same holds for Swedish Kalmar, with its historic city quarters at 5-minute walk from the ship's landing, as it also happens in Turku and Copenhagen. Cruise ship moorings are central even elsewhere in Europe and North America – witness Venice, with ships riding at anchor off the waterfront of Piazza San Marco, and Montreal's Old Port cruise ships that park directly at the historic waterfront promenade. Only in large international ports are the ships docked off-centre, making access to downtown time-consuming. Thus, impacting from Baltic Sea cruise tourists upon the port city or town is direct and focused.

3. Impacting beyond city cores: in spite of limited land time, Gotland and Visby cruise tourists diffuse extensively, directly or indirectly, thus bringing the impacting well beyond the city. They may break out of Jaakson's infernal tourist bubble in spite of land programmes, but unfamiliarity with a foreign language and local navigation often force them back in. Organized bus tours move the tourists deep into the hinterland – still in the tourist bubble, though (Jaakson, 2004).

'Gotland beyond Visby' is a standard bus tour for Visby and parts of Gotland, whereby visits are made to various parts of the Visby region and its Historical Museum, the Lummelunda Caves towards the north, the interior countryside with the Roma Monastery ruins, medieval churches, Gotland's botanical marvel – the flowery grazing meadows, Viking ship tombs, coastal lookouts, craft studios and, weather permitting, a picnic en route. Similarly, Stockholm abounds with boat and bus sightseeing covering the central metropolitan area. Longer excursions exist – the Birka archeological boat tour westward into lake Malaren, assorted castle and eastbound archipelago tours. These forays generate indirect economic multipliers of unknown dimensions, while the tourists browsing the downtown commercial core clearly produce individualized direct economic impacting. Sometimes the tourists even 'unbubble' in international downtown Stockholm (Jaakson, 2004).

Hinterland penetrations occur not only in Stockholm and Gotland or Visby but also around the Baltic Sea coast. In Kalmar, it involves excursions to the famous glassworks at Orrefors and Kosta–Boda; in the case of Rostock, Germany, bus tours are arranged to the Pomeranian Lake District or Berlin further south for a glimpse of modern German architecture and, of course, for photographing the famous cold war geopolitical flashpoint, Checkpoint Charlie – a must for history aficionados.

The Future of Baltic Sea Cruising

One can argue that the international segment of the cruise ship traffic favours big tonnage designed for the big open seas, such as the Atlantic Ocean or the rough North Sea. As a result, the narrow waterways of the Baltic including smaller ports have gradually become difficult to navigate, and port space limitations make big ship port visits increasingly impractical: to navigate the M/S *Constellation* (GRT = 90,000 t) through the Stockholm archipelago to the central harbour basin is difficult under the best of circumstances, even with the best of river pilots! The much smaller M/S *Costa* (GRT = 53,000 t) must ride at anchor off the port of Visby. Clearly, smaller ports in smaller inland seas impose their own, specific size limitations or . . . ? Only by downsizing the cruise ships can Baltic Sea cruises be developed in the future.

In the downsizing of the ship, the cruise must follow suite. To make the redesigned future Baltic Sea cruise operationally viable requires more sophisticated market segmentation analyses, and more imaginative itinerary creativity.

In recent years, the interest in Baltic Sea culture and theme voyages has grown on the sailing level, but above all beyond the coast, in the hinterlands.

The Helsinki-based Kristina cruises represent one future cruise model with suitable ship dimensions, modest passenger capacity and convenient cruise time of 4–6 days. But the M/S *Kristina* lacks thematic discovery enthusiasm – she simply carries passengers between ports,

offers 6-hour land visits and hoards passengers back on board, in time. This contrasts sharply to the culture-specialized tour programmes promoted by a new generation of travel agencies-cum-tour producers.

The Favorite Culture and Theme Travel Company of Stockholm (Favorit Kultur Och Temaresor, 2004) is one such newcomer. Its travel register identifies 'serious' Baltic tours. The theme offered incorporates tantalizing cultural experiences, such as the Finnish landscape painting school of the early nineteenth century (3-day tour), or historic Baltic city tours of Vilnius–Riga–Tallin (6 days). Passenger and ferry services may be engaged, but sometimes the group even flies! The Russian river tour company, Fremad Russia Ltd, is also a newcomer, successfully operating the St Petersburg–Ladoga–Onega–Moscow canal route (Fremad Russia, 2004). Another uses the waters between Sweden and Germany, with focus upon Bornholm Island and the south-eastern corner of the Swedish province of Scania, Osterlen, with a ferry connect to Bornholm, an island stay and island tour (4 days).

Clearly, the standard 'round the Baltic Sea' cruise, the mainstay of international cruises in the Baltic since the early 1970s, needs a critical reassessment from which might spring new, diverse tourist developments in the future.

Actually, we are seeing the new beginnings – already!

References

Ambrosiani, B. and Clarke, H. (1996) *Towns in the Viking Age.* Leicester University Press, Leicester, UK, 210 pp.

Appleyard, D., Lynch, K. and Myer, J. (1964) *The View From The Road.* MIT Press, Cambridge, Massachusetts, 64 pp.

The Baltic: A Special Issue (1980) *Ambio* 9(3–4). Royal Swedish Academy of Sciences, Pergamon Press, Oxford.

Baltic Line/2/KRYSS-93 (1993) Published by Baltic Lines, Stockholm, 129 pp.

Baltic Tourism Cooperation (BTC)/Baltic Tourism Commission (1993) Cruise Ship Survey Document. Norrkoping, Sweden.

Braudel, F. (1973) Histoire économique du monde méditerranéen, 1450–1650. Toulouse, France, 686 pp.

British Tourist Board (1976) Drive-as-you-please tourist programme for Britain.

Brockhaus, der Grosse (1997) Enzyklopädie, Teil 9, 'Hanse', p. 481.

Burgess, A. and Haskell, F. (1967) *The Age of the Grand Tour*. Crown Publishers, New York, 136 pp.

Campbell, C.K. (1967) An approach to research in recreational geography, Occasional Papers, No.7. Department of Geography, University of British Columbia, Vancouver, pp. 85–90.

Cruise Europe Port Statistics (2002) Statistics 2000–2002. *Cruise Europe News Bulletin* 9(4), 8. Port of Reykjavik, Iceland.

Defert, P. (1967) Le taux de fonction touristiques: mise en point et critique. *Cahiers Du Tourisme*, C-13. Chet., Aix-En-Provence, France.

Encyclopedia Britannica Macropedia (1981) Coastal geomorphology, Vol. 2, Baltic Sea, p. 667; Baltic States History, p. 669, etc.

Favorit Kultur Och Temaresor (2004) Stockholm, 144 pp. Bornholm, p. 33; Insjofinland, p. 37; Aland and Kokar, p. 39; Balticum, Vilnius, Riga and Tallin – the rediscovered pearls of the Baltic, p. 40.

Fremad Russia Ltd (2004) River cruises brochure, St Petersburg.

Hufvudstadsbladet (1926) Helsinki. Advertisement of scheduled sailings for Finska Ångfartygsbolaget, 26 June.

Infrastructure in the Baltic Sea region, March 1992, Cooperation in the Baltic Sea area. Report from the Second Parliamentary Conference, Nordic Council, at the Storting, Olso, Norway, April 1992.

Jaakson, R. (2004) Beyond the tourism bubble? Cruise ship passengers in port. *Annals Of Tourism Research* 31 (January).

Jansson, C. (1996) Över Östersjon till Gotland: Passagerartrafiken genom tiderna (crossing the Baltic toward Gotland: passenger traffic through the centuries). Kristianstad Boktryckeri AB, Kristianstad, Sweden, 334 pp. Swedish text.

Jarnhammar, L. (1994) Stockholms Skargard Tur Och Retur. Swedish text.

Kiel Hafenamt Kreutzfahrtschiffsliste (2004–2003–2002) Kiel Hafenamt, Deutschland.

Klein, R. (2002) *Cruise Ship Blues – the Underside of the Cruise Industry*. New Society Publishers, Gabriola Island, British Columbia, Canada.

Langewiesche, W. (2004) A sea story. *The Atlantic Monthly*, 293(4).

Lundgren, J. (2001) Canadian tourism going north: conceptualizations and tourist functions. In: Sahlberg, B. (ed.) *Going North: Periheral Tourism in Canada and Sweden*. 161 pp. European Tourism Research Institute (Etour), Ostersund, Sweden, pp. 13–45.

Nord-Ostsee-Kanal Passagierschiffpassagen 2003. Website Print-out.

Olsson, C.G. (1996) Svensk Kustsjofart 1840–1940 (Swedish coastal shipping 1840–1940); Svensk Kustsjöfart 1840–1940 (Swedish coastal shipping 1840–1940); Sjöhistorisk Årsbok 1996–1997, 287 pp. Publicerad Av Foreningen Sveriges Sjofartsforening I Stockholm. Printed at Centraltryckeriet I Boras, Sverige. Swedish text.

Pearce, D. (1987) *Tourism Today: A Geographical Analysis*. Longman Scientific and Technical, UK. Co-published in the US with John Wiley & Sons, New York, 229 pp.

Postan, M.M. (1967) *An Economic History of Western Europe 1945–64*. Methuen and Co. Ltd, London, UK, 382 pp.

Urry, J. (1990) *The Tourist Gaze: Leisure and Travel in Contemporary Societies*. London, UK, 176 pp.

Viking Line (1989) History document, 1959–1989. Mariehamina, Åland, 48 pp. Swedish text.

Visby Port Cruise Statistics (1978–1992, 2001–2002). Documents prepared by the Hamnkontoret (Port Administration Offices), Visby.

Worthington, B. (2003) Changes in an Estonian resort. *Annals of Tourism Research* 30 (April), 369–385.

14   The Alaska Cruise Industry

John M. Munro[1] and Warren G. Gill[2]

[1]Simon Fraser University, Department of Economics, Burnaby, BC, Canada
V5A 1S6; [2]Simon Fraser University, Department of Geography,
Burnaby, BC, Canada V5A 1S6

Introduction

Alaska is one of the world's principal cruise destinations and is the second most important
North American market after the Caribbean
(CLIA, 2001; Butler, 2003). Activity is seasonal
between May and September and is largely configured into 1-week segments on three principal
itineraries. About 805,000 passengers were on
28 major cruise ships[1] visiting Alaska in 2004
producing almost 1.5 million embarkations
and debarkations (NorthWest CruiseShip
Association, Vancouver, BC, 2004, personal
communication). Canada's third largest city,
Vancouver, British Columbia, has historically
been the principal homeport for these cruises
and the jumping off point for the sheltered, spec-
tacularly scenic 'Inside Passage' route to the
north. In the last 4 years Seattle, Washington,
has captured a 37% (and growing) share of the
trade as a result of cruise line innovation, creative marketing, a new solution to restrictive US
law and the turmoil in US tourism following the
terrorist attacks of 11 September 2001.

In common with almost all the world's
cruising regions, the Alaska cruise industry rep-

resents an extreme divergence between localized
impact and local policy control. The industry
produces a service using mainly imported factors of production (ships, crews, supplies),
which it then sells to buyers, almost all of whom
are from outside the region. Yet certain regional
facilities and access to regional environmental
capital are necessary to the success of the product. Resolution of the tensions and conflicts that
inevitably arise has involved various national
and regional public policy measures, cruise
industry organizations and other tourism interests. This activity occurs against a backdrop of
an intensely competitive travel industry where
alternatives to cruising abound and there are
other competing cruise destinations. Policies
that raised the costs of cruising so that Alaska
became an uncompetitive destination for the
cruise industry or for individual companies
would result in service reductions. So far, judg-
ing by the rapid growth of the Alaska cruise
industry, this has not happened.

The Alaska cruise industry of today grew
out of a regional Canadian and US shipping
industry that used ships registered in each country and crewed by each country's nationals.
While much smaller in size, this pioneer industry had a larger local economic impact per passenger than does today's international cruise
industry because it was regionally based.
Apparently, any environmental impacts were
ignored. The recent tremendous growth in the

---

[1]These large ships dominate the Alaska cruise industry but service is also provided by 14 small or 'pocket'
cruise ships and five ferries operated by the state-
owned Alaska Marine Highway System.

industry has focused attention on both sides of the border on economic and environmental issues, with pollution being a major public policy concern in Alaska (and perhaps soon in British Columbia), while Seattle vies for an even greater share of the economic benefits.

There is a substantial literature on the economic impact of tourism on regional economies. This literature emphasizes the spending of tourists on accommodation, meals, sightseeing and other retail goods and services and uses various techniques of economic impact analysis such as multipliers and input–output modelling to assess the impact of tourism.[2] The cruise industry might seem to offer less regional economic impact than shore-based tourism because the main expenditure items, accommodation and meals, are provided on board, not in the local economy. This may be true for ports of call during cruises. However, for cities that are terminals for cruise ships, the potential economic impacts are much larger. The extension of the cruise experience through pre- or post-cruise land-based excursions can also magnify the impact in specific regions.

The chapter begins with a review of the evolution of the Alaska cruise industry. Both Canadian and US entrepreneurs and firms played roles in the development of this market, although the context today is multinational. This leads to a discussion of the economic impacts of the Alaska cruise industry on the various regions along its routes. The chapter concludes with observations on the prospects for expanding the economic impact of this industry.

Policy Environment

The operational shape of the Alaska cruise industry has been strongly influenced by US national maritime policy. An 1886 statute, the Passenger Vessel Service Act, restricts transportation between US ports to ships built, registered and crewed in the USA (US House of Representatives, 1998). Only two operating deep-sea cruise ships meet these specifications because costs are lower

with other arrangements.[3] The cruise industry typically builds its ships in Europe, registers them in Liberia, Panama or the Bahamas and operates them with diverse international crews.[4] Consequently, this US statute means that the international cruise industry must have a Canadian port of call in their Alaska cruise itineraries; geography and port facilities have made Vancouver the most suitable port. Companies are permitted to turn their Alaska vessels around in ports such as Seattle and San Francisco, but they must schedule a call somewhere in British Columbia, usually in either Vancouver or Victoria, to do this. From Seattle, it has historically been problematic to schedule a 7-day round trip to Skagway and meet this constraint.[5] From San Francisco, it is impossible, and ships homeported in San Francisco, only one or two in most years, operate on 12-day round-trip schedules to Skagway. These schedules are believed to be less attractive to the market.

As a result, Vancouver has historically been the homeport for the great bulk of modern Alaska cruise activity. Seattle, which in the first half of the twentieth century was an important point of departure for Alaska, until recently only played a minor role in the development of the modern Alaska cruise. The significant infrastructure that developed to service the cruise industry seemed to add to Vancouver's locational advantage (Marti, 1990); however, there have been dramatic changes since 2000 that have made Seattle very competitive for return trip 7-day cruises.

Other countries, including Canada, also restrict their domestic shipping business to national vessels but it is curious that the US restriction has been retained after the domestic deep-sea passenger shipping industry that it was supposed to protect has withered away. The explanation is that any loosening of the passenger legislation would be perceived as the

---

[2]Dwyer and Forsyth (1998) provide a general discussion of cruise tourism's economic impacts.

[3]According to Buchholz and Carol (1993), 20–25% lower.

[4]Wood (2000) argues that the cruise industry has the most globalized labour force in the world.

[5]'Problematic' in the sense that the voyage to southeastern Alaska is in outside waters, not the scenic British Columbia Inside Passage, and there is little slack in the schedule.

Fig. 14.1. *Princess Kathleen* in the Inside Passage *circa* 1950. Photo: CPR.

first step in weakening the similar protection for intranational freight transportation contained in the Merchant Marine Act of 1920 (well known as the 'Jones Act'). That protection is important and a powerful lobby has so far resisted all moves to rationalize these old protectionist laws.

The Alaska Cruise

The great bulk of activity in the Alaska cruise industry is mass market and involves the promotion of the ship and the cruise as a resort experience (Douglas and Douglas, 2004). Although a strictly seasonal market, the Alaska cruise represents about 8% of the overall North American cruise industry. For many of the major firms Alaska cruises are a major focus of activity. In 2004, Princess, Holland America (both divisions of Carnival) and Royal Caribbean/Celebrity all had six or more ships engaged in the trade, while Norwegian had four.[6] Specialty lines such as Crystal, Radisson and Silversea were also represented by single ships.

Unlike sun cruises to the Caribbean, the Alaska experience is focused on scenery, eco-tourism and history. For many Americans – who make up 80% of passengers – Alaska is the 'Last Frontier' and rings with the call of the wild, the rambunctiousness of gold rushes and the mysteries of native people. Relatively recently occupied by Europeans, the north-west coast still retains for many a sense of the unexplored. The Inside Passage route, some 1600 km (1000 miles) through British Columbia and the Alaska Panhandle, is largely sheltered and offers a spectacular view of a drowned fjord coast (see Fig. 14.1).

The early days: gold rushes, staples and tourism

The history of the Alaska cruise includes the line voyage, servicing the resource hinterland, and the pleasure cruise. As early as the 1880s 'quite a few pleasure travelers discovered that this route from San Francisco or Portland to Southeast Alaska possessed some of the grandest scenery on the continent' (McDonald, 1984, p. 2). Naturalist John Muir found Glacier Bay in 1879 – now a US National Park and World Heritage Site – and tourism to this landscape of great natural beauty and scientific interest began soon

---

[6]For a company like Princess Cruises, Alaska has represented about 20% of annual deployment vs 34% in the Caribbean (Brown, 2001).

Fig. 14.2.   Alaska cruise brochures 1936 to 1971. Photo: Greg Ehlers.

after (National Park Service, 1997). Excursions to view other glaciers were also recorded in the 1880s (McDonald, 1984) as steamship services expanded with the discovery of gold at Juneau. The main force in the development of transportation service to Alaska was, however, the Klondike gold rush of 1897/98. The gold of Canada's Yukon was only practically accessible through Alaskan ports and a frenzied trade immediately developed commandeering every available, but not necessarily seaworthy, vessel to provide passage to the fortune seekers. When the rush was over in 1900, 'most of the spur-of-the-moment steamship companies faded from the scene, but the Alaska coastal route had become an established one' (Newell and Williamson, 1959, p. 84). The Alaska Steamship Company was one of the survivors, providing passenger sailings from Seattle until 1954.

Canadian companies such as Union Steamship, Canadian Pacific and Grand Trunk Pacific (later Canadian National) provided service from Vancouver. These routes initially formed part of an extensive network developed on the British Columbia coast to service the burgeoning resource industries centred on fishing, forestry and mining. The ships provided supplies to, and shipped cargo from, the many camps along the coast that operated as staging points for resource exploitation in nearby areas.

There was early recognition of the value of tourism (see Fig. 14.2). Pacific Coast Steamships promoted summer Alaska excursions in 1906 as the 'Totem Pole Route' featuring 'glaciers' and 'a thousand islands en route' along the 'Inside Passage – sea sickness unknown' (Newell and Williamson, 1959, p. 24). Prior to the First World War, Grand Trunk advertised trips to Prince Rupert and Stewart in British Columbia as 'an ideal vacation trip through the "Norway of America"'. In 1922 Canadian Pacific's new ship *Princess Louise* began sailing the 'tourist run to Skagway, upon which she was employed for no less than 40 years' (Hacking and Lamb, 1974, p. 256).[7]

Following the Second World War, the traditional transportation function provided by the steamship companies was increasingly under

---

[7]*Princess Louise* was built to replace *Princess Sophia*, lost with all aboard on Vanderbilt Reef in the Lynn Canal south of Skagway on 25 October 1918 in the Pacific coast's greatest maritime disaster. Of the 353 people on board (including 50 women and children) were 'crews of many ice-bound river steamers, miners, trappers, businessmen and a few late season tourists' (Turner, 1977, p. 115). Coates and Morrison (1990) argue that the loss of so many key seasonal workers on *Sophia* furthered the economic and social decline of the Yukon.

siege. Consolidations and technological change in the resource sector reduced the number of small communities requiring passenger and freight service. New air services such as Queen Charlotte Airlines, using wartime amphibians, soon drew the bulk of the remaining up-coast passenger traffic (White and Spilsbury, 1988). What remained was the seasonal summer tourist service, for which Canadian National constructed a purpose-built ship, *Prince George*, and the CPR refitted the *Princess Kathleen* (Turner, 2001). By the 1960s the Alaska cruise was reduced to the CPR's *Princess Patricia*, which continued in this service – with winter charters to Princess Cruises for Mexican Riviera cruises from 1965 to 1967 – until 1981, and the *Prince George*, which operated under CN auspices until 1975 (and briefly ran again to Alaska in 1982), and the small ships of Alaska Cruise Lines.

The contemporary Alaska cruise

The tremendous growth of the Alaska cruise market from 38 sailings for 22,800 revenue passengers in 1970 to 436 sailings generating 1,491,976 passengers through the ports of Vancouver and Seattle in 2004 parallels the overall development of the cruise industry. Ships have become much larger and their cruise product more sophisticated with ever larger and more sumptuous facilities and services.

One unique element that has marked the expansion of the Alaska market has been the focus on extensive land tour packages to supplement the cruise experience. While the CPR and the White Pass and Yukon Route had historically promoted such packages, it was the development by Chuck West of Alaska Cruise Lines of motor coach and rail tours to the Alaskan hinterland in the 1960s that became a key for further growth (West, 1993). His company, Westours, operated two former Union Steamships and two other small vessels to provide access from Vancouver to his land excursion business and several Alaska hotels he owned. By 1970 he had overextended his operation. On a business trip to Amsterdam he met an official of Holland America Line. As West recalled, 'The Dutch possessed the one cruise tour component that was vital to the future of Westours and

I had not been able to supply – large efficient ships' (Dickinson and Vladimir, 1997, p. 30). Holland America purchased Westours and entered the Alaska market, later moving their head office to Seattle in 1973.

In the late 1960s both P&O and Princess began offering cruises to Alaska (Bannerman, 1976; Hacking, 1990) and after their merger in 1974 they further developed their own land tour capability. Others joining the market in the 1970s and 1980s were Sitmar (which often homeported a ship in San Francisco), Costa, Cunard, Royal Viking and Regency. The Alaska cruise business grew tenfold from 1970 to 1985. To meet this demand Vancouver completed a new cruise terminal in 1986 at Canada Place and later refurbished a second terminal in 1994.

Land tours remain an important distinguishing feature of the Alaska cruise and some companies have substantial land tourism facilities, as shown in Table 14.1. The 7-day 'Glacier Route' cruises across the Gulf of Alaska that originate either in Vancouver or Seward or Whittier, Alaska, with passengers flying the other leg, account for about one-third of trips. These cruises offer much greater opportunities to market land packages to Denali National Park and other interior Alaska destinations than do return trips. Since their inception by Princess in 1989 they have also had the added benefit of reducing terminal congestion in Vancouver. Competition between cruise lines now focuses on land excursion capacity as well as type and quality of ship. A proposed joint venture between P&O Princess and Royal Caribbean was in part predicated on reducing costs through the joint utilization of Princess's land assets in Alaska (and perhaps gaining access to Glacier Bay cruises), areas where Royal Caribbean was weak (P&O Princess Cruises, 2001).

As elsewhere in the cruise industry, large 'economy of scale' ships (Dawson, 2000, ch. 7) have come to dominate the Alaska cruise by offering a product directed to extracting maximum return from a captive audience. Ship size grew from 20 major ships with an average size of 26,204 gross registered tonnage (GRT) in 1990 to 28 major ships with an average 74,077 GRT in 2004 (*Harbour & Shipping*, 1990, 2004). Passenger growth into the 1990s was steady, with dramatic increases observed after the Open Skies Agreement of 1995 permitted more US

Table 14.1. Land excursion capacity 2001.

	Princess	Holland America	Royal Caribbean
Guest rooms			
Alaska interior	1001	894	–
Alaska south-east	–	551	–
Yukon	–	585	–
Total	1001	2030	–
Railcars	–	–	–
Cars	10	13	2
Daily capacity	880	858	160
Motorcoaches	219	192	6
Capital employed	US$160m	US$200m	US$10m
Balcony cabins per week	1824	864	1845
Glacier Bay cruises	77	101	–

Source: Ball (2001).

direct flights into Vancouver International Airport, thereby reducing the need to bus passengers from nearby US airports.

This rapid escalation in numbers of passengers and ship size has not been without problems. Environmental concerns in the 1980s prompted the US National Park Service to restrict cruise ship access to Glacier Bay (a prime sightseeing area; see Fig. 14.3), and the number of permits authorized remains a hotly contested issue (Frantz, 1999). In addition, the limited capacity of small Alaskan ports of call to absorb ever-larger ships and numbers of visitors has raised questions about the environmental and social impacts of the cruise industry on these communities. When combined with terminal capacity restrictions in Vancouver, these issues forced the cruise lines to expand beyond the preferred Saturday and Sunday departures to almost all days of the week.

The supply and quality of terminal facilities are very important influences to the cruise industry (Marti, 1990). In an attempt to attract some of the growth in the Alaska market, the Port of Seattle completed new cruise ship berths in part in 1996, but did not receive any cruise homeport activity until 2000.[8] Since then the rise of Seattle as an Alaska homeport has been nothing short of remarkable, with 562,000 passengers passing through the port in 2004. Vancouver attempted to stem the erosion of trade to Seattle by expand-

ing the Canada Place terminal for the 2002 season to accommodate larger ships and provide for more weekend sailings but Seattle countered by building two new berths for the 2004 season.

The shift to Seattle as southern homeport is the result of both innovation and world events. The presumption had always been that the increased round-trip distance to Seattle (~480 km or 300 miles) created a locational disadvantage *vis-à-vis* Vancouver – with or without the effect of the Passenger Vessel Services Act – given that the market demanded as much time as possible in Alaska. Unable to secure a weekend berth in Vancouver in 2000, Norwegian Cruise Line (NCL) was forced to reconsider some of the basics of their Alaska cruise operation in order to meet the market 'requirement' of visiting three Alaska ports and viewing a glacier within a 7-day trip. To achieve this they placed a faster-than-normal 25-knot ship in Seattle and then made the key decision to avoid the fabled Inside Passage by travelling directly to and from Alaska on a route outside Vancouver Island. This 'Outside Passage' route in the north Pacific can be rough and is almost entirely devoid of land scenery for the 2 sea days of the voyage, but saves considerable time.[9] The Passenger Vessel Services Act was observed by using Victoria, British Columbia,

---

[8]This was only the second time since the early 1950s that Seattle had been used as a homeport for Alaska cruises.

[9]NCL has recently engaged in a form of geographical amputation in their promotional literature by reducing the Inside Passage to the area within the Alaska Panhandle heralding that 'the dramatic beauty of this 274–mile pristine waterway is unequaled anywhere on earth' (Norwegian Cruise Line, 2003).

Fig. 14.3. *Statendam* class ship in Glacier Bay. Photo: Holland America Line.

on Vancouver Island as a 'service call' port, stopping for a few hours in the evening before proceeding to Seattle. Victoria can thus be seen as the agent in the relative decline of Vancouver. The cost to the British Columbia economy of having cruise ships stop in Victoria for a few hours instead of spending all day in Vancouver at the beginning and end of a cruise is substantial (see Fig. 14.4).

Whether this would have been such an important innovation without the events of 11 September 2001 is unclear. With many Americans afraid to travel far after the terrorist attacks, the cruise lines scrambled to position ships away from Europe and closer to the USA. Holland America quickly announced the deployment of its new fast ship, *Amsterdam*, from the Mediterranean to Alaska for the 2002 season and NCL added another ship, with Princess joining in with the 2600-passenger post-PANAMAX *Star Princess* in 2003. In 2004 both Holland America and Princess added very large ships and Celebrity relocated one from Vancouver. The 'Outside Passage' has been a great success, accounting for essentially all of the astounding 56% growth in the Alaska market since 1999 (see Fig. 14.5). The pressure

on Alaska destinations is so great that Princess has reduced the 'glacier experience' for Seattle passengers to Tracy Arm, previously a very secondary choice.

In the post 11 September world, Seattle has developed a significant 'drive market', as only 74% of passengers arrive by air (John C. Martin Associates, 2004). Pricing may also be an incentive for cruise lines and passengers in choosing Seattle because the Port of Seattle, which has a favourable taxation regime and federal subsidies unavailable to Vancouver, only charges US$7.50 per passenger, compared with US$11.00 in Vancouver (Constantineau, 2004a). This advantage is likely offset by the increased cost of sailing the additional distance to Seattle, but cheaper air fares within the USA help make Seattle more price-competitive.

Economic Impacts

General economic impacts

For any region, the economic impact of the cruise industry is likely less than would be generated by the same number of land-based

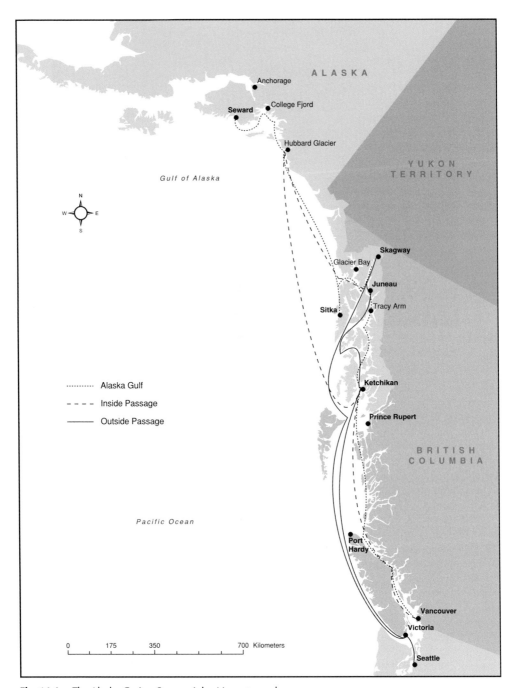

Fig. 14.4. The Alaska Cruise. Source: John Ng cartographer.

tourists. A cruise is essentially a self-contained, fully prearranged vacation experience; indeed, that feature is one of the most important marketing devices for cruise companies. How much spending stimulus this form of tourism delivers to a regional economy depends on onshore spending by passengers before, during and after the cruise.

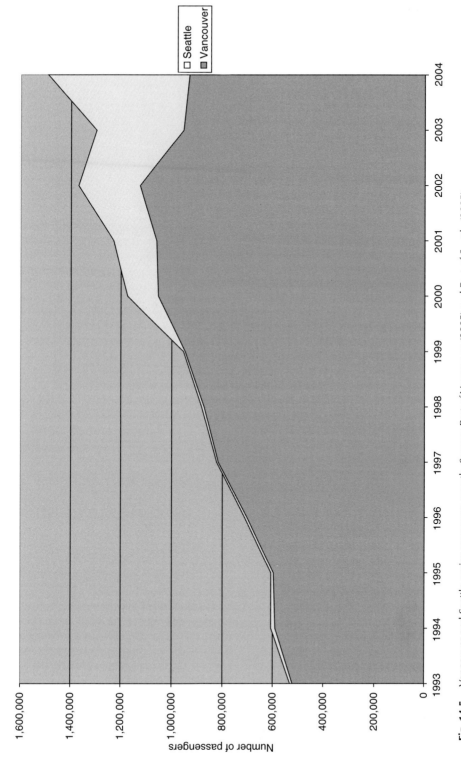

Fig. 14.5. Vancouver and Seattle cruise passenger growth. Source: Port of Vancouver (2005) and Port of Seattle (2005).

Fig. 14.6. Princess, Holland America and Royal Caribbean ships at Canada Place, Vancouver, BC, 2002. Source: Vancouver Port Authority.

In addition to passenger spending, cruise ships purchase services from local port authorities. There is considerable research interest in the economic impact of ports. Most of this is generated by port authorities and port-related industries, which presumably wish to assure governments and the general public that they are important for local and regional economies. This desire for recognition may be stimulated by a desire to protect certain benefits and powers conferred on ports such as local tax abatements, local taxing powers and the ability to borrow against the public credit of the metropolitan area. Port economic impact studies are also used to inform decisions concerning port development and infrastructure investment (Cowan and Brooks, 1995).

Cruise ships interface with ports in much the same way as cargo ships. They must be docked, unloaded, supplied and provisioned, repaired, loaded and undocked (Fig. 14.6). Some of these functions are more or less important for cruise ships than for cargo ships, but because cruise ships spend more time in port as a percentage of their annual operation, the port interface is more frequent. Also, cruise ships have far larger crews than cargo ships, and crew members' personal spending ashore is an important supplement to passenger spending. The regional economic impact of all these expenditures is influenced by a number of key parameters:

1. The number of days the average cruise passenger spends in the region is determined by such factors as personal choice,[10] whether a city is the origin and/or destination of the cruise, and how many regional ports are visited on the cruise and for how long.

---

[10]According to an earlier survey (InterVistas Consulting, 1999), 65% of passengers spent some time in Vancouver; however, the average time spent by them is only around 2 days.

2. Average cruise passenger expenditures per day are determined by average passenger income, personal tastes and choices and port arrival/departure travel mode.

3. Average expenditures per crew member depend on the number of visits to each port and average salary levels of crew members. These vary by occupation, by nationality and by ship.

4. Cruise company expenditures depend on vessel size and characteristics (expenditures per vessel by cruise companies increase as the size of ships increases) and vessel schedule and cruise marketing.

5. Multipliers to extend the economic impact of initial expenditures across the regional economy depend on the interindustry structure of the regional economy and spending stream leakages. For example, a large proportion of the goods sold to Alaska cruise passengers and cruise companies is imported. However, passengers and companies also purchase services and these have a much lower import component, and so involve smaller leakages from the regional spending stream.

Cruise tourism spending has widely dispersed impacts throughout national and regional economies. According to a study prepared for the International Council of Cruise Lines (BREA, 2003), every state in the USA experiences a larger economy with more spending higher gross domestic product (GDP) and more employment because of the cruise industry. Across the whole of the USA, the total (direct, indirect and induced) employment effects of the cruise industry are 279,000 jobs or around 1 job per 1000 population. The largest relative employment impact is in Alaska with 25 jobs per 1000 population. Florida is second (7 jobs per 1000 population) and Washington third with around 2.6 jobs per 1000 population. These three states account for almost 59% of total national cruise-related employment, and for Alaska and Washington it is the Alaska cruise that accounts for most spending and employment impacts.

British Columbia impact estimates

A recent study for the Port of Vancouver (InterVistas Consulting, 2001) estimated 2001

British Columbia tourism spending by Alaska cruise passengers at CAN$138 million. Crew spending added a further CAN$41 million. Cruise companies spent CAN$147 million on supplies and services purchased in British Columbia. This total spending of CAN$326 million generated 2970 direct person-years of employment in British Columbia and added CAN$148 million to provincial GDP. Applying multipliers to account for indirect and induced effects of this spending increases the employment impact to 6100 person-years and the GDP impact to CAN$277 million.[11] A later study (BREA, 2004) estimates a total of 10,400 jobs in British Columbia derived from the cruise industry, about the same per capita employment impact as for Washington.[12]

Alaska impact estimates

The typical cruise ship, whether on a 7-day Vancouver–Vancouver or Seattle–Seattle round trip or a Vancouver–Seward one-way trip, spends about 30 hours in Alaskan ports (usually three ports). While this totals more time than the average ship spends in Vancouver, Seattle, or Seward, passengers have no option to extend their time in these ports, except in Seward, the origin and destination for tours to interior Alaska. Cruise company spending in Alaskan ports is much lower than in Vancouver or Seattle.

There are two recent studies of the economic impact of the cruise industry on Alaska. The BREA (2003) study estimated the total cruise industry impact on the Alaska economy as a result of purchases of US$595 million with employment at 16,455 and wages totaling US$546 million. An earlier study (McDowell Group, 2000) prepared for several south-eastern Alaska cities that are important cruise ship

---

[11]The British Columbia employment and GDP estimates are derived from the study's (InterVistas Consulting, 2001) estimates for Western Canada.

[12]Direct cruise spending in British Columbia was CAN$160 per capita, much larger than the US$96 estimated for Washington. Since the same consulting firm prepared the two source reports, the lower employment impact in British Columbia may lie in a less regionally favourable employment structure in British Columbia rather than in different methodology.

ports was based on spending surveys and did not extend initial spending and resulting employment through the whole economy. For the major (because it is included in all itineraries) port of Juneau, the study showed spending by passengers, crew and companies amounting to US$83 million, US$6 million and US$2 million, respectively. Cruise industry employment effects for all south-eastern Alaska ports were estimated at over 2000 person-years.

Washington impact estimates

Until Seattle became a homeport for some Alaska cruise vessels, the industry would have had an economic impact on Washington's economy somewhat similar to its impact on the Oregon economy. The Seattle location of Holland America's head office would have augmented this, as would Washington's closer general economic connections to Alaska and Seattle's proximity to Vancouver, but clearly the recent success in selling Seattle as a southern homeport has greatly increased cruise industry economic impacts in Washington. The BREA (2003) Washington estimates of 16,455 total jobs based on total spending of US$586 million are impressive.

Environmental impacts of the Alaska cruise

Any assessment of the regional economic benefits of the Alaska cruise industry should consider environmental costs. The major environmental concern is marine pollution from discharge of wastewater from cruise ships. Most Alaska cruise vessel time is spent in port or in inner coastal waters and so the industry mainly operates in USA or Canadian territorial waters. Various federal and state statutes and regulations apply to these discharges. Environmental groups argue that the standards and practices of the industry are insufficient to prevent damage to the marine environment while the cruise industry and related tourism interests say that new technologies and protocols have greatly reduced the impact of cruise ship operations on the marine environment.

Another environmental concern is the congestion effect created when thousands of passengers descend on a small town or city or a wilderness area. This seems to be a growing concern in Alaska. The courts have ordered the cruise lines to reduce their trips to Glacier Bay, arguably the premier scenic attraction on the Alaska cruise itinerary. While members of the Alaska congressional delegation are now attempting to eliminate this restriction through federal legislation, the issue will not be forgotten. It is also a concern in the small cities of south-eastern Alaska and in the wilderness areas of central Alaska that are often added to an Alaska cruise trip. Tourism is Alaska's second largest industry in terms of employment (after government) and GDP (after oil and gas) but harmonizing its growth with preserving the attractions that create demand for travel to Alaska will not be easy.[13]

Conclusions

After over a century of evolution the Alaska cruise has become a significant contributor to the tourism economies of Alaska, British Columbia and now Washington State, although it can be argued that as the major supply point for Alaska, Seattle has always shared in Alaskan success. Since the establishment of a contemporary cruise industry dedicated to tourism in the late 1960s there has been continued growth in passengers, economic impact and environmental surveillance. Results from various economic impact studies indicate a significant impact in both GDP and jobs, but also suggest substantial potential for greater returns. For continued growth the challenge will be to develop new ports of call as the Alaska ports become saturated with visitors and concerns about environmental degradation increase. Another contentious issue is the Passenger Vessel Services Act, which encouraged the use of Vancouver as the principal homeport. Any significant change here could direct even more homeport activity to Seattle. Any economic sector built on trade restrictions risks, in the long run, the removal of this protection. This is what seems to be happening to Vancouver's status as preferred southern homeport.

---

[13]For discussion see the National Parks Conservation Association website: http://www.npca.org

Fig. 14.7. *Regal* and *Dawn Princess* at Skagway, 1997. Photo: Warren Gill.

While Alaska cruises are a relatively small part of British Columbia tourism (probably not more than 10% of tourism GDP and employment), this part of the sector has grown more rapidly than total tourism and the potential is there for more growth. Another option for growth, which would also reduce the industry's impact on Alaska, is the Cruise BC initiative that involves developing British Columbia coastal ports, such as Campbell River and Port Hardy, as ports of call, just as they were in the earlier days of the Alaska service ships (Vancouver Port Authority, 2004). In 2004 both Celebrity Cruises and NCL called at Prince Rupert with a Seattle-based ship in order to comply with the Passenger Vessel Services Act (Constantineau, 2004b,c). Whether this augurs well for greater diversity in the Alaska cruise is unclear; the mainstream US market remains focused on Alaska, with the long journey through British Columbia waters being just a means to an end.

Given the importance of passenger spending in determining economic impact, a key strategy for southern regions is to extend pre- and post-cruise stays in British Columbia and Washington and to develop tourist products that encourage higher levels of expenditures. In British Columbia, shore packages in Vancouver are common and some lines offer excursions to Victoria, Whistler and the British Columbia interior. The marketing task is to make these and similar attractions more central to the Alaska cruise experience (see Fig. 14.7).

In Alaska the cruise industry is a large part of the tourism industry, which is the second largest employer in Alaska and the second largest contributor of value-added income to Alaska's gross state product. Overall, the wilderness and scenic attractions of Alaska are relatively more important to the cruise industry than those in British Columbia.[14] Thus, solving the environmental problems of the cruise ship operation is essential if Alaska is to continue to enjoy the economic benefits of this industry. However, increasing the economic impact of the Alaska cruise industry may prove challenging as some have argued that the Alaska market may be saturated (Cartwright and Baird, 1999). The sustained expansion over the past 30 years and the recent dramatic increase in the Seattle-based trade would seem to belie that assertion. Cruise companies have already shown they can successfully adapt to the limitations of south-east Alaska ports by developing new products, such

---

[14]Ships are in Alaska longer and the greatest scenic attention is given to various Alaska attractions.

as Glacier Route cruises, the Outside Passage and deep interior land excursions.

Moreover, the need to balance the costs of higher environmental standards for cruise ships with the pressures of a highly competitive environment inside the cruise industry and in the leisure market overall should be the highest priority in the short term for both Alaska and British Columbia.

References

Ball, C. (2001) Princess Alaska. Analyst presentation on board *Grand Princess*, 12 May. Available at: http://www.poprincesscruises.com/

Bannerman, G. (1976) *Cruise Ships: The Inside Story.* Saltaire, Sidney.

BREA (Business Research and Economic Advisors) (2003) *The Contribution of the North American Cruise Industry to the US Economy in 2002.* Prepared for the International Council of Cruise Lines.

BREA (2004) *The Contribution of the International Cruise Industry to the Canadian Economy in 2003.* Prepared for the NorthWest Cruiseship Association, the Vancouver Port Authority and the St Lawrence Cruise Association.

Brown, D. (2001) USA cruise market demand. Analyst presentation on board *Grand Princess*, 12 May. Available at: http://www.poprincesscruises.com/

Buchholz, T.G. and Carol, C.M. (1993) All at sea. *Forbes* 152(11), 174.

Butler, M. (2003) *Worldwide Cruise Ship Activity.* World Tourism Organization, Madrid.

Cartwright, R. and Baird, C. (1999) *The Development and Growth of the Cruise Industry.* Butterworth Heinemann, Oxford.

CLIA (2001) Cruise industry records 16% growth in 2000. *Cruise News and Specials, Cruise Lines International Association*, 5 March. Available at: http://www.crusing.org.cvpc/news/news.cfm? NID = 69

Coates, K. and Morrison, B. (1990) *The Sinking of the Princess Sophia: Taking the North Down With Her.* Oxford University Press, Toronto.

Constantineau, B. (2004a) Competition from Seattle threatens Vancouver's share. *The Vancouver Sun*, 30 October, G3.

Constantineau, B. (2004b) Rail tour to cater to cruise ships. *The Vancouver Sun*, 27 January, F5.

Constantineau, B. (2004c) Artists set to cash in on cruise-ship traffic. *The Vancouver Sun*, 26 April, D3.

Cowan, J. and Brooks, M. (1995) Port economic impact studies: an examination. *Proceedings, Canadian Transportation Research Forum*, pp. 400–413.

Dawson, P. (2000) *Cruise Ships: An Evolution in Design.* Conway Maritime Press, London.

Dickinson, B. and Vladimir, A. (1997) *Selling the Sea: An Inside Look at the Cruise Industry.* John Wiley & Sons, New York.

Douglas, N. and Douglas, N. (2004) *The Cruise Experience: Global and Regional Issues in Cruising.* Pearson Education Australia, French's Forest, NSW.

Dwyer, L. and Forsyth, P. (1998) Economic significance of cruise tourism. *Annals of Tourism Research* 25, 393–415.

Frantz, D. (1999) Sovereign Islands – a question of regulations: Alaskans choose sides in battle over cruise ships. *New York Times*, 29 November, A1.

Hacking, N. (1990) Ship and shore. *Harbour & Shipping* 73(4), 30–31.

Hacking, N.R. and Lamb, W.K. (1974) *The Princess Story: A Century and a Half of West Coast Shipping.* Mitchell Press, Vancouver.

Harbour & Shipping (1990) Alaska cruise ship issue. *Harbour & Shipping* 73(4), 26.

Harbour & Shipping (2004) Annual Alaska cruise ship issue. *Harbour & Shipping* 87(5), 24.

InterVistas Consulting Inc. (1999) *1999 Vancouver-Alaska Cruise Passenger Study*, Vancouver.

InterVistas Consulting (2001) *Port Vancouver Economic Study*, Vancouver.

John C. Martin Associates (2004) *The Economic Impacts of the 2003 Cruise Season at the Port of Seattle.* John C. Martin Associates, LLC 2938 Columbia Avenue, Suite 602 Lancaster, Pennsylvania 17603.

Marti, B.E. (1990) Geography and the cruise ship port selection process. *Maritime Policy and Management* 17, 157–164.

McDowell Group (2000) *The Economic Impacts of the Cruise Industry in Southeast Alaska*, Juneau.

National Park Service (1997) *Glacier Bay.* US Department of the Interior, GPO 1997– 417-648/ 60038.

Norwegian Cruise Line (2003) *Freestyle Alaska 2004.* Brochure 360776 9/03 700M DB AK 04.

P&O Princess Cruises (2001) Proposed DLC combinations with Royal Caribbean Cruises Ltd. Available at: http://www.poprincesscruises.com/presframes. htm/RCPcirc.pdf

Port of Seattle (2005) Available at: http://www.port seattle.org/seaport/statistics/cruisepassengers. shtml

Turner, R.D. (1977). *The Pacific Princesses: An Illustrated History of the Canadian Pacific Railway's Princess Fleet on the North-west Coast.* Sono Nis Press, Victoria.

Turner, R.D. (2001) *Those Beautiful Coastal Liners*. Sono Nis Press, Victoria.

US House of Representatives (1998) Effect of the Passenger Services Act on the domestic cruise industry. Subcommittee on Coast Guard and Marine Transportation and Infrastructure, Committee on Transportation and Infrastructure, Washington, DC, 29 April. Available at: http://commdocs.house.gov/committees/Trans/hpw105-65.000/hpw105-65_1.htm (5 February 2002)

Vancouver Port Authority (2004) Vancouver's cruise business adapting to change. Available at: http://www.portvancouver.com/media/news200 40422-1.html (22 April 2004)

Vancouver Port Authority (2005) Available at: http://www.portvancouver.com/statistics/2004_statistical.html

West, C.B. (1993) *Mr. Alaska: The Chuck West Story, 50 Years of Alaska Tourism from Bush Pilot to Patriarch*, 2nd edn. Weslee Publishing, Seattle, Washington.

White, H. and Spilsbury, J. (1988) *The Accidental Airline: Spilsbury's QCA*. Harbour Publishing, Madeira Park, BC.

Wood, R.E. (2000) Caribbean cruise tourism: globalization at sea. *Annals of Tourism Research* 27, 345–370.

15 The Cruise Industry and Atlantic Canada: A Case Study

Nancy Chesworth

Mount St Vincent University, Department of Business and Tourism, Halifax, Nova Scotia, Canada, B3M 2J6

Introduction

The presence of the cruise industry in Atlantic Canada is a recent phenomenon. The ports of the east coast of Canada represent a relatively new market for the industry (Fig 15.1). This chapter presents a case study of the cruise industry in the four Atlantic Provinces. A brief history of the region is provided as background to aid the reader in better understanding the position of the Atlantic Provinces in the cruise industry.

Background

Ships have been bringing people to Canada's east coast for millennia. Evidence of fishers and adventurers blown off course by storms in the North Atlantic finding themselves off the coast of Newfoundland or Nova Scotia, and perhaps further south, is found in songs and legends of Ireland, Wales, Iceland, England and Scotland. Long before Columbus set sail, the Vikings left rocks inscribed with runes and an abandoned settlement dated to AD 1000, at L'Anse aux Meadows, Newfoundland.

Paleo-Indians and later the Mi'kmaq, Malaseet and Beothuk were established in eastern Canada as long as 10,000 years ago (Choyce, 1996). There is little trace of the earliest inhabitants of the region. The Vikings apparently had some contact with the Beothuk.

The recorded history of Canada begins with the east coast. Abundant fish made for easy fishing on the Grand Banks off southern Newfoundland, which first attracted the attention of Basque fishers at least as early as 1504. The French attempted settlement in 1604 on a small island in the St Croix River in New Brunswick. The following year they moved across the Bay of Fundy to the less exposed and more fertile shores of the Annapolis River in Nova Scotia. A fort, Port Royal, was constructed and farming commenced. The French named what is now New Brunswick, Prince Edward Island (PEI) and Nova Scotia, L'Acadie. In the ensuing centuries, treaties signed between France and Britain, at the conclusion of various wars in Europe handed L'Acadie, or Acadia, back and forth between them. In the course of passing the area back and forth, several forts were built.

Fort Anne, in Annapolis Royal across from the remnants of the French settlement of Port Royal, was begun in 1708, and Fortress Louisbourg, on Cape Breton island in 1719, Fort Beausejour, in 1751 at the end of the Bay of Fundy in New Brunswick. The Halifax Citadel was built by the British from 1828 to 1856 to defend against the possibility of an invasion from the USA which had declared independence from Britain in 1776. In 1758 Louisbourg fell to the British. The following year, Wolfe defeated Montcalm at Quebec; thereafter, Acadia and Quebec were

© CAB International 2006. *Cruise Ship Tourism* (ed. Ross K. Dowling)

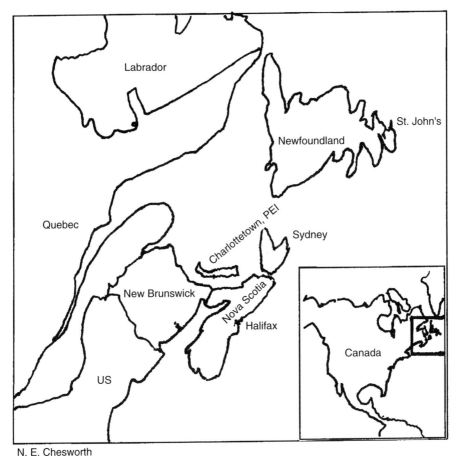

N. E. Chesworth

Fig. 15.1. Map of Atlantic Canada. Source: Nancy Chesworth.

British territory. Although the French settlers in Acadia were deported, largely to Louisiana, some returned to rebuild. Their descendants celebrated 400 years of Acadian culture in 2004.

Settlement of the region had been intercontinental until those loyal to Britain fled north during the Revolutionary War in the USA. They were followed later by a group known as the Planters from the New England area of the USA. Intracontinental migration between Canada and the USA has continued since, albeit on a less intensive scale. English, Scots, Irish, Germans and other Europeans came over the centuries for many reasons. Some migrated in hope of a better life, others fled persecution, famine and forced displacement. Still others were lured by the promise land grants. In the process of settlement, the native Beothuk population of Newfoundland was wiped out. The population

of Mi'kmaq and Malaseet peoples was decimated and their cultures all but obliterated.

Canadian confederation in 1867 established Canada as a nation. Newfoundland and Labrador became the tenth Canadian province in 1949. Until that time New Brunswick, Prince Edward Island and Nova Scotia were collectively known as the Maritime provinces. With the addition of Newfoundland and Labrador, the four are now referred to as the Atlantic provinces.

The demise of the age of wooden sailing ships brought the end of prosperity in the region. Thereafter fishing, farming and forestry were the mainstays of the region's economy until the 1980s. Lumbering is still a major industry in all but Prince Edward Island, which relies on farming and fishing as its economic mainstays. Fishing was the traditional way of life for generations of families in small communities scattered along the rugged coasts of all of the provinces. The collapse of the fishery in the 1980s caused economic hardship in all four provinces, but especially in Newfoundland. The loss of the fishery meant retraining for some, and migration to western Canada for many others. Unemployment in the region averages between 8% and 16% higher than anywhere else in Canada other than Quebec (Statistics Canada, 2004). Unfortunately, there is little incentive for those seasonally unemployed to upgrade their skills or find full-time work as the unemployment insurance system has created a culture of dependency in some and usury in others (Crowley, 2000).

Tourism in the Region

In many countries, tourism is promoted as the panacea for unemployment and the answer to economic problems. The Atlantic provinces, being the poorest in Canada (Statistics Canada, 2004) have been encouraged by the government to develop tourism as a means of counteracting the economic losses resulting from the decline of the traditional industries. Tourism has certainly grown in the Atlantic region; however, the climate dictates a short tourism season and the problems that go with seasonality.

Rich in history, scenic beauty, traditions and culture, the Atlantic provinces are among the less discovered tourism areas of the world. Each province has its own flavour but, like the small island countries of the Caribbean, from the outside, the Atlantic provinces all look the same. All four offer a variety of activities such as whale watching, sea kayaking, hiking, birding, historic forts and other sites, festivals and cultural events based on heritage and culture, among others. They share a common heritage, culture, climate and image. In addition, Atlantic Canadians are proud of what they perceive as a better quality of life than found in other parts of Canada. They are also pleased with the region's reputation of hospitality to visitors. Over time this attitude has taken on the character of a culture of niceness; not only is one expected to be nice to tourists but part of being nice includes the tacit agreement that one should always be in favour of anything that might produce jobs and money. Even constructive criticism is frowned upon or summarily discounted.

In promoting tourism, each province markets what it sees as its unique attributes, usually to similar or the same markets. Newfoundland's focus is on whales, icebergs and spectacular fjords. Nova Scotia highlights the Cabot Trail, Peggy's Cove with its iconic lighthouse and the city of Halifax. PEI depends on the popularity of *Anne of Green Gables* and its beaches. New Brunswick, traditionally a pass-through province and not a destination, has found success by featuring one-day adventures centred primarily on Acadian culture, lighthouses and the Bay of Fundy and the use of whales as a featured image. Beyond the main icons featured in advertising, each province has its lesser known unique features and attractions.

Rather than marketing themselves as a distinct region, the provinces continue to compete with each other for tourists and tourist dollars. The lack of cooperative effort means that old rivalries continue. The idea of a union of the three Maritime provinces as a means of increasing political clout, economic benefits and economies of scale has been put forth many times. Last proposed in 1996, by the then premier of Nova Scotia, John Savage (*The Mail Star*, 1996), the idea of Maritime union apparently met with some opposition (*The Chronicle Herald*, 1996).

Perhaps the only benefit of the relative lack of economic development in eastern Canada is that much has been preserved rather than bulldozed to make way for new construction. The entire region, especially when compared with the eastern seaboard of the USA, looks quaint, or at the least cute, especially to American visitors. A typical comment from one woman passenger who had toured Charlottetown, PEI was that she felt she had stepped back in time (Stewart, 2004). Atlantic Canadians are well aware of the quaint image of the region and many work hard to preserve it. An example of this is the recent vote to continue to ban shopping on Sunday in Nova Scotia, other than in convenience stores and small specialty shops. Nova Scotia has thus distinguished itself by remaining the only place in North America where this is so.

The major port cities are far more affluent than the small towns and villages, whether or not they have port facilities. Indeed, Halifax is frequently referred to as 'a have city in a have-not province'. In recognition of the disadvantaged status of the region, the federal government established the Atlantic Canada Opportunities Agency to find ways to encourage and develop new businesses. Overall the region is still less well off economically than the rest of Canada, leaving the four provinces open to any scheme to improve the economy and create jobs. Thus the growth of the cruise industry in the region has been greeted with unbridled enthusiasm largely on the part of the press (*The Daily News*, 2004).

The Infrastructure Issue

The largest ports in the area are found in Halifax, Saint John, Sydney, St John's and Charlottetown. Ports in smaller towns such as Lunenburg, St Andrews, Corner Book and L'Anse aux Meadows do not have wharves capable of accommodating large cruise vessels. Passengers are taken ashore by tender, which is time consuming and more expensive than gangway access. Smaller ships can sometimes access smaller ports, provided the harbour has enough depth.

Like the provinces, the ports have their similarities and distinctive features. All are, in North American terms, old ports in old cities and towns with architecture indicative of past wealth and practicalities as well as current business interests. They are all working ports reflecting the gritty, pragmatic life of those who depend on the sea for a livelihood, whether on working ships or servicing them.

Halifax, with the second largest natural harbour in the world, is the largest container port on the east coast of Canada, handling international shipping as well as construction and service for offshore oil rigs. As the main east coast port, Halifax already had piers large enough to accommodate cruise ships when they began to utilize the port in increasing numbers in the 1990s. Until trans-Atlantic passenger liners for the most part became cruise lines in the late 1960s, passenger vessels frequently called at Halifax on the way to or from Europe. Beautifying the dock area for visual accommodation of passengers was never a consideration until representatives of the cruise lines impressed upon those concerned, the need for attractive docks and reception areas for cruise visitors.

Theoretically, making the dock area attractive will lure passengers off the boats to sightsee, shop, and it is hoped, to find reason to return for a longer land-based visit. Consequently, some ports have invested millions of dollars to upgrade port facilities and infrastructure, with the expectation that revenue from shore-going passengers will grow and that cruise ships will continue to arrive, and in increasing numbers.

The port of Halifax has spent CAN$4.2 million to refurbish the warehouse on Pier 20 and link it with the likewise refurbished Pier 21. Pier 21 was used from 1928 to 1971 as a processing centre for immigrants arriving by sea. It is now a combination museum and interpretative centre, and attracts many cruise visitors. The revamped Pier 20 is the staging point for sightseeing tours, provides visitor information and features an assortment of kiosks and shops catering to the cruise passenger.

For the inshore fishery the federal government built the docks that are available to the cruise ships in Sydney and Charlottetown. With the decline of the fishery, the Department of Fisheries and Oceans has moved to divest itself of responsibility for wharves in all provinces. Sydney and Charlottetown are faced with the question of whether or not to invest millions of dollars to lengthen their docks, as they are too short to accommodate many of the cruise vessels. Len Parsons of the Charlottetown Development Corporation said that although the Coast Guard wharf is long enough to accommodate most cruise ships, its location is not convenient to the downtown area; consequently, the previously mentioned addition to the existing dock is under consideration. Charlottetown undertook a revitalization programme in its harbour area in the early 1980s, which included the construction of dock and marina facilities, several small shops and restaurants. Plans are being made to add to the assortment of shops and amenities available to the cruise visitors, primarily in hopes of attracting more ships and to provide more facilities for cruisers (L. Parsons, 29 August 2004, personal communication).

Betty MacMillian, Chair of the Atlantic Canada Cruise Association (ACCA), said that Saint John has invested over CAN$12 million to tear down a warehouse on the wharf used for cruise ships, and to compensate for the effect of the world's highest tides, purchased an elevating device to allow passengers to disembark and re-embark without having to climb up or down a steep gangway. Additional millions are to be spent to build facilities and shops on the dock for the use of cruise passengers (B. MacMillian, Saint John, 2004, personal communication).

The port of St John's in Newfoundland is a special case. The entrance to the harbour is through a narrow passage between granite cliffs, known as 'The Narrows'. Mr Leo Brown, Assistant to the Harbour Master, stated that the channel is 11.8 m deep allowing most ships to enter the harbour. Unfortunately, new larger cruise ships such as the *Queen Mary 2* with a draft of 10.3 m would find the passage risky. The harbour pilot, harbour master and ship's captain all play a role in deciding whether a ship can safely enter a harbour. Ultimately, the decision rests with the captain. Once in the harbour, there is the issue of dock length. Piers ten and eleven, both 150 m long are used as berths for cruise ships. While this length is sufficient for those ships currently calling at the port, both of these berths would be necessary to accommodate the *Queen Mary 2*, or a vessel of similar size (L. Brown, St John's, 28 August 2004, personal communication). Ironically, with the widened passage and adequate dock, the *Queen Mary 2* could enter the harbour, but not leave. In some spots within the harbour, the water is not deep enough for the ship to turn safely.

St John's also benefits from smaller capacity ships occasionally using St John's as a homeport. These ships cater to a different market, more in keeping with the allocentric or venturer described by Plog (2004). Passengers spend one or more nights in hotels in the City of St John's before and/or after cruising to small outports along the coast of Newfoundland and Labrador and as far north as Iqaluit, just below the Arctic Circle. The economic impact of these passengers rivals that of those on a much larger ship (Todd Lehr, August 2004, personal communication). Deborah Cook, Tourism Development Coordinator for the City of St John's, and Richard Parsons, Executive Director of the ACCA based in St John's, are working to encourage home porting of smaller, more ecologically oriented ships as well as European based cruise lines (August 2004, personal communication).

Shoreside Services

In the late 1980s and early 1990s, people disembarking from a cruise vessel in most of Atlantic Canada's ports were largely left to their own devices as to what to do while ashore. In Halifax, a meet-and-greet programme was put into effect, taxi drivers given special training, a free shuttle to shopping areas in the city was made available and a few tours were offered, usually using school busses to transport cruisers to Peggy's Cove and a few points of interest in the city. In Saint John, there was little direction given to passengers. Complaints, presumably from passengers, brought to the attention of port authorities by the cruise lines, brought marked changes. Aside from the infrastructure investments noted above, agencies in each port interested in developing and attracting the cruise lines now ensure that a full-blown Atlantic Canada welcome is laid on for arriving ships. In almost every port, pipers in full kilt meet each ship, and vessels arriving on a first-time port call are treated to a commemorative welcome ceremony. On leaving the ship, cruisers are greeted by volunteers wearing vests indicating that they are there to help the visitors. These volunteers also provide tourist information and act as ambassadors for the city or town. Available options include an array of excursions on comfortable motorcoaches, tours offered by licensed taxi, limousines and private vehicle, walking tours, shopping opportunities and other activities. Most shoreside tours are purchased aboard ship before disembarking.

To their credit, most ports recognize the value of crew spending and goodwill. For the ship's crew, the larger ports provide transportation or directions to local shopping malls and opportunities for participation in organized or individual activities and sports. Smaller ports have more difficulty providing for the expectations of cruise passengers on ships carrying several hundred or more people. For a small community, the influx of a large number of people suddenly injected into the community can put pressure on fragile infrastructure and cause stress for residents. Most small communities are not equipped to deal with the demands of mass tourists who require more infrastructure and special services that an independent traveller who, instead of expecting the community to cater to their desires, fits into the community and uses existing facilities. Tour operators in small ports cannot afford to have a fleet of motorcoaches available for a few large cruise ship visits. Smaller ships with a passenger load of 47–150 visiting smaller ports can be effectively accommodated.

Enticing the Ports

The main enticement to encourage ports to accommodate ships, passengers and crew is the amount of money passengers spend ashore. The second incentive is held to be the possibility of repeat land-based visits by passengers. Recognizing that cruise ship visitors spend considerably less than land-based visitors, most ports and their surrounding communities are anxious to determine how much the average passenger spends ashore. Indeed, ports everywhere want to know how much a person spends ashore in order to determine whether expenditures made to accommodate the ships are beneficial.

Fees for dockage, ships' pilots and assorted ship services are part of the revenue realized by any given port. In addition, a head tax is charged for each person going ashore. The Caribbean countries and Mexico, which have many years of experience with cruise ships and passenger spending estimates, have repeatedly tried to impose a head tax on each person going ashore. An attempt by 13 Caribbean countries to charge a tax of US$15 per head fell apart when the cruise industry threatened to stop visiting islands that did so. Many islands charge between US$3 and US$5 per person. The small island country of St Lucia collects US$6.50 per passenger (Wise, 1999). A recent agreement between the Caribbean Hotel Association, the Caribbean Tourism Organization and the Florida Caribbean Cruise Association spurred by ongoing friction between cruise lines and hotel and resorts in the Caribbean is aimed at addressing the inequities between the little tax revenue collected from cruise ships and the income, social security and occupancy taxes paid by the hotels (Springer, 2004). Whether this will prove to be a sincere effort on the part of the cruise industry is the subject of speculation (Springer, 2004).

In Mexico and Belize in the western Caribbean, the number of cruise passengers and ship calls have increased dramatically. So has bitterness over the small amounts spent by cruisers. This led to calls for a head tax of up to US$30. Here again the hotel industry has pointed out their costs and community commitment in contrast to the lack of same on the part of the cruise lines (Stevenson, 2004).

Per person fees in Atlantic Canada are in line with those charged in the Caribbean. For example, Halifax charges CAN$7.24 a head, and Saint John, CAN$6.43, making these bargain rates for the cruise lines over the last several years. However, as the US dollar continues to decline, the head tax could become an issue.

The impact of spending by the ship's crew is sometimes not included in research. Crew have different needs, but their spending is still significant. Keeping in touch with family, shopping for personal items and attending to personal needs that cannot be dealt with aboard ship are a few of the things crew look for in port. Over time, crew expenditures become consequential. Crew are also important because their positive or negative word-of-mouth recommendations can affect disembarking passengers' attitudes towards the location as well as spending ashore (Klein, 2003) (see Table 15.1).

The other incentive promoted by the cruise industry to encourage ports to accommodate cruise ships and passengers is the opportunity to showcase their destination and to encourage repeat land visitation and a longer stay. If the Cruise Line Industry Association's (CLIA) claim of a repeat passenger rate of 52% is accurate (CLIA, 2002), it seems reasonable to conclude that repeat cruisers prefer a cruise vacation to a land-based vacation. Thus far, the small amount of research done on this issue indicates that few cruisers return to a destination by land. The 'best guess' offered was 10%, while the study done in 2003 by Corporate Research for the Halifax Port Authority found that when asked about the likelihood of a repeat visit, 29% of those surveyed would definitely return, and 44% said they would probably do so. The author has not been able to learn whether the interview question specified that the passengers would return on another cruise, or by land. Moreover, intentions are one thing, and conversion rates another.

Table 15.1. Passenger spending estimates from intercept surveys.

Location	Year	Amount per person (CAN$)
Halifax	2003	102.00 to 117.00
	2002	90.00
	2000	83.00
St John's	2003	72.55
	2002	69.30
	2001	111.00
Charlottetown	2003	66.48
Saint John	1999	85.00
Average – all ports	2002	57.00

Note: Estimates are based on the assumption of 95% of passengers going ashore.

The Atlantic region is primarily a motoring destination. As noted previously, these provinces are known for their scenery and cultural and historical attractions. It seems unlikely then that those who favour a cruise vacation where the emphasis is on entertainment and limited decision making other than when and how much to eat or whether to go ashore or not, would subsequently partake of a motoring vacation with the myriad decisions and responsibilities entailed in that choice. Added to that is the fact that the perceived travel distance from the USA, where most cruise tourists originate (Irving, 2000), is generally considered by most Americans to be too great to be worth the effort to drive. The higher cost of fuel provides a further disincentive. In fact, the Atlantic region is easily accessed by air from Boston or New York in less than 2 h. Were the region to promote the ease of fly–drive packages, some increase in visitation by previous cruisers might result.

There has so far been no reaction by Hotel Associations in Atlantic Canada to the increasing number of cruise tourists. Unlike Caribbean destinations, the Atlantic region has a growing meetings, conventions and special events sector and easy connections to large population centres. In addition, year-round business travel and recent promotion of four-season travel in the region are helping to compensate for traditional low occupancy rates in the off season.

Do cruise ships really need ports of call?

Cruise ships are sometimes referred to as condominiums floating on their side. But with recent upgrading and in particular the newly launched ships, they are more like floating suburban towns with all the amenities. Other than civic services, everything a passenger wants is already on the ship: food, shopping, activities, entertainment, gambling, spas and a variety of other services and amenities. The cruise ship has a captive market. The myriad services and amenities enable and encourage passenger spending and create profit for the cruise lines. If passengers never disembarked, the ship would retain all the profit from on-board spending. But, people want and expect to see the ports on the itinerary. Therefore, any port call must generate profit for the ship. Onshore shops are charged fees to be listed on the 'approved list' or on maps of the town, and tours are marked up, selling at up to three times the original cost (Klein, 2003).

In some Caribbean ports, prices in many shops magically rise on the day one or more ships are to call. The cruise lines practice of marking up the cost of tours and excursions puts pressure on vendors to deliver a value equivalent to the price paid by the passenger aboard ship for a tour that ordinarily costs far less (Andrea Gray, July 2004, personal communication). To date, tour operators and shopkeepers in the Atlantic region, while feeling the pinch of having to deliver more with less, have yet to band together to limit undercutting each other and enabling them to survive and profit as suggested by Ross Klein in 2003. Although shopping and tours are the two major shoreside activities, there is less opportunity to spend if on a tour, or in port for a short time. Some ships appear to have cut the length of time in ports that are not profitable, particularly in small ports that have little shopping available.

Mausi Reinbold, formerly of Tourism Halifax, noted that the cruise industry in Atlantic Canada got a huge boost from the first Gulf War when cruise lines moved ships from the Mediterranean. Canada and Canadian ports being perceived as safe, appealed then as now, to a clientele afraid of travel to distant places (Mausi Reinbold, August 2004, personal communication). Apart from the need to cater to fearful customers and the attraction of visiting a variety of places on the cruise itinerary, the cruise industry has four reasons to be interested in ports in Atlantic Canada: (i) construction of more ships means more ports are needed; (ii) more ships mean more passengers; (iii) repeat cruisers tired of the same itineraries mean more destinations are needed; and (iv) most important is the effect of the cabotage law on ships taking on passengers in the USA.

Santangelo (1984) accurately predicted both the growth of the cruise industry and the diversification of itineraries. The increase in the number and size of ships has forced the cruise lines to expand on itinerary offerings. More ships mean a need for more ports simply because most harbours were not built to accommodate large numbers of cruise ships. Bermuda, for example, places limits on the number of ships in port at any given time, partly due to berthage and the size of the harbour and also because of the volumes of tourists flooding ashore. Indeed, some ports were hard pressed to accommodate ships arriving before the building boom. The increase in the number of cruise ships is thus a factor in the growth of the cruise industry in Atlantic Canada.

Those new to the cruise ship experience are usually attracted to the Caribbean, Mexico or Hawaii or to the spectacular coast of Alaska. However, for experienced cruisers or those limited to vacationing in the North American summer months, hot or cold destinations may be unappealing. For those who dislike tropical climates, the temperate summers of the Atlantic Provinces are an added incentive. In addition, passengers leery of getting off a ship in a strange-looking foreign country have the comforting image of Canada as friendly and safe.

For repeat cruisers, choices in itinerary are rather limited. An intercept survey for the Port of Halifax of cruisers visiting Halifax in 2003 showed that 80% had visited the Caribbean on a cruise, 48% Alaska, 46% Mexico, 30% the New England area of the USA and/or eastern Canada, 32% in Europe (Corporate Research Inc., 2004). The number who had previously cruised Atlantic Canada was not reported. Considering the number of people who have cruised elsewhere, the Atlantic provinces represent a new itinerary for the cruise lines to attract repeat cruisers who might otherwise start searching for other vacation alternatives.

The need for alternative ports and itineraries is not the only reason the cruise ship industry has expanded to include Atlantic Canadian ports. The USA Passenger Services Act of 1889 (the cabotage law) is undoubtedly the main impetus for the growth of the cruise industry in eastern Canada's ports. The act states that a foreign vessel taking on passengers in a port of the USA must call at a foreign port before returning to the USA. The intent of this law is to protect the US cruise industry. Although the majority of cruise ships are owned and operated by Americans and up to 93% of passengers (Irving, 2000), on the ships are American residents, all of the major cruise lines operating on the eastern seaboard except for the Mayflower line, are flagged in less developed countries, thus avoiding US taxation. The galvanizing impact of the destruction of the World Trade Center on the travel habits of the American public led the cruise industry to establish home ports along the east coast of USA among other locations. Atlantic Canada's ports then are more than just a handy option. Ships can stay within the letter of the law by calling at a Canadian port while providing passengers with the added fillip of travelling to a foreign country. Clearly, the cabotage law means that the cruise lines could not operate on the eastern seaboard at all without the ports of eastern Canada.

However, considering the cost of fuel, the Atlantic province's ports are an increasingly expensive alternative. The escalating price of fuel alone would dictate that a ship embarking cruisers in a US east coast port would realize considerable savings if it remained in US waters because of the distance travelled. Being well aware of this, the cruise lines have lobbied, so far unsuccessfully, to have the cabotage law repealed. The current climate of fear of terrorism in the USA serves as an additional inducement for repeal, with the argument that keeping ships in US waters would protect them from terrorists in supposedly less secure ports. The fact that Atlantic Canada's ports are as secure as any is easy for the cruise industry to ignore. In reality, cruise ships are vulnerable, no matter where they are located.

Research Needed Here

Amounts reportedly spent per person in the ports of Atlantic Canada vary widely. Unfortunately, all of the studies done in the region on passenger spending have used intercept interviews as the data collection method. The inaccuracies inherent in this method mean that the resultant data are highly questionable. Further, leakage factors are not taken into account, although two recent studies have accounted for the mark-up on tours imposed by the ships. Other factors are not included. Some of these are: the increased cost to individual businesses due to the need to hire additional staff to deal with the volume of shopping cruisers, shoplifting and fees demanded by the cruise lines to participate in their 'approved' store programme; increased demands on police services; and other community services such as garbage removal, sewage, electricity, and potable water, air and water pollution, upgrading and repairs to infrastructure.

In their zeal to promote the cruise industry as highly beneficial, port authorities have thus far focused only on the expected benefit of passenger spending and repeat visitation. The negative impacts or disbenefits to accommodating cruise ships are ignored. The result is an unbalanced and misleading picture of the benefit of hosting cruise ships. As Klein (2003) points out, there is a need for cities to accurately assess the costs of cruise ship visits to determine if cruise ships are beneficial, or if the cities and ports are subsidizing them (see Table 15.2).

The real impact of the cruise industry on Atlantic Canada can only be determined by a cooperative venture that would include the participation of all stakeholders. Unfortunately, the cruise lines seem to have little interest in sharing research efforts, or in providing access to passengers in such a way that accurate, meaningful data could be collected. A balanced research design should include an assessment of the multiplier, leakage, carrying capacity, environmental and social impacts, the psychographics and demographics of those taking a cruise holiday that includes the region on the itinerary, as well as the factors mentioned earlier. Until careful, accurate research is conducted the question of whether or not the Atlantic region benefits from the cruise industry, or subsidizes it, will remain unanswered. Ultimately, it is unlikely that such thorough research will ever be carried out. The well-meaning people who represent their ports, cities and towns, are primarily interested in negotiating the best deal for their port. Research other than on passenger spending is of little interest. The importance of such research and the need for strategic contingency plans for both growth and contraction of the cruise industry in the Atlantic region are unfortunately not well understood.

Conclusion

As noted in the beginning of this chapter, the Atlantic provinces have a history of competing with each other. The consequences of competition instead of collaboration and cooperation are a weaker economy, willing self-exploitation and resignation to the status quo. Richard Parsons stated that the goal of the ACCA is to work together for the good of the cruise industry in the whole region. The ACCA seems to be making at least some headway in that regard at present, however, when the cabotage law is repealed, as it almost certainly will be, the various ports in the region will find themselves fighting for whatever market share remains. The old rivalries will undoubtedly rise again. As Wise (1999) put it: the lack of a common vision, a will to work together for the good of all, ultimately works in favour of multinational corporations which can easily pit one province or port against another as they have done in the Caribbean. The

Table 15.2. Cruise ship port calls: ships/passengers.

Port	1990	1995	2000	2004
Charlottetown, PEI	NA	NA	20:7,728	28:1,948
Halifax, NS	33:24,423	39:30,257	94:138,371	122:212,000
Saint John, NB	4:1,989	12:12,226	67:101,410	60:138,842
St John's, NF	3:253	4:259	20:8,014	19:9,236

Sources: ACCA; Port of Halifax; Saint John Port Authority; Port of Charlottetown; City of St John's.

question for the future is: can the ACCA develop the strength of purpose to stand together for the good of all and sustain the industry in the Atlantic region, or will history continue to repeat itself?

References

Choyce, L. (1996) *Nova Scotia: Shaped by the Sea.* Viking, Toronto.

Corporate Research Inc. (2004) *2003 Port of Halifax Cruise Ship Study.* Corporate Research Inc., Halifax, Nova Scotia, Canada.

Crowley, B. (2000) Atlantic Canada and the zero sum economy. Speech given to United Alternative Conference, 29 January 2000. Available at: http://www.aims.ca/commentary/ua.html

Cruise Line Industry Association (CLIA) (2002) Passenger statistics Available at: http://www. CLIA.com

Irving, J. (2000) East coast gaining in popularity with cruises. [national edition] *The National Post.* Don Mills, Ontario, 14 July, A4.

Klein, R. (2003) Cruising – out of control: the cruise industry, the environment, workers and the maritimes. Canadian Centre for Policy Alternatives, Halifax, Nova Scotia, Canada. Available at: http://www.policyalternatives.ca/ns/index.html

Plog, S. (2004) *Leisure Travel: A Marketing Handbook.* Pearson Education, Upper Saddle River, New Jersey.

Santangelo, R. (1984) What's happening in the cruise industry. *Journal of Travel Research* 23(2), 3–5.

Springer, B. (2004) A new phase for the Caribbean? *Amsterdam News*, 6 May 2004. Available at: http://www.breakingtravelnews.com/20040506171353200

Statistics Canada (2004) Unemployment rate. Available at: http://www.statcan.ca/english/subjects/labour/LFS/lfs-en.htm

Stevenson, M. (2004) Cruise industry faces a Caribbean revolt. *The Globe and Mail*, 10 September, A4.

Stewart, D. (2004) Cruise ship visitors love quaint island with 'beautiful' weather. *The Guardian*, 20 May, A2.

The Chronicle Herald (1996) Savage to downplay maritime union. 7 May 1996, A6.

The Daily News (2004) Cruise ships leave $15 m behind. 26 March, p. 17. Halifax, Nova Scotia, Canada. Accessed via Proquest, 23 July 2004.

The Mail Star (1996) January 19. In: Choyce, L. (ed.) *Nova Scotia: Shaped by the Sea – A Living History.* Penguin, Toronto.

Wise, J. (1999) How cruise ships short change the Caribbean. *Fortune* 139(6), pp. 44–46.

16 The Changing Geography of Cruise Tourism in the Caribbean

York University, Faculty of Environmental Studies, 4700 Keele Street, Toronto, Ontario,
Canada M3J 1P3

Introduction

With over 18 million cruise passenger arrivals in 2003, the Caribbean accounts for approximately 50% of the world's total cruise capacity placement (Dwyer and Forsyth, 1998, p. 393). In fact, cruise tourism is 'the only industry in the world in which the Caribbean is the dominant market' (Anonymous, 2003b).

While there is a long history of tourists travelling on passenger and freight ships in the Caribbean region dating back to the 19th century, the modern era of cruise travel in the Caribbean – in the sense of dedicated passenger ships travelling on a circuit to multiple destinations solely for the purpose of tourism – did not begin until the mid-1960s when the first transatlantic lines[1] began regular Caribbean cruises during the winter season.

> December 19, 1966 is recognized as a landmark because on that date a series of cruises was launched that, for the first time, was created and packaged as a mass-market product and sold on a year-round basis. The ship, the *Sunward* of the Norwegian Caribbean Line (later renamed the Norwegian Cruise Line), sailed from Miami to Nassau with 540 passengers on the first three- and four-day cruises to be offered year-round between Miami and the Bahamas.
>
> (Showker, 2004, p. 3)

By 1970, with most transatlantic lines being involved in cruising within the Caribbean region (Lawton and Butler, 1987, p. 338), there were 1.6 million cruise passenger arrivals in the Caribbean (CTRC, 1985, p. 31).[2] The period 1970–1973 was termed the era of the 'cruise revolution' by the Cruise Lines International Association (CLIA), a promotional organization of cruise lines, because of the high rates of growth in numbers of ships involved, cruises offered, ports of call and passengers (Santangelo, 1984, pp. 3–5).

In fact, 'with the exception of Bermuda, all Caribbean islands recorded an increase in cruise traffic between 1970 and 1973' (Lawton, 1986, p. 163). The pattern in Bermuda was a result of government policy to restrict the number of cruise ships in port to three at any given time

---

[1]Now almost completely replaced by airplanes, transatlantic ships conveyed passengers between Europe and North America; most had direct routes, although some made tourism-related calls, e.g. to Bermuda.

[2]It is important to note that 'cruise passenger arrivals' refers not to how many individual tourists travelled on cruise ships, but rather to the number of ports of call visited multiplied by the number of individual tourists on the ships. That is, one individual passenger on a ship visiting five ports of call counts as five arrivals. There is also disagreement as to whether the numbers were based on the number of passengers on a ship's manifest or the number of passengers who disembark at individual ports of call; current figures refer to the number of passengers on a manifest.

because cruise growth, combined with stay-over tourist and resident population increases, had 'overtaxed infrastructure, thereby detracting from its [Bermuda's] traditionally amicable environment' (Lawton and Butler, 1987, p. 338).

The 'first oil crisis' of 1973 and the subsequent recession in the USA, however, resulted in a downturn in numbers of Caribbean cruise passengers, with negative growth rates of 1.7% in 1974 and 1.8% in 1975 for the Caribbean as a whole (Centaur Associates, 1980, p. 47). As a result, cruise lines used three strategies to save fuel:

1. More time was spent in port and/or certain ports of call were eliminated in order to minimize distance travelled (Waters and Patterson, 1975, p. 35).
2. Longer cruise circuits from Miami were reduced to shorter excursions of seven days or less, e.g. to the Bahamas and the United States Virgin Islands (Waters and Patterson, 1975, p. 35); as a result, some ports of call had major increases in arrivals (e.g. Cozumel, Cayman Islands, Jamaica, Haiti), while others had decreases (e.g. Antigua, Grenada, Trinidad).
3. San Juan, Puerto Rico, was developed as a port of embarkation to further reduce transport costs (Lawton and Butler, 1987, p. 339).

Growth resumed after 1975, attributable in part to the popularity of the television series *The Love Boat* and post-recession recovery (Bannerman, 1982, p. 10; Centaur Associates, 1980, p. 47). This recovery led to an expansion of cruise fleets through new, rebuilt and lengthened vessels; in turn, however, there was a temporary oversupply in carrying capacity that was soon corrected by increased marketing and discounted prices.

By 1980, Caribbean cruise arrivals had risen to 3.8 million, a figure which would continue to grow, with minor exceptions, annually, reaching 14.9 million in 2002. The exceptions were 1981 (3.5 million or −5.7%) and 1982 (3.2 million or −3.8%) because of the 'second oil crisis' and 1999 (12.1 million or −2.2%) because of damage to port facilities in several Eastern Caribbean islands resulting from damage from Hurricane Lenny. While the events of 11 September 2001 resulted in downturns for particular destinations, the overall picture was

continued growth, with 15.9 million arrivals in 2002 and 18.0 million in 2003 (see Table 16.1).

Given this overall picture of the growth of cruise tourism in the Caribbean, this chapter will analyse the geography of these cruise arrivals in terms of ports of origin and destination ports and show how the patterns have changed over time.

Ports of Origin for Caribbean Cruises[3]

With the shift from transatlantic ships to dedicated cruise ships, New York's previous dominance as the main port of origin for Caribbean cruises had been replaced by Miami by 1970 (Stansfield, 1977). Mescon and Vozikis (1985) provide three reasons for this shift: (i) continued modernization of port facilities; (ii) popularity of Florida as a recreational and retirement area; and (iii) proximity to the Caribbean.

It is argued, however, that there are three other reasons: (i) the decrease in the number of scheduled transatlantic crossings[4] (with New York as the primary North American port for such crossings); (ii) the increasing availability at decreasing costs of air travel (following the introduction of commercial passenger jets in the mid-1960s); and (iii) the increasing propensity of North Americans to travel.

By 1976, Stansfield (1978, p. 16) argues that the major ports of origin for Caribbean cruises, in order of importance, were Miami, San Juan, Port Everglades, New York, New Orleans, Curaçao, Baltimore, Galveston, Norfolk and Tampa. He (1978, p. 17) defines ports of origin such as New York as 'hinged' ports in that they 'occupy a "hinge" position between the vacationer's workaday world and their vacation environment', while others such as Miami and Port Everglades are 'embedded within a major

_____
[3]Time series data on ports of origin over an extended time period are not available; therefore, it is necessary to highlight particular years.
[4]Gray (1970, p. 170) notes that the transatlantic liner passenger trade between North America and Europe dropped from 64% of the total traffic (or 892,000 passengers) in 1953 to 5% (or 338,000) in 1969, a pattern which was mirrored in the financial ruin of several transatlantic steamship companies (Lawton and Butler, 1987, p. 336).

Table 16.1. Cruise passenger arrivals (in '000).

Destination	1970	1971	1972	1973	1974	1975	1976	1977	1978	1979	1980	1981	1982	1983	1984	1985	1986
Bahamas[a]	351.9		420.9	462.4	386.7	421.3			449.6	476.2	577.6	596.9	719.6	854.1	907.8	1136.5	1495.6
Bermuda	90.0						131.9		131.7	140.4	117.9	104.7	124.2	120.8	111.4	142.8	132.2
Eastern Caribbean	559.9	646.5	988.1	1235.0	1292.8	1290.2	1341.0	190.1	1613.3	1825.7	2056.4	2009.0	1582.5	1507.3	1635.4	1727.7	2261.3
Antigua & Barbuda	18.7	37.7	63.8	52.5	28.3	23.2	32.4	36.0	51.9	70.2	107.1	113.2	66.8	52.0	66.8	100.8	122.4
British Virgin Islands	0.2			2.0	0.7	0.9					38.1	33.4	28.3	13.9	24.8	22.1	15.7
Dominica									7.3	7.8	7.4	5.5	2.4	6.1	3.2	6.6	11.5
Dominican Republic		4.5							156.0	195.4	183.1	162.6	141.6	98.9	96.0	92.8	131.1
Guadeloupe	15.2	26.4	22.7	51.0	55.0	53.3	48.7		78.0	43.2	49.7	25.2	32.0	34.4	64.5	69.2	64.4
Haiti	28.6	42.5	92.3	87.6	129.9	196.7	201.8		187.5	169.3	159.7	117.1					40.0
Martinique	99.3	118.6	179.3	203.3	161.5	143.5	170.4	153.2	143.8	181.7	203.4	202.5	168.0	158.6	135.5	153.0	214.2
Montserrat	1.4	1.8	1.1	1.9	2.1	1.7	1.2		3.9	3.1	4.1	5.1	9.1	3.6	4.3	7.4	9.3
Puerto Rico	136.6	163.8	261.2	344.3	411.1	415.6	412.3		434.6	430.0	501.1	531.2	444.1	411.2	436.0	419.3	484.6
St Kitts & Nevis	4.0	1.8	3.1	1.4	4.0	4.8	3.1	0.9	2.1	1.0	5.8	10.9	11.1	22.8	34.1	31.5	27.0
St Maarten									121.1	105.5	106.4	92.9	73.0	112.7	146.1	313.9	
US Virgin Islands	251.4	253.9	364.6	491.0	500.2	450.5	471.1		548.2	602.9	691.4	695.2	586.2	632.8	657.5	678.9	827.2
Southern Caribbean	333.1	288.7	394.9	514.0	488.7	500.2	539.9	294.8	675.5	619.1	679.1	528.3	425.2	382.7	431.4	513.8	626.0
Aruba	44.7	27.5	45.4	44.5	62.3	57.8	67.7		98.0	95.6	107.1	113.2	66.8	52.0	66.8	100.8	122.4
Barbados	79.6	79.2	100.1	116.5	119.5	98.5	99.4	103.7	126.0	110.1	156.6	138.8	110.8	102.5	99.2	112.2	145.3
Bonaire	4.4	2.9	1.2	5.1		4.1	6.0		2.6	5.0	2.9	12.0	6.8	0.3	2.9	2.7	2.5
Curaçao	110.9	75.2	105.4	155.6	182.6	180.1	175.7	191.1	178.0	174.0	169.0	128.4	110.0	107.1	122.5	108.8	125.9
Grenada	41.3	48.7	94.1	132.3	57.6	85.5	106.4		116.3	138.7	145.6	77.6	62.1	50.2	34.2	90.7	113.9
St Lucia	36.1	42.9	37.3	46.5	43.1	53.5	69.1		68.0	54.3	59.0	18.9	33.8	33.3	37.2	55.0	58.8
St Vincent & Grenadines	16.1	12.3	11.4	13.5	23.6	20.7	15.6		20.9	20.7	32.5	33.4	28.9	34.4	64.0	34.0	38.1
Trinidad & Tobago									65.7	20.7	6.4	6.0	6.0	2.9	4.6	9.6	19.1
Western Caribbean	86.5	68.2	72.8	92.9	95.9	176.2	190.9		193.7	208.6	194.1	217.7	352.7	386.8	434.6	520.2	548.7
Belize		0.9	0.3	0.4	0.7	3.3	8.8										
Cayman Islands	0.3	0.9	1.0	1.0	2.5	22.5	40.6		45.1	49.0	60.7	78.0	158.3	177.2	203.6	258.7	270.9
Cozumel																	
Jamaica	86.2	66.4	71.5	91.5	92.7	150.4	141.5		148.6	159.6	133.4	139.7	194.4	209.6	231.0	261.5	277.8
Total	1421.4	1003.4	1876.7	2304.3	2264.1	2387.9	2203.7	484.9	3063.8	3270.0	3625.1	3456.6	3204.2	3251.7	3520.6	4041.0	5063.8

[a]At first port of entry only.
Note: Some historical data could not be found; recent figures in italics are estimates because exact data are not yet available.
Source: CTO and its predecessor organizations.

tourist region. The environs of these two ports are a significant part of the total vacation experience.' Island ports of origin are clearly embedded, e.g. San Juan, Curaçao and Montego Bay. He describes other ports of origin such as Baltimore, Norfolk and Galveston as hinged ports in that they are ports of departure for the convenience of accessibility rather than any significant inherent vacation function in addition to the cruise experience. Finally, he labels New Orleans and Tampa Bay as being transitions between hinged and embedded.

By 2001, this pattern had strengthened. While New York remains the major hinged port of origin for 137 cruise ship calls and 220,000 cruise arrivals in 2001 (Ebersold, 2004), it is a minor origin compared with the major southern ports of origin: Miami (684 calls; 1,710,000 passengers), Port Canaveral (359; 885,000), Fort Lauderdale (473; 877,000), San Juan (346; 717,000), Tampa Bay (145; 274,000), New Orleans (54; 124,000) and Galveston (85; 150,000) (Ebersold 2004). The Florida ports and San Juan can be described as embedded,

1987	1988	1989	1990	1991	1992	1993	1994	1995	1996	1997	1998	1999	2000	2001	2002	2003
1434.2	1505.1	1644.6	1853.9	2020.0	2139.4	2047.0	1805.6	1543.5	1687.1	1751.1	1729.9	1981.5	2512.6	2551.7	2802.1	2970.2
153.4	158.3	131.3	112.6	128.2	131.0	154.7	172.9	169.7	181.7	181.9	188.3	195.6	209.7	180.0	200.2	226.1
2778.8	3183.1	3211.4	3543.6	3903.6	3968.0	4087.0	4287.6	4445.1	5067.5	5821.5	5968.4	5173.4	6130.5	6340.3	5979.5	6503.5
153.3	198.6	208.0	227.3	255.6	250.2	238.4	236.0	227.4	270.5	285.5	336.5	328.0	429.4	408.8	309.7	385.7
28.4	38.4	71.6	96.7	78.8	87.6	113.2	82.4	122.1	159.6	104.9	105.1	180.7	188.5	202.5	180.8	180.8
12.1	7.5	6.0	6.8	65.0	89.8	87.8	125.5	134.9	193.5	229.9	244.6	202.0	239.8	207.6	125.0	177.0
166.7	100.0	100.0	100.0	100.0	50.0	27.8	50.1	30.5	110.9	270.8	392.7	283.4	183.2	208.2	247.0	398.3
68.7	65.2	86.3	130.0	261.2	245.7	262.5	313.6	419.2	589.5	470.1	334.3	292.7	392.3	392.3	392.3	392.3
								225.4	250.4	238.4	246.2	243.3	304.5	357.4	354.1	354.1
296.7	385.5	368.2	421.3	417.0	398.9	428.7	419.9	428.0	408.4	386.8	414.6	339.1	290.1	201.3	207.4	268.5
10.1	10.8				5.6	8.8	11.0									
666.4	766.6	800.1	893.0	949.9	1019.2	968.1	976.9	1001.1	1025.1	1227.4	1243.4	1148.6	1301.9	1350.8	1202.9	1234.6
31.4	53.6	36.6	33.9	52.8	74.0	83.1	112.9	120.9	85.8	102.7	154.1	137.3	164.1	252.2	166.6	166.6
389.1	450.9	472.0	515.0	502.2	469.7	659.9	718.6	564.3	657.4	886.0	881.4	615.6	868.3	867.8	1055.0	1171.7
955.9	1106.0	1062.6	1119.6	1221.1	1277.3	1208.7	1240.7	1171.3	1316.4	1619.0	1615.5	1402.7	1768.4	1891.4	1738.7	1773.9
717.5	792.7	823.0	1051.8	1153.0	1155.3	1336.1	1376.8	1521.6	1573.6	1670.8	1727.5	1659.0	2168.6	2151.9	2125.1	2086.0
86.1	81.1	70.3	130.0	133.2	216.6	251.1	257.1	294.0	316.8	297.7	257.8	289.0	490.1	487.3	582.2	542.3
228.8	290.3	337.1	362.6	372.1	299.7	428.6	459.5	484.7	510.0	517.9	506.6	432.9	533.3	527.6	529.3	559.1
3.4	7.8	7.1	4.5	12.5	28.2	17.4	11.9	10.7	14.9	20.4	20.2	14.8	43.5	40.5	42.1	44.6
107.0	124.2	117.3	158.6	156.6	160.1	182.9	160.5	171.7	173.1	214.7	231.0	220.7	309.4	300.1	318.4	279.4
127.2	136.0	120.7	183.2	196.1	195.9	200.1	200.8	249.9	267.0	246.6	265.9	245.5	180.3	147.4	135.6	146.9
83.8	79.5	104.3	101.9	162.8	164.9	154.4	171.5	175.9	182.2	310.2	372.1	351.2	443.6	490.2	387.2	393.2
65.7	62.7	49.7	78.6	88.0	63.0	69.0	70.5	85.3	63.2	31.4	34.9	47.7	86.2	76.5	70.3	65.0
15.5	11.1	16.5	32.4	31.7	26.9	32.6	45.0	49.4	46.4	31.9	39.0	57.2	82.2	82.3	60.0	55.5
563.6	683.3	848.0	747.5	965.3	1265.0	1985.5	2133.1	2204.9	2444.4	2668.9	2808.2	3138.0	3501.2	3698.6	4817.5	6235.7
					1.5	5.9	13.3	7.9	0.2	2.7	14.2	34.1	58.1	48.1	319.7	575.2
271.7	315.6	403.9	361.7	474.8	614.0	606.0	599.4	682.9	800.3	866.6	871.4	1035.5	1030.9	1214.8	1574.8	1819.0
						744.0	925.4	908.9	985.7	1087.9	1248.9	1304.1	1504.6	1595.4	2057.6	2708.9
291.9	367.7	444.1	385.8	490.5	649.5	629.6	595.0	605.2	658.2	711.7	673.7	764.3	907.6	840.3	865.4	1132.6
5647.5	6322.5	6658.3	7309.4	8170.1	8658.7	9610.3	9776.0	9884.8	10954.3	12094.2	12422.3	12147.5	14522.6	14922.5	15924.4	18021.5

while Galveston is hinged; New Orleans probably remains as a transition between hinged and mixed.

The events of 11 September 2001, however, had three distinct impacts on ports of origin. First, the number of passengers at the major ports of origin soon increased as Americans reacted to the terrorist attacks by reducing international air travel and vacationing closer to home, including taking Caribbean cruises. In 2003, Miami (735 calls; 1,865,000 passengers) continues as the leader, followed by Port Canaveral (451; 1,116,000), Fort Lauderdale (544; 1,078,000), San Juan (225; 571,000),

Tampa Bay (213; 418,000), Galveston (203; 377,000) and New Orleans (143; 297,000) (Ebersold, 2004). Perhaps because it necessitates a flight over open ocean, San Juan alone has seen a decline in both calls and passengers.

Second, there appears to be an increased use of more hinged ports in order to attract travellers who prefer to drive rather than fly to a port of origin: 'most cruise lines redeployed their ships to ports that were within driving distance of a large enough population that sufficient passengers could be had without relying on the air lines' (Klein, 2003, p. 4). While other US ports have been used in the past as ports of origin to the Caribbean, diversification seems to be the coming pattern. In the 2004/05 cruising year, for example, ports of origin for Bermuda include Baltimore, Norfolk and Philadelphia; Bahamas cruises include Baltimore, Jacksonville and New York; while cruises to various parts of the Caribbean include Baltimore, Houston, Key West, New York and Norfolk (Showker, 2004).

Third, even before 11 September 2001, cruise lines big and small had been suffering hard times. In 2000, two small cruise lines (Premier Cruises and Commodore Cruises) had gone bankrupt. In 2001, fuel costs rose further and there was a decline in the US economy; compounded by several new, large ships having come on line recently, the results were empty berths and a price war. September 11 resulted in immediate massive cancellations of travel plans, but by the 2001 Christmas season, numbers began to increase followed by a better than anticipated winter season. The immediate cancellations, however, were so large that two small cruise lines (American Classic Voyages and Renaissance Cruises) went out of business in 2001, followed by two more (Regal Cruises and World Explorer Cruises) by 2003 (Showker, 2004, p. 10). This speeded up the consolidation in the cruise industry that had begun in the 1990s (Weaver, 2003, p. 101). As a result, while there are 20 companies operating cruise ships in the Caribbean in 2004–2005, the industry is dominated by three 'supercarrier' companies, two of which own several cruise lines:

1. Carnival Corp.: Carnival Cruise Lines (18 ships), Costa Cruises (4), Cunard Line (1), Holland America Cruise Lines (7), P&O Cruises (2), Princess Cruises (9), Seabourn Cruise Line (2) and Windstar Cruises (2).
2. Royal Caribbean International: Celebrity Cruises (8), Royal Caribbean International (17).
3. Star Cruises: Norwegian Cruise Lines (6) (Showker, 2004).

The remaining 17 companies mainly run boutique (or niche) and sailing ships with small capacities. The outcome is that decisions affecting ports of origin are, for all intents and purposes, almost totally in the hands of three companies.

Destination Ports for Caribbean Cruise Ships

Historically, there has been a wide array of Caribbean ports of call, as evidenced by Lawton and Butler's (1987, pp. 342–343) data on potential cruise routes based on ship itineraries in the *New York Times*. Their data show that there were 33 expected ports of call during the 1955–1956 cruising year,[5] 35 in 1965–1966, 48 in 1975–1976 and 45 in 1985–1986. Various explanations can be suggested why there are differences in the list of ports in the 4 years. For example, Freeport (Bahamas) is not in the 1955–1956 list because it did not exist then, while Havana is only on the 1955–1956 list because of the subsequent US embargo of Cuba. Cozumel appears for the first time on the 1975–1976 list because it did not have a cruise dock in earlier times. Others seem to be the case of one small ship (e.g. there is a recurring figure of 165 passengers, or a multiple of 165, in the data) visiting a different set of islands in the different time periods.

There is, however, a high degree of stability in the ports listed over the four time periods in their study (see Table 16.2). For example, of the 33 potential ports of call for 1955–1956, 29 (87.8%) were still listed in 1965–1966, 28 (84.8%) in 1975–1976 and 29 (87.8%) in 1985–1986. The same pattern holds true for the other time periods. Indeed, overall there are 17 ports which occur in only 1 year, all of them minor destinations visited apparently by small ships, with the exception of Havana (79,661), which is listed only for 1955–1956. If these 17 ports were to be considered outliers and removed from the list, the degree of stability is generally even higher.

_____

[5]It is not exactly clear when the '1965–1966' cruising year (and subsequent such time periods) began and ended, but presumably it was centred on the winter high season. These data, therefore, are not directly compatible with the calendar year data – the common time period used in Caribbean tourism statistics – presented elsewhere in this paper. Another type of data is also used, but less frequently, namely number of cruise ship calls per port of call per year; while interesting, it is slightly problematical given the wide variation in the passenger capacity of ships, particularly in recent years.

Table 16.2. Stability of potential ports of call.

Base year	Number of potential ports of call (outliers removed)	Number of potential ports of call from base year also listed in the other years			
		1955–1956	1965–1966	1975–1976	1985–1986
1955–1956	33 (29)	–	29 (26)	28 (27)	29 (25)
%			87.8% (89.7%)	84.80% (93.1%)	87.80% (86.2%)
1965–1966	35 (34)	26 (26)	–	30 (30)	33 (30)
%		74.30% (76.5%)		85.7% (88.2%)	94.3% (88.2%)
1975–1976	48 (40)	31 (31)	31 (30)	–	39 (37)
%		64.6% (77.5%)	64.6% (75.0%)		81.30% (92.5%)
1985–1986	45 (41)	25 (24)	29 (31)	38 (38)	–
%		55.60% (58.3%)	64.40% (75.6%)	84.40% (92.7%)	

Source: Lawton and Butler (1987, pp. 342–343).

Another argument for the effect on changes in the array of ports of call with the growing dominance of Miami as a port of origin could be derived from Gray's (1970, p. 17) contention that, in 1964, about 70% of all Caribbean cruises were classed as short excursions to the Bahamas or Bermuda, with Miami and New York, respectively, as the main ports of origin.

Other data, however, suggest that this argument is incorrect. In particular, Lawton and Butler (1987, pp. 342–343) provide expected arrivals data derived from cruise ship itineraries and passenger capacities of the ships involved (rather than actual arrivals) (see Table 16.3a). While these data are potential cruise passenger numbers as compared to Gray's '70% of all Caribbean cruises' figure and, therefore, are not directly comparable, they suggest a very different pattern for the mid-1960s than does Gray. In 1955–1956, Nassau was indeed the largest potential port of call in 1955–1956 (72,727), but Bermuda was only fifth (48,401); these two ports accounted for 121,128 potential passengers, or 19.4% of the total of the 622,991 for the 33 ports listed.[6] This proportion doubled in the next time period, when Nassau was also the largest potential port of call in 1965–1966 (412,221 potential passengers), Freeport was second (148,339), but Bermuda was only fifth (72,352); these three ports accounted for 632,912 potential passengers, or 42.6% of a total of 1,486,868 for the 35 ports listed.[7] In the third time period, 1975–1976, this proportion declined significantly, when both Nassau and Freeport dropped in numbers; the former remained the largest (301,648), while the latter was fifth (82,934). Bermuda was probably fourth (approximately 100,000).[8] These three ports accounted for approximately 484,582 potential passengers,

or 20.6% of a total of 2,352,255 for the 48 ports listed.

These proportions would be substantially reduced if it were assumed that these data represent some (unknown) correlation with the number of cruises (as implied by Gray's figure) because it is highly likely that a large proportion of the Freeport passengers would also visit Nassau on short 3–4-day cruises. In fact, G.P. Wild's data (2002) on cruise ship calls for 1976 (not 1975–1976) present the same problem, with, for example, Freeport and Nassau being listed separately (see Table 16.3b). Nevertheless, the patterns in the two sets of data are quite similar. It is suggested, therefore, that, while the Bahamas and Bermuda were important ports of call, they were not as dominant as Gray contends.

It is interesting to note that, despite the dramatic increases in the total number of potential cruise passengers over the Lawton and Butler's four time periods – from 622,991 in 1955–1956 to 5,458,883 in 1985–1986 – the number of potential ports of call only increased from 33 to 45. This suggests that ports of call with a history of cruise ship calls generally continue to receive cruise passengers, but in seemingly ever-growing numbers.

The destination data provided to this point appear to present a very clear and simple picture of continued and dramatic growth, but these data are mainly based on *potential* numbers of cruise passengers (based on maximum capacity of individual ships) and cruise calls collected from advertisements and forecasted routes. Moreover, they provide only snapshots taken for particular time periods. The more detailed, but not totally complete time-series data on actual cruise passenger arrivals per annum (since 1970 in most of the 26 destinations for which data were available) presented in Table 16.1, however, suggest that growth in cruise arrivals has been widespread and dramatic, but that much more complex patterns exist that warrant examination.[9] The data will be examined in terms of both the major cruise destination sectors (Bahamas, Bermuda, Eastern Caribbean,

---

[6]Havana (79,661) was second, Curaçao (59,351) third and La Guaira, Venezuela (52,641) fourth.

[7]The US Virgin Islands (159,181) was third and San Juan (113,455) was fourth.

[8]'Approximately' is used because there appears to be an error in Lawton and Butler's data (1987, p. 342), with Bermuda being listed with only 14,127 potential passengers in this time period; therefore, an estimate of 100,000 is used here. The US Virgin Islands (281,282) was second, San Juan, Puerto Rico (204,603) third, and La Guaira, Venezuela (136,185) fourth.

[9]Four notes are in order in Table 16.1. First, data are provided only for member countries of the Caribbean Tourism Organization (CTO) and, with the exception

Table 16.3. Leading Caribbean cruise destinations (1975–1976 and 1976).

	(a) Number of potential passengers, 1975–1976[a]				(b) Number of calls, 1976[b]		
Rank	Destination	Cruising sector	Number	Rank	Destination	Cruising sector	Number
1	Nassau (Bahamas)	Bahamas	301,648	1	St Thomas (USVI)	Eastern	640
2	US Virgin Islands	Eastern	281,282	2	San Juan (Puerto Rico)	Eastern	427
3	San Juan (Puerto Rico)	Eastern	204,603	3	Nassau (Bahamas)	Bahamas	397
4	La Guaira (Venezuela)	Southern	136,185	4	La Guaira (Venezuela)	Southern	301
5	Bermuda	Bermuda	100,000	5	Port-au-Prince (Haiti)	Eastern	203
6	Martinique	Southern	91,665	6	Curaçao	Southern	201
7	Freeport (Bahamas)	Bahamas	82,934	7	Martinique	Southern	196
8	Barbados	Eastern	82,931	8	Montego Bay (Jamaica)	Western	169
9	Curaçao	Western	77,169	9	Cozumel (Mexico)	Western	168
10	Grenada	Southern	76,396	10	Freeport (Bahamas)	Bahamas	162
11	Port au Prince (Haiti)	Eastern	72,151	11	Grenada	Southern	159
12	Montego Bay (Jamaica)	Western	70,166	12	Puerto Plata (Dom. Rep.)	Eastern	149
13	Cap Hatien (Haiti)	Eastern	61,041	13	St Maarten	Eastern	145
14	Cozumel (Mexico)	Western	55,542	14	Cap Hatien (Haiti)	Eastern	123
15	Guadeloupe	Eastern	47,228	15	Bermuda	Bermuda	120
16	Port Antonio (Jamaica)	Western	36,480	16	Barbados	Eastern	114
17	Aruba	Western	36,395	17	Port Antonio (Jamaica)	Western	101
18	St Lucia	Southern	35,140	18	Guadeloupe	Eastern	95
19	St Maarten	Eastern	33,068	19	Grand Cayman (Cayman Is.)	Western	85
20	Trinidad	Southern	27,675	20	St Lucia	Southern	83
21	Grand Cayman (Cayman Is.)	Western	20,909	21	Trinidad	Southern	76
22	Cartagena (Columbia)	Western	16,622	22	Aruba	Western	68
23	Antigua	Eastern	14,627	23	Ocho Rios (Jamaica)	Western	63
24	St Vincent	Southern	14,250	24	Playa Del Carmen (Mexico)	Western	63
25	Santo Domingo (Dom. Rep.)	Eastern	14,212	25	Belize	Western	44
26	Belize	Western	9,929	26	Roatan (Honduras)	Western	37
27	Kingston (Jamaica)	Western	5,894	27	Cartagena (Columbia)	Western	32
28	Panama Canal	Western	5,848	28	Antigua	Eastern	28
29	Ocho Rios (Jamaica)	Western	3,700	29	Santo Domingo (Dom. Rep.)	Eastern	23
30	St Kitts	Eastern	3,390	30	St Croix (USVI)	Eastern	21
31	Bonaire	Western	1,690	31	St Vincent	Southern	21

[a]Source: Lawton and Butler (1987).
[b]Source: Stansfield (1978).

Southern Caribbean and Western Caribbean) and individual destinations.

Bahamas

The pattern for the Bahamas has been a bit of roller-coaster ride, with generally rising numbers, from 351,900 cruise arrivals in 1970 until reaching a peak in 1992 at 2,139,400. The numbers declined to 1,543,500 in 1995 as a result of the economic recession in the USA. It is suggested that, because so many cruises to the Bahamas were short 3- or 4-day trips and because such a large part of the market for Bahamas cruises is first-time cruisers, for many people such vacations were either unaffordable or expendable during this period. Hepple (2003) attributes the decline to cruise lines developing new itineraries in the Western and Southern Caribbean and to Key West, Florida, being opened as a destination for short cruises. The continuous upswing in numbers since then – reaching 2,970,200 in 2003, an increase of 508.0% since 1970 – is a direct result of three factors. First, the government passed legislation designed to encourage ships to stay longer in port (e.g. allowing on-board casinos to remain open while in port) and to increase the overall volume of traffic by offering incentives to the cruise line companies.

of Cozumel, are not broken down by port. Second, data are not available for all destinations for all years. Third, these data were gathered from material published by the CTO (and its predecessor organizations); while they may vary from other sources referenced here, it is assumed that they are the most accurate available, since over time revisions to parts of various time series were published. Fourth, the 'total' figures are based only on available data; for example, for unknown reasons, data for 1977 are rare and, therefore, the totals shown are underestimates of the actual figures. The author has collected similar time-series data on cruise calls for these same destinations, but they are not presented here for two reasons. First, data are not available for a greater number of years. Second, the great – and growing – variability in the size of ships masks patterns; for example, ships range from 'boutique' sailing ships with 100 or fewer passengers to megaships with nearly 3800 passengers.

Second, two new ships – *Disney Magic* (1998) and *Disney Wonder* (1999) – began twice-weekly cruises to the Bahamas. Third, 'private islands' were developed by Disney and Holland America, on which passengers are provided with a day of beach activities and facilities. Such private island experiences have numerous benefits for the cruise lines; for example, the one day not in a port results in reduced overall port costs, sales of goods and services being captured totally by the company and controlled environments. In turn, there are both costs (e.g. lost port taxes and charges, sales of goods and services) and benefits (e.g. avoidance of overcrowding and pollution) for the destination port not visited.

Lawton and Butler's (1987, p. 342) hypothesis that the Bahamas would continue to grow as a cruise destination as a part of 'the further development of the Miami hinterland' has not held true entirely. While Miami is a major port of origin for the Bahamas, other ports (including Baltimore, Jacksonville and Port Canaveral) now also serve as hinged ports of origin for the Bahamas (Showker, 2004).

Bermuda

With a history of hosting cruise ships dating back to the 1930s, Bermuda has seen an overall increase in cruise arrivals, rising from 90,000 in 1970 to 226,100 in 2003, an increase of only 151.2%. The road to that point, however, has been rocky. While data for years earlier than 1970 are not available, the 1960s saw rapid growth, culminating in 'one frenzied weekend in August 1969, [when] six cruise ships deposited 5000 tourists in the colony, choking Hamilton's streets' (McDowall, 1999, p. 186). The result was a government policy to restrict the number of cruise ships and passengers per day (with none being allowed on Sunday). The maximum numbers have increased over time as docks and other facilities have been improved. As with many other cruise destinations, the most important variable, however, has been the cyclical effects of exogenous economic patterns, e.g. downturns caused by the energy crisis of the late 1970s and the 1990s recession in the USA.

Eastern Caribbean

Until the aftershocks of the events of 11 September 2001, the Eastern Caribbean has seen almost continuous growth from 559,900 cruise arrivals in 1970 to 6,503,500 in 2003, and increase of 1061.5%. Overall, the only major downturn was in 1999, largely due to damage caused by Hurricane Lenny.

The pattern of cruise arrivals for a number of Eastern Caribbean countries has been affected by a variety of natural, social and economic factors. Perhaps the most dramatic single event was the virtual cessation of cruise ship arrivals – and most air arrivals – in Montserrat after a volcanic explosion in 1996 which resulted in most of the island's population being permanently evacuated.

Natural disasters have, however, severely affected other islands. Dominica, for example, had an erratic pattern in the 1980s with the numbers of ships and passengers fluctuating wildly (e.g. lows of seven calls and 2400 arrivals in 1982, and highs of 38 calls and 12,080 arrivals in 1987). There were many reasons for this low level of performance, including lack of suitable berthing facilities (including on the Roseau waterfront where a dock was destroyed by Hurricane Allen in 1980), shopping and restaurant facilities, and local tour companies capable of handling large influxes of arrivals. Construction of two piers, one at Cabrits National Park and the other in Roseau, and a deliberate government policy to encourage cruise tourism led to 130 calls and 65,000 arrivals in 1991. Despite reaching a peak of 244,600 arrivals in 1998 and a trough of 125,000 in 2002 following the events of the previous September, the numbers appear again to be on the rise, with 177,000 in 2003. The government seems to want to encourage as many cruise arrivals as possible, given the fragile state of the economy due the declining banana industry: on one day near Christmas in 2003, four cruise ships visited the island, with the first docking at the cruise pier in Roseau, the second at the Roseau container dock, the third at anchor off the town and the fourth at Cabrits.

The US Virgin Islands presents an interesting case where direct political affiliation with the USA encourages cruise arrivals, to a large extent through special duty-free allowances allowed to Americans visiting the islands. Long the leader in cruise arrivals in the Eastern Caribbean (as correctly hypothesized by Lawton and Butler [1987, p. 342]), they rose from 251,400 arrivals in 1970 to 1,773,900 in 2003. In 2002, cruise arrivals accounted for US$453.4 million in estimated expenditures. The average per capita expenditure of US$260.77 is approached only by Bermuda's figure of US$226.43; in comparison, the figure for Dominica is a mere US$27.70 (CTO, 2003).

With Port-au-Prince and Cap Hatien having been important cruise destinations in the 1970s, Haiti saw all forms of tourism drop off dramatically with its growing political instability in the 1980s. The picture changed, however, with the provision of a safe and secure 'private island' by Royal Caribbean International which uses Labadee, a fenced-in, private beach facility near Cape Haitien, for day excursions. Advertisements for these cruises always mention Labadee without reference to Haiti; in fact, passengers do not enter any other part of Haiti as they are lightered to shore directly from a ship anchored off the beach. The number of arrivals has been around 350,000/year for 2001–2003.

Southern Caribbean

Growth in cruise arrivals in the Southern Caribbean has been dramatic, but less so than for the Eastern Caribbean, with an increase of 526.2% from 333,100 in 1970 to 2,086,000 in 2003. The same 1980 hurricane that hit Dominica resulted in similar damage which stalled St Lucia's small but growing cruise business. New berthing and shopping facilities at Point Seraphine in Castries harbour and, again, a deliberate government policy to encourage cruise arrivals, led to 393,200 arrivals in 2003. Further redevelopment of the harbour area, including relocation of a container facility is currently underway in order to facilitate even more cruise ships. Similarly, with arrivals of 542,300 in 2003, a doubling since 1994, Aruba is planning to move its container terminal out of Oranjestad to alleviate the crowded conditions of the downtown area on cruise arrival days. Likewise, Barbados has recognized that it must improve port facilities if it is to expand arrivals beyond the approximately 500,000/year figure that it has hovered around since 1994. Other southern ports, such as Bonaire and St Vincent, remain minor destinations, partly because of the lack of adequate port facilities.

Western Caribbean

The most dramatic growth in cruise arrivals has been seen in the Western Caribbean which rose a remarkable 7108.9% from 86,500 arrivals in 1970 to 6,235,700 in 2004. As with the Bahamas, however, this is not entirely a result of Lawton and Butler's (1987, p. 342) hypothesis about the growth of Miami's hinterland; other ports (including Fort Lauderdale, Galveston, Key West, New Orleans, Port Canaveral and Tampa Bay) now act as hinged ports of origin for the Western Caribbean (Showker, 2004).

With a long history of cruise tourism dating back to passengers travelling via banana cargo boats to vacation in Port Antonio in the late 19th century, Jamaica has seen its cruise arrivals rise 1213.9% from 86,200 in 1970 to 1,132,600 in 2003, with activity now focused on Montego Bay and Ocho Rios.

Even more dramatic have been Cozumel (2,708,900 in 2003) and the Cayman Islands (1,819,000 in 2003), both of which have grown regularly and rapidly since the 1980s. Mexico has had a deliberate policy to promote tourism in parts of Yucatan other than Cancun, including cruise tourism to Cozumel (Clancy, 2001). With the exception of a relatively serious decrease immediately following the 1991 Gulf War and minor decreases in 1993 and 1994 due to the American recession, the Cayman Islands have seen almost continuous and dramatic growth since the mid-1970s when it became government policy to promote cruise tourism. The environmental impacts of both the ships themselves (e.g. cruise lines being successfully prosecuted for the deliberate dumping of garbage in territorial waters) and the passengers (e.g. traffic congestion caused by the almost simultaneous arrival of several cruise ships in George Town) resulted in a policy creating a limit of no more than three cruise ships or 5500 passengers per day (Wilkinson 1997, p. 116). The policy, like another earlier policy to limit beach development, was not adhered to and numbers

have been allowed to continue to grow. A recent policy framework report came to the following conclusion:

> Clearly, the policy should be to limit numbers so that the experience is a good one and they do not dominate and deter stayover (and upscale cruise) visits. Unfortunately, hard information is not available; the scale of the problem and the relevant threshold is difficult to define. *The real concern is that this growth is happening without a clear understanding of the impacts or a long-term strategy for managing visitors.* The old policy limit of 5500–6000 passengers/day is ignored; the port is working to thresholds of up to 14,000 passengers/day for the next two-three years.

> (The Tourism Company, 2002, p. 54)

Perhaps the most interesting case in the Caribbean as a whole, however, is Belize. A minor destination until 2001 when it attracted only 48,100 arrivals, a boom in the 'ecotourism' market for day trips saw 319,700 arrivals in 2002 and 575,200 in 2004.

The results for the Western Caribbean, in particular, support Stansfield's (1978, p. 16) hypothesis that the number of destination ports of call would not decrease in the future if numbers of passengers and size of ships increased (as could be expected with transatlantic type or cargo ships). The reason, according to Stansfield (1978, p. 16), is that 'the unique physical/cultural environmental complexes of close neighbors throughout the Caribbean plus the tendency for older, established tourist objectives to become "common", i.e. socially contaminated by crowds, thus spurring the desire of wealthier and more sophisticated tourists to search out "undiscovered", uncrowded, "off-the-beaten-path" places'.

Conclusion

Is Caribbean cruising likely to continue to grow at rates similar to those of recent years? In the short to middle term, the answer is likely to be 'yes', for three reasons. First, Caribbean governments seem either unable to control cruise tourism (and to increase their economic benefits from cruise ships) through to the failure to band together to implement an across-the-board and higher landing tax (Anonymous, 2003a) or, with the exception of Bermuda, unwilling to limit the number of cruise calls and passenger arrivals, as appears to be the case in many islands.

Second, for the cruise lines, cruising is profitable business: in 2002, Carnival Corp. had a net income of US$1.02 billion on revenues of US$4.37 billion, Royal Caribbean Cruise Ltd US$254 million on US$3.15 billion, P&O Princess US$301 million on US$2.45 billion and Star Cruises US$82.6 million on US$1.57 billion (Klein, 2003, p. 6).

Third, the cruise lines have already invested a great amount of money in growth: at least 15 cruise ships (with a total capacity of 36,251 passengers *per cruise*) destined in whole or part for the Caribbean market are either currently under construction or soon to begin (see Table 16.4). This conclusion is also that of the Government of Barbados (2001, p. 29), with caveats concerning the social and economic effects of cruise tourism:

> The forecast is that it [cruise tourism] will continue to grow in the short to medium term as more and larger ships leave dockyards worldwide. However, there is a concern that Barbados does not benefit even from this phenomenal growth as much as it could; particularly, when coupled with the effect that cruise may have on stayover tourism which from all indications provides an overall better net effect to the society and to the country.
>
> The strategy being proposed for cruise tourism in Barbados, therefore, seeks to increase the net economic benefits from cruise tourism while reducing congestion both at the port and on island. For this sector to be sustained, we must also focus on determining the carrying capacity of the country for this specific activity as well as encouraging wider participation from the cruise industry in the social and economic development of the Barbadian society.

In the long term, the answer as to whether Caribbean cruising is likely to continue to grow at rates similar to those of recent years is 'no': such growth cannot continue forever. There are environmental – biophysical, economic and social – limits to growth, particularly in such fragile marine and terrestrial ecosystems that exist in the Caribbean region. For example, one cruise ship produces:

- 10 gal. of sewage/passenger/per day, 90 gal. of grey water, 2.3 kg. of solid waste;

- 15 gal. of toxic waste/day (e.g. dry cleaning sludge, photofinishing chemicals, paint waste and solvents, print shop waste, fluorescent lamps, batteries);
- 7000 gal. of oily bilge water/day;
- 1000 tonnes of ballast water (often containing non-native species) per release when entering harbour (to offset consumed fuel and for stability during voyages);
- diesel exhaust emissions equivalent to 12,240 automobiles.

(Klein, 2003, pp. 12–13)

Given the negative impacts of cruise ships, including pollution, reef damage, crowding, traffic, etc., Stansfield's contention (1978, p. 18) that 'cruise passengers place a lighter burden on the limited resources and fragile ecologies of many smaller islands and thus may be more welcome in many locales than other types of tourists' seems to be of dubious validity given current and projected cruise ship and passenger numbers.

Barring some major disaster (e.g. an act of terrorism aimed at a cruise ship), the patterns of ports of origin and destination seem likely to continue. While worldwide airline travel is back to pre-2001 levels and is likely to continue to grow as the airline industry recovers from the bankruptcy of many airlines, the number of hinged ports of origin will continue at its current level or increase, particularly if cruise lines find that they attract a broader customer base. On the other hand, Miami and the other Florida ports of origin will continue to dominate for two reasons: they are embedded in a land-based tourism region that continues to grow in importance and rising fuel prices will favour cruises that originate nearer to destinations.

In terms of the patterns for destinations, size does matter. That is, destinations that have berthing facilities capable of handling the new megaships will continue to grow dramatically, as will destinations that make no attempt to control the numbers of cruise calls and arrivals. Destinations that are currently minor are likely to continue in that way, unless boutique and sailing ships choose to visit them rather than busier ports.

The question that remains unanswered is whether the benefits of cruise ships to the Caribbean out-weigh the biophysical, social and economic costs. That topic merits extensive research.

Table 16.4. Cruise ships under construction or on order by major companies.

Company	Cruise line	Ship	Due date	Tonnage	Passengers	Cost (US$ million)
Carnival Corp.						
	Carnival Cruise Lines	Carnival Miracle	2004	86,000	2124	375
		Carnival Valor	2004	110,000	2974	500
		Carnival Liberty	2005	110,000	2976	450
	Costa Cruises	NA	2006	NA	3800	450
	Princess Cruises	Crown Princess	2004	110,000	2600	450
		NA	2006	88,000	1950	330
	Holland America Cruise Lines	NA	2005	85,000	1848	400
		NA	2006	84,000	1800	400
	Cunard	Queen Victoria	2005	85,000	1968	400
Royal Caribbean International						
	Celebrity Cruises	NA	2005	85,000	1950	350
	Royal Caribbean International	Mariner of the Seas	2004	137,300	3114	600
		Jewel of the Seas	2005	88,000	2000	400
		NA	2006	88,000	2000	400
		'UltraVoyager Class' I	2006	160,000	3600	NA
		'UltraVoyager Class' II	2007	160,000	3600	NA
Star Cruises						
	Norwegian Cruise Lines	NA	2005	NA	2400	NA
		NA	2006	NA	2400	NA

NA = not available.
Source: Competition Commission (2002); Cyberspace Cruise Magazine (2003); Sarna (2003); Sea Cruise Enterprises (2003).

References

Anonymous (2003a) Levy on hold. *Cruise Job Link.* Available at: www.cruisejoblink.com/00news room121/n01.ht

Anonymous (2003b) Parle: ships could cause hotels serious problems. *Barbados Daily Nation,* 7 July.

Bannerman, G. (1982) Growth in cruise ships prompts discount prices. *Globe and Mail,* 29 October, B10.

CTO (Caribbean Tourism Organization) (2003) *Caribbean Tourism Statistical Report: 2002–2003 Edition.* CTO, St Michael, Barbados.

Caribbean Tourism Research and Development Centre (CTRC) (1985) *Caribbean Tourism Statistical Report 1984.* CTRC, Christ Church, Barbados.

Centaur Associates (1980) *Analysis of the North American Cruise Industry.* United States Maritime Administration, Washington, DC.

Clancy, M. (2001) *Exporting Paradise: Tourism and Development in Mexico.* Pergamon Press, Amsterdam.

Competition Commission (2002) P&O Princess Cruises plc and Royal Caribbean Cruises Ltd: a report on the proposed merger. Presented to Parliament by the Secretary of State for Trade and Industry, London.

Cyberspace Cruise Magazine (2003) Cruise ship order book. Available at: www.cybercruises.com/orderbook.htm

Dwyer, L. and Forsyth, P. (1998) Economic significance of cruise tourism. *Annals of Tourism Research* 25(2), 393–415.

Ebersold, W.B. (2004) Cruise industry in figures. *Business Briefing: Global Cruise 2004.* Available at: www.bbriefings.com/pdf/858/ACF7B5.pdf

G.P. Wild (International) Limited (2002) *Cruise Industry Statistical Review.* G.P. Wild (International), Haywards Heath, UK.

Government of Barbados (2001) Green Paper on the Sustainable Development of Tourism in Barbados: A Policy Framework. Ministry of Tourism, Bridgetown, Barbados.

Gray, H.P. (1970) *International Travel: International Trade.* Heath Lexington Books, Lexington, Massachusetts.

Hepple, J. (2003) Tourism history. Bahamas ministry of tourism. Available at: tourism/bahamas/org

Klein, R.A. (2003) *Cruising – Out of Control: The Cruise Industry, The Environment, Workers, and the Maritimes.* Halifax, Canadian Centre for Policy Alternatives, Nova Scotia, Canada. Available at: www.policyalternatives.ca

Lawton, L.J. (1986) The spatial development of the Caribbean cruise ship industry. Unpublished MA thesis, Department of Geography, University of Western Ontario, London.

Lawton, L.J. and Butler, R.W. (1987) Cruise ship industry – patterns in the Caribbean 1880–1986. *Tourism Management,* 26, 329–343.

McDowall, D. (1999) *Another World: Bermuda and the Rise of Modern Tourism.* Macmillan, London.

Mescon, T. and Vozikis, G.S. (1985) The economic impact of tourism at the port of Miami. *Annals of Tourism Research* 12(4), 515–528.

Santangelo, R.A. (1984) What's happening in the cruise industry. *Journal of Travel Research* 23(1), 3–5.

Sarna, H. (2003) Royal Caribbean announces world's biggest ship. *Cruise News,* 21 October. Available at: www2.i-cruise.com/cruisenews.htm

Sea Cruise Enterprises (2003) New cruise ships entering service. Available at: www.seacruiseent.com/scesite/newcruiseships.html

Showker, K. and Sehlinger, B. (2004) *The Unofficial Guide to Cruises,* 8th edn. John Wiley & Sons, Hoboken, New Jersey.

Stansfield, C.A. (1977) Changes in the geography of passenger liner ports: the rise of south-eastern Florida ports. *Southeastern Geographer,* 17 May, 25–32.

Stansfield, C. (1978) A note on cruiseship traffic patterns in the Caribbean. *Revue de Tourisme* 4, 15–20.

The Tourism Company (2002) Focus for the Future: a tourism policy framework for the Cayman Islands. A report prepared for the Ministry of Tourism, Government of the Cayman Islands, London.

Waters, S.R. and Patterson, W.D. (1975) *The Big Picture: World Travel Trends and Markets.* Travel Comminications, New York, pp. 73–74.

Weaver, A. (2003) The McDonaldization of the cruise industry? Tourism, consumption, and customer service. Unpublished PhD thesis, Department of Geography, University of Toronto, Toronto.

Wilkinson, P.F. (1997) *Tourism Policy and Planning: Case Studies from the Commonwealth Caribbean.* Cognizant Communications Corporation, Elmsford, New York.

17 Paradise and other Ports of Call: Cruising in the Pacific Islands

Ngaire Douglas[1] and Norman Douglas[2]

[1]*Southern Cross University, School of Tourism and Hospitality Management, PO Box 157, Lismore, NSW 2480, Australia;* [2]*Pacific Profiles, PO Box 229, Alstonville, NSW 2477, Australia*

Introduction

According to the Cruise Lines International Association (CLIA), in 2003 South Pacific cruising accounted for only 1.55% of world capacity. The figure for the Pacific Islands increases to 4.31% if the islands of Hawaii (2.76%) are included, and increases further if trans-Pacific cruising, which takes into account both island and mainland destinations, is included, but still amounts only to 4.44% (CLIA, 2004). The figures, however, are misleading, since they are based only on CLIA's member organizations, and P&O Cruises Australia, the major player in South Pacific cruising, is not represented. In 2003 the company claims to have carried 61,000 passengers on cruises to the South Pacific and with additions to its fleet expects to increase that number to 150,000 (P&O Cruises, 2004a). A July 2004 survey by the International Cruise Council of Australasia shows that, in 2003, 64,580 Australians took cruises from Australia to the South Pacific Islands, including New Zealand (ICCA, 2004). However, the Malaysia-based Star Cruises claims to have carried 55,000 passengers mainly on South Pacific cruises in 2003 while two of its vessels were deployed to the region for a period of some weeks during the SARS epidemic (personal communication, July 2004).

Two evident conclusions may be derived from these figures: one is their incompatibility; the second is that viewed from an international perspective they are quite modest. But in terms of regional tourism they are of considerable importance. Cruising to the Pacific Islands is of great historical significance, to both the development of tourism in the region and the evolution of the region's tourism imagery. Cruising to and among the islands represented the very foundation of organized tourism in the region, both in the islands of Hawaii and those of the South Pacific (Fig. 17.1). Although Hawaii is referred to from time to time, the major emphasis in this chapter is on the South Pacific. Discussions on Pacific cruising cannot be fully understood without being placed in a historical framework. The earliest cruises in this region, 'far from being short-lived novelties, proved to be the precursors of very durable activities indeed' (Douglas and Douglas, 2004a, p. 74).

Historical Overview

P&O has been credited with introducing travel by ship as a leisure and recreational activity rather than merely a means of transport in 1844. Within 40 years the Queensland-based

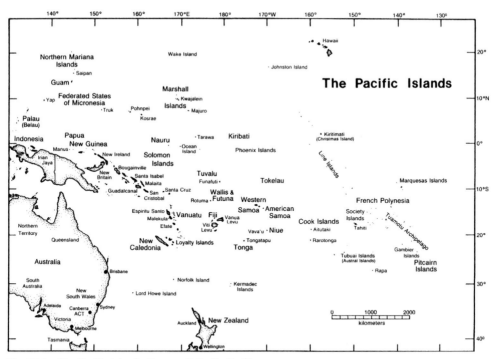

Fig. 17.1. The Pacific Islands. Source: © Pacific Profiles.

trading firm Burns Philp & Company (BP) and the Union Steamship Company of New Zealand were offering cruises to the islands of the Western and Eastern Pacific, respectively. For both companies it was a way of drawing public attention to their other services and extending their influence in their main areas of operation; of enhancing their public profile (McLean, 1990, p. 39). As excursion services became more frequent, staff members at the islands' branches of both companies organized shore activities for passengers.

In February 1884, BP advertised its first cruise from Thursday Island in the Torres Strait north of Australia to Port Moresby in Papua. This brief voyage, the importance of which was long overlooked, heralded not only the beginning of cruising in the Islands region, but also the effective beginning of tourism there. The Union Steamship Company, BP's counterpart in New Zealand, responded soon after with two cruises to the Eastern Pacific Islands on a far more extensive itinerary, visiting Fiji, Samoa and Tonga. Though successful, they were appar-

ently not followed up until 1898, when the company placed a new steamer on its excursion service, omitting Fiji, but taking in the Cook Islands and Tahiti, timing its arrival at the latter to coincide with the Bastille Day celebrations (Union Steamship Company, 1898).

Advertisements for the early cruises promised adventure and exotic delights, but the primary aims were to load/unload cargo and deliver mail. The presence of excursion passengers was profitable but largely incidental, although from these first tentative steps into tourism, both companies developed large travel departments. However, the remarkable number of island ports visited by BP and Union ships in the first decades of the 20th century, illustrates the extent of their trading, cargo and mail activities rather than their need to keep passengers amused. None the less, for some years the very novelty of this kind of travel to the Islands was reward enough for many, since there was little in Australia to compare with the 'colourful savages' of Melanesia and many New Zealanders evidently relished the prospect of spending a few weeks in the middle of the year cruising the tropical islands as an alternative to their often bleak winter.

By the beginning of the 20th century BP's cruising itinerary included, in addition to Papua and New Guinea (then separately administered), Vanuatu (then the New Hebrides), Solomon Islands, Lord Howe Island and Norfolk Island. Regular ports of call included, in addition to the capital towns, Port Moresby, Tulagi (Solomon Islands) and Port Vila, many remote outstations in Melanesia. Lord Howe and Norfolk, administered by Australia, were part of BP's Vanuatu route, until they developed their own importance as the company's schedule of 'conducted tours' grew (Buckley and Klugman, 1981, p. 269). BP, then, effectively dominated both trade and passenger routes in Melanesia for the first decades of the 20th century. Union's base in New Zealand made it favourably placed to similarly dominate much of Polynesia, and its visits to the Cook Islands and, later, Western Samoa, were aided by these islands being under New Zealand's administration. Capitalizing on their early achievements in cruising and responding to the worldwide growth in travel, both companies began to produce travel-related literature in impressive quantities.

As early as 1917 Union became a subsidiary of P&O, when the latter acquired all of Union's ordinary shares. The move aroused some popular controversy in New Zealand (McLauchlan, 1987, p. 66), and was part of an early expansionist phase during which P&O took over other companies also, among them the British India Steam Navigation Company in 1914 and Orient Line in 1917. As is the case today, the 'merged' companies continued to operate under their own names and – at least in Union's case – there is no indication that P&O was responsible for any significant change in policy. There is no existing evidence that a takeover of Burns Philp by P&O was ever considered. Although both P&O and Orient had been sending ships to Australia for decades (Howarth and Howarth, 1994), it was December 1932 before P&O made its entry into Pacific cruising with a brief holiday excursion to Norfolk Island one of its new 'Strath' class of luxury passenger vessels. The following day, Orient's *Oronsay* began a short cruise to New Caledonia, later pronouncing it a complete success (Orient Line, 1943, p. 35).

Enthused by passenger response to these cruises, company representatives were despatched to various parts of the South Pacific to check out port facilities and onshore attractions with a view to establishing a series of cruise itineraries for the Australian winter. Suva, Fiji, and Noumea, New Caledonia, the first pioneered as a tourist port of call by the Union Steamship Company, the second by the French organization Messageries Maritimes, were brought into P&O's orbit. They have remained on most Pacific Islands cruise itineraries ever since, although they invariably fare poorly on passenger satisfaction surveys: Suva generally because of the overbearing persistence of souvenir sellers and 'duty-free' merchants; Noumea generally because of the industrial nature of the harbour and the perceived 'arrogance' of the resident French. P&O also added Port Moresby, Samarai and Rabaul in Papua New Guinea, Port Vila in Vanuatu and Tulagi in Solomon Islands to its ports, all of them in BP territory. Within a few months of P&O's first cruise to Norfolk Island Burns Philp, P&O's agent in Australia, 'was in the incongruous position of promoting the growing cruise activities of its major competitor in the region, carrying vivid poster-style advertisements and articles on P&O's port visits in its house journal, *The BP Magazine*' (Burns Philp, 1933, p. 13; Douglas and Douglas, 1996a, p. 9).

P&O with its larger vessels introduced a marked change in Pacific cruising. The company, uninvolved in island trading, did not need to call at the majority of BP's small stations, and with passenger numbers far greater than that of many BP ships, a higher degree of onshore organization was required. This was most likely to be found at the rapidly growing port towns in the South Pacific. Passenger priority, therefore, rather than cargo priority influenced the choice of ports of call for P&O, a development that pointed the way to the long-term future of cruising in the region. Thus was established the fundamental South Pacific 'cruise circle' – Sydney, Noumea, Port Vila, Suva and return – which, with occasional modifications has remained the main framework of regional cruising ever since (Douglas and Douglas, 2004a, pp. 101–102).

Hosts and Guests in the South Seas

The sudden appearance of the larger P&O vessels with their several hundreds of passengers was regarded as ominous by some observers, including Sir Hubert Murray, Lieutenant Governor of Papua, who wrote to the captain of the *Strathaird* strongly suggesting that tourists were causing some social disruption within the Papuan community and encouraging beggary among the children. Entrepreneurial Melanesians had quickly become aware of the cash value of both their artefacts and themselves as photographic subjects and raised prices accordingly when the steamer was in. Murray thus became an early participant in the continuing debate on the effects of tourism on indigenous cultures (Douglas, 1996, pp. 82–83). At an even earlier time, Basil Thomson, former Prime Minister of Tonga, noted that in Fiji vendors of traditional artefacts were endeavouring to make them look old by 'dyeing [them] for the white tourists in Suva', and that any one of the group of 'innominate Melanesians' that hung about the wharf in Suva 'will carry a bag or camera for sixpence, though he will inevitably demand two shillings' (Thomson, n/d *c.* 1905, p. 9, 6). In the Pacific Islands 'boat day' has continued throughout the decades to be an occasion for economic opportunism, from the lei sellers of Honolulu to the minibus drivers of Vanuatu to the bullying vendors of hastily carved swords and masks in Fiji.

By the mid-1930s in Suva, which had been receiving tourists since the late 19th century and had its first tourist guide published in the early years of the 20th century by the Canadian–Australian Royal Mail Steamship Line, there were diversions enough. The practice of bidding farewell or greeting passenger ships with a brass band, already established in Honolulu, was introduced about this time. Organized drives could be taken to the hinterland, and at least one hotel – the Grand Pacific – had been built two decades earlier essentially for tourists by the Union Steamship Company: its interior design reflected this. Noumea provided, as it still does, 'an outpost of French culture' in the Pacific: there is little evidence that, during this period, visitors to the capital of New Caledonia were given any opportunity to visit Melanesian villages. In far less developed Vanuatu and Solomon Islands onshore entertainment was often restricted to watching the loading and unloading of cargo and having afternoon tea with the plantation manager or mission sisters. In their small capitals, Port Vila and Tulagi, passengers were often invited to the

Resident Commissioners' houses for tea (Douglas and Douglas, 1996a, p. 11).

The Matson Line

The Matson Navigation Company, based in San Francisco and with an aggressive policy towards both freight and passenger services in the Pacific, contributed its vessels to the Pacific's leisure traffic, and helped to demonstrate to North Americans that the Islands did not begin and end with Hawaii. Destinations such as Fiji, the Samoas and French Polynesia were included on Matson's trans-Pacific itineraries and added to the company's growing store of tourist images of 'Paradise' (see below). Matson absorbed an earlier operator in the Pacific, the Oceanic Steamship Company, in 1926 and 6 years later replaced the latter's older ships on trans-Pacific service with two attractive modern vessels, *Monterey* and *Mariposa*, specially built for the Pacific run. Each carrying 715 passengers, two-thirds of them in first class, *Monterey* and *Mariposa* were regarded by many prospective passengers in the region as the definitive Pacific cruise ships, against which the smaller excursion vessels of Burns Philp and Union failed to measure up. Aided by Matson's belief that, despite the economic depression, 'the affluent would respond to the new luxury liners to explore the exotic islands and ports of the Pacific', especially if encouraged by a vigorous promotional campaign, they quickly became identified with the region's ultimate cruise experience (Stindt, 1991, p. 83).

Faced with the competition, Union, a long-time and bitter rival of US companies, especially over mail contracts, withdrew its ships from the trans-Pacific service in 1936. 'More passengers', wrote Matson's historian, 'switched from British [*sic*] operated vessels to the new US flag liners'. Passenger traffic also boomed on the trans-Tasman service 'as travellers in those countries wanted to experience the luxury, service and cuisine of the American ships' (Stindt, 1991, p. 62). The majority of Matson's Hawaiian and trans-Pacific voyages were promoted as 'cruises', indicating that, among its passengers, travel largely for leisure rather than merely transport was a very significant factor. Along with the rest of Matson's organization, *Monterey* and *Mariposa* were turned to US government service following the outbreak of war in the Pacific on 7 December 1941. The vessels bearing the same names that cruised the Pacific under Matson's flag between 1956 and 1970 were newer and smaller ships and were only moderately successful.

The Imagery of Pacific Cruising

'So, I said, why can't *Fairstar* go to some of those unspoilt Island paradises for a change?' (Phil Young, managing director, P&O Australia, 1996, personal communication).

As Pacific tourism in general was later to do, early cruising in the region benefited enormously from the growth of the myth of Paradise and the romantic imagery associated with it. The concept of a paradise in the Pacific Islands was first applied to Tahiti by the French explorer Bougainville in 1768, but enthusiastically hijacked by commercial interests in the Hawaiian Islands in the mid-19th century. By the end of the century the slogan 'Paradise of the Pacific' was being applied freely to Hawaii and images appropriate to it were widely disseminated (Douglas and Douglas 1996b, pp. 19–23). The term Paradise and related expressions not only helped drive the success of Pacific cruising throughout its history, but became in time almost inseparable from any tourism references to the islands, surviving many decades of overuse. In 2004 despite its growing weariness it was still being used as a marketing theme – 'Discover Paradise' – by the South Pacific Tourism Organization (SPTO, 2004a).

It is fair to say that the widespread dissemination of tourism imagery of the South Pacific Islands began with the advertisements and brochures of BP and Union Steamships. In 1911 a second edition of BP's lavish tourist publication, *Picturesque Travel*, added – to what were still basically cargo runs – the gloss of promotional language that helped to define Melanesia for many tourists in terms that anticipated the travel brochures of a much later era. The Solomons was made up of 'wild islands', yet at each anchorage 'one is free to wander through the native villages', comforted by the fact that the 'picturesque simplicity of the natives is not yet destroyed by influence of civilisation' (Burns Philp, 1911). By the late 1920s a new publication – *The BP Magazine* – was exploiting the myth of the South Seas for all it was worth. Full-page advertisements for the company's cruises spoke of the 'Wonder Isles' and 'The Enchantment' of the Pacific and invoked the writings of Tennyson and Robert Louis Stevenson (Burns Philp, 1928, 1929, 1933). For its part the Union Steamship Company in 1912 enlisted the talents of Beatrice Grimshaw, a prolific writer of both fact and fiction with Pacific settings, to enhance its promotional literature. In Grimshaw's hands the islands of the Eastern Pacific became – quoting Rudyard Kipling – 'The Islands of the Blest', where the 'sweet-eyed, brown-skinned Island races' were unlike any other people in the world, 'their lives one long dream, one endless holiday' in a 'Paradise of Laziness' (Grimshaw, 1912, pp. 1, 4).

Matson, already experienced at the game, gave visual expression to the Paradise theme on posters, postcards and menu covers. The main emphasis in Matson's trans-Pacific advertising was on the major destinations, Australia and New Zealand, but 'The South Seas', as the Islands region was popularly known, was prominently featured on the company's brochures. Matson's perception of the South Pacific was influenced to a great extent by its experience of Hawaii, to which it had been operating services from San Francisco since 1901, and the tourist imagery of which it helped to define, if not invent. P&O also succumbed to this form of promotion, most notably during the latter part of the 20th century, applying the term Paradise generously throughout its Pacific-oriented brochures; to its cruise region as a whole, or to randomly chosen islands, or to individual cruises which were given titles such as 'Bonjour Paradise', 'Escape to Paradise', 'French Pacific Paradise', 'Precious Paradises' and so on. One of the company's most recent additions to its increasing number of small island calls is Ouvea in the Loyalty Group, 'the closest island to paradise' (P&O Cruises, 2004b, p. 25). On the previous page of the same brochure Apia, the traditionally scruffy capital of Samoa, is described as 'so perfectly paradise, you'll never want to leave'. A brochure for *Pacific Princess*, a rechristened Renaissance Cruise Line vessel and now P&O's premium product in the South Pacific, assures prospective passengers that the ship is where 'South Pacific Paradise comes to you' (P&O/Princess, 2004).

For all its predictability, the notion of the Pacific Islands as 'Paradise' clearly dies very hard indeed. As recently as June 2004, Gavin Smith, P&O Cruises' managing director in Australia, announced the Pacific fleet's new itineraries with the words: 'Never before has P&O Cruises offered a mix of so many destinations, many of them remote island paradises where our passengers can experience the real magic of the South Pacific' (P&O Cruises, 2004a). The destinations may be new, but the promotional language has barely changed for more than a century.

Second World War and after

The hostilities of the Second World War affected vast areas of the Pacific and Asia which had been relatively safe from the Europe-centred conflict of the First World War. The effects on all forms of shipping were grim. The P&O group alone lost 182 ships, eight of them from P&O's own passenger fleet. Losses were heavy also for BP, less so for the Union Steamship Company. The requisitioning and refitting for war service of Matson passenger vessels by the US Government made them far too costly to return to normal cruise services and new, smaller vessels were built (Worden, 1981, p. 121).

Cruising in the South Pacific was slow to resume after the disruptions to shipping caused by the war. BP's early command of the Southwest Pacific as a cruise region was gradually overtaken by P&O. BP finally withdrew from passenger shipping completely in 1968 (Fig. 17.2). Its New Zealand counterpart, the Union Steamship Company, abandoned passenger services in 1973, when its popular *Tofua* was 'sold to foreigners' (Brewer, 1982, p. 229), presumably the most ignominious of fates.

The rebirth of cruising was not helped by the post-war increase in air travel, especially later developments which included wide-bodied jet aircraft. None the less, a number of lines made seasonal cruises in the islands region either between line voyages to and from Europe – many of which carried assisted migrants to Australia – or as part of a trans-Pacific voyage to New Zealand and Australia from the west coast of the US. Matson helped to repopularize destinations such as Tahiti and Samoa, generally omitted from cruises out of Australia because of their distance. Ironically, however, Matson

Fig. 17.2. Burns Philp's popular *Bulolo* was withdrawn in 1968, ending the company's cruise services. Source: Norman Douglas collection.

ceased passenger services in 1970, on the eve of a strong revival of cruising.

P&O's Pacific

P&O's seasonal cruise presence in the South Pacific gained considerably by its use of vessels such as *Himalaya*, *Oriana* and *Canberra*, the superships of their day, for which many Australian cruisers developed strong emotional attachments. In 1974 the company's presence was further strengthened by the acquisition of the Los Angeles-based Princess Cruises which sent ships to Australia, New Zealand and the Pacific Islands during the American winter. Against this formidable combination, other players in the South Pacific cruise game appeared feeble, though all had their devotees, in particular Lauro Lines' *Achille Lauro* and Sitmar International's *Fairstar*. Later the CTC charter group would offer a budget challenge to P&O with their reconstituted Black Sea ferries.

P&O's acquisition of the ailing Sitmar International in 1988 including *Fairstar*, which had been cruising in the region since 1973 on well-established itineraries, opened a new era in South Pacific cruising (Fig. 17.3). This was far less because of *Fairstar*'s quality – it was built as a troop carrier and was for many years a migrant ship before it turned to full-time cruise activity – than its reputation. Until its eventual retirement in 1997, *Fairstar* bore much of the evidence of its origin, with cramped, badly ventilated and poorly decorated cabins and ill-designed bathrooms, but these were of little concern to the majority of its passengers. In the 15 years between its entry into the South Pacific and P&O's takeover, the 'Fun ship' developed a notoriety quite unmatched in South Pacific cruising (Fig. 17.4). 'It says a good deal for *Fairstar*'s reputation that it was the only Sitmar vessel not renamed by P&O after the take-over' (Douglas and Douglas, 2004a, p. 103).

Perhaps more importantly for the geography of Pacific cruising, changes to the marketing of *Fairstar* had occurred before its acquisition by P&O, including a revamping of its earlier itineraries. Cruises of between 24 and 45 days were eliminated and a fortnight or less became standard, resulting in the removal of some popular island destinations including

Fig. 17.3. P&O celebrated 50 years of Pacific Islands cruising with an unlikely picture. Source: Norman Douglas collection.

Tonga, which saw its cruise visitors reduced by more than 90% over a 13-year period. Other itinerary modifications also took place as a result of discussions between Sitmar's new marketing manager, Phil Young, and operations manager, Luigi Nappa, a former *Fairstar* staff captain. Against opposition from Sitmar's head office, Young and Nappa went scouting for 'unspoilt' destinations as an alternative to the larger ports of call and tested the market with the inclusion of Dravuni, a southern outlier in Fiji. When the passenger response exceeded expectations a number of other 'unspoilt island paradises' followed including Champagne Bay, 'Mystery Island' (Inyeug) and Lamen Bay in Vanuatu, Lifou in New Caledonia's Loyalty Group and Yasawa–I–Rara, Rotuma and Kioa in Fiji, though by no means all of them on every cruise. P&O acquired both Nappa and Young along with *Fairstar* in 1988 and the innovations continued. The company has jealously guarded

Fig. 17.4. P&O's 'Fun ship' promotion was revived in 2004 for a new market. Source: Courtesy P&O.

their 'exclusive' discoveries against attempted intrusions by other cruise ships.

A number of the new ports did not succeed, their social and cultural bases seemingly having been inadequately researched in the first place. Rotuma was dropped after one call when local jealousies and the prevalence of rough seas made it untenable. One landing at Kioa, in an isolated part of Fiji and as unlike Paradise as one could imagine, was sufficient. 'We realised the impact on the local community would be too great', according to P&O Australia's then operations manager (L. Nappa, 1999, personal communication). Later, the first visit to Lamen Bay was notable for the degree of misunderstanding between P&O and the local Islanders. The successful ones have been maintained on a regular but infrequent basis, as local conditions made it inappropriate to call at them too often. In passenger surveys they have proved generally more popular than longer established ports such as Noumea or even Port

Vila, a long time passenger favourite. Surveys conducted in 2003 showed that, on itineraries which included both, small ports such as Lifou were beginning to displace Port Vila as a favourite call for South Pacific cruisers. For its 2004/05 season, with two new vessels to find itineraries for, P&O was offering several new ports – most of them quite small 'beach calls' – in both Vanuatu and New Caledonia. With countries such as Papua New Guinea and Solomon Islands generally avoided by cruise ships in recent years because of social and political instability, destination planners are experiencing a shrinking range of choices.

Beach calls and visits to small villages are also the speciality of a number of well established small ship or expeditionary cruising companies in the South Pacific. Among these are Blue Lagoon Cruises and Captain Cook Cruises in Fiji which offer short duration cruises mainly through the Yasawa Islands in Western Fiji, and Melanesian Tourist Services and Trans Niugini Tours in Papua New Guinea which offer in the main cruises on the Sepik River (Douglas and Douglas, 2004b). The promotional activities of these companies tend to be directed mainly to the European and North American markets and the products are priced accordingly. All appear to have suffered an economic downturn as a consequence of international tensions in recent years. Up to date and accurate passenger figures are difficult to obtain. All of these enterprises, however, help to bring a measure of the revenue from tourism directly to village communities and grass-roots entrepreneurs, a contribution also made by much larger organizations such as P&O Cruises at their small ports of call.

Landings at small ports in ships large or small, however, can be problematic. The best time to cruise in the South Pacific is during the middle months of the year when monsoons, cyclones and heavy seas are out of season. However, cruise companies based in the US or the UK prefer to send their ships to this region during the northern hemisphere winter which coincides with the November to April southern hemisphere monsoon and generally wet season. Landing during these times, especially at ports requiring tenders, may be extremely difficult, even unsafe. Passengers and Islanders alike are frequently disappointed at a captain's decision not to land at a small port, in the interests of

safety. 'Mystery Island' in Vanuatu and Lifou and Amedee in New Caledonia have been the subject of eleventh hour alterations a number of times when weather conditions were deemed unsuitable.

Conclusion

A new importance has been accorded to cruising in the Pacific in recent years. There are illustrations of this at the infrastructural level as well as at the level of planning and economics. Improvements to cruise terminals in Sydney at long last illustrate the city's position as the region's major hub and, once again, a cruise terminal for Brisbane is being planned: industry optimists predict its completion by mid-2006. A dedicated terminal in Noumea gives further evidence of its significance – if not its popularity – as a cruise destination, and has apparently encouraged other regional ports to take cruising seriously rather than taking it for granted. The South Pacific Tourism Organisation (SPTO), based in Suva, Fiji has belatedly recognized the importance to tourism of the cruise sector and the need to 'develop and implement a regional cruise shipping strategy', making the curious claim that 'there is a paucity of studies and little data available on the subject' (SPTO, 2004b). Cruise ships have been visiting Fiji for over a century. Cruising in the Hawaiian Islands is effectively dominated by Norwegian Cruise Line (NCL) – a subsidiary of Malaysia-based Star Cruises – under its NCL America brand. The introduction of NCL's US-registered, 2000-passenger *Pride of Aloha* not only reaffirmed the company's faith in the USA, but relieved it of the necessity of having to include remote Fanning Island (Kiribati) in its Hawaii cruises in order to comply with regulations relating to the operations of foreign flagged vessels in US waters. By mid-2006 the company expects to have three vessels of similar size operating in Hawaii.

In the Eastern Pacific Tahiti has emerged as a new hub, with the vessels of four cruise companies based there for several months of the year, and visiting from Papeete other islands in French Polynesia as well as the Cook Islands and Samoa. French Polynesia's Tourism Minister has acknowledged that the cruise sector cannot be ignored, claiming that 'cruise ship passengers represent a turnover of 11 billion French Pacific francs (US$112 million) for French Polynesia, or a fourth of tourist spending.' The Minister announced further incentives for cruise companies to position ships in the French Territory (SPTO, 2004c).

The most evident fact about the state of cruising in the South Pacific in the early 21st century is the dominance of P&O Cruises. The company's regional fleet, long dependent on one ship (most recently *Pacific Sky*), has been increased to three, with an acquisition from the defunct Renaissance Cruise Line (*Pacific Princess*) followed by the rehabilitation and renaming of an older vessel from Carnival's extensive collection (*Pacific Sun*). Encouraged by an International Cruise Council of Australasia survey that showed cruising out of Australia increased by 32% between 2002 and 2003, the company expects to fill all the additional berths in its expanded fleet. Of 78 cruise ship movements scheduled for Sydney between September 2004 and September 2005, 61 are P&O or Princess vessels (Sydney Ports Corporation, 2004). Modifications to itineraries to take in additional ports in New Zealand and Australia and the seasonal repositioning of its vessels reflect not only greater consumer choice, but also P&O's long-held intention to keep out competition. The company has seen a number of potential rivals fade away, and arguably made a strong contribution to the demise of its most recent and most determined competitor, Norwegian Capricorn Line (Douglas and Douglas, 2001), although its press releases invariably 'welcome competition'. The founder of Norwegian Capricorn Line, Sarina Bratton, has re-emerged with Orion Expedition Cruises, using a sophisticated 106 passenger vessel. Orion, by concentration mainly on Australian coastal cruising and Antarctica, wisely avoids duplicating P&O's Pacific itineraries (Orion Expedition Cruises, 2004).

P&O's promotional approach to the Pacific has changed relatively little over the past two decades, although with more vessels it is now possible – and desirable – to distinguish more precisely between markets and design promotion accordingly. The industry watcher, however, cannot help but notice that, though ostensibly embarrassed by the roistering reputation of *Fairstar* and having tried hard to overcome it (Douglas and Douglas, 2004a, pp. 157–158),

P&O, now one of the Carnival Corporation's 13 brands, has resurrected the full-scale 'Fun Ship' promotion, originally a Carnival theme, and bestowed it upon one of *Fairstar*'s successors, *Pacific Sky*. In cruising, it appears, some traditions are hard to overcome. P&O may not have pioneered cruising to the South Pacific, as it once claimed (P&O Cruises, 2001, p. 17), nor invented the marketing language for it but, at least for the foreseeable future, the company's pre-eminence is obvious enough.

References

Brewer, N.H. (1982) *A Century of Style: Great Ships of the Union Line, 1875–1976*. A.H. & A.W. Reed, Wellington.

Buckley, K. and Klugman, K. (1981) *The History of Burns Philp: The Australian Company in the South Pacific*. Burns Philp & Co., Sydney.

Burns Philp & Co. (1911) *Picturesque Travel*. Burns Philp & Co., Sydney.

Burns Philp & Co. (1928) *The BP Magazine* 1(1).

Burns Philp & Co. (1929) *The BP Magazine* 1(4).

Burns Philp & Co. (1933) *The BP Magazine* 5(3).

Cruise Lines International Association (2004) *Cruise Industry Overview: Marketing Edition*. Cruise Lines International Association, Spring.

Douglas, N. (1996) *They Came for Savages: 100 Years of Tourism in Melanesia*. Southern Cross University Press, Lismore, New South Wales, Australia.

Douglas N. and Douglas, N. (1996a) P&O's Pacific. *Journal of Tourism Studies* 7(2), 2–14.

Douglas, N. and Douglas, N. (1996b) Tourism in the Pacific: historical factors. In: Hall, C.M. and Page, S.J. (eds) *Tourism in the Pacific*. International Thomson Business Press, London, pp. 19–35.

Douglas, N. and Douglas, N. (2001) The short, unhappy life of an Australia-based cruise line. *Pacific Tourism Review* 5(3–4), 131–142.

Douglas, N. and Douglas, N. (2004a) *The Cruise Experience: Global and Regional Issues in Cruising*. Pearson Education Australia, French's Forest, New South Wales, Australia.

Douglas, N. and Douglas, N. (2004b) Small ship cruising in the South Pacific: from muddy rivers to blue lagoons. In: Novelli, M. (ed.) *Niche Tourism: Contemporary Issues, Trends and Cases*. Butterworth-Heinemann, Cambridge.

Grimshaw, B. (1912) *The Islands of the Blest*. Union Steamship Company, Dunedin.

Howarth, D. and Howarth, S. (1994) *The Story of P&O: The Peninsular and Oriental Steam Navigation Company*, rev. edn. Weidenfeld & Nicholson, London.

ICCA (International Cruise Council of Australia) (2004) *The Australia Cruise Industry: A Summary*. International Cruise Council of Australia, Sydney.

McLauchlan, G. (ed.) (1987) *The Line that Dared: A History of the Union Steamship Company*. Four Star Books, Mission Bay.

McLean, G. (1990) *The Southern Octopus: The Rise of a Shipping Empire*. New Zealand Ship and Marine Society & Wellington Harbour Board Maritime Museum, Wellington.

Orient Line (1943) *Orient Line: Australian Annals*. Orient Line, Sydney.

Orion Expedition Cruises (2004) *Orion Expedition Cruises*. Orion Expedition Cruises, Milsons Point, Australia.

P&O Cruises (2001) *P&O Cruises South Pacific 2002 Season*. P&O Cruises, Sydney.

P&O Cruises (2004a) *P&O Cruises Offers an Ocean of New Ports*. Press release, 24 February.

P&O Cruises (2004b) *P&O Cruises South Pacific and Queensland: August 2004–October 2005*. P&O Cruises, Sydney.

P&O/Princess (2004) *Pacific Princess November 2004–April 2005*. P&O Cruises, Sydney.

SPTO (South Pacific Tourism Organisation) (2004a) Available at: www.tcsp.com

SPTO (South Pacific Tourism Organisation) (2004b) *Market Intelligence Report 2: Cruise Shipping Market Segment, Summary*. South Pacific Tourism Organisation, Suva.

SPTO (South Pacific Tourism Organisation) (2004c) *Weekly Newsletter Update*, 19–22 May.

Stindt, F. (1991) *Matson's Century of Ships*. Privately published, Modesto, California.

Sydney Ports Corporation (2004) *Cruise Schedule*. Available at: www.sydneyports.com.au

Thomson, B. (n/d. *c.* 1905) *Fiji for Tourists*. Canadian–Australian Royal Mail Steamship Line, London.

Union Steamship Company (1898) *Off to Tahiti!: Trip to the South Sea Islands*. Union Steamship Company, Dunedin.

Worden, W.L. (1981) *Cargoes: Matson's First Century in the Pacific*. The University Press of Hawaii, Honolulu.

18 The Antarctic Cruise Industry

Thomas Bauer[1] and Ross K. Dowling[2]

[1]Hong Kong Polytechnic University, School of Hotel and Tourism Management, Hung Hom, Kowloon, PR China; [2]Edith Cowan University, Faculty of Business and Law, School of Marketing, Tourism and Leisure, Joondalup, WA 6027, Australia

Introduction

The Antarctic continent surrounds the geographic South Pole and extends to 13.9 million square kilometres, 98% of which are covered by a thick layer of ice (Fig. 18.1). It is the highest, coldest, driest and remotest of all the continents and its ice cover holds 90–95% of the world's fresh water reserves. Over 2000 years ago, the Greeks had postulated that a giant southern continent must exist to 'balance' the Northern Hemisphere. Until 1895, no human had set foot on the continent. The published reports of early explorers like Shackleton and Scott as well as modern adventurers have stimulated interest in this remote region in the minds of 'ordinary' people, some of whom are now visiting the region as paying tourists.

It is a continent of great beauty. Its coastal regions feature an abundance of wildlife and visitors are attracted by the prospects of encountering whales, seals, flying seabirds such as the wandering albatross and, of course, penguins. Towering snow and ice-covered mountains fall off steeply into the ice-choked seas, floating icebergs the size of large buildings or at times the size of small countries and glaciers calving into the sea, all provide visitors with unsurpassed vistas. Bransfield and Gerlache Straits provide ocean access to some of the most magnificent cold-climate scenery in the world. The highlight of any cruise in the Antarctic peninsula region is the passage through the Lemaire and Neumayer Channels, narrow ocean passages flanked by high, snow-covered mountains. The first author has captured many of these images on the CD-ROM and video productions of *Voyage to Antarctica: A Celebration of Beauty*.

Unlike any other major landmass, Antarctica is not owned or controlled by any particular country. Argentina, Australia, Chile, France, New Zealand, Norway and the UK all lay claims to parts of Antarctica (some of them overlapping), but their claims are not universally accepted. South of 60° S latitude, the Antarctic is managed under the Antarctic Treaty of 1959 and its associated instruments. These include:

- Convention on the Conservation of Antarctic Marine Living Resources;
- Agreed Measures for the Conservation of Antarctic Fauna and Flora;
- Convention for the Conservation of Antarctic Seals;
- Protocol on Environmental Protection to the Antarctic Treaty (Madrid Protocol).

Antarctic Tourism

Antarctic shipping began with the navigator Captain James Cook, who in 1773 took his ships *Resolution* and *Adventure* across the Antarctic Circle but did not actually see the continent.

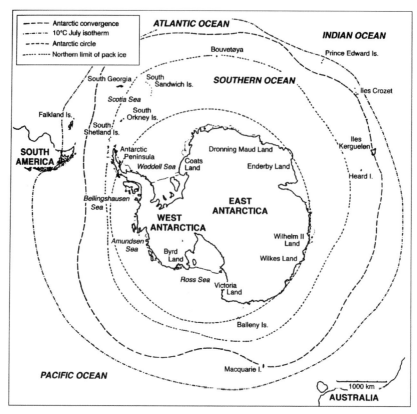

Fig. 18.1. Antarctica.

Later sealers and whalers plied their trade in Antarctic waters. In the early part of the 20th century the travel firm of Thomas Cook advertised a cruise to the Ross Sea but for unknown reasons, perhaps a lack of paying passengers, it did not take place. As global tourism increases, experienced travellers are seeking new and remote places to visit. Mirroring the increase in the interest in nature-based tourism activities among the travellers of the world, the number of voyages to Antarctica has increased significantly in recent years (Bauer and Dowling, 2003). The region is governed by the Antarctic Treaty System, which in Recommendation VIII-9/1975 acknowledges that 'tourism is a natural development in this Area and that it requires regulation' (Heap, 1990, p. 2602). Some environmental organizations have called for the establishment of Antarctica as a 'World Park', which would allow controlled tourism activities while others have policies that would prohibit any tourism from taking place.

Antarctic visitor arrivals increased rapidly during the last decade of the 20th century and the early part of the 21st century but it is still the least visited continent on earth. It is a remote destination with a fragile and at times hostile environment where the conduct of tourism is only possible through the close cooperation between governments, tour operators, the industry association, tourists and guides. To date, tourism in the south has been managed in an exemplary way and much can be learned from the way it is handled that can also be applied to tourism management elsewhere. Of particular interest is the establishment of the International Association of Antarctica Tour Operators (IAATO) in 1991, which aims to manage tourism in the south in a sustainable and responsible way.

As a consequence of the number of tourists visiting the Antarctic, there has been an attendant increase in the number of sites visited. This rose from 36 in 1990 to nearly 200 just 7 years later (National Science Foundation, 1997). One of the main reasons for the increase in ship-based tours during the 1990s was the ready supply of Russian research vessels. These had become available at reasonable charter rates after the Government of Russia could no longer afford to fully fund the oceanographic research activities of its research institutes. This in turn forced institutes such as the P.P. Shirov Institute of Oceanology in Moscow to look for outside funding, and when tour operators approached them with the idea to use these ice-strengthened vessels in the Antarctic tourist trade, they were willing to do business. Today Russian-flagged vessels account for a large proportion of voyages to Antarctica (Fig. 18.2).

Antarctica is the southernmost frontier of shipping. In McMurdo Sound, at the southern extreme of the Ross Sea in latitude 77° 40′ S, is where the southern ocean ends – this is as far south as ships can go. An icebreaker of the US Coast Guard is the first vessel to arrive each season to cut through the winter ice to open up a 10-nautical mile channel of open water that allows ships to deliver supplies to Antarctica's largest settlement, McMurdo Station. Tourist vessels such as the M/S *Bremen* (ice-strengthened) and the icebreaker *Kapitan Khlebnikov* also pay sporadic visits carrying passengers to this remote region of the world. Meanwhile in the waters along the Antarctic peninsula 165+ cruises take place during the Antarctic summer months from November to March, carrying over 20,000 passengers per season.

Ship-based Tourism

While sightseeing, overflights of Antarctica are possible and some adventurous travellers visit the interior of the continent; the bulk of Antarctic tourism is cruise ship-based. Getting to Antarctica is a major challenge. The most common route takes the traveller from Ushuaia on the shores of the Beagle Channel in southern Argentina to the islands off the west coast of the Antarctic peninsula. Regular commercial cruising began in 1966 when tourism pioneer Lars-Eric Lindblad first chartered the Argentinean vessel *Lapataia* to take 94 passengers across the stormy waters of Drake Passage to the Antarctic peninsula region, 1000 km to the south of Cape Horn. Today most Antarctic cruises depart from Ushuaia, the southernmost town in the world.

During the last decade the city has substantially upgraded its port infrastructure and as a consequence Antarctic tourism is now a significant contributor to the local economy. Cruises to the Antarctic peninsula usually last between 10 and 20 days (depending on whether South Georgia is included in the programme or not),

Fig. 18.2. Cruise ships in Port of Ushuaia, Tierra Del Fuego, Argentina. Left to right: *Kapitan Dranitsyn*; *Professor Multanovskiy*; *Marco Polo*. Source: Ross K. Dowling.

but on shorter voyages no more than 5–7 days are spent in Antarctic waters. After their visits to the sites in the peninsula, tourist vessels regularly round the famous Cape Horn where tribute is paid to the sailors who lost their lives rounding the Horn (Fig. 18.3). Until recently ships were able to approach Cape Horn to within 2–3 nautical miles but during 2004–2005 the Chilean administration demanded that ships observe Chile's 12-nautical mile territorial boundary, thus only providing tourists with a distant view of this magnificent landmark.

Cruise ships visiting the Antarctic vary in degrees of size and luxury. They range from yachts with 4 passengers to vessels carrying 1000 or more passengers. The most popular ships visiting Antarctica carry between 50 and 160 passengers. Since there are no berthing or landing facilities in Antarctica, operators depend on inflatable rubber dinghies (zodiacs) to transport passengers ashore (Fig. 18.4). Tourism activities are restricted to the southern summer months (November to March) when the region is relatively ice-free. This makes it possible for ice-strengthened vessels to land passengers. Visitor numbers increased as the number of ships capable of negotiating the southern waters increased. In the online version of its newsletter, IAATO (2005) provides the following estimates for the 2004–2005 season (Table 18.1).

Fig. 18.3. Cape Horn, tip of South America. Second author in foreground. Source: Ross K. Dowling.

As Table 18.2 shows, Antarctic visitor numbers have grown significantly during the last decade and arrivals are set to increase even more in the decades to come as new market segments such as tourists from Asia are tapped.

The following ships landed passengers in Antarctica during the 2003/04 season: *Akademik Ioffe, Akademik Vavilov, Akademik Shokalskiy, Andrea, Bremen, Clipper Adventurer, Discovery, Endevour, Explorer II, Grigory Mikheev, Hanseatic, Kapitan Khlebnikov, Marco Polo, Nordnorge, Orion, Orlova, Polar Pioneer, Polar Star, Professor Molchanov, Professor Multanovskiy, S/V Golden Fleece, S/V Pelagic, S/V Pelagic Australis, S/V Tooluka, Saga Rose, The World, Ushuaia, Vistamar, World Discoverer.*

Spatial Distribution

Antarctic tourism is highly concentrated at only relatively few locations, mainly in the Antarctic peninsula region including the South Shetland Islands. Only limited tourism takes place on the sub-Antarctic islands of South Georgia, Falkland Islands (Islas Malvinas), Macquarie Island (Australia) as well as the Campbell and Auckland island groups to the south of New Zealand. A few ships each season venture into the Ross Sea where they undertake landings at places such as Cape Adare, Terra Nova Bay and, ice conditions permitting, also at McMurdo Station. Even fewer cruise ships sail along the coast of the Australian Antarctic territory.

Cruise Tourists

A survey of tourists was carried out in 2001 on one trip organized by the US-based company Quark Expeditions, which specializes in taking tourists to Polar Regions (Dowling, 2002). A summary of the findings is presented here. The trip, from 26 January to 2 February 2001, was undertaken on board the Russian icebreaker *Kapitan Dranitsyn*, which departed and returned from Ushuaia, Tierra del Fuego, at the bottom of South America. The 91 passengers comprised organized groups from Australia (44%), France (27%) and the USA (22%) as well as a number of individuals from several other countries. The

Fig. 18.4.   Cruise passengers landing by zodiacs on the Antarctic mainland. Source: Ross K. Dowling.

passengers were all well travelled and mainly older persons (47%, 40–59 years; 36%, 60+) and there were more females (69%) than males (31%). This research reports on a survey of 55 of the 91 passengers.

The principal reason given why they travelled to the Antarctic was to view one of the last surviving, relatively untouched areas of the world. The element of adventure and the 'unknown' was also a magnet. The chance to return home and be able to talk about somewhere most people only dream of going was also part of their decision to visit. Sample comments from respondents included 'to see the landscape and wildlife', 'the chance to improve my awareness of this vast unknown continent', 'for an adventure

holiday and to see the historical sites', 'to go, as near as possible, where Scott, Amundsen, Shackleton and Mawson had gone, and try to experience something of what they did'.

Before travelling to the Antarctic the tourists expected to see a range of features. These included icebergs and glaciers, historic sites and wildlife. The visitors' expectations were met in regard to the icebergs and glacial features but their expectations of viewing the research stations and islands were far exceeded. In addition, while they expected to view penguins they did not expect to see them in such abundance. At several sites the tourists were able to view hundreds of thousands of penguins. Items that did not meet the tourists' expectations included

Table 18.1.   Summary estimates for Antarctic visitation in the 2004/05 season.

Type of tourism	Number of departures	Number of passengers (excluding officers, staff, crew)
IAATO sea-borne traditional tourism in the Antarctic peninsula	165	16,535
IAATO sea-borne traditional tourism Ross Sea continental voyages	5	383
IAATO sailing vessels/yacht operators	7	37
IAATO fly/cruise	4	130
IAATO large ship cruise only in the Antarctic peninsula	4	4,358
Non-IAATO large ship cruise only	1	669
Non-IAATO small ship/yacht peninsula	17	1,124
Non-IAATO large ship with landings in the Antarctic peninsula	8	4,088

Source: IAATO (2005).

Table 18.2. Antarctic tourist trends – landed 1992–2005 (includes ship and land-based passenger numbers; 1997–1998 onwards includes commercial yacht activity).

Year	Passengers
1992/1993	6,704
1993/1994	8,016
1994/1995	8,120
1995/1996	9,367
1996/1997	7,413
1997/1998	9,604
1998/1999	10,013
1999/2000	13,826
2000/2001	12,248
2001/2002	11,588
2002/2003	13,571
2003/2004	19,772
2004/2005	22,297

Source: IAATO (2005).

Fig. 18.5. Passengers disembarking down gang-plank on to zodiacs to be transferred to Antarctic mainland. Source: Ross K. Dowling.

the fact that on their particular trip fewer whales were seen than expected. While they also expected to see penguins the tourists were often disappointed to find the penguins 'dirty and smelly' covered in penguin poo. In addition, a number of tourists had expected to land and walk on the pack ice, as illustrated in the tour brochure; however, due to the relative warmth of the polar summer, the ship did not reach the pack ice, which was further south than usual. Therefore this expectation could not be fulfilled.

In regard to the trip itself, the respondents made a number of observations about the ship and the shore landings. A number of them indicated that some landings were awkward for those not so mobile or agile (Fig. 18.5); however, the majority of respondents were satisfied with facilities and services on the ship. Similarly, most of the respondents were satisfied with facilities and services in relation to the landings. It appeared that more respondents were more satisfied with the landings than with the ship.

As a result of their visit the tourists nominated a number of changes in their attitude to the continent. All respondents agreed that as a result of their visit their knowledge of the Antarctic had increased significantly. They also noted that their knowledge had increased in relation to Antarctic research, wildlife, history and marine life. The majority of respondents stated that they found the overall condition of

the Antarctic to be pristine, and a repeated statement was that they 'had a new-found respect for the Antarctic and wanted its perceived fragile environment to be protected'.

The knowledge gained from their tour came from a variety of sources. These included the zodiac landings, the ship's on-board lecturers, videos and library material. Many respondents commented on the fact that a key source of information was gained from casual discussions with expedition staff both on and off the ship, at meal times, on the bridge or during the landings (Fig. 18.6).

The tourists were more than satisfied with the number of landings made on the Antarctic peninsula and surrounding islands, with 11 landings made in 6 days. These were the highlights for the visitors who were more satisfied with the landings than the ship. Tourists commented on the different and unique natural features of each site, some being stunningly beautiful natural areas with others rich in wildlife.

Fig. 18.6.   On the bridge of the *Kapitan Dranitsyn*, Antarctica. Foreground: Captain Agafonov; background: passengers viewing scenery. Source: Ross K. Dowling.

Respondents were particularly taken by Brown Bluff, as it was the first point that they actually set foot on the Antarctic mainland. Paulet Island was noted as being very smelly due to the presence of hundreds of thousands of breeding penguins. Paradise Harbour was described as aptly named as it was extremely beautiful. Visits to bases and refuges were also highly valued with respondents having visited Argentine and British bases as well as a Ukrainian station (Fig. 18.7). Port Lockroy, a 'working' UK base, was noted as an important site with respondents glad to see the British maintain the historical site and open it to tourists.

The only adverse comments made in relation to the shore visits were that some landings were awkward for those not so mobile or agile. Others were that on this particular trip the group did not land at several advertised sites due to the inclement weather at those places. The respondents were also asked to respond to a number of prepared statements in relation to their Antarctic visit (Table 18.3). The majority agreed with the statements, finding the condition of the Antarctic excellent, the staff helpful, the landings well managed and enjoying the scheduled

activities. A small minority of respondents chose the 'middle ground' in relation to the landings and activities while a minority disagreed that the condition of the Antarctic was excellent.

After having visited the Antarctic, the visitors ranked the importance of various aspects of their trip (Table 18.4). They noted that most important for them was to see the continent, its wildlife, natural beauty, historical sites and remoteness. When asked what was the 'best' part of their trip, their comments included 'being up close and personal with the wildlife and icebergs', 'the shore landings by zodiacs', 'the vastness of the continent', 'the icebergs were awesome' and 'the incredible heights of the mountains and the overall beauty left me spellbound'. The most popular destination was the aptly named Paradise Harbour. A typical comment was that 'it showed all the magnificent features of nature in one place, I never wanted to leave'.

In an overall summary of the trip the majority of respondents stated that their trip exceeded their expectations. A repeated comment was the notion that the Antarctic was a 'special' environment, which humans did not have the right to alter. The view was also shared that one could

Fig. 18.7.   Antarctica. Foreground: Gentoo penguins; centre: *Kapitan Dranitsyn*; background: dramatic
Antarctic landscape. Source: Ross K. Dowling.

only truly appreciate the size, beauty and harshness of the continent by seeing it first hand.

The current management mix of guidelines
and operator-provided education seems likely to
continue but with larger ships now plying the
Antarctic, it may be necessary to limit the number of landing sites that some of the larger ships
can visit.

Impacts of Antarctic Tourism

Tourism in the Antarctic is frequently portrayed
as an activity that is threatening the Antarctic
environment. However, the continent is still a

relatively pristine area and the operation of
some of the scientific stations has previously
been cited as having despoiled the environment.
Generally though, Antarctica is the least disturbed continent but the growth in the tourism
industry is adding new challenges for wildlife,
increasing the potential for disturbance and disease introduction. To overcome some of these
problems it has been suggested that remediation
of contaminated sites, removal of wastes and
disused buildings, prevention of exotic species
and disease introduction, and use of alternative
energy systems should be considered by all
national Antarctic programmes (Australian
Antarctic Division, 1995).

Table 18.3.   Tourist opinions on their Antarctic visit, 2001.

	1	2		3	4	5
Statement	Strongly agree	Agree	% SA & A	Neutral	Disagree	Strongly disagree
The condition of the Antarctic was excellent	36	15	**93**	0	4	0
The lecturers and other staff were helpful	45	10	**100**	0	0	0
The landings were well managed (quality)	42	9	**93**	4	0	0
I enjoyed the scheduled activities	40	10	**91**	5	0	0

Table 18.4. Tourists' satisfaction with facilities and services provided in the Antarctic, 2001.

	Satisfied					Dissatisfied		
	1	2	% SA&A	3	4	5	NR[a]	NA[b]
Ship								
Officers and crew	41	14	100	0	0	0	0	0
Bridge visits	39	16	100	0	0	0	0	0
Lecture theatre	26	29	100	0	0	0	0	0
Expedition lecturers	48	6	98	0	0	0	1	0
On-board facilities	35	16	93	4	0	0	0	0
Library	21	24	82	9	0	0	1	0
Landings								
Landing craft	46	9	100	0	0	0	0	0
Crew assistance	47	8	100	0	0	0	0	0
Wildlife viewed	44	10	98	1	0	0	0	0
The natural environment	49	5	98	1	0	0	0	0
Landing sites	37	12	89	6	0	0	0	0

[a]NR = no response.
[b]NA = not applicable.

Antarctic tourism activities can be placed into perspective when it is realized that the effects of the tourist industry on the Antarctic may be estimated as 0.52% of the total human impact (Headland, 1994). The other 99.48% can be attributed to scientists and their support staff. It is also sometimes overlooked that Antarctic tourism is highly concentrated at several high-profile sites in the Antarctic peninsula region and that the rest of Antarctica is practically never visited by tourists. This concentration of tourism activities raises questions of the potential for overvisitation of certain sites, but one should not infer from this that all of Antarctica is under threat from tourist visits. As Bauer (2001) notes, the abundance of many species of Antarctic wildlife is also often ignored and, unlike at other prime wildlife destinations such as the Galapagos Islands, Antarctic wildlife populations are substantial.

Environmental impacts

Beck (1994) points out that all human activities in Antarctica, whether conducted by scientists, tourists or others, exert environmental impacts, but it has also been observed that cruise ship passengers ashore in the Antarctic are well behaved and do not drop litter, know-ingly trample vegetation or interfere seriously with wildlife (Stonehouse, 1994). Supporting this view, the Australian Antarctic Division's field equipment and training officer, Rod Ledingham, states that '[t]he environmental impact [of tourism] is minuscule compared with that of long-term expeditions in national operations' (Whelan, 1996, p. 86), and he adds that 'the population of the region's government bases average . . . about 200 times that of the tourists, none of whom drives a vehicle, eats, sleeps or excretes on the continent' (1996, p. 87). Whelan (1996, p. 87) concludes: 'I believe that both scientists and tourists have the right to visit Antarctica, but everyone should adhere to the rigorous environmental standards required to protect our planet's last great wilderness'. These comments are in line with the observations of the authors who have participated in 16 voyages to Antarctica as either guides and/or lecturers (Bauer and Dowling, 2003, Plate 2).

Because of the high visitor concentration at only relatively few landing sites, the impacts of tourism at the most visited sites need to be monitored. Furthermore, there is the risk of general pollution by sewage, waste, oil, fuels and noise from ships and zodiacs.

To minimize the potential impact of tourism operations, tour operators must satisfy the environmental impact assessment procedures that are specified under the *Protocol on Environmental Protection to the Antarctic Treaty*. Under the protocol any human activity that has more than a minor or transitory impact is subject to the completion of an initial environmental evaluation (IEE) or, where appropriate, a comprehensive environmental evaluation (CEE). As tourism to Antarctica booms, ensuring responsible travel there becomes increasingly important for the industry and governments alike (Smailes, 2004).

Marine incidents

Antarctica is largely a pristine area and concern has been raised in some quarters that tourist shipping may pose a serious environmental risk to the environment. Since tourism began, there have been several marine incidents, the most famous one involving the Argentinean supply vessel *Bahia Paraiso*, which on 28 January 1989 ran aground off the US Palmer Station. All crew and passengers were evacuated before the ship sank spilling 600,000 l of fuel into the pristine waters. By Antarctic standards, the damage done to the environment was substantial. In 2002, IAATO (2002, e-mail communication) pointed out that since 1991, when the organization was established, seven shipping-related incidents have occurred in Antarctica. These include three temporary groundings of ships: one that was beset in the ice; two with propeller damage; and one oil leak that resulted in the spillage of a small amount of gearbox/TEBO pressure oil. None of these marine incidents led to environmental damage. Given that up to 2002 there had been some 800 tourist voyages, the number of incidents has been very small. All vessels are required to have the Convention on the Prevention of Pollution on Ships (MARPOL), Safety of Life at Sea (SOLAS), Shipboard Oil Pollution Emergency Plans (SOPEP) and other international conventions in place in order to operate in Antarctic waters. Environmental impacts of ships in Antarctica include emissions from engines (air pollution), noise that may interfere with the wildlife (mainly from outboard engines used on

the inflatable zodiacs), discarding of waste (although this is prohibited inside the Antarctic Treaty area south of 60° S latitude).

As larger ships with 1000 or more passengers start visiting the region (even though they do not land passengers), there is also increased concern of the potential for a large-scale marine accident. Should a large vessel be disabled by hitting an uncharted rock, the damage to the environment could be substantial. Ships carry oil slick containment equipment, but how effective this would really be in Antarctica is untested. Of course there is also the danger to human life in a region where only very limited rescue facilities exist and where the nearest hospital able to deal with large numbers of insured passengers is perhaps 2–3 days' sailing away.

To date, all indications are that tourists and tour operators have complied with industry guidelines and Antarctic Treaty recommendations. Beginning with Lars-Eric Lindblad and continuing with IAATO members, tour operators have been proactive in their measures to protect the resource on which their businesses depend – the Antarctic environment. Consequently, the negative environmental impacts caused by ship-based Antarctic tourism have been negligible.

Conclusion

Cruise tourism in the Antarctic is cold-climate tourism that takes place in a setting without a local population and without tourism infrastructure. It is wilderness tourism at its best offering thousands of environment-sensitive visitors the chance to visit the world's last great frontier (Fig. 18.8). As in all other cruising regions, the possibility of a serious marine incident exists, but at this stage of its development Antarctic cruise shipping does not pose an unacceptably high risk to the environment. As long as responsible best practices in the preparation and execution of cruises are used, Antarctic cruise shipping will continue to be a sustainable activity.

Fig. 18.8. Passengers aboard the *Akademik Sergei Vavilov* admire the scenic beauty of the southern end of the Lemaire Channel in the Antarctic Peninsula. Source: Thomas Bauer.

References

Australian Antarctic Division (1995) *Looking South: The Australian Antarctic Program in a Changing World*. Kingston, Tasmania.

Bauer, Th.G. (2001) *Tourism in the Antarctic: Opportunities, Constraints and Future Prospects*. The Haworth Hospitality Press, Binghamton, New York.

Bauer, T. and Dowling, R.K. (2003) Ecotourism policies and issues in Antarctica. In: Fennell, D.A. and Dowling, R.K. (eds) *Ecotourism Policy and Planning*. CAB International, Wallingford, UK, pp. 309–330.

Beck, P. (1994) Managing Antarctic tourism – a front burner issue. *Annals of Tourism Research* 21(2), 375–386.

Dowling, R.K. (2002) Tourism in Antarctica. *Journal of Tourism* 5(1), 123–132.

Headland, R.K. (1994) Historical development of Antarctic tourism. *Annals of Tourism Research* 21(2), 269–280.

Heap, J. (ed.) (1990) *Handbook of the Antarctic Treaty System*, 7th edn. Polar Publications, Scott Polar Research Institute, University of Cambridge.

IAATO (2005) Available at: http://image.zenn.net/REPLACE/CLIENT/1000037/1000115/application/pdf/IAATONnewsletterMay2005.pdf

National Science Foundation (1997) *Notes from the Seventh Antarctic Tour Operators Meeting*. National Science Foundation, Arlington, Virginia.

Smailes, B. (2004) Heat is on as Antarctic business booms. *Cruise Passenger* 16, 35–37.

Stonehouse, B. (1994) Ecotourism in Antarctica. In: Cater, E. and Lowman, G. (eds) *Ecotourism: A Sustainable Option?* John Wiley and Sons, London, pp. 195–212.

Whelan, H. (1996) Antarctica's new explorers. *Australian Geographic* 42, 80–97. Available at: www.antdiv.gov.au/information/aboutus/division.asp

19 Round-the-world Cruising: A Geography Created by Geography?

Robert J. McCalla[1] and Jacques J. Charlier[2,3]

[1]Saint Mary's University, Department of Geography, Halifax, Nova Scotia, Canada, B3H 3C3; [2]University of Paris-Sorbonne, Department of Geography, France, 75005; [3]University of Louvain-la-Neuve, Department of Geography, Belgium 1348

Introduction

Cruise shipping is one of the fastest-growing segments of the tourism industry with one of the highest growth rates, be it for demand or for supply (Casteljon and Charlier, 2000; Charlier, 2004; Hall, 2004; Peisley, 2004; Wild and Dearing, 2004). In most cases, cruise ships perform relatively short cruises, with their average duration slightly less than 7 days. Approximately half of the cruises offer a standard 7-day product, allowing for the much-demanded Saturday or Sunday departures and arrivals. Other popular products are of a shorter duration, i.e. 3–4 or 4–5 nights, whereas there is a more limited demand and offer for 10–11 or 14-night cruises. Prices for these longer cruises are more or less proportional to their duration, or even somewhat higher given that they are often offered aboard vessels ranking high in the star system of cruise travel guides such as the *Berlitz Guide* (Ward, 2004). However, in a limited number of cases, some cruise lines arrange much longer voyages that fall into two main categories: (i) repositioning trips, from one world area to another because of the seasonal character of offer and demand for cruising (Charlier and Arnold, 1997 and Chapter 2, this volume); and (ii) what is often described as world cruises (or grand voyages), the most glamorous of which are the round-the-world (RTW) cruises dealt with more in this chapter.

Little has been written about the RTW segment of the cruise industry, and we hope that this chapter will be a valuable addition to the growing body of academic literature dealing with cruise shipping. Its economic importance should not be overestimated, though, and we want to make it clear that this is a marginal segment, and that the bulk of the demand and offer in the cruise industry is for much shorter cruises. We must also immediately indicate that the very long voyages whose geography will be explored below are divided into several shorter segments and that, actually, most passengers stay aboard for shorter periods (2 or 3 weeks) than the 3–4-month-long or so (round the) world cruises under review here.

This chapter proceeds with an overview of how world cruises, especially RTW ones, fit into the overall cruise industry in terms of seasonality and ships dedicated to it. We focus particularly on the RTW cruise season of 2003/04 with the development of the theme that the ships operating RTW cruises define collectively a geography of operations that to a great extent is constrained by the world's geography.

World Cruising in Context

As shown previously (Charlier, 2000), there are several distinct geographical areas where cruises are offered, in some cases year-round and in other cases only on a seasonal basis – a category into which the RTW cruise falls. In 2004, the theoretical number of bed-days offered aboard the 250 cruise ships or so with a capacity of at least 50 lower berths identified by the Swedish consultancy ShipPax (2004) amounted to 105 million of which 102 million were effectively made available if one discounts the 2.7% of the capacity temporarily laid off for various reasons, including the seasonal lay-off of a series of small, older vessels plying the Mediterranean.

As seen in Table 19.1, cruises in North and Central American waters amounted to 57.2% of the world's theoretical offer on a yearly basis, be it in year-round markets like the Caribbean (39.8%) and the Mexican Riviera or Panama (7.2%), or in seasonal markets like Alaska (6.9%) or the north-east Atlantic (3.3%). Even if the share of North and Central America remains by far the highest, there are another two main regional areas for cruising: Europe (24.1%) and the Asia-Pacific region (10.5%).

Within Europe, one finds a year-round market like the Mediterranean (17.8%) and a seasonal market like north-west Europe (6.3%, including transatlantic crossings; included here because most of the islands called at when the crossings are not direct are European islands). The other two year-round markets are the South-east and Far East (5.3%), and the South Pacific and Hawaii (5.2%).

Only the South Pacific and Hawaii cruise area offers a significant number of cruises in the southern hemisphere, but with much less offer during the local winter season, as the detailed capacity figures provided in Table 19.1 on a quarterly basis. The figures also show that there is a series of other smaller regional markets mainly located in the southern hemisphere, such as South America and the Antarctica (2.6%), and Africa (excluding its Mediterranean façade, but including the Macaronesian islands) and the Indian Ocean (1.7% as a whole), again with a limited offer in the southern hemisphere winter. Last and least, there are the world cruises, accounting for 1.2% of the world's theoretical offer in 2004, but with major seasonal contrast and a peak at 4.2% during the first quarter (when South America and the South Pacific are also peaking). Ideally, these world

Table 19.1. Quarterly capacity by regional cruising area, 2004 (% bed-days, lower berths).

	First quarter	Second quarter	Third quarter	Fourth quarter	Year overall
North/Central America	**63.30**	**54.31**	**52.03**	**59.61**	**57.15**
Caribbean/Bahamas	54.46	33.27	25.52	47.31	39.81
Mexican Riviera/Panama	8.83	6.02	4.53	9.39	7.15
Alaska	0.00	12.11	14.86	0.04	6.90
North-east Atlantic	0.01	2.91	7.13	2.77	3.29
Europe	**5.80**	**31.88**	**38.66**	**18.46**	**24.11**
Mediterranean	5.74	22.20	23.90	18.46	17.84
North-west Europe/Transatlantic	0.06	9.68	14.77	0.00	6.27
Asia-Pacific	**12.20**	**8.81**	**8.10**	**13.15**	**10.53**
South-east Asia/Far East	5.14	5.25	4.87	5.82	5.27
South Pacific/Hawaii	7.06	3.56	3.23	7.33	5.26
Rest of the World	**13.10**	**3.28**	**0.71**	**5.67**	**5.52**
South America/Antarctica	6.49	0.90	0.29	3.19	2.64
Africa/Indian Ocean	2.43	1.64	0.38	2.27	1.66
World cruises (incl. RTW)	4.18	0.73	0.04	0.20	1.22
Subtotal active fleet	**94.41**	**98.28**	**99.50**	**96.79**	**97.31**
Laid-up vessels (temporarily)	5.59	1.72	0.50	3.21	2.69
Grand total cruise fleet	**100.00**	**100.00**	**100.00**	**100.00**	**100.00**

Source: Adapted from ShipPax's *Pocket Guide 2004*.

cruises should have been regionalized and the capacity of these ships allocated to the markets where they are effectively sailing, but they have been kept apart here in order to distinguish clearly this particular type of offer from the more conventional, much shorter cruises in these areas. In this way, we focus on world cruises, especially the RTW variety, as a distinct subject.

The seasonality of these regional cruise markets is shown on a monthly basis in Fig. 19.1. It is clearly shown that, as Europe expands its cruise offerings in the summer months, North and Central America and the rest of the world (including world cruises) contract their offerings. This expansion–contraction complementarity is explained on the macro-geographical level by interregional ship migrations between continents taking roughly one-third of the world cruise fleet from one continent to another, and at the meso-geographical level through intraregional repositionings (Chapter 2, this volume).

In order to quantify further the seasonal importance of the world cruises, an intensity index, similar to the well-known location quotient, has been computed (Table 19.2). The index is determined by dividing the monthly shares of world cruises by their average for the year 2004 as a whole (1.2% for all world cruises and 0.8% for the RTW variety). For each of the months of the first quarter, the index is higher than 3.000 indicating a very high concentration of such cruises by the industry overall, especially by certain cruise lines (see below). Technically, there is a shoulder season in April (or at least during the first half of that month), when the index is still higher than 1.000. Also, since some of the world cruises start by mid-December, the index for that month is already nearing 0.500. Because of the shoulder season phenomenon both before and after the first quarter of the year, we will often refer to 2004 world cruising as the 2003/04 season when considering the detailed itineraries of the RTW cruises explored below.

Ships and Shipping Lines Involved in World Cruises

A search of the World Wide Web, published cruise company brochures and travel agent catalogues (especially Cruise Travel International 2004 and ShipPax 2004) elicited 14 ships that *advertised* a world cruise during the 2003/04 season (Table 19.3). Ten of these cruises we categorize as RTW; the other four, although advertised as world

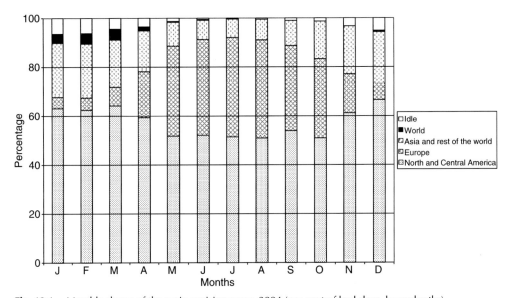

Fig. 19.1. Monthly shares of the main cruising areas, 2004 (per cent of bed-days, lower berths).

Table 19.2. Monthly cruise capacity for world cruises, especially round-the-world cruises, 2004.

	All world cruises			Of which round-the-world cruises		
	Lower berths	% of world total	Intensity index	Lower berths	% of world total	Intensity index
January	311,984	3.77	3.093	202,788	2.45	3.182
February	339,706	4.32	3.544	220,809	2.81	3.650
March	381,284	4.44	3.642	247,835	2.89	3.753
April	134,220	1.59	1.306	87,432	1.04	1.351
May	29,388	0.32	0.265	20,150	0.22	0.286
June	28,440	0.32	0.265	0	0	0
July	11,284	0.12	0.099	0	0	0
August	0	0.00	0.000	0	0	0
September	0	0.00	0.000	0	0	0
October	0	0.00	0.000	0	0	0
November	0	0.00	0.000	0	0	0
December	53,444	0.58	0.479	35,154	0.38	0.494
Overall	1,289,704	1.22	–	814,168	0.77	–

cruises, were in fact circumnavigations of a continent only or were restricted sailings within one or two oceans. The average gross registered tonnage (GRT) and average number of lower berths of RTW cruise ships amounted, respectively, to 40,181 GRT and 946 lower berths, whereas the figures for the other four ships performing non-RTW world cruises were 54,607 GRT and 1299 lower berths. Not only were these four ships larger than the ten RTW ships but they were also much younger (average building year was 1999, against 1982 or 1983 for RTW ships). The main reason for different average sizes may be port constraints limiting the size of RTW vessels more so than non-RTW cruise ships. The difference in average ages is probably because very few cruise ships built recently are capable of making true RTW cruises (the exception is *Queen Mary 2*, but see below). Moreover, the older vessels employed in RTW cruises have excellent sea-going characteristics much valued by their passengers. There is no strict size or age limits to RTW and non-RTW ships. *Oriana*, for example, has already performed RTW cruises in the recent past, and the *Delphin Renaissance* is due to offer RTW cruises in 2006/07 after performing non-RTW world cruises in 2003/04 and in 2004/05.

Within both the RTW and the non-RTW ships one finds panamax-sized vessels. Vessels in the 69,000–77,500 GRT bracket, like P&O's *Aurora*, Crystal's *Crystal Serenity* and Cunard's *Queen Elizabeth 2*, are among the RTW ships, and P&O's *Adonia* and *Oriana* are listed among the non-RTW ships. Thus, size, per se, does not seem to be a distinguishing feature of RTW vessels. Also, within both groups there are smaller 'handy-sized' vessels ranging from 20,000 to 40,000 GRT. Being panamax-sized is a quasi *sine qua non* condition to qualify as an RTW ship, because most RTW cruises intend to use the Panama Canal shortcut, although there are exceptions from time to time. For example, in the 2003/04 season Saga Shipping's *Saga Rose*, the third smallest RTW vessel, bypassed Panama by sailing around Cape Horn (see below). The other notable exception of avoiding the Panama Canal during an RTW cruise was the sailing of the former Compagnie Générale Transatlantique's *France*, in 1971 and 1972 via the Horn route. In this case, the *France* was an overpanamax vessel.

It is highly unlikely that today's largest cruise ship, Cunard's recently launched *Queen Mary 2* (142,200 GRT), will ever offer a true RTW cruise although it has the capability. The ship is an overpanamax vessel and, thus, would need to follow the Horn route in a world circumnavigation (Charlier, 2004). Given her size, and the limited market for world cruising, it is unlikely that such a routing would be commercially viable. However, the *Queen Mary 2* is designed to undertake long voyages besides

Table 19.3. Technical characteristics of the cruise ships performing world cruises in 2003/04.

Ship	Cruise line	Year built	Gross registered tonnage	Length (m)	Beam (m)	Draft (m)	Lower berths	Total berths	Berlitz rating (%)
A: round-the-world cruises									
Albatros	Phoenix Reisen	1973	28,518	205.5	25.2	8.9	824	1,000	–
Astor	Transocean	1987	20,606	176.5	22.6	5.8	590	656	72.5
Aurora	P&O Cruises	2001	76,152	270.0	32.2	7.9	1,878	2,290	77.4
Black Watch	Fred Olsen Lines	1972	28,668	205.5	25.2	7.3	775	821	71.5
Crystal Serenity	Crystal Cruises	2003	68,870	250.0	32.2	7.8	1,096	1,140	87.8
Deutschland	Deilmann Rederei	1998	22,496	175.4	23.0	5.8	604	613	–
Maxim Gorkiy	Phoenix Reisen	1969	24,220	194.7	26.6	8.3	650	880	69.3
Prinsendam	Holland America Line	1988	37,845	204.0	28.9	7.1	766	843	83.5
Queen Elizabeth 2	Cunard Line	1969	70,327	293.5	32.0	9.9	1,660	1,791	68.7–87.1
Saga Rose	Saga Shipping	1965	24,108	188.9	26.6	8.3	620	747	71.2
B: other world cruises									
Adonia	P&O Cruises	1998	77,499	261.3	32.3	8.1	2,022	2,342	76.9
Delphin Renaissance	Delphin Seereisen	2000	30,277	181.0	25.5	6.0	698	777	–
Oriana	P&O Cruises	1995	69,153	260.0	32.2	7.9	1,760	1,804	76.5
Seven Seas Voyager	Radisson Seven Seas	2003	41,500	206.5	28.8	7.0	714	768	85.2

transatlantic crossings and conventional cruises, and she might, in future, offer non-RTW world cruises to Asia and Australia via the Suez Canal and/or the Cape of Good Hope.

In general, though, being panamax-sized is a must for world cruises. As a consequence, in the late 1960s, Cunard's *Queen Elizabeth 2* was conceived in a dual role of transatlantic liner and world cruiser, meaning that her length and beam are somewhat smaller than for her great predecessors on the North Atlantic, Cunard's *Queen Mary 1* and *Queen Elizabeth 1*, as well as Compagnie Générale Transatlantique's *Normandie*.

World cruises in general and RTW in particular are offered only by a few cruise lines, most of which are European-based. To offer a world cruise requires much expertise, not found in all the world's cruise lines. European lines have developed this expertise partly based on their need to deploy their vessels at a time when cruising is at its lowest level in European waters (see Table 19.1). Most of the major US-based lines have no need to redeploy their ships elsewhere in the northern hemisphere winter when cruising is at its peak in what is their backdoor, i.e. the Caribbean and the Mexican Riviera or Panama canal. Holland American Line (part of Carnival Corporation) and Crystal are exceptions to this generality, but both only contribute one ship to world cruising.

Consequently, the leaders in this highly particular segment are either British or German lines, even though they also cater to significant numbers of North American customers, especially on the British vessels. The industry leader is by far P&O Cruises, with three panamax-sized ships in 2003/04, one of which (*Aurora*, the newest of the trio) performed a world cruise qualifying technically as an RTW cruise. One German line, Phoenix Reisen, operated two RTW cruises in 2003/04 aboard its *Albatros* and *Maxim Gorkiy*, whose combined capacity is smaller, however, than for the one P&O ship *Aurora*. Otherwise, world cruises are one-ship operations for the other lines, with Transocean's *Astor*, Fred Olsen's *Black Watch*, Crystal's *Crystal Serenity*, Deilmann's *Deutschland*, Holland America's *Prinsendam* and Saga Shipping's *Saga Rose* offering RTW cruises, and Delphin Seerederei's *Delphin Renaissance* and Radisson

Seven Seas' *Seven Seas Voyager* operating non-RTW cruises.

World cruising vessels can also be distinguished by their Berlitz rating (Ward, 2004). At the top end of the ratings are vessels scoring in the 80% category (Table 19.3). Cunard's *Queen Elizabeth 2* falls into this category but only in its Grill class where it is rated at 87.1%, slightly below the 87.8% featured by Crystal's *Crystal Serenity*, currently ranked as the most luxurious ship in service. Two other world cruises are offered aboard ships whose Berlitz rating is higher than 80%: the non-RTW vessel, Radisson's *Seven Seas Voyager* (85.2%); and the RTW ship, Holland America's *Prinsendam* (83.5%). This ranking for the *Prinsendam* is less than her previous rating when she was known as the *Royal Viking Sun*, the then highest rated luxury ship in the world.

At the lower end of the ratings are RTW ships rated in the high 60s and low to middle 70s. Interestingly, the *Queen Elizabeth 2* also scores in this lower range in its Mauritania class. The RTW German ships, *Maxim Gorkiy* and *Astor*, and the British ships, *Saga Rose*, *Black Watch* and *Aurora* all have lesser ranks than their luxurious competitors. It is likely that the not yet rated *Deutschland* of Deilmann Rederei probably deserves a Berlitz rating above the 80% mark, and Phoenix's not yet rated 'new' *Albatros* should be rated in the low 70% range, which is slightly better than the even older ship of the same name she replaced in 2003, whose ranking was well below 70%.

RTW cruising is therefore not just an affair of luxurious ships and very high fares. There is a tale of two stories with highly rated vessels on the one hand (generally newer and larger) and lower rated ships on the other hand.

Finally, world cruises are often an affair of tradition, with the same lines and the same ships (or their successors) at the forefront. Table 19.4 lists all ships for which world cruises, both RTW and non-RTW, were advertised since the 1999/2000 winter season. Repeaters (ships and companies) are shown in bold. Particularly of note are the repeat cruises made each year by the Phoenix's *Albatros* (two different vessels of the same name) and *Maxim Gorkiy*, P&O's *Oriana*, Cunard's *Queen Elizabeth 2*, Saga's *Saga Rose* and Transocean's *Astor*. Other companies, besides the ones associated with the

Table 19.4. Round-the-world and other world cruise ships, 2000/04.

Ship	Cruise line	GRT	2000	2001	2002	2003	2004
Adonia	P&O Cruises	77,499	X	X	X	No	Yes
Albatros (former)	Phoenix Reisen	24,803	Yes	Yes	Yes	Yes	X
Albabros (current)	Phoenix Reisen	28,518	X	X	X	X	Yes
Astor	Transocean Tours	20,606	Yes	Yes	Yes	Yes	Yes
Asuka	NYK Line	28,717	Yes	No	Yes	Yes	No
Aurora	P&O Cruises	76,152	X	X	Yes	Yes	Yes
Black Watch	Fred Olsen Lines	28,668	No	No	No	No	Yes
Christopher Columbus	Hapag-Lloyd	28,717	No	Yes	No	No	No
Crystal Symphony	Crystal Cruises	51,044	Yes	Yes	Yes	Yes	Yes
Crystal Serenity	Crystal Cruises	68,870	X	X	X	X	Yes
Delphin	Delphin Seereisen	16,214	Yes	Yes	Yes	Yes	Yes
Delphin Renaissance	Delphin Seereisen	30,277	X	X	X	X	Yes
Deutschland	Deilmann Reederei	22,496	Yes	No	Yes	Yes	Yes
Europa	Hapag-Lloyd	28,497	Yes	Yes	No	No	No
Maxim Gorkiy	Phoenix Reisen	24,220	Yes	Yes	Yes	Yes	Yes
Nippon Maru	MOSK Cruises	21,903	Yes	Yes	Yes	No	No
Oriana	P&O Cruises	69,153	Yes	Yes	Yes	Yes	Yes
Prinsendam	Holland America Line	37,845	X	X	Yes	Yes	Yes
Rotterdam	Holland America Line	59,652	Yes	Yes	No	No	No
Royal Princess	Princess Cruises	44,348	No	Yes	No	No	No
Seven Seas Voyager	Radisson Seven Seas	41,500	X	X	X	X	Yes
Queen Elizabeth 2	Cunard Line	70,327	Yes	Yes	Yes	Yes	Yes
Saga Rose	Saga Shipping	24,108	Yes	Yes	Yes	Yes	Yes
Seabourn Sun	Seabourn Cruise Line	37,845	No	Yes	X	X	X
Silver Wind	Silversea Cruise Line	16,927	No	Yes	No	No	No
Victoria	P&O Cruises	28,891	Yes	No	No	No	No

Note: X = ships taken from service or not yet built.

ships named, which have offered world cruises each year since 2000, are Crystal, Delphin Seereisen and Holland America. Two Japanese vessels, NYK Line's *Asuka* and MOSK Cruises' *Nippon Maru*, do not qualify in our list of *winter* world cruises, as the grand voyages they offered during 3 of the 5 years under review were, actually, long *summer* cruises in the Pacific Basin.

Considering that there are approximately 250 cruise ships in the world operated by about 50 different companies, the world cruise club is, indeed, selective and exclusive, much like the passenger market it caters to.

The Geography of RTW Cruises, 2003/04

The RTW cruise itinerary can be described both geographically, the *where*, and temporally, the *when*. Geographical descriptors include embarkation and disembarkation ports, directions, longitude and latitude ranges, waters cruised and ports called. Time descriptors include beginning and end dates and duration. By analysing these two broad characteristics we can see both common characteristics and unique distinctions that differentiate one cruise from another.

Embarkation and disembarkation ports

Table 19.5 illustrates the embarkation and disembarkation ports of various ships. The majority of cruises begin at a European port. In 2004 seven cruises began on that continent, the other three began in North America. Not all RTW cruises end their cruises in their embarkation ports. *Queen Elizabeth 2* does not even end on the same continent that belies the designation of RTW voyage. *Queen Elizabeth 2* begins her cruise in New York and ends it in Southampton. Three other vessels, *Deutschland*, *Crystal Serenity* and *Prinsendam*, are also not truly performing RTW cruises although the *Deutschland* at least starts and ends in the same sea (the Mediterranean). The other two begin on one side of North America and end on the other, thus avoiding passage through the Panama Canal, even though they are panamax-sized and capable of making the voyage.

The most popular embarkation and disembarkation port is Southampton. The only other multiple embarkation port is Los Angeles. Southampton is also the most popular end point of RTW cruises. New York is the port of disembarkation for two cruises (the same two that began in Los Angeles). The other cruises start and end uniquely in ports of Europe. The embarkation and disembarkation ports of the various ships are indicative of the markets the ships serve. *Albatros*, *Astor*, *Deutchland* and *Maxim Gorkiy* cater primarily to German-speaking passengers. *Aurora*, *Black Watch* and *Saga Rose* cater to British passengers. *Crystal Serenity* and *Prinsendam* focus primarily on the American market. Finally, the *Queen Elizabeth 2* is aimed at an English-speaking market of primarily American and British passengers.

Direction and latitudinal range

Table 19.6 depicts direction and range of RTW cruises. Only one of the cruises is from east to west; all the others take a westerly track, which is the preferred direction in past years also. The exception is the *Maxim Gorkiy*, which is also the only cruise that is in both North Pacific and North Atlantic waters. She makes the passage from Tokyo to Honolulu in the Pacific and from Halifax to Ponta Delgado (Azores) in the Atlantic. In the Pacific Ocean, the *Maxim Gorkiy* quickly moves from northern waters to tropical ones with port calls at Guam and the Marshall Islands before arriving in Honolulu. The westerlies in the Atlantic Ocean assist her in its passage but she must fight against the north-east trades in the Pacific passage. All the other ships, by taking a western circumnavigation, are helped by the winds. North of the equator in both the Atlantic and Pacific oceans, crossings are assisted by the north-east trades, whereas south of the equator, ships take advantage of the south-east trades.

Most RTW cruises make an equatorial circumnavigation; however, their polar range is restricted even though all cruises operate in both the northern and southern hemispheres. The greatest north–south extent of any of the cruises is made by the *Saga Rose* at 112° latitude, ranging from 50.90° N (Southampton) to 61.17° S (Elephant Island). The most limited

Table 19.5. Embarkation and disembarkation ports.

Ship	Embarkation port	Disembarkation port
Albatros	Monte Carlo	Monte Carlo
Astor	Nice	Nice
Aurora	Southampton	Southampton
Black Watch	Southampton	Southampton
Crystal Serenity	Los Angeles	New York
Deutschland	Genoa	Piraeus
Maxim Gorkiy	Bremen	Bremen
Prinsendam	Los Angeles	New York
Queen Elizabeth 2	New York	Southampton
Saga Rose	Southampton	Southampton

range is 71° by the *Maxim Gorkiy*. Although she has the most northerly penetration of any of the cruises (53.08° N at Bremen, her start and end points), the *Maxim Gorkiy* only ventures to 18.17° S (Madagascar) in the southern hemisphere. Only the *Maxim Gorkiy* and *Crystal Serenity* do not go to Auckland, which greatly limits their southern extent. For the most part RTW cruises operate between 40° N and 36° S with some extensions in the northern hemisphere to embarkation and disembarkation ports, and in the southern hemisphere to call at New Zealand ports or southern Australian ports and, on one occasion, to make a foray to the Antarctic continent margin. These southern hemisphere extensions are only possible because in January and February, the time when most of the cruises are making their southern latitudes calls, the southern hemisphere is experiencing its summer season.

Waters cruised

By dividing the world into 30° latitude and longitude blocks, one can get an appreciation of those parts of the oceans most frequented by RTW cruise ships. No block was visited by all ten RTW ships in 2003/04, but two of the blocks – 0–30° N longitude and 60–90° W latitude, and 30–60° N longitude and 0–30° W longitude – were visited by nine of the vessels. The former area encompasses the Caribbean Sea and the Panama Canal. The latter takes in the entrance

Table 19.6. Direction and range of round-the-world cruises, 2003/04.

Ship	Direction of travel	Latitude range	
		Most northerly	Most southerly
Albatros	Westbound	Monte Carlo 43.73° N	Auckland 36.92° S
Astor	Westbound	Nice 43.42° N	Auckland 36.92° S
Aurora	Westbound	Southampton 50.90° N	Auckland 36.92° S
Black Watch	Westbound	Southampton 50.90° N	Launceston 41.41° S
Crystal Serenity	Westbound	New York 40.70° N	Cape Town 33.93° S
Deutschland	Westbound	Genoa 44.41° N	Milford Sound, NZ 44.68° S
Maxim Gorkiy	Eastbound	Bremen 53.08° N	Toamasina, Madagascar 18.17° S
Prinsendam	Westbound	New York 40.70° N	Dunedin 45.87° S
Queen Elizabeth 2	Westbound	Southampton 50.90° N	Christchurch 43.55° S
Saga Rose	Westbound	Southampton 50.90° N	Elephant Island 61.17° S

to the Mediterranean Sea at Gibraltar and the west coast of Europe. Conversely, there were vast areas of the world's oceans not visited by RTW cruise ships. These include the North Pacific waters, the Arctic waters and many of the southern hemisphere quadrants above 30° S. The exceptions are the quadrants encompassing New Zealand and Australia and those around the tip of Africa and the Cape of Good Hope. Figure 19.2 shows quite well the importance of the 0–30° N band where between 150° W and 150° E longitudes in each of the quadrants at least half of the 2003/04 RTW cruise ships passed.

Ports called

No port was visited by all ten RTW cruise ships. Auckland, Sydney and Singapore received eight of the ships; Hong Kong and Bangkok received seven. The ships missing Auckland and Sydney were the *Maxim Gorkiy* and *Crystal Serenity*, which opted to visit north-east Asia (Taiwan and Japan) rather than Australia–New Zealand in their itinerary. However, they both stopped at Singapore and Hong Kong. The two ships that bypassed Singapore were the *Black Watch* and

Saga Rose. They were the only two to make a southern Indian Ocean crossing from Australia to Mauritius, thus missing South-east Asia and the Indian subcontinent entirely. The itinerary of the *Saga Rose* was unique among the cruise ships. Not only did she make the southern Indian crossing but she was also the only ship to visit Antarctic waters, the west coast of South America, and Easter Island.

Ports called at by at least half of the RTW ships are shown in Table 19.7. These 11 ports

Table 19.7. Favoured ports of call, round-the-world cruises, 2003/04.

Port	Number of calls
Singapore	8
Auckland	8
Sydney	8
Hong Kong	7
Funchal, Canary Islands	7
Bangkok (Laem Chabang)	7
Mumbai	6
Honolulu	6
Pago Pago, American Samoa	5
Yokohama/Tokyo	5
Acapulco	5

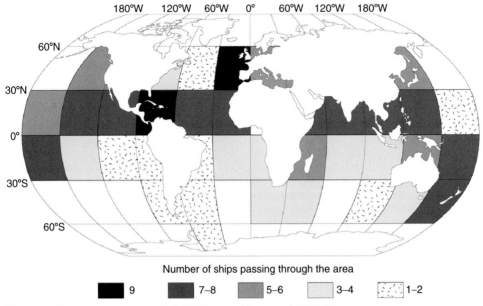

Number of ships passing through the area

■ 9　■ 7–8　■ 5–6　□ 3–4　░ 1–2

Fig. 19.2. Ocean areas through which RTW cruise ships passed, 2003/04.

define the favoured cruising stops of the RTW voyages. Yokohama, Hong Kong, Bangkok, Singapore and Mumbai represent ports of call in Asia. Sydney and Auckland were the most frequented ports in Australia–New Zealand. Honolulu and Pago Pago were way-stops on the crossing of the Pacific Ocean. Acapulco was visited by at least half the ships and represented the most popular port of call on the west coast of the Americas. Funchal was a favoured stop in the eastern Atlantic for ships coming up from the South Atlantic or crossing the Atlantic. None of these ports is in the US mainland, which is quite surprising given the American dominance on the passenger lists of some RTW cruises. As they are mainly catering to British or German passengers, four of the ships – *Black Watch*, *Astor*, *Albatros* and *Saga Rose* – did not even call in the US mainland. The remaining ships divided their west coast calls among Los Angeles (3 calls), San Francisco (2) and San Diego (1), whereas on the east coast, calls are made at either New York (3) or Fort Lauderdale (3).

Timing and duration

The start and end dates and duration of the cruises are shown in Table 19.8. All RTW cruises took place in the northern hemisphere winter with some even starting before the turn of the calendar year. They all ended in the spring. These start and end dates allowed for the escape of European and American residents (the majority of RTW passengers) from the harshness of the winter season. It is not surprising that all cruises sailed south and into the tropics as soon as possible, and continued into the southern hemisphere. By the time the ships returned to their ports of disembarkation in the northern hemisphere the season had changed to spring with warmer less harsh conditions.

As Table 19.8 shows cruises ranging from 80 to 159 days with an average duration of 115 days. Different cruise lengths mean different itineraries were followed with more or less ports visited and with more or less time spent in them. For example, the 80-day world cruise of the *Aurora* made only 24 port calls; the 159-day cruise of the *Deutschland* featured 71 calls. *Aurora* was in most ports for only 10 h or less, arriving in the morning and leaving in the early

evening. *Deutschland*, on the other hand, was in some ports for 48 h and even 71 h in one case (Honolulu) to allow for a change of passengers for those who opted to purchase only partial itineraries. Also, not all ships cruise at the same speed, thus affecting the cruise duration.

Table 19.8 shows the duration of the entire RTW voyage. However, all RTW cruises allow passengers to join and leave the cruise at critical key intermediate ports. Thus, the RTW voyage can be seen as a series of segments. These segments may be as long as 76 nights (Valparaiso to Southampton on the *Saga Rose*) or as short as 18 days (Southampton to Montego Bay on the *Black Watch*). It is important that the intermediate embarkation and disembarkation ports be close to large international airports to allow for the convenient transfer of passengers. Thus, places such as Singapore, Auckland, Mumbai and Sydney are intermediate embarkation and disembarkation ports for at least half of the RTW cruises offered in 2003/04.

In summary, RTW cruises have much common geography in terms of ports of embarkation and disembarkation, direction and latitudinal range, waters cruised and ports called, and duration, but there is a great deal of uniqueness offered by individual voyages. Not all RTW cruises are the same; each has its distinctive geography. This uniqueness is a form of differentiation and marketing of the RTW trips, especially in the German and British markets where the competition is the stiffest.

Geographical Influences Determining RTW Cruise Itineraries

Not only is there a geography created by the collective offerings of the RTW cruise voyages but the world's geography is also a contributing factor to *where* and *when* the voyages go. As has already been mentioned, an overriding macro-geographical factor is the world's climate. Cruising is a local warm season experience. Another overriding factor explaining the RTW cruise route is the arrangement of the continents and the necessity to get around them or through them. Vital 'choke points' must be negotiated. Also, the sheer size of the world's oceans and the positions of key islands within that vastness are important factors in planning

Table 19.8. Timing and duration of round-the-world cruises, 2003/04.

Ship	Start	End	Duration
Albatros	21 December 2003	25 April 2004	127 days
Astor	19 December 2003	10 April 2004	118 days
Aurora	11 January 2004	1 April 2004	80 days
Black Watch	5 January 2004	20 April 2004	106 days
Crystal Serenity	19 January 2004	5 May 2004	106 days
Deutschland	20 November 2003	14 April 2004	159 days
Maxim Gorkiy	20 December 2003	6 May 2004	140 days
Prinsendam	20 January 2004	7 May 2004	109 days
Queen Elizabeth 2	5 January 2004	20 April 2004	106 days
Saga Rose	5 January 2004	21 April 2004	107 days

the RTW cruise route. Cruise ships must stop for resupply; but just as importantly, passengers want to stop to experience the character of the ports and their immediate surroundings. Finally, the infinite variety of physical and human geography attractions and which ones to include in the itinerary will determine more precisely on a micro-scale the ports of call and even the duration of the cruise. Moreover, RTW cruises are for real sea lovers, also interested in seascapes as opposed to landscapes.

Climate as a factor

All RTW cruise voyages begin in the northern hemisphere winter at ports of embarkation north of 30° N but they quickly proceed to southern warmer waters. Of the 11 most visited ports (Table 19.7), 7 are within 30° N and S of the equator. The fact that only one of the RTW cruises, the one performed by the *Saga Rose*, made its way into Antarctic waters in January means that the cruise is climate-controlled. It is risky business, even at the height of the warm season, to make this journey. This fact is evidenced in the *Saga Rose*'s promotional material (2004): 'The itinerary in Antarctica depends on weather and ice conditions and is at the Master's discretion.' The climatic restriction means that, at that time of the year, no RTW cruises included northern waters such as the Gulf of Alaska, the Baltic Sea, the coast of Norway or the Arctic Ocean in their itinerary. These are popular cruising areas at other, warmer, times. There could be RTW cruises in the northern

hemisphere's summer, but the demand for more lucrative, shorter cruises is too high at that time. There is no need to escape the cold in the northern hemisphere summer. However, just because a water is tropical does not guarantee that many cruise ships will sail there. As shown in Fig. 19.2 the waters off tropical South America are infrequently visited. Also no cruise ship ventures into the Gulf of Guinea in West Africa.

Choke points

The Americas, Africa and the European-Asian landmass present formidable barriers to RTW cruising. The world's two major canals, Panama and Suez, and its most important straits for shipping, Malacca and Gibraltar, are used by most of the RTW cruises to overcome the formidable land barriers. However, not all RTW cruises use these important choke point waters (see Table 19.9).

Panama was used by seven of the vessels. The exceptions were the *Prinsendam* and *Crystal Serenity*, which both began their world cruises on the US west coast but ended them on the US east coast, thus avoiding the Panama Canal; also the *Saga Rose*, which used Cape Horn, was the only ship to venture into this famous but treacherous waterway.

The Suez Canal and the Gibraltar Strait were transited by six vessels; the other four (*Queen Elizabeth 2*, *Black Watch*, *Crystal Serenity* and *Saga Rose*) opted for the Cape of Good Hope route as the way to get around Africa. This route is not as formidable a water passage as

Table 19.9. Number of round-the-world cruises using important choke point waters, 2003/04.

	Westbound	Eastbound	Overall
Panama Canal	6	1	7
Strait of Malacca	7	1	8
Suez Canal	5	1	6
Strait of Gibraltar	5	1	6

Cape Horn, nor is it as far south as Cape Horn and thus not as time-consuming to make the journey. Also Cape Town and other ports of southern Africa are attractions in their own right. However, these four cruises bypassed Mediterranean ports by opting for the more southern route to overcome the African land mass. It may also be that the Suez Canal and the Mediterranean Sea were seen as security concerns to be avoided.

The Strait of Malacca was used by eight of the vessels. As already mentioned, only the *Black Watch* and *Saga Rose* avoided it and the related call in Singapore. In both cases the vessels proceeded directly from Fremantle to Mauritius without making a northern foray into Southeast Asian waters. Again, we see the unique itinerary of the *Saga Rose*, reflecting its willingness to offer a unique itinerary in the highly competitive British market, as well as the fact that, as Cunard's former *Sagafjord*, this vessel earned a high reputation for her seaworthiness and comfort at sea.

The only other way to get around the large land mass of the northern hemisphere is through the north-west and north-east passages of Arctic waters. However, given the timing of the cruises this option is not possible, and even in the best of weather in the northern hemisphere summer season few cruise vessels venture into these waters, especially those of the size of the RTW vessels under study here.

Panama, Suez, Malacca, Gibraltar, Cape of Good Hope and Cape Horn are all important water passages in planning the RTW itinerary. They allow links between the oceans; except for the Cape routes, they shorten distances (and thus save time); they are attractions in their own right. To overcome the Americas two options are available: Panama and Cape Horn. The favoured option is Panama. To overcome Africa, Suez and

the Cape of Good Hope are available. Suez is favoured but the Cape route is viable on the one hand because of the tourist attraction of southern Africa, and on the other hand because some passengers and cruise lines have concerns about sailing in the near and Middle East. To get from the Pacific to the Indian Ocean most cruise lines choose Malacca, but it is possible to make the journey by following a course around southern Australia. The choices made here are some of the most important in defining the geography of RTW cruises.

Overcoming the vastness of the oceans

The sheer size of the oceans is both a plus and a minus to the world cruise itinerary. In a positive sense, the oceans' size and individual characteristics give exotic flavours to the voyage. The oceans allow for the RTW cruise to exist at all. Conversely, the oceans are a physical and psychological challenge to overcome. In traditional cruising operations, such as in the Caribbean or the Mediterranean, ships call at a new port almost every day. In RTW cruising, ships also make frequent port calls, but these stops may not, and cannot, be made every day given the distance required to circumnavigate the globe and the limited time in which to do so. As a rule, the ships making the fastest circumnavigation stop the least and have the longest legs at sea. They are also those whose average cruising speed is the highest. However, when the ships are in South-east Asian waters they often visit a different port every day; when in Australian waters, port calls are usually made every second day.

But, there are certain areas in the circumnavigation where the time between ports is greater than 5 days and may be as long as 8

(Table 19.10). These long-distance legs are necessary, but they are minimized as much as possible by using strategically located islands that become stepping stones across the oceans' vastness. This is particularly the case of the Pacific Ocean. The Hawaiian Islands, the islands of French Polynesia, Samoa Islands and Fiji all have RTW cruise ships stopping at them. In the Indian Ocean, Mauritius, the Seychelles and the Maldives also see RTW cruise ships. The Atlantic sea-crossing is shortened with stops at Madeira or the Canary Islands in the eastern North Atlantic, at Barbados, Antigua and Barbuda, or Guadeloupe in the eastern Caribbean, or St Helena in the South Atlantic.

Table 19.10 shows that many of the longest crossings are found in the Pacific Ocean. There are many combinations of islands used to cross the Pacific, but in general there are two preferred routes (Fig. 19.3): one uses the Hawaiian Islands; the other uses the islands of French Polynesia. In the former case, RTW ships use US west coast ports (San Francisco, Los Angeles or San Diego) and pass through the Hawaiian Islands either on their way to Australia–New Zealand by way of the Samoa Islands, Tonga or Fiji. If the ships are bypassing Australia–New Zealand they pass by way of Guam on their way to or from Japan and north-east Asia. RTW ships using the French Polynesian Islands are all on their way to Australia–New Zealand. These ships do not make US west coast calls; nor do they stop in the Hawaiian Islands. By taking a more southern track across the Pacific and not going to the US west coast they shorten significantly their world RTW journey although the individual link from the Americas to French Polynesia may be very long. The Panama–Marquises passage by the *Black Watch* is the longest single sea link of any of the ships, whereas the Acapulco–Nuka Hiva passage by the *Astor* and *Albatros* is longer than any of the US west coast passages to Hawaii.

Attractions

In planning the RTW cruise itinerary there are literally hundreds of thousands of places that could attract a cruise ship. The decision of which places to visit is constrained by the foregoing factors, but there are still many options open. The varied physical world attracts cruise ships and passengers. Examples abound: the Great Barrier Reef, the fjords of New Zealand's

Table 19.10. Crossing the oceans: the longest legs (at least 4000 km = 5 days).

Ship	To/From	Distance (km)	Time[a]
Pacific Ocean			
Black Watch	Panama/Nuku Hiva	6932	8 days, 16 hours
Crystal Serenity	Lahaina/Guam	6234	7 days, 19 hours
Albatros, Astor	Acapulco/Nuku Hiva	5212	6 days, 12 hours
Deutschland	San Diego/Honolulu	4195	5 days, 6 hours
Queen Elizabeth 2, Aurora, Prinsendam	Honolulu/Pago Pago	4194	5 days, 6 hours
Queen Elizabeth 2	Los Angeles/Honolulu	4118	5 days, 3 hours
Atlantic Ocean			
Prinsendam	Funchal/Fort Lauderdale	6079	7 days, 14 hours
Aurora, Deutschland	Funchal/Bridgetown	4835	6 days, 2 hours
Albatros	Funchal/Pointe-à-Pitre	4824	6 days, 1 hour
Astor	Funchal/Saint Johns (Antigua and Barbuda)	4806	6 days
Crystal Serenity	St Helena/Rio de Janeiro	4000	5 days
Indian Ocean			
Black Watch, Saga Rose	Fremantle/St Louis (Mauritius)	5893	8 days, 9 hours

[a]Based on an average speed of 18 knots.

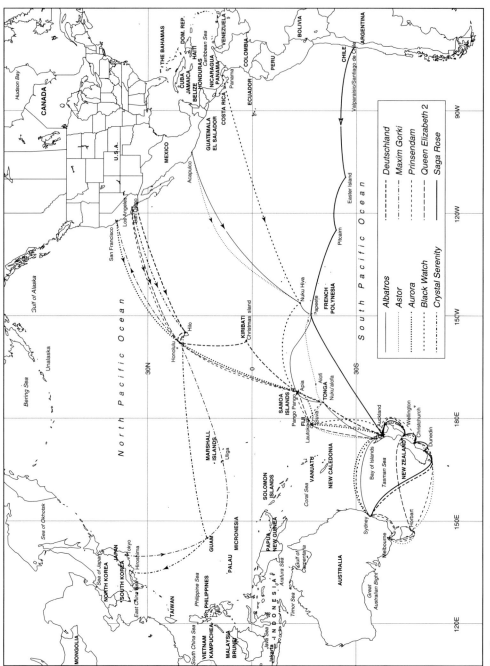

Fig. 19.3. Pacific crossing, RTW cruise ships, 2003/04.

South Island and the tropical beaches of the South Pacific islands are all high on the list of places to visit. The unique itinerary of the *Saga Rose* taking her into Antarctica and Easter Island is primarily explained by the physical attractions of these places. But physical geography alone does not determine the cruise itinerary. Cultural attractions, including airports to allow for transfers, are just as important. What else explains visits to some of the world's greatest cities such as Hong Kong, Mumbai or Tokyo?

Some RTW cruises allow for land excursions to, for example, the Great Pyramids of Egypt, the architectural ruins of Greece or the temples of Thailand. It is difficult to categorize the itineraries of RTW cruise ships by the physical and cultural features that the ships allow the passengers to experience. It is highly doubtful that a passenger would choose to go on an RTW cruise simply because the ship will be going to one or two places the passenger wants to visit. The choice to make an RTW cruise depends more on the company offering the cruise, the ship itself and its on-board amenities, and the total itinerary of the cruise or the particular interest in a given segment. Individual attractions are all part of the total package. A passenger wishing to visit a certain place does not need to take an RTW cruise to go there.

In sum, the world's geography determines to a great extent the routings of RTW cruise ships. The world's climate, the configuration of the continents and the oceans with important choke points, and overcoming long distances across the oceans are major macro-geographical factors at work to explain the RTW cruise routes. Actual ports of call and the shore-based excursions should be seen as micro-scale phenomena in explaining the exact RTW cruise ship itinerary.

The World according to RTW cruising

An RTW cruise can only give a selective flavour of the world. How much of the world can one see in 100 days, especially at an average speed of 18 knots? What type of world is represented in the RTW cruise experience?

As a generalization the world of RTW cruising is a water world, a warm world, a world of selected ports and islands. As such, the RTW world does not represent the variety of the earth; nor does it try to. However, even in the world it represents there are large gaps.

Consider the water world. RTW cruise ships miss out large areas of the world's seas. The most obvious gaps are the Arctic Ocean and the southern oceans bordering on Antarctica. Also missing or infrequently visited are the waters of western South America and the West African coast in the Gulf of Guinea, the Black and the Baltic Seas and the Gulf of Alaska and other North Pacific areas.

The warm world of RTW cruising is under-represented in the waters around South America, Africa and western Australia, and in the eastern Pacific Ocean. Primarily the warm world is in the Caribbean Sea, the South-western Pacific and the waters joining the Indian and the Pacific oceans.

The world of islands of RTW cruising is concentrated in South-east Asian waters, the South Pacific and the Caribbean. Many of the islands of the Mediterranean are not visited by cruise ships. This is true of Malta, Sardinia, Corsica, Sicily, Crete and Cyprus. Only Samos, Santorini and Rhodes are called at by at least one ship. The islands of the high latitudes are excluded also, such as Greenland, Iceland and the Falklands. Finally, a glaring exception to the world of RTW cruise shipping island stops is the Galapagos Islands where there are government restrictions on the companies allowed to call at the Islands.

A dependence on an RTW cruise to experience the variety of the world gives a geographically biased view of that world. Even within the warm water world of islands and mainland ports of call, the RTW cruise is selective. Although much is seen, even more is missed.

Conclusion

World cruising is a small segment of the very large cruise shipping business. In bed-days it consumed only 1.2% of the theoretical yearly capacity of the industry in 2004. There were only 14 ships offering world cruises in 2003/04, and of these only 10 offered RTW voyages. The RTW ships vary by age, size and luxury rating. They are mostly European-owned and -operated. They have a long-established tradition of serving a very select market.

Notwithstanding the small size of the world cruise segment, especially the RTW portion, there is a very definable geography, seasonality and duration to it. For the RTW portion in 2003/04, ports of embarkation and disembarkation were few; almost all cruises were westbound; their latitudinal range was limited; ports of call were many, but only a few were called at by the majority of the ships; all RTW cruises were in the northern hemisphere winter with a shoulder season extending into the spring; all lasted at least 80 days but most were in the range of 3–4 months.

These descriptive characteristics are largely determined by the world's geography. Climate, choke points and the position of key islands in the vast oceans are macro-geographic factors at work influencing the RTW routing and timing. RTW cruising is not representative of the Earth's variety, and even within its world, much is missed. There is still much of the world that world cruises can explore – new seascapes and landfalls abound, and they exist within and outside the geographical constraints discussed in this chapter. Because of the new opportunities, the future of world cruising would seem secure for the small market segment to which it appeals.

References

Casteljon, R. and Charlier, J. (eds) (2000) *El renacer de los cruceros: la mundializacion de los negocios turisticos y maritimos*. Fundacion Portuaria, Madrid.

Charlier, J. (2000) An introduction to the geography of cruise shipping. In: Casteljon, R. and Charlier, J. (eds) *El renacer de los cruceros: la mundializacion de los negocios turisticos y maritimos*. Fundacion Portuaria, Madrid, pp. 16–28.

Charlier, J. (2000b) De la norme panamax à l'essor des overpanamax. *Acta Geographica* 121, 102–111.

Charlier, J. (2004) The cruise shipping industry in the corporate mergers and the overpanamax eras. A comparison with the container shipping industry. *BELGEO* 4, 433–460.

Charlier, J. and Arnold, P. (1997) Les complémentarités saisonnières du marché mondial des croisières. *Bulletin de la Société Belge d'Etudes Géographiques* 66, 181–198.

Cruise Travel International (2004) *Le Grand Livre des Croisières 2004*. Cruise Travel International, Anvers Island, Palmer Station.

Hall, D. (2004) Ocean cruising: market dynamics, product responses and onshore impacts. In: Pinder, D. and Slack, B. (eds) *Shipping and Ports in the 21st Century: Globalisation, Technological Change and the Environment*. Routledge, London, pp. 99–130.

Peisley, T. (2004) *Global Changes in the Cruise Industry 2003–2010*. Seatrade, Colchester, UK.

Saga Rose (2004) *The Ultimate Adventure aboard* Saga Rose. Saga Shipping Company, Folkestone, England.

ShipPax (2004) *Pocket Guide 04*. ShipPax, Halmstad.

Ward, D. (2004) *Ocean Cruising and Cruise Ships 2004*. Berlitz Publishing, London.

Wild, P. and Dearing J. (2004) *Outlook and New Opportunities for the Cruise Industry to 2014*. G.P. Wild International, Haywards Heath, UK.

20 The Norwegian Coastal Express: Moving Towards Cruise Tourism?

Ola Sletvold

Finnmark University College, Department of Tourism and Hotel Management Studies, Follums v 31, 9509 Alta, Norway

Introduction

The Coastal Express, 'Hurtigruten', is one of a handful of Norwegian tourism products that are well known internationally. Branded as the Norwegian Coastal Voyage (NCV), it is basically an 11-day round-trip sailing journey along the coast from Bergen in the south-west to Kirkenes in the north-east on the Russian border. It calls at 35 different ports, larger towns and small fishing villages, on islands and in fjords (see Fig. 20.1). The route has been exactly the same for 70 of its 110 years. The NCV, now jointly run by two companies located in north Norway, over the years has served a combination of transport functions – mail, goods and passengers – and tourists have been a recognizable passenger group throughout its history. However, it is especially during the last decade that the tourist market has emerged as its most important source of income.

This account shows how the Coastal Express has developed from a form of transport with some seasonal tourism to a full-blown coastal voyage, and how it seems to be developing further in the direction of the cruise ship business. It discusses what kind of tourism the trip represents and examines the peculiar combination of being a tradition-based social institution and a tourist service. Finally, it looks at the process of becoming more distinctly a tourism and cruise supplier, and illustrates how such a transformation is evident in different fea-

tures of the Express's products. This chapter is not based on any primary empirical data but on research previously presented in Norwegian, in addition to consultancy and company reports and own observations while travelling the Express throughout a number of years.

A Brief History of the NCV

'Hurtigruten' is a cultural–historical phenomenon whose life extends over four periods: (i) the establishing of the route until roughly 1935; (ii) its institutionalization up to the mid-1970s; (iii) its decline until approximately 1990; and (iv) its tourism rejuvenation from that time onwards.

In 1891, the national steamship advisor in Norway came up with the idea of providing an express shipping service between Trondheim and Hammerfest (see Fig. 20.1). Two steamship companies were offered the route. However, they both rejected it, as sailing during the dark and stormy winters was virtually impossible. Subsequently, a north Norwegian company rose to the challenge. Since for some time it had been keeping accurate notes on courses, speeds and times taken to sail the route, it felt that the service would be viable. The government signed a 4-year contract with it, thereby providing the company with the backing for a weekly service between Trondheim and Hammerfest during the summer and Trondheim and Tromsø during the winter. In the beginning there were nine

N

Fig. 20.1. Sailing route. Source: http://www.
cruisenorway.com/sailingschedule.html

ports of call on the route. The first 68-hour continuous sailing was achieved in July 1893
(http://www.hurtigruten.com).

The initial threefold aim of the route was
primarily to improve the quality of mail and
goods handling and people mobility. In an area
of the country with few roads and no railway,
sea transport had been slow, local and fragmented. Compared to that situation, tourism

cruise sailings in summer were quick and more
direct. At the turn of the century, the western
coast and its northernmost point constituted
a well-known tourism destination. Following
royal visits to the North Cape, Thomas Cook &
Sons started their summer cruises there in 1873
(Johnson, 1992), thus introducing organized
tourism in tandem with an explorer type of
tourism that for some years had made use of the
existing transport routes.

Sailing during the night and in dark winter
for some time gave the Express a competitive
advantage over the dominating steamship companies that were based in the south. The birth
of the future Coastal Express, therefore, also
belongs to the north–south dimension of
Norwegian history (Bratrein and Niemi, 1994).
The name of the Express – 'Hurtigruten' – literally
meaning 'the fast route' refers to the speed
of the transport that was a result of keeping to
the main shipping lane and leaving traffic to the
deeper fjord ports and the outer island regions to
local ship companies. The route proved to be
an important infrastructural improvement.
Governmental concessions, permits and financial support of the Express demonstrated a political willingness to more than lip service
inclusion of the northern periphery in a nation
that was in the process of establishing itself as a
sovereign state. The union with Sweden was dis-
solved in 1905, and the Coastal Express contributed towards integrating the distant north in
the new nation state (Furre, 1991; Bratrein and
Niemi, 1994, p. 198). From a longer-term perspective, Hurtigruten represented the modernization of an 800-year-old trade and transport
tradition (Sandnes, 1977; Nedkvitne, 1988).

Early in the 40-year period until the 1930s,
the system was established that still exists. Its
main elements were a fixed number of ports of
call, daily departures, a sufficient number of
ships and the involvement of only a few companies. This situation meant that industrial modernity came to the north, represented by the
clock-like rhythm of the traffic, as well as the
planning and coordination with local routes. It
fostered reliability, and thus popular trust, and
was always underpinned by the necessary governmental regulation and financial support.
From the very start, the Express adapted to the
summer tourism and in the spring ships got some
fresh white paint. First-class cabins and the

upper deck seasonally became tourist territory and sometimes a temporary pool was installed (Stavseth, 1983). Yet the role of tourism was not fully politically accepted until 1935 when the distribution of the standard product was established. The companies then received governmental approval to organize and sell the typical full trip tickets through general agents abroad. In addition to passenger, mail and goods transportation, tourism was finally legitimized as one of the functions of the Express.

During the second period, the Express became institutionalized, in the sense that its coming and going was taken as a natural, matter-of-fact aspect of daily life along the coast (Scott, 1995; Sletvold, 1997). Even so, the 1940–1945 war was a definite setback. As many as 14 ships carrying 700 people were lost, and replacements made during and after the war were unsatisfactory in size and speed (Johnson, 1994). The classical era started with a generation of specially designed ships from around 1950. This fleet represented the material basis for the Express as a societal institution. People along the coast became familiar with these vessels, so much so that their daily passing became part of people's external landscape and the interiors became known through own travel. Currently, these ships have all been taken out of regular service and either sold or erected as museums. Yet each of them sailed a total itinerary equal to 7–8 times the distance to the moon (Johnson, 1994), with remarkable regularity and very few accidents. Several machine-like metaphors have been used to describe their qualities: the 'perpetuum mobile of the coast', 'a large Paternoster work', a 'rotation work', the 'eternal pendulum traffic' (Johnson, 1992, 1994; Bakka, 1997). Additionally, organic images have been used that further illustrate the institutional character of the route: 'the spine of the coast' and its 'artery' (Johnson, 1994).

The late 1970s became the start of a period of decline. Having been instrumental in the modernization of the coast, the Express itself became a victim of modernity. The sea-based combined transportation of mail, people and packages seemed outdated. Technological developments in the handling of goods, innovations in hydrofoil and catamaran boats for passenger traffic, and not least large government investment in roads, railways and airports made the Express a rather slow alternative. The number of flight passengers in north Norway reached the size of the Coastal Express traffic in 1976 – half a million people. During the following 20 years the quantum of air traffic doubled five times, whereas the amount of Express traffic halved.

Throughout this period of decline, tourists had become gradually more important for the economics of the route. Since 1990, the strategy of concentrating on goods and tourism, including meetings, conferences and cruises, has become increasingly articulated. The fleet has been totally and radically renewed and capacity has doubled several times. The number of passengers has grown twofold since the lowest years and, with 550,000 passengers in 2002, traffic is not just back to where it was before the beginning of the period of decline, but is rising (Econ, 2004). Table 20.1 illustrates the development since 1990. The percentage change in traffic from year to year shows a remarkable steady growth with only minor setbacks. The summer seasons are mostly booked to capacity, sometimes with the result that local port-to-port passengers are not accepted.

Since the late 1980s, only two companies have been involved in the running of the NCV. Both are located in north Norway and both are regionally owned. They are dominant travel and transport providers with diversified activities. They have full control of the product development and international distribution of 'Hurtigruten'.

Table 20.1. Development of traffic 1991–2003. Per cent change in number of passengers above previous year.

1991	1992	1993	1994	1995	1996	1997	1998	1999	2000	2001	2002	2003
0.8	−3.6	6.4	27.0	−8.8	11.6	11.0	7.7	−1.8	−2.7	6.0	22.5	−3.4

Source: Econ (2004).

The Norwegian Coastal Voyage as a Tourism Product

Whether the NCV is a cruise or not depends on the understanding of that term, since there seems to be no accepted common definition (Douglas and Douglas, 2004). Certainly the NCV meets the minimum criterion of being a water-borne round trip; yet it is not ocean-going, nor is the recreation of passengers its only purpose. The companies are strategically specific in preferring the term 'voyage' to differentiate it from other cruises (Nilsen *et al.*, 2004).

There is a mix of passengers on board the NCV. In a cost–benefit analysis that reflects the companies' way of thinking, customers are classified into three groups (Econ, 2004). Firstly, there are the round-trip tourists, going either northbound or southbound for 5 days or taking the full 11-day tour. This is an internationally composed group. Even so, there are relatively more Norwegian round-trippers nowadays than there were 15 years ago. The main international markets are Germany, Great Britain and the USA. Secondly, there are port-to-port passengers travelling shorter distances. These are mostly Norwegians, although some short-haul, point-to-point journeys are popular among foreign tourists. Thirdly, there are conference groups staying on board for a certain number of days. Three product types are linked to these categories. The experience-oriented voyage is a kind of cruise product; yet it has some unique characteristics. The tourist or experience motivation is found in round-trip passengers as well as in some of the destination or port-oriented groups. However, a large portion of the latter looks only for the transport element. The conference product is normally port-to-port, but may be coupled with experience motivation as well. However interesting the topic under discussion, it is hard not to notice the passing through landscapes and the calling at ports even during meetings. This larger setting for conferences figures prominently in the marketing material directed towards this specific market (Emma Publishing, 2004). Thus, combining the facts that the NCV is a round trip and that a large group of passengers are recreation- or experience-motivated, it seems clear that it is a kind of cruise. On the other hand, the companies' strategy of labelling

it a 'voyage' seems to work, since in a recent survey only 8% had considered a cruise as an alternative when buying their NVC voyage (Nilsen *et al.*, 2004).

Experience-oriented travel is largely an April–September seasonal product. Demand during the winter is far below berth capacity. Figure 20.2 illustrates the distribution of different passenger types in 2001/02. According to Lian *et al.* (2002), port-to-port passengers dominate the total picture with some 84% of the annual total. In summer, experience-oriented groups make up nearly 50%, and round-trip tourists represent nearly 70% of the annual bednights. They account for two-thirds of passenger income.

For all passenger transport the accommodation elements of cabins and meals are basic. Some of the segmentation and competition in cruise markets are based on quality and price differentiation concerning these elements, and cruise suppliers have met and developed global, expanding and composite markets (Douglas and Douglas, 2004). Accommodation seems to be important in the inclusive round trips of the NCV. These passengers are given priority over other groups in the choice of cabins and they always have reserved seating during meals. All the same, accommodation is not the competitive advantage of the NCV, nor are other facilities offered on board decisive product elements. They constitute a kind of hygiene factor where standards must be met for satisfactory quality assessments. But they are secondary to the nature and culture elements in the product, both for the tourists' motivation in selecting this particular product and for the reputation it has in the market (Econ, 2004).

The NCV is basically a nature-as-landscapes-and-seascapes sightseeing product. Its roots are found in a romantic interest in nature as spectacle (Towner, 1996; Wang, 2000). During the cruise, different tourist gazes are continually offered of changing vistas of natural scenery as the ships move along their itineraries. The views vary between seasons because of the ever-mutating length of daylight. Some waters are narrow, some are too open for comfort, some are colourful, some are barren. Most natural scenes are different southbound from what they are northbound, because of the sailing direction or due to the time of day of passing through a

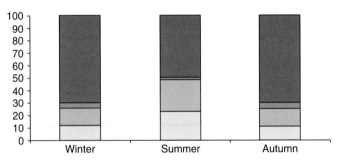

Fig. 20.2. Distribution (%) of passenger types seasonally: winter, summer and autumn 2001/02. From top down: port-bound traffic; experience-oriented short-distance travel; round-trip passengers; conference passengers. Sources: Lian *et al.* (2002); cf. Econ (2004).

particular landscape. For much of the trip one can observe cultivated land, farms, quays, bridges and settlements, as the NCV ships move in waters close to the mainland. However, apart from these closer looks at the built environment, nature sights are in principle not markedly different from what is offered by any cruise ship that goes north in the summer (there are on the average a hundred such visits to the North Cape Island annually), or from any land-based transportation along the coast.

The unique attraction of the Coastal Express has been, and will be, found in a combination of five features. Firstly, concerning the experience of nature and landscapes, it offers that old-fashioned mobility associated with travelling by ship (Urry, 2000). On a ship one experiences a slowing down of the separation between time and space (Giddens, 1991) that might otherwise trouble the post-modern tourist. It is closely connected to the sensual experience of movement, something that is probably still intact for the NCV. The size of a ship influences the sensing of motion. These vessels' berth capacity is less than 700 and their gross registered tonnage (GRT) only 11,000. The largest cruise ships are ten times this size (Dawson, 2000). In rough weather, being at sea is therefore bodily experienced in a more direct way in an NCV vessel than on board a bigger cruise ship. Thus, the opportunities for more varied sensescapes (Urry, 2001) are greater. Walking the decks, with the wind, the smell of the sea, the sound of seagulls and the movements of the ship, together represent a pleasant, multi-sensory, corporeal experience. The rela-

tively slow speed of the Express is also different from most cruises. The normal average velocity is only 16 knots, a little below the maximum in order to have some reserve for maintaining the schedule.

Secondly, the regularity and rhythm of the Express as a working ship seems to be another fascinating aspect of the product. In a series of interviews that focused on what tourists regarded as the NCV tradition (Sletvold, 2001), most answers were related to the rhythm of the voyage and to the fact that this represented history and the flow of time. Tourists talked of the change experienced between short port visits and moving towards the next port, as well as the well-defined and predictable regularity of life on board – the working ship aspects that structured what happened. Several other surveys confirm that cruise passengers highly value the transport function of a traditional sea voyage, something that gives an added dimension to the NCV that ordinary cruises can never really offer (Econ, 2004).

The function of a working ship is serving ports of call. Thirdly, therefore, the very fact the ship stays quayside for 1–5 hours gives tourists the chance of briefly witnessing daily life and ordinary people in various towns and fishing villages on average three times a day. Moreover, at many of the port stops the cruise is programmed with organized excursions to natural and cultural attractions, sights that form part of the local land-based tourism industry. Together these elements make the NCV cruise a much more extrovert product with much more tourism industry and local society involvement than many ordinary cruises that focus on on-board activities (Klimov and Sletvold, 2003). The NCV excursions are not part of an inclusive tour and do not represent the kind of company-controlled onshore visits that can be seen in other sections of the cruise industry. This side of the NCV product therefore also distances it from the standardizing tendencies towards McDonaldization (Ritzer, 2000) that Weaver (2003) has observed in greater parts of the cruise industry.

Fourthly, for the cruise tourists there is a cultural product element in the experiences of local port-to-port travellers: families, students and people going to the nearest town, conference groups, someone coming home from the hospital. The tourists are no longer separated from these short-distance travellers or given designated deck areas as they once were in earlier times, and although cabin prices naturally differ, there are no longer defined fare 'classes'. The coexistence with the port-to-port travellers, and even the mingling with them, is a little programmed or programmable product aspect, something hardly experienced on normal cruises. Today tourists dominate the ships in the main season of April–September. However, in the quieter periods of the year other passengers are more important, reflecting the old duties of the NCV.

Lastly, there is also an art element in the product. To have ships and ship technology that could meet the special needs of performing the fundamental duties was central for the pre- and post-Second World War period. The ships that built the Express's reputation in Norway since the 1950s were specially designed for functionality, speed and strength. Those were the days when things were made to last, so durability in the choice of materials was needed. Nevertheless, the aesthetic side of life received some attention because in all the ships artists were given the task of decoration. Probably the most valuable artistry of these features, inspired by fishermen's lives at home and at sea and by legendary coastal personalities, became especially popular among all kinds of passengers. Practically everyone was pleased that whole wall panels were removed and saved before the old ship was sold and that, in addition to contemporary art, they now adorn the newest ship of the fleet. Again, that is a sign of the tradi-

tional orientation of this showcase of Norwegian identity. Art on-board passenger ships is hardly something special for the NCV. Yet the conscious links to a tradition of decoration that has a regional geographic reference make it stand out from the general offerings of cruise art.

To sum up, the NCV cruise is quite different from the kind of self-contained space of many other cruises. Weaver (2003, p. 62; cf. Dann, 2000) claims that a cruise ship could even be regarded as 'a vehicular total institution'. By contrast, the NVC cruise is not introvert and solely oriented towards on-board entertainment under company control; rather, it is extrovert and open towards the society that the ships serve. The place and space produced encompass a diversity of ports, land-based attractions and close-up stretches of coastal landscapes, as well as somewhat unplanned, and not necessarily company-controlled, meetings with fellow passengers and ordinary Norwegians (Klimov and Sletvold, 2003).

Moving Towards Cruise Tourism?

In one sense the NCV has been a cruise line all its life. From the very start it took on-board tourists in competition with other cruise companies. However, cruise tourism has developed immensely in quantity and character, being differentiated and democratized during the last few decades (Douglas and Douglas, 2004), whereas the principal character of the NCV and the essential elements in the product remained unchanged until the late 1980s. The Coastal Express has since then been making moves towards cruise tourism in several ways. Because it had been run on government permit and support, these changes have their background in the political process. It has also therefore been a difficult strategic endeavour for the NCV companies. The task includes a more definite promotional orientation towards tourism markets, with image building and branding as cornerstones. It has been a lengthy and heavy investment period, geared towards a total renewal of the fleet for a doubling of passenger capacity. It includes a change in price policy, where the round trip in the domestic market is no longer sold as, or considered, an upper-class product.

And it includes portfolio and product development where the companies diversify into other parts of the tourism industry and move into cruise production in a narrower sense.

The background is to be found in the long-running discussion within the companies and in the public political sphere concerning the future of the Coastal Express. During the 1980s, the cost of subsidizing the Express came under scrutiny because the number of passengers and amount of goods kept going down. In the worst year (1988) only 250,000 passengers took a trip, as the traditional ships seemed to have become an inefficient and outmoded transport alternative to many. For some in the decision-making process, an obvious alternative was to downsize the route to a goods transportation line. Although this option was proposed by the government in 1990, hard and very efficient lobbying from the companies, in alliance with other stakeholders in the coastal regions of Norway, succeeded in making this a politically unacceptable solution. In the end, Parliament authorized a 1.8 billion NOK agreement with the Express companies for a 12-year transition period, after which the Express was to be managed as a commercial enterprise (Johnson, 1994; OVDS, 2003). Thus, instead of reducing the activity towards running a goods line, the companies over the last decade have made the biggest investment in tourism in the whole of Norway in their renewal of the fleet. The investment process is probably still (2004) not finished, as the companies have been discussing ordering two more ships.

Since 2002, the government pays for services rendered, i.e. mail and goods transported on a daily basis all year round. Household consumer items comprise the main type of goods for northbound sailings, and frozen fish the principal item for southbound sailings. For some of the most distant ports the Express is still the most reliable transporter, and for some journeys it is the shortest and fastest. Dependence on the Express rises the further north one goes (Econ, 2004). From a government point of view, the public pays for these transport services only and should not finance the cruise facilities. However, it is the transport that builds the material foundation for the cruise product. There is obviously a synergy effect. In a cost–benefit analysis line of thinking there are advantages to both customer

groups (Econ, 2004). Besides the value of maintaining the Express as a part of coastal transport structure, there is also the importance of keeping it up as a carrier of coastal cultural history and a sign of the unity of modern Norway.

In his book on cruise ships and design, Dawson (2000) describes a link between the main cruise markets and what he terms 'Scandinavian design'. One chapter is entitled 'Norwegian-style cruising comes to America', something that refers to the entry of Norwegian entrepreneurs into the American cruise market. They brought with them a different tradition in the exterior and interior designs of ships that for some time influenced the development of the cruise industry. This tradition, according to Dawson, goes back to the Coastal Express ships of the 1930s, which are recognized as combining function with beautiful design (Dawson, 2000, p. 79ff.). In a wider context, the Scandinavian influence also seems to have come from ferry and short sea traffic.

The first boats in the 1990s' generation of NCV ships were met with some scepticism concerning their design and size, the arrangement of deck spaces and the choice of colours and materials (Sletvold, 1997). The new ships were four times larger in tonnage than the traditional ships, with 2–3 times the berth capacity. The exterior in particular was a definitive break with what was seen as the reliable and enduring traditional look of coastal vessels. As interpreted with a land-based gaze, some thought it was too much of an adaptation to tourism production. Such critics said they were reminded of large international ferries and cruise ships. They were taller and had unfamiliar deck proportions. However, after more than 10 years, peoples' mental image of the fleet seems to be dominated by the new ships and there are no objections or protests, even though some, in a somewhat nostalgic mood, lament the passing of the traditional smaller vessels.

Clearly the exterior and interior of the ships are influenced by international trends in passenger ship construction and design (cf. Dawson, 2000). They are built for a larger number of passengers, more decks have been added and greater space is allocated to tourism activities. The ticket counter is like a hotel lobby, and some ships additionally have passenger lifts. Even if the furniture, interior lightening, walls and floors are claimed to be the best in contemporary Norwegian design, the materials are the same as in other sea-borne tourism: glass, brass and wood, polished and shining surfaces. To some degree the situation reflects the necessity of raising standards, but tourism functionality seems to be more design-dependent than transport-oriented. In the newest ships there are Jacuzzis, saunas, fitness facilities and even swimming pools – product elements that have nothing to do with the basic functions of transport. Added weight is given to art on board – in panels, paintings, sculpture and textiles. In general, the ships reflect some of the contemporary art scene in the country, although some of the ships specifically aim at addressing regional culture. Following established tradition, artists are given the opportunity to present inspirations from, and impressions of, northern coastal landscapes and the lives of their people. Again, the presentation of, and reflection on, identity seems evident. The latest innovation is seasonal art sales galleries, possibly another influence from cruise development.

While these matters concern cruise tourism's characteristics being imported into a traditional transport route, the other way that the NCV companies move towards tourism implies leaving domestic waters behind in a literal sense. The two companies have both expanded and diversified. One is a leading hotel owner and participant in tourism development on Spitsbergen and Svalbard, thus doing (more successfully) what the pioneer Richard With did in 1895: it offers cruises on one of the traditional boats to the archipelago and organizes land excursions there (http://www.tfds.no). The other NCV company has expanded with a tour operation branch in mainland Norway under the label 'Coastal Experiences'. In the low winter season it further takes its most modern ship into the special cruise market of sailing between Chile and Argentina and Antarctica. It claims to have obtained a market share of approximately 20% of this niche traffic (OVDS, 2003). Moreover, the voyage from Norway to Chile has itself become a 2-week special cruise.

The new system thus makes it possible for the companies to still run the NCV like the traditional transport of delight (Urry, 2001). The NCV tourism product has even strengthened its port element. In some harbours its quay location for some years was moved out of the town centres to goods terminals in order to have more efficient goods handling. Such a reduction in experience quality has been reversed. The tourists are once more being brought to the centres of the towns. In addition, the list of excursions has been expanded. At the same time it has become possible for the companies to compensate for the lower guaranteed income and greater capital costs by harvesting in bigger and more profitable cruise markets during the winter season. With the additional ships that are about to start cruising, overall capacity will exceed what is needed for running the Express. Consequently the ties to only serving national infrastructure functions are being loosened. However, the coastal cruise should retain its specific qualities as long as the coast of northernmost Norway continues to be inhabited to the same extent as it is at present.

Conclusion

An examination of the NCV has shown that, besides bearing minimum cruise characteristics, the product is a unique combination of qualities that reflects some central aspects of Norwegian national identity. Coastal Norway today retains a traditional closeness to nature, linked to a historical dependence on nature. Although people live in a well-integrated modern society, until now many have preferred rather small communities and towns that have some urban qualities, while still giving immediate access to relatively unspoiled nature, such as the ports along the route. The tradition of the daily coming and going of the NCV ships, the rhythm of its itinerary and the presence of other passengers represent qualities that are valued by tourists. Combined with the experience of coastal scenery and attractions in the ports and on excursions, these qualities constitute a unique cruise product. However, the institutionalization of a transport tradition implies a certain regional nostalgia, which has made the careful move towards cruise tourism a somewhat lengthy transition. The companies running the NCV want to uphold the qualities of the voyage at the same time as they have been expanding into other tourism production, including cruises outside Norwegian waters. It seems the Coastal Express allows them to have their cake and eat it.

Acknowledgement

The author expresses gratitude to Graham M.S. Dann for comments on an earlier version of the manuscript.

References

Bakka, D. (1997) *Hurtigruten, Sjøveien mot nord.* Seagull Publishing, Bergen, Norway.

Bratrein, H.D. and Niemi, E. (1994) Inn i riket. Politisk og økonomisk integrasjon gjennom tusen år, In: Einar-Arne, D. (ed.) *Nord-norsk kulturhistorie*, bind 1. Gyldendal, Oslo, pp. 146–209.

Dann, G. (2000) Overseas holiday hotels for the elderly: total bliss or total institution? In: Robinson, M. (ed.) *Reflections on International Tourism: Motivations, Behaviour, and Tourist Types.* Business Education Publishers, Sunderland, UK, pp. 83–94.

Dawson, P. (2000) *Cruise Ships: An Evolution in Design.* Conway Maritime Press, London.

Douglas, N. and Douglas, N. (2004) *The Cruise Experience: Global and Regional Issues in Cruising.* Pearson Education Australia, Frenchs Forest, New South Wales, Australia.

Econ (2004) *Hurtigrutens økonomiske betydning: Econ-notat nr 2004–028.* ECON Analyse, Oslo.

Emma Publishing (2004) Advertisement attachment for the Hurtigruten in the daily newspaper *Dagens Næringsliv*, Oslo, 12 August 2004.

Furre, B. (1991) *Vårt hundreår: norsk historie 1905–1990.* Det norske Samlaget, Oslo.

Giddens, A. (1991) *Modernity and Self-identity.* Polity Press, Cambridge.

Johnson, P.E. (1992) *Hurtigruta.* Cappelen, Oslo.

Johnson, P.E. (1994) *Med Hurtigruta nordover.* Boksenteret, Oslo.

Klimov, D. and Sletvold, O. (2003) *Movement on a Place and a Place in Movement: Two Cruise Trips Compared.* Paper presented for the 13th Nordic Tourism Research Symposium, Stavanger.

Lian, J.I., Eidhammer, O., Rideng, A. and Strand, S. (2002) *Utredning av transportstandarden for kysten Bergen: Kirkenes, TØI rapport 609/2002.* Transportøkonomisk Institutt. Oslo.

Nedkvitne, A. (1988) *Mens bønderne seilte og jægterne for: nordnorsk og vestnorsk kystøkonomi 1500–1730.* Universitetsforlaget, Oslo.

Nilsen, R.E., Kristensen, H., Hågensen, M. and Røsok, A.K. (2004) *Hurtigruten: OVDS.* Bachelor thesis, Finnmark University College, Alta, Norway.

OVDS (2003) *Annual Report.* Ofotens og Vesteraalens Dampskibsselskab, Narvik.

Ritzer, G. (2000) *The McDonaldization of Society.* New Century Edition. Pine Forge Press, Thousand Oaks, California.

Sandnes, J. (1977) *Norges historie, bind 4: Avfolkning og union 1319–1488.* Cappelen, Oslo.

Scott, W.R. (1995) *Institutions and Organizations.* Sage, Thousand Oaks, California.

Sletvold, O. (1997) Hurtigruta: moderne tradisjon. In: Jacobsen, J.K.S. and Viken, A. (eds) *Turisme: Fenomen og næring.* Universitetsforlaget, Oslo, pp. 153–159.

Sletvold, O. (2001) Hurtigruten: transport, tradisjon og turister. In: Viken, A. (ed.) *Turisme: Tradisjon og trender.* Gyldendal Akademisk, Oslo, pp. 166–178.

Stavseth, R. (1983) *Nordover med Hurtigruten: Historie og hverdagsbilder gjennom nitti år.* Tanum-Norli, Oslo.

Towner, J. (1996) *An Historical Geography of Recreation and Tourism in the Western World 1540–1940.* John Wiley & Sons, Chichester, UK.

Urry, J. (2000) *Sociology Beyond Societies: Mobilities for the Twenty-first Century.* Routledge, London.

Urry, J. (2001) Transports of delight. *Leisure Studies* 20, 237–245.

Wang, N. (2000) *Tourism and Modernity: A Sociological Analysis.* Pergamon Press, Oxford.

Weaver, A. (2003) The McDonaldization of the cruise industry? Tourism, consumption, and customer service. PhD thesis, University of Toronto, Toronto, Canada.

Web sites

http://www.cruisenorway.com/sailingschedule.html

http://www.hurtigruten.com/index.asp

http://www.tfds.no/index.php?c=65&kat=Sitemap&p=9

21 The Structure and Operation of Coastal Cruising: Australian Case Studies

Sacha Reid[1] and Bruce Prideaux[2]

[1]University of Technology, School of Leisure, Sport and Tourism, Sydney, PO Box 222, Lindfield, NSW 2070, Australia; [2]James Cook University, School of Business, PO Box 6811, Cairns Mail Centre QLD 4879, Australia

Australians have had a long affinity with the sea. The first aboriginal settlers arrived by sea perhaps as long as 40,000 years ago (Flannery, 2002) in primitive ocean-capable water craft. In the late 18th century, the first European settlers arrived in Australia by sea. Sea remained the primary method of travel to Australia until replaced by long-range passenger jets in the 1960s. From the time of the first European settlement, most Australians have lived on or near the coast, and until the growth in railway passenger services that linked the various colonial capitals by the end of the 19th century, the nation relied almost exclusively on coastal steamers for intra- and interstate travel. Even as late as the 1950s, scheduled coastal passenger ships operated between many regional ports and state capitals. By the 1960s, however, scheduled domestic airline services, long-distance coaches and private cars had replaced coastal passenger liners. Coastal cruising did not cease altogether and the long tradition of maritime travel was maintained by passenger ferry services providing services to nearby islands or beach resorts for both residents and for recreationalists. In recent years there has been a significant increase in activities of this nature, particularly as the popularity of travel has increased.

While the growing significance of ocean cruising as a leisure activity has attracted con-siderable interest by researchers, investigation into the structure and operation of the coastal cruise industry has received relatively less atten-tion. However, in many coastal destinations coastal cruising activities are an important ele-ment of the tourism industry. This chapter examines the structure of coastal cruising and offers a comparative framework that can be used to examine the structure, operations and future potential for coastal cruising activities. The chapter draws on a number of Australian exam-ples to illustrate aspects of the framework, which has the capability of being applied in any coastal setting.

In recent decades the rapid increase in pop-ularity of ocean cruising has attracted consider-able attention from academics. Commencing with the first special issue devoted to cruising, which appeared in 1996 in the *Journal of Tourism Studies* (Vol 7.2), there has been a grow-ing number of journal articles and books (Hooper, 1991; Peisley, 1992; Dickson and Vladimir, 1997; Cartwright and Braid, 1999; Cudahy, 2001; World Tourism Organization, 2003; Douglas and Douglas, 2004) reporting on aspects of ocean cruising. In Australia, a num-ber of government organizations have acknowl-edged the potential contribution that this market segment has to the tourism industry and have developed a range of policy initiatives at federal, state and local levels. As early as 1992 the federal government acknowledged the potential of developing ocean cruise operations from ports along the Australian coast in the first federal attempt to develop a national tourism strategy. This document, 'Tourism – Australia's Passport to Growth: A National Tourism Strategy', was followed in 1994 by 'Towards a National Cruise Shipping Strategy' and in 1995 by 'National Cruise Shipping Strategy', the nation's first cruise ship strategy.

On a state level, Victoria released 'The Victorian Cruise Shipping Strategy 1998–2001' in 1998, aimed at building on the growth of interest in ocean cruising by encouraging investment in cruise facilities in the state. Tourism Queensland, in collaboration with the Department of State Development, also followed this lead and in 2000 released 'Queensland Cruise Shipping Plan' designed to encourage homeporting of ocean cruise ships in Queensland ports. To date, the focus of all levels of government has been largely directed towards ocean cruising with the apparently less glamorous coastal cruising sector being left to the administration of various state government regulatory authorities. In spite of this neglect, coastal cruising has become one of the key sectors in a number of destinations, including Cairns and the Whitsunday's in Queensland.

Because the focus of government attention has been directed towards ocean cruising, a number of inconsistencies in policy and data collection in relation to coastal cruising have emerged. For example, cruising is defined as occurring when 'vessels undertaking scheduled, deep water cruises of 2 days or more with a passenger capacity of 100 persons or more' (Commonwealth Department of Industry, Tourism and Resources, 1994, 2004; Cruise Lines International Association, 1995; Tourism Queensland, 2000). However, the Great Barrier Reef Marine Park Authority (1999) defines passenger-carrying vessels of 70 m or more in length as cruise boats. Vessels or cruise activities that are not classified within these definitions are excluded from statistical data-sets. This situation contrasts to the international understanding of marine tourism that, according to the Cruise Line International Association (1995), recognizes that apart from ocean cruising there are other significant components of the marine tourism industry including ferries and short

tour operators as well as a range of smaller vessels that are unsuitable for deep-water voyages. The scale of coastal cruising in Australia is significant but the paucity of data collection precludes an accurate assessment of passengers carried and revenue generated.

Coastal cruising takes a number of forms including sailing, sightseeing cruises, ferry trips, diving and a range of other leisure and recreational activities. These are discussed in great detail later in the chapter. Coastal cruising constitutes an important activity in a diverse number of regions including Alaska (Bull, 1996; Dwyer and Forsyth, 1996), the Caribbean (Riley, 1992; Wood, 2000), Mediterranean, Pacific and island nations such as the Philippines and Indonesia. In coastal destinations that have access to significant marine resources, such as offshore islands or coral reefs, coastal cruising has become a major focal point for tourism activity. Although the data is now quite dated, Hooper (1991, p. 11) found that the 'coastal cruise industry [in the Whitsunday's and Far North Queensland] caters to 48,000 passengers each year and turns over approximately $30 million'. Since Hooper made this estimate the industry has grown substantially in visitor numbers and operators. By 2002, the total number of visitors to the Great Barrier Reef Marine Park was 1.6 million, of who 839,000 originated in Cairns (Great Barrier Reef Marine Park Authority, 2004). With the price of individual trips ranging between AUS$65 per person to AUS$180, the economic impact of this sector on the regional economy is substantial. In a study of the contribution of the Great Barrier Reef to the economies of Cairns and its hinterland, funded by the Association of Marine Tour Operators (Hassal and Associates, 2001), it was estimated that marine tourism directly and indirectly contributed AUS$732 million per annum to the regional economy and generated 6000 jobs based on input and output tables for the Cairns–Port Douglas area.

Clearly there is a need to examine coastal cruising to identify its structure, operational characteristics and the major drivers behind its growth. In many countries, marine public transport networks connect coastal settlements and offshore islands to major urban areas, enabling the tourism industry to capitalize on these networks to develop tourism-specific activities including sightseeing and transfers. Another sector of domestic marine recreation that has been developed as a tourism resource has been the private coastal cruising clubs that operate from many destinations including Berkshire, UK (Dinghy Cruising Association, 2001) and Florida, in the USA (Windjammers of Clearwater, 2001). In many destinations, extensive marinas have been developed to service the large number of motorized and non-motorized pleasure craft that make up this sector of the marine tourism industry. Aside from the literature previously discussed, other studies of coastal cruising have examined a range of issues including environmental impacts (Kesgin and Vardar, 2001; Isakson *et al.*, 2001) and safety issues (Wang, 2001). Few references are made to coastal cruising as a tourism activity.

The difference between ocean-based cruising and other forms of vessel-based marine tourism relates to the size of the vessel, the proximity of the cruise to land and the shorter duration of tours in comparison with ocean-based cruises. In many respects the structure of coastal cruising is determined by the same range of factors that determine the structure of ocean cruising including the characteristics of the generating region serviced, the nature of the resource in the destination region and the standard of infrastructure available in the destination. For example, the structure of the Florida-based cruise industry is largely determined by the attractiveness of cruising as an activity to domestic US tourists and to a lesser extent European visitors; the ability of Miami to homeport cruise boats; the provision of sufficient facilities such as hotels and airport capacity for passengers in transit to and from cruises; and the availability of safe sea lanes and short-term stopover ports during cruises. In their study of the Whitsunday's region in Australia, Reid *et al.* (2002) noted the importance of backpackers as the principle market for the commercial coastal cruising in the region, the significance of easily accessible coral reefs as the major resource that attracts tourists, and the easy access to the region by air, long-distance coach and self-drive motor vehicles.

Based on a definition developed by Reid *et al.* (2002) the structure of coastal cruising is defined within the following parameters:

- operates at distances out to 100 km from the coastline;
- includes, but is not limited to, powered and non-powered vessels, moored platforms servicing the tourism industry, submersibles of any form, novelty cruises and bareboat charters;
- includes, but is not limited to, day trips and overnight cruises;
- is primarily for recreation, including recreational fishing, diving and sailing.

The definition incorporates all non-ocean cruise activities currently undertaken in Australian waters.

The operation of the coastal cruising industry in any specific area can be classified according to a number of operational and activity characteristics of the industry including tourist-specific activities, vessel type, specific purpose of vessel, duration of activity and on-board facilities. These are illustrated in the framework outlined in Table 21.1. More traditional classification criteria such as length, weight, passenger numbers, range of vessel and crewing were considered; however, as these relate mainly to classifications used for purposes such as vessel registration, insurance and berthing procedures, these criteria were rejected in favour of descriptors that more closely reflect the tourist-related activity undertaken by vessels in this sector.

By applying the operational and activities characteristics outlined in Table 21.1 as a template it is possible to compare and contrast elements of coastal cruising between destinations on an international scale.

Research for this chapter identified three specific structures of coastal cruising based on geographical characteristics of destinations overlaid by the tourism and residents transport tasks undertaken by the marine transport industry. These are depicted diagrammatically in Figs 21.1–21.3. Geography is a major factor in determining a transport network structure. In some destinations, coastal ferry services operate regular scheduled passenger services in parallel with land transport modes, while in others there is little marine transport. The existence, or absence, of offshore islands is a further factor, as are the scenic values of the coastline, degree of development of marine recreation and use of marine resources such as coral reefs and fish

Table 21.1. Framework of operational and activity structure of coastal cruising.

Type of vessel
  • Engine-powered
  • Sail-powered
  • Alternate power sources
Activities
  • Diving and snorkelling
  • Fishing
  • Whale and dolphin watching
  • Privately owned luxury boat (either motor- or sail-powered)
  • Moored platform
  • Submersible
  • Human-powered such as a kayak
  • Other marine sports (including parasailing)
  • Coral viewing
  • Inshore and offshore cruising
  • Ferry boat services to offshore islands
  • Water taxi services
  • Charter boat operations
  • House boats
Length of activity
  • Day
  • Overnight
  • Extended
On-board facilities
  • Restaurant
  • Recreational facilities (including diving and fishing gear)
  • Research facilities
  • Accommodation
Passenger characteristics
  • Sociodemographic
  • Segmentation membership
Geographic structure of cruising
  • Localized cruising activities
  • Activities located away from the port
  • Scheduled ferry service

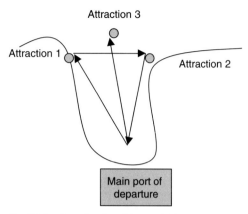

Fig. 21.1. Localized cruising activities.

mine the structures that most commonly represent coastal cruising operations.

The first conceptual model (Fig. 21.1) illustrates a coastal destination where the attractions that are of interest to tourists are situated either within the boundaries of the destination or nearby. Maritime transport services for tourists often incorporate two elements: a scheduled public transport service for residents on which is superimposed services that are primarily designed to meet the transport needs of tourists and a range of commercial cruising activities. Sydney, Australia, is a typical example of this form of spatial organization. Sydney harbour and its spectacular scenery, attractions located on the harbour foreshore and nearby beach settlements generate considerable coastal cruising activity. The Sydney Ferry Service, established in the late 19th century to provide scheduled public transport to Sydney residents, now services 41 ferry terminals (Sydney Ferries,

stocks. The actual size of the tourism element as distinct from domestic usage patterns is determined by the interplay between the demands of visitors for marine tourism activities, the nature of the resource in the destination, and the standard of infrastructure available in the destination.

When developing the conceptual models of the marine tourism transport network illustrated in Figs 21.1–21.3, particular note was made of the direction of passenger flows, types of activities undertaken and spatial relationships that were evident. Together these deter-

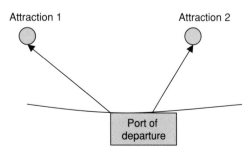

Fig. 21.2. Sydney Ferries network map. Source: Sydney Ferries (2004a).

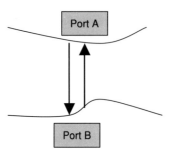

Fig. 21.3. Activities located away from the port.

2004a) operating a network of scheduled ferry services that is illustrated in Fig. 21.4. A small number of these terminals service popular tourist attractions such as Manly, Taronga Park Zoo and Homebush, site of the 2000 Olympics. In the financial reporting year 2002/03, Sydney Ferries transported approximately 13.3 million passengers (State Transit Authority, 2003). The size of the tourism task is not known as no distinction is made between tourists and residents except for the ticket type discussed later in this chapter. Aside from the ferry service, commercial cruising activities are provided by over 100 companies and include harbour cruises, charter cruises and night-lights charters. Because both the domestic passenger task and commercial cruise operations are largely harbour-focused,

vessels built for this market are short-range and designed for inshore rather than offshore operations. Other cities with this spatial structure of coastal cruising include Melbourne and New York.

In Sydney, tourists constitute a significant market; therefore, a vigorous marketing programme that targets both domestic and international visitors, as well as local residents, has been developed by the ferry service and commercial operators. Advertising strategies have targeted commuters and tourists with slogans such as 'getting there is half the fun'. Operators also use websites as a marketing tool. The Sydney Ferry Service operates an innovative website that incorporates trip-planning tools, which allows tourists to develop an itinerary that incorporates major Sydney sights that are accessible by ferry transportation (Sydney Ferries, 2004b). Sydney Ferries has also developed a range of services specifically for the leisure tourist market including tourist or visitor fare rates, dedicated harbour cruises and multi-destination passes.

Another example of a destination that has an activity profile centred around localized activity with maritime services that provide transport for both domestic and international passengers is Hong Kong, where Star Ferries operates services between Hong Kong Island,

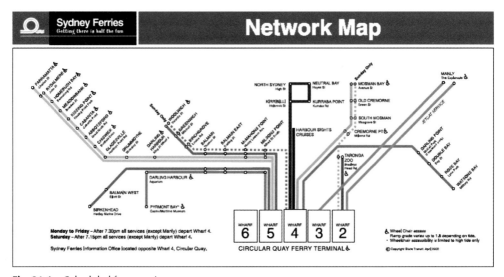

Fig. 21.4. Scheduled ferry service.

Kowloon and adjacent localities (Reiber, 2003). Established in 1898, Star Ferries has become a tourism icon and in 2002 the company transported 26 million passengers averaging 72,000 people per day (Star Ferries, 2002). Apart from tourists who purchase harbour sightseeing tickets, the number of tourists using Star Ferries is not known. Sightseeing tours incorporate a hop-on–hop-off service with four stops at major attractions located around the harbour. In Sydney and Hong Kong, the public transport task of the service provider has been expanded to incorporate the leisure tourist market.

The second conceptual model of coastal cruise operations, illustrated in Fig. 21.2, shows the use of marine transport to service offshore locations that lie some distance beyond the destination. These services are primarily tourist-focused and not used for scheduled marine public transport services. Cairns in North Queensland is an example of a destination that has a coastal cruising industry designed to transport tourists to distant offshore attractions, in this case the Great Barrier Reef. The Whitsundays region of Queensland is another example.

In the case of Cairns, there is a wide range of vessels that transports tourists to islands and diving sites on the Great Barrier Reef. In 2003, approximately 839,000 commercial passengers travelled from Cairns to locations on the reef including several small resort islands with overnight accommodation, diving and snorkelling sites, semi-submersibles, limited recreational fishing sites and anchored pontoons on the reef (Great Barrier Reef Marine Park Authority, 2004). A wide range of vessels undertakes this task including traditional monohull and more recent multihull high-speed catamarans. To support this large sector of the cities' tourism industry a substantial boat building and repair industry has also been established. In addition to the commercial sector a large recreational boating sector has emerged, but the size of this sector is unknown.

In the Whitsundays region, numerous offshore islands provide a perfect setting for the emergence of a large island resort sector that complements shore-based resort accommodation. In this region coastal cruising is based at Shute Harbour and a growing number of marinas. Coastal cruise activities in this region

include day trips to the Great Barrier Reef and offshore resort islands, limited recreational fishing, diving and snorkelling, whale watching and bare boat charters. Itineraries include both day and overnight trips. The extensive number of islands and relatively calm seas has created ideal conditions for sailing, and in the late 1990s a large sailing boat sector also emerged offering both day and overnight trips.

A third type of coastal cruising is based on the operation of scheduled ferry services between ports as illustrated in Fig. 21.3. Unlike the structure of regular passenger services described in Fig. 21.1 that operate in the near vicinity of the destination, Fig. 21.3 describes ferry passenger services that connect one or a number of ports and may operate over considerable distances. Services of this nature may include elements of tourism traffic as well as other passenger movements. There are many examples of this form of coastal cruising in the Mediterranean, between many ports in the other parts of Europe, as well as Asia and the Caribbean. In Asia, for example, the Busan (South Korea) to Fukuoka (Japan) Hydrofoil, operated by the Kyushu Railway Company trading as Beetle, carried 300,000 passengers in 2003. Ferry services have patterns of operation including overnight or day-only services, may or may not include accommodation and range in size from small to very large vessels. The factor that differentiates this form of coastal cruising from ocean cruising is the scheduled public passenger transport nature of the service. Vessels operating ferry services cannot be described as leisure vessels offering inclusive holidays.

In the Australian context there are only a limited number of coastal cruising activities that fall into this category, primarily because of the popularity of car and air travel. The most significant service is the Tasmania to Melbourne and more recently Sydney Ferry Service operated by the Spirit of Tasmania/Port of Devonport Corporation. This service operates both day and night voyages and offers limited cabin accommodation on the overnight services. The scale of this service is similar to many of the services that operate in Europe and Asia. During the reporting period 2002–2003, TT-Line – the company that operates this service – has grown exponentially with a 45% increase in visitor numbers to 504,350 passengers (Spirit of

Tasmania, 2003). Research conducted by the organization indicates that 181,566 of these passengers are visitors or tourists (25.8% of all tourists to Tasmania) who contribute approximately AUS$326 million to the state of Tasmania. Therefore, the ferry service that they operate is a significant contributor to the tourism industry and the economy of Tasmania (Spirit of Tasmania, 2003).

Conclusion

While there has been considerable research into ocean cruising, the coastal cruising sector has been largely overlooked. Research into the market size, product development and other issues affecting coastal cruising warrants further investigation. Specifically, the economic impact of this market has not been extensively analysed, and there is a case for including coastal cruising as a subcategory of ocean cruising. The adoption of the definition and classification of coastal cruising suggested in this chapter, or a similar definition and classification, will be one positive step to recognize the significance of this sector in overall marine tourism.

Recognition of the role of coastal cruising in marine tourism will also assist policymakers, both in Australia and globally, to develop appropriate policies and strategies to enhance the development of marine tourism in specific destinations. The structure of the coastal cruising industry suggested in this chapter may also be beneficial in providing an analytical framework when developing coastal cruising products. Investigation as to the market segments of coastal cruising could also assist product developers in developing products that satisfy current and potential tourists and visitors' expectations. Additionally, the impact of coastal cruising on host communities requires further exploration.

References

Bull, A. (1996) The economics of cruising: an application to the short ocean cruise market. *Journal of Tourism Studies* 7(2), 28–35.

Cartwright, R. and Baird, C. (1999) *The Development and Growth of the Cruise Industry*. Butterworth-Heinemann, Oxford.

Cruise Lines International Association (1995) *The Cruise Industry: An Overview*. Marketing Edition, July, Cruise Line International Association, New York.

Cudahy, B. (2001) *The World Cruise Ship Phenomenon in North America*. Cornell Maritime Press, Centreville, Maryland.

Commonwealth Department of Industry, Tourism and Resources (2004) Niche markets. Available at: http://www.industry.gov.au/content/itrinternet/cmscontent.cfm?objectID=F294F506-96C7-EC89-7E8ED5CAD0751824

Dickson, B. and Vladimir, A. (1997) *Selling the Sea: An Inside Look at the Cruise Industry*. John Wiley & Sons, New York.

Dinghy Cruising Association (2001) Available at: http://www.dca.uk.com

Douglas, N. and Douglas, N. (2004) *The Cruise Experience: Global and Regional Issues in Cruising*. Pearson Education, Sydney.

Dwyer, L. and Forsyth, P. (1996) Economic impacts of cruise tourism in Australia. *Journal of Tourism Studies* 7(2), 36–43.

Flannery, T. (2002) *The Future Eaters*. Grove Press, Berkeley, California.

Great Barrier Reef Marine Park Authority (1999) *Cruise Shipping Policy for the Great Barrier Reef Marine Park*. Available at: http://www.gbrmpa.gov.au/corp_site/key_issues/tourism/documents/cruise_ship_policy.pdf

Great Barrier Reef Marine Park Authority (2004) Visitor Days to the GBRMPA Cairns Planning Area 1999–2002. Available at: http://www.gbrmpa.gov.au/corp_site/key_issues?tourism

Hassal and Associates (2001) *Socio-Economic Impact Assessment of the Contribution of Marine Tourist Operations to the Cairns-Douglas Region*. Association of Marine Park Tourism Operators, Sydney.

Hooper, P. (1991) *The Performance of Ocean Cruising in Australian and Future Prospects*. Institute of Transport Studies, Sydney.

Isakson, J., Persson, T. and Lindgren, E. (2001) Identification and assessment of ship emissions and their effects in the harbour of Göteborg, Sweden. *Atmospheric Environments* 35, 3659–3666.

Kesgin, U. and Vardar, N. (2001) A study on exhaust gas emissions from ships in Turkish Straits. *Atmospheric Environments* 35, 1863–1870.

Peisley, T. (1992) *The World Cruise Ship Industry in the 1990s*. The Economist Intelligence Unit, London.

Reiber, B. (2003) *Frommer's Hong Kong: With Macau and Insider Shopping Tips*, 7th edn. John Wiley & Sons, New York.

Reid, S., Slaughter, L. and Prideaux, B. (2002) Coastal cruising: targeting the backpacker market in the Whitsunday region, Australia. In: Pforr, C. and Carlsen, J. (eds) *Tourism and Hospitality on the Edge*. Proceedings of the 2002 CAUTHE Conference, Promanco, Fremantle.

Riley, C. (1992) The Atlantic–Caribbean cruise industry. *Progress in Tourism, Recreation & Hospitality Management* 15, 313–328.

Spirit of Tasmania (2003) Annual report 2002–2003. Available at: http://www.spiritoftasmania.com.au/mediaroom/downloads/annrpt0203.pdf

Star Ferries (2002) Annual report. Available at: http://www.starferry.com.hk/new/en/report.asp

State Transit Authority (2003) Annual report. Available at: http://www.sta.nsw.gov.au/commonpdfs/report/2003/2003_annual_report.pdf

Sydney Ferries (2004a) Available at: http://www.sydneyferries.nsw.gov.au/

Sydney Ferries (2004b) Available at: http://www.131500.info/newJourney.asp

Tourism Queensland (2000) *Queensland Cruise Shipping Plan*. Tourism Queensland and Queensland Government, Department of State Development, Brisbane.

Wang, J. (2001) The current status and future aspects in formal ship safety assessment. *Safety Science* 38, 19–30.

Windjammers of Clearwater (2001) Available at: http://www.windjammersofclearwater.org

Wood, R. (2000) Caribbean cruise tourism globalization at sea. *Annals of Tourism Research* 27(2), 345–370.

World Tourism Organization (2003) *World Cruise Ship Activity*. World Tourism Organization, Madrid.

22 Adventure Cruising: An Ethnography of Small Ship Travel

Valene L. Smith

*California State University Chico, Department of Anthropology, Chico,
CA 95929-0400, USA*

Adventure cruising is identified by the US travel industry as a new niche market that is rapidly increasing in popularity (Niche Cruises, 2004). The wide range of destinations and types of travel available to the US public has created trends of in-fashion travel and activity that parallel the cyclical nature of sports (Readman, 2003). Many upscale US passengers are currently wearied of the 'floating resort' megaships or superliners that host 2000 or more multigenerational, multicultural passengers. These behemoths have become destinations *sui generis* and the shore stops are crowded ports; even the so-called 'private islands' have faked authenticity (Khelladi, 2003). Carnival Cruises advertises its 'fun ships' as party ships for dining, dancing, drinking, gambling and shopping, which is an appealing lifestyle, 'supported by high-tech games, sliding down a huge waterslide, playing miniature golf or going ice skating on a ship at sea' (Sasso, 2004).

Cruising has attained such status among some Americans that a coterie of cruise passengers make it their goal to sail aboard the inaugural cruise of every major vessel, and thus can speak knowingly about the details of architecture, decor and amenities of each new ship. However, urban living and job stress often mandates quieter vacations. Elderly passengers complain that the size of such ships requires long walks even to eat, and single passengers feel lost in the crowd. To meet some of these concerns, a number of cruise lines are introducing 'spa vacations' to offer individual travellers more

personalized attention. One of the adventure cruise companies provides in their advertising a list of distinctions between standard cruising and adventure cruising (Table 22.1).

This chapter analyses the adventure cruise niche in terms of its four different types: nostalgia cruises (sailing ships and paddle wheelers); long-haul ferries; yachts; and expedition cruises, including icebreakers. Each cruise type involves distinct differences in itinerary and destination(s) as well as in lifestyle and activities, and marketing strategies differ due to considerable variation in cost. Adventure cruising is virtually unreported in the scholarly tourism literature, and this article provides a baseline for further research. Adventure cruising is expected to further expand, both in Europe and into the Pacific-Asian ethnic market in the near future, thus adding further dimension to this topic. In fairness, it should be noted that the author has been a participant–observer in every type of cruise facility described in this chapter, and for lack of citations, draws heavily on personal data. This repeats the anthropological format of participant–observer concept introduced by the Australian authors of *The Cruise Experience* (Douglas and Douglas, 2004).

A Brief Global Perspective

The Age of Discovery instilled in Europeans a strong association with seafaring as an alternative occupation to farming or fishing. The advent of steam-powered vessels in the mid-19th

Table 22.1. Comparisons between megaships and adventure cruising.

Megaships	Adventure cruising
Thousand or more passengers	50–100 passengers
Pre-set ports of call	Expeditionary stops using zodiacs/helicopters
Cruise Director and one general lecturer	Several naturalist guides in diverse specialities who lead shore excursions
Emphasis on on-board amenities and shopping	Emphasis on destination participant activities
Floor shows, casinos, games, dancing	Lectures, videos, well-stocked library
Shore excursions are optional expense	Shore excursions included
Pre-assigned dining and/or buffets	Open single seating

century facilitated European travel and tourism to overseas colonies, and also heightened trade and whaling. Small ship cruises developed soon thereafter in Europe, thanks to its many inland seas and gulfs including the Mediterranean, Adriatic, Aegean, the Dalmatian Coast, the Baltic Sea and coastal Norway.

Prior to the Second World War, European nations developed prestigious national cruise companies (Douglas and Douglas 2004), and their wealthy citizenry toured the continents while the indigent travelled on lower decks as emigrants. Meanwhile, in the 1920s and 1930s, the Americans drove their 'tin Lizzies', to visit their National Parks. The American Automobile Association estimated that in 1935, 40,000,000 Americans (one-third of the population) took at least one autovacation per year (Haynes, 1936).

Following the Second World War, reconstruction and recovery dominated Western Europe while Americans who had in general profited from the war began to vacation overseas, travelling by ship or air, first to Europe and often to visit relatives 'back home'. In the 1970s travel to and within the USA was too expensive for most Europeans, so they searched for winter 'second homes' along the Mediterranean shores. Instead, Americans turned on their televisions to the *Love Boat* series inaugurated by Princess Cruises, and the now retired members of the American 'Depression kids' (born 1915–1930) became the first generation of Caribbean and Alaskan cruisers. Demand has subsequently spawned increasingly larger, more luxurious ships but the market for marine mass tourism may have peaked as of January 2005. No new construction of megaships is currently planned and the industry silently worries about a possible terrorist attack on a vessel.

Uniqueness of US cruising

The USA is geographically favoured with two coastlines that offer especially desirable seasonal sailing, thus keeping many vessels actively occupied throughout the year. Ships operating from Florida and the Gulf Coast gain access to subtropical Caribbean islands and the warm waters of the Gulf Stream. Cruise itineraries from November through March host winter travellers from Canada, the USA and Europe, the latter often by negotiated cheap air fares, that include islands of diverse nationalities and ethnicities. Duty-free shopping, excellent water sports and good deep-sea fishing are important winter attractions for these 'snowbirds'.

The Caribbean cruise tourism industry was well documented by the mid-1990s (Wilkinson, 1997). Most Caribbean cruises are 1 week long, and each ship has a homeport from which it sails late Saturday afternoon. The itinerary is described as *short haul, fast turn-around*, for the distance travelled in the week is often not more than 600 miles, with 3 or 4 shore stops, and returns to homeport on Saturday morning. The crew has at most 4–5 hours to take on supplies and ready the ship for the arrival of the next complement of passengers in early afternoon. Few crew have much, if any, shore leave.

In April each year, most vessels, especially the megaships, leave the Caribbean for a transition voyage through the Panama Canal and north to Alaska for their summer itineraries. Passengers often travel at substantially reduced rates during these 'off-season' voyages. The vessels return to the Caribbean in late September. This south-bound sailing is favoured because September is the least foggy month on the West coast. Also, the ship is sailing with the southward flow of the California current, for the smoothest passage of the year.

In Alaska the same 'short haul, fast turnaround' applies, with a slight modification to accommodate two 'home ports': Vancouver, British Columbia in the south and either Juneau or Skagway in the North. Passengers cruise between the two, in a 4–5-day span viewing mountain scenery and watching for whale, seals, eagles and bear. In addition, the ships make shore stops at several Alaskan coastal towns for sightseeing and shopping. These Alaskan communities have only a few blocks of flat land, with mountains rising steeply behind. With a minimum of three megaships docking every day all summer, with a minimum of 6000 visitors, the main street is heavily trafficked with tourists weaving in and out of the many curio shops. Each town has one or more galleries that specializes in indigenous crafts and fine art, but there are few customers.

The cruise companies try to inject some Alaskan adventure into their programmes, and offer half-day optional tours for kayaking, helicopter flights over the glaciers, halibut fishing and salmon bake lunches (prepared by Native Americans). These shore excursions create local employment but add appreciably to the cost of the vacation. Arriving at the terminus of their cruise, passengers usually fly back to their boarding city. Crews are obtained through hiring agencies that screen potential employees from economically depressed countries including eastern Europe and the Philippines (Wood, 2000). Contracts are written for 4–6 months, hours are long and wages are notoriously low. Most stewards rely on passenger tips for their income.

Long-haul itineraries – around South America and/or around the world – are usually made by mid-sized vessels (500–1000 passengers) or by luxury small ships such as the Seabourne line. The itinerary is customarily divided into segments, so passengers can fly into one port, sail through their favoured area and fly home after 2–3 weeks. The fare, based on cost per mile and higher staff per passenger ratios, is higher than for short haul, plus the connecting air fares. Several such vessels are among the 30 expected to visit peninsular Antarctica in winter 2004/05 (IAATO, 2004). Reflective of the substantial distances involved, a 10-day large ship Antarctic visit may cost as little as US$6000 (in 2005) in contrast to expedition cruising to the same areas, for a minimum of US$9000 (see below). However, the former makes no shore stops to visit penguin rookeries or even to 'set foot' on the continent.

In addition to the itineraries and services outlined above, many small regional operations serve special needs, such as coastal cruising in Glacier Bay (Alaska) to see waterline glaciers 'calve', to watch bears feed on spawning salmon in Katmai National Park (Alaska) or for whale watching along both coasts. Counterparts to these regional cruises operate in many areas of the world and need not be identified here.

Adventure Cruising

To adventure is defined as 'a bold undertaking in which hazards are to be met' (*Webster's*, 1998), and suggests that an out-of-the-ordinary cruise might encounter some surprises, and possibly some danger. Chaucer in the 14th century advised 'take the chance, try the risk' and we have been adventuring ever since. The hazard is not necessarily harmful – it could be a stirring experience, even a shipboard romance. Most readers will agree we individually live amidst constant 'dangers': a computer glitch; 'catching' some other person's cold or flu; lost baggage; or an autowreck. Europeans routinely ride trains; many Americans have never been on a train and consider it a major adventure. Imagine the sense of adventure of Thomas Cook's first escorted train tour, to attend a temperance meeting. *Adventure is what we perceive it to be.* Travel writers and marketing agencies have instilled in the public the belief that to travel on a small ship is more adventurous than sailing on a superliner or megaship. *Therefore, so be it.*

The Passengers

The dominant population who now support adventure cruising are the baby boomer generation, born 1946–1964 (Smith and Brent, 2001, p. 118) who are newly retired or nearing retirement, well educated, in good health and with highly successful careers. Many shy the admission that they are ageing, preferring to self-test their strength and energy in active sports and at health clubs, and quite openly benefit from cosmetic surgery. These adventure travellers have the financial resources to support their motivation for small group travel, which is frequently high-end in cost. They seek the advantage of using vessels of up to 110 passengers as a floating hotel, with emphasis on nature study and shore-based activities including birding, hiking, snorkelling, scuba diving and kayaking. Most small ships carry zodiacs to facilitate landing in uninhabited areas, and naturalist guides escort shore parties on a range of activities. This group of adventurers plans ahead, makes their reservations early, and many sailings are totally booked months before departure.

Forms of Adventure Cruising

Nostalgic cruising includes sailing vessels and paddle wheelers, and is a form of heritage tourism. The world literature is filled with legends of great sailing ships and the exploits of their captains – men such as Magellan and Captain Cook, and even Captains Bligh and Henry Hudson. Reconstructed sailing ships are tourist attractions in many harbours worldwide, and entertainment centres such as Mystic Seaport (located in Connecticut USA) are heritage sailing destinations.

To sail aboard a tall ship recaptures some of that early drama, especially if aboard one of the historic three- or four-masted schooners. Windjammer Cruises has successfully operated 'barefoot cruises': in the Bahamas for over 40 years, using vessels such as the S/V *Mandalay* dating to 1923, and the S/V *Yankee Clipper* built

in 1927. Being the only armour-plated sailing vessel in the world, it became the racing craft for the wealthy Vanderbilt family. The *aficionados* enjoy the prevailing informality of being 'part of the crew' aboard these vessels, listening for orders from the 'Bosun's whistle', and best of all, at a price that is often no more than US$100 per day. Upscale by contrast, the legendary S/V *Sea Cloud* (Fig. 22.1) was built in 1931 by American financier E.F. Hutton as a wedding gift to his bride, Marjorie Merriwether Post, heiress to the cereal fortune, and also the inventor of fast frozen food processing.

Marjorie as owner of the world's most luxurious sailing ship (Fig. 22.1) used it to entertain royalty, motion picture stars and leading political figures. Her suite still boasts a real fireplace (on a wooden hulled ship!), marble tubs and solid gold toilet fixtures. Until the Second World War, the ship attained fame as the floating US Embassy – anchored in St Petersburg harbour – while her second husband, Joseph Davie, was Ambassador to the Soviet Union. Later, when Mr Davie served in a similar capacity to Belgium, Marjorie relocated the ship to Antwerp and continued the lavish lifestyle. The ship was built in Kiel, Germany, and the preponderance of her passengers are German. In addition to many operational crew, the *Sea Cloud* carries 27 sailors for the sole purpose of handling the extensive canvas sails. When she is fully rigged and racing before the wind, every passenger is helplessly caught in reliving the drama of early explorers whose daring voyages mapped our planet.

Paddle Wheelers

Steamboat 'round the bend' was the traditional call that announced the pending arrival of a paddle wheeler on the Mississippi River, or one of its tributaries. These big wooden-storied flat-bottom boats (Fig. 22.2), with either a stern wheel or two side wheels, became the artery of early USA. Samuel Clemens became a cub pilot aboard the river ship *Paul Jones* in 1857, earned his licence in 1859 and served 2 more years, until steamboat services ceased operation during the US Civil War (1861–1865). Clemens' pilot experiences created the memorable novels *Tom Sawyer, Huckleberry Finn* and the descriptive

Fig. 22.1. *M/V Sea Cloud*. Courtesy of Sea Cloud Company.

Fig. 22.2. *Delta Queen* Steamboat. Courtesy of Delta Queen Steamboat Company.

Life on the Mississippi, written under the pen name Mark Twain.

The vessels were uniquely constructed for river passage, with the long gangway suspended forward, to permit the boat to pull in close to shore and drop the gangway on land for easy access to a plantation, mill or town. In the historic South, their outbound cargo was cotton and tobacco, and inbound they brought supplies to plantations and farmsteads. They carried mail and people, and they also brought news and entertainment, as so well described in the Jerome Kern and Oscar Hammerstein II musical, *Showboat*.

The US Civil War was originally divisive but ultimately decisive, in ending slavery and uniting the warring sides into 'one nation under God'. Many US citizens are students of civil war history and participate in the military re-enactments. Uniformed 'soldiers' set up encampments, horses haul in cannons and supplies, and the battles rage (no injuries); the ladies in long dresses and bonnets set up and staff the souvenir stands! Battles are held regularly throughout the country, often hundreds if not thousands of miles from the original site, and some participants travel from one site to the next. Steamboats began to operate for tourism as early as 1890 (see history, www.deltaqueen.com), and their marketing strategies have satisfied several generations of enthusiastic repeat clients. The company has maintained the architectural design and decor of the late Victorian era. Now home-based in New Orleans, the ships ply the Mississippi and Ohio rivers with three vessels. There are replays of traditional 'steamboat races'; there are 'theme cruises' for Christmas, fall colours and 4 July. Especially notable are the spring pilgrimage sailings, which coincide with the Natchez Trace azalea festival when many ante-bellum homes are open just 1 or 2 days a year for visitors. The ships are also scheduled to be docked in Louisville as overnight accommodations for cruise passengers to attend the famed Kentucky Derby horse race.

In 2000, the American Steamboat Company reintroduced steamboating to the Columbia River where it historically played a major role in the development of the Pacific North-west following the Lewis and Clark Expedition of 1802–1805. The shore excursions by motor coach visit a variety of landmarks including a Native American reservation, a hellcat ride on the Snake River, and a tour of the Visitor Centre at Mount St Helen's volcanic crater. This company has also recreated tourist coastal steamboat service from Seattle to Skagway, Alaska, reviving the very important route to the gold rush sites of 1898. The gracious ambience of both steamboat companies is supported by repeat clientele who appreciate the added heritage of southern cuisine and western seafood.

Yachts

Yachts are relatively small pleasure watercraft, which have provided owners, their families and friends the opportunity to literally tour worldwide. However, the focus here is the commercialization of yachting as a form of adventure tourism. The expense of maintaining a yacht has increased perceptibly in recent years with higher costs for fuel and, in urban areas, excessive rental fees for anchorage in sheltered marinas. Yacht Rental dealers arrange charters of vessels of varying size, either as bare boat or with captain and crew. The owner gains some income to offset maintenance and possibly some tax deductions. Sea Dream Yacht Club, created in 2001 by Atle Brynestad (founder of luxurious Seabourne Cruises), specializes in charters of 'boutique mega-yachts' for the 'active affluent clientele'. Ward (2004) describes the experience 'like having your own private yacht in which hospitality and anticipation are art forms practiced to a high level . . . the SeaDreams provide the setting for personal indulgence and refined, unstructured and languorous living at sea in a casual setting'. Services in 2004 were advertised at US$450 per person per day.

Some larger yachts in the range of 300–400 feet in length are periodically rented out to favoured tour companies for specific longer voyages, and do not have to fit the constraints of the purely commercial operations. In one such example, the owner sailed with the ship from the home-port in Greece to Mumbai, India; a 50-person tour sponsored by the National Geographic Magazine boarded there and sailed south to Sri Lanka and north to Chennai (formerly Madras), while the owner toured India by land for 2 weeks. When we disembarked, the owner rejoined the ship and returned to Greece. This convenient arrangement is expandable for the reciprocal benefits to both parties in long-haul ferries.

Ferries

Ferries are customarily described as watercraft that transport people and goods from one shore to another. Two such services are long-haul and make multiple interesting stops, which identy them as services of adventure tourism. Best known is the Norwegian *hurtigrute (ferry service)*, which operates along the 1250-mile fiorded coast from Bergen to North Cape and Kirkenes. The service began in 1891 with freighters and a limited number of cabins, and has gradually evolved into modern passenger liners with staterooms and facilities. For the traveller, the adventure still lies in the scenic grandeur and the shore stops, for each town is unique, and the activities and people differ each time at the same stop. Further, if one so chooses, they can select an itinerary that makes a stop in the off-the-beaten track Lofoten Islands, then join another ferry a few days later. Norway enjoys a high standard of living, and onshore costs are high by US standards. However, the price for the ferry is realistic and offers good value (www.norwegiancoastalvoyages.com).

A comparable ferry service carries passengers and goods along the west coast of Greenland but its existence is scarcely known. Most Americans know Greenland as the 10th-century home of famed Viking Eric the Red, who probably also set foot in the Americas. The disappearance of the Viking from Greenland in the 15th century remains something of a scientific mystery (see Diamond, 2005). In 1721, the Royal Greenland Trading Company resettled in Greenland with Danish immigrants, and slowly instituted shipping services until they became routine ferry service daily during the summer from Narsarssuaq (site of a US-built Second World War airstrip) in the south to Upernavik in the north. Winter services vary according to ice conditions. Under Home Rule in 1986, the ferry service was transferred to Greenland and the Arctic Umiaq Line (www.aul.gl). The ferries have been enlarged, modernized and offer extensive holiday packages with local sightseeing (Fig. 22.3). The line advertises itself thus: '[W]atch whales and icebergs pass by as you travel along our coast with

Fig. 22.3.   Greenland Ferry. Courtesy of Arctic Umiaq Line.

the local population.' The Greenland ferry is an exceptional adventure tourism destination at modest cost.

Expedition Travel

To date, expedition travel is almost exclusively a US product, and is operated by three US-based companies – Lindblad, Zegrahm and Quark. The term *expedition* applied to tourism appears to have been introduced by Quark in 1991 when they began to formally advertise their specialization in Arctic tourism using Russian icebreakers. However, the distinctions between adventure cruising and expedition cruising are poorly defined. If adventure cruising suggests there may be hazards, expedition cruising suggests that we have set forth with a purpose – e.g. to explore and/or to learn something – and are prepared with personnel and equipment for that purpose (*Webster's*, 1998). One difference is clear – expedition travel is identified with a greater range of on-board lecturers as an integral part of that learning experience. Normally the staff would include a geologist, an ornithologist, a marine biologist and several other individuals with expertise in various aspects of natural and/or ethnographic history. If geographic conditions permit and sites of interest prevail, there are usually two and sometimes as many as four expedition 'stops' per day, to snorkel or dive, to walk in the rainforest, to climb a volcano, and/or to photograph wildlife and birds. If there are 4 hours 'free' during the day, there will be at least one lecture by an on-board naturalist. In the evening, there are appropriate videos in the staterooms, and early to bed for wakeup call is often at 6 AM for an early morning landing. There is no casino, no dancing and no entertainment other than one's own but there is a well-stocked library.

Marketing a programme of this type is selective, and the overall educational level among passengers is very high. Target audiences are alumni of leading universities, which, if serving as a sponsor, will add a scholar of note from that campus. Other supporters include special interest organizations such as World Wildlife, Nature Conservancy and Audubon. The atmosphere aboard is collegial, although in some 15 years I have met only two other professors aboard who were not lecturers probably because of the high per diem cost. (I am a full-fare expedition passenger and willingly pay for the seminar quality education.) One evening the cruise director jokingly addressed the audience as, 'You doctors, lawyers, techies and robber barons', and everyone laughed for it was an honest, revealing analysis of our position(s) in life.

This lifestyle confirms the definition by Sharpley (1994, pp. 29–32): 'Adventure tourism involves an experiential physical activity by the traveler. It is a business enterprise that is usually small in scale and often localized.'

Expedition travel (although it was then termed 'adventure') began with the l969 launch of the *Lindblad Explorer*, the first ship constructed with an 'ice-hardened' hull to sail in Antarctic waters during the Austral summers, and elsewhere throughout the year. The ship soon had a loyal following, including the Second World War veterans who voyaged from the Solomon Islands to New Guinea, dropping commemorative wreaths at battle sites. The 'little red ship' as she was affectionately known roamed the globe with her 114 passengers and 60 crew; the service ratio was 1:6, and notable lecturers were added to the complement. Eric Lars Lindblad was a 20th-century Thomas Cook expanding horizons, and his company is still in operation headed by his son, Eric. In 2005, Lindblad Travel continues to operate worldwide, using a variety of leased vessels after the *Explorer* was retired. The small ship concept proved so popular that the *World Discoverer* entered service in 1974, operated by Society Expeditions. Although the ship was a great passenger favourite, the company gradually overextended. In 1990, six employees left, to form a new entity, Zegrahm Expeditions (www.zeco.com). The latter has been very successful, and added a new sector, Eco-Expeditions, in which it has taken the lead in aerial charter expeditions to remote regions, including the first

Circumnavigation of North America by Air (2005).

Europeans have pointed out that there are no expedition-type tours available to them from European operators. Peter Deilmann operates river boats in Europe and occasionally charters a vessel such as the *Hanseatic* for Arctic touring. However, the ship lacks the ice-hardened hull so Europeans are more apt to travel on icebreakers. Because of manifest concerns with differences in language, cuisine, lecture material and ethnicity, the US expedition operators accept only European clients who are personally known to them. This is rational, not prejudicial. I asked for space on a Costa (Italian) ship, and was denied because I am not fluent in Spanish – 'the trip is for Latins only' (the dining hours are those of Spain, and the primary entertainment is ballroom dancing). There is a growing market for expedition travel in Europe.

Icebreakers

Icebreakers are predominantly industrial ships, used to clear shipping lanes for the convenience of freighters and supply vessels, including the Baltic Sea, the US Great Lakes and Canada's Arctic North. The Russian icebreakers that are currently used for tourist expeditions to the Arctic and Antarctic are remnants of a Soviet industrial fleet. Explorers had sought for several centuries to find a northern route (Northeast Passage) from the Atlantic to the Pacific, to save half the travel distance and time. In the early 1930s, the Soviets initiated the Northern Sea Route, creating an icebreaker-escorted 'train' that would take supplies to the then developing new mines of Siberia. It is said that some 14 new cities were being created, each with a population nearly 100,000. Construction materials and food flowed east, the minerals moved west to Murmansk and, with rail links, to Soviet manufacturing plants. Each 'train' was led by a non-nuclear icebreaker of 25,000 Bhp (British horsepower) that could cut ice to a depth of some 8–9 feet. This 'engine' had several cargo vessels tied in tandem (using 3-inch heavy hawser), then a second icebreaker of the same category was tied to the last freighter; this was then attached to yet another string of cargo vessels, ending with a final ice-breaker. Crew members have described the navigational skill required to maintain the exact distance between the ships – if one went too fast, it could overtake and ram the vessel in front; if lagging behind, the strain could break the hawser. Two companies were involved – the western company, Poseidon, was based in Murmansk and operated east to the mouth of the Lena River; there cargo might be shifted to the eastern company, based in Valdivostok.

The 1991 collapse of the Soviet Union terminated this marine highway, leaving the mines inoperative, the cities dwindling, the vessels idle and the crew out of work. The Siberian and Kamchatka coasts are virtually abandoned. Owners of the *Kapitan Khlebnikov*, the 25,000-Bhp ice-breaker based in Vladivostok (Fig. 22.4), sought a new market in the Americas. They relocated officers and crew out of their cabins into quarters below deck, and hastily installed better toilet and shower facilities, beds and furniture and hired an Austrian chef. Quark picked up the option, and Arctic expedition cruising began in earnest. By comparison to other cruise vessels the ship is uncomfortable. The metal frame is always cold, the one small dining room is very crowded and meal service is rushed as the crew must also use the same dining room (manageable only because the crew work by Moscow time, and passengers live by sun time according to their longitude). There is no lounge, only a small library and a lecture hall. The saving grace is the very wide bridge and the Captain's open-bridge policy. Most passengers spend most of

their time standing at windows on the bridge watching for polar bear, whale and walrus. If the ship is cutting ice, many passengers are outside on front deck, bundled in parkas and laden with cameras for it is a fascinating, if noisy, operation. The ship carries two large helicopters for use in scouting open water and leads; both transport passengers to shore locations, including (in the North) Inuit villages and scenic locations; zodiacs are quiet and are used to approach walrus or photograph the ship as it cuts ice or cruises among icebergs.

In 1993, Quark offered a circumnavigation of Greenland, at the then monstrous price of US$22,000. Starting from the the Second World War US-built airstrip at Sondre Stromfiord on the West coast, the *Khlebnikov* sailed anticlockwise south, then north along the east coast and reached the northern tip of Greenland before becoming beset. There it sat in the ice for 3 days, while passengers watched airplanes fly overhead to consider their plight, and the cruise director, the indomitable Mike Messick, plied passenger cooperation with barbecues on the ice, volleyball matches and champagne. After considerable international negotiation, the Danish and Canadian governments agreed to permit the 'mother of all ships', the nuclear-powered icebreaker *Yamal* to enter these restricted waters. With its tremendous 75,000-Bhp engines, the two vessels worked to create an open pond large enough for the *Yamal* to turn around, then the *Khlebnikov* was tied to her stern. After some hours, both ships cleared the

Fig. 22.4.   I/B *Khlebnikov*, Ellesmere Island. Photo: Valene Smith.

heavy pack ice, and went their separate ways – the *Yamal* to homeport in Murmansk, and the *Khlebnikov* to Longyearben in Svalbard, to an airstrip to fly her passengers home. It was an expedition that is now recorded in polar history books.

For the benefit of readers who might be considering a journey on either ship (both are operational in 2005, and expect to be for some years yet to come), there is a significant difference between the ice-cutting mechanisms of the two ships. *Khlebnikov* has a long prow, which is pushed by the power of the engines out onto the icepack ahead of the ship. When the ship is stopped by the ice, the weight of the towering seven storeys that form the cabin area of the ship comes crashing down on the ice and (hopefully) cracks or breaks the ice, forming an open water area. In the situation described above, the *Khlebnikov* made 27 runs (backing up and rushing forward on full power onto the ice), before abandoning the operation and admitting they were 'stuck'. In addition to the weight, the ship has three other techniques for working through the ice – the ship carries water as ballast in tanks and the captain or engineer can shift the weight of the water from one side to the other. This 'rocking motion' often supports the downward plunge. Moreover, steam from the engine is forced out at waterline through small holes – and on immediate contact, the hot air melts the surface ice (visible in Fig. 22.4). Also at waterline, the ships hull is covered in a band of 'slippery' paint that supposedly reduces ice friction. Needless to say, when working through heavy ice, the ship is in constant motion; passengers are asked to hold fast to anything but not to a doorjamb lest you lose a finger if the door slams shut. The worst factor about the ship is its round hull, well designed like Amundsen's *FRAM* for Arctic ice, but when in open water and rough seas, the ship can wallow and roll as much as 60°. A voyage from Europe or even from Capetown to the Antarctic is only for the hardiest of sailors.

Yamal has a normal hull, and relies solely on her tremendous nuclear engine power to cut 12–15 feet in ice, the thickness depending on its age. All icebreakers carry Ice Captains whose years of Arctic experience is invaluable in selecting routes, and are informative to passengers. *Yamal* is, none the less, a remarkable vessel, and carries enough fuel for 5 years, enough water for 3 years, and food for 2 years (almost everything served aboard is pre-frozen). She has pulled alongside a stricken city and supplied electricity and water for an extended period of time.

Yamal and *Dranitysen* (25,000 Bhp) are based in Murmansk and provide Arctic expedition cruising services to the Europeans. *Yamal* makes several trips each summer to the North Pole, and also operates in the high Arctic during the winter, taking European adventurers and explorers north to ski, to dogsled, etc. It is truly expedition travel.

In August 2004, from the New Siberian Islands east to the Lena River, the Northern Sea Route should have been ice-free. Instead, 100-year-old pack ice filled the channels, and the *Yamal* was reduced to 3 miles per hour. The ship was destined for the World Heritage Site of Wrangel Island, and Cruise Director Mike Messick and 104 passengers were frantic and made no landings for 5 days. Instead, the helicopters were busy with passenger flights to photograph the ship 'cutting ice'. Expedition cruising requires patience and flexibility!

Conclusion

Cruising has become a preferred lifestyle because it requires so little energy for most passengers. Their principal obligation is to select the ship and travel style that fits their individual needs and preferences. Once aboard, passengers can be as indolent or active as they wish. And the ship can literally traverse the 71% of the earth's crust that is water. We can travel from the Tropics to the Arctic; we can pull alongside and gaze at the Namib – one of the world's driest deserts and be saddened by the wrecked ships and lives lost on the so-called Skeleton Coast. We can marvel at man's ingenuity as we transit locks and canals, and admire beautiful new bridge design. Given the increasing hassles at airport security, flying has lost considerable charm.

However, lest we forget, despite all the modern technology of satellite communication, sonar, radar, global positioning system (GPS), diving gear to repair broken propellers (yes, even on the *Yamal*) – we must remember: the sea is forever the master. The *tsunami* of 26 December 2004 is a sombre reminder of the power of the ocean. Ice laid claim to the *Titanic*; an uncharted reef in the Solomon Islands claimed the *World Discoverer*, fortunately without loss of life although she still seeps fuel into the sea. Her resting place is too remote for salvage; the indigenous islanders would like to see her pulled offshore and sunk, to eventually create a historic diving site like the *President Cleveland* in Vanuatu. This would create more heritage marine tourism.

To enjoy the richness of our planet mandates its stewardship. The ships on which we travel have impacts on the sea and its biota, and also on the people who live around its shore. They need and deserve protection from human pollution, misuse and overuse. As passengers, we have an obligation to ensure that our chosen cruise operation meets the highest possible standards.

References

Diamond, J. (2005) *Collapse: How Societies Choose to Fail or Succeed.* Penguin Group, New York.

Douglas, N. and Douglas, N. (2004) *The Cruise Experience: Global and Regional Issues in Cruising.* Pearson Hospitality Press, French's Forest, New South Wales, Australia.

Haynes, N. (1936) *Hotel Life.* University of North Carolina Press, Historical Statistics of the United States, Chapel Hill, North Carolina.

IAATO (2004) *1992–2005 Antarctic Tourist Trends – Landed.* Available at: www.iaato.org

Khelladi, Y. (2003) *Cruise-Ship Stop That Dares Not Speak its Name.* Available at: www.kiskeya-alternative. org/cangonet/cango2000/0359.html

Niche Cruises (2004) *Sales Guide.* Niche Cruising Marketing Alliance, Everett, Washington.

Readman, M. (2003) Golf tourism. In: Hudson, S. (ed.) *Sports and Adventure Tourism.* Haworth Hospitality Press, New York, pp. 165–202.

Sasso, N. (2004) Descriptive Commentary in Carnival Cruise Advertising Brochure. Carnival Cruise Lines, New York.

Sharpley, R. (1994) *Tourism, Tourists and Society.* Elm Publications, Huntingdon, Virginia.

Smith, V. and Brent, M. (eds) (2001) *Hosts and Guests Revisited: Tourism Issues of the 21st Century.* Cognizant Communication Corp., Elmford, New York.

Ward, D. (2004) *Berlitz Ocean Cruising and Cruise Ships.* Berlitz Publishing, Princeton, New Jersey.

Webster's (1998) *New World Dictionary of the English Language,* 3rd college edn. Simon & Schuster, New York.

Wilkinson, P. (1997) *Tourism Policy and Planning: Case Studies from the Commonwealth Caribbean.* Cognizant Communication Corp., Elmford, New York.

Wood, R.F. (2000) Caribbean cruise tourism globalization at sea. *Annals of Tourism Research* 27(2), 345–370.

23 Off the Beaten Track: A Case Study of Expedition Cruise Ships in South-west Tasmania, Australia

Claire Ellis[1] and Lorne K. Kriwoken[2]

[1]Formerly *University of Tasmania, School of Management, Tourism Programme, Hobart, Tasmania, Australia;* Currently *Tourism Tasmania, GPO Box 399, Hobart, Tasmania 7001, Australia;* [2]*University of Tasmania, School of Geography and Enivronmental Studies, Private Bag 78, Hobart, Tasmania 7001, Australia*

Introduction

Significant growth has occurred in the cruise industry and it has been considered one of the fastest-growing segments in tourism (Wild and Dearing, 2000, p. 316). The growth of the cruise industry is supply-led and as cruise ship-building continues, the industry is expected to grow rapidly. With this growth, the market is becoming increasingly competitive. There are a wide variety of types and sizes of ships, modes of operating and itinerary structures as companies seek to differentiate themselves within the market and create new market niches.

One of these niches is the expedition cruise ship market. However, there is no established agreement between academics or within the industry on different niches within the cruise ship industry. Douglas and Douglas (2004, p. 117) discuss 'small ships' and argue that although the industry sometimes classifies these as carrying 500 passengers or less, a more appropriate figure may be 300 passengers. Mancini (2000) lists small ships as carrying 200–500 passengers. Small ships can also be distinguished by their 'informality and ecological interests' and limited cruising area (Douglas and Douglas, 2004, p. 117). The distinction between small ships, adventure ships and expe-

dition ships is unclear (Douglas and Douglas, 2004, p. 127) and industry advertising often uses the terms interchangeably. This chapter uses the term 'expedition cruise ships' and characterizes these by their style of operations, which explore new locations, get off the beaten path and often have an ecotourism focus, with on-board lecturers and expedition teams providing an educational flavour.

Expedition cruise ships account for a small portion of the estimated 10 million passengers who travelled on cruise ships in 2000 (Kester, 2002, p. 337) partly due to their small passenger numbers. Because of their mode of operation they tend to take approximately 100–150 passengers, so do not include all types of 'small' or 'adventure' ships. This small size is an essential part of expedition cruising as a ship must disembark passengers in locations with often no wharf or jetty. Instead, manoeuvrable, fast, zodiac-style craft are used to transfer passengers ashore. Despite the small size of expedition cruise ships, their interest in finding new unspoilt, previously unvisited locations with a strong natural or cultural appeal means that the impact of their visits may be significant. For planning purposes the sites visited can also be difficult to control.

This chapter uses a case study of planning and management of expedition cruise ships to the Tasmanian Wilderness World Heritage Area (TWWHA) and argues that scoped research on environmental impacts should play a pivotal role in determining whether expedition cruise ships should be granted permits to operate in these highly sensitive marine ecosystems. The chapter first discusses the growth of the cruise market and places expedition cruise shipping in context. This is followed by an overview of the Tasmanian cruise ship industry. The planning and management requirements for the TWWHA are then introduced with a specific focus on the Bathurst Harbour–Port Davey region. The chapter concludes with a discussion on how an environmental impact study of expedition cruise ships in the region has significantly improved management of the marine area and enabled the finalization of the *Guidelines for the Preparation of Licences for Commercial Vessels Operating in Port Davey–Bathurst Harbour*.

The Growth of the Cruise Market

The international cruise market is dominated by the North American region, both in terms of passengers and the cruise location of the Caribbean. The North American domestic market is characterized as a mature market with slow growth. The cruise industry is becoming increasingly global in terms of passengers and locations. For instance, the Asia-Pacific is now third in terms of market share and is growing quickly (Kester, 2002). Cruise ships have also been growing in terms of size and the new 'floating resort'-style ships that offer a wide variety of entertainment and activities encourage passengers to spend their time on board to increase spending, whilst the shore visits are less important. With this growth in cruise ship size has come economies of scale, and smaller ships have had to develop new itineraries and different styles to compete effectively.

The development of new itineraries and diversification into new locations has also been encouraged by the high level of repeat passenger in the cruise ship market. Figures vary and it has been suggested that 50–60% of cruise passengers were repeat passengers, but specific studies show variation and Petrick and Sirakaya's survey (2004, p. 473) of two Caribbean cruises had

a repeat level of 37%. Definitional differences exist between researchers and may account for some of these variations in statistics. For instance, whether the repeat behaviour is with the same company or same ship, and the use of the term 'cruise' can vary between operators. Despite these distinctions, researchers acknowledge that the cruise market has a relatively high level of repeat business compared with other tourism segments. Brand loyalty is highly valued in tourism as it is often more desirable and less expensive to retain tourists than seek new ones (Petrick and Sirakaya, 2004). Cruise ship operators actively promote and value brand loyalty and the development of new itineraries for a ship is a useful mechanism to attract repeat business.

Australia has not traditionally been a major location for cruise ships, but it is an appealing destination for the 'explorer' segment (Miller and Grazer, 2002, p. 228) and this may grow with the preference for safe locations with recent terrorism and international travel uncertainty. As well as attracting international visitors to cruise in Australia, the International Cruise Council Australasia stated that 'the global cruising market was up 11 per cent in 2003 compared with the previous year, while Australia's cruise market grew 32 per cent in the same period' (Allen, 2004). In 2005, more than 250,000 passengers are forecast to take a cruise (Anon, 2004). Australians may be attracted to a domestic cruise by the type of holiday and facilities and also by the fact that the ship can offer an itinerary that visits remote or difficult areas not easily possible to visit or view by land.

For expedition ships, Tasmania, the island state of Australia, is ideal for inclusion in a cruise ship itinerary in a geographic sense. Tasmania is situated between the mainland of Australia and Antarctica, and is also relatively close to New Zealand and sub-Antarctic islands, such as Macquarie Island. As a destination, Tasmania is also appealing with 334 offshore islands, a diverse range of accessible areas for cruising and a wide variety of natural and cultural values. Exploring offshore islands and viewing rugged coastlines from the sea are the type of attractions that expedition ship companies seek and use to separate themselves from other cruise ship niches.

Tasmania's Cruise Industry

Tasmania's tourism industry has been undergoing rapid growth, with a 13% increase in visitors in 2003/04 (Tourism Tasmania, 2004), and the island is becoming increasingly popular as a holiday destination, featuring unspoilt wilderness, scenic beauty, historic areas and fine food and wine. International knowledge, particularly of its natural attractions, has increased the number of expedition cruise ship operators assessing the potential of the State for future itineraries. Cruise ship companies are also actively encouraged to visit and make multistop visits by Cruise Tasmania, a marketing consortium consisting of Tasmania's main ports and Tourism Tasmania (J. Abel and C. Ellis, Hobart, 2003, unpublished data). The consortium highlights new cruise destinations, activities and attractions and has an itinerary planner to assist cruise line decision makers and planners in identifying new opportunities to present to an ever-expanding base of new and repeat clients. Cruise ship visitation has been almost 50,000 per year and this accounted for over 30% of all international visitation to Tasmania in 2001/02 (J. Abel and C. Ellis, 2003, unpublished data).

Large cruise ships depend on wharfs where space can be at a premium and they often utilize structured shore trips that require considerable advance planning and booking. Because of the needed infrastructure, port calls of larger ships are often in locations where a permit process already exists, and within Tasmania there are four ports (Hobart, Launceston, Devonport and Burnie) that regularly accommodate cruise ships with over 500 passengers. In addition to pilotage requirements, additional planning processes are required to ensure that social and environmental sustainability issues are incorporated (Dobson et al., 2002; Jaakson, 2004).

In contrast, smaller expedition cruise ships do not require port facilities, have their own on-board guides and shallow drafts allow them to get close to shore. They can potentially access various areas outside established harbours. If the site visit is not within a national park boundary, no permits are usually required. Potentially cruise ships have the ability to visit peripheral areas with little infrastructure and this can assist in more widely distributing the tourist dollar. Garrod and Wilson

(2004) argue that marine ecotourism in peripheral areas can encourage sustainable development by supporting these regional economies. However, their case study used locally based marine ecotourism operations. From the viewpoint of a host community, expedition ships may not provide significant economic benefit to a local area as they frequently do not rely on bus tours or incorporate shopping trips, may not visit commercial attractions and have their own expedition team, thus minimizing the need for local guides at each stop. Despite this, compared with other types of cruise ships, expedition ships are generally considered some of the most 'eco-friendly' and some of the strongest supporters of sustainable tourism.

At least twelve different Tasmanian sites have been accessed by international cruise ships in the last few years, of which six were ports. Cruise Tasmania also advertises seven anchorages in addition to the existing ports. One of these is Port Davey, the only safe cruise ship anchorage to access the wild and remote TWWHA (Fig. 23.1).

Tasmanian Wilderness World Heritage Area

The TWWHA, which has internationally and nationally significant natural and cultural values, was formally recognized under the World Heritage Convention in 1982 and again in 1989 when the World Heritage Area (WHA) was expanded. The TWWHA currently represents 20% of Tasmania's land mass (1.38 million ha) and therefore plays a critical role in Tasmania's environmental, economic, social and political spheres. The TWWHA Management Plan has the overall objective to 'identify, protect, conserve, present and where appropriate, rehabilitate the World Heritage and other natural and cultural values of the world heritage area and to transmit that heritage to future generations in good or better condition than at present' (TPWS, 1999).

Specific management objectives for the terrestrial and marine components of the southwest region have been formulated in the Melaleuca–Port Davey Advisory Committee

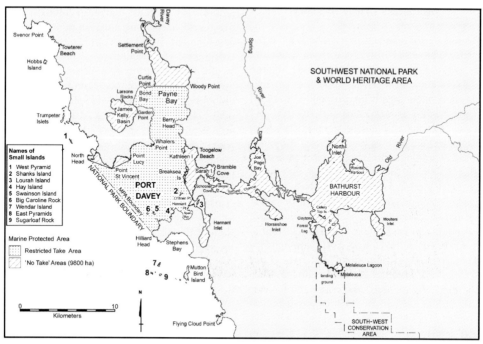

Fig. 23.1. Port Davey, Bathurst Channel and Bathurst Harbour, TWWHA.

(MPDAC), which has the mandate to 'provide appropriate recreational opportunities and facilities for visitors consistent with the protection of wilderness quality and the natural cultural values of the area' (TPWS, 2003, p. 6). The MPDAC also has specific requirements to, *inter alia*, 'protect, maintain and monitor the marine and estuarine ecosystems'. Despite the remote location, approximately 4000–5000 people visited the area in 2000, of which approximately 3000–4000 flew in to the airstrip at Melaleuca, 500 walked in and the remainder visited by sea (TPWS, 2003). These data are known to underestimate private boating visitation, however, as there is little means of collating data on private sea-borne visitors. The busiest tourist season for Port Davey is during January, immediately after the completion of the Sydney–Hobart yacht race.

Whilst the natural and cultural values of the TWWHA are significant, few ships choose to visit Port Davey, partly due to frequent inclement weather, rough seas and the limitations on safe anchorage sites. The exposed southern coastline of Tasmania and potentially rough seas of the Southern Ocean can contribute to an uncomfort-

able journey to Port Davey. However, once a ship has arrived, the enclosed waters of Port Davey and Bathurst Channel (Fig. 23.2) form a large, very scenic area suitable for cruise ships, similar in nature to Milford Sound, New Zealand. Bathurst Channel, which connects Bathurst Harbour to the coast at Port Davey, has a depth varying between 15 m and 40 m. Therefore navigational issues limit the size of ships that can enter and the distance up the Channel they can travel. Between Port Davey and Bathurst Channel there is a shallow 12 m sill, but the waters of Port Davey are generally over 20 m deep.

Port Davey, Bathurst Channel and Bathurst Harbour form the largest estuarine system in Australia, fed by unrestrained rivers (Davey, Spring, North and Old Rivers), with no road access and have not experienced significant human impact (Edgar and Cresswell, 1991). Water currents and circulation patterns in Bathurst Channel and Bathurst Harbour are complex. It is one of only three large Australian estuaries where the water remains well stratified for long periods of time. The estuary is characterized by a dark freshwater layer, which is the result of staining from tannins, leached from the

Fig. 23.2.   The enclosed waters of Port Davey and Bathurst Channel form a large, scenic area.

surrounding peat soils and buttongrass plains. This dark layer of water overlies the bottom layer of clear tidal marine water and prevents much of the sunlight from penetrating into the lower stratified layers. The layers of water also differ in their salt content creating a halocline, with the mid-layer (the halocline) gradually changing in salinity levels from the fresh surface water to the bottom saltwater layer. The depth of the halocline in Bathurst Harbour–Port Davey is difficult to determine precisely as it requires accurate measurement of nitrate and oxygen levels; however, it is believed that the halocline decreases in depth towards the western outlet of Bathurst Channel and ceases to exist outside Breaksea Island, Port Davey. During winter, when rainfall is highest, the dark brackish water is known to reach a depth of up to 6 m. During summer, when expedition cruise ships are most likely to visit, the low input from freshwater rivers causes the halocline and the dark layer of tannin-stained water to virtually disappear for short periods through much of the Bathurst Harbour and Bathurst Channel (Edgar, 1989).

In addition to the stratification of the estuary, the waters of Bathurst Channel and Bathurst Harbour are believed to exhibit the lowest nutrient levels of any estuaries in Australia. This is a result of the surrounding nutrient-poor soils, geology, plankton commu-

nities, lack of human-induced pollution and highly stratified marine system, which minimizes upwellings or water disturbances.

The limited penetration of light and the varying concentrations of marine water, resulting from the halocline and the stratified waters, have allowed invertebrate communities, normally found in waters over 50 m deep, to thrive in shallow waters and replace some plant communities (Edgar and Cresswell, 1991). Such communities are composed of sponges, lace corals, sea squirts and anemones, sea pens, sea whips, soft corals and bryozoans (Last and Edgar, 1994). The invertebrate communities vary. Some fauna live on rocky areas and are quite resistant to the strong currents that can flow in narrow sections of the Channel and significant wave action that naturally occurs in the area. Other fauna live in fine sediment zones and are sensitive to disturbance, including any potential turbulence created by passing ships. The fish found in Bathurst Harbour–Port Davey are also affected by the halocline and stratified water column, and expected assemblages of shallow water species are not present, possibly due to the lack of seaweeds. Instead, the fish found in the area are more like those found in deeper waters rather than estuaries. The most common fish in Bathurst Harbour and Bathurst Channel are sharks and skates.

The aquatic organisms are also unique as they include relict fauna from over 80 million years ago, when Gondwana split and elements from the ice age that are extinct elsewhere can still be found in the Port Davey–Bathurst Harbour. For instance, a unique species of ice fish has been found in Port Davey and it appears to have links to species in Patagonia and New Zealand. A recent finding in Bathurst Harbour has identified a new species of skate (*Dipturus* sp.) also believed to be a relict from Gondwana species, and now restricted to the habitat of Bathurst Harbour and Macquarie Harbour. Close relatives to this skate have been identified in New Zealand in waters 1000 m deep.

Given the unique nature of the estuary, it has been the focus of much debate regarding a Marine Protected Area (MPA) designation. In 1999, the Marine and Marine Industries Council (MMIC) was set up with the mandate to create an MPA Strategy for Tasmania. MMIC identified the Tasmanian Resource Development and Planning Commission (RPDC, 2002) as the appropriate body to conduct an inquiry and propose specific recommendations for MPA proposals. The strategy had the primary goal to 'establish and manage a comprehensive, adequate and representative system of marine protected areas, to contribute to the long-term ecological viability of marine and estuarine systems, to maintain ecological processes and systems and to protect Tasmania's biological diversity' (Tasmania, 2000, p. 8). The RPDC was asked to assess the proposal for an MPA at Port Davey–Bathurst Harbour as part of the strategy. The RPDC submitted a Final Recommendations Report in July 2003 and the Port Davey–Bathurst Harbour MPA was declared on 3 February 2004 (RPDC, 2003).

The RPDC inquiry examined four options for the MPA designation ranging from strict 'no-take reserves' to multiple use zones. The final decision divided the MPA into two broad zones: sanctuary (no-take areas) and habitat protection (restricted-take areas) (Fig. 23.1). Sanctuary zones prohibit fishing and other extractive uses in order to preserve the ecological integrity of the area and to ensure its use as a benchmark area. The habitat protection zone allows low-impact fishing including abalone diving, rock lobster fishing and hand lining. Trawling, netting, long lining and fish trapping are not permitted.

In both the sanctuary and habitat protection zones recreational activities are allowed to continue with appropriate permits. Activities can potentially include ocean kayaking, scuba-diving, recreational boating and cruise ship visitation. Because the area is a National Park and WHA, licences must be obtained for commercial vessel operations (including cruise ships), but private, commercial fishing and all other types of boating are exempt. Few cruise ship operators have requested access to Port Davey. However, since 1999 expedition ship companies have requested and been granted permits to visit limited zones within the area.

Environmental Impacts

Cruise ships often access areas of high natural wave action, such as tropical coral reef areas, yet little research had been undertaken concerning the potential impact of turbulence on benthic communities in soft sediment zones that occur at some sites within Bathurst Channel. Potential physical damage from cruise ships such as anchor damage, grounding or wrecks has been examined (Smith, 1988) along with the impact of turbulence on pollution dispersion by cruise ships (Loehr *et al.*, 2001). The assessment of potential cruise ship impacts has often been based on the length, draft and/or speed of vessels, but these were not considered sufficiently precise to be used in the cruise ship permit process in the sensitive marine environment of Port Davey and Bathurst Channel.

To identify the most significant variables that determine a ship's turbulence, a team of experts was drawn from the Australian Maritime College, Tasmanian Aquaculture and Fisheries Institute, Department of Primary Industries, Water and Environment – Nature Conservation Branch and the Parks and Wildlife Service, CSIRO, Maritime and Safety Tasmania, Hobart Ports Corporation and University of Tasmania. Their brief also broadly incorporated an assessment of cruise ship access to Bathurst Channel and potential environmental impacts. The research was complex and logistically difficult. Ships similar in proportion to expedition ships were needed to traverse over current metres in specific estuarine areas. The work was supported by Heritage Expeditions, a New Zealand cruise ship operator, and a research grant from the Cooperative Research Centre for Sustainable Tourism.

The study addressed environmental aspects and was conducted in two stages: first, the creation of a model based on existing theory to predict the turbulence created by a specific ship; and second, to partially validate the model results using full-scale tests. This enhanced the certainty of the modelled results. This full-scale testing was undertaken initially in a similar estuarine system (Port Huon) outside the WHA. After demonstrating the accuracy of the model, full-scale testing in Bathurst Channel was conducted using underwater video cameras and other techniques (Ellis *et al.*, 2004). Wave–wake erosion on channel banks was also assessed and found to have an insignificant environmental impact compared with naturally occurring wave action.

The results of the ship's trials confirmed the modelled results. Subject to speed and navigation restrictions, if the modelled output of a specific ship met the identified criteria, it was determined that the ship was able to navigate within permitted sections of Bathurst Channel with no identifiable disturbance. Wind conditions were also taken into account. Navigation was restricted to the centre of the main deepwater channel and turning (at a specified location near Joe Page Bay) did not create propeller turbulence that caused suspension of sediments. The process of anchoring, and swinging at anchor, under low wind conditions was also assessed and appeared to cause little impact. Although the research was only indicative, a significant margin of error was added and the research team made its recommendations to the Tasmanian Parks and Wildlife Service.

Using the results of this research, the *Guidelines for the Preparation of Licences for Commercial Vessels Operating in Port Davey–Bathurst Harbour* was finalized (TPWS, 2002). All applications for an expedition cruise ship visit to Bathurst Channel will now be assessed using the model (which requires specific ship dimensions as input). The permit process will also limit the number of cruise ships that can visit over a 2-year period to seven. An overall ship limit of 120 m and/or draft of 7 m have been included as restrictions to the permit process. A pilot is required and all cruise ship-

ping must stay in the deepest section of the channel and use the single identified anchorage site (if needed).

Specific research such as that outlined above may have further application within the cruise industry, as expedition cruise ships seek new areas away from the traditional grounds of tropical coral reefs and as the value of estuarine and shallow marine areas becomes more acknowledged. However, the decision-making process regarding access rights of cruise ships in remote, pristine or underdeveloped areas needs further examination.

Conclusion

As expedition shipping appears to be expanding in Tasmania, mechanisms for determining appropriate areas for visitation need to be enhanced. For ships wishing to visit a National Park, a mechanism for determining where ships may visit is feasible. Cruise ship visitation to Port Davey and Bathurst Channel highlights some of the difficulties in determining permit approvals. Although this area was physically unusual, the research demonstrates how little understanding there was concerning the environmental impact of visitation to this area. In this case, it was decided that small cruise ships with limited numbers of passengers visiting occasionally had no discernible marine impact. Expedition ships may also bring significant benefits, and other Tasmanian sites visited only by expedition ships, small enough to visit peripheral rural areas, have reported positive social impacts from the occasional visits (J. Abel and C. Ellis, Hobart, 2003, personal communication). Further research is required to analyse the extent of social and economic impacts associated with expedition ship visitation.

Expedition cruise ship companies often conduct ecotours and access sites of high natural and cultural value. In areas where the marine conservation values are high or the area is sensitive to disturbance, an appropriate planning mechanism is needed to license cruise shipping. This research was complex and the resulting permit process was time-consuming. However, the results allow the potential effect of each proposed cruise ship visit to be assessed objectively, and for clear and consistent guidelines for licences to be developed. The clarification of the licensing process has now permitted Cruise Tasmania to develop an appropriate marketing plan for expedition cruise ships, particularly in peripheral regions. It has contributed to the discussion of marine and estuarine environmental impacts associated with shipping. In addition, this research assisted a number of stakeholders to achieve consensus concerning cruise ship access to Port Davey and assisted in the development of an environmentally sustainable marine tourism industry in Tasmania.

References

Allen, L. (2004) Luxury liners cruising along in Asia-Pacific market. *Australian Financial Review*, 17 June 2004.

Anon. (2004) Princess takes delivery of 'Sapphire'. *Lloyds Cruise International*, p. 5.

Dobson, S., Gill, A. and Baird, S. (2002) *A Primer on the Canadian Pacific Cruise Ship Industry*. Available at: www.sfu.ca/coastalstudies/Cruise Ship.pdf

Douglas, N. and Douglas, N. (2004) *The Cruise Experience*. Pearsons Education Australia, New South Wales, Australia.

Edgar, G. (1989) *Hydrological and Ecological Survey of the Port Davey–Bathurst Harbour Estuary, 1988–1989*. Department of Zoology, University of Tasmania, Hobart.

Edgar, G.J. and Cresswell, G.R. (1991) Seasonal changes in hydrology and the distribution of plankton in the Bathurst Harbour Estuary, South-western Tasmania, 1988–89. *Papers and Proceedings of the Royal Society of Tasmania* 125, 61–72.

Ellis, C., Barrett, N. and Schieman, S. (2004 submitted) Wilderness cruising: turbulence, cruise ships and benthic communities. *Journal of Marine Environment* 2(1), 1–2.

Garrod, B. and Wilson, J.C. (2004) Nature on the edge? Marine ecotourism in peripheral coastal areas. *Journal of Sustainable Tourism* 12(2), 95–120.

Jaakson, R. (2004) Beyond the tourist bubble? Cruise ship passengers in port. *Annals of Tourism Research* 31(1), 44–60.

Kester, J. (2002) Cruise tourism. *Tourism Economics* 9(3), 337–350.

Last, P.R. and Edgar, G.J. (1994) *Wilderness Ecosystems Baseline Studies Interim Report 1994: Invertebrate Community Delineation and Mapping of Bathurst Harbour*. Wilderness Ecosystems Baseline Study, Hobart.

Loehr, L., Mearns, A. and George, K. (2001) *Cruise Ship Waste Disposal and Management. Initial Report on the 10 July 2001, Study of Opportunity of Currents and Wake Turbulence Behind Cruise Ships*. Alaska Department of Environment Conservation. Available at: http://www.state.ak.us/dec/press/cruise/documents/reports2001.htm

Mancini, M. (2000) *Cruising, A Guide to the Cruise Line Industry*. Delmar Thomson Learning, New York.

Miller, A and Grazer, W. (2002) The North American cruise market and Australian tourism. *Journal of Vacation Marketing* 8(3), 221–234.

Petrick, J.F. and Sirakaya, E. (2004) Segmenting cruisers by loyalty. *Annals of Tourism Research* 31(2), 472–475.

RPDC (Resource Planning and Development Commission) (2002) *Background Report: Inquiry Into the Establishment of a Marine Protected Area Within the Davey and Twofold Shelf Bioregions*. Resource Planning and Development Commission, Hobart, Tasmania, Australia.

RPDC (2003) *Inquiry into the Establishment of Marine Protected Areas Within the Davey and Twofold Shelf Bioregions: Final Recommendations Report*. Resource Planning and Development Commission, Hobart, Tasmania, Australia.

Smith, S.H. (1988) Cruise ships: a serious threat to coral reefs and associated organisms. *Ocean & Shoreline Management* 11, 231–248.

Tasmania (2000) *Draft Tasmanian Marine Protected Area Strategy*. Marine and Marine Industries Council, Hobart, Tasmania, Australia.

TPWS (Tasmanian Parks and Wildlife Service) (1999) *Tasmanian Wilderness World Heritage Area: 1999 Management Plan*. Tasmanian Parks and Wildlife Service, Hobart, Tasmania, Australia.

TPWS (2002) *Guidelines for the Preparation of Licences for Commercial Vessel Operations in Port Davey–Bathurst Harbour, May 2002*. Tasmanian Parks and Wildlife Service, Hobart, Tasmania, Australia.

TPWS (2003) *Draft Melaleuca Port Davey Area Plan*. Department of Tourism, Heritage and the Arts, Hobart, Tasmania, Australia.

Tourism Tasmania (2004) Tasmanian visitor survey, 2003/2004. Tourism Tasmania, Hobart. Available at: http://www.tourismtasmania.com.au/research/tvs2004_resultsjunfinyear.html

Wild, P. and Dearing, J. (2000) Development of and prospects for cruising in Europe. *Maritime Policy Management* 27(4), 315–333.

Part IV

Interactions: Economic, Social and Environmental Impacts

Introduction

Part III explored the supply side of cruising through a number of global examples. In Part IV the industry's interactions with the economic, social and natural environments are explored in nine chapters. The first identifies the importance of on-board revenue centres and the introduction and development of a range of new revenue sources. The next three discuss economic elements in relation to a destination region, ports and the day-cruise industry. Socio-cultural aspects are discussed in relation to local communities (host) and cruise tourist (guest) interactions in the Eastern Caribbean and Baja California, Mexico. The industry's environmental record is investigated and some suggestions are advocated in relation to industry self-regulation and voluntary guidelines versus command and control regulation. This interesting section of the book is then completed by a report on the impact of cruise tourism on the island of Cozumel, Mexico.

Introducing this part is the first of two chapters in this book by the legendary Ross Klein (Canada). Professor Klein is an outstanding academic author on cruise tourism and is known throughout the world for his informative website www.cruisejunkie.com and his recently established International Centre for Cruise Research (www.cruiseresearch.org). In Chapter 24 he identifies the importance of on-board revenue as an integral part of the cruise line's bottom line and explores the traditional on-board revenue centres and the introduction and development of a range of new revenue sources. In Chapter 25 Greg Ringer (USA) presents an interesting account of the economic growth of the Alaskan cruise industry and its social and environmental impacts.

The following two chapters, by contributors from Florida, USA, examine the economic impacts of cruising. In Chapter 26 Bradley Braun and Fred Tramell (Orlando) explore the nature and sources of the impact from cruises on a port's local/regional economy with reference to the definition and measurements of economic benefits.

Next (Chapter 27) Lori Pennington-Gray (Gainesville) illustrates the nature of the day-cruise industry as a form of specialty cruises and examines the significance of economic contribution to the State of Florida. Pennington-Gray suggests several recommendations that might improve the position of the day-cruise industry.

Social impacts are the focus of the following two chapters. In Chapter 28 Lydia Pulsipher and Lindsey Holderfield (USA) argue that cruise tourism in the Eastern Caribbean is creating an ever-wider chasm between tourist and island and contributing to misperceptions and disappointments on the part of both hosts and guests. In Chapter 29 Lynnaire Sheridan and Gregory Teal (Australia) claim that cruise tourism is a heady mix of reality and fantasy and is continuously portrayed as bringing prosperity and development, but this does not correspond seamlessly with the local reality as in the case of Ensenada.

The environmental impacts of the cruise industry are presented in two chapters. In the first (Chapter 30) Jamie Sweeting and Scott Wayne (USA) suggest that major cruise lines have done much to respond to the challenge of preserving the environment on which their business depends. They argue that the cruise industry has the opportunity to become a model for the shipping and tourism industries if it continues to show leadership in piloting and implementing leading practices to address the environmental impacts. This contribution is augmented by Chapter 31 in which Suzanne Dobson and Alison Gill (Canada) suggest that the cruise industry inevitably affects the marine environment and requires some form of regulation to guide its activities and procedures. The authors examine the debate over industry self-regulation and voluntary guidelines versus command and control regulation.

The final chapter in this section comprises a report on the impacts of cruise tourism on the island of Cozumel, Mexico. Helle Sorensen's Chapter 32 deals with challenges domineering the core of the USA over Mexico when cruise lines seek to maximize profits and increase passenger numbers with little regard to the wishes of the little island of Cozumel.

This then leads us to the final section, Part V on Industry Issues.

Beggars in Ensenada, Baja California, Mexico in 2004. The migration of such people to cruise ship port communities can be a source of cultural conflict for tourists and locals alike. Source: Lynnaire Sheridan.

24 Turning Water into Money: The Economics of the Cruise Industry

Ross A. Klein

*Memorial University of Newfoundland, School of Social Work, St John's,
Canada NL A1C 5S7*

How does one describe the modern cruise industry? Its image is rooted in the days of classic ocean liners plying the oceans of the world with impeccable service, gourmet food and a truly all-inclusive product. But cruise ships today are quite different than this image, most significantly in regard to being 'all-inclusive'. In contrast to the past when ships were used mainly for transportation and drew their income almost entirely from the cruise fares, cruise lines today rely heavily on on-board revenue. Centres for on-board revenue include, among other things, rock-climbing walls, ice-skating rinks, virtual reality centres, and daytime recreation programmes for children; for adults there are bars, casinos, shops, art auctions and much more.

The modern cruise industry has been profitable, in effect turning water into money. Carnival Cruise Line, for example, began with a single ship in 1972, which curiously ran aground on its maiden voyage. The company turned to profitability 3 years later. In 2006, Carnival Corporation operates 12 brand names, has 83 ships with accommodations for 150,000 people (assuming two people per cabin). Its net profits in 2004 were approaching US$1.85 billion, with revenues of close to US$10 billion. Carnival's closest competitor, Royal Caribbean Cruises Limited (RCCL), operates three cruise lines. In 2006, it operates 30 ships with accommodations for 64,000 passengers (based on two per cabin). Its net profits are proportionally modest when compared to Carnival, but are still significant.

Historical Context

The cruise industry is the largest growing segment of the leisure travel industry. In the 35 years from 1970 to 2004, the number of passengers carried increased by 2200% – from 500,000 to close to 11 million North Americans per year. These increases are fuelled in large part by construction of new ships. In the first 5 years of the millennium, the industry added 100,000 new beds, increasing capacity by approximately 50%. To the surprise of some analysts, the industry has managed to keep its ships full, and continue to maintain occupancy rates of 104% or 105%. Some of the megaships can have occupancy rates approaching 120% (meaning there are more than two people per cabin).

It is not just the growth in the number of people cruising. The size of ships has also ballooned. In the 1970s and early 1980s, the typical cruise ship accommodated between 500 and 800 passengers. There were some exceptions, such as Cunard's *Queen Elizabeth 2* that was built in 1969 and accommodates 1600 passengers, and Norwegian Cruise Line's (NCL's) *Norway* (built originally as the SS *France* in 1962) that accommodates 2000 passengers. However, both of these vessels were built for transatlantic crossings and intended primarily for transportation rather than pleasure cruising.

The size of ships built exclusively for the cruise market began to grow in the 1980s. In 1985, Carnival Cruise Line introduced the *Holiday*, the first of three superliners. At 46,000 t, it was the largest ship ever built for vacation cruises. It accommodated 1500 passengers. Three years later, Royal Caribbean Cruise Line introduced the *Sovereign of the Seas*, a ship weighing in at 73,192 t and accommodating as many as 2850 passengers.

The next wave of growth came in the late 1990s with the introduction of megaships. Carnival Cruise Line was first with its Destiny-class vessel in 1997. The 101,000-t ship accommodates 3300 passengers. Princess Cruises followed a year later with its first Grand-class vessel – 109,000 t and accommodation for 2600 passengers. In 1999, Royal Caribbean International introduced the first of its Voyager-class vessels. At 143,000 t, the ship can carry over 3800 passengers. With crew, almost 5000 people are on board the ship.

In 2006, Royal Caribbean introduces its next wave of megaship – its Ultra Voyager-class. The US$720-million ship weighs 160,000 t, roughly 15% larger than Voyager-class ships, and carries more than 5000 passengers and crew – close to 6000 when booked to full capacity. But the *Ultra Voyager* will be the largest for only a short time. Carnival Cruise Line's 'Project Pinnacle' will run 170,000–180,000 t. Passenger capacity will be 10% greater than the *Ultra Voyager*; with crew the ship will carry as many as 6500 people. When Carnival's ship comes to fruition, likely in 2008 or 2009, it will claim both the largest size and capacity. It is interesting to compare these new ships with those with which the companies started. RCCL's first ship, *Song of Norway*, was built in 1970; it weighed 18,000 t and carried 724 passengers. Carnival's first ship, *Mardi Gras*, was introduced in 1973. It weighed 27,300 t and accommodated 1024 passengers.

As it has grown, the cruise industry has consolidated. This began in the late 1980s and hit its peak in 2002 when Carnival Corporation won a bidding war with Royal Caribbean for takeover of P&O Princess. This left three companies controlling more than 95% of the cruise

market in North America (GAO, 2004). Carnival Corporation is the largest with 53% of the market. It operates 12 cruise lines: Carnival, Holland America, Windstar, Costa, Cunard, Seabourn, Princess, P&O (UK), Swan Hellenic, Aida, P&O (Australia) and Ocean Village (UK). RCCL controls 33.4% of the market with its three brands: Royal Caribbean International, Celebrity Cruises and Island Cruises (a joint venture with First Choice Holidays). Star Cruises holds just under 9% of the market with Star Cruises, NCL and Orient Line.

With growth has come change. A recent report from the US Federal Trade Commission succinctly captures the changes:

> Cruising has evolved from a minor offshoot of the oceanic passenger industry of the past into a broad-based vacation business . . . . Today's cruise ships, bearing a far stronger resemblance to floating luxury hotels, or even amusement parks than to traditional ocean liners, offer their thousands of passengers amenities such as full scale, 'Main Street'-style shopping districts, multiple restaurants, spas, basketball courts, and even ice skating rinks and rock-climbing walls.

(Federal Trade Commission, 2002)

This reflects the increasing importance of on-board revenue to the cruise line's bottom line. Amenities and experiences are no longer part of the 'all-inclusive' package, but have become a critical part of the cruise line's income. On-board sales today are a significant proportion of the money turned over by a cruise ship. According to Royal Caribbean's Vice President for Commercial Development, John Tercek, US$100 million of that company's US$351 million profit in 2002/03 was derived solely from shore excursions. A typical Royal Caribbean ship can generate close to half a million dollars in tour income with a single call at St Petersburg, Russia (Peisley, 2003). The amount generated by shore excursions continues to increase as cruise lines introduce a range of higher-priced boutique tours.

Making Money

Consumers buy cruises today for less than they would have paid 15 or 20 years ago. Prices have scarcely recovered from the first Gulf War in 1991, which coincided with a period of new construction and led to cruise lines lowering prices in order to fill ships. Although prices have from time to time inched up, they have been pushed back at times of international unrest and economic uncertainty. In order to make up for the lost revenue, cruise lines turned to on-board revenue centres. By the early 1990s, most major cruise lines had corporate managers of on-board revenue. Modern cruise ships were on their way to becoming 'little more than floating bedfactories with shops and restaurants attached. Time spent at sea is simply a matter of getting from A to B with an emphasis on cajoling those trapped inside into spending their money on shopping, drinks, and other extras' (Ashworth, 2001).

Traditional on-board revenue centres

The two largest sources of income on modern ships are bars and casinos (Dupont, 2004). In contrast to the 1970s and 1980s when cruise ship bars charged relatively little for beverages – they passed on to passengers duty-free prices – cruise ships today price their soft drinks, wine, beer and liquor comparable to major hotels. There are a range of bars, including wine bars, piano bars and any number of theme bars. And in all, as a norm, only 20% of revenues from sales represent actual costs for the product (Huie, 1995). Beverage sales are maximized by prohibiting passengers from bringing soft drinks or alcohol on board (Klein, 2002).

Casinos are a relatively recent large revenue centre. Over the years they have grown in size with larger ships, and because they are an effective source of income casinos take up proportionately more space. Many of the casinos, like other revenue centres on cruise ships, are operated by a concessionaire rather than by the cruise line itself. The concessionaire pays for the space and shares a proportion of the revenues.

Often the third-largest centre for revenue is art auctions. First introduced by NCL in the mid-1990s, they are commonplace today. Passengers are attracted to auctions by the offer of free champagne and often for the entertainment value. They are shown serigraphs, lithographs, signed prints, etc., including from well-known artists such as Picasso, Dali, Erte and Chagall. The auctioneer provides background about the art, and emphasizes the excellent price available, suggesting that pieces may be had for as much as 80% off shore-side prices. *USA Today* cited a number of people who dispute this claim. In one case, the same piece of art bought on the ship was found at the neighbourhood K-Mart and was being sold for a fraction of the price. No matter whether this is correct, art auctions are big business. Park West Gallery, only one of the on-board art auctioneers, reported selling 200,000 pieces of art in 2000 (Yancey, 2001).

Other traditional sources of income include bingo, spas, shops, photography and communication services. Like casinos, the space devoted to on-board shops has increased significantly. Rather than a small shop carrying a few sundries and some duty-free items, ships today can have as much as 'a four-storey-tall shopping mall deep in the bowels running a considerable length of the ship' (Cochran, 2003). The same is true for spas, which have expanded into large-scale operations. Steiners Leisure Limited provides services to the majority of cruise ships, although some cruise lines have experimented with in-house operations.

Communication services used to be limited to telephone. Internet cafés were introduced in the late 1990s, wireless Internet connections in 2002 and cell phone service the following year, beginning with Costa Cruises and following on NCL in 2004. When NCL announced that it would introduce wireless telephone service, some lamented that passengers taking a cruise to relax and to get away from the routines of home will now be bothered by having to listen to someone talk about their stock options as they are on deck by the pool getting some sun. Colin Veitch, CEO of NCL, dismissed the concern: 'Are you going to be annoyed by sitting next to the pool and having somebody talking on their cellphone? Probably not any more annoyed than just having a noisy person next to you', Veitch said. 'People will just get used to it' (Pain, 2004).

Time will tell whether wireless telephones present a problem. In the mean time, it will be a lucrative source of on-board revenue, but it also influences the nature of the cruise product and the cruise experience.

New on-board revenue centres

The late 1990s saw the introduction of a range of new revenue sources. Many, such as rock-climbing walls and ice-skating rinks, have been given considerable attention. These are part of a growing group of activities and recreation options offered for an additional fee. They include golf driving ranges, virtual reality games, pay-per-view movies, in-room video games; and fees for yoga, certain fitness classes, and for wine tasting and a range of 'optional' activities (such as a culinary workshop for US$395). And it goes further. NCL offers same-day delivery of select newspapers on some of its ships – for US$3.95 a day, and in 2003 it introduced the concept of 'premium' entertainment for which passengers pay extra (Smart, 2004). Cruise ships have minibars, automated teller machines (ATMs), and every other revenue centre found at a hotel or resort.

One area in which income has significantly grown is from food. In contrast to the late 1990s, when Princess Cruises was criticized for charging extra for Hagen Dazs ice cream and Royal Caribbean was criticized for charging at its Johnny Rockets restaurant, cruise ships today have a range of food options, and most charge an extra fee. Passengers can spend money at cafés for pastries and premium coffees, and at 'extra-tariff' restaurants; an alternative to the normal dining venue where charges can range from US$3.50 to US$30 or more, plus beverages and tip. These optional dining experiences are available across the industry, from the à-la-carte supper club on the *Carnival Legend* to the Todd English restaurant on the *Queen Mary 2* that charges a US$30 reservation fee.

The most recent generation of on-board income is seen in NCL America's charge of a US$10 service fee per passenger per day, which is paid through the passenger's on-board account. Previously, many cruise lines automatically charged passenger on-board accounts for gratuities, but the passenger had the option to raise or lower the amount of the charge. NCL America's fee is mandatory. Whether mandatory or not, money paid to a cruise ship as a service fee or as a gratuity is a source of income to be used to pay staff, and presumably to support other activities. Many workers report that they earn less money under this system than they did when they were paid tips directly by passengers.

Onshore revenue

A major source of on-board revenue is derived from onshore activities, particularly from shore excursions and port shopping programmes. Shore excursions are land-based tours sold by the cruise ship. They are convenient for passengers, 50–80% of whom buy an excursion in each port, and provide solid revenue to the cruise line – as little as one-half to one-third of the shore excursion price is paid to the person providing the shore excursion. For example, a shore excursion costing a passenger US$60 may yield the in-port provider US$20 or less (Klein, 2002; Sandiford, 2003). The cruise line and its shore excursion concessionaire share the remainder. This leaves the shore excursion provider in the uncomfortable position of being paid US$20 for a product that passengers expect US$60 of value. If passengers are disappointed, they blame the port; not the cruise ship.

North American-based cruise lines generally use one of three companies to run their shore excursion programme: International Voyager Media, On-Board Media or the PPI Group. The concessionaires arrange the excursions, hire port lecturers and handle shore excursion sales. The model is slightly different in Alaska where the major cruise lines operate their own tour companies. Carnival Corporation, through Westours and Princess Tours, operates more than 500 motor coaches and 20 domed railway cars in Alaska (Klein, 2005).

The same companies that provide shore excursion programmes also offer port lectures and port shopping programmes. Along with lectures on shore excursion options, passengers learn about shopping, are provided a map with preferred stores and are advised that they will get the best prices at the recommended stores. These on-board promotions evolved into a mini-industry by the mid-1990s, and continue to thrive today. They formalized a system whereby the cruise line captures significant income it had been missing. 'What used to happen is that the tour directors on a major line would earn a quarter of a million dollars a year in royalties from port merchants' (Reynolds, 1995). Now, the money is shared between the concessionaire and the cruise line, with the concessionaire increasingly being squeezed by the cruise lines. The largest, On-board Media, is owned by Louis Vuitton Moet Hennessey (LVMH); it operates shops on board many ships. Like the PPI Group and International Voyager Media, On-board Media offers art auctions.

A cruise ship may also derive income from onshore, but not from on-board sources. Take, for example, Panama's introduction in 2000 of a 5-year scheme whereby cruise ships are paid a bounty for every cruise passenger landed at a Panamanian port – the amount escalates to a maximum of US$12 per passenger as more passengers are landed. The effect is that Panama shifted from receiving no port calls when the plan was announced to dozens of cruise ship stops by 2003. Some ports use cash incentives for reaching a target number of passengers. San Juan, Puerto Rico, rebates US$360,000 to the cruise line for every 120,000 passengers landed (Guadalupe-Fajardo, 2002); Bahamas refunds half of its US$15 per passenger head tax if a company brings half a million visitors in a year, and Jamaica has a scheme whereby US$7 of its port fee may be rebated (O'Hara, 2003). Ports appear willing to offer incentives to ensure that cruise ships continue to visit. Cruise lines benefit in the end.

Private islands

Private islands are another way to generate income. NCL was the first to introduce the concept. The innovation provided an alternative to landing passengers in already congested ports. It could also be used on Sundays when passengers would often complain about shore-side shops being closed.

The private island has several economic benefits. For one thing, passengers on a private island are a captive market. The cruise line runs all beverage sales and concessions, such as tours, water activities, souvenirs and convenience shops. It has no competition; so all money spent on the island contributes to its revenue and profit. An added benefit is that passengers tend to enjoy the experience. This provides a positive impression of the cruise line and is an indi-rect source of increased revenue in the form of future passenger referrals (Lloyd's List, 1991).

Private islands also contribute to the economic bottom line of the cruise line because of their location. Most are located in the Bahamas or Haiti. With a stop at the island, ships are able to save fuel by cruising at a slower speed between two primary ports. Rather than sailing non-stop from St Thomas to Miami, a ship may reduce speed between the two ports with its scheduled stop at the private island. The ship saves money and at the same time increases passenger satisfaction.

Saving Money

As just seen, reducing costs is as effective a means of improving the economic bottom line as is generating income. This has been a key force driving consolidation in the industry. There are clear benefits from economies of scale. Both Carnival and Royal Caribbean projected savings of US$100 million a year from the synergies achieved by their merger with P&O Princess. Carnival's experience indicates that actual savings are exceeding expectations. There are a number of other ways that the industry has been effective in turning water into money.

'Offshore' registration

Like the shipping industry generally, the cruise industry is largely foreign-registered. Even though the corporate offices for most major cruise lines are in Miami, Florida, and the clientele served is largely North American, the companies and their ships are registered in places like Panama, Liberia, Bermuda, and the Bahamas. This arrangement provides several benefits to the corporation. The most visible is that the companies operate free of US, Canadian and other countries' taxes. Except for tax on tour operations owned and operated in the USA (mainly Alaska), neither Carnival Corporation nor RCCL pays any income tax. P&O Princess, which is registered in the UK, reportedly had a tax rate in 2002 of 5% based on its worldwide income – 72% of its income is from North America (Sesit, 2002).

A second benefit of foreign registration is that cruise lines operate independent of the labour laws other than in the country where a ship is registered. The result is that there is no minimum wage on most cruise ships, no limit to the number of hours permitted in a workday and limited regulation of worker contracts. Wages for most cruise ship workers are very low by North American and European standards; they can work 12 months straight without a vacation, 10–14 hours per day, and receive as little as US$300 or $400 a month (see ICONS, 2000; International Transport Workers Federation, 2000; Nielsen, 2000). There have been several unsuccessful efforts by the US Congress to bring cruise lines operating out of US ports under US labour laws; however, in each case the legislation failed. During hearings before a House committee, the President of the International Council of Cruise Lines went so far as to threaten that the industry would relocate its ships to foreign ports if the USA attempted to legislate labour standards on cruise ships (Glass, 1993). The threats mixed with effective lobbying appeared to work.

Liability issues are also affected by foreign registry of the companies and the ships. In the absence of national legislation, claims related to accidents, injuries and deaths on the high seas are governed by maritime law. In many cases, passengers find that assumptions about liability common on land are not applicable at sea. The matter is made even more complex by the industry's use of concessionaires for many on-board services and products, and the schism on some ships between the company selling the cruise and the company operating the ship. Unbeknownst to many passengers, the cruise line is usually not responsible for the actions of its concessionaires, including malpractice by the physician on board.

Port relations

Many ports have a love–hate relationship with the cruise industry. They feel on the one hand that they are not getting their fair share of cruise tourism revenues; but on the other hand ports recognize the money they make from cruise tourism and are hesitant to speak up for fear that cruise ships will pass them by.

Although income is rarely at the level claimed by the cruise line, it is still significant. The situation is a classic buyers market, with the cruise lines doing the buying. The result is that they are able to play ports off against one another and can expect ports to go out of their way to attract or keep them.

This is reflected in the willingness of many ports to build new and expensive terminals. They want to attract passengers; but more importantly they want to keep the cruise lines happy. Much of the development at ports like Phillipsburg, St Maarten and St John's, Antigua, was directed by the industry through the Florida Caribbean Cruise Association. In time, St Maarten invested more than US$60 million based on recommendations from industry studies and input from cruise lines and the FCCA (Gill, 2003). Ports in the USA and Canada often receive their advice from one of a few consultants with close links to the cruise industry (Klein, 2003a). They, too, are spending lots of money on ports. Vancouver invested US$130 million in its cruise terminals between 2000 and 2003. Ketchikan, Alaska, is committed to a US$100 million project that will see seven berths by 2010; the first phase, costing US$28 million, was completed in 2005. And New York City is at the early phases of a US$200 million project, which will be completed in 2017. But new terminals do not guarantee continued cruise business. Since 2002, Vancouver has lost more than a quarter of its cruise business to Seattle. In 2004, St John, New Brunswick, was near completion of a US$12 million cruise terminal project when it learned that it would have one-third less visitors in 2005 because the *Voyager of the Seas* was being redeployed from Canada to Bermuda.

In some places the cruise lines themselves are taking over ownership and/or management of cruise terminals. Costa has its own terminal at Savona (outside Genoa) and is in a co-management arrangement for the terminal at Naples; both Carnival and Royal Caribbean operate their own port facilities in Belize City; and Carnival has arrangements in Turks, Caicos and Cancun for construction of its own terminal. These arrangements provide income (and direct savings, as in Belize, when a cruise terminal operator receives a portion of the per passenger fee collected by the port), but more significantly they free the cruise line from dependence on a terminal operator that may raise fees or fail to provide services.

A different, but perhaps ideal, arrangement is found at the purpose-built port at Hoonah, Alaska. It was built by a private partnership using public funds, turned over to the local aboriginal community and then leased back to the partnership for a nominal fee. The port has agreed to refrain from implementing any tariffs, head taxes, tonnage or similar user fees or charges for the use of the dock facility. It is a moneymaker for the local community and both a revenue source and cost savings for the cruise ship.

One way in which ports have tried to capture a larger proportion of cruise tourism revenues is to raise per passenger fees. Only some have been successful. Competition between ports, and knowledge that ships can easily stop someplace else, has generally kept charges modest. They are as low as US$2 per passenger at some islands in the Caribbean. Where port fees have risen, governments often offer volume discounts or rebates. Port fees range from nothing at some ports in Hawaii to US$65 per passenger in Bermuda.

The cruise industry has an interest in keeping ports charges down in order to keep the cost of a cruise vacation as low as possible. In 2003, the industry vehemently opposed a Caribbean Tourism Organization (CTO) initiative to charge a US$20 passenger levy for all cruise ships travelling to the Caribbean. The proposed levy, to be included in passenger tickets, would be used to finance Caribbean tourism programmes that improve the competitiveness of Caribbean tourism. The idea was to make investments that make the Caribbean more tourist-friendly generally. Through the Florida-Caribbean Cruise Association, the industry confronted and criticized the CTO, lobbied individual governments and ultimately broke the solidarity of Caribbean small island states by selectively offering economic incentives. Grand Cayman received US$26 million for a new cruise terminal. Other islands did not make out as well, but they received enough that they broke ranks with the group. The levy failed. In 2004, the CTO, Caribbean Hotel Association and Florida-Caribbean Cruise Association entered into a partnership to work on common concerns.

Whether the small island states of the Caribbean fare better in this format remains to be seen.

Environmental practices

As discussed in a separate chapter in this book, the cruise industry has recently embarked on a progressive initiative with regard to shipboard wastes (see Klein, 2005 for a critical analysis of the initiative). Until now, however, it would have been easy to conclude that the industry's approach to the environment was that it was more cost-effective to pollute or pay fines than to be 'green'.

The USA began stricter enforcement for pollution offences in 1993, following a number of unsuccessful attempts to have the problem addressed by the state where offending ships were registered. It complained to the International Maritime Organization's Marine Environmental Committee in October 1992 that it had reported pollution violations to the appropriate flag states 111 times, but received responses in only about 10% of the cases (Lloyd's List, 1993). In the 5 years that followed, the USA charged 104 cruise ships with offences involving illegal discharges of oil, garbage and/or hazardous wastes (GAO, 2000). And in the next 5 years, 1998–2002, it fined the three major cruise companies US$50 million for environmental violations. And still, violations have not entirely stopped (see www. cruisejunkie.com/envirofines.html).

Despite the negative press, the cruise industry has presented a united front with regard to the environment. It has promoted an environmentally green image through the International Council of Cruise Lines, and takes every opportunity possible to reinforce that image. But the industry has also taken a stance against legislation such as the Clean Cruise Ship Act of 2004, and similar legislation in individual US states. It instead favours a voluntary approach to environmental regulation through use of a Memorandum of Understanding (MOU). Three states in the USA have adopted MOUs; Canada as well has adopted a voluntary protocol. This sort of approach is more convenient and cost-effective for the cruise ship – it avoids arrest because requirements and standards are not legislated – but is not always the best for local interests (Klein, 2003b; OECD, 2003). Judgements of what arrangement is best depend on the vantage point taken.

Labour

Cruise ships take advantage of the world labour market and are able to draw a workforce that sells its labour for a fraction of what would be required by North American and European standards. A study done by the International Transport Workers Federation in 2000 found that more than half of cruise ship workers reported a monthly income of less than US$1000; 16% earned less than US$500. Only 12% reported an income of over US$2000 (Klein, 2002). With low labour costs, the industry is able to generate favourable profits.

The challenges posed to a cruise line by regulations that govern wages and work conditions are made visible when comparing US-flagged vessels and those registered outside the US NCL. The USA prices its product more than the equivalent product with NCL, because of increased labour costs associated with wages and work conditions; it has a mandatory service charge; and yet it struggles with keeping standards of service comparable to its foreign flagged ships. How successful NCL America is with its US-flagged ships remains to be seen, but they have nevertheless demonstrated the value of labour drawn from developing countries and illustrated the scale of profits drawn from that labour.

Turning Water into Money

The cruise industry has proven economically successful. Companies such as Carnival and Royal Caribbean made profits early and built on their success. They used their profits to grow new capacity, and effectively created expanding demand that kept pace with new ship construction. As income from passenger fares decreased in 1990s, the industry shifted to revenue centres on board to make up the difference. While accurate figures for on-board revenue are difficult to locate – cruise lines do not make such information public – the income is significant. Lloyd's List reported in 1997 that the Sun Princess had a weekly on-board revenue of US$6 million (Lloyd's List, 1997). A 1999 report stated that 'daily onboard

revenues at NCL were expected to be $220 per passenger, just $2 below Carnival's average for all of its lines, including the pricey Cunard and Seabourn, and $10 under No. 2 operator Royal Caribbean' (Connor, 1999). On-board revenue is obviously a major source income.

On-board revenue, whether from on-board sources or from those onshore such as shore excursions, is just one element in the cruise industry's economic success. The industry has also been successful in reducing and minimizing costs. Savings have been achieved through consolidation and mergers. Cruise lines have also maintained their profitability by keeping labour costs low, by cutting unnecessary costs (such as use of bunker fuels rather than fuels that are more environmentally 'green'), and by gaining concessions and incentives from ports. The industry is seen by many ports as a 'cash cow'; it is seen by many holidaymakers as a reasonably priced vacation; and it is seen by its investors and owners as a good investment.

References

Ashworth, J. (2001) A ship that thinks it's a conference centre. London Times, 14 July.
Cochran, J. (2003) The ship hits the fans. MSNBC, 24 November. Available at: www.msnbc.com/m/pt/printthis_main.asp?storyID=995770
Connor, M. (1999) Norwegian line would fit nicely with Carnival. Reuters, 2 December. Available at: biz.yahoo.com/rf/991202/92.html
Dupont, D.K. (2004) Casinos boost onboard spending. Miami Herald, 1 May.
Federal Trade Commission (2002) Statement of the Federal Trade Commission concerning Royal Caribbean Cruises Ltd/P&O Princess Cruises plc and Carnival Corporation/P&O Princess Cruises plc, FTC File No. 021 0041, 5 October 2002. Available at: www.ftc.gov/os/2002/10/cruisestatement.htm
GAO (General Accounting Office) (2000) Marine Pollution: Progress Made To Reduce Marine Pollution By Cruise Ships, But Important Issues Remain. General Accounting Office (Doc No. GAO/RCED-00-48), Washington, DC.
GAO (2004) Maritime Law Exemption, February 2004. General Accounting Office (Doc No. GAO-04-421), Washington, DC.
Gill, J. (2003) Cruise tourism . . . St Maarten's golden goose. Caribbean Cruising (Second Quarter), 19–20.
Glass, J. (1993) ICCL gives ultimatum to House of Representatives subcommittee on relocation of foreign-flag ships. Lloyd's List, 15 May, p. 3.

Guadalupe-Fajardo, E. (2002) Incentives package to cruise lines extended to 2004. *Caribbean Business*, 25 April. Available at: www.puertoricowow.com

Huie, N. (1995) F&B spending on the rise. *Cruise Industry Quarterly* Fall, 95.

ICONS (International Commission on Shipping) (2000) *Inquiry into Ship Safety: Ships, Slaves, and Competition.* International Commission on Shipping, Charlestown, New South Wales.

International Transport Workers Federation (2000) The dark side of the cruise industry. *Seafarers' Bulletin* 14.

Klein, R.A. (2002) *Cruise Ship Blues: The Underside Of The Cruise Industry.* New Society, Gabriola Island, British Columbia.

Klein, R.A. (2003a) *Charting A Course: The Cruise Industry, the Government of Canada, and Purposeful Development.* Canadian Centre for Policy Alternatives, Ottawa, Canada. Available at: www.cruise junkie.com/ccpa2.pdf

Klein, R.A. (2003b) *The Cruise Industry and Environmental History and Practice: Is A Memorandum of Understanding Effective for Protecting the Environment.* Bluewater Network, San Francisco. Available at: www.bluewaternetwork. org/reports/rep_ss_kleinrep.pdf

Klein, R.A. (2005) *Cruise Ship Squeeze: The New Pirates Of The Seven Seas.* New Society, Gabriola Island, British Columbia.

Lloyd's List (1991) Exclusive destinations concept an economic necessity for 1990s: out-islands the in-thing. *Lloyd's List*, 18 October.

Lloyd's List (1993) U.S. cracks down on marine pollution. *Lloyd's List*, 17 April, p. 3.

Lloyd's List (1997) Boost for group's annual results. *Lloyd's List*, 17 April, p. 6.

Nielsen, K. (2000) The perfect scam: for the workers life is no carnival, believe it or not. *Miami New Times*, 3–9 February.

OECD (2003) *Voluntary Approaches to Environmental Policy: Effectiveness, Efficiency, and Usage in Policy Mixes.* Organization for Economic Co-operation and Development, Paris.

O'Hara, T. (2003) Ante upped for cruise ships. *Keys News*, 13 September.

Pain, J. (2004) Cruise lines to cellphone users: all aboard. *Fort Wayne Journal Gazette*, 26 July. Available at: www.fortwayne.com/mld/journal-gazette/business/9245650.htm

Peisley, T. (2003) Shore excursions make impressive profits. *Cruise Business Review*, 5 December.

Reynolds, C. (1995) Into the beckoning arms of paying port merchants. *Los Angeles Times*, 17 September, L-2.

Sandiford, K. (2003) Port authority: carrying the wallets of thousands of fun seekers, the cruise industry receives a warm welcome from the theme park named Halifax. *The Coast*, 14–21 August. Available at: www.thecoast.ca/archives/140803/feature.html

Sesit, M.S. (2002) U.S. tax proposals may squeeze multinationals. *Wall Street Journal*, 9 August, C 14.

Smart, G. (2004) Stormy seas ahead. *MSNBC*, 29 January. Available at: msnbc.msn.com/id/3860856/

Yancey, K.B. (2001) Cruise lines draw profits from selling works of art. *USA Today*, 9 February.

25   Cruising North to Alaska: The New 'Gold Rush'

Greg Ringer

*University of Oregon, International Studies Program and Department of Planning,
Public Policy and Management, Eugene, OR 97403-1209, USA*

Introduction

More than 6000 years after humans reputedly first reached the North American continent by land, Vitus Bering led a Russian expedition aboard two ships to explore Alaska in 1741. Four decades later, Captain James Cook arrived by boat to map Alaska's extensive coastline for Great Britain. Soon thereafter, intrepid Russian colonialists sailed from Siberia to establish the first European settlement on Kodiak Island, and almost 30,000 adventurous goldseekers disembarked from steamships in 1897 in transit to the Yukon and Klondike mines. Today, almost one million visitors reach Alaska by boat each year during the brief summer season (May–September). Although many come aboard ferries of the state's famed Alaska Marine Highway System, most sail on one of 32 vessels owned by 12 cruise lines that now ply the inland waters of Alaska and the Canadian Pacific – and their popularity is growing almost exponentially.

Alaska's inbound cruise arrivals now account for almost half of all visitors to the state, and their numbers are increasing at an annual rate of 10% as more ships dock each year from San Francisco, Seattle, and Vancouver, British Columbia. Indeed, so popular has this niche become, both regionally and internationally, that the marine advocacy group, Oceana, estimates cruise passengers (85% of them US residents) will more than double to 20 million by the year 2010, as more families and younger travellers try a cruise vacation. To meet this anticipated demand, the International Council of Cruise Lines (ICCL), a consortium of 16 of the world's leading cruise lines,[1] expects to christen 38 new cruise ships in the next few years, thereby increasing its own fleet capacity by 45%. Many of these vessels will be added to those previously repositioned to serve Alaska after the September 2001 attacks (Klein, 2002; Alaska Travel Industry Association, 2004; Cruise Lines International Association, 2004; Morton, 2004).

The advent and rapid growth of cruise tourism presents both opportunities and challenges for destination communities in Alaska and the Pacific North-west (Fig. 25.1). Air pollution, illegal dumping of sewage and solid waste, inadequate treatment equipment, damage to coral reefs and sensitive marine environments from inappropriate anchorages and recreational activities aboard cruise ships, and falsified records are only a few of the regulatory infractions for which

---

[1]ICCL members include Carnival Cruise Lines, Celebrity Cruises, Costa Cruise Lines N.V., Crystal Cruises, Cunard Line Limited, Disney Cruise Line, Holland America Line, Norwegian Cruise Line, Orient Lines, Princess Cruises, Radisson Seven Seas Cruises, Regal Cruises, Royal Caribbean International, Royal Olympic Cruises, Seabourn Cruise Line and Windstar Cruises. The vessels owned by these companies represent approximately 90% of the North American cruise line industry.

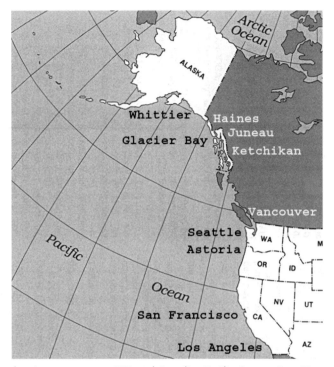

Fig. 25.1.   Selected cruise ports, western USA and Canadian Pacific. Source: Greg Ringer, 2004.

cruise lines have paid millions of US dollars in fines. The socio-economic and cultural costs are equally significant, particularly in the isolated coastal and island communities increasingly attractive to cruise visitors because of their rural lifestyles and local traditions (Ringer, 1998; Hawaii Tourism Authority, 2004).

Subsistence practices among indigenous Alaskan natives are now threatened by environmental and cultural mismanagement, while social systems are overwhelmed in communities where the ratio of passengers to residents is often 11:1 or greater. Economic benefits remain equally uncertain, as villagers spend money preparing for cruise tourists who may not come, or will spend less than land-based tourists and independent travellers if they do arrive. In other ports, the noise of sightseeing helicopters and float planes, the stress on humpback whales and wildlife from tour boats, conflicts over trail use, and the '[f]loods of cruise passengers threaten to overtax the limited facilities and supplies' (Earthjustice, 2003, p. 2). Meanwhile, the ports of Juneau and Seattle must incur additional

expenses for security measures mandated by the Maritime Transportation Security Act of 2002 to directly monitor cruise ship passengers, crews and baggage while docked. As a result, the Port of Seattle continues to lose money every year on the cruise business (Zuckerman, 1999; Schroeder, 2005; Meadahl, 2003; Brown, 2004).

At the same time, there can be no denying the positive impacts of cruise travel for both passengers and local people. Economically, the influx of ships and people pumped US$958 million into Alaska in 2003 in wages and purchases, and another US$103 million in tax revenue, moorage fees and marketing. Money spent by cruise visitors while ashore added an additional US$230 million in income to state businesses and governments. As a result, cruise travel is now 'the largest sector of the tourism industry in Southeast Alaska, and has a significant economic impact in the region' (Schmid, 2003, p. 1; McDowell Group, 2004; Northern Economics Inc., 2004).

In Juneau, Alaska's state capital, the cruise tourism boom has successfully revitalized the town, helping to fund restoration of a downtown historic shopping district, and to diversify the local economy through job creation and business partnerships. Where cruise visits have disturbed wildlife or disrupted residents, State and community officials have tried to mitigate the impacts through established 'best practices', and the designation of more socially and ecologically sensitive routes, landing sites and viewing areas. For this reason, annual opinion surveys conducted by the city tourism office consistently show strong support among community members for the cruise visits. Despite legitimate concerns about growing ship and passenger arrivals, many residents and local governments throughout south-east and south-central Alaska appear equally cognizant of the practical benefits of cruise tourism (Alaska Division of Community and Business Development, 2001).

Socio-economic Impacts

Although the state of Florida accounts for the majority of embarkations at US ports – 69% of an estimated 7.1 million passengers in 2003 – the western states of California, Oregon, Washington and Alaska, as well as Canada's Pacific provinces, are experiencing equally significant socio-economic impacts. Ports in Astoria, Oregon; Seattle; and Vancouver, British Columbia, now share a growing segment of the national cruise ship market, as Alaska prospers as a cruise destination in spite of increased worries over personal safety and high unemployment (Fig. 25.2).

Attracted by its abundant and accessible natural scenery, wildlife and native culture, the North West Cruise Ship Association recorded in excess of 800,000 passenger arrivals in Alaska in 2004 – 110,000 more than reported only 3 years earlier – and the state is ranked among the five most profitable for cruise tourism in the USA. With nearly 8% of the total worldwide cruise market, the industry claims that every summer, 'one of every five cruise ships on the planet is navigating Alaska's Inside Passage to Ketchikan, Juneau and other outposts [and an] Alaska cruise is now the world's third most popular voyage, trailing [only] the Caribbean and Mediterranean runs' (Lynch, 2004, p. E1; Alaska Travel Industry Association, 2004). 'With our many natural attractions, colorful history and native cultures, Alaska is a perfect cruise destination', said Governor Frank Murkowski. 'The cruise business is an important part of our diverse economy' (International Council of Cruise Lines, 2004, p. 2).

Most US 'cruisers' come from the east coast or midwest and consequently, embark on their 7–11 day journey to the 'Last Frontier' from a major coastal gateway, such as Los Angeles, San Francisco and Vancouver, British Columbia. A growing number, however, sail from smaller 'drive-to' markets in close proximity to larger populations in the Pacific North-west, including Seattle. So popular are these sailings regionally that Idaho and Oregon American Automobile Association travel agents alone booked 37% more Alaskan cruise vacations in 2004 than the previous year (AAA Oregon/Idaho, 2004).

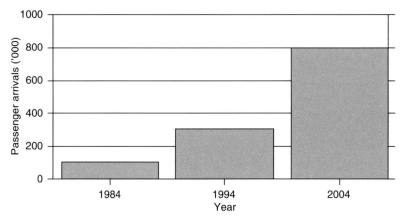

Fig. 25.2. Alaska cruise passenger arrivals. Source: Alaska Travel Industry Association, 2004.

The majority of passengers are married and middle-aged (50 years or older). Since Alaskan cruises tend to be relatively expensive, costing an average of US$10,000 a person for a week-long cruise, those who sail aboard the cruise ships are also moderately affluent, with median household incomes of US$75,000 and more. Passenger surveys further indicate that Alaskan cruisers prefer to travel in pairs or parties of two, and the majority are women.

Popular ports of call include Juneau; Sitka, once the political center of Russian America in the 19th century; Ketchikan, Alaska's 'First City' as cruise ships transit the Inside Passage north; Skagway, a former gold rush town; Haines, terminus for the Alaska State Marine Highway; Hubbard Glacier, in the Wrangell–St Elias National Park (the largest protected area in the USA); and Whittier, gateway to Anchorage and Denali National Park. As a destination market, Alaska attracts more than 90% of all US port-of-call passengers – and this total does not include those who sail on small cruise ships, or 'pocket cruises' that typically carry 50–100 passengers on day cruises for whalewatching and to view scenic sights like Prince William Sound, the Malaspina Glacier, College Fjord and Glacier Bay National Park (Vipond, 2004).

Because of passengers' varied interests and itineraries, the major lines employ a practice called 'vertical integration'. By purchasing businesses in all segments of the Alaskan tourism industry (including investments in land- and water-based tour companies in the primary destinations, gift and souvenir shops, hotels and restaurants), cruise lines strive to satisfy every desire of the growing number of users. In this manner, both cruise companies and Alaskan communities derive considerable revenue from a wide range of ancillary support and recreational activities, such as 'flightseeing', fishing, birdwatching and wildlife viewing, and wilderness accommodations, as well as related spending in food sales, environmental management, marine maintenance and infrastructure development.

With multiplying passenger numbers and jobs – the Alaska cruise industry now employs almost 19,000 workers or 7% of the total cruise-related workforce in the USA – marine tourism impacts virtually every part of the state's economy, from construction to agriculture and trans-portation. In ports from Astoria to Skagway, 'industry and passenger spending in the United States rose from $10.3 billion in 2000 to $12.9 billion in 2003 – a 25 per cent gain' (Business Research & Economic Advisors, 2004, p. 1). The International Council of Cruise Lines further reports that cruise ships and their vendors contributed more than US$694 million in direct purchases, salaries, taxes and services to the state's economy in 2004. Nearly two-thirds of this amount comes from crew and passengers, the latter spending US$140 each per visit or '31 per cent of all passenger and crew spending in the United States' (Business Research & Economic Advisors, 2004, p. 1; Sacks, 2004).

The Juneau Convention & Visitor Bureau (2004, Juneau, Alaska, personal communication) reported almost 850,000 cruise arrivals in 2004 from both large and 'pocket' cruise lines (a 9% annual growth rate), while in Ketchikan, between one and five ships now anchor each day in the summer season, with 508 stops by 34 ships recorded by the Ketchikan Visitors Bureau (2004). Aboard were a total of 681,096 passengers, nearly triple the number reported a decade earlier, when a total of 27 cruise liners stopped in port.

The decline of the timber industry in Haines in the early 1990s led to similar growth in tourism, with the town targeting the cruise ship market early by identifying the industry's infrastructure needs and nearby attractions, and then spending US$1.5 million to expand the Port Chilkoot dock facilities and transportation networks. The result, at least initially, was continued increases in both ships and passengers, from 58 stops (27,000 passengers) in 1990 to a peak of 184,134 passengers on 13 vessels (157 stops) in 2000 (Cerveny, 2004; Gilbertson, 2004; Mazza, 2004).

In addition to the growth of cruise tourism in Alaska, neighbouring states in the USA and the Canadian province of British Columbia have also profited as cruise travel attracts more passengers to the Pacific North-west, already the second-largest source of cruise passengers in the country, with 1.18 million reported in 2003. Seattle, a major port of embarkation for visitors from across the USA is now reputedly the third-largest cruise port in the nation in terms of passengers, with 172,500 passengers boarding in 2003 (many of them regional and local residents).

On average, seven cruise ships now stop briefly in Seattle each week from May to September, with 149 cruises recorded in 2004 and annual income of almost US$ 200 million, and the city is homeport for four international companies – a remarkable turnaround for a city that rarely saw a cruise ship before 2000. Perhaps more significant for local workers, jobs in the cruise industry are also increasing, with nearly 2000 positions either directly or indirectly servicing the cruise lines in 2003, each paying approximately US$39,500 a year. Anticipating further expansions in the Alaska cruise market, with 185 ships and 375,000 passengers expected to dock in Seattle in 2005, as faster ships make it possible for those based in Los Angeles and San Francisco to explore Alaska, the Port of Seattle is now redeveloping its harbour facilities to accommodate more cruise ships, and establishing itself as administrative headquarters for cruise lines on the west coast through a combination of ship repair facilities and management support services.

With Portland considered too inconvenient for cruise ships because of its location inland on the Columbia River and its lack of inner-city moorings, the San Francisco–based '[c]ruise ship stopovers bring economic hope' (Associated Press, 2004a, p. D13) to the small coastal community of Astoria, Oregon, as well. In a town where dilapidated shops and houses were the norms only a few years ago, the arrival of cruise ships headed north to Alaska has helped initiate an economic revival. Following rehabilitation of Astoria's historic hotels and renovated waterfront, and sparked by the arrival of Norwegian Cruise Lines in 1997, companies now stop in Astoria so that passengers can enjoy walking tours and excursions to Mount St Helens, an active volcano, or to seaside towns nearby (Tobias, 2004).

In 2004, a total of eight ships docked – including three on the same day in late September, with 6000 passengers altogether in a city of only 10,000 persons – and 14 vessels are scheduled to visit Astoria in 2005, evidence of the growing popularity of both the town and cruise tourism. Although the stopovers are relatively brief, averaging 6–8 hours in length from berth to departure, tourism has increased by half since 2002 and the cruise stops are quite

lucrative for the local community, with each passenger spending approximately US$150 while ashore. In time, the city's goal is to become a 'jump-off spot where Oregon cruisers could get on and off ships . . . [instead of a] pit stop for California cruisers' (Lynch, 2004, p. E2).

Along the Canadian Pacific coast, cruise travel is equally strong, as revenue and total passengers are driven higher by the Alaskan cruise market. Although Vancouver's role has changed since cruises to Alaska began in the 1950s, as more cruise lines homeport in Seattle, the city remains a prominent beneficiary of Alaska's popularity and the US Passenger Services Act (1886), which generally allows only US-owned, -built and -crewed ships to transport domestic passengers directly between US ports. Since most of the Alaskan cruise ships are foreign-owned and -manned, they must make an intermediate stop outside the USA en route to and from Alaska and the contiguous USA. For this reason, in part, more than two dozen ships now either depart from, or visit, Vancouver each year in transit to Alaska, and the 368 port calls scheduled for 2004 earned an estimated US$1.9 million in direct and indirect benefits (Dobson et al., 2002; Marine Transportaion Security Act, 2002; Lynch, 2004).

Accompanying the economic contributions, however, are growing conflicts – from Astoria to Alaska – related to the changing dynamics and behaviour of tourists, the congestion and strains on local residents and infrastructure, and the potential loss of social and cultural identity as communities evolve into tourist destinations, and local people are forced to make the difficult transition from lifestyles defined by resource extraction (fishing, timber, mining) to those of a tourist attraction. Local entrepreneurs complain that the permit process utilized by cruise ships in Glacier Bay is unfair to local business owners, while operators in Haines are unable to profitably compete against the tours pre-sold by the cruise ships, as independent travel to Alaska declines in interest – only 23% of those who visit south-east Alaska now label themselves 'independent travelers', compared to 40% in 1989 (McDowell Group, 2002; Cruise Junkie.com, 2004a).

Aggravating the situation, many working-class residents have been displaced by higher housing costs associated with the economic rebirth and gentrification of Alaska's coastal communities, and wages in the cruise sector remain significantly less than those historically paid in the logging and fishing industries. In addition, the instability of the domestic and international tourism markets, along with the hostility of the cruise industry to visitor taxes and cruise cap measures, and its willingness and ability to transfer ships and stops to more lucrative routes on short notice, add to the difficulty of relying on tourism as a sustainable source of income, as the people of Haines are learning.

In 2002, the total number of cruise visitors declined by almost 79% after Royal Caribbean International cancelled 52 dockings in Haines, the *Norwegian Sky* cancelled 19 port calls, and the *Universe Explorer* reduced its visits by one, dropping the total number of arriving cruise passengers to only 37,192 for the season. Two years later, Holland America Line announced plans to withdraw 8 of the company's 17 planned cruise stops in 2005 and shift them to neighbouring Skagway, where passengers could connect directly to the company's bus tours and lodges. The result will be a further reduction in passenger numbers, with only 14,400 passengers expected to arrive next summer – the lowest number since cruise ships began stopping in Haines in the early 1990s – and an equal decline in income. As a result, there is now considerable out-migration of younger residents and families for affordable homes, jobs and schools elsewhere (Morphet, 2002; Williams, 2004).

Health and Ecological Impacts

In addition to the economic displacement and behaviour transformations associated with the development of cruise tourism in many of these towns, there are risks associated with cruise ship sanitation and public health. Since many Alaskans rely on the natural environment for subsistence, as well as recreation and transportation, this is an issue of great concern, and one which the Alaska Department of Environmental Conservation (ADEC) highlighted in 1999 when it established the Alaska Cruise Ship Initiative to address impacts caused by cruise ships in state waters (ADEC, 2002).

All Alaskan cruise ships must comply with Federal and State environmental laws, including the Clean Water and Clean Air Acts, and the Oil Pollution Control Act. Despite these efforts, sewage-borne illnesses, similar to the recent outbreaks of Norwalk-like viruses on several cruise ships in the Caribbean and the Mediterranean that affected more than 3000 passengers and crew, have resulted in cancelled port stops and shortened itineraries in Alaska as well. Yet, this highly contagious virus is spread, in part, by raw sewage dumped into the oceans by cruise boats, which 'generate as much as 30,000 gallons of raw sewage [in addition to 7 t of garbage and solid waste, 15 gallons of toxic chemicals, 7000 gallons of oil and bilge water, and air pollution equivalent to the exhausts of 12,000 automobiles] every day' (Klein, 2002, p. 1).

Although diesel engine emissions from cruise ships are regulated in Alaska (Cruise Ship Air Emissions Working Group, 2000), air pollution also remains a serious public health problem. While compliance has certainly improved since 1999, when 13 ships from six companies were fined by the US Environmental Protection Agency (2004) for violating air quality standards in Glacier Bay, Juneau and Seward, ships from Holland America Line continue to be cited every year for violating air opacity regulations in Alaskan ports (though most fines were suspended after the company promised to comply).

In addition, while cruise ships are legally barred from releasing plastics and untreated grey water (waste water from sinks, baths, showers and laundries) in Alaska state waters, and may only release untreated sewage in the Alexander Archipelago of Alaska while travelling at least 6 knots an hour and a mile offshore, neither the US nor the Canadian governments regularly monitor discharges in the Inland Passage or Gulf of Alaska. Nor are cruise ships required to have a permit to dump or to monitor water quality where they discharge, or even to report the contents of their release (Friends of Misty Fjords Wilderness, 2004).

As a result, no one knows whether the illegal sewage discharge in Juneau in May 2001 by the *Norwegian Sky*, where '[f]ecal coliform counts were 3500 times the allowable federal standard and total suspended solids 180 times the standard' (London, 2002, p. 39), was an anomaly in terms of seriousness? Unlawful grey water and waste water discharges were clearly the industry norms, however, as evidenced by similar citations against three other vessels while docked in Juneau only a month later, and the subsequent dumping of 40,000 gallons of sewage sludge in Juneau's harbour by Holland America Line's *Ryndam* in 2002 (Cramer *et al.*, 2003; Cruise Junkie.com, 2004b).

Nevertheless, ADEC determined that same year, after nearly 2 years of research and advisory input, that Federal and State regulations were adequate in controlling potential hazards to the marine and terrestrial environments. Although 'the high levels of faecal coliform found in cruise ship discharge testing during the 2000 cruise ship season in Alaska' (Dobson *et al.*, 2002, p. 13) increased concern over industry impacts to wildlife and human health, ADEC advisers noted that every cruise ship entering Alaskan waters is equipped with primary or secondary treatment facilities. They argued, therefore, that normal ship operations should not ordinarily release harmful amounts of chemicals or particulates. Consequently, the state was urged only to restrict chlorine discharges, a caustic disinfectant regularly used in shipboard treatment systems, and to address the possible impacts of waste water dumping by cruise ships and state ferries in slow-moving water.

An equally serious environmental threat stems from the release of ballast water into state waters. Frequently laden with non-endemic, invasive marine species, bacteria and diseases transported from foreign ports, the impacts can include the decimation and extinction of native plants and wildlife, and it is a growing problem in west coast ports. Yet, only California regulates ballast discharges at present, though the US Environmental Protection Agency is currently developing sewage and grey water disposal standards for cruise ships in Alaskan waters under Title XIV: Certain Alaskan Cruise Ship Operations (33 U.S.C. 1902 Note), with sampling initiated in the summer of 2004.

Furthermore, while some 'cruise lines have worked to develop – and implement – state-of-the-art waste treatment equipment . . . no government programs exist to verify the efficiency and benefits of new technologies' (Ocean Conservancy, 2004, p. 3), and US and international laws continue to permit ocean-going vessels to dump treated sewage anywhere at sea

and untreated sewage more than 4 knots from shore (though the cruise ship industry standard is 12 knots). Thus, while cruise travel in Alaskan waters is certainly better managed, and the ocean and marine wildlife better protected, by Federal and State legislation than elsewhere in the country, it remains primarily the responsibility of local communities to determine whether fishing and swimming in coastal waters remain safe for public consumption and use (Ocean Conservancy, 2002a; Cruise Junkie.com, 2004b).

Fortunately, 'this pollution can be stopped for the costs of a can of soda per passenger per day' (Oceana, 2002, p. 2). Unfortunately, many communities are restrained from taking effective action against polluters by political barriers, as well as budget constraints. Every cruise ship now operating on the Alaska route flies a 'flag of convenience', indicating that it is registered outside the USA. As such, these ships are immune from stronger US labour and environmental laws, even though they operate in US waters.

Enforcement efforts against illegal actions by cruise ships are further impeded by misinformation among cruise ship passengers, most of whom mistakenly believe that environmental safeguards are in place aboard most ships, and consequently are unaware that sewage is dumped daily at sea. However, a strong majority (80%) of tourists opposed this practice when informed, and 60% expressed a willingness to pay more to ensure cleaner, 'eco-friendly' cruises. More specifically, cruise customers want companies to upgrade existing ship-based, waste-treatment systems, and favour more stringent inspections and frequent, independent monitoring of cruise ship practices (Reece, 2003; ADEC, 2004).

The Future

There is no doubt that many Alaskans share these sentiments, as Governor Tony Knowles himself indicated in June 2001, when he signed legislation giving Alaska state regulators direct authority over the cruise industry. Designed to give greater protection to Alaska's marine resources, including 'the world's largest populations of wild salmon and other species that are important to commercial, sport, and subsistence users' (M. Brown, Commissioner, Alaska Department of Environmental Conservation, Juneau, 2002, personal communication), the industry-funded law created, for the first time, a set of enforceable environmental standards and a verified programme for monitoring and documenting ship discharges and emissions in state waters effective January 2004. Although small cruise ship operators now seek an exemption from the waste water pollution law, arguing against the high expense of the equipment required, violations of the Marine Visible Emissions Standards have declined from a total of 15 in 2000 to only 2 Notices of Violation in 2003, as a direct result of the approximately 260 opacity assessments conducted each year on large cruise ships in south-east and south-central Alaska ports (Associated Press, 2004b; Eastern Research Group, Inc., 2004).

This effort accelerated in December 2003, when the International Council of Cruise Lines and Conservation International announced a 'joint initiative to protect biodiversity in top cruise destinations and promote industry practices that minimize the cruise industry's environmental impact' (ICCL, 2003, p. 1). It was critical, the Ocean Conservation and Tourism Alliance proclaimed, that actions be taken immediately by the cruise industry to 'pioneer conservation solutions that are scientifically, economically and culturally sound . . . [noting that] approximately 70% of cruise destinations are in the biodiversity hotspots' (ICCL, 2004, p. 2). With an initial commitment of US$1.2 million, the partnership, in consultation with scientific experts in conservation and cruise tourism, urged companies to become better environmental stewards by acting quickly to: (i) establish 'best practices' and improved technology for waste water purification and disposal; (ii) increase environmental education for vendors, crew members and cruise guests to highlight critical environmental challenges and support opportunities; and (iii) create collaborative 'destination partnerships' between local communities, governments and cruise companies to assure quality experiences for both residents and visitors, and long-term protection for the natural and cultural environments of the cruise destination.

Actions already undertaken include the installation of a US$4.5 million electric shore-power plug-in system in Juneau, where cruise ships may disconnect their engines while docked, thereby reducing both noise and air pollution. The City and Borough of Juneau (CBJ) have also joined with cruise lines and tour operators to institute Tourism Best Management Practices, 'a model management program for sustainable tourism' (CBJ, 2004, p. 1) that addresses the concerns of local residents, government leaders and the industry.

> Our vision is to work with leaders in the tourism industry and demonstrate how the industry and conservation community can work together to produce mutually beneficial results. The goal is to not only protect the places tourists visit but also maximize positive contributions to conservation in high biodiversity areas where the cruise industry operates.
>
> (ICCL, 2004, p. 3)

The recently proposed Clean Cruise Ship Act of 2004 is another step in protecting the marine environment enjoyed by cruise passengers. Among its provisions are those that would ban all cruise ship discharges within 12 miles of US shores, require cruise lines to reduce air emissions and harmful impacts on ocean ecosystems by outfitting all ships with the latest environmental technology, and ensure greater enforcement efforts by the US National Oceanic and Atmospheric Administration and other Federal agencies to ban or limit waste water discharges in marine protected areas and sensitive environments. While some existing treatment plants in Alaska would be 'grandfathered' into the new law, due to the investments already made in improvements under existing law, the net goal would be zero pollutants by 2015 in all US waters (Conservation International, 2003; Currey, 2003; Alaska Conservation Foundation, 2004; Ocean Conservancy, 2004).

In conclusion, for the people of Alaska, the social and environmental problems brought by the cruise industry are still seen as manageable, and cruise passengers continue to be welcome in most ports for both personal and economic reasons. Whether they will remain as guests, however, will depend upon the cruise lines, and the practices that they employ, as Alaskans strive to sustain both their communities and their marine environments in the 21st century.

References

AAA Oregon/Idaho (2004) *AAA Travel Agency Sales Strong for 2004: Cruises, European Destinations Once Again Top Agents' List.* Available at: www.aaanewsroom.netArticles.asp?ArticleID=309&SectionID=4&CategoryID=8

ADEC (Alaska Department of Environmental Conservation) (2002) *Alaska Cruise Ship Initiative: Part 2 Report.* Division of Statewide Public Service, Juneau.

ADEC (Alaska Department of Environmental Conservation) (2004) *Assessment of Cruise Ship and Ferry Wastewater Impacts in Alaska.* Commercial Passenger Vessel Environmental Compliance Program, Juneau.

Alaska Conservation Foundation (2004) *Alaska Oceans Programs: Current Issues on Alaska's Oceans.* Available at: www.alaskaoceans.net

Alaska Division of Community & Business Development (2001) *2000 Southeast Alaska Commercial Recreation Provider Survey.* Presented to the AWRTA Conference, Alaska Division of Tourism, Juneau.

Alaska Travel Industry Association (2004) *2004 Tourism and Visitor Industry Forecast.* The Alaska State Chamber of Commerce, Juneau.

Associated Press (2004a) Cruise ship stopovers bring economic hope to Astoria. *The (Eugene) Register-Guard,* 29 September, D13.

Associated Press (2004b) Small cruise ships say waste laws sink profits. *Anchorage Daily News,* 5 March, D1.

Brown, C. (2004) Glacier Bay ship numbers could grow, Norton says. *Anchorage Daily News,* 27 April, B3.

Business Research & Economic Advisors (2004) *Cruise Industry Economic Impact Topped $25 Billion in 2003.* International Council of Cruise Lines, Arlington, Virginia.

CBJ (City and Borough of Juneau) (2004) *2004 Tourism Best Management Practices.* CBJ, Juneau.

Cerveny, L.K. (2004) *Preliminary Research Findings from a Study of the Sociocultural Effects of Tourism in Haines, Alaska.* US Department of Agriculture, Forest Service, Pacific Northwest Research Station, Portland, Oregon.

Conservation International (2003) *A Shifting Tide: Environmental Challenges and Cruise Industry Responses.* CI, Washington, DC.

Cramer, E.H., Gu, D.X. and Durbin, R.E. (2003) Diarrheal disease on cruise ships, 1990–2000: the impact of environmental health programs. *American Journal of Preventive Medicine* 24(3), 227–233.

Cruise Junkie.com (2004a) Your resource for the other information about the cruise industry. Available at: www.cruisejunkie.com

Cruise Junkie.com (2004b) Environmental violations in Alaska, 1999–2003. Available at: www.cruise-junkie.com/alaskafines.html

Cruise Lines International Association (2004) Double-digit passenger growth buoys CLIA member cruise lines' 2nd quarter passenger, occupancy figures. *Cruise News,* 2 September.

Cruise Ship Air Emissions Working Group (2000) *Alaska Cruise Ship Initiative: Part 1, Final Report (Activities and Work Products up to June 1, 2000).* Division of Statewide Public Service, Juneau.

Currey, S. (2003) Cruising toward a cleaner industry. *Coast Lines* 13(1), 24–26.

Dobson, S., Gill, A. and Baird, S. (2002) *A Primer on the Canadian Pacific Cruise Ship Industry.* Simon Fraser University and Canada Department of Fisheries and Oceans, Pacific Region, Vancouver, British Columbia.

Earthjustice (2003) *Cruise Ships: Impacts on the Island of Molokàii.* Earthjustice, Honolulu.

Eastern Research Group, Inc. (2004) *Generic Sampling and Analysis Plan for Large Cruise Ships in Alaska Waters.* US Environmental Protection Agency, Engineering and Analysis Division, Washington, DC.

Friends of Misty Fjords Wilderness (2004) *FMFW Appeal to the Commissioner of Alaska as an Adversely Affected Party!* Alaska Department of Natural Resources, Ketchikan.

Gilbertson, N. (2004) Southeast Alaska: a tale of two economies. *Alaska Economic Trends* 3, 1–14.

Hawaii Tourism Authority (2004) *Benefits & Impacts of the Cruise Industry in Alaska.* HTA, Honolulu.

ICCL (International Council of Cruise Lines) (2004) Alaska received $694 million in direct spending and 18,500 jobs from U.S. cruise lines in 2003. ICCL, Arlington, Virginia.

ICCL and Conservation International (2003) International Council of Cruise Lines and Conservation International announce joint initiative. PRNewswire, Washington, DC.

Ketchikan Visitors Bureau (2004) Cruise ships: past arrival data. Available at: www.visit-ketchikan.com/cruise_ship_info/shipinfo.html

Klein, R. (2002) *Cruise Ship Blues: The Underside of the Cruise Industry.* New Society Publishers, Gabriola Island, British Columbia.

London, T. (2002) *Blowing the Whistle and the Case for Cruise Certification.* Oceans Blue Foundation, Seattle.

Lynch, J. (2004) Northwest cruises are gaining speed. *The (Portland) Oregonian* 4 July, E1–E2.

Marine Transportation Security Act (2002) SI 1994/40. Canada Ministry of Transport, Ottawa, Canada.

Mazza, R. (2004) *Economic Growth and Change in Southeast Alaska.* US Department of Agriculture, Forest Service, Pacific Northwest Research Station, Portland, Oregon.

McDowell Group (2002) Southeast Alaska tourism and the new Alaska travelers survey. Working together: tourism in Southeast Alaska conference. Alaska Department of Community and Economic Development, Juneau.

McDowell Group (2004) *Economic Impact of the Cruise Ship Industry in Alaska, 2003*. North West Cruiseship Association, Juneau.

Meadahl, M. (2003) BC cruising for tourists en route to Alaska. Media release. Simon Fraser University, Vancouver, British Columbia.

Morphet, T. (2002) Businesses brainstorm response to RCI pullout. *Chilkat Valley News* 30 (51), 2.

Morton, T. (2004) *The Clean Cruise Ships Act, S.2271/H.R. 4101*. Oceana, Seattle.

Northern Economics Inc. (2004) *Alaska Visitor Arrivals, Summer 2003*. Alaska Department of Community and Economic Development, Anchorage.

Oceana (2002) Cruise ship regulations help cut water pollution. *Environment News Service*, 18 December.

Ocean Conservancy (2002) *Cruise Control: A Report on How Cruise Ships Affect the Marine Environment*. TOC, Washington, DC.

Ocean Conservancy (2004) *Cruise Ships and Clean Oceans*. TOC, Washington, DC.

Reece, K. (2003) Environmentalists urge cruise ships to clean up. *KOMO TV-Seattle Local News*, 20 May.

Ringer, G. (ed.) (1998) *Destinations: Cultural Landscapes of Tourism*. Routledge, London and New York.

Sacks, A. (2004) *The Alaska Tourism Satellite Account: A Comprehensive Analysis of the Economic Contribution of Travel & Tourism*. Global Insight, Allentown, Pennsylvania.

Schmid, C. (2003) Cruise-ship industry activist, author to speak in Juneau. *Juneau Empire Online*. Available at: www.juneauempire.com/stories/011503/loc_ speaker.shtml

Schroeder, R. *et al.* (2005) Tourism growth in Southeast Alaska: Trends, projections and issues. In: L. Kruger and R. Mazza, eds. *Social Conditions and Trends in Southeast Alaska. General Technical Report PNW-GTR 653*. US Department of Agriculture Forest Service, Pacific Northwest Research Station, Portland, Oregon.

Tobias, L. (2004) Bicentennial brings boom times: rising tourism is a mixed blessing for the town of Astoria. *The (Eugene) Register-Guard*, 18 September, D3.

US Environmental Protection Agency (2004) *Cruise Ship Water Discharges*. Environmental Protection Agency, Washington, DC.

US Passenger Services Act of 1886 (1886) SI 1886. US Congress, Washington, DC.

Vipond, A. (2004) *Alaska by Cruise Ship: The Complete Guide to Cruising Alaska*, 4th edn. Ocean Cruise Guides, Delta, British Columbia.

Williams, S. (2004) Holland America drops dockings. *Chilkat Valley News* 33(4), 1.

Zuckerman, S. (1999) Come again, but leave your tour at home: Alaskan towns take stand against tourism's excesses. *Tide Pool* 48, 1–2.

26 The Sources and Magnitude of the Economic Impact on a Local Economy from Cruise Activities: Evidence from Port Canaveral, Florida

Bradley M. Braun[1] and Fred Tramell[2]

[1]University of Central Florida, College of Business Administration, Department of Economics, PO Box 161400, Orlando, FL 32816-1400, USA; [2]University of Central Florida, College of Business Administration, Institute for Economic Competitiveness, PO Box 161400, Orlando, FL 32816-1400, USA

Introduction

Cruise activities at a port represent exciting opportunities for increasing local and regional economic exports. Ports earn revenue from providing services to ships and passengers. Cruise lines and passengers spend money in a port's regional economy that has been earned elsewhere. Hence, cruise activities help to increase the number of jobs and income within a port's impact region. Local governments also benefit from increased tax revenues that result from economic growth. The magnitude of the benefits depends on the value added by a region's economy, which in turn determines the amount of local job creation. Value added and jobs depend on the sources and nature of cruise industry spending. Cruise spending in a local economy is influenced by fleet size, passenger capacity, length of cruise itinerary, a ship's flag, a port's attractiveness as port of call, the overall size of the homeport's industry cluster and the underlying structure of the local economy (Davis, 1983).

This chapter explores the nature and sources of the impact from cruises on a port's local and regional economy. We begin the discussion with a general description of the North American Cruise Line (NACL) industry, Port Canaveral and the minimum requirements of a cruise port. The chapter continues with a discussion of economic benefits, including how they are defined and measured. Next, we describe the relative economic impact of cruises over the last decade at Port Canaveral, Florida. The chapter ends with a summary of the sources and nature of economic impact from cruises.

Cruise Activities in North America and at Port Canaveral

Although the roots of cruising can be traced back to the 19th century, it was not until the 1970s that cruising evolved into the vacation experience with which it is associated today. By 1990, the North American cruise fleet stood at 120 ships and carried 3.64 million passengers. Ten years later, the fleet had expanded to 163 ships and carried 6.88 million passengers (ICCL, 2001, pp. 9–10). The perception of enormous economic gains from serving as a port of call, or even more so as a homeport, has prompted many port cities to compete fiercely for a share of the NACL industry's vacation market. Likewise, Port

Canaveral has exploited the opportunity for economic gain from cruises. Fortunately, the increasing NACL fleet size and the mobility of ships have allowed footloose cruise operators to position or reposition their ships to the most profitable itineraries and homeports. Port Canaveral has thus evolved from a port of call in the early 1970s to the second-largest North American cruise port in 2004 (Fig. 26.1). The nature of economic gain depends on myriad factors. To help illustrate these economic concepts, the story of the NACL industry and Port Canaveral is told.

According to the Cruise Line International Association, the NACL industry is defined as 'those cruise lines that primarily market their cruises in North America'. The NACL, which comprises about 80% of the global market, offers cruises with destinations throughout the globe, with 72% of the world's total originating from a US port. In turn, 48% of the world's total originates from a port in the state of Florida (ICCL, 2004, p. 13).

From 1990 to 2000, the NACL fleet grew by 35% from 120 to 163 ships. At the same time, capacity nearly doubled from 83,500 berths in 1990 to 158,400 berths in 2000. The simple explanation for the difference in growth of fleet size and capacity is the size of most new cruise ships. From the 1970s through the early 1990s, cruise ships tended to be both slow and small, typically accommodating fewer than 1000 passengers. Most of the cruise ships added to the fleet since 1997 have capacity in excess of 2000 berths. Port Canaveral illustrates the trend to larger, faster and more stable ships. In 1990, there were four ships at the Port, with an average capacity of 1240 berths. By 2000, Port Canaveral had six homeported ships with an average capacity of 2080 berths. In 2004, the fleet numbered ten, with an average capacity of 2297 berths. Underlying this shift was a repositioning to other ports of three older ships with average capacity of 1142 berths, and the addition of four new ships with average capacity of 2616 berths. In addition to a repositioning of smaller ships to niche and seasonal markets, the NACL industry added some smaller new ships to the fleet, including a number of newly constructed river boats. The most successful of these niche markets are the one-day cruises

Fig. 26.1. When the US Congress authorized the construction of Port Canaveral in 1945, it could not have been expected to later become the world's second-busiest cruise port. The tourism-based regional economy of Orlando, Florida, and the public infrastructure investments by the Port Authority and the State have helped make the cruise industry the most significant economic activity at Port Canaveral.

to nowhere, also called gaming boats. Port Canaveral had one-day cruises to nowhere from the early to mid-1980s. Since 1998, Port Canaveral has been homeport to two gaming ships.

A Decade of Cruises at Port Canaveral

In 1994, Port Canaveral was homeport to a fleet that varied between three and four ships. The fleet sailed itineraries that averaged 3.5 days and had an average capacity of less than 1500. Infrastructure investments enabled Port Canaveral to double the size of the fleet to eight ships in 1999. The expansion of the fleet in the late 1990s included Disney's twin mega-class ships, which increased the fleet's average itinerary to 3.54 days in 1999. By 2000, the average itinerary had grown to 4.5 days, while average ship capacity had grown to over 1700 berths. In 2004, there were ten ships in the fleet, including eight mega-class ships. The itineraries of mega-class ships have increased ship capacity to 2297 berths, increased the average cruise length to 4.63 days and decreased the average length of stay of passengers in the local economy to 1.25 days. Underlying this shift in itinerary length and capacity was a repositioning of older and smaller ships to other ports. Changes within Port Canaveral's cruise industry reflect the overall trend in the North American Cruise Industry of sailing larger ships for longer periods of time.

The changes in the industry have allowed cruisers to enjoy a more extensive choice of cruises in terms of length and destination. At the same time, the changes to the industry have altered the nature of the impact from cruises at Port Canaveral (see Fig. 26.2).

Requirements of a Homeport

The minimum requirement for a region to enter the cruise market as a homeport is deep-water shipping infrastructure and warehouse space to process passengers and baggage. While the largest ship at Port Canaveral, the mega-class *Mariner of the Seas* with 3807 berths, requires a 35-feet deep basin, the smallest ship, the *SunCruz VIII* gaming boat with a 1000 passenger capacity requires just 20 feet.

As the smallest ships require less channel depth, so too are their requirements smaller for additional capital investment to process passengers, baggage and supplies. The smaller ships, such as those sailing 'cruises to nowhere', face only the cost of boarding passengers and supplies, which are both nominally lower. The small ships can operate with little more than a small lounge on shore with a gang plank. In contrast, to effectively compete for multi-day cruises, it is crucial for a homeport to have reachable ports of call and adjacent feeder airports. A port's terminals need to be both functional and aesthetically pleasing, with state-of-the-art infrastructure.

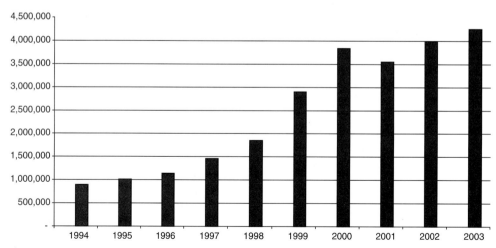

Fig. 26.2.   Cruise passengers at Port Canaveral (embarking and disembarking).

Additionally signage, baggage handling, parking, ground transportation terminals and covered gangways are all expected to be in place. A major hurdle for an aspiring port is the price tag attached to a mega-class cruise ship terminal – US$32.5 million per year to build and operate, including debt service (Canaveral Port Authority, 2004). Whether the investment is sound depends on the sources of revenues, the nature of costs and the net economic gain as measured by value added and jobs.

Economic Impact of Cruise Activities

The benefits of cruise activities at a port derive from income that is spent within the local economy that was originally earned elsewhere. The money that flows from fees on dockage, wharfage, passengers and parking benefit a port directly. Direct purchases by cruise lines and passengers from local businesses create income and jobs. Local governments benefit from increased tax revenues associated with cruise operations and the resulting economic growth. In many instances, fees flow directly to a quasi-governmental port authority rather than directly to a state or local government, which may be financially supporting infrastructure investment. For example, since 1995 the Canaveral Port Authority has invested approximately US$50 million in cruise ship facilities (Braun et al., 2002).

The economic benefits derived from cruise activities are measured by impact analysis, which is normally based on an input–output model. An input–output model calculates changes to income, value added and employment in a region's economy caused by an initial injection of spending. Spending by cruise lines and cruise passengers in the impact region represents the potential direct economic impact of the cruise industry at a port.

While this chapter focuses on direct value added, cruise activities not only directly provide income and jobs but also stimulate a ripple effect of broad economic interactions that produces additional jobs and generates additional regional income (Archer, 1976; Braun, 1989, 1990). These indirect or induced effects arise as a result of the fact that the expenditures of the cruise industry to some extent become income

to the affected local firms. However, this income is received for goods or services rendered. To produce and distribute the requisite goods and services demanded by cruise lines, local firms must purchase additional inputs including labour services. This second round of impacts, albeit indirect impacts, is part of the total economic impact on the region. However, the process continues with additional rounds that diminish in economic magnitude. The summation of all rounds of indirect economic impacts constitutes the cruise industry's multiplier effect. The size of the multipliers depends on the underlying structure of the local or regional economy. In this chapter, we focus on the direct value added associated with cruise-related spending, with the understanding that the output impact, via the multiplier process, is higher (see Fig. 26.3).

An economic impact analysis of the cruise industry must identify, measure and distinguish between the gross value of the goods which are consumed as part of cruise activities and that part of the gross value which is contributed by the cruise industry. In essence, many goods that are part of a 'cruise package' have value prior to their purchase by the cruise lines or cruise passengers. However, as goods and services reach the ultimate consumer, additional costs are incurred that may be associated with additional processing of the goods, or merely by the costs associated with distribution of the product or service. The value added only measures that part of the total value created or added within the local economy. More formally, value added by an organization or industry is revenue less non-labour costs of inputs. Revenue can be imagined to be the product of price and quantity, and costs are usually described by capital (structures, equipment, land), materials, energy and purchased goods and services. Value added is a measure of output that is potentially comparable across economies both large and small.

To summarize, value added is found by identifying cruise-related spending, subtracting the amount of cruise-related purchases from non-local providers and subtracting the costs incurred by local sources to distribute and produce goods and services. The value added by a local economy from cruise activities depends on the unique characteristics of the industry, its ports of call and its homeport. The most important factors of cruise industry impact include the

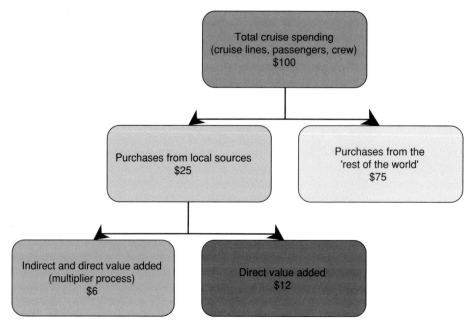

Fig. 26.3. Cruise-related spending.

fleet size, passenger capacity, length of itinerary, ship flag, attractiveness of the port as port of call and the overall size of the industry cluster. To illustrate these factors, we investigate the experience of Port Canaveral over the last decade.

Economic Impact of the Cruise Industry at Port Canaveral

In this section we describe the economic impacts of cruise-related spending at Port Canaveral in 1994, 1999 and 2004 (see Table 26.1). In 1994, Port Canaveral was a small port with a small fleet. It had a small distribution infrastructure, which was not integrated with the cruise line supply chain. Only a small portion (20%) of cruise line spending was directed to local providers. By 1999, Port Canaveral had a larger fleet, higher passenger capacity and longer itineraries. By that time, the Port's regional economy appears to have been integrated fully into the cruise line supply chain. As a result, a large proportion of goods purchases went to local providers located in the Port's regional economy. The integrated supply chain was further strengthened by industry clustering both in cruises and in the overall tourism sector.

The total value of cruise spending grew fourfold from US$323 million in 1994 to over US$1.7 billion in 2004. While spending by both cruise lines and passengers was up in nominal terms, the relative amounts did change. As a per cent of total cruise spending, purchases by cruise lines increased from 78% in 1994 to 85% in 2004, and passenger spending fell from 22% in 1994 to 15% in 2004. At the same time, inflation-adjusted cruise line spending per passenger per day declined from US$87 in 1994 to US$73 in 2004, indicating an increase in the efficiency of the fleet (see Table 26.2). The critical turning point for these values coincides with the introduction of the first mega-class ships and the expansion of the fleet at Port Canaveral.

Cruise lines at the Port spent over US$1.4 billion in 2004 on goods, services and wages. Of total cruise line spending, 80% was for goods and services and 20% for wages. However, because not all purchases were made from local firms and not all wages were paid to local residents, only a portion of total cruise-related spending actually entered the Port's regional economy.

Table 26.1.   Direct economic impact of cruise industry at Port Canaveral, Florida.

	US$ in millions		
	1994	1999	2004
Cruise line spending			
Local			
Goods	34.48	465.04	724.72
Services	15.49	120.25	187.39
Subtotal	49.97	585.29	912.11
Rent	1.03	5.65	6.12
Wages	14.90	28.61	32.20
Subtotal	15.93	34.26	38.32
Non-local			
Goods and services	126.84	225.89	250.13
Wages (shore-based)	7.45	31.30	36.90
Wages (crew)	53.26	110.02	202.13
Subtotal	187.55	367.21	489.16
Passenger local spending	69.75	131.96	248.13
Total spending	323.20	1,118.72	1,687.72
Total local spending (direct economic impact)	135.65	751.51	1,198.56

Direct local spending by the cruise industry at Port Canaveral

In 1994, about half of total cruise line spending (US$65 million) went to local providers, while in 2004 nearly 80% (US$950 million) went to local providers. As a per cent of total spending by cruise lines for goods, local sources increased from 33% in 1994 to 84% in 2004. Services purchased from local sources as a per cent of total service spending by cruise lines increased from 16% in 1994 to 19% in 2004.

Table 26.2.   Port Canaveral economic variables.

	1994	1999	2004
Total revenue passengers	1,070,343	2,902,479	4,253,569
Average cruise length (days)	3.50	3.54	4.63
Average stay (days)	1.50	1.50	1.25
Cruise line spending per passenger (US$)	236.80	339.97	338.44
Passenger spending per day (US$)	67.66	96.04	73.10

Wages paid to local residents as a per cent of total wages paid decreased from 20% in 1994 to 12% in 2004, while wages paid to non-residents as a per cent of total wages paid increased from 70% in 1994 to 75% in 2004. The shift in the relative wages of ship versus shore-based cruise workers reflects the increase in the efficiency of the fleet (see Table 26.1).

Cruise passenger spending within the Port's region rose from US$70 million in 1994 to nearly US$250 million in 2004. Port Canaveral is well positioned as a port of call with its Atlantic beaches, and Kennedy Space Center just a few miles to the north. Less than 50 miles to the west, and connected by a high-speed motorway, is Orlando and the largest concentration of theme parks, resorts and hotels in the world. Unlike cruise line spending, nearly all passenger spending goes to local sources. The average amount of spending per passenger rose slightly from US$130 in 1994 to US$169 in 2004. This relatively small increase is owing to a reduction in the amount of time the average passenger remained in the Port region, which fell from 1.5 days in 1994 to 1.25 days in 2004. While over 80% of passengers sailing through the Port on cruises of 4 days or less extended their stay by an average of one and a half additional hotel nights in central Florida, only 40%

on longer cruises extended their stay by an average of one and a half additional hotel nights in central Florida. Again, this change coincides with the introduction of the mega-class ships, with their longer itineraries (see Table 26.2).

The Value Added by the Cruise Industry at Port Canaveral

Of the US$1.4 billion in cruise line spending in 2004, nearly two-thirds (US$950 million) was spent locally by cruise lines. Of the amount of cruise line local spending, only 40% (or US$369 million) was value added by the local economy. The impact from cruise line purchases of goods appears to be confined to the distribution of goods by businesses located in the Port's region. In contrast, most purchases by cruise lines on services tend to be from local providers, such as the port authority. A large proportion of the value of services is added at the regional level. Over the last decade, the relative size of value added from cruise line purchases as a portion of total cruise local spending on goods and services has remained at approximately 30%. A constant per centage of value added indicates that, other than the increase in magnitude of cruise line spending, the underlying economic structure has changed little in regard to the distribution and production of goods and services.

In addition to the spending of cruise line employees that is captured in the value added of cruise line spending described above, non-resident ships' crews at Port Canaveral spent a portion of their wages in the local economy (i.e. US$202 million in 2004). The amount of value added for ships' crews has grown from US$4 million in 1994 to US$15 million in 2004. As a portion of total value added of cruise-related spending, the importance of local spending by ship crews has declined from 5% in 1994 to 3% in 2004.

In 2004, cruise passengers spent nearly US$250 million. In contrast to cruise line purchases, the total amount of passenger spending is local by definition. Of the US$250 million spent locally by passengers in 2004, nearly 85% (or US$210 million) was value added. As a portion of total value added of cruise-related spending, the overall importance of passenger local spending has declined from 46% in 1994 to 35% in 2004 (see Table 26.3).

Table 26.3. The value added to the Port Canaveral economy from the cruise industry.

Value added	US$ in millions		
	1994	1999	2004
Cruise line local spending	42.32	245.85	368.85
Ships' crews local spending	3.99	8.24	15.13
Cruise passengers local spending	39.85	111.64	209.82
Total value added	86.16	365.73	593.80

Summary Sources of Impact from Cruises

In an attempt to generalize the observations made from Port Canaveral's experience over the last decade, we summarize the important concepts from the previous section. The economic benefits of the cruise industry derive from two sources: (i) spending by cruise lines for supplies, services, labour and items for resale on board the ship; and (ii) spending by cruise passengers off-ship for hotels, meals, entertainment and local transportation. The benefits to a port's surrounding community from these potential sources of economic impact in terms of value added depend on the unique characteristics of its local cruise industry and the underlying structure of its local and regional economy.

Cruise Line Spending

It is obvious that the benefit to a port's impact region is less than the total value of cruise line spending. First, many purchases by cruise lines cannot be satisfied from local sources. Thus, it is correct to consider as potential impact only the value of purchases that are made from businesses located within a port's impact region. Second, a large portion of wages are paid to ships' crews, who may not reside shore-side in the port community. Thus, it is correct to consider as potential impact only the wages paid by cruise lines to local resident employees, and the amount of wages spent locally by non-resident ships' crews.

The million-dollar question is the value that ports, local businesses and workers add to the goods and services that cruise lines purchase. It is the value added that makes both income and jobs grow within a local port community. Value added depends on myriad factors but is fundamentally constrained by the ability of a port's regional economy to satisfy the demands of the cruise industry. The local economy must have the public and private infrastructure in place to support the distribution and production of the types of goods and services purchased by cruise lines. The basic cruise-related spending categories include goods, services and labour.

More than half of cruise line spending is for goods; therefore, the economic impact associated with the purchase of goods is potentially large. However, the value added to an economy depends on the amount of production and distribution that is done by local firms. In general, the more localized is production and distribution, the higher is the value added and the number of jobs created within the regional economy. Cruise line purchases of goods in order of importance are food and beverages, fuel, hotel products, office supplies, water and goods for resale. Other than water few, if any, regional economies are capable of producing the wide range of products demanded by cruise lines. Where local production is deficient, the potential impact from the purchase of goods is confined to the distribution of goods by businesses located in the region. Small ports with small fleets, such as Port Canaveral in the early 1990s, are unlikely to have a distribution infrastructure that is integrated with the cruise line supply chain. The result is that a small portion of the value of goods distribution is added at the regional level. On the other hand, ports with large fleets, high passenger capacity and long itineraries, such as Port Canaveral in the first decade of the 21st century, are more likely to have an integrated supply chain in the regional economy. The result is that a large proportion of the value of goods distribution is added at the regional level. An integrated supply chain can be further strengthened by industry clustering both in cruises and in the overall tourism sector.

Services make up nearly 20% of cruise line spending. In order of importance they include port services, ship agents, ground transportation, ship maintenance, travel and entertainment, telecommunications, medical and financial expense. Unlike goods, most purchases by cruise lines on services tend to be from local providers. The most important services are related to cruise logistics. The minimum infrastructure requirements needed to be a cruise port are such that a large amount of services must be produced and distributed by local providers, including the port authority. The result is that a large proportion of the value of services is added at the regional level.

Labour also represents nearly 20% of total spending. Cruise ilnes employ ship-based crews and shore-based support staff. Nearly three quarters of wages are paid to ship crews, with the remainder paid to shore-based support staff. The important thing to keep in mind is that it is the amount of wages paid to, and spent by, cruise line employees in the regional economy that will add value. Shore-based support staff who are local residents are likely to spend a large amount of their income in the community, while those who are not residents spend little if any. A large fleet and short itineraries increases the number of resident shore-based staff, and thus increases value added. In contrast, most wages of foreign crews are remitted home. However, a small portion of wages paid to foreign crews is spent locally on items such as transportation, financial services, communication services, personal services, entertainment and retail (Braun et al., 2002). The result is that only a portion of wages paid by cruise lines adds value to the port's local or regional economy.

Passenger spending

Cruise passengers generally spend both time and money in ports of call and homeports. In the case of a port of call, the amount of time and money spent by cruise passengers depends on the length of stay and the amenities available both on and off the ship. Amenities include sightseeing, visiting beaches, shopping, eating, gambling and other entertainment. In the era of the great mega-class ships with all their amenities, the challenge for ports of call is to coax passengers to disembark and open their wallets.

Just like any port of call, the amount of time and money spent by cruise passengers in the homeport depends primarily on the opportunities for off-ship leisure activities. In addition, it also depends on the length of a cruise. The shorter a cruise is, the more likely it is for a passenger to extend his or her stay in the local area. The objective of a homeport as port of call is to coax passengers to stay off-ship and to open their wallets. Again, the amenities include sightseeing, visiting beaches, shopping, eating, gambling and other entertainment.

Conclusion

The cruise industry in North America and at Port Canaveral has experienced dramatic changes. A newer and larger fleet with higher passenger capacity has resulted in an increase in quality and efficiency, and a reduction in costs. At the same time, the overall magnitude of cruise-related spending has mushroomed.

The potential benefits to a community seem large given the amount of total cruise-related spending. However, the actual benefits to a port's regional economy are much lower. First, not all spending goes to local providers. Second, much of the value added of the products and services purchased is contributed at the local level. At the same time, because of the export nature of cruise activities, cruise-related purchases are a significant engine for growth in income and employment to a port's local and regional economy. The issue facing port communities is whether the potential benefits from cruise activity can justify the costs of building, maintaining and operating the infrastructure. To enter the cruise industry, a port must possess a minimum of public and private infrastructure. To compete in the mega-class market requires substantial investments in public and private infrastructure. A certain critical mass in both cruising and other tourism-related activities is necessary for a regional economy to become integrated into the industry supply chain.

The economic benefit for small ports with small ships is relatively more dependent on passenger spending. Passenger spending is constrained by a lack of tourism-related infrastructure and amenities. At the same time, cruise line spending is constrained by a lack of distribution infrastructure. On the other hand, larger ports have more of both passenger and cruise line spending. In relative terms of importance, cruise line spending is higher for larger ports with larger fleets. Both passenger and cruise line spending could be constrained by a lack of tourism-related infrastructure and links to the industry supply chain.

While larger ships provide a higher quality of cruises, they also have lower costs per passenger. The impact from spending by passengers on ships sailing longer cruises is less as time spent in the homeport is decreased. However, the higher volume of demand for goods and services locally could offset the relative decline in passenger spending. For example, it took the addition of two mega-class ships before Port Canaveral was integrated into the industry supply chain. It is not clear whether two mega-class ships is one too many or not enough for critical mass. Critical mass depends in part on a region's overall tourism sector, which is quite large at Port Canaveral. The question is whether or not a small port can attract a mega-class ship without being integrated into the industry supply chain and enjoy the same level of costs.

The issue of net economic gain is complex and dependent on myriad variables unique to each geographic location. A port region must assess the potential impact based on expected fleet size, passenger capacity, length of cruise itinerary, a ship's flag, a port's attractiveness as port of call and the overall size of the homeport's industry cluster.

References

Archer, B. (1976) The anatomy of a multiplier. *Regional Studies* 10, 71–77.

Braun, B. (1989) The impact of Port Canaveral on the economies of Brevard County and the Central Florida Region. *IMPACT*, University of Central Florida, Orlando, Florida.

Braun, B. (1990) Measuring the influence of public authorities through economic impact analysis: the case of Port Canaveral. *Policy Studies Journal* 18(4), 4, 1032–1044.

Braun, B., Xander, J. and White, K. (2002) The impact of the cruise industry on a region's economy: a case study of Port Canaveral, Florida. *Tourism Economics* 8(3), 317–324.

Canaveral Port Authority (2004) Port Canaveral 22(4).

Davis, H. (1983) Regional port impact studies: a critique and suggested methodology. *Transportation Journal* 23(2), 61–71.

ICCL (International Council of Cruise Lines) (2001) *The Contribution of the North American Cruise Industry to the U.S. Economy in 2000.* ICCL, Arlington, Virginia.

ICCL (2004) *The Contribution of the North American Cruise Industry to the U.S. Economy in 2003.* ICCL, Arlington, Virginia.

27 Florida's Day Cruise Industry: A Significant Contributor to Florida's Economy?

Lori Pennington-Gray

University of Florida, Center for Tourism Research and Development, Department of Tourism, Recreation and Sport Management, PO Box 118209, Gainesville, FL 32611 8209, USA

Introduction

The cruise industry is one of the fastest-growing segments of the leisure travel industry. Since 1970, the cruise industry in the USA has grown by more than 1800%, with an estimated 500,000 people taking a cruise (CLIA, 2004). In the last decade, the number of North Americans taking cruises grew from 4.5 million in 1990 (Peisley, 2004) to over 8 million in 2003 (CLIA, 2004). Experts expect this growth to continue.

Today over 175 cruise ships embark from more than 23 US ports (Angelo and Vladimir, 2004). US ports handled an estimated 7.1 million cruise embarkations during 2003, accounting for 72% of global embarkations and represented an increase of 9.4% from 2002 (BREA, 2003).

The state of Florida's ports handled approximately 4.7 million embarkations, accounting for two-thirds of all US cruise embarkations (BREA, 2003). According to the Business Research and Economic Advisors' report (2003), Florida's cruise industry represented US$4.6 billion in direct spending and 130,750 jobs paying US$4.7 billion in income. Florida's market accounted for more than 35% of the industry's direct expenditures in 2003. Interestingly, the state of Florida is home to at least ten cruise line corporate or administrative offices. Undoubtedly, Florida is the heart of the cruise industry in the USA.

Specialty Cruises: The Riverboat Cruise in North America

The cruise industry is made up of a wide array of experiences, ranging from large vacation cruise lines to specialty cruises. One specialty line that is fairly unique to the USA is riverboat cruising. According to Garrison (2004), riverboats have a romantic aura surrounding it, which dates back to the 19th century. Aside from a means of transportation, riverboats provide an opportunity to gamble for a limited time on board. Tables and slots are opened when the riverboat sails down the river or around the lake. In recent years, many riverboats have become 'stationary' (moored to the dock) to allow for longer gambling periods and therefore more revenues back to the states. Today, several states have riverboat gambling, including Iowa, Illinois, followed by Missouri, Indiana, Louisiana and Mississippi.

The riverboat experience is a specialty cruise experience that focuses on gambling as a primary purpose for the experience.

The Day Cruise Industry as a Form of Specialty Cruises

In addition to the riverboat specialty line, casino cruises or day cruises are a segment of the cruising market that also primarily focuses on the gambling experience. Most cruise research suggests that typically 'people do not take a cruise to gamble' (Dickenson and Vladimir, 1997, p. 273); however, in the day cruise industry (DCI) the opposite is true. Most people cruise only to gamble. Casino cruises or 'cruises to nowhere' sail into international waters literally to no particular destination in order to allow their passengers to gamble. Casino cruises exist in several states within the USA, including Texas, Massachusetts, Georgia and Florida.

Florida has the largest number of casino cruises in the USA. The first port to receive a day cruise in Florida was Port Everglades. Now, Florida hosts 16 vessels across every major port on the Florida peninsula (except the panhandle) (Fig. 27.1). The cruise ships range in size from the 1800-passenger *Ambassador II* cruise ship all the way down to the yacht-sized *SunCruz Casino* boat, which carries just 150 passengers.

Day cruises typically set sail either once or twice a day and offer opportunities to participate in slots, video poker, blackjack, craps, roulette and Caribbean stud poker. Some casinos also offer baccarat, mini-baccarat, sportsbook, poker, pai gow poker, let it ride and bingo. Tables and slots only open once the vessel is in international waters. International water is defined as 3 miles offshore on the Atlantic side and 9 miles offshore on the Gulf of Mexico. Each boat sets its own minimum gambling age: on some boats it is 18 and on others it is 21.

The Florida Day Cruise Association (FDCA) estimates the economic impact of the industry to be approximately US$1 billion a year; however, no formal study has been conducted to measure the real impact. Estimates from several ports in the state are known and therefore these numbers were used to project the total impact. The Canaveral Port Authority makes US$5 million a year off charges to gambling boats (Byrd, 2004).

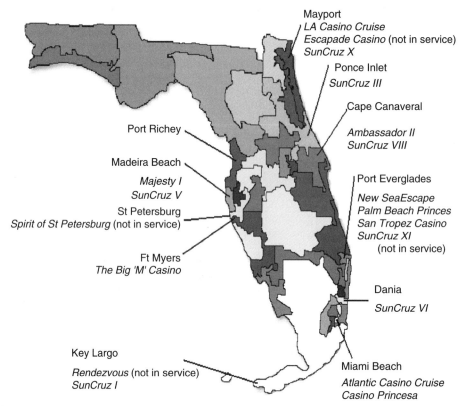

Mayport
LA Casino Cruise
Escapade Casino (not in service)
SunCruz X

Ponce Inlet
SunCruz III

Cape Canaveral
Ambassador II
SunCruz VIII

Port Richey

Madeira Beach
Majesty I
SunCruz V
St Petersburg
Spirit of St Petersburg (not in service)

Port Everglades
New SeaEscape
Palm Beach Princes
San Tropez Casino
SunCruz XI
        (not in service)

Ft Myers
The Big 'M' Casino

Dania
SunCruz VI

Key Largo
Rendezvous (not in service)
SunCruz I

Miami Beach
Atlantic Casino Cruise
Casino Princesa

Fig. 27.1. Locations of vessels in Florida. Source: L. Pennington-Gray, S. Holland, J. Zhang, D. Mulkey and A. Hodges, unpublished data (2003).

It is fairly interesting that the value of the DCI has not been documented. In addition, it is odd that a profile of the industry is lacking from academic textbooks and manuscripts. Thus, the purpose of this chapter is to profile the DCI in Florida and discuss some of the challenges and issues associated with the industry.

This chapter will: (i) address the challenges that the industry has faced in recent years; (ii) discuss implications of these challenges; (iii) profile the day cruise participant; (iv) report the economic contributions of the industry; and finally (v) provide some food for thought in the conclusions.

Challenges Facing the Day Cruise Industry in Florida

The DCI has been a target for the Florida Cabinet and State Legislature since its incep-

tion. In early 2000, the State Legislature proposed a rule that threatened the existence of the industry. Specifically, Governor Jeb Bush and the Cabinet decided to ban 'cruises to nowhere' from docking on state-owned lands (Yardley, 1999). At the time, 17 vessels in the state docked on state-owned lands, representing 100% of day cruise vessels. The Legislatures' argument was that it is within the rights of the government to put restrictions on public lands when it is in the interest of the public, and since Florida voters had repeatedly rejected casino gambling, the policy was appropriate. The DCI filed an appeal and on 18 October 2001, the District Court of Appeal ruled unanimously in favour of the DCI.

Later that same year, the DCI again received attention from the Florida Legislature, this time as a method of paying for smaller classroom sizes, which Floridians approved in the previous election (Ulferts and Bousquet, 2002). Although

Governor Bush had opposed new forms of gambling in the state of Florida, he said he was going to 'allow ideas to come forth for a while . . . [because] we have a duty to comply with this constitutional amendment' (Ulferts and Bousquest, 2002, p. 1A). The DCI was stated as an option.

Finally, late in 2000, the DCI was under scrutiny again by the Florida Legislature because of lack of regulation in international waters. Their argument was that when vessels were outside of US boundaries, 'unregulated gambling quickly becomes crooked' (Thompson cited in Meyers, 2002, p. 4). The Florida Attorney General even stated that 'when a cash-rich business like a casino boat has little oversight, it becomes attractive to people looking to laundered money, such as drug dealers (Glogau cited in Meyers, 2002, p. 4). The push by the Legislature was to either look into government regulation of some sorts or disband the industry.

Implications of These Challenges

As a result of being a target, several implications arose. The Florida Day Cruise Association was established in the spring of 1994, 'as a non-profit organization, formed to facilitate the examination, consideration, promotion or opposition of issues of concern to the Association'

(www.daycruiseassociation.com/buildingan association). As a result of the proliferation of government activity in 2000 the FDCA mobilized with a purpose. Several owners and operators came together explicitly to protect the industry. One of the primary objectives was to have the Executive Director complete a Code of Ethics for the industry (Fig. 27.2). Moreover, the FDCA hired five additional lobbyists to support their year-round lobbyist who had been hired since 1995.

Finally, in 2003 the University of Florida's Center for Tourism Research and Development compiled a *Description of the Day Cruise Industry*. The content of the report included economic contributions of the Florida DCI. The information included basic economic indicators but was not an overall economic impact study. The purpose of the report was to describe the economic contributions of the industry to legislatures in the state of Florida. The method of data collection included personal correspondence with each of the owners and operators of all the day cruises in the state of Florida. Most of the owners and operators participated in the study. Each owner was asked to provide figures related to a variety of categories over the past year or two. Three categories of ships were created: small, medium and large. Missing data were determined using the mean values in each

---

Whereas we agree:
1. To always treat our customers with the utmost care and courtesy.
2. To maintain all equipment on each cruise ship, in keeping with proper safety regulation established to ensure the safety of our workers and our customers.
3. To fulfill commitments to our customers to the best of our ability.
4. To observe all applicable laws or regulations of state, federal and other regulatory bodies, and to conduct only operations as we are competent to perform.
5. To promote the best interest of tourism, economic development and recreation in the state in which we occupy.
6. To participate in fair and honest advertising of services.
7. To avoid untrue or misleading statements concerning a competitor or their methods of operation.
8. To use accurate methods of operation and equipment for each ship.
9. To respond promptly to complaints by customers and settle disputes in a fair and reasonable manner.

Fig. 27.2.   Code of Ethics. Source: www.daycruiseassociation.com/aboutthedca/codeofethics

category and projected to represent the total population in the category. For example, if three owners responded on behalf of three medium-sized ships, but there were five ships in the medium category, the average in each category would be used to determine the totals for each category. After the projections were made, several key informants in the industry double-checked numbers for accuracy. These numbers provide the data for this chapter.

Profile of the Day Cruiser in Florida

The popularity of day cruising has grown tremendously in the last two decades. More recently, passenger loads have been increasing over the last 5 years, although the rates of growth have slowed (Table 27.1). A slight decrease in visitation occurred in 2002. This is probably a result of the events of 11 September 2001. Because the terrorist attacks occurred in September, decreases were not fully recognized until the busier spring season in 2002. Passenger load reports for 2003 indicated a rebound with passenger loads equal to those prior to 11 September 2001 (L. Pennington-Gray, S. Holland, J. Zhang, D. Mulkey and A. Hodges, 2003, unpublished data). On an average, 27% of the visitors are from outside the county of port within the state of Florida, 8% are USA residents (outside the state of Florida) and 6% are international visitors (L. Pennington-Gray et al., 2003, unpublished data).

The busiest months of the year for the DCI are March (10.7% of annual sales), February (9.1% of annual sales) and April (9.1% of annual sales); these months account for approx-

imately 30% of the annual sales. The off-peak times for the industry are December (6.8% of annual sales), November (7.3% of annual sales) and September (7.3% of annual sales). In general, spring is the peak season and fall is the shoulder season (Table 27.2).

Economic Contribution

The description of the economic contribution of the industry will be presented in eight categories: (i) labour issues; (ii) annual vendor purchases; (iii) fees paid to ports; (iv) vehicle and vessel leases; (v) fees to all private marinas; (vi) local fees and taxes paid; (vii) state fees and taxes; and (viii) federal fees and taxes. The following model represents the variables included in the economic contribution of the DCI (Fig. 27.3). The combinations of all these categories represent the economic contribution made by the industry to the state of Florida.

Labour issues

One of the largest economic contributions to the Florida economy is through the hiring of local residents. The total number of employees in the Florida DCI was 2854 full-time employees and 266 part-time employees in 2002 (Table 27.3). The total payroll for the industry was estimated at US$73,151,158 in 2001, with unemploy-

Table 27.1. Passenger loads for 1998–2002 in Florida.

Year	Passenger load	Number of vessels	% change
1998[a]	1,077,616	10	–
1999	3,100,105	16	187.7
2000	3,651,734	16	17.8
2001	3,544,329	16	2.9
2002	3,503,500	16	1.2

[a]Note: 1998 not all vessels reporting.
Source: L. Pennington-Gray, S. Holland, J. Zhang, D. Mulkey and A. Hodges, unpublished data (2003).

Table 27.2. Percentage of annual sales by month and ranking.

Month	Average % of sales
January	8.1
February	9.1
March	10.7
April	9.1
May	9.0
June	7.7
July	8.6
August	8.8
September	7.3
October	7.8
November	7.3
December	6.8
Total	100

Source: L. Pennington-Gray, S. Holland, J. Zhang, D. Mulkey and A. Hodges, unpublished data (2003).

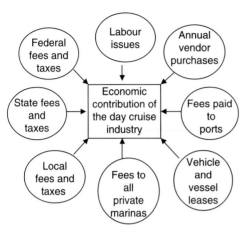

Fig. 27.3. Proposed model of economic contribution.

Table 27.4. Annual vendor purchases in 2002.

Vendor purchases	Totals for 2002 (US$)
Food and beverage	15,750,802
Fuel	6,357,531
Lube oils	113,038
Supplies	4,155,910
Maintenance and repairs	5,350,110
Outsourced labour	14,569,882
Other (marketing, casino, insurance, gift shop purchases, dry docks, accounting services, legal services)	36,493,079
Total vendor purchases	82,792,354

Source: L. Pennington-Gray, S. Holland, J. Zhang, D. Mulkey and A. Hodges, unpublished data (2003).

ment taxes totalling an estimated US$240,000 (L. Pennington-Gray *et al.*, 2003, unpublished data). Payrolls decreased slightly due to lower passenger loads in 2002 (probably as an after effect of the 11 September 2001 terrorist attacks). Also, relocation of ships within the state has allowed for more efficient use of employees. In addition, many of the ships offer full-time employees medical, dental, 401K plan, life insurance, disability insurance, personal days, paid vacation, holiday premium pay, free cruises, birthday bonus days and other benefits.

Annual vendor purchases

Moreover, owners and operators contribute to the economy through the purchases of goods and services locally (Table 27.4). These goods and services include: (i) food and beverage; (ii) fuel; (iii) lube oils; (iv) maintenance and repair; (v) outsourced labour; (vi) and other. The largest

Table 27.3. Employee numbers and payroll.

Employment	Employee number	Payroll (US$)
Full-time employees in 2001	2854	73,151,158
Part-time employees in 2002	266	63,311,717

Source: L. Pennington-Gray, S. Holland, J. Zhang, D. Mulkey and A. Hodges, unpublished data (2003).

annual vendor purchase was 'other' purchases, which included advertising and promotions, dry docks, insurance and accounting services as examples, followed by food and beverage. Total estimated vendor purchases exceeded US$82.8 million in 2002.

Fees paid to ports

An additional contribution to the economy comes in the form of fees that operators in the DCI pay. Typically these fees are paid to the ports. The Florida ports that receive fees include: (i) Port Canaveral; (ii) Port of Palm Beach; and (iii) Port Everglades. Fees consist of dock rentals, dockage fees, wharfage fees, office rent, stevedoring and line handling fees, and valet parking fees. A wharfage fee is the fee or duty paid for the privilege of using a wharf for loading or unloading goods. A stevedoring or line handling fee is a fee charged to attach the vessel to the dock. Overall estimated fees to ports represented US$17.3 million in 2001 and over US$17.8 million in 2002 (Table 27.5). In each category the fees increased over the previous year.

Vehicle and vessel leases

Another category of economic contribution is vehicle and vessel leases (Table 27.6). Leases to vehicles represented over US$51,000 in 2001.

Table 27.5. Fees paid to ports in 2001 and 2002.

Fees paid to ports	Totals for 2001 (US$)	Totals for 2002 (US$)
Dock rental fees	2,170,479	2,533,125
Dockage fees	2,087,329	2,096,314
Wharfage fees	8,075,610	8,102,928
Office rents	780,218	903,595
Stevedoring/line handling	4,015,694	4,035,349
Parking	159,926	159,926
Totals to ports	17,291,257	17,833,239

Source: L. Pennington-Gray, S. Holland, J. Zhang, D. Mulkey and A. Hodges, unpublished data (2003).

This number dropped to one-third in 2002. This drop is reflective of a decrease in vehicles leased by one company. Vessel leases represented US$6.3 million in 2001 and US$6.7 million in 2002. The total category of leases was US$6.4 million in 2001 and close to US$6.7 million in 2002.

Fees to all private marinas

Of the total day cruise fleet in operation (total 16) in the state of Florida, 10 operate out of private marinas. This number is a taxable number, with a 6% state sales tax (some counties may add a county sales tax that is a voted number). Therefore, the total fees paid to landlords of marinas were US$4.7 million in 2001 and US$4.9 million in 2002 (L. Pennington-Gray et al., 2003, unpublished data). Taxes represented approximately US$282,000 in 2001 and US$294,000 in 2002 (L. Pennington-Gray et al., 2003, unpublished data).

Local fees and taxes paid

Another economic contributor to the Florida economy is local fees and taxes. The following

Table 27.6. Leases of vehicles and vessels.

Leases	2001 (US$)	2002 (US$)
Vessel leases	6,315,998	6,657,122
Vehicle leases	51,109	17,403
Total	6,369,108	6,676,527

Source: L. Pennington-Gray, S. Holland, J. Zhang, D. Mulkey and A. Hodges, unpublished data (2003).

fees and taxes are paid locally by owners and operators of the DCI: (i) occupational taxes; (ii) tangible personal taxes; (iii) property taxes; and (iv) valet parking fees (Table 27.7). An estimated total of US$1.1 million was paid locally in fees and taxes in these categories. Fees to Bayfront Park Management Trust in Miami were the largest category followed by property taxes. The Bayfront Park Management Trust was created in 1987, by the Miami City Commission, to manage Bayfront Park 'for the purpose of insuring maximum community utilization and enjoyment' (http://www.bayfrontparkmiami.com/pages/bpmt.html). Fees by one of the vessels docked at Bayfront Park account for this fee.

State fees and taxes

One of the more important contributions to the state are fees and taxes. Approximately, four vessels indicated that they charged an admission fee. A 6% state sales tax is charged on the admission fee (Table 27.8). Total admission taxes were US$531,740 in 2002. The state sales tax paid on the total goods sold in state waters was US$667,383 in 2002. In addition to goods sold, total liquor taxes paid in 2002 were US$130,546. An additional fee is the state pilot fee. State pilot fees are a fixed rate of fees paid to a person duly qualified, and licensed by authority, to conduct vessels into and out of a port, or in certain waters. State pilot fees were US$3,474,726 million in 2002.

State taxes on the purchases of new vessels totalled to almost US$63,000. In 2002, only one new vessel was purchased in the state. Fuel taxes

Table 27.7. Local fees and taxes paid in 2002.

Fees and taxes	Total US$ paid in 2002
Occupational taxes	50,566
Tangible personal taxes	72,538
Property taxes	166,150
Valet parking	43,953
Fees to Bayfront Park Trust (in Miami from one vessel)	615,000
Miami parking surcharge	150,000
Totals for 2002	1,100,209

Source: L. Pennington-Gray, S. Holland, J. Zhang, D. Mulkey and A. Hodges, unpublished data (2003).

Table 27.8. State fees and taxes in 2002.

State fees and taxes	Totals for 2002 (US$)
Sales tax on total goods sold inside state waters	667,383
Admission tax	531,740
Liquor tax	130,546
State corporate income tax	175,875
Professional taxes	7,305
Intangible taxes	16,440
Vessel purchase taxes	62,778
State pilot fees	3,474,726
Fuel taxes	89,502
Unemployment taxes	239,688
Total	5,397,985

Source: L. Pennington-Gray, S. Holland, J. Zhang, D. Mulkey and A. Hodges, unpublished data (2003).

Table 27.9. Federal fees and taxes in 2002.

Federal fees and taxes	Totals for 2002 (US$)
Excise taxes	10,922,916
Coastguard inspection fees	13,800
Totals	10,938,718

Source: L. Pennington-Gray, S. Holland, J. Zhang, D. Mulkey and A. Hodges, unpublished data (2003).

were approximately US$90,000. State corporate income taxes were US$175,875. Unemployment taxes to the state for 2002 were almost US$240,000. Total state fees and taxes for 2002 equated to US$5,397,985.

Federal fees and taxes

Finally, federal fees and taxes are a large economic contribution, although outside the state of Florida. These fees and taxes consist of excise taxes and coastguard inspection fees. Total estimated excise taxes paid in 2002 by owners and operators of the DCI was US$10,922,916 (Table 27.9). Excise taxes are governmental levies on specific goods produced and consumed inside a country. They differ from tariffs, which usually apply only to foreign-made goods, and from sales taxes, which typically apply to all commodities other than those specifically exempted. The other federal fee is a coastguard inspection fee. These fees were US$13,800 in 2002. The total federal fees and taxes were US$10,938,718.

Total contribution

Undoubtedly, the DCI is a significant economic contributor to the Florida economy. In summary, payroll in 2002 exceeded US$63 million. Annual vendor purchases were almost US$83 million in 2002. Leases of vehicles and vessels represented almost US$7 million in 2002. An estimated US$5 million were paid in private

marina leases. State fees and taxes were over US$5 million; other local fees and taxes were in excess of US$1 million. Federal fees and taxes were almost US$11 million. Finally, fees paid to ports were almost US$18 million.

Conclusions: Food for Thought?

After examining the economic contribution to the state of Florida, it would be difficult to argue that Florida's DCI is not a significant contributor to Florida's economy. However, the question still remains: is this a significant enough contribution to the economy to avoid being targeted by elected officials? The future of the DCI remains in the hands of those involved with the industry, e.g. owners, operators, patrons and supporters. There are several recommendations that might improve the position of the DCI.

Continued measurement of the economic impact of the industry is necessary. A thorough economic impact study should be conducted by a reputable research company that will document the direct, indirect and induced impacts of the industry. Total jobs generated by the industry and total wages generated by the industry also should be documented. This will help to justify the industry's impact on legislators and others who may target the industry for elimination.

With the growing focus on social factors associated with gambling, the industry needs to move towards integrated management techniques to address these issues. Social marketing programmes that partner with the Florida Council on Compulsive Gambling would be a step in the right direction. For example, promotional pieces on websites (e.g. www.daycruiseassociation.com) that educate the patron on compulsive gambling would indicate that the industry is interested in promoting social responsibility.

Hiring a public relations officer for the DCI is also another recommendation that might lead to greater knowledge and more positive images of the industry. This public relations officer could help to put together press releases to go out to both travel writers as well as travel sections of newspapers and magazines. Profiling the fun of the industry and possibly new and creative partnerships (e.g. Florida Council on Compulsive Gambling example above) would be a good way to have travel writers pick up the story on the industry.

A national association is needed. Currently, a national association does not exist. Several states have casino cruises that could bring together people to form a larger united front to help with attacks against the industry as well as help with a comprehensive marketing programme for the industry. The FDCA is the only organized association. Owners and operators of cruise casinos from Texas, Massachusetts, Georgia, Florida and other states could come together to create this national association. The primary goal would be educational, particularly to educate the public on the industry. Several other objectives would also be critical to the formation of the association. These objectives might include such things as lobbying government legislatures, public service announcements, public relations, environmental policies adopted by the industry and several others.

The DCI needs to position itself along with the International Council of Cruise Lines (ICCL) and Cruise Line Industry of America (CLIA). This would be beneficial for several reasons. Primarily, membership in these organizations would increase awareness of the DCI. In addition, several critical initiatives that are occurring with ICCL and/or CLIA, such as the United Nations Environment Program (UNEP), are important for the DCI to be involved with. The UNEP report focuses on sustainable tourism issues, primarily sustainable environmental practices, for cruise ships. These practices are very important for the casino cruise industry to be up to date on and reacting to. It is essential that the DCI position itself as an ally with these organizations.

These are merely a few recommendations that could help to strengthen the position of the DCI in the USA, particularly Florida. In an industry that is not well organized beyond the borders of the state of Florida and is rather small (a few owners and operators), these recommendations are critical to the future of the industry.

References

Angelo, R.M. and Vladimir, A.N. (2004) *Hospitality Today: An Introduction*. Educational Institute of American Hotel and Lodging Association, Lansing, Michigan.

Business Research & Economic Advisors (BREA) (August 2003) *The Contribution of the North American Cruise Industry to the US Economy in 2002*. International Council of Cruise Lines, Arlington, Virginia.

Byrd, A. (2004) Gamers push port to top cruise spot in the country. *Orlando Business Journal*. Available at: http://www.bizjournals.com/orlando/stories/2000/11/27/story6.html on October 11, 2005

CLIA (2004) *Cruise Industry Overview*, marketing edition, Spring 2004, Available at: http://www.cruising.org/press/overview

Dickenson, B. and Vladimir, A. (1997) *Selling the Sea: An Inside Look at the Cruise Industry*. John Wiley & Sons, New York.

Garrison, L. (2004) *The Changing History of Gambling on Rivers and at Sea*. Available at: http://cruises.about.com/cs/shipactivities/a/cruisecasinos.htm

Meyers, J. (2002) Sea of trouble: gambling cruises avoid government rules. *The Boston Herald*. Available at: http://web.lexis-nexis.com/universe/document

Peisley, T. (2004) *By Cruise Liner*. Available at: http://www.celestia.co.uk/wexas/p3_bycruise-liner.htm

Ulferts, A. and Bousquet, S. (2002) Class size cost could revive gambling option. *St Petersburg Times*. Available at: http://web.lexis-nexis.com/universe/document

Yardley, W. (1999) Casino ships fight ban from state land. *St Petersburg Times*. Available at: http://web.lexis-nexis.com/universe/document

28   Cruise Tourism in the Eastern Caribbean: An Anachronism in the Post-colonial Era?

Lydia M. Pulsipher[1] and Lindsey C. Holderfield[2]
[1]University of Tennessee, Department of Geography, Knoxville,
TN 37996-0925, USA; [2]Upper James River Roundtable Highland County,
Virginia, USA

Introduction

In this chapter we argue that cruise tourism, as it is developing in the Eastern Caribbean, is creating an ever-wider chasm between the tourist and the islander and contributing to misperceptions and disappointments on the part of both hosts and guests. The cruise tourism product, as it is designed by cruise companies and island governments, provides tourists with an impoverished experience and leaves island people disempowered in their own places and underpaid for the wear and tear on their societies and psyches that tourism brings. Whereas in the past, tourists in the Caribbean would spend at least a few days and nights in an island hotel and have at least some encounters with island people and places; now most visitors to the region come on cruise ships, visiting individual islands for at most a few hours. Moreover, most cruise passengers in the Eastern Caribbean now tend to stay on-board ship for the duration of the trip, discouraged from venturing ashore by the cruise company and by their own mistaken ideas about the islands. The few that disembark often spend their time in harbour-side shopping centres filled with international franchise shops and restaurants (Herme, Colombia Emeralds, Laura Ashley, Burger King or Kentucky Fried Chicken). Or they may take an island tour organized by the cruise company, rather than by island entrepreneurs.

Some of this withdrawal by the tourists from contact with island people and places is the result of the effort by cruise companies to limit the time passengers spend on island, thus to retain for themselves most of the money that tourists spend during the period of their cruise. Some of it is the result of tourist's own ignorance of the Eastern Caribbean and misperception of it as a place of abject poverty and petty crime where strangers may be endangered. But island people are also at fault for not adequately and proactively defining and marketing their islands as modern societies worth visiting for their own sake. Too often island marketers push the idea that the islands are bits of paradise where visitor can and should remain detached, while resting from the stresses of the real world. The tours they offer are too often bland and nearly devoid of intellectual content, focusing on nothing more than smiling faces, pretty vistas, a few scraps of inaccurate history and trivializing comments about local people. We argue that cruise tourism as it is presently constructed in the Eastern Caribbean does not serve either the tourists or the islands well. In fact, cruise tourism may be the final deteriorating stage in a tourism strategy that once held great promise for both regional development and international understanding.

For North Americans, famously in need of greater understanding of the world beyond their shores, a cruise that took them to former British, French, Dutch and Danish islands in the Eastern

Caribbean could be an enlightening first introduction to foreign places – places that differ strikingly from North America in their histories, in their racial and cultural make-up, in their linguistic traditions, in their built environments, in their perspectives on world politics and in their markedly lower levels of mass consumption. For people in the Eastern Caribbean, visits by hundreds of thousands of affluent North Americans could provide not only a chance to earn an income but also an opportunity to show the wider world that their small societies are vibrant, modern and well functioning, and have much to contribute as models for others. Unfortunately, little of this is happening. Instead cruise tourists are staying on board or partaking in only brief island visits of an hour or two. Caribbean people, meanwhile, not only lose income as cruise tourism expands and passengers retreat from on island experiences but also have allowed themselves to be marginalized in their own places by the cruise industry, to be inaccurately stigmatized as poor and ignorant, and to be blocked from interacting as equals with visitors to their homelands.

The social, political and economic features of the modern Eastern Caribbean

According to a number of measures, the islands of the Eastern Caribbean should present a particularly attractive destination for *stopover tourists* (those who spend at least one night on island) as well as cruise tourists. First location: the islands form an ethereally beautiful archipelago that arcs hundreds of miles from Puerto Rico to the South American continent; and most individual islands are accessible by air and sea. Second, the Creole culture of the region – architecture, cuisine, music, dance, language, literature, religion and folklore – is a rich and exuberant blend from the Americas, Africa, Europe and Asia that could provide plenty of appeal for the traveller. Third, and central to our point in this chapter, by all the usual measurements the Eastern Caribbean is a relatively prosperous place, firmly in the global middle class. Yet, it is this feature of the region that seems not to be registering with potential visitors, with the cruise industry or even with policymakers and promoters of tourism within the region.

The extent to which these islands have escaped the poverty-stricken status of 50 years deserves illustration. Since the Second World War, through a combination of aid from former colonial powers (and Canada, much less so the USA) and enlightened locally driven social policy, Eastern Caribbean physical and social infrastructures have improved steadily. All children now have the opportunity to finish technical or regular high school and most eventually go on for further career training or university degrees. Literacy rates for people below 70 years of age average close to 95% (Table 28.1, column 5; UNDP, 2003). There is basic health care: mothers receive pre- and post-natal care, nearly all babies are born in hospitals, and infant mortality rates are low (much lower than they were as recently as the 1970s and lower than in several parts of the USA in 2003, see Table 28.1, column 4). Community clinics provide regular services to those suffering chronic disease, such as diabetes and hypertension. Life expectancies are in the high 70s (UNDP, 2003) and elderly care is provided by family, neighbours and increasingly by the state. Partly because children are now healthier, people are choosing to have smaller families; the overall annual rate of population increase for the Eastern Caribbean (1%) is on a par with the industrialized countries.

Not only has the basic state of human well-being drastically improved over what it was in the 1960s but also the island physical infrastructures have advanced markedly. Hard-surfaced roads reach into the remote countryside. The housing stock has been drastically upgraded (usually paid for by emigrants who send money to upgrade family homes), and electricity, running water and telephone service are available in virtually every home. Banking services are widely offered. Computers are popular, and in some islands well over 10% of the population has home Internet access (UNDP, 2003). Cable and satellite TV is widespread, meaning Caribbean people routinely keep in touch with events in Boston, London, Istanbul and across the world. Every day, taxi drivers waiting for fares, shoppers and vendors in markets and patrons in rum shops can be heard chatting about the latest events in Iraq, Paris or South-east Asia. Many of their observations are based on personal experience, because Eastern Caribbean people travel widely.

Table 28.1. Human well-being rankings of countries in Eastern Caribbean, 2003.

Country (1)	GDP per capita, adjusted for PPP[a] in 2001 $US (2)	Human Development Index (HDI) global rankings, 2003[b] (3)	Infant mortality per 1000 live births, 2003 (4)	Adult literacy (%), 2001 (5)	Life expectancy at birth, 2003 (6)
Antigua and Barbuda	10,170	56 (medium)	17	89	73.9
Bahamas	16,270	49 (high)	16	95.6	67.2
Barbados	15,560	27 (high)	13.2	99.7	76.9
Dominica	5,520	68 (medium)	16	96.4	72.9
Grenada	6,740	93 (medium)	17	94.4	65.3
Guadeloupe	9,000 (1997 est.)[c]	N/A (high)	7.6	90[e]	77.7[e]
Martinique	10,700 (2001 est.)[c]	N/A[d] (high)	8	93[e]	79.4[e]
Netherlands Antilles	11460 (N/A) (2002 est.)[e]	N/A[d] (high)	13	93[e]	75.6[e]
St Kitts and Nevis	11,300	51 (high)	28	97.8	70
St Lucia	5,260	71 (medium)	14	90.2	72.2
St Vincent/Grenadines	5,330	80 (medium)	19	89	74
Trinidad and Tobago	9,100	54 (high)	19	98.4	71.5
USA	34,342	3 (high)	10	99	76.9
World (for comparison)	7,160	Not applicable	55	Not available	66.7

[a]PPP = purchasing power parity.
[b]The high, medium and low designations indicate where the country ranks among the 175 countries classified by the United Nations; the only country in the Western Hemisphere to rank low is Haiti.
[c]Data from *United Nations Human Development Report 1998* (data not available in 2003).
[d]N/A = data not available.
[e]Data from *CIA World Factbook, 2003*.
Source: United Nations Human Development Report 2003.

A number of Eastern Caribbean islands are in the most prosperous cohort on the United Nations Human Development Index (United Nations Development Programme, 2003; see Table 28.1, column 3). And per capita GDP figures (between US$5330 and US$16,270, adjusted for purchasing power parity; UNDP, 2003) put the islands in income brackets well above the averages for most of Latin America, Southern and Eastern Europe, South-east Asia, much of East Asia and all but Hawaii in the Pacific Islands (Table 28.1, column 2). The Caribbean also ranks high in the extent to which women are empowered to participate in society. On the United Nations Gender Empowerment scale (UNDP, 2003) which measures the extent to which a country gives women access to participation in civil society, Barbados, the Bahamas and Trinidad/Tobago outrank Japan, Italy, Portugal, Greece and all of the new Central

European countries that joined the European Union (EU) in May, 2004. Across the Eastern Caribbean, it is now common for women to be ministers of government and to head local businesses and institutions. An indication of the extent to which females are being empowered is the fact that according to a United Nations study on fertility behaviour Caribbean countries are among the few on earth where girl children are actually preferred over boys (United Nations Population Study, 1987) and where female literacy is higher than male literacy (Seager, 2003, pp. 76–77).

This general progress in human well-being is the result of diligent efforts by island elected officials (discussed further below). The progress is also the result of widespread civic responsibility exercised by local organizations such as the Rotary and Lions clubs, libraries, chambers of commerce, gourmet cooking clubs, garden societies, village clean-up associations, local radio and television stations, newspapers and active churches. All of these organizations are strong advocates of participatory democracy, i.e. citizens meet regularly to educate one another about important skills for living and about social and environmental issues, they rotate leadership roles, and they continuously design and implement solutions to local problems. The media announce and promote civic events, interview officials and local citizens regularly, include editorials on local and international issues, and encourage individual citizen participation by providing call-in and write-in venues.

As a result of all this public and private action to raise standards of living and improve social relationships, Caribbean people are for the most part comfortable in their own place, competent in their self-governing, and well informed about local, regional and global affairs. Caribbean people, themselves, travel widely, often migrating for several years to work and study abroad. Many of these sojourners abroad send home substantial remittances and return on regular visits. Some eventually return to reside permanently in the islands of their birth, bringing with them skills and financial assets. Returning emigrants report that overall the quality of life on their home islands actually exceeds that of the far more materially endowed societies where they have been working, because island life is enhanced by strong community and family support and by the healthful and beautiful island environments (L.M. Pulsipher's personal conversations with returning migrants, 1970–2004).

In short, the Eastern Caribbean exhibits many features that should make it a nearly perfect tourism destination, especially for people first venturing outside the USA. But oddly enough, North Americans, who now constitute about 50% of the stopover tourists coming to the Eastern Caribbean and about 70% of those coming to the larger Caribbean on cruises (according to the Caribbean Tourism Organization (CTO, 2004), 8.5 million in 1997, 7 million a year in the post-11 September era through 2003), appear to be withdrawing from any direct contact with these well-functioning places. While they are attracted to the beauty and romanticism of the Caribbean as portrayed in tourism advertising, increasingly tourists are choosing not to experience the islands personally but to view them only from a distance. More and more North American tourists are choosing ocean-going cruises in very large ships rather than trips to resorts or villas in the Eastern Caribbean. This choice is reflected in the recent marked increase in the size of Caribbean cruise liners (Fig. 28.1) (Wood, 2000, p. 349). Because the size of the ships now makes docking in small ports difficult, passengers often are not even offered the option of disembarking or the option of going to shore on a lighter proves unattractive. When a means to go ashore is provided, only about 15% of passengers do so (Holderfield, 2002). Interviews with cruise passengers (Holderfield, 2002; L.M. Pulsipher, 1993–1995, unpublished data) reveal that many have only viewed the islands and their inhabitants from the ship's deck, or have spent only an hour or two in waterfront tourist shops or on hasty island tours. They return home with an ill-defined feeling of regret, even guilt,[1] about what they perceive to be the abject poverty of the region. Like this Knoxville, Tennessee hairdresser interviewed by Pulsipher in 1994, many tourists express shame about their trip to what had been billed in the tourist literature as 'Paradise':

> You work in the Caribbean? Oh, I went there on a cruise last year and I got so depressed, that I never want to go back. The people are so poor! They didn't have any schools or hospitals! There were 1500 of us on that ship and when we got off in those little islands, the people just crowded around, shouting to sell us things or to take us on tours. After a while, I just stayed on the ship so I wouldn't feel so guilty.

One has to ask why such misconceptions of the islands are carried away by these visitors. We argue that several circumstances conspire to lead impressionable US tourists to these erroneous and stultifying conclusions about the

---

[1]Shame and its counterpart, guilt, are here defined as the emotional reaction that occurs when we find ourselves breeching our deepest values. Stronger than embarrassment, guilt is felt when we act in what we perceive to be a socially inappropriate way (Kaufman, 1985; Fossum and Mason, 1986).

Fig. 28.1. Two cruise ships docked at St Johns, Antigua, in 2000. Together they hold more than 3000 passengers. During high season, as many as 12 such ships will call at St Johns per week. There are auxiliary docks for days when three or four ships arrive. Passengers first pass through a low-rise shopping centre of foreign-owned franchise shops and then come to a street where vans hired by the cruise companies take them on tours of various types.

Caribbean region. Part of the explanation lies in the basic geographic ignorance of the US public – virtually every recent survey of the US public has shown that the citizenry has little or no knowledge of the world beyond their borders (Trivedi, 2002), and part of it lies with the avaricious practices of the cruise industry that (we think) cynically and purposely misleads their cruise passengers so as to enhance cruise ship profits. But also a substantial part lies with Caribbean societies who allow themselves to passively cooperate with an industry that perpetuates for visitors to the Caribbean what geographer James Blaut (1992) has called 'a colonizers' model' (see discussion below) – the idea that the people outside the developed world are benighted by lack of schooling, not very competent or prosperous, and vaguely in need of help from the 'developed world'. By not seizing control of how they are depicted by the tourism industry, and by not better organizing the contexts in which island people and cruise passengers encounter each other, Caribbean societies have tacitly accepted a role defined by the colonial mind set in which visitors are encouraged to view the islands much as they might view Disneyworld, as places that deserve only a bland

and cursory look. Visitors are not encouraged to see the islands as complex real places to be experienced with intellectual engagement. Unlike host societies in Europe, South American cities, South-east Asia or Hawaii, where residents assertively instruct tourists on how to think about the place, Caribbean island people do not seize the opportunity to educate their visitors.

Tourism as a development strategy

Over the last 50 years, Island governments have successfully turned former dependent plantation economies, once managed from Europe and North America, into more self-directed, self-sufficient and flexible entities that can adapt quickly to the perpetually changing markets of the global economy. The 1960s and 1970s saw the final demise of plantation crops such as sugar, cotton and copra. Some islands (Dominica, St Lucia, St Vincent) turned to producing 'dessert' crops such as bananas and coffee that were sold for high prices under special agreements with the European countries that once held them as colonies (Grossman, 1998). Now these protections are disappearing as the trade rules within the EU make such agreements illegal. Other island countries turned to the processing of special natural resources, for instance: petroleum in Trinidad and Tobago, bauxite in Jamaica, the assembly and finishing of such high-tech products as computer chips and pharmaceuticals in St Kitts-Nevis and the processing of computerized data in Barbados. By the 1960s, a number of Eastern Caribbean islands were combining one or more of these strategies with efforts to encourage tourism; and it is important to note that, although the strategy was never well thought out, from the beginning tourism was embraced as a development strategy because island governments thought bringing visitors to the islands for a stay of a week or more (referred to as *stopover visits*) would foster 'clean' and significant economic development for island people. Already in 1931, a British official in Trinidad observed that it would be wise to supplant the old plantation crops of the islands with a new lucrative crop, 'the tourist crop', which he felt would bring in a 'handsome sum' to island revenues (Gilmore, 2000, p. 37). Thus, we can see that early on tourism was associated in Caribbean minds with the colonial plantation system. Furthermore, it has often been observed that the Caribbean tourism industry as it developed after the Second World War resembles the plantation system before it in that tourism depends on foreign investment, foreign management, cheap local labour, the exporting of profits and lopsided island infrastructures that favour outsiders over local people (Pattullo, 1996; Gilmore, 2000). Little surprise then that tourism also perpetuated among Caribbean people an archaic subservient and now clearly dysfunctional attitude towards themselves and towards tourists and tourism.

Tourism gained interest as a development strategy in the Eastern Caribbean in the 1960s and spread in the 1970s as islands, recently independent or about to become so, searched for ways to be more economically self-sufficient. Tourism was promoted to island people as a 'clean export' (way to earn foreign currency). It was imagined that unlike the extractive plantation economy, tourism would bring passive, prosperous outsiders to island locations to enjoy the scenery, slicked-up versions of local culture (festivals, costumes, dance and music performances) and some rum punch. Their presence would create non-agricultural jobs paying living wages (Pulsipher's interviews with businessman, Reginald Osborne, and Chief Minister, Willie Bramble, Montserrat, 1973). The visitors would willingly pay substantial hotel fees, leave large tips, and perhaps – though this was not an overtly stated potential benefit – the visitors might even facilitate migration to the USA for those with whom they made friends (the authors' personal observations of tourism promotion within the region, and of encounters between visitors and Caribbean people; also see Archer, 1985).

To entice these stopover visitors some islands sought large hotel development, as was the case in Antigua and Barbuda, Barbados, Guadeloupe, Martinique and St Martin. Some islands, such as Anguilla, Antigua and Barbuda, Dominica, St Lucia, Montserrat and Nevis, opted for small intimate resorts in natural settings that charged a wide range of rates from modest (US$100–150 per night per person) to pretentious (US$500–1000 per night per person). A few, Antigua and Barbuda, Mustique, St Barts, Montserrat, added high-end residential tourism to their repertoire. (The reader will notice that Antigua and Barbuda tried all of the strategies at once.) In the case of residential tourism, wealthy expatriates were encouraged to build grand villas and reside on island for several months every year. Islands earned money first from extended hotel visits by residential investors as they organized the building of their homes, and then from the construction of the villas. Most villas required the importation of high-end materials but concrete blocks and stone were usually available locally, and in many islands skilled (if elderly) stonemasons were available to work themselves and to train a new generation of craftsmen. Once owners or renters occupied the villa, island business people earned regular income from the consuming habits and domestic service needs of the villa occupants. By one estimate in 2000, the owners and/or renters of a completed villa who stayed on island most of the year spent close to US$60,000 per annum for taxes and the materials and services to support their daily lives (Pulsipher, 2002).

For some islands, all types of tourism and related activities, such as building and facilities construction, eventually contributed to as much as 90% of the gross national product (GNP), as was the case in Antigua and Barbuda in 2003

(OECS High Commission, 2004). In the Bahamas, Barbados and St Martin, in the mid-2000s tourism is 60% of GDP and in the Bahamas the industry directly or indirectly employs half of the population. Tourism is the main industry in Grenada, St Lucia, St Vincent and the Genadines, and in St Kitts-Nevis tourism is part of a trinity of industries along with IT and electronics manufacturing (*CIA World Factbook*, 2004).

In the relatively well-managed islands, such as St Martin, Montserrat, Nevis and Barbados, the era of stopover tourism along with other development strategies transformed island infrastructures and raised standards of living significantly, as the human well-being data presented earlier show. In others, most notably Antigua and Barbuda, while living standards have increased, corruption and mismanagement resulted in tourism not fulfilling its promise. Projects repeatedly failed (e.g. the Royal Antiguan Hotel, built with local tax money), or did markedly less well for the island than expected or actually fleeced local people. In the latter case, the gambling industry in Antigua, first touted as a way for the island to gain income from tourists, was by the early 1990s making less than US$100 per capita from tourist customers, yet was gaining most of its income from the gambling addictions of Antiguan workers and business people (L.M. Pulsipher, conversation with USA gambling executive, 1990). Also, Antiguan revenue and tax structures were manipulated to consistently deprive ordinary citizens of the full benefits of tourism income while island officials became wealthy (Holderfield, 2002). In a number of islands (Antigua again prominent among them), heavy borrowing to build hotels, airports, water systems and shopping centres to support tourism left island citizens with huge debts to pay off. For example, in the early 2000s, Antigua and Barbuda, St Kitts-Nevis, St Lucia and Dominica all had external debt exceeding 25% of total GDP (*CIA World Factbook*, 2004).

Overall, by the year 2000, Caribbean people had a more reasoned view of what tourism could do for their islands. Host countries now recognize that stopover tourism is difficult to regulate, in part because it is a complex multinational industry. They also better understand the extent to which tourism markets are controlled by external organizations: travel agencies, airlines, hotel and restaurant conglomerates, food jobbers and entertainment promoters. The Caribbean press regularly takes note of the fact that rapid growth of the industry in an unregulated environment led to overbuilding and to countless poorly developed projects in St Croix, St Kitts-Nevis, St Thomas, Antigua and Barbuda, St Martin and beyond (see http://www.caribbeannewspapers.com). None the less, tourism is now a mainstay of island economies and most islands would like it to stay as such; but when conceptualizing how to portray themselves to visitors, Caribbean people still have not thrown off the mantel of colonialism. In private conversations, Caribbean citizens involved in tourism – often highly educated and widely travelled people themselves – recognize that their US visitors are usually uninformed about the world outside the USA and are inexperienced in visiting foreign places. They are aware that tourists often need guidance in how to relate to the islands. Yet few see this need as something they can ameliorate themselves by speaking authoritatively to tourists about Caribbean places and by proactively managing the encounters between tourists and island people.

For example, the disenchanted Knoxville woman quoted above was referring to an experience in Grenada. There cruise ships often pull up to banana-loading docks, passengers disembark and wend their way through the fruit-loading facilities to a wire gate, where on the other side wait a dozen or more vendors of spice baskets and bottled extracts – all local products worth sampling. But rather than being greeted in a welcoming fashion, the visitors are confronted by a cacophony of voices pleading with them to buy those goods or take an island tour, or accept the company of a guide who will show the way to shops and the open market. Now, in fact, this vivid scene (the vendors are often dressed in Caribbean folk costumes) is reminiscent of dockside arrivals in the Caribbean described by sojourners in the 17th and 18th centuries and might conceivably be promoted as a living history portrayal, but it is not, and no one helps the cruise tourists see this experience as positive. Many assume that these few dozen people represent how Grenadians live today, and that Grenadians are desperate. With no help in understanding the situation, many are actually frightened to venture further. They retreat to the ship or to a cruise company-managed tour, thus missing the chance to enjoy an island with a distinctive character and with some 100,000 modern, well-educated, modestly well off, and gracious citizens (L.M. Pulsipher, 1990–1993, personal observation while lecturing on the *Sea Cloud*, for Lindblad Tours).

The Ascendance of Cruise Tourism in the Eastern Caribbean

Cruise tourism, now the fastest growing component of mass tourism worldwide and the largest cruise market (Wood, 2002, pp. 420–422), began to gain ground in the Eastern Caribbean in the 1980s. By 1990, Antigua and Barbuda, Brabados, Grenada, Martinique, St Vincent and the Grenadines and the US Virgin Islands hosted

more cruise passengers than stopover tourists (Table 28.2, see also Holder, 1993, pp. 209–210; Wood, 2000, p. 348). During the 1990s the international cruise industry aggressively promoted the Caribbean region and increased the number of cruise ships to 71 and ship capacities to over 3000 (Royal Caribbean's *Voyager of the Seas* can carry 3840, the Princess Line's *Grand Princess* can carry 3300; Fig. 28.2). By late in the decade there were roughly 10 million tourist arrivals in (all) Caribbean ports per year (Wood, 2000, p. 348). But, despite this emphasis on the Caribbean region, the cruise industry no longer promotes the Caribbean as the actual destination; rather the islands are the mere backdrop for the cruise experience and the destination is now the ship itself. Cruise line brochures speak of the Caribbean as an exotic place best observed from the deck of a cruise ship (cruise line brochures cited in Wood, 2000, p. 359); and

Table 28.2. Stopover visits and cruise arrivals in the Eastern Caribbean, 2003.

Destination (stopover)	I. Period	Tourist arrivals	% Change 2003/02	Destination (cruise)	II. Period	2003	% Change 2003/02
Anguilla	Jan.–Dec.	46,915	7.1	Anguilla	–	–	–
Antigua and Barbuda*	Jan.–Oct.	182,423	12.8	Antigua and Barbuda	Jan.–Jul.	220,308	2.6
Bahamas*	Jan.–Dec.	1,428,599	1.8	Bahamas	Jan.–Dec.	2,970,174	6.0
Barbados	Jan.–Nov.	474,248	5.6	Barbados	Jan.–Nov.	467,848	4.1
British Virgin Islands[P]	Jan.–Jul.	184,777	–4.3	British Virgin Islands[P]	Jan.–Jul.	178,699	57.3
Dominica	Jan.–Nov.	66,252	8.9	Dominica	Jan.–Jun.	96,105	5.4
Grenada	Jan.–Oct.	117,758	7.6	Grenada	Jan.–Oct.	95,063	–4.4
Martinique	Jan.–Nov.	405,128	–0.6	Martinique	Jan.–Dec.	286,218	38.0
Montserrat	Jan.–Oct.	5,966	–13.4	Montserrat	–	–	–
Saba	Jan.–Sep.	7,808	–2.3	Saba	–	–	–
St Lucia	Jan.–Dec.	276,948	9.3	St Lucia	Jan.–Dec.	393,262	1.6
St Maarten*	Jan.–Dec.	427,587	12.3	St Maarten	Jan.–Sep.	785,706	6.2
St Vincent and G'dines	Jan.–May	28,137	–7.2	St. Vincent and G'dines	Jan.–May	34,317	–34.1
Trinidad and Tobago	Jan.–Sep.	303,788	4.9	Trinidad and Tobago	Jan.–Apr.	33,477	–18.2
US Virgin Islands	Jan.–Dec.	618,703	3.5	US virgin islands	Jan.–Dec.	1,773,948	2.0
Totals		4,575,037				7,335,125	

*Non-resident air arrivals.
–No cruise figures are reported
[P]Preliminary figures.
Source: Caribbean Tourism Organization. Data supplied by member countries and available as of 5 January 2006.

Fig. 28.2.   A 2000 passenger cruise ship docked in St Johns, Antigua, looms over a quiet street. On a good day, a thousand passengers or more will decide to come ashore and range through the town looking for souvenirs or a short tour.

Caribbean people, the majority of whom are the descendants of African slaves, are rarely depicted in brochures and are only a tiny minority on the crews of cruise ships plying their home waters (Wood, 2002, p. 423). The most common origin of Caribbean cruise ship employees is the Philippines (Wood, 2000, p. 356; L.M. Pulsipher, 1990–1993, field notes, aboard the *Sea Cloud*).

The cruise industry's success in drastically increasing the number of passengers floating through the Caribbean, but rarely actually alighting, was based on marketing strategies that targeted middle class North Americans rather than the upper middle class that had been the mainstay of stopover tourism in the past. And it became the overtly stated goal of the cruise industry to take business away from Caribbean hotels and (by extension, though not overtly stated) from Caribbean citizens. Dickinson and Vladimir (1997, p. 140) in their inside look at the cruise industry quote Rod McLeod, an executive with Royal Caribbean as saying the aim of his industry is to gain passengers by taking 'people out of hotels within our destination areas. And if we could empty out some Miami Beach hotels, some Puerto Rican

hotels, some in Jamaica – all the better' (cited in Wood, 2000, p. 359).

The expansion of cruise tourism at the expense of stopover tourism was planned and established by the cruise industry well in advance of the terrorist attacks on 11 September 2001 and the subsequent economic recession. New ships were ordered in the 1990s, and the strategies for supplanting hotel tourism with cruise tourism were laid at the same time (see 1997 quote of Royal Caribbean executive, above). For a while after 11 September the Caribbean cruise industry, like all travel industries, experienced a sharp decline in part because of the industry's dependence on airline connections, and also because of economic recession and fear of terrorism. None the less, by 2002 cruise passengers in the Caribbean nearly equalled the peak year of 1997. By 2002, the industry was capitalizing on the US fear of terrorism by marketing the region as a relatively safe travel experience – one that would be yet safer if passengers refrained from actually disembarking (McCabe, 2002). The strategy of hinting that staying aboard ship would be safer than going ashore meant, of course, that the cruise companies generated more income from shipboard bars, casinos and shops.

A typical cruise to the Eastern Caribbean now occupies from 3–10 days, depending on the cruise line, the distance travelled and the time of year. The trip will cost between US$159 and US$8000 with 8-day trips for under US$1000 being by far the most popular. Several of the cruise days are spent 'at sea' meaning there is no stop in an island. The longer trips include two to three stops in island ports for about 8 h each during which passengers will be free to disembark for 3–5 h. According to reports by colleagues and our experience, as well as survey data from Antigua, by 2000, only 10% to 15% of the passengers were disembarking in any given port. One of the island visits is likely to be to a so-called 'private island', meaning an uninhabited island (or in some cases a walled off and depopulated portion of an inhabited island) owned or leased by the cruise company. On the 'private islands' passengers can disembark and have a highly controlled and constructed experience devoid of contact with citizens of the region. One such island is Half Moon Cay, Bahamas, billed by the Holland America Line as a resort on 'a white sand mile-long beach' where one can have a 'total experience' of all 'that can be found in the West Indies: paradise rediscovered' (cited in Wood, 2000, p. 361).

The financial features of Caribbean cruise tourism

In the case of Caribbean cruise tourism, the main way for island governments to realize revenue is a 'head tax' ranging from US$4 (USVI) to US$15 (Bahamas and Jamaica) per passenger from each of the large ships that visits the island (CTO, 2000). Such small per capita fees can provide substantial cash income for islands because many ships carry a thousand or more passengers and some islands host up to 10 or 12 ships per week, during the high season. Although the funds must go first to support expensive infrastructure facilities for cruise tourists, in theory, most of this money goes into general revenues to support the island community. It is frequently rumoured, though difficult to substantiate without tourism records being made public, that at least in Antigua and Barbuda, if not elsewhere in the Caribbean, corruption prevents much of the head-tax money from contributing to

tourism infrastructure development and maintenance let along general revenues (Kurlansky, 1992; Lazarus-Black, 1994; Pattullo, 1996; Holderfield, 2002). Of course, the head tax was originally intended as only a small portion of the earnings that would accrue to islands from cruise tourism. It is the spending by tourists while they are on island that is supposed to go to local entrepreneurs and non-profit organizations providing guided tours, shops, interpreted historical sites, museums, nature trails, restaurants and other services. In fact, however, evidence has been mounting for years that, worldwide, cruise passengers are notorious low spenders in ports of call. On average per-passenger spending on most islands in the 1990s was less than US$15 (in South-East Asia it can be as low as US$5 per person); hence only minimal earnings ever accrued to island entrepreneurs and non-profits (Gayle and Goodrich, 1993). In Antigua and Barbuda, it is common for tourists to visit the well-managed free museum in St Johns, the capital, and leave behind only tiny contributions of a US$1 or US$2 (L.M. Pulsipher, conversations with founder of the museum, Desmond Nicholson, 2003). By 2003, cruise arrivals in Antigua and Barbuda exceeded stopover visits by 17% and earnings from cruise tourism were declining. Already in 2000, fewer passengers disembarked and per capita spending by those who did disembark was also in decline (Antigua and Barbuda Ministry of Tourism, 2000). In the Eastern Caribbean as a whole in 2003, cruise arrivals (7,335,125) exceeded stopovers (4,575,037) by 38% (see Table 28.2; CTO, 2004).

Cruise tourists' low expectations and low commitment to the tourism experience

Our discussion above shows a growing tendency for Eastern Caribbean cruise passengers to maintain a distance from the host cultures. This tendency to remain aloof from the host society was true even during the heyday of resort-based Caribbean tourism, but the tendency is apparently growing despite the fact that now Eastern Caribbean societies have much to offer the visitor.

In this section we use survey data collected on the island of Antigua in 2000 as a case study of how cruise passengers regard island visitations. Because international cruise ship passengers are a fairly homogenous group (Orams, 1999), we believe that visitors to Antigua are sufficiently representative of Caribbean cruise ship passengers for our purposes. Of the 60 respondents to the survey 60% made no effort on their own to acquire information about the islands they would be visiting. Just over half, 53%, indicated that the cruise company provided them with information prior to their departure from home. Thirty-eight per cent indicated that they sought further information on their own prior to departure.

In an effort to evaluate the visitor's general knowledge of attractions on Antigua, the respondents were given a list of 14 of the most well-developed and popular island attractions and asked to indicate which they had heard of and which they planned to visit during their shore excursion. Though several of the 14 attractions received high name recognition on the survey, there was a disconnection between name recognition and comprehension. Eighteen per cent of the respondents indicated that they had not heard of the very site they were standing in at the time of the survey and 13% indicated that they did not plan to visit it (Holderfield, 2002). The fact that more than 60% of respondents made no effort, before their vacation, to learn about Antigua on their own reveals their overall disinterest. The information provided by the cruise companies mainly consisted of brochures promoting the cruise and then, once onboard, daily itineraries placed outside each cabin door the night before arrival in port. The brochures included some basic data about the island such as the currency used, the language spoken and the annual temperature and rainfall averages. No information was given about the geography of the island, its recent history, type of government, economic activities, human well-being rankings or current issues. And, typically, the information on the port of call of the day was overshadowed by announcements about on-board activities: meals to be served, games, movies, dance parties and up-coming cocktail-hour activities (cruise brochures, daily itineraries as analysed by Holderfield, 2002; Pulsipher's personal experience working on cruises, 1991–1993). Thus, the ability of this information to educate the passengers

about the island(s) to be visited was minimized, with the ship being promoted as the dominant competitor for the attention and money of the passengers.

Respondents to the above mentioned survey were participating in a cruise company-organized 'historic tour of the island' that lasted just less than 2 h of the at least 6 h available for onshore activities. The tour included Lord Nelson's Dockyard and Shirley Heights, two of Antigua's most well-developed historic attractions. Understandably, given the paucity of the information provided to them in advance, it is not surprising that the passengers brought with them a low level of knowledge about the places they were visiting and demonstrated little interest in learning more about them. They rarely ventured from the structured itinerary. After the 2-h tour, in their remaining time on island, these tourists could have visited a number of other island attractions with a local taxi driver. Antigua is a relatively small island with a good road system (like many Eastern Caribbean islands) that provides access to varied environments and cultural attractions. Local drivers are knowledgeable, many having been formally trained for the job of tourism guide. Instead, upon completion of the tour, most cruise ship passengers returned to dockside franchise shops or to the ship with hours to spare.

Conclusions and Suggestions for Change

Rather than suggest that the cruise industry must change its stripes in order for the cruise tourism product in the Eastern Caribbean to be improved for all concerned, we argue for a proactive stance on the part of the Eastern Caribbean host societies. As the advertised destinations of Caribbean cruises, and as those who have the most to gain from a reformed industry, Eastern Caribbean island countries are the logical instigators of change.

Geographer James Blaut (1992, pp. 17–30) observed that despite the extensive post-colonial critique of the last several decades, despite widespread acknowledgement that across the globe modern political and economic issues are closely linked to patterns established during the colonial era, most Westerners still carry with them a 'colonizer's model of the world'. That is to say, as in colonial times, the idea remains prevalent among the general public that Western developed societies are superior to others on all the important indices (per capita income, well-being, education, values, industriousness and standards of living) and that all places outside the developed world are somehow inadequate and in need of Westernization. There is the further implication, again with strong colonialist strains, that non-Western places exist to be consumed in ways that best suit the consumers, who are none other than people from Western developed societies. In this paper, it is our contention that the cruise industry, as presently constructed in the Eastern Caribbean, is the embodiment of the 'colonizer's model of the world'. The cruise industry sees the Eastern Caribbean as a place to be consumed on terms set by the cruise industry, which takes thousands of visitors there each year for great profit, yet pays little for the privilege and leaves only small revenues for host societies. The industry is able to dictate the terms of trade because it is lodged well outside the region in the developed economies of North America and Europe; the passengers (the sources of revenue) come from these economies; and there are no international regulations to ensure that the small societies of the Eastern Caribbean earn a fair profit and are properly compensated for the costs they bear. Furthermore, the industry has the power to define how cruise tourists shall view Eastern Caribbean societies, and it subtly depicts these societies as poor and even dangerous, in order to keep cruise passengers and their money on board.

What can Eastern Caribbean societies do to remedy the situation? We suggest nothing short of a revolution in the ways Caribbean people view themselves and depict themselves to others. The colonizer's model of the world can last only so long as the victims allow colonizing perceptions of them to persist. We would urge Caribbean people in general, and especially those in the region who promote tourism as a development strategy, to take off the velvet gloves when dealing with cruise companies, none of which are based in the region.

Here is a set of actions that could begin to change the terrain:

- Adopt the point of view that visitors to the Caribbean are enjoying a privilege for which they should prepare by reading and studying about the region (Pulsipher, 2002).
- Design fee structures that will bring in enough revenue to provide truly enlightening locally devised island visits.
- As a condition for operating in the region, demand not only that island people be hired as crew but also more importantly that island scholars be hired as shipboard regional experts who will be trained to give holistic and realistic interpretations of the islands.
- Take control of the publishing of brochures and other tourism-related materials about the islands, using such materials to engage potential visitors intellectually. Pique their curiosity about the realities of the islands they will visit, depict actual citizens who deal with real social, political and economic issues.
- Encourage on-island trips for cruise passengers to places that will reinforce the perception that these islands, in addition to being beautiful places, are well-functioning societies with schools, legislative assemblies, hospitals, university campuses, experiment stations, development projects, cultural performances and also beautiful natural and historical heritage sites.
- Encourage questions and debates and provide skilled (and paid) island experts to manage discussions with visitors on how the island residents make a living, how they are tied into the global economy and the consequences such ties hold for island people.
- See to it that there are systems in place to adequately compensate all island people who support these services to tourists for their time and intellectual contributions.

Our experiences in the Eastern Caribbean cruise industry have shown that when tourists are provided with these insights, they get excited about their Caribbean travel experiences and wish to become further engaged with the places they visit. They almost immediately begin to talk of coming back for a week or more on particular islands. Two examples will suffice here to illustrate how engagement with island people and issues can bring lasting benefits. During a short

Fig. 28.3. A quiet side street in Soufriere, St Lucia, the hometown of Derek Walcott, the 1992 recipient of the Nobel Prize for Literature. With unpractised eyes, cruise passengers almost inevitably conclude that this is a scene of grinding poverty. It is not. When helped to analyse the Soufriere landscapes, cruise passengers noted that the people are not major consumers, but they have a modern hospital, several fine schools, bookstores, several large churches, and many small shops where one can buy such delicacies as hand-made chocolate. Statistics show Soufriere to be a healthy place: life expectancies here are long, infant mortality low and literacy rates high.

introductory lecture, on the first evening out of Antigua on a 10 day Sven Lindblad-sponsored cruise through the Eastern Caribbean aboard the *Sea Cloud* (Fig. 28.3), a wealthy and well-connected passenger asked one of the authors (Pulsipher, the paid shipboard lecturer), if he was correct in his observation that the islands were poor in comparison to the USA. And, if this were so, was not the USA implicated in some way in the poverty. What ensued was a cruise-long exploration and discussion of what constitutes poverty, how the various Caribbean islands rank globally (see material on this topic above) and how consumers in the developed world (including tourists) benefit from wage differentials and cheap resources acquired abroad. With some prompting by the lecturer, when these passengers alighted in an island, they sought out local people who might be kind enough to enlighten them further on these topics (Figs 28.4 and 28.5). They were eager to find local newspapers and to talk with merchants, vendors and passersby to see what were the local issues of the moment. They became intensely

observant of island landscapes and cultural features, looking now for subtle signs of well-being or need, of economic and social isolation or connections to the wider world. At the end of the day, they rushed back to cocktail-hour discussions aboard ship with stories of people they had met, of insights they had collected. Fortunately, this particular voyage was blessed with an enlightened cruise director, who upon observing the interest level of the passengers in local affairs, accepted the idea of inviting local people on board for dinner and evening discussions with the passengers.[2]

---

[2]The *Sea Cloud* is a four-masted yacht that plies the world ocean at the high end of cruise offerings. This particular trip and the one described in the following paragraph were sponsored by the Sven Lindblad Agency of New York in the early 1990s and were planned by Kevin Shafer and Lydia Pulsipher in conjunction with the *Seeds of Change Exhibit* (Columbus 500th anniversary) at the Smithsonian Museum of Natural History in Washington, DC.

Fig. 28.4. The *Sea Cloud*, a four-masted yacht once built by the broker E.F. Hutton for his wife Marjorie Merriweather Post, is now a luxury cruise ship that occasionally plies the Eastern Caribbean. It often calls at Soufriere, St Lucia and is one of a very few ships that employs Caribbean lecturers who treat *Sea Cloud* passengers to careful explanations of Caribbean social and economic history and modern daily life.

Fig. 28.5. The fishing village adjacent to Soufriere figures prominently in Derek Walcott's epic poem *Omeros*, for which Walcott won the Nobel Prize for Literature in 1992. Without help from a knowledgeable cruise lecturer, passengers tend to conclude that this is a very poor village even though a modern hospital and large, well-maintained school are within site of the shoreline.

On another occasion, as the result of the suggestion of a particularly savvy island primary school teacher who was also a friend of the cruise lecturer (Pulsipher), about 20 cruise passengers were brought to a small country primary school on the island of Montserrat. The school included a preschool class for children aged three through five. As it happened, the visitors were treated to a telephone etiquette lesson for the preschoolers. The children manned a phone bank along one side of the room. A phone would ring and a child would answer, 'Hello! Good morning. May I help you?' which is the common phone greeting in the Eastern Caribbean. The teacher on the other end of the line would ask to speak to a member of the child's family, and the child would first reply and then pretend to find the person. The idea that tiny toddlers should learn such manners made immediate sense to the guests, even as they realized that in their own cultures such lessons were too rarely given. The cruise passengers went on to observe a recitation in English grammar and a geography class in which the topic was local issues related to solid waste management. For the rest of the cruise, passengers were abuzz with comments on how schools in the USA might well emulate Caribbean schools in their curriculum and pedagogical techniques.

The visit with charming and mannerly preschool and primary school children on a remote Caribbean island and the cruise-long discussions about real island issues instigated by a curious passenger are only two examples of the sorts of tourism exchanges that can go a long way towards dispelling the colonizer's model of the world. In both cases, those involved completely changed their ideas about the Caribbean and became boosters for the region. Personal communications with the passengers in the years since confirm that the experience had lasting effects. Some applied their insights to analysis of their own home communities, others returned for longer stays in the Eastern Caribbean region, a few even decided on extended stays during retirement.

From the perspective of citizens in the Eastern Caribbean, replicating such experiences for the masses of cruise tourists now visiting the region would be difficult and probably unwise. But, if tourism is to be a major component of island development strategies, and if Caribbean people are to adequately address the 'Development for whom?' question – meaning how can tourism fulfill *first of all* the needs of Caribbean people – then finding a way to maximize the benefits of cruise tourism should receive careful attention by Caribbean tourism planners. Were cruise tourists to be approached as intelligent potential allies in furthering the economic and social well-being within the region, then by extension Caribbean tourism planners might wisely reorder their priorities in dealing with the cruise industry.

References

Antigua and Barbuda Ministry of Tourism (2000) *Visitor Arrival Records, and Mode of Transportation Records.*

Archer, E. (1985) Emerging environmental problems in a tourist zone: the case of Barbados. *Caribbean Geography* 2(1), 45–55.

Blaut, J.M. (1992) *The Colonizer's Model of the World.* The Guilford Press, New York/London.

Central Intelligence Agency World Factbook (2003, 2004). Available at: http://www.cia.gov/cia/publications/factbook/index.html

CTO (Caribbean Tourism Organization) (2000) Caribbean tourism statistical report 2000–2001. Available at: http://www.onecaribbean.org/information

CTO (Caribbean Tourism Organization) (2004) Tourism performance summary. Available at: http://www.onecaribbean.org≤javascript:ol ('http://www.onecaribbean.org')

Dickinson, B. and Vladimir, A. (1997) *Selling the Sea: An Inside Look at the Cruise Industry.* John Wiley & Sons, New York.

Fossum, M.A. and Mason, M.J. (1986) *Facing Shame.* W.W. Norton and Company, New York/London.

Gayle, D.J. and Goodrich, J.N. (eds) (1993) *Tourism Marketing and Management in the Caribbean.* Routledge, London.

Gilmore, J. (2000) The tourist crop. In: Gilmore, J. (ed.) *Faces in the Caribbean.* Monthly Review Press, London, Latin America Bureau, New York.

Grossman, L.S. (1998) *The Political Ecology of Bananas: Contract Farming, Peasants, and Agrarian Change in the Eastern Caribbean.* The University of North Carolina Press, Chapel Hill, North Carolina.

Holder, J.S. (1993) Caribbean tourism organization in historical perspective. In: Gayle, D.J. and Goodrich, J.N. (eds) *Tourism Marketing and Management in the Caribbean.* Routledge, London.

Holderfield, L. (2002) Heritage tourism as a revitalization strategy in Antigua, West Indies. Massachusetts thesis, The University of Tennessee, Knoxville, Tennessee.

Kaufman, G. (1985) *Shame: The Power of Caring.* Schenkman Publishing Company, Cambridge, Massachusetts.

Kurlansky, M. (1992) *A Continent of Islands: Searching for the Caribbean Destiny.* Addison-Wesley Publishing Company, New York.

Lazarus-Black, M. (1994) *Legitimate Acts and Illegal Encounters: Law and Society in Antigua and Barbuda.* Smithsonian Press, Washington, DC.

McCabe, K. (2002) This isn't your grandparents' cruise: trends for 2003. *USA Today,* 20 November 2002. Available at: http://www.cruisemates.com/articles/CMpress/USAToday112002.html

Orams, M. (1999) *Marine Tourism: Development, Impacts, and Management.* Routledge, London. OECS (Organization of Eastern Caribbean States) High Commission, Ottawa, Canada, 2004. Available at: http://www.oecs.org/ottawa/ecs.html

Pattullo, P. (1996) *Last Resorts: The Cost of Tourism in the Caribbean.* Cassell Wellinton House, London.

Pulsipher, L.M. (2002) A proposal for knowledge-based tourism in Montserrat. Presented at the University of the West Indies Country Conference, Montserrat, 2002. Available at: http://www.uwichill.edu.bb/bnccde/montserrat/conference/papers/pulsipher.html

Seager, J. (2003). *The Penguin Atlas of Women in the World.* Penguin, New York, London, Camberwell, Toronto, New Delhi, Auckland, Johannesburg.

Trivedi, B.P. (2002) Survey reveals geographic illiteracy. *National Geographic Today,* 20 November 2002. Available at: http://news.nationalgeographic.com/news/2002/11/1120_021120_GeoRoperSurvey.html

United Nations Development Programme (2003) *Economic Growth and Human Development*: Addendum. Available at: http://www.undp.org/hdr2003

United Nations Population Studies (1987) Fertility behaviour in the context of development: evidence from the world fertility survey. *Population Studies,* No. 100. New York.

Wood, R. (2000) Caribbean cruise tourism: globalization at sea. *Annals of Tourism Research* 27(2), 345–370.

Wood, R. (2002) Caribbean of the east? Global interconnections and the South-east Asian cruise industry. *Asian Journal of Social Science* 30(2), 420–440.

29 Fantasy and Reality: Tourist and Local Experiences of Cruise Ship Tourism in Ensenada, Baja California, Mexico

Lynnaire Sheridan and Gregory Teal
Edith Cowan University, Faculty of Business and Law, School of Marketing, Tourism and Leisure, Joondalup WA 6027, Australia

Introduction

Cruise ships are isolated from the world, so the operator has a unique opportunity to create idyllic vacation experiences. The cruise operator carefully styles and shapes the passenger experience from well before they board the ship, and continues throughout the journey. The management of experience includes the glossy marketing brochures through to on board talks where the tourists are 'primed' prior to shore visits. The goal is to ensure that guests achieve positive experiences that match the product and its marketing. This requires that guests interpret the cultural environment of the destination through a specially designed looking-glass, or tourist gaze (Urry, 2002), promoted by the operator.

The tourist gaze is constructed around, and by multiple sources, including the cruise company, the cruise ship, marketing and the voyage. However, the destination participates in this construction by catering, in numerous ways, to the cruise operators and the tourists. Powerful economic, political and media actors also attempt to manage the perception of cruise tourism among local residents. Here too, there is a heady mix of reality and fantasy. Cruise tourism is continuously portrayed as bringing prosperity and development, but this does not correspond seamlessly with the local reality.

Thus, there are two fantasies (at least) at work in cruise tourism: (i) that of the cruise and its passengers; and (ii) that of the destination and its residents. While neither fantasy matches the reality, they are vital elements in sustaining cruise tourism, and they are linked in mutually sustaining ways. As we shall see, there is a dependency between the cruise industry and the destination, but one whose terms are largely determined by the industry.

This chapter explores the interface of fantasy and reality in cruise tourism by examining the cruise experience vs the realities of tourism in Ensenada, a medium-size city in Baja California, Mexico. Research for this chapter is based on extended ethnographic fieldwork conducted by the first co-author, including a cruise on one of the cruise ships sailing to the port of Ensenada. In addition, the authors have read and analysed almost all newspaper articles from Ensenada on cruise tourism over a period of 2 years. This combination of closely following one cruise ship, indeed participating in one of the cruises, as well as tracking the reporting, analysis and opinion from the destination allows us to describe and interpret the different but interactive sides of cruise tourism. The first part of this chapter discusses the constructed image of the community by the cruise operator for consumption by the tourist. The subsequent section

examines the image of the cruise industry constructed by local business, government and
media for the local community. The final discussion addresses the cracks in the image, interactions between tourists and locals that do not
conform to the fantasy.

Crafting the Fantasy: Cruise Ship Operators and the Tourist Gaze

Cruise ships, due to their sheer size and economic potential, have a strong presence in small-
to medium-size destination communities (Fig.
29.1). However, it would be a shock to many
locals in these communities to find out that the
ship – not their community – is often the primary
tourist destination and that, in fact, the shore is
largely an extension of the ship rather than con-
stituting a unique identity. On board, and earlier,
the cruise operator manages and controls the
image and experience of the onshore destinations to achieve visitor satisfaction, i.e. to ensure
that the destination meets expectations and provides continuity to the on-board experience. This
is so that the operator can maintain a high level
of return clients as well as remaining attractive

in its market segments, in a highly competitive
industry. Thus, there is a seamless web between
marketing, the on-board experience and expectations of the onshore experience.

With the ship as the primary destination,
cruise operators may consider onshore destinations to be inconsequential and readily interchangeable. The host community is often of so
little importance that – ironically – it is rarely
mentioned or not even named. This is especially the case if the passengers' perceptions of
the destination based on their previous exposure to media reports do not fit with the operator's ideal destination. Los Angeles Times
journalist Paisley Dodds (2003) reported that
Royal Caribbean, for example, did not inform
tourists that they were going to Haiti, the western hemisphere's poorest nation. The word
'Haiti' could evoke an image contrary to 'fun'
cruise. Tourists were therefore told that they
were going to a private island off the coast of
Hispaniola, the island that Haiti and the
Dominican Republic share.

In the case of Ensenada (population
370,000), Baja California, there are generally two
cruise ships that visit the city, each on a twice-
weekly basis. This community is the only Mexican

Fig. 29.1.   Cruise ships dominate Ensenada's landscape. Source: Lynnaire Sheridan.

shore destination. On one cruise it is the only shore visit while the alternative cruises also visit one or two ports in mainland USA. Management of the image of Ensenada as a destination begins with the pre-trip literature provided to passengers, which is identical to the material available on the web. This literature places the emphasis on the ship, and in particular its fun, food and facilities. The cruise ship itself is the primary destination while Mexico, rather than the specific destination community, adds some exotic flare.

Pre-trip and on-board literature

Details of the specific onshore destination are only very briefly provided on a trip summary page. The tour descriptions contain a little information about the community but are activity focused. In promotional and pre-trip literature the only reference to the community is:

> On your [number] day getaway, you'll visit Ensenada, which has grown from a sleepy fishing village to become a popular beach resort and one of Mexico's most successful cities. Among its most popular locations are the pristine beaches, the waterfront promenade, the fashionable shops of Avenida Primera and a winery . . .

This idyllic description of the onshore destination is quite contrary to the reality. Up until the early 1990s, this community was one of the world's most important tuna fishing ports and is still the largest port in Baja California (Peterson, 1998). So 'sleepy fishing village' would not adequately represent the fishery industry, nor could the mid-sized city be considered a 'popular beach resort' with 'pristine beaches'. Water temperatures are too cold for swimming even in midsummer, while coastal pollution would make most tourists wary (Fig. 29.2).

In the literature provided by the operator for the passengers and prospective passengers there is no discussion of Mexican culture or unique features of the destination community. The emphasis is on a limited number of tourist attractions and generic activities, such as golf, that are not place-specific. Even on board, as observed by the researcher, reference to the onshore destination was scant. The on-board shore excursion brochure states:

Fig. 29.2. So-called 'pristine' beach. Source: Lynnaire Sheridan.

> Going ashore is half the fun of going on a cruise. And we've got some optional excursions at every port that are bound to intrigue you and offer a little something different in the way of excitement.

While the importance of the shore destination is emphasized, adjectives are not used to describe the destination but to describe the 'fun' or 'excitement' of activities. Tours are described but the place is not.

The on-board newspaper the day prior to visiting the onshore destination refers only to a travel talk (logistics, shopping and tours) that will discuss disembarkation, and states:

> Travel Talk: Join your Cruise Director [name] for important information about Ensenada, ID required to go onshore, the BEST shopping, information on the shore excursions.

The on-board newspaper for the morning that the ship is to dock in port simply mentions that it will be docking. In a four-page newspaper that is the only reference to the destination, the rest is about on-board activities, shopping and tours. The only related comment is as follows:

Welcome to Ensenada, Mexico. Overlooking beautiful Todos Santos Bay, Ensenada is a congenial blend of fishing port, tourist centre and industrial complex. With an estimated population of 370, 000 you'll find that it can accommodate your every need and can be quite cosmopolitan.

As can be seen, pre-trip and on-board literature, overall, has very little reference to the onshore destination. Indeed, Ensenada is mentioned no more than three times. Much of the image of the destination was pre-established by individuals' pre-existing images of Mexico, and then shaped on board during the Travel Talk. This shaping says little about the destination, and much of what is said is highly superficial and distorted. This shaping is also intended to orient passengers towards onshore activities inline with the cruise operator's overall strategy of management of the visitor experience.

On-board travel talk

Creating the 'right' image, that is, as determined by cruise operators, of the onshore destination is important for matching tourist expectations with the marketing strategy of the cruise opera-

tor. It also has a direct economic benefit for the ship as sales of onshore tours (run by local companies) generate commissions. There is also direct payment for promotion of onshore tourist businesses on the cruise ship. In this case study, for example, the cruise ship operator promotes onshore retail outlets on board for a fee of US$500 per store per ship visit, approximately US$1000 per week from each business. In addition to contributing to creating the desired image – as the cruise operator controls which onshore businesses will be promoted – this contributes to fomenting economic dependency by the local destination on the cruise operators, a process which we explore in greater detail later.

A tourist's natural concern for personal safety seems to have been an important element in the 'recommended product' promotional strategy conducted by the operator. A clever balance is achieved between disconcerting the tourist, in order to persuade them to purchase recommended tour products or shop only in 'safe' stores, while assuring them that there is no personal risk in order to achieve a positive visitor experience. In other words, it could be interpreted that there would be no risk, provided that the tourist conforms to the guidelines, shops or itineraries suggested by the operator (Fig. 29.3).

Fig. 29.3. Competition for tourist dollars is fierce. This stall utilizes the on-board fear-based marketing to promote their sales. Source: Lynnaire Sheridan.

While a fun vacation experience is promoted in the marketing brochures, careful creation of the 'you will be safe but need to be shopping savvy' destination image clearly occurs on board during pre-disembarkation talks. According to the Cruise Director during the pre-disembarkation talk:

> You came on a cruise so that you could go somewhere like Mexico and feel safer. To go somewhere and know someone – you know us – you came with us. So let's say, I mean, you get the cab and you get out in the middle of nowhere and the cab blows a flat tire and the cabbie jumps out of the cab and runs into the woods. What do you do? Who do you call? Do you call the embassy? Do you call the cops? What do you do? We set up a local number so you can be taken care of. We will come and take care of you. We will come and get you bring you back to the ship. You're going to be ok.

In the operator's travel brochures cruising is not promoted as a 'safe vacation', safety is not mentioned, yet it is continually brought up during the travel talk. The scenario of the taxi is presented and infers a general unreliability about getting around independently off the ship in Mexico, in contrast to using a recommended product so that you can 'feel safer'.

Shortly after this talk the onshore tour manager was introduced and stated:

> . . . we come to Ensenada twice a week so we've got this down. We know what's going on. We work with these tour operators for years and they've got all these tours lined up for you so we make it very easy for you . . . You want to come away, maybe go to a different country like Mexico and you've never been before and you want to feel safe about getting off of the ship, going out and doing something – take one of our organized shore tour excursions. With our tour operator we're in contact with them, we know what's going on at any given time, where you are. You can feel safe about that.

Again safety rather than convenience are emphasized with the tourists being cocooned while participating in onshore activities that, to a considerable extent, are managed directly or indirectly by the cruise operator.

The Cruise Director then continued with his discussion and emphasized the activity of onshore shopping. He tried to create demand for a product (silver) by recommending it as a qual-

ity purchase, but then created a general distrust of local store owners by implying dishonest practices, such as stamping 925 on products other than silver. He then proceeded to elevate certain stores above others by inferring that they are honest, although it is never mentioned to the tourist that these stores pay considerably to have exclusive on-board promotion. In the words of the Cruise Director:

> Now I wanna talk about shopping . . . the two things you really want to shop for here; number one is great deals on silver cause they mine silver not too far from here. Now a lotta people go 'I know, you look for the 925 stamp, I know' hey, they know that too now. So pretty much everything has a 925 stamp. My towels have a 925 stamp. So the thing is what you want to do is go to a store where they will give you a receipt – this being the trick – with their store name on it so you can walk back in and return something. A receipt with their store name on it. The best store in town for jewellery is [store name provided]. There's no question. Ahh they've got some great necklaces in there recently, great choice of earrings, toe rings, beautiful stuff. [Store name] have about eight locations, it's a wonderful store. I really like it. It is the silver jewellery store. Without question. [Store name]

The speech by the Cruise Director prepared tourists for a contrived experience of the onshore destination. Overall, the cruise ship tourist is lightly informed about the destination community and is then guided towards products and activities that generate funds for the cruise ship company in response to the suggestion that the local community is generally safe but local people will 'rip off tourists'. It means that even when passengers are onshore at the destination, they are in a world shaped so as to be largely an extension of the ship.

Conforming to an Image: Local Communities, Business and Cruise Ships

While cruise passengers may not know much about their onshore destination, the ships and their passengers are very important to the host community. Local businesses and government, together with media, shape the all-important locals' perspective of cruise ship tourism. They try to maintain community support for this niche of tourism, even when the apparent economic benefits are limited to a few businesses and infrastructure costs are shared with taxpayers (Fig. 29.4).

According to media reports, in 2002 Ensenada received approximately 10,000 cruise passenger arrivals per week (*El Mexicano*, 2002a). In that year alone, according to the Ensenada Tourism Promotion Office, 450,000 tourists arrived by cruise ship travelling with Carnival, Royal Caribbean and Celebrity Cruises. This establishes Ensenada as the second most important cruise port in Mexico (Mendoza, 2003).

What is really important to the local community is passenger spending and the potential economic benefits of cruise tourists to the city. The media claims that the average onshore expenditure for 2002 was US$40–45 per passenger, bringing in well over US$13 million (Ybarrola Mejía, 2002a). The Port Authority (which

Fig. 29.4. Street artist Oscar Zapala sells paintings of cruise ships to the tourists. Ironically, most of his paintings depict destruction of the cruise ships in a 'Titanic' style. This, he claims, is a subtle reference to the making of the movie in Baja California's Fox Studios rather than the community's attitude towards cruise tourism. Source: Lynnaire Sheridan.

receives docking fees) is more upbeat, it claimed that each adult passenger spends an average of US$85 in Ensenada (*El Mexicano*, 2002b).

While the media predominately 'demonstrates' the economic benefit of cruise ships to Ensenada, there is some contestation and debate particularly from within tourism planning circles. The interim President of the Municipal Committee of Tourism and Conventions of Ensenada warned that Ensenada's tourism industry should not depend upon, nor be overly confident in, cruise tourism (Ybarrola Mejía, 2002b).

Reconsidering the economic benefits, most cruise ships that dock in Ensenada cater to the lower end of the market, and carry passengers who are likely to spend minimal amounts of money onshore. At times Ensenada does receive upmarket cruise ships, such as *The World* (essentially a floating condominium) but, in any case, the ships stay between 10 and 16 hours, time alone limits onshore spending (*El Mexicano*, 2002c). Moreover, with many organized social activities on the ship, a destination like Ensenada may have difficulty competing with the services offered on board including casinos, spas, golf ranges, tennis and swimming pools (*El Mexicano*, 2002d). Some passengers do not leave the ship while it is docked in Ensenada and make no contribution to the local economy.

Nevertheless when the Viking Serenada stopped using Ensenada as a port of call in 2002, locals were not encouraged to re-evaluate the worth of cruise tourism to the host community. Instead, the local tourism industry, tourism promoters, local and State government officials, and the State Governor lobbied until the cruise line executives met with them. In June 2003, *Monarch of the Sea* and *Ecstasy* each began calling in to Ensenada 2 days a week, on the understanding that the authorities and the business sector assured the cruise executives that Ensenada would continuously become better as a cruise destination. The Secretary of Tourism for the state declared that

> Everyone in Ensenada has the responsibility to see that the tourists who visit the City return to their country with a big smile and recommend that others visit Ensenada and Mexico. This will allow for information about Ensenada to be passed by word of mouth and that for each

tourist that returns to his or her country, three more will come back here.

(*El Mexicano*, 2003)

The dependency on the cruise industry is such that criticism of Ensenada by cruise operators was placed back on to the entire community. The habits and behaviours of all residents (not just those benefiting from cruise tourism) would have to be conducive to cruise ships. At the same time infrastructure would have to match the requirements of cruise operators. One regional tourism official, for example, pressed the Ensenada municipal government to restore the tourist lookout on the local scenic drive, as well as to revitalize the visitor information office, to improve services and to upgrade the professionalism of employees in the industry.

Such upgrades require considerable spending by local taxpayers in order to cater to the potential needs and wants of the fickle cruise ship industry; however, media images of the cruise industry are usually so convincing that the local community rarely questions such spending. For example, one representative of the Tourist Promotion Office of Ensenada declared:

> I believe that this (the cruise industry) represents a big opportunity for Ensenada to rejuvenate itself, it is the obligation of everyone to try to present a safe, clean city, with quality services so that the passengers will come back on another cruise, and that others will hear about and come to Ensenada.

(*El Mexicano*, 2002a)

Journalists, jointly with business and government, are often engaged in this mobilization, by writing in positive ways about the cruise industry and by presenting its impacts invariably as positive, indeed, necessary for the good of Ensenada and its citizens. Over and over again, articles in the press reiterate that the cruise industry benefits everyone:

> [Ensenada] is celebrating, no one doubts it, because with the arrival of the cruise ships, the affluence of the visitors to the commercial zone increases considerably and with it the economic spill-over effects increase for the benefit of all people of Ensenada.

(Ybarrola Mejía, 2003)

There are undoubtedly economic benefits in terms of employment and income generation, particularly in the service and hospitality sector. At the same time, it is also clear that those benefits are not evenly distributed. Yet, even though some local representatives of the tourism industry occasionally mention the risks of being so dependent on the cruise industry, these same players nevertheless call upon towns and cities in the region to redouble their efforts to be continuously and increasingly attractive to this industry. As the journalist covering the cruise industry for one of Ensenada's major daily papers expressed, upon the recovery of the industry in 2003 came:

> . . . the challenge of the quality of service, attention to clients, the image of the cit, and the variety of its products and services, is placed in front of the view of the large ship companies of the world.

(Ybarrola Mejía, 2003)

In Ensenada, the public is called upon to support public and business efforts to accommodate the cruise industry without questioning the real community benefits of cruise tourism. In contrast to the 'fantasy' of widespread economic benefits for the city (created by business and government in the media), locals are increasingly expected to invest taxpayer dollars in infrastructure that, if successful in attracting ships, will benefit the few businesses catering to cruise tourism. In the media, Ensenada is presented as very important to the cruise ship, but this is not an accurate presentation of the unequal relationship between this onshore destination and the ship. The geographic mobility of the cruise ship means that the ship always has the upper hand. While the cruise product is dependent upon local places, it is not dependent upon any one specific location. Ensenada is interchangeable with any onshore community that is more inviting, or perhaps compliant, to the needs of the cruise operator.

Cracks in the Image: Managing the Interface Between Tourists and Locals

While local people are regularly informed by the media, in very few circumstances do the local people have an opportunity to board the ship and very rare would be the local who has actually participated in the cruise experience. This essentially means that local residents, and even tourism planners, have little idea of how their community is portrayed by the cruise operator's on-board presentations or of how the passengers' perception of their community is constructed and managed by the operator. Locals only contribute to the shaping of the tourist experience from arrival onwards and perhaps have an opportunity to gently remould the image that the tourist has been presented on board.

In her book *They Came for Savages: 100 Years of Tourism in Melanesia*, Ngaire Douglas illustrates some of the serious and negative long-term consequences of tourism when tourists hold inappropriate preconceived ideas about local communities (Douglas, 1996). Images are often so strong that preconceived notions may merely be reinforced rather than re-evaluated or challenged during the tourist experience. It is therefore a tough battle for the local community to balance an image that is acceptable to the tourist (and their preconceived ideas) and yet is also at the same time acceptable to the local community as realistic and, dare it be said, authentic.

In Ensenada, the business community satisfies the cruise tourists and perhaps minimizes negative impacts on the local community using three principal strategies: (i) minimal re-education of cruise tourists with a view to broaden positive tourist perceptions of Ensenada; (ii) the creation of a tourist precinct within which tourist–resident interactions can, in part, be managed to promote positive experiences on both sides; and (iii) restricted entry by locals to entertainment establishments during cruise ship visits.

The re-education of tourists is limited to the representation of Ensenada by tour guides on tours endorsed by the cruise ships, where the history and culture of Ensenada may be explained in greater detail, and by a free weekly newspaper aimed at cruise tourists. The newspaper presents a more multidimensional image of Ensenada than that presented on board by the cruise operators. It outlines the full spectrum of natural and cultural attractions, as well as information about the region and traditional foods, crafts and culture. This alliance between

the local newspaper and tourism businesses aims for independent return visits by cruise tourists. Ideally, return visitors would stay overnight, creating economic benefits for hotel sector and the supply chain, and would also spend money in a variety of businesses and not just those recommended on the cruise ship.

The tourist precinct, in contrast to re-education initiatives, is an ambitious project only made possible because of the close collaboration between an exclusive group of tourist business owners in Ensenada. With assistance and support from the local municipality, this tourist zone is composed of one street parallel to the waterfront, with well-presented tourist shops, and another cross street which is focused on entertaining, such as bars and restaurants. On one level, the precinct satisfies the needs of both the tourist and a segment of the local population. For the tourist this precinct is clean, well lit, within easy reach of the cruise ship, and they are comfortably surrounded by other tourists. For the local person the precinct offers alternative entertainment venues, although somewhat expensive for the average income earner. This, itself, might select the 'right' sort of local for the cruise tourists to see (Fig. 29.5).

The precinct separates tourists from those locals not involved in tourism-related business, thereby potentially minimizing negative impacts on both sides. Tourists are safe and catered for in the precinct; very few are observed leaving the immediate area. The more adventurous tourists, or those that have accidentally strolled into the locals' cheap bar district will soon feel the stares; a little discomfort should encourage most of them back into 'their part of town'. For the locals, avoiding tourists means avoiding the congested precinct on the days that the cruise ships are in port. At the same time, the precinct helps to keep tourists in a specific area and away from the general activities of town where crowding might annoy locals and where tourists might see things (everyday life) that snap them out of the fantasy–reality that has been created for their consumption by the cruise operator.

In creating the precinct, the local government tourism department, along with local businesses, profiled cruise ship tourists in order to understand them better and encourage visitor satisfaction and local economic benefits in the

Fig. 29.5.   Ensenada's tourist precinct presents only the 'best' of the city to the tourist. Source: Lynnaire Sheridan.

tourist zone. According to the study, in 2001 visitors most enjoyed shopping (61%), followed by food and drinks (28%), trips or excursions (15%), beaches (3%), recreational activities (3%) and other (8%). Perhaps, more important is what the tourists did not like: begging children, aggressive sales people and street selling (together making up 32% of dissatisfaction), followed by recreational activities (15%) or lack thereof (Ajamil *et al.*, 2002).

Overall, the most unpopular part of a visit to Ensenada identified by cruise passengers was dealing with beggars. This is also a nuisance for local people. The following scenario, witnessed by the researcher, took place in a local store; an angry local resident entered the store and said:

> They beg, beg, beg and it is never enough . . . Give one peso and they want 20 plus then they are everywhere and on top of you.

The shopkeeper then said:

> Yes, and they are bad for tourism because they annoy tourists.

Ironically, from observation, begging is closely aligned with the cruise ship industry. The cruise ship arrives in town twice a week and the beggars (as do the street sellers) arrive in town on cruise ship days (Fig. 29.6). The beggars themselves are usually migrants from other parts of Mexico (distinguishable by their clothing and physical characteristics) who deliberately target cruise ship destinations in order to make a living. This annoys locals both because many of them are also approached by the beggars and because they feel it creates a negative image of their city and one which may interfere with the cruise ship industry and local business.

The precinct does provide, however, a space for control over undesirable activities such as begging. Regulation has had moderate success in controlling the activities of beggars and dealing with other 'problems', such as drink driving. In terms of begging, however, the more successful campaign has been the tourism industry's English language billboards in the precinct asking tourists not to give money to beggars. These businesses assure visitors that these children would be at school if they were not forced to beg for money on cruise ship day. If tourists refuse to give money, things will change but, ironically, seeing beggars (although being disgusted by it)

Fig. 29.6. A popular bar on cruise ship day. In the foreground a street seller offers generic 'tropical' bags and backpacks. Source: Lynnaire Sheridan.

may be part of the expectation that cruise ship tourists hold when visiting Mexico. Nevertheless, a tourist zone (as opposed to dispersed tourism) makes managing this issue easier from both the government and the business perspective.

The local government only deals with community-based problems and ignores inappropriate behaviour by tourists. This then obliges the local businesses to manage tourists. Local entertainment businesses, such as discos and bars, rely on cruise tourists and locals. It is crucial that these businesses maintain a positive image in the eyes of the cruise industry and the local community. However, cruise tourist expectations and local behavioural codes are not always compatible. Cruise tourists hold an image of Ensenada as a 'party town' with few rules, limits or restrictions. To locals, the subsequent drunken and public sexual behaviour in the street by cruise tourists is highly inappropriate. Encouraging 'improper' behaviour by Americans and satisfying the cruise tourist may not be conducive to local patronage. This has

led to locals being 'locked out' of events at local bars on cruise ship days.

One local male bar tender stated that locals are not allowed on the premises while cruise tourists are in town because:

> The local parents let their daughters go to [name of very popular bar] and so they need to protect the reputation of the place because when the US tourists from the boat are there they flash their boobs and behave in ways that locals would be shocked by. The local people wouldn't come to our bar if they knew what goes on during a cruise ship day.

For the tourism worker, not only is there the economic advantage brought by cruise tourists, but also cultural conflicts. For example, one day the field researcher entered a bar on a cruise ship day with a female American friend. Our waiter guided us upstairs with his hands on our backs where we were welcomed by the all-male staff. It was a very touchy experience – the staff placing their hands on our shoulders, arms and waist. Very flirtatiously 'You off the cruise ship?' he asked. 'No' we said. 'Great, I take you out later then' – we laughed to play along. Soon a waiter offered to take our photo with our camera – our waiter joined us wrapping his arms around us.

Later, we started chatting in Spanish to our waiter. He immediately stood at a greater distance from us and was no longer flirtatious. After he realized the researcher was living locally and was not a tourist, he then said that he lost his girlfriend through working in the bars because he has to act flirtatious in order to get tips. He is studying engineering at the local university. He believes that working at the bar teaches one a lot about people – who is going to be fun or annoying. He said 'For example these "prom" girls are going to be a mess [there was a group of girls celebrating their graduation from high school; they are legal to drink in Mexico but underage in the US] – a girl outside was completely drunk – she just kissed me out of the blue – they come to drink'.

Nevertheless, local workers continue to be willing to 'put up with' cruise tourists because of the economic rewards, particularly the tips, that they can earn. They can 'suspend' their perceptions of negative impacts if the economic benefits compensate. Restricting entry of locals into bars on cruise ship day could be considered an effective impact management strategy as only workers, those who are then economically compensated, witness culturally inappropriate tourist behaviour and, overall, the broader community is unaffected. It is a case of 'out of sight, out of mind'.

Conclusion

Cruise tourism in Ensenada, Baja California thrives on constructed fantasies. The cruise ship 'creates' an onshore destination; it just happens to be called Ensenada. The fictitious Ensenada is presented on board as safe, but only if you follow ship recommendations. This 'Ensenada' is an extension of the ship. It bolsters visitor satisfaction, as the contrived reality matches the marketing brochures, and generates earnings for the cruise operator through commissions from 'recommended' onshore tour sales and kickbacks for promoting particular stores.

For the consumption of the local community, Ensenada's tourism businesses, government and media have created a 'cruise ship' fantasy. Cruise ships equal money. These ships float around in the ocean waiting to be welcomed by a host community so they can dock and leave their money. In order for them to dock, however, the community must behave in a way that would attract these ships. This links into community pride, Ensenada is 'important' if it attracts these big cruise ships.

Working within these two fragile fantasies, local tourism businesses manage the interface between cruise ships and the local community. Conflict management is successful, separating tourists from the locals does appear to reduce negative local perceptions of cruise tourists and their behaviour. While tourism businesses do reap the economic benefits of cruise tourism, they too are trapped in a fantasy as they believe that their dependency on the cruise ships is only for a limited time. They believe that cruise tourism is a good exposure for Ensenada and it will generate independent return visits. Ironically, the cruise tourists never really visited Ensenada. They simply spent some time in an outdoor extension of the ship. Ensenada, the constructed destination, is just as interchangeable for the tourist as the operator; it never had any intrinsic values that they would return to visit.

References

Ajamil, B. *et al.* (2002) *Encuesta a Pasajeros de Cruceros Turisticos: Resultados camparativos 1997–2001.*

Dodds, P. (2003) Cruise-ship stop that dares not speak its name. *Los Angeles Times*, 27 April 2003. Available at: www.latimes.com/news/printedition/asection/la-adfg-cruise27apr27,1,2628671.story

Douglas, N. (1996) *They Came for Savages: 100 Years of Tourism in Melanesia.* Southern Cross University Press, Australia.

El Mexicano (2002a) Ensenada, en la mira de navieras. 4 November.

El Mexicano (2002b) Reactivará la economia el arribo de cruceros. 19 November.

El Mexicano (2002c) Diversos arribos registró el Puerto. 15 December 2002.

El Mexicano (2002d) Arribó lujoso crusero que solo aloja a condóminios. 20 December.

El Mexicano (2003) Dejan cruceros gran derrama económica. 13 June.

Mendoza, A. (2003) *Se irían turistas. El Vigia*, 21 November.

Peterson, W. (1998) *The Baja Adventure Book.* Wilderness Press, Berkeley, California.

Urry, J. (2002) *The Tourist Gaze.* Sage, London.

Ybarrola Mejía, F. (2002a) *Prevén la llegada de Nuevo crucero. El Mexicano,* 28 December.

Ybarrola Mejía, F. (2002b) *Cruceros no deben ser base turística. El Mexicano,* 10 December.

Ybarrola Mejía, F. (2003) *Retornan cruceros turísticas al Puerto. El Mexicano,* 8 June.

30 A Shifting Tide: Environmental Challenges and Cruise Industry Responses

James E.N. Sweeting[1] and Scott L. Wayne[2]

[1]Conservation International, The Center for Environmental Leadership in Business, Travel and Leisure, 1919 M Street, NW, Washington, DC, 20036, USA; [2]SW Associates, 2527 I Street, NW, Washington, DC, 20037, USA

Introduction

Over the last 2 years, the state of the world's oceans has been at the forefront of public attention:

- In the summer of 2004, the US Commission on Ocean Policy released its final report, *An Ocean Blueprint for the 21st Century*, to the US Congress and the President.
- In June 2003, The Pew Oceans Commission issued a report entitled *America's Living Oceans: Charting a Course for Sea Change*, the most comprehensive look at the nation's seas in the last 30 years.
- Soon after the Pew Report, Conservation International (CI) convened the Defying Oceans End Conference, which brought together nearly 150 experts from more than 20 countries to develop an approach to articulating a global plan of action.

None of these studies or action plans specifically pointed to the cruise industry as a major contributor towards maritime pollution. At the same time, though, the leaders of the cruise industry do recognize that any level of environmental impact can be a problem for their business, because the very nature of their product depends on a clean and a healthy natural environment. Clean oceans are essential to the cruise experience – passengers simply do not want to sail on polluted waters or visit contaminated beaches. Furthermore, good environmental practices allow the industry to expand its market and tap into the growing international demand of informed and concerned tourists seeking environmentally and socially responsible travel choices.

The cruise ship industry is one of the fastest growing and most visible sectors of the travel industry. For many years, the cruise industry has had a negative image in people's minds regarding environmental issues – one of a polluter, spilling oil and dumping garbage at sea. Cruise ships do have an environmental impact and the industry's high growth rates may mean even more impact. However, a number of the leading cruise lines have responded by implementing practices and procedures to address their environmental impacts.

This chapter focuses on the two major cruise line companies that represent nearly two-thirds of the cruise market: Carnival Corporation (2002) and Royal Caribbean Cruises Ltd, each of which includes two or more subsidiaries. The authors also received input and support from Radisson Seven Seas Cruises and the International Council of Cruise Lines (ICCL). Most of these companies' business is based in the Caribbean, the Mediterranean and Alaska, areas that are considered priorities for many conservation organizations. Because of this focus, much of the data and examples in this document come from these companies and destinations. In addition, this chapter centres principally on ships' operations and not on the impact of cruise passengers when ashore or on issues related to port development. These are vital topics for both further research and action.

The major cruise lines have done much to respond to the challenge of preserving the environment on which their business depends. Royal Caribbean, Carnival Corporation and several other cruise lines are implementing leadership practices, testing and refining new technologies and developing management programmes to address and mitigate environmental impacts. In some cases, cruise ship companies have taken actions that go well beyond existing regulations and/or common shipping practices. Nevertheless, key challenges remain for the cruise industry to minimize their environmental footprint. Many of these challenges and industry responses are detailed in this chapter.

New practices and technologies are continually being developed to address the most pressing environmental impacts of shipping, with the cruise industry playing an important role in developing and testing new equipment. Many cruise lines are using new technologies and practices on some, but not all of their ships. The authors contend that companies should apply the best possible technologies and practices, and develop and communicate management plans across their entire fleets. The cruise ship industry has the opportunity to become a model for the shipping and tourism industries if it continues to show leadership in piloting and implementing leading practices.

Finally, a key conclusion of this study is that there is a pressing need for further study on the impacts of cruise ship activity on the environment. Although much is known in general about the effects of air pollution, oily water or untreated waste, there is little data on the specific impacts of cruise ships. There is a dearth of information on impacts in the Caribbean, which is home to more than half of the cruise industry's activities. Non-governmental, academic and scientific organizations all play an important role in conducting research, in cooperation with the cruise industry, to better understand the potential and actual impacts of cruising and to determine the most effective and sustainable responses.

The State of the Cruise Industry

Since its beginning in the 1960s, the modern cruising industry has rapidly evolved from mainly exclusive journeys for the rich to popular vacations for everyone. Today, the cruise industry is one of the world's fastest growing tourism segments. The number of cruise ship passengers has grown nearly twice as fast as world international tourist arrivals over the last decade (WTO, 2001) and is expected to grow at 8.5% per year over the next decade (Table 30.1). Bob Dickinson, President of Carnival Corporation says 'We're in such an embryonic stage that it's silly. I can't see the end. I can't even see the end of the beginning.'

Nearly two-thirds of the cruise industry is concentrated in just three corporations: Royal Caribbean Cruises Ltd, Carnival Corporation and Norwegian Cruise Line (Table 30.2). In response to the growing demand for cruises, these and other cruise line companies are expected to add as many as 49 new ships to their fleets between 2002 and 2005, at a cost of approximately US$12 billion (Cruiseserver, 2003).

Table 30.1. Growth of the cruise industry.

Year	Number of passengers worldwide
1970	500,000
1998	9.5 million
2010	14.2 million (estimate)

Source: GAO (2000); Toh (2000).

Table 30.2. The largest cruise ship companies.

Company	Approximate number of ships	Approximate global market share (%)
Royal Caribbean Cruises Ltd	28	22
Carnival Corporation	71	41
Norwegian Cruise Line	11	9

Source: ICCL, CLIA, G.P. Wild Ltd, Cruiseserver (2003).

Much of this growth in the cruise industry is occurring in destinations that are located in biodiversity hotspots, which are among the most diverse and threatened environments on Earth (Fig. 30.1). About 70% of cruise destinations are in the hotspots, such as the Caribbean, the Mediterranean, Western Mexico, the Panama Canal Zone and the South Pacific (Fig. 30.2).

Of this total, a full half of the world's cruise passengers depart from USA ports for the Caribbean. In 2003, the North American cruise industry alone contributed US$25.4 billion to the US economy, a US$5 billion increase over 2002 (ICCL, 2004). Because of the significance of the North American cruise industry, this study focused on US federal and state laws for its legal and policy analysis.

Environmental impact and regulations

With the cruise industry's predictions of continued rapid growth over the next decades, it will be increasingly important to understand and address the potential environmental impacts of cruising. While the cruise industry is growing at a rapid pace, it still represents only a tiny fraction of the world shipping industry. In January 2001, passenger ships, which include cruise ships and ferries, made up only about 6% of the world shipping fleet (LMIS, 2003). The 115 plus ships of the ICCL (2003) members, which account for about two-thirds of the world's cruise ships, comprise less than 5% of all passenger ships and only 0.2% of the world's trading fleet. Thus it is important to look at the cruise industry in a broader context. While cruising may have a

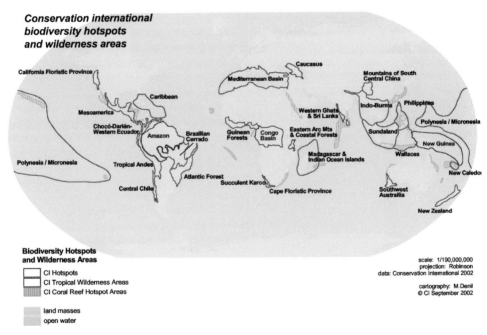

Fig. 30.1. Biodiversity hotspots. The biodiversity hotspots concept is a prioritization system, adopted and refined by Conservation International, which allows conservationists to focus their efforts on the regions where the threat is the greatest to the largest number of species. Hotspots are designated as such because they harbour a great diversity of endemic species (those found nowhere else in the world) and, at the same time, have been significantly altered and impacted by human activities. The 25 terrestrial biodiversity hotspots (see map) contain 44% of all plant species and 35% of all terrestrial vertebrate species in only 1.4% of the planet's land area. For more information on biodiversity hotspots, see www.biodiversityhotspots.org. Source: Conservation International.

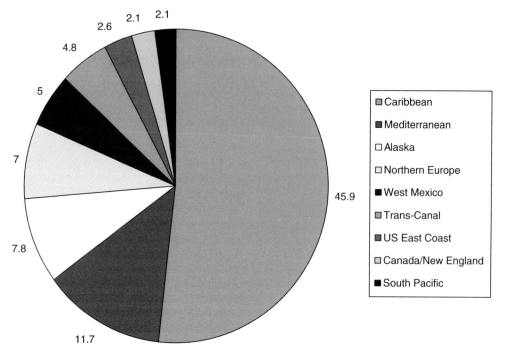

Fig. 30.2. Where the cruise ships go (%).

relatively minor environmental impact compared to the full shipping industry, it is an impact none the less. And in certain ports, for example in the Caribbean or Alaska where cruise ships may represent a major portion of activity, the local environmental impacts can be significant.

Because a cruise ship will probably be in a number of national and state jurisdictions, as well as international waters, during a typical cruise, the cruising industry is regulated by a series of international treaties, national and state laws that control discharges and emissions and specify waste management procedures. The International Maritime Organization (IMO, 2005) develops and oversees conventions and treaties that apply to cruise vessels and other types of ships in all international waters. The principal treaty governing cruise ship activity is the 1973 International Convention for the Prevention of Pollution from Ships (MARPOL), which was modified in 1978 and has subsequently been updated by various amendments.

Over the last decade there have been a number of examples of cruise lines not abiding by these laws and regulations. For instance, in April 2002, Carnival Corporation was fined

US$18 million for the deliberate falsification of oily bilge record-books, related to the discharge from a few ships of oily bilge water through separators with disabled oil content meters. In July 2002, Norwegian Cruise Line was fined US$1 million for falsification of oily bilge water records by the previous owner aboard one of its ships. In 1998 and 1999, Royal Caribbean Cruises Ltd was fined US$9 million and US$18 million, respectively for discharging oil-contaminated bilge waste (GAO, 2000). While many of these incidents are attributed to accidents caused by human error or mechanical failure (ICCL, 2002), it is essential for the cruise industry to demonstrate a commitment to compliance with international, national and state regulations. This commitment is also important in order to maintain credibility regarding the cruise industry's environmental performance.

Industry Response

In June 2001, ICCL and its members adopted a set of practices and procedures entitled *Cruise Industry Waste Management Practices and*

Procedures. These practices primarily build on the regulations of the IMO and the US Environmental Protection Agency (EPA).

The major cruise companies and some smaller companies, such as Radisson Seven Seas, have corporate programmes for implementing the ICCL practices and procedures, and, in some cases, exceeding these standards. All of the major lines have programmes that include environmental awareness training for their crews, screening of vendors who handle shoreside offloading of wastes and testing of technologies to minimize or eliminate waste. Each of these programmes is continually evolving to integrate the latest technologies and management practices.

Key Environmental Challenges and Cruise Industry Responses

The cruise industry faces a number of key environmental challenges related to its activities and operations in the world's oceans, particularly in and around priority conservation areas. There is significant potential for wide-ranging negative environmental impacts from mishandled waste and pollutants or poorly planned and implemented management processes. Although the major cruise lines have made progress in addressing and mitigating these impacts, there is still work to be done to fully minimize the effect of cruising on the natural environment. Furthermore, due to a serious lack of data related to the specific impacts of cruise ships in sensitive environments, there is a real need for more study on these issues.

This section looks at the challenges raised by several key issues – wastewater, hazardous waste, solid waste and oily bilge water. Under each issue, both the potential impacts and the implications for the industry, as well as current industry responses are discussed.

Wastewater

Challenge

Cruise ships generate two kinds of wastewater: grey water and black water. Grey water is wastewater from the sinks, showers, galleys and cleaning activities aboard a ship. It can contain a variety of substances including detergents, oil and grease and food waste. More than 1 million gallons (3.785 million litres) of grey water are typically produced on a 7–10 day cruise, which makes it the largest source of liquid waste generated by cruise ships (Ocean Conservancy, 2002). While the standards for discharging grey water vary at the international, national and local levels, this waste can legally be pumped overboard almost anywhere the ship sails.

Black water is sewage – wastewater from toilets, urinals and infirmaries (Box 30.1). A cruise ship generates an estimated 8000–21,000 gal. (30,280–79,5000 l/30–80 metric tonnes) of black water per day (Royal Caribbean, 2001).

A key impact of wastewater discharges is the introduction of excessive nutrients into a marine environment. Excessive nutrients can overstimulate the growth of aquatic plants and algae, a process known as eutrophication. When eutrophication is prolonged in tropical waters, corals can be smothered and die beneath a thick cover of algal growth. This, in turn, affects fish and other organisms that depend on the reef ecosystem, leading to a decrease in animal and plant diversity and affecting use of the water for fishing and swimming (EPA, 2003a). Wastewater can also contain bacteria, such as faecal coliform, which can cause serious human health problems.

In 2000, the Bluewater Network, a nonprofit environmental organization, petitioned the US EPA (2003b) on behalf of 53 organizations, asking for 'an in-depth assessment . . . of waste streams from cruise ships'. Subsequent studies by the EPA, ICCL and the Science Advisory Panel of the State of Alaska have looked at the composition, dispersion and impact

---

Box 30.1. According to the International Maritime Organization (IMO) Annex IV of MARPOL

'It is generally considered that on the high seas, the oceans are capable of assimilating and dealing with raw sewage through natural bacterial action and therefore the regulations in Annex IV of MARPOL 73/78 prohibit ships from discharging sewage within 4 miles of the nearest land, unless they have in operation an approved treatment plant. Between 4 and 12 miles from land, sewage must be comminuted and disinfected before discharge.' (MARPOL, 2000)

of grey water and black water discharged from cruise ships. The studies concluded that the current practices of the major cruise lines were resulting in high dispersion levels with minimal negative impacts on the environment. The faster a ship sails, the more extensive the dispersion of grey water. In fact, high bacteria counts were found when grey water was not discharged and instead held in tanks near warm engine compartments, which helped accelerate bacterial growth. In July 2001, Alaska established a programme that regulates cruise ship wastewater discharges (ADEC, 2003).

Response

Cruise lines that are members of the ICCL have agreed to discharge grey water and treated black water only while the ship is underway, proceeding at a speed of not less than six knots. The companies have also agreed that wastewater will not be discharged in port or less than four nautical miles (7.4 km) offshore, or the distance dictated by local laws.

Although grey water can legally be discharged almost anywhere, some cruise lines have adopted more restrictive policies. For example, Royal Caribbean, in keeping with the company's environmental commitment to act 'above and beyond compliance', has a policy that prohibits discharge of grey water less than 12 nautical miles (22.22 km) from land (Royal Caribbean, 2001). Carnival Cruise Lines has a similar internal management policy. Holland America and other lines also adhere to a 'zero discharge' policy in harbours, special areas and protected pristine environments such as Glacier Bay National Park in the USA.

The USA Clean Water Act mandates the use of a marine sanitation device (MSD) on all vessels that are equipped with installed toilets, to prevent the discharge of untreated or inadequately treated black water. An MSD uses physical, chemical and/or biological processes to allow effluent to be discharged with characteristics that are similar to effluents from wastewater treatment plants on land.

In addition to the standard MSDs, many cruise ships are using or experimenting with other advanced water treatment technologies to break down and separate contaminants in the wastewater. For example, Celebrity Cruises uses a reverse osmosis process by Rochem (similar to that used to make bottled water) to clean wastewater so effectively that it meets the most stringent discharge standards, including those in Alaska (Celebrity Cruises, 2002). The MSDs on Royal Caribbean International ships use physical and chemical processes to break down the wastewater. Carnival Cruise Lines is testing a Rochem ultrafiltration system on one of their ships for wastewater; MSDs that use biological treatment processes are installed throughout their fleet. Radisson Seven Seas and Princess Cruises are using Hamworthy systems that utilize membrane bioreactors to break down and screen the wastewater. Holland America is using ZENON membrane bioreactors on six of their ships.

Hazardous waste

Challenge

In their waste management systems, cruise ships maintain separate processes for hazardous and non-hazardous materials. Hazardous waste is any solid or liquid waste that can or does pose a serious present or potential threat to human health or the environment (Box 30.2).

The Convention on the Prevention of Marine Pollution by Dumping of Wastes and Other Matter (LDC) of 1972 was amended in 1996 to 'prohibit the dumping of any wastes or other matter with the exception of those listed in Annex 1'.

These are:

1. Dredged material;
2. Sewage sludge;

Box 30.2. According to both International Council of Cruise Lines (ICCL) and International Maritime Organization (IMO) definitions, hazardous waste from cruise ships includes:

- waste from photo processing, including X-ray development fluid;
- dry-cleaning waste fluids and contaminated materials;
- print shop waste fluids;
- fluorescent and mercury vapour lamp bulbs; and
- certain batteries.

3. Fish waste or material resulting from industrial fish-processing operations;
4. Vessels and platforms or other man-made structures at sea;
5. Inert, inorganic geological material;
6. Organic material of natural origin (MARPOL, 1986.

Only 16 countries, representing less than 11% of the world's gross shipping tonnage, have ratified this Convention. Nevertheless, the members of the ICCL have agreed not to discharge any hazardous substances at all, even outside territorial waters.

If mishandled, any of the above-mentioned hazardous materials can cause serious damage to plant and animal species, as well as threaten human health. For example, the silver in waste from photo processing can cause death or reproductive failure in fish, shellfish and other marine organisms. Dry-cleaning sludge and print shop wastes contain chemicals that can be toxic to aquatic mammals. Also the anti-foulant paint that has been painted on ship hulls to kill any form of marine life that comes in contact with them, contains the chemical compound tributyltin, which is extremely toxic to lobster and mollusks such as mussels, clams and oysters. Through the IMO, the shipping industry and governments have recently agreed to phase out the use of these paints.

Response

As the potential for serious harm to biodiversity and human health is so great from hazardous materials, the cruise lines indicate that they are exercising extra caution to comply with and exceed current regulations. It is standard industry practice to offload hazardous wastes in port for either recycling or disposal, in much the same way as land-based generation of the same wastes. For example, in the Caribbean, hazardous wastes are offloaded to one of the 15 ports with approved facilities and hazardous materials contractors. Waste management firms are inspected and audited to ensure compliance with applicable laws and requirements. Carnival reviews, for example, insurance, licenses and procedures of each vendor to ensure full compliance with environmental regulations.

The ICCL's 'Waste Management Practices and Procedures' are very specific as to the management and handling of hazardous substances. Most substances must be landed ashore for processing and recycling in accordance with US federal laws. The major cruise lines also have individual corporate programmes to review and revise operational procedures, to reduce hazardous chemical use and substitute with more benign substances. In 2000, Royal Caribbean eliminated the use of 99 different chemicals. Carnival Corporation maintains a list of prohibited chemicals for their fleet.

Waste is carefully processed to separate out hazardous materials. On Royal Caribbean ships, for example, batteries, electronic parts and butane lighters found in trash bins are removed for separate processing and disposal. On Carnival ships, aerosol cans are segregated from the solid waste, depressurized and drained. Any remaining propellant is collected in a sealed container and landed ashore as a hazardous waste.

The cruise lines have also adopted a number of specific practices for different types of hazardous wastes:

- Carnival Corporation and Royal Caribbean offload photo processing waste onshore and are experimenting with complete digitalization.
- For dry-cleaning operations, Celebrity Cruises has installed a filtration system that removes the most toxic chemicals from the process.
- ICCL members are beginning to use alternative printing inks, such as soy-based and non-chlorinated hydrocarbon-based inks in their print shops. Royal Caribbean ships now use water-based instead of chemical-based printing plates.
- Photocopier and laser printer toner cartridges are offloaded for recycling by all Royal Caribbean and Carnival Corporation ships.
- Excess or expired over-the-counter medicines are offloaded for disposal in an environmentally responsible manner. Carnival donates some older pharmaceuticals to animal shelters, aquariums and animal rehabilitation facilities.
- Batteries, fluorescent bulbs and mercury lamps are separated from waste and recycled

or offloaded as a hazardous waste. Carnival ships, for example, annually recycle nearly 7200 lb (3273 kg) of batteries and 18,000 fluorescent lamp bulbs. P&O Princess collects old batteries from passengers at on-board photo shops.

Solid waste

Challenge

Solid waste generated on a ship can include glass, paper, cardboard, aluminium and steel cans, incinerator ash, plastics and kitchen grease. On average, each cruise ship passenger generates at least 2 lb (about 1 kg) of solid waste per day and disposes of two bottles and two cans. With some ships carrying more than 3000 passengers, the amount of waste generated in a day can be massive.

Much of this non-hazardous waste is not easily biodegradable or does not biodegrade at all (Table 30.3). Marine mammals, fish, sea turtles and birds can be injured or killed from entanglement with plastics and other solid waste. Animals may also get sick or die from ingesting these objects.

Through the IMO, most of the world's shipping countries have agreed to a complete ban on dumping all plastics into the sea, at any distance from land. Other types of garbage, such as paper products, rags, glass, metal, bottles, crockery, lining and packing materials can be legally discharged 25 miles (40.23 km) from shore. No discharging of any type of garbage is permitted in 'special areas', which are bodies of water deemed to require additional protections beyond the normal discharge requirements (EPA, 2003a).

The entire Caribbean is considered a 'special area', but an exception is made for food waste that can be discharged 12 or more nautical miles (22.22 km) from shore (EPA, 2002). And any food waste that has passed through a grinder can be discharged 3 miles (4.8 km) from shore.

Response

As with hazardous waste, the ICCL members' waste management practices are very specific as to the management of solid waste. The practices are based on IMO regulations and USA laws such as the Federal Water Pollution Control Act. ICCL member cruise lines have 'zero-discharge' policies, in effect, meaning that they have committed to not discharging certain types of wastes and discharging others only after they have been treated properly.

Wastes such as glass, cardboard, aluminium and steel cans are processed on board through crushing, reuse and/or recycling and incineration. Incineration is used primarily for food waste, contaminated cardboard, some plastics, trash and wood. Incinerator ash is periodically tested for toxicity and, if it is determined to be non-hazardous, can be disposed at sea in accordance with international regulations. Hazardous ash must be disposed of onshore. Royal Caribbean Cruises Ltd and Carnival Corporation land all ash ashore and test the ash regularly to ensure that hazardous substances are not present; as their policies are not to incinerate hazardous materials.

Most of the major cruise lines have begun to implement shipboard recycling programmes, to reduce the generation of solid waste. Carnival's recycling programme achieves a recycling rate of nearly 65%, which is much higher than most land-based communities. An average of 170,000 lb (77,111 kg) of cardboard, aluminium cans, plastics, glass and steel are recycled each month from Carnival's fleet (Carnival Cruise Line, 2003). Prior to sending waste to a facility, each vendor is checked to ensure that they are in full compliance with local, state and federal environmental regulations. Royal Caribbean's Vision-class ships sort, crush and offload about 450 lb (204

Table 30.3. Estimated time required for waste to biodegrade or dissolve at sea.

Paper bus ticket	2–4 weeks
Cotton cloth	1–5 months
Rope	3–14 months
Woollen cloth	1 year
Painted wood	13 years
Tin can	100 years
Aluminium can	200–500 years
Plastic bottle	450 years

Source: Hellenic Marine Environment Protection Association (HELMEPA) (IMO, 2003).

kg) of aluminium cans for recycling per week-long trip.

The major cruise lines also minimize and prevent waste generation through product purchasing practices that emphasize products with recycled content and less packaging. Holland America uses recycled paper for all on-board printed materials. In some cases, disposable packaging is eliminated before products are even brought on board, or replaced with reusable packaging materials. Some of the cruise lines have eliminated plastic cups, straws, stirrers and packaging, and introduced bulk dispensers in place of individually packaged condiments.

To minimize the use of plastics, Princess Cruises has worked closely with suppliers to replace plastic with other biodegradable materials or eliminate or reduce packaging materials. The company has been able to reduce plastic waste by approximately a third, or seven million pieces of plastic, each year over the last few years. Royal Caribbean has begun cleaning and reusing plastic pails, for holding items such as laundry soap, using as tote buckets for tools or for the collection of spent batteries for recycling.

Oily bilge water

Challenge

The discharge of untreated oily bilge water into the ocean can contribute to marine pollution. On a ship, oil often leaks from engine and machinery spaces or from fittings and engine maintenance activities and mixes with water in the bilge, the lowest part of the hull of the ship. A typical large cruise ship will generate an average of 8 metric tonnes (2228 gal. or 8434 l) of oily bilge water for each 24 h of operation (ACSI, 2002).

To maintain ship stability and eliminate potentially hazardous conditions from oil vapours in these areas, the bilge spaces need to be flushed and periodically pumped dry. However, before a bilge can be cleared out and the water discharged, the oil that has accumulated needs to be extracted from the bilge water. This process involves pumping the oily water out of the bilge and, in accordance with international and national laws, passing it through an oily water separator (OWS) before further processing. Any oil that is extracted from the bilge

water can then be reused, incinerated and/or offloaded in port, although most ports lack adequate facilities to receive the extracted oil (AAPA, 2001).

An OWS can usually treat from 1 to 10 t (0.9–9 metric tonnes/up to 2600 gal. or 9842 l) of bilge water each hour. IMO regulations require that the oil content of any discharged water be less than 15 parts per million and that it should not leave a visible sheen on the surface of the water. A single pint of oil can leave a sheen of oil across as much as one acre of ocean surface (AAPA, 2001). If a separator is faulty or deliberately bypassed, untreated oily bilge water could be discharged directly into the ocean. Some discharge incidents over the past few years have been due mainly to human error or malfunctioning equipment. As mentioned above, a number of cruise lines have been charged in relation to this issue in recent years. For example, in 2002, Carnival Corporation was fined US$18 million for deliberate falsification of oily bilge record-books, related to the discharge from a few ships of oily bilge water through separators with disabled oil content meters. And in 1998 and 1999, Royal Caribbean Cruises Ltd was fined US$9 million and US$18 million, respectively, for discharging oil-contaminated bilge waste.

Discharging oil or oily water into the ocean can hurt or kill marine life and severely damage coral reefs. Diesel fuel is acutely toxic to fish, invertebrates and seaweed, although in open water it dilutes quite rapidly. Spills can be particularly toxic to crabs and shellfish in shallow, confined near-shore areas because these organisms bioaccumulate the oil, often over a period of several weeks after exposure. Oily contaminants may also concentrate on the sea surface, which is an important area for the early development of the eggs and larvae of many fish and other marine species. Because there is only a limited understanding of the risks caused by long-term chronic oil discharges, such as from oily bilge water, into coastal marine environments in the Caribbean and elsewhere, there is a pressing need for further study of these issues.

Response

Despite the recent incidents of illegal bypass pipes and falsified logbooks, the ICCL and the major cruise companies do seem to be taking the issue of oily bilge water seriously. For example, Royal Caribbean's current discharges of oily bilge water contain less than 5 parts per million of oil, which far exceeds international standards (Wright, 2002). In addition, the company's use of gas turbine engines on its Celebrity ships reduces oily bilge water because they are based on a combined gas turbine and steam turbine system, rather than diesel fuel system.

All cruise ships are required under US law to use some form of OWS or store the oily water for offloading in a port. Most cruise ships separate the oil from the water to create a sludge, which is then either incinerated or offloaded. Holland America and several other cruise lines now often use two OWSs to prevent accidental discharges from equipment malfunction.

Conclusion

The practices and procedures detailed in this chapter demonstrate that the major cruise lines have begun to respond effectively to the environmental challenges of the past decades. Nevertheless, much remains to be done to ensure that the rapidly growing demand for cruising does not overwhelm the very assets of a pristine environment that attract people to cruises and cruise destinations. Cruise lines should continue to pilot and implement leading practices for addressing environmental impact and seek partnerships with non-governmental and scientific organizations to better understand their impact. The major cruise lines find themselves at an important crossroads of expanding their business while also factoring in the protection of the natural environment that their customers enjoy. The cruise industry has the opportunity to become a model for the shipping and tourism industries as it continues to show leadership in piloting and implementing leading practices, thus encouraging others, such as its destination partners to take steps too.

Ocean Conservation and Tourism Alliance

On 10 December 2003, the industry took such a leadership position with the creation of the Ocean Conservation and Tourism Alliance – a joint initiative between the ICCL and CI. This partnership is focusing on the protection of biodiversity in top cruise destinations and the promotion of science-based industry practices to minimize the cruise industry's environmental impact.

The Ocean Conservation and Tourism Alliance has established several priority areas on which they are focusing their efforts including: best practices for wastewater management, establishing destination partnerships and promoting environmental education among crew, passengers and vendors.

As a first step, the advisory committee established a panel of scientific experts in conservation, environmental technologies and cruise industry environmental practices. Headed by Dr Sylvia Earle, an internationally recognized marine biologist, National Geographic Explorer-in-Residence and former Chief Scientist for the US National Oceanic and Atmospheric Administration (NOAA), the science panel is tasked with determining best practices for cruise ship wastewater management, identifying ways of accelerating the development of those systems, and subsequently encouraging their adoption on board cruise ships. Detailed recommendations from the panel are expected in 2006.

Creating awareness of conservation issues among cruise industry passengers and crew is another important element. The Alliance will work to develop appropriate education and awareness materials for cruise passengers and crew, including a 2-year public education plan concerning environmental conservation and biodiversity.

The Alliance will also promote vendor education. Obviously, where there are tourists, services spring up to meet their needs and desires and someone will be ready to provide tourists with the wide variety of experiences and adventures they are seeking. The Alliance will examine the feasibility of applying its resources to CI's Responsible Marine Tourism Initiative, which brings together marine recreation providers, their major contractors and other interested parties to implement and monitor responsible marine recreation.

Acknowledgements

This chapter is primarily based on an independent interim summary report financed by

The Ford Motor Company and published by Conservation International in March 2003, as well as on details about the subsequent OCTA partnership between CI and the cruise industry.

References

ACSI (Alaska Cruise Ship Initiative) (2002) *Report of the Work Groups: Wastewater and Solid Waste Handing, Air Emissions, Oil Spills Environmental Leadership*. Alaska, USA.

ADEC (Alaska Department of Environmental Conservation) (2003) *Cruise Ship Waste Disposal and Management*. Available at: http://www.state.ak.us/local/akpages/ENV.CONSERV/press/cruise/cruise.htm

AAPA (American Association of Port Authorities) (2001) *Green Ports: Environmental Management and Technology at U.S. Ports*. Alexandria, Virginia.

Carnival Corporation (2002) *Press Release Seakeepers, Eco-Friendly Dry Cleaning are the Latest Carnival Cruise Lines' Fleetwide Environmental Programs*. Miami, Florida.

Celebrity Cruises (2002) *Press Release*. Available at: http://www.celebritycruises.com/pressrelease.asp?s = 9C928E4A35&xref = 17094

Cruiseserver (2003) *Marine Pollution: Progress Made to Reduce Marine Pollution by Cruise Ships, but Important Issues Remain*. GAO Report to Cong-ressional Requesters (GAO/RCED-00-48). Available at: http://www.cruiseserver.net/travelpage/other/new_build.asp

EPA (Environmental Protection Agency) (2003a) *A Vessel Sewage Discharge Program*. Available at: http://www.epa.gov/owow/oceans/vessel_sewage/

EPA (Environmental Protection Agency) (2003b) *Federal Register, IMO Special Areas, August 21, 1995*. Washington, DC.

GAO (2000) *Marine Pollution – Progress Made to Reduce Marine Pollution by Cruise Ships, but Important Issues Remain, GAO Report to Congressional Requesters* (GAO/RCED-00-48). Available at: http://www.gao.gov/new.items/rc00048.pdf

ICCL (International Council of Cruise Lines) (2002) *Cruising Toward Sustainability: An Environmental Performance Report for the International Cruise Industry*. Arlington, Virginia.

ICCL (International Council of Cruise Lines) (2004) *Press Release*. Arlington, Virginia.

IMO (International Maritime Organization) (2005) *Prevention of Pollution by Garbage from Ships*. Available at: http://www.imo.org/Environment/mainframe.asp?topic_id = 297

LMIS (Lloyd's Maritime Information Services) (2003) *Website of the Maritime International Secretariat Services*. Available at: http://www.marisec.org/shippingfacts/keyfactsnoofships.htm

Ocean Conservancy (2002) *Cruise Control: A Report on How Cruise Ships Affect the Marine Environment*. Washington, DC.

Royal Caribbean (2001) *Environmental Report*. Available at: http://www.royalcaribbean.com/asp/rc/nw/rcnw_aboutusintro.asp?s = F8050E44F3

Toh, A. (2000) *Plan for Second Cruise Center Needs Scrutiny: PSA chief*. Shipping Times, Singapore.

US Resource[Q8] Conservation and Recovery Act (1996) Section 1004, Article 4. *The Convention on the Prevention of Marine Pollution by Dumping of Wastes and Other Matter, 1972, as amended in 1996*. Washington, DC.

WTO (World Tourism Organization) (2001) *Initial Report on the Cruise Industry*. Madrid, Spain.

Wright, C.W. (2002) *Email message to Scott Wayne*. Royal Caribbean Cruise Lines, Miami, Florida.

31 Environmental Policy Challenges for the Cruise Industry: Case Studies from Australia and the USA

Suzanne Dobson and Alison Gill

Simon Fraser University, Department of Geography, Burnaby, BC, Canada, V5A 1S6

Introduction

The international scope and dynamic nature of the cruise industry poses environmental policy challenges for both governments and corporations. The industry has gained momentum since the 1980s with many new and larger ships entering the market accompanied by an expansion of routes and destinations. In 2004, the worldwide cruise ship fleets contained over 230 vessels (US Environmental Protection Agency, 2004). According to a 2001 World Tourism Organization report (WTO, 2001), the number of global cruise passengers over the past decade has increased at almost twice the pace of overall international tourist arrivals. The WTO (2001) has also estimated that North American and European demand will surpass 12 million passengers by the end of 2010. Environmental issues and concerns surrounding the activities and procedures of cruise ships have increased proportionately with their rise in popularity and size.

The cruise industry inevitably affects the marine environment and requires some form of regulation to guide its activities and procedures. Cruise vessels travel through both domestic and international waters bearing international flag state status, crews and guests. Their travel patterns and international status require cruise vessels to adapt to a complex mix of legislation and regulations ranging from the international level to local level demands from specific port

locations. Over the last 40 years governments have made considerable progress advancing and implementing environmentally responsible legislation and policy guidelines. However, current debate argues that ongoing progress will not be accomplished by government intervention alone (Furger, 1997; Freeman and Soete, 1997; Luke, 1997; Sinclair, 1997). Other institutions also have a role to play and many of today's institutions, such as environmental non-governmental oganizations (ENGOs), corporations, supranationals, classification societies and investors, have developed their own environmental mandates (Furger, 1997). Table 31.1 displays the traditional institutions which have played a role in policymaking for the cruise industry and highlights the emerging institutions recently assuming a role in the policymaking process.

There can no longer be any doubt that environmental policies have impacted on corporate and community economic development strategies in addition to transforming traditional policymaking in government and governance structures. In response to both public and private sector pressures a variety of environmental policy mechanisms has emerged within the cruise sector. However, these policy mechanisms are geographically diverse exhibiting locational differences that reflect political, cultural, environmental and economic attributes of place. This has resulted in distinctive mixes of policy mechanisms.

Table 31.1. Examples of traditional and emerging institutions in the cruise ship industry.

	Civil society	Corporations	Governments
Traditional institutions	Coastal communities	Princess Cruises (P&O cruises)	Local
			Provincial or State
		Holland America	Federal
		Carnival Cruises	Port Authorities
		Royal Caribbean Cruise Lines	
Emerging institutions	Civil society	Membership alliances	Supranationals
	Aboriginal groups	International Council of Cruise	International Maritime Organization
	NGOs		
	Interest groups	Lines	
		North-West Cruise Ship Association	Classification Societies

Source: Dobson (2006).

In this chapter, we examine the debate over industry self-regulation and voluntary guidelines versus command and control regulation. In line with Sinclair's (1997) argument, we believe that policy mechanisms exist on a regulatory continuum with pure self-regulation and strict command and control regulation at opposite ends. We feel that a variety of policy instruments within the regulation continuum can be combined to more effectively accommodate place-specific characteristics in the environmental regulation of the cruise ship industry.

Command and control is the dominant form of environmental regulation in most countries and until recently has been the most common government response to environmental pollution (Sinclair, 1997). It 'requires polluters to meet specific emission-reduction targets and often requires the installation and use of specific types of equipment to reduce emissions' (European Environment Agency, 2004). From a management perspective, it is based on the prescription of rules and standards and the use of sanctions to enforce compliance with them. However, there is widespread agreement from regulators, industries and communities that command and control has been too burdensome and expensive. Along with diminishing benefits from command and control regulations, compliance is increasingly difficult to measure, and the cost of their enforcement is rising (Furger, 1997; Steger, 1993). Consequently, there has been a search for regulatory alternatives to improve the environmental performance of the industry – especially

self-regulation (Gunningham and Rees, 1997; Sinclair, 1997).

Industry self-regulation is a form of market-based incentives that relies on economic and social motivations to encourage environmental protection and cost-effectiveness. Gunnigham and Rees (1997, p. 364) define industry self-regulation 'as a regulatory process whereby an industry level (as opposed to a governmental or firm-level) organization sets rules and standards (codes of practice) relating to the conduct of firms in the industry'. The goal of industry self-regulation for environmental purposes is to reduce damaging processes involved with operation of their industry for the good of the public. 'Pure' industry self-regulation, on the one end of Sinclair's (1997) continuum, would be regulation and enforcement which is carried out independent from direct government involvement. The common criticism to industry self-regulation arises from the abuse of the use of the term by industry to portray an environmentally responsible image while continuing to pollute and act in its own self-interest (Beder, 1997; Gunningham and Rees, 1997). Increased and unbiased monitoring and enforcement would help in ensuring industry credibility; however, questions, concerning whose responsibility monitoring and enforcement should be and at what cost to the public, remain.

Using two case study examples, Juneau, Alaska and Sydney, New South Wales, we explore the significance of place in determining the type of environmental policy that is adopted to regulate the cruise industry. The empirical examples used in this study are drawn from a larger body of research examining environmental regulation in the cruise industry (Dobson, 2006) which employed key informant interviews and document analysis to compare regulation in several ports in the USA, Canada and Australia. Before discussing the specifics of the case studies we present a general overview of environmental policy mechanisms that affect the cruise industry.

An Overview of Environmental Policy Mechanisms

Shipping in international waters is regulated under the United Nations Convention on the Law of the Sea (UNCLOS). While controversial, and as yet not signed by all nations (and only recently in Canada), 200-mile (320 km) exclusive economic zones and 12-mile (20 km) territorial seas have been established around signatory nation states. The International Maritime Organization (IMO), a branch of the United Nations, exists as the main supranational body governing, among other things, environmental regulation of the shipping industry through the International Convention for the Prevention of Pollution from Ships (MARPOL). The Convention consists of a series of Articles and six Annexes prohibiting the dumping or discharging of certain items including oil, hazardous waste, plastics, sewage and other toxins. Although the IMO establishes the environmental guidelines for MARPOL, it does not enforce them. Nation states have to ratify MARPOL's annexes and are responsible for their implementation, monitoring and enforcement (Furger, 1997).

The Convention and Annex I entered in full force in 1983. Currently, all the Annexes have been ratified except for Annex IV (sewage) and Annex VI (air pollution) which is still awaiting ratification by countries with enough tonnage for the Annex to enter into force. A country's tonnage is calculated based on the total tonnage of the ships flagged by that country. As such, countries like Panama, Liberia and the Bahamas, which possess over 30% of the world tonnage, become crucial signatories for the ratification of MARPOL's Annexes. Both Annexes are scheduled to be ratified in 2005. Annex IV, however, similar to Annex

III (harmful substances) is an optional annex meaning that a country can ratify MARPOL without having the domestic regulations in place to meet Annex IV's regulations. Annex IV's official title is 'Regulations for the Prevention of Pollution by Sewage from Ships' and is the most applicable to cruise ship's wastewaters and the environment. Annex IV's regulations with regards to onshore treatment facilities were the main reason why some countries had not ratified the Annex. In 2001, Regulation 10 stated that:

> The Government of each Party to the Convention undertakes to ensure the provision of facilities at ports and terminals for the reception of sewage, without causing undue delay to ships, adequate to meet the needs of the ships using them.
>
> (Sustainable Development Networking Programme, 2005)

Unfortunately not all the ports of call for many cruise ships had the necessary onshore sewage treatment facilities. The MARPOL Annex was revised on 1 April 2004 with more lenient regulations for sewage and the onshore reception requirements. Annex IV is scheduled to enter into force on 1 August 2005 with Australia as a signatory country but the USA has yet to sign. International law has been effective in stimulating improvements in environmental practice in the shipping industry, although issues continue with regards to effective monitoring and enforcement procedures for ships due to the sheer size of the oceans and the coastlines.

Federal and state/provincial laws in many instances incorporate regulations very similar to those of MARPOL at the international level and include a variety of measures for environmental protection. For example, cruise ships that operate in American waters must comply with US environmental laws, including the Clean Water Act, the Clean Air Act and the Oil Pollution Control Act. Similar laws in Canada, including the Canadian Environmental Protection Act, the Shipping Act, the Oceans Act and the Fisheries Act, all regulate against pollution and harmful environmental practices. State and provincial governments have additional environmental legislation that regulates activity in the near coastal zone.

In addition to international and federal regulation, the cruise industry associations, for example, the International Council of Cruise

Lines (ICCL) has set its own voluntary environmental policies for the member cruise lines. ICCL has 16 member cruise lines and includes the majority of the cruise ships travelling in the world today such as Royal Caribbean Cruise Lines, Princess Cruise Lines, Holland America, Carnival Cruise Lines and Celebrity Cruise Lines. In most destinations, ICCL's environmental standards for its cruise lines, assuming they are adhered to, exceed or at least match international and federal legislative requirements (ICCL, 2003). As a result of these industry-based regulations, the aforementioned cruise ship companies have agreed to the following environmental practices: no discharge of black water (treated or untreated sewage) in port; no discharge of grey water (sink or shower water) in port; discharges of treated black water and grey water conducted when vessels are more than 10 miles (15 km) from port call and proceeding at 6 knots or faster; and, legal discharges are not conducted when a cruise vessel is within a mile from any surrounding shore. ICCL's voluntary practices and procedures cover high volume wastes (garbage, grey water, black water, oily residues and bilge water), pollution prevention and the smaller quantities of hazardous waste produced on board. The ICCL standards for environmental performance were set at a level consistent with the standards outlined in the *International Management Code for the Safe Operations of Ships and for Pollution Prevention* (ISM Code) and MARPOL's mandated *Waste Management Manual* (ICCL, 2003). In other words, any violations of the ICCL standards would be considered violations of IMO Conventions and could be punished by the port state. Again, the main concern is not the effectiveness of the standards themselves, but whether the ships are adhering to the practices and procedures with which they have agreed. This highlights the importance of monitoring and enforcement issues.

Cruise ships must also meet the requirements of classification societies, which are private, third party organizations whose main function is to inspect the ship at regular intervals to ensure whether its seaworthiness and the ship's structure and machinery are being maintained as required by classification societies' rules. Classification societies will also inspect cruise ships for compliance with international

safety regulations including Safety of Life at Sea (SOLAS) and MARPOL. Major classification societies include the American Bureau of Shipping, based in the USA; Lloyd's Register of Shipping, in the UK; Det Norske Veritas, in Norway; Bureau Veritas, in France; and Registro Italiano Navale Group, in Italy. Lloyd's Register is the premier classification society for passenger ships, with over 47% of the world passenger fleet currently classified with them. Environmentally, classification societies have been known to acknowledge certain cruise ships with 'green certification' or to require compliance with the International Standards Organisation (ISO) 14001 series of environmental management systems.

Port locations have to adapt their policies to accommodate the presence of the cruise ships, and there is considerable variation in the degree to which ports implement and enforce regulations. In some locations such as Canada and in some coastal states in the USA, the federal and state/provincial governments have been divesting policy decisions for the cruise ship industry to both the international and local level. In these locations, the voluntary standards set by the cruise industry are the policy mechanism followed with little monitoring and enforcement efforts. Other locations, such as Alaska and New South Wales, have assumed the primary role in dictating cruise regulations, monitoring and enforcement, yet have come to that decision through different pressures and have had varying degrees of success. In the two comparative case studies presented here, we examine why at the local level, differing approaches to environmental policymaking have arisen.

The Case Studies

The case studies have been selected to provide contrasting policy responses to managing environmental quality relating to the cruise sector. On the one hand in Sydney, New South Wales, the development of command and control regulation has restricted industry innovation, whereas in Juneau, Alaska, it has resulted in the development of technological innovation and self-regulation by the industry. The case studies offer evidence to suggest the reasons for this differing response.

Juneau, Alaska, USA

Juneau, the capital of Alaska, with a population of 30,711, received 547 port calls in 2003 and exists as the most popular cruise destination in the North Pacific market. It is not surprising that Juneau and the State of Alaska have some of the strictest cruise ship specific regulations for sewage and grey water anywhere in the world. Both the federal and the state governments have imposed regulations for discharging sewage in port and in state waters.

In the USA, the Clean Water Act applies to all point-source pollution including vessels, but provides a permit exception for discharges of sewage from ships; effluent from properly functioning marine engines; laundry, shower and galley sink wastes. Under Section 312 of the Act dumping of sewage into the navigable waters of the USA, within 3 miles (5 km) of shore, is prohibited and all vessels must possess working marine sanitation devices (MSDs). Beyond the 3-mile limit raw sewage can be legally dumped into the ocean. Grey water can currently be discharged anywhere but Alaska or the Great Lakes. However, the cruise lines have opted to collect and hold grey water for discharge until ships are underway and operating at a speed of more than 6 knots to disperse it. Under ICCL policy, the discharge occurs at least 12 nautical miles from land. The US Coast Guard has primary enforcement authority as well as the responsibility to certify compliance. However, they have been criticized for their lack of emphasis on, and ability to address, environmental issues (General Accounting Office of the United States, 2000).

Citizen concern over cruise ships in Juneau began with the increasing number of ships in the early 1990s and the sprawl of tourists into the city of Juneau. It was impossible not to notice the large cruise ships in port in Juneau, which during the summer cruise season was receiving up to seven ships in a day. The city became overcrowded with thousands of tourists, souvenir shops and tour buses. The social interruptions created a disdain for the cruise companies and passengers, which led to further concerns surrounding the impacts of such vessels.

Environmental concerns existed before 1998, but many of the institutions in Juneau's policy community agree that the Royal Caribbean Cruise Line felony counts were the catalyst that began the environmental movement, which eventually resulted in many environmental policies changes. In 1998, Royal Caribbean Cruise Ltd (RCCL) pleaded guilty to 21 felony counts for purposefully dumping hazardous wastes from their photo shops, dry-cleaning facilities and bilge water tanks into many US waters – including Alaska's Inside Passage. RCCL agreed to pay a fine of US$18 million. In 1999, the State of Alaska filed suit again against RCCL for another incident where they illegally dumped oil and hazardous waste into state waters, which resulted in a judgement of a further fine of US$6.5 million. The spill and resulting fines attracted the attention of local ENGOs demanding to know what exactly the cruise ships were discharging in the water, where and what laws existed to regulate the industry. The ENGOs discovered that although many laws existed to regulate oil and bilge water, sewage and grey water remained largely underregulated. This gave rise to great concern not only among citizens in Juneau but throughout Alaska resulting in protests and demonstrations.

The increased pressure led to the Alaska Cruise Ship Initiative (ACSI) (1999), enacted by the State's Alaskan Department of Environmental Conservation (ADEC) with cooperation from the US Coast Guard, US Environmental Protection Agency, members of the South-east Conference, industry representatives and concerned local citizens. The ACSI represented an institutional reengineering response to address the RCCL spill as well as the increasing public pressure to address environmental concerns. It did not demand new policy reforms but recommended a study to determine the scale and scope of the perceived problem. By committing to the study, the state responded to the negative press and sentiment in Alaska without agreeing to take action.

The ACSI carried out a series of tests in 2000 including wastewater monitoring. It boarded 21 large cruise ships twice in the 2000 season to test overboard samples against the common parameters used to assess the level of sewage treatment. It was determined that the current MSDs were not working up to standard and also showing alarming test results from sewage and grey water discharges. Almost all the ships tested had effluent levels of faecal coliform that were above the legal standard (Klein, 2002). Grey water tests also showed that the bacteria and faecal coliform counts in grey water were as bad, if not worse, than those found in sewage.

In the face of great citizen concern about these results and pressure from ENGOs, response by both the government and the cruise industry was rapid. By the summer of 2001 wastewater discharges in Juneau (and throughout Alaska), were regulated by both new federal and state bills. In addition, state law passed in 2001 included smaller cruise vessels and addressed grey water discharge as well as sewage.

As a result of these federal and state regulations, cruise ships have three options:

1. They must hold their wastewaters and only discharge them once outside of Alaskan waters (3 nautical miles) where they are excluded from the sampling and effluent standards.
2. They can discharge when at least a nautical mile from shore and travelling at a speed of at least 6 knots. In this scenario the wastewaters must meet the state effluent standards.
3. They can install advanced wastewater treatment systems that meet the stringent requirements that enable them to be certified by the US Coast Guard for continuous discharge.

Alaskan state law has also put measures in place for a verified compliance programme for testing, sampling and reporting of wastewater and air emission as well as a requirement that the cruise companies pay for that programme.

ICCL first responded to the federal and state regulations controlling sewage and grey water in Juneau by introducing new industry guidelines to be followed by its member lines, which matched or exceeded the federal and state regulation for the North Pacific Coast. Second, individual cruise companies, including Princess Cruise Lines and Holland America, began a research and development effort to improve their current wastewater technologies and MSDs (Alaska Department of Environmental Conservation, 2004; Princess Cruise Lines, 10 July 2003, personal communication). Within a year of the Alaskan regulation, Holland America announced in 2001 that it had discovered Zenon, a new wastewater processing system developed by Zenon Environmental Inc. that turns black water and grey water into near drinking water quality (Alaska Department of Environmental Conservation, 2004). Other cruise companies have been developing similar technology with other companies such as Rochem, Alpha-Laval, Hamworthy and Hydroxyl.

The approximate cost of installing this new technology is US$ 3 million per ship and requires rigorous testing. When cruise vessels choose to install this new technology it has to be certified by the US Coast Guard. Ships can then continuously discharge anywhere in Alaska. In order to become certified, test results from at least five effluent samples over a 30-day period must satisfy strict wastewater levels, including having no more than an average faecal coliform level of 40 colonies per 100 l of water (US Coast Guard, 15 July 2003, personal communication). Once certified, the ships must continue sampling bimonthly for faecal coliform, chlorine, BOD, TSS and pH. Since the passage of the law in 2001, 32 large vessels representing over 90% of the North Pacific cruise fleet, were registered for continuous discharge (Alaska Department of Environmental Conservation, 2004).

Sydney, New South Wales, Australia

Sydney is the largest city in Australia with over four million residents. It is the largest cruise ship destination in the country with 78 port calls in the 2002–2003 season. Sydney currently has both a domestic and an international cruise ship market with Princess Cruise Lines being its most frequent visitor. Australia is a signatory to the UNCLOS and has also ratified Annex IV of MARPOL, which places regulations on the discharging of sewage. Australia thus requires that cruise vessels possess a working MSD or an adequate holding tank for sewage. Annex IV also requires treated sewage to be discharged between 4–12 nautical miles from shore while travelling at a speed of at least 6 knots. Australia has used many international laws to aid in its creation of Commonwealth and state law. For example, regulations concerning sewage and environmental protection from dumping are based on an international convention that aims to prevent pollution that is harmful to human health and marine life, damages amenities or interferes with other legitimate uses of the sea. However, the legislative approach to marine pollution response in Australia is not uniform as states possess the power to regulate their coastal and inland waters in different ways (AMSA, 1998). On 30 June 1995 Sydney's port became an independent port corporation. Many countries' governments and ports have made the decision to privatize ports to become more commercially focused and efficient (Palmer, 1999). Ironically the corporatization of ports comes at the same time as International Law gives port states the central role in monitoring for environmental protection (Palmer, 1999).

In Sydney, most of the regulations for sewage and grey water exist in the state's and the port's legislations. The principal marine pollution act in New South Wales is the Marine Pollution Act 1987 (NSW MPA). Sydney Port has been delegated those responsibilities, but is subject to the Ports Corporatisation and Waterways Management Act 1995 (NSW PCAWMA). Under the PCAWMA the minister has general responsibility for marine safety, including the protection of the environment in connection with the use of vessels in state waters. There is a range of other legislation that relates to the environment in New South Wales. The Protections of the Environment Operations Act 1997 (NSW POTEOA) exists as the main environmental protection act in NSW. It includes a prohibition on polluting any waters and renders the Environmental Protection Authority the appropriate regulatory authority for the Act.

Organized public concern for the environmental quality of Sydney Harbour was first raised in 1989 in association with 'Clean Up Australia Day'. Ian Kiernan, an Australian yacht racer who had encountered many polluted oceans throughout the world during his sailing career, initiated this event. 'Clean Up Sydney Harbour Day' in 1989 received an enormous public response with more than 40,000 people donating their time and energy to clean up the harbour (Clean Up Australia Online, 2004). An annual Clean Up Australia Day followed that heightened environmental stewardship for marine environments. As a result, environmental measures were stressed to the governing institutions and environmental regu-

lation was introduced in 1990 when the Waterways Authority took on the responsibility for cleaning Sydney Harbour as a major environmental initiative (Waterways Authority, 2003). Sydney Ports has established a no-discharge zone in port and in inland waters.

As a result of these government regulations there is no organized environmental opposition to cruise ships in Australia. In the eyes of the public, the current structure adequately regulates the environment, so there is no institutional pressure for change and the current governing institutions are content with their regulations, infrastructure and technology (Barwil Shipping Agency, 4 April 2003, personal communication; Sydney Ports, 28 April 2003, personal communication).

Discussion

The case studies described illustrate two differing policy responses to environmental issues relating to the cruise industry. On the one hand in Juneau, command and control mechanisms were complemented by industry self-regulation that sought to go beyond regulatory compliance. In the case of Sydney, stricter command and control regulations without any industry self-regulation have adequately protected the marine environment, but are argued to stifle technological innovation. In this discussion we consider why, despite the fact that the same cruise ship companies (and in some instance the same ships) are involved, there have been differing responses in different places. This discussion is set within the broader debate over the benefits of industry self-regulation versus command and control regulation in enhancing environmental quality.

In Juneau, the series of events leading up to legislative action demonstrate how place-based institutions (e.g. ENGOs, political agents) used the cruise ship violations to advance their own agendas. The process by which environmental policy changes occurred was not without controversy leading to many rumours concerning the motivation for regulatory changes. Some people, including ENGOs and many citizens, argued that the motivations were purely environmental, suggesting that potential damage to the fragile and unique characteristics of the environment in

Alaska was too great a risk to ignore (Earth Island Institute, 18 July 2003, personal communication). However, it is noteworthy that both a federal bill (that applied only to Alaska and no other state) and a state bill for the State of Alaska were passed in an unusually short-time period. This led to speculation regarding political motivation. It was seen by some as a power struggle between federal and state governments, with each body seeking to exert its power over the marine environment (Alaska State Representative, 17 July 2003, personal communication; Environmental Protection Agency, 16 July 2003, personal communication).

Others suggested that the political motivation was related to individual politicians positioning themselves for election on a clearly hot topic concerning the environment (Alaska Department for Environmental Conservation, 15 July 2003, personal communication). Yet others believed that the dependency of Juneau on the cruise ships and their feelings that the city was been taken over and controlled by foreign entities was the motivation (Royal Caribbean Cruise Lines, 15 July 2004, personal communication). We are not suggesting that the environmental reasons for the new policies were not important, but rather noting that environmental degradation has been often overlooked in the political arena – regardless of the severity of the impact – without additional motivation for action. For example, this can be seen in the case of oil exploration and extraction in Alaska, which poses many challenges and impacts to the environment. The Alaskan Governor Knowles received a substantial amount of negative press and pressure from environmentalists, but continued his effort to establish BP Amoco as an oil company monopoly in Alaska. Gary Cook, a Greenpeace climate change campaigner, reported the following quote after Knowles received a BP employee of the year award in the year 2000:

> BP Amoco could not have asked for a better supporter. However, long-term environmental interests could not have found a worse advocate. It's time for Governor Knowles and other Alaskan politicians to realize it is not in the long-term interests of its citizens, or the environment, to keep drilling for new sources of oil.
>
> (Alaskan Governor receives BP employee of the year award, 2000)

Indeed, political motivation aside, there are obvious correlations between the pressure by the ENGOs for action and the creation of a political environment conducive to wholesale policy changes for the cruise ship industry.

The case of Juneau also offers support to Freeman and Soete's (1997) argument that a combination of pressure including ENGO and consumer pressure can, together with command and control regulation, promote sustainable innovations within corporations. The notion of industry self-regulation has been popularized by increased free trade and the globalization of capital. The basic corporate argument for industry self-regulation suggests that the old mentality of short-term gain at the expense of long-term protection has reached its limits, turning the fears of degradation into current realities, especially for companies requiring dwindling natural resources for their operations (Escobar, 1996). Rondinelli and Berry (2000) believe the greening of corporations represents a move towards the ethical behaviour of a company towards its society. They define corporate citizenship 'as practices that meet a company's responsibilities to its stakeholders, including employees, shareholders, customers and suppliers as well as to the communities in which it is located' (Rondinelli and Berry, 2000, p. 73). Many organizations can see immediate and direct business benefits from proactive environmental management in the form of lower costs, less risks and liabilities and more efficient operations (Rondinelli and Berry, 2000). Business for Social Responsibility (1998) points out that public demands for enforcement of regulations and for increased disclosure by investors, regulators and public interest groups have also played a strong role in increasing corporations' sensitivity to their social responsibilities.

In the case of Juneau, the ENGO, namely Oceana and the Earth Island Institute, was very effective in targeting cruise ship consumers and local citizens regarding their environmental concerns. A loss in consumer respect (reputational capital) can lead to a huge loss in profits. As Sonnenfeld and Mol (2002, p. 1324) observe, 'Most economic actors have to be put under pressure before "voluntarily" contributing to environmental improvements.' According to a representative of NWCL (18 March 2002, personal communication), cruise corporations claim they can see the new relationships being formed between the environment, their reputation, their customers, their stakeholders, their comparative advantage and their profits. Further, to avoid being accused of violating their own environmental regulations, cruise companies strive to exceed their own voluntary guidelines. The pressures placed on the industry in Juneau, by ENGO activism, the media and consumers – and subsequently by legislation – stimulated the cruise industry to introduce self-regulation that demonstrated beyond compliance behaviour. The development of industry policies by ICCL and NWCA for all of North America followed, which establish proper procedures for cruise ship dumping with regulations that either match or exceed the highest legislation in the North American market.

Further, the industry also responded to the situation in Juneau by developing innovative technology in the form of advanced on-board wastewater treatment facilities. The new innovative technology was arguably developed as an indirect response to the happenings in Juneau, but as Freeman and Soete (1997, p. 201) point out: 'Necessity maybe the mother of invention, but procreation still requires a partner'. Once legislation has been set, beyond compliance behaviour can have marketing, reputation and economic value. While costly to install, the new technology does reflects a commitment to environmental compliance while undoubtedly anticipating that the investment is worthwhile. Other market-based mechanisms that the cruise industry has implemented in various global markets to 'voluntarily' respond to environmental concerns include best practice management, eco-labelling and green marketing.

As with Juneau, in the case of Sydney, early concern for the environmental quality of the harbour was brought to the publics' attention through the efforts of ENGOs. However, these concerns were generic and not focused specifically on the cruise industry but rather shipping and the health of Sydney Harbour in general. A representative of Sydney Waterways feels Ian Kiernan's Clean Up the Harbour campaign was the catalyst that brought the issue over the environmental health of the harbour to the attention of Sydney's citizens (Sydney Waterways, 24 April 2003, personal communication). Thus, there were no focusing events that created neg-

ative emotions towards the cruise industry or placed specific pressure on it to change. This could be a factor of the size of the city and the relative importance of the cruise sector to the overall economy of Sydney. Compared to Juneau, where the cruise industry is the major economic activity and has a significant physical and social presence in the community, in Sydney its influence is dwarfed by other shipping activity in the harbour.

The main difference between the two case studies is that the introduction of command and control regulation in Juneau stimulated industry response to go beyond compliance, whereas the reverse is true in Sydney. There is a frustration expressed by the shipping agents towards Sydney's no-discharge policy. A shipping agent organizes a ship's entry into port and informs them of the laws and regulations they must adhere to in and around the port. In essence, the shipping agents are the mediators between the ships and the government. While regulations in Sydney meet international standards for environmental control they are seen to stifle innovation and discourage beyond compliance behaviour (Barwil Shipping Agency, 4 April 2003, personal communication). The Barwil Shipping representative (4 April 2003, personal communication) commented that there are no incentives given by the port to ships for beyond compliance behaviour and although some ships have the newest technologies, they cannot use them. In Juneau, cruise vessels with the state-of-the-art wastewater systems are certified to discharge continuously. In Sydney, those same vessels are not exempt from the zero discharge rule that applies to Sydney Harbour.

Sydney Ports' argument for disallowing continuous discharge from the advanced wastewater systems is that the new treatment systems, despite their ability to turn sewage and grey water into near drinking water quality, produce excess nutrients (Sydney Waterways, 24 April 2003, personal communication). As a result it has held on to its no-discharge policy in port regardless of the lack of monitoring presently occurring (Barwil Shipping Agency, 4 April 2003, personal communication). The new systems cannot be used in Australia and has become a financial liability, because ships with this new technology not only must cover the cost of installing and operating the system but must also pay for sewage disposal.

Consequently, cruise companies have been deploying older ships with the older technology to Australia. Arguably receiving the older ships poses more of an environmental hazard than simply sewage disposal. The shipping companies feel that Australia's stubbornness towards change is actually posing a degree of harm to the environment that has not as yet drawn the attention of ENGOs (Barwil Shipping Agency, 4 April 2003, personal communication).

Conclusions

Much debate still exists surrounding what type of policy and mix of policy mechanisms will invoke environmentally responsible behaviour and stimulate science and technological innovations (Furger, 1997; Gunningham and Rees, 1997; Sinclair, 1997). Many feel that the current neo-liberalism era requires strong command and control regulations to limit the footloose and fancy-free behaviour of corporations (Schmidt, 2000; Klein, 2002). Others feel that regulation stifles innovation and advocates for less regulation and more industry self-regulation (Gunningham and Rees, 1997; Rondinelli and Berry, 2000). There is no doubt that there is a growing trend in environmental policymaking in many locations to leave corporations to respond to market mechanisms (Furger, 1997; Gunningham and Rees, 1997).

Global variability with respect to environmental stewardship within the cruise industry has raised questions over the degree of concern held for the environment and the overall effectiveness of industry self-regulation. Unfortunately, as ENGOs often claim, the voluntary nature of the self-imposed regulation is weak and does not solve the credibility issues with the cruise industry. The cruise industry has been caught and charged, on several occasions, with deliberate illegal discharges of sewage and bilge water into the marine environment (Klein, 2002). As a representative of Earth Island Institute observed, some ENGOs claim this confirms that cruise companies are convicted felons and as such should not be trusted to self-regulate (Earth Island Institute, 4 July 2003, personal communication). Further, as in

the case of Australia, cruise companies have not been deploying their state-of-the-art ships to all their markets. This can be explained on the basis of regulatory constraints that lead to additional costs for the cruise lines if ships with newer technology are used. However, this together with the fact that new ships are currently being built without the advanced wastewater systems, has led to speculation, especially in the ENGO community, concerning the degree of commitment that the cruise industry really has towards good environmental management. It would appear that cruise ships have developed efficient voluntary regulations for their activities in locations with institutions advocating for environmental awareness (such as the British Columbia–Alaska route), however deploy their older ships with less advanced technology to locations without institutions pressuring for increased environmental accountability (Barwil Shipping Agency, 4 April 2003, personal communication).

This reality brings the corporate mindset under scrutiny and makes command and control mechanisms more necessary in some locations than others. However, self-regulations may be the only 'real' option available to some destinations as a regulatory requirement is only as strong as its monitoring and enforcement and many destinations do not have adequate resources to enforce regulations even if they are legislated. Some ENGOs and suprana-tionals have challenged both industry and government's ability to regulate the cruise industry and have turned to certification programme efforts for third party monitoring. The International Standards Organization (ISO) 14000 series is the most notable example of certification effort. ISO has incorporated environmental management systems into a wide variety of corporations and organizations including cruise ships. These standards serve a double purpose of pressuring corporations to incorporate environmental standards to demonstrate compliance, and conversely as a marketing strategy for corporations to earn comparative advantage (Prakash, 2000). Voluntary third party certification for the cruise industry is in its infancy, but with more time and effort, it could be a valuable policy instrument for increased monitoring and enforcement.

In conclusion, there does not appear to be a universal solution that adequately promotes effective and efficient environmental policymaking in the cruise sector for all locations. It is not necessarily a matter of command and control versus self-regulation (Sinclair, 1997). As demonstrated in the examples presented, the mix of environmental policy options that a place selects will reflect the geographical essence of that place, including not only environmental character but also social, political, economic, historical and cultural attributes. These findings support Sinclair's (1997) argument that a preferred solution is to employ a number of 'regulatory variables' to 'fine-tune' regulatory options to suit the specific circumstances of particular environmental issues – and we would add, 'places'. Future environmental policy approaches, cannot be ones that attempt to reverse the market changes that have taken place or that the cruise industry functions within. We believe government intervention and regulation of environmental policy in the cruise industry should be more pragmatic and place emphasis on the values inherent in industry self-regulation, local knowledge, certification and innovation.

References

Alaska Department of Environmental Conservation (2004) Commercial passenger vessel environmental compliance program: frequently asked questions. Available at: http://www.state.ak.us/dec/water/cruise_ships/pdfs/cruisefaqs.pdf

AMSA: Port Reform and the National Plan (1998) Thompson Clarke Shipping, Sydney, Australia.

Beder, S. (1997) *Global Spin: The Corporate Assault on Environmentalism*. Scribe Publishing, Australia.

Business for Social Responsibility (1998) Available at: http://www.bsr.org/

Clean Up Australia Online (2004) About us: the clean up story. Available at: http://www.cleanup.com.au

Dobson, S. (2006) Place, institutions and the environmental policy-making process: a comparative analysis of the Australian, Canadian and, American Pacific cruise ship industry. PhD thesis, Simon Fraser University, Burnaby, British Columbia, Canada (in press).

European Environment Agency (2004) EEA multilingual environmental glossary. Available at: http://glossary.eea.eu.int/EEAGlossary/C/command-and-control

Escobar, A. (1996) Constructing nature: elements for a poststructural political ecology. In: Peet, R. and Watts, M. (eds) *Liberation Ecologies: Environment,* *Development, Social Movements*. Routledge, London, pp. 46–69.

Freeman, C. and Soete, L. (1997) *The Economics of Industrial Innovation*, 3rd edn. MIT Press, Cambridge, Massachusetts.

Furger, F. (1997) Accountability and systems of self-governance: the case of the maritime industry. *Law and Policy* 19(4), 445–472.

General Accounting Office of the United States (2000) Marine pollution: progress made to reduce marine pollution by cruise ships, but important issues remain. Report to Congressional Requesters. Washington, DC.

Gunningham, N. and Rees, J. (1997) Industry self-regulation: an institutional perspective. *Law and Policy* 19(4), 363–409.

ICCL (International Council of Cruise Lines) (2003) ICCL Industry Standard E-01-01 (Revision 2): cruise industry waste management practices and procedures. Available at: http://www.iccl.org/policies/environmentalstandards.pdf

Klein, R. (2002) *Cruise Ship Blues: The Underside of the Cruise Industry*. New Society Publishers, Gabriola Island, British Columbia.

Luke, T. (1997) *Ecocritique*. University of Minnesota Press, Minneapolis, Minnesota.

Palmer, S. (1999) Current port trends in an historical perspective. *Journal of Maritime Research* (online journal). Available at: http://www.jmr.nmm.ac.uk/index.php

Prakash, A. (2000) Greening the firm: the politics of corporate environmentalism. In: *Academy of Management Review*. Cambridge University Press, Cambridge, pp. 3–9.

Rondinelli, D.A. and Berry, M.A. (2000) Environmental citizenship in multinational corporations: social responsibility and sustainable development. *European Management Journal* 18(1), 70–84.

Schmidt, K. (2000) *Cruising for Trouble: Stemming the Tide of Cruise Ship Pollution*. Bluewater Network, California. Available at: http://www.bluewaternetwork.org/reports/rep_ss_cruise_trouble.pdf

Sonnenfeld, D.A. and Mol, A.P.J. (2002) Globalization and the transformation of environmental governance: an introduction. *American Behavioral Scientist* 45(9), 1318–1339.

Sinclair, D. (1997) State-regulation versus command and control? Beyond false dichotomies. *Law and Policy* 19(4), 529–555.

Steger, U. (1993) The greening of the board room: how German companies are dealing with environmental issues. In: Fisher, K. and Schot, J. (eds) *Environmental Strategies for Industry: International Perspectives on Research Needs and Policy Implications*. Island Press, Washington, DC, pp. 47–159.

Sustainable Development Networking Programme (2005) *MARPOL Optional Annex Annex IV: Regula-*

tions for the Prevention of Pollution by Sewage from Ships. Available at: http://www.sdnpbd.org/sdi/treaty/oceans_their_living_resources/ww173.htm

Waterways Authority (2003) Background on environmental services. Avaiable at: http://www.waterways.nsw.gov.au/hbrcleanhist.html

WTO (World Tourism Organization) (2001) Tourism statistics. Available at: http://www.worldtourism.org/newsroom/Bulletin/more_bulletin/B010500.html

US Environmental Protection Agency (2004) Cruise ship water discharges. Available at: http://www.epa.gov/owow/oceans/cruise_ships/

32 Cozumel: The Challenges of Cruise Tourism

Helle Sorensen

Metropolitan State College, Department of Hospitality, Meeting, and Travel Administration, Campus Box 60, PO Box 173362, Denver, CO 80217,USA

In travel guidebooks of the 1950s there was no mention of Cozumel Island, which lies 19 km off the Yucatan Peninsula in Mexico. Since Jacques Cousteau discovered the underwater wonders of the reefs off the west coast of Cozumel and filmed a documentary in 1961, Cozumel has been very popular among divers. The island has also evolved as one of the most visited cruise destinations in the Caribbean. The challenges of a small island evolving from a little-use dive destination to a heavy-use cruise destination are substantial. Onsite qualitative fieldwork and quantitative research suggest that Cozumel's exploding cruise tourism only fractionally benefits the island. Therefore, the cruise growth is engulfed in controversy. Three controversial issues stand out:

1. The construction of cruise ship piers. Figure 32.1 shows Cozumel's oldest cruise pier on the northern tip of Paradise Reef. A second pier was constructed even closer to Paradise Reef. Pier opposition contends that this pier was built so close to Paradise Reef that the coral ecosystem suffers serious stress (CEC, 1997). While this debate was still hot on the table, the plan for a third pier in the same area was underway.
2. Cozumel's exponential growth of cruise tourism. Within a short period of 10 years, the number of cruise tourist arrivals increased from 743,965 in 1993 to 2,708,913 in 2003 (MGTO, 2000; CTO, 2004). The challenge is the management of this 264% growth.

3. The economic life in Cozumel, where foreign cruise lines control the island's cruise tourism.

This chapter examines these issues of a domineering core's creation of cruise tourism on a small peripheral island.

Methodology

Inadequate longitudinal Cozumel tourism data makes it difficult to measure change over time. Illustrating what Cozumel was like in the 1960s (before cruise tourism) and the types of changes that have occurred later is therefore a challenge. It is equally difficult to pinpoint which changes are caused by cruise tourism, because impacts may not be fully evident for several years after completion of the last two piers. In an attempt to conduct retrospective research, qualitative methods of participant-observation and semi-structured interviews were conducted in Cozumel in December 2000, January 2001 and June 2004. Dive shop owners, local residents, tourists and divers were asked to volunteer to participate. Two key informants were identified from the diving community and local residents. The observations took place specifically in the area of the cruise ship piers and during a cruise to Cozumel on a major cruise line. Semistructured

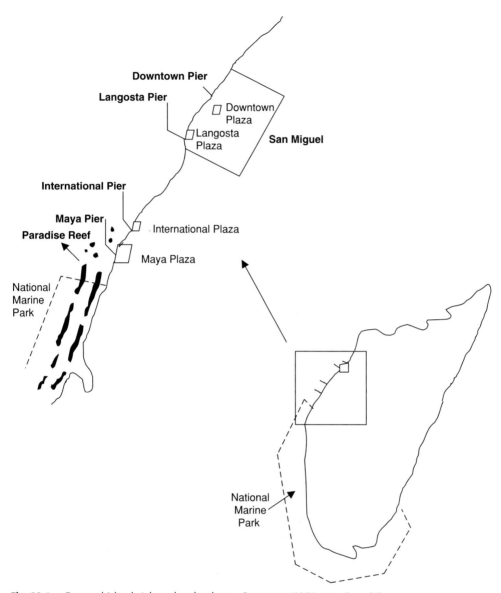

Fig. 32.1.   Cozumel Island. Adapted and redrawn: Semarnap (1996, map 3, p. 14).

interviews allowed the informants to speak spontaneously, while keeping some structure in the interview. Identities of persons are omitted, and anonymity is secured through a coding system. The first tourist interviewed is assigned the code TOU1, a second dive interviewee DIV2 and a third local person LOC3.

Maya Pier Project

Since Cousteau's popularization of Cozumel diving in the early 1960s, divers have explored the enormous wealth of sea life inhabiting Cozumel's 20 coral reefs. Jacques Cousteau named this 50-km long island as one of the top diving spots in the world. In the 1960s, many local people participated in tourist activities. For example, fishermen allowed tourists to join them at night in catching crabs (Davies, 1969), and Casa Denis was the only restaurant in San Miguel (LOC4). Another long-time tourism participant is the owner of a jewellery shop (LOC1). This Cozumel native has made jewellery and figurines since the early 1960s.

Cozumel has evolved as one of the most popular cruise destinations in the Caribbean. LOC4 explains that the addition of Cozumel as a cruise destination in 1968 was a major turning point in the island's tourism history. As can be seen in Fig. 32.1, Cozumel has four piers. Ferries use the Downtown Pier to transport passengers between Cozumel and mainland Mexico. Three cruise ship piers are within a few miles south of the Downtown Pier. The oldest International Pier outgrew its capacity by the late 1980s, so the Maya Pier was constructed and completed in 1998 (Burkett, 1998). The Langosta Pier was completed 6 months later in early 1999 (LOC4, LOC6, LOC7).

Cozumel's rapid cruise development could not have happened without the investments of the core area of Mexico. According to the core/periphery concept, the core is in the centre of a geographical area surrounded by peripheries (Greenberg and Park, 1994). Rural areas are the peripheries that depend on the core for economic development. On the other hand, core areas are often accused of exercising too much control over their peripheries. This can be seen in the case of Cozumel that is on the periphery of Mexico. Since the Mexican government has more power than state and municipal governments (Merino, 1987), coastal developments and control over coastal resources have been exercised by federal agencies.

Cozumel's cruise growth can be attributed to Mexico's 1989–1994 tourism plan. This plan reflected the core's need to control tourism developments and modernize existing peripheral tourism areas (Casado, 1997). The core also sought to provide jobs and disperse the flow of workers throughout the peripheries. In 1994, the Mexican government contracted Consortium H to construct the Maya Pier and Maya Plaza, complete with a terminal, access road, shops and restaurants. This construction endeavour was named the Maya Pier Project

(CEC, 1997). The proposed site received considerable international attention, because 'Paradise Reef used to extend much farther than its present encompassing state. The first pier (International Pier) was built off the northern tip of the reef, and as a likely result, the coral below it died' (Marx, 1997). Figure 32.1 shows that the 550-m Maya Pier cuts through the first ridge of Paradise Reef, even though the 1989–1994 tourism plan emphasized preservation of natural resources (Casado, 1997).

Pier opposition contends that the Maya Pier was built so close to Paradise Reef that the delicate coral ecosystem suffers serious stress (CEC, 1997). Jacques Cousteau's son, Jean-Michel, raised awareness of the Paradise Reef issue when it was declared 'dead' by Mexico's National Institute of Ecology in order to justify the construction (Cousteau, 1996). The University of Wisconsin contradicted the claim that Paradise Reef was 'dead' with a study that found 30 species of hard coral in this thriving near-shore fringe reef (Burkett, 1998). This healthy and living reef boasts '83% of the hard coral species typically found in the waters off the coast of Cozumel' (Burkett, 1998). DOP2 further explained:

> Somebody was sent by a person from an office in Mexico City. That person took pictures of dead coral, of a really deserted area and said, 'here are pictures of the area where the pier is going to be built. Nothing is going to get hurt.' Of course, people in Mexico City don't know anything about the way our underwater environment works.

Three non-governmental organizations (NGOs) presented this pier controversy to North American Free Trade Agreement's (NAFTA) Commission for Environmental Coorperation (CEC) in 1996. CEC monitors ecological protection in the member nations of Mexico, Canada and the USA. Part of CEC's mission is to ensure that the three governments live up to their own environmental laws (Marx, 1997). The NGOs claimed that the primary goal of ecological balance was disregarded in the permitting process because of the failure to file a required Environmental Impact Assessment (EIA) that would examine the effects of the *entire* pier construction project (CEC, 1997). The Secretariat of Environment, Natural Resources and Fisheries (Semarnap) criticized the NGOs for only *assuming* the pier would cause reef damage and for not providing any proof of actual damage (Semarnap, 1996). Semarnap further criticized the NGOs for only presenting their claim to international organizations such as NAFTA and not to regional or national courts. The dilemma with both NAFTA and CEC is that they cannot enforce environmental law but can only promote environmental protection and conservation.

Consortium H insisted that the Maya Pier would cause no damage because the proposed site was devoid of reefs. However, Fig. 32.1 clearly shows the pier between two coral patches. When Consortium H later claimed that the pier would hurt less than 3% of the 180-m wide reef, the Mexican government required Consortium H to institute a Species Rescue Programme. Under this programme, 24,000 organisms and 30 coral aggregations were transplanted into similar environments along Paradise Reef (Semarnap, 1996). The flora and fauna that was attached to the marine floor were 'cemented onto 34 reinforced concrete structures' (Semarnap, 1996, p. 36). Semarnap considers the transplantation a success, with a less than 10% mortality rate. However, cruise lines were not informed about the Species Rescue Programme and destroyed the unmarked reef area (Marx, 1997). Consortium H was also required to institute a Continuous Monitoring Programme between 1996 and 2000 with the purpose of monitoring the overall health of Paradise Reef. Semarnap (1996, p. 37) insists that a 'suitable construction method' has 'effectively mitigated' impacts by the Maya Pier construction.

When applying the core/periphery concept on a larger global scale, the core of Mexico can also be considered a periphery of the USA. Mexico's cruise developments in Cozumel heavily depend upon the investments and needs of the US core and the growing popularity of the cruise product in the USA. This has led to the USA dominating Mexico's cruise tourism. In Cozumel, it is a common knowledge that Carnival Cruise Lines, the largest cruise line in the USA, has owned and operated the Maya Pier since 2002 (LOC4, LOC5, LOC6, LOC7). This gave Carnival Cruise Lines priority docking. This domination has escalated into control over the Maya Plaza. According to the locals, Carnival

Cruise Lines owns the plaza. All the Maya Plaza stores and restaurants rent their space from Carnival Cruise Lines. The third Langosta Pier was constructed by San Miguel almost simultaneously with the Maya Pier.

Impact on Reef Ecosystem

Cozumel's main attraction has always been its beautiful reefs. Paradise Reef is world famous for its abundant marine life. The Mexican Constitution states that coasts and beaches, which cover a width of 20 m, are the public property of Mexico and therefore cannot be purchased or owned (Merino, 1987). The reefs from the Downtown Pier to the southernmost point of Cozumel entered federal protection in 1980, which means commercial fishing, undersea sports fishing and commercial coral collection were prohibited. The proposed Maya Pier site was within this zone (CEC, 1997). The Mexican government declared the protected zone as a National Marine Park in 1996. Since Mexican law also states that Mexico has control over marine resources, the government used its power over peripheral Cozumel to move the limits of the marine park south of the proposed site before the pier was constructed. Figure 32.1 illustrates the new boundaries of the National Marine Park, which covers approximately 85% of Cozumel's dive sites. DOP2 explains all piers are outside the park because:

> The damage from the cruise ships is very visible. The crew would throw in their lines as soon as they got to the dock and fishing in a national park. Even when the pier was within the national park, nobody did anything about it. No one said anything to the crew about fishing within a national park. Around 1993 there was trash and fishing lines everywhere from the cruise ships.

Paradise Reef is the closest reef to San Miguel and is therefore the most frequented by divers. This is also the most trafficked reef, because boats ply its waters on the way to other reefs. This constant dive boat traffic makes protection of Paradise Reef a challenge because the 1-km long Paradise Reef is in shallow water. DOP2 seems convinced that coastal protection is questionable:

. . . whether we want it or not, and the people are, like, 'No, we don't want it'. But the last thing I heard was that if we want it or not, it is going to be built. That's the way people are here. We fight, we jump, we scream, and at the end we just shut up. Because it's like any place. Money talks. That's the way it is, and it's very scary.

The controversy did receive extensive international media attention for a few years. Jean-Michel Cousteau, Coral Reef Alliance and Greenpeace were among the voices on behalf of Cozumel. After the construction was partially completed, few voices were expressed, media attention disappeared, and research evaporated. It is possible that the supreme power of the Mexican president became evident, as expressed by Merino (1987, p. 40): 'bribes have contravened many . . . protection measures. Many resources involving programmes and plans have been diverted in order to justify personal or group interests.'

Indeed, the government may have justified their own self-interest by moving the park limits. The new limits may also have interfered with marine life. DOP1 insists that the behavioural pattern of the shark changed and its habitat disrupted: 'the Caribbean reef shark used to be seen everywhere at a depth of 24 m, but now it can be seen only at 30–35 m'. The pier may also impact the reef storm barrier that protects the shoreline from erosion and provides ships with safe harbour (Marx, 1997). Intensive tourism development in a previously tranquil coastal area can cause irreversible damage to a thriving coral reef. Coral is a delicate ecosystem that does not have the ability to recover from major damage. For example, cruise ship anchors may dislodge chunks of coral heads every time they are pulled back up. Coral is a slow-growing organism that takes many years to recover from excessive damage. One of the worst impacts of a pier is the blocking out of sunlight, because solar energy powers these ecosystems. Marx (1997, p. 15) argues that Paradise Reef shows 'signs of potential decline in reef health' while Semarnap (1996) insists that Paradise Reef is in excellent health due to a strong south-to-north current. The reefs off the west coast of Cozumel are part of the Belizean Reef system, the second largest reef in the world. This reef system stretches from the northern tip of the Yucatan Peninsula to Honduras.

An example of US core domination over peripheral Mexico is Cozumel's catamaran and cattle boat businesses. A catamaran is a 140-passenger snorkelling boat. Most catamarans belong to cruise lines from the USA. A major US cruise line that averages 11 dockings in Cozumel each week year-round offers three catamaran trips per ship per day. The cattle boat is a 40-passenger dive boat. DOP2 explained the difficulty in managing 40 divers, because beginners linger at the surface and advanced divers go to the bottom immediately. DOP2 is a small-scale local operator with six passenger boats. The latest *snuba* idea (a combination of *snorkel* and *scuba*) is promoted by the cruise lines and has become quite popular. A snuba programme takes uncertified, and hence inexperienced, people on brief diving trips. The catamarans and cattle boats are owned by the cruise lines and these excursions are arranged by the ships without the use of local operators. The dilemma is that Paradise Reef is ideal for novice divers, because of its light to moderate currents and easy accessibility.

Catamarans and cattle boats do not have the permission to enter the marine park (DOP2). Instead, they go to the closest and most abused Paradise Reef. Reef damage near the cruise ships is greatest because of a high volume of divers and 'the cruise passengers are the worst divers, they are the most destructive' (DIV1). However, it could be argued that these 'destructive' divers wreck one small area that has little interest to the serious diver. If reef damage can be confined to Paradise Reef, the remainder of Cozumel's reefs may be saved from excessive damage. Experienced divers avoid Paradise Reef anyway, because 'you don't want a crowd. You don't want a bunch of people around you. You're not there to see other divers. You're there to see the coral and the invertebrates' (DIV1).

Impact on Cozumel Culture

Cozumel's divorce from its original cultural environment attracts the mass-market cruise tourists. For example, Señor Frogs is one of the first establishments that greets cruise tourists as they disembark the ship. DOP2 explained the altered culture:

While working on this pier I have influenced the tourism in that cruises bring a lot of people. The people aren't here to get really close to the culture. It is somehow affecting the way of living, like transportation. When we have cruise ships in town, taxi drivers only want to take people that are going to pay with dollars rather than taking people that live here and because we pay in pesos. But people on the cruise ship usually get ripped off. And people get ticked off because they will be waiting for transportation and the taxi drivers will just be waiting there for the people with the money to get off the cruise ship. The culture around the piers is affected.

Population growth also attests to a transformed culture. Most of Cozumel's population lives in San Miguel, the only town on the island. The population explosion from 3000 in 1965 to 75,000 in 2003 (LOC4) 'is due to cruise ship workers and hotel workers from Mexico City. And cruise workers' families live here, because cruise ships dock here longer than anywhere else' (LOC1). Discontent with this population boom is expressed by LOC1, because he has seen some local businesses being replaced by outside competition: '[. . .] didn't make it. He had language problems. He couldn't communicate well with his dive customers. Competition drove him out. I don't know where he is.' Shops have also attracted non-Cozumel workers: 'I moved here 15 years ago from Mexico City and moved my family here a few years later. It's safe here, a much nicer place to be, no crime, no pollution' (LOC5).

The staggering growth of cruise ship arrivals has affected Cozumel culture the most.

Figure 32.2 shows Thursday as the day in the week with the highest concentration of ships. On Thursdays, eight cruise ships dock during the high season period between November and April. Two ships dock in the May–October low season. With three piers accommodating two ships each, two ships cannot dock on high season Thursdays. Two ships anchor by San Miguel or Paradise Reef and tender its passengers to the piers. Additionally, on Wednesdays and Fridays the piers are filled to near capacity. Cozumel receives cruise ships every day all year-round, except Sunday, receiving very little relief from the crowds in San Miguel. The problem with crowding is exacerbated by San Miguel's narrow cobblestone sidewalks with large sales signs and sharply dressed sales people in front of the stores. TOU1 has noticed the crowds:

> Where are you going to walk? It's not big enough for this many people. There just didn't used to be as many people around. They didn't used to have a stoplight. They certainly didn't have an oriental rug store. There was no need for it, and I don't know that there is now. I don't understand how there are even eight ships in here with all those passengers.

Cozumel went from no cruise tourists in 1965 to receiving 55,542 cruisers in 1975, which increased to 484,486 in 1985 (Lawton and Butler, 1987). This cruise growth continued at an exponential rate to 2,708,913 in 2003 (CTO, 2004). With an average of 50,500 cruise tourists flooding San Miguel each week

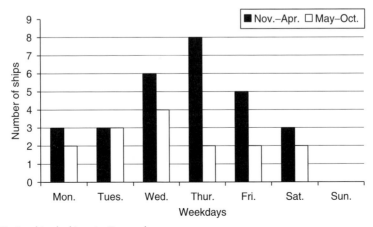

Fig. 32.2. Cruise ship dockings in Cozumel.

year-round, this small area is overstressed. Figure 32.3 shows that each Thursday year-round, San Miguel gets invaded by about 19,000 cruise tourists. Cruise interviews revealed that shopping, convenience and low-cost vacation were a priority among the passengers. With over 2.7 million cruise tourists annually, TOU1 expressed:

> I can't stand to be downtown. It's so crowded. They're stepping on you. You can't walk comfortably. It's just too crowded down there. And there is a lot more of aggressive salesmen. I've never faced that before. Not here.

The counterargument of Cozumel's cruise crowds resembles that of the 'destructive' divers. Cruise shoppers are confined to certain shopping areas. The crowd arrives at about the same time in early morning hours. In a few hours, the cruise visitors go for shopping and return to their ships. LOC4 seems to tolerate the crowds: 'there are too many people here but they are only here for a few hours, they leave by 6 pm'. One could ask why capacity is allowed to be exceeded on Thursday and why the arrival of ships is not spread out more evenly throughout the week to include the no-use Sunday. The challenge is that most cruises depart US ports on Saturday afternoon and arrive Cozumel by Thursday morning.

Semarnap (1996) reports that 50% of Cozumel's residents were in favour of the pier. Interviews and observations support Semarnap's statistic. Local people generally agreed that Cozumel receives too many cruise tourists. At the same time, the locals can tolerate the cruise tourists for a few hours, because the cruise tourists are the reason why some of them have a job. A different story can be told of Cozumel's original residents, the Maya Indians. In 2001, some Mayans were selling their handicrafts by the Downtown Plaza. The Mayans spread out their wares on beautiful blankets on the pedestrian street. Today, they are nowhere to be seen. LOC1, LOC4 and LOC6 were convinced that the Mayans have been squeezed out of competition. One is left to ponder how the Mayans now sell their handicrafts, and how they deal with such an altered way of life.

Impact on Cozumel Economy

Mexico seems to have been successful in developing a popular tourism product in Cozumel. Semarnap (1996) reports that 'tourism' is Cozumel's first major industry and employer, followed by 'construction'. Manufacturing and selling of handicrafts and water sports equipment is third. A major turn of events is the appearance of 35 international jewellery stores, most of which line the oceanfront by the Langosta Pier in San Miguel. All these jewellery stores are owned by a man from New York City (LOC1, LOC4). This person opened his first inter-

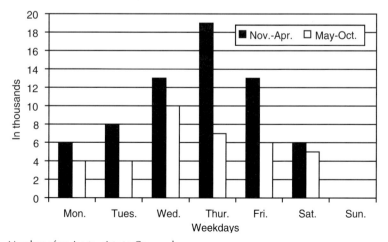

Fig. 32.3.   Number of cruise tourists to Cozumel.

national jewellery store in the mid-1990s in Cozumel. He employs people from all over the world, but especially from Mexico City. This pattern of US ownership and employees having migrated from Mexico City is obvious throughout the international jewellery stores.

The economic leakage, the profits from tourism activities that leave Cozumel, from international jewellery sales is significant. If a cruise visitor spends US$1000 on a diamond necklace, nearly the entire amount leaks out of the local economy, because the store is foreign owned, managed by foreigners and mostly staffed by temporary non-locals. A conversation with an employee attests to this leakage. LOC2 arrived from Mexico City 4 months earlier to make jewellery sales, save money for a university education and return to Mexico City. Since most of LOC2's income will be spent outside Cozumel, not much trickles into the local economy. LOC1 maintains that LOC2 will earn university tuition fast, because jewellery store sales people earn 30% commission. 'They make more money than doctors. They keep offering discounts: 10, 20, 30% off and they still receive 30% commission.'

The international jewellery stores resemble a virtual monopoly over Cozumel's economic life. The monopoly has been created through a US$500 kickback system that is arranged and regulated by the cruise lines (LOC1). Under this system, a store pays US$500 per ship per day in order to get their store promoted on the ship. LOC4 calls the system a form of advertising fee. According to LOC4, each international jewellery store pays US$30,000 per ship per year in advertising fee. In a sales pitch on board the ship, cruise workers direct passengers to certain stores, convincing them of special cruise discounts. Methods of persuasion include a Cozumel travel briefing on board the ship, but the briefing only covers which shops to use. Another method is the distribution of a shopping map that only marks the location of the 35 international jewellery stores. In case the first two methods fail, cruise tourists will eventually stumble across a whole forest of promotional sidewalk signs. LOC1 calls the kickback system a big scam, because all the money goes back to the cruise line. LOC1 does not participate in the programme, and in the eyes of the cruise ships 'I don't exist and I never will'. However, local

businesses do exist. Small jewellery stores, restaurants and souvenir shops are plentiful. None of them participates in the kickback system. One of these businesses is the Casa Denis restaurant, serving Yucatan and Mayan dishes. The current owner's grandfather opened the restaurant in 1945, serving customers in the backyard.

Local businesses compete fiercely with three new pier shopping plazas. Cozumel has four plazas. The Downtown Plaza is an open-air marketplace, filled with local shops and restaurants, such as Casa Denis. There are no international jewellery stores in the Downtown Plaza. Carnival Cruise Lines owns the Maya Plaza that opened in 2003. The plaza's stores and restaurants rent their space from Carnival Cruise Lines. It is clear from Fig. 32.1 that the Maya Plaza is the largest plaza in Cozumel. Maya Plaza resembles a small self-contained village. This open-air plaza is surrounded by a wall and has security guards at two entrance gates. There are 35 shops, seven of which are international jewellery stores. There are three restaurants and bars. The entry into the Maya Plaza leads a cruise tourist past two restaurants and bars before leading to the shops. The point here is that the Maya Plaza seems to be deliberately designed to keep the cruise tourist from venturing into San Miguel. The closest exit gate funnels the cruise tourist through the plaza past the shops. The same can be said about the Langosta and International Plazas, which were opened a few years earlier than the Maya Plaza and are privately owned.

The plazas are clearly designed for the cruise tourist only. The economic leakage from these plazas is obvious. All signs are written in the English language. The restaurants display menus in English with American food items, such as hamburgers and chicken fingers. The prices are the same, or higher, than in the USA. The Maya and International Plazas close when there are no cruise ships. The international jewellery stores in San Miguel close every Sunday, because Cozumel receives no cruise ships on Sundays.

Cozumel does enjoy employment opportunities as one direct economic benefit from cruise tourism. Several local people eagerly described how they worked on the pier construction projects and now work in the stores. As LOC7 explained:

Cozumel has jobs. It's the new place to be. Minimum salary all over Mexico is 800 pesos per week, but in Cozumel you receive good tips because there are many tourists. Some receive commission.

Discussion of Study

This chapter has shown that cruise lines seek to maximize profits and increase passenger numbers with little regard to the wishes of Cozumel. One challenge is the domineering core of the USA over Mexico. This core's short-term interests in cruise sales profits indicate that sustaining Paradise Reef is insignificant. The fact that the reef was claimed dead in order to justify pier construction raises some questions: Should the powerful Mexican government, whose primary driving force is economic gain, be required to take care of their environment? Is it the goal of environmentalists to preserve Paradise Reef to benefit their own diving experiences? Should a change in the Mexican coastal management style be imposed?

It is important to remember that impacts by cruise tourism are challenging to pinpoint, because the relationship between tourism, nature, culture and economics is highly interdependent and complex. Exceptional diving and exciting cruising have provided an alluring environment. Cozumel's unprecedented growth rate is centred around the cruise product, and the economy was quickly dominated by foreign firms. However, cruise tourism occurs within a small area of Cozumel, leaving the rest of the island relatively undisturbed. Therefore, it could be argued that Cozumel manages cruise tourism quite effectively.

Knowing how to manage tourism and its inevitable crowds is exactly the key to success. Developing Cozumel's west coast is not necessarily a 'bad' thing. A seemingly uncontrolled cruise tourism development has brought jobs and prosperity for some, but this development practice does not measure qualitative costs, such as crowding and economic leakage. Perhaps this is the reason why the controversy over Cozumel's piers only received extensive international media attention during the construction stages. The lack of continuing research is striking. After the Maya Pier was completed, debate

abruptly ceased, and a follow-up study of the expected reef damage and impacts by the piers has yet to be done.

If cruise tourism is to continue to flourish in Cozumel, it must continue in a sustainable way. The basic seed corn of Cozumel's tourism industry is the stunning natural environmental quality of the destination. The protection of this environment should be in the interest of business, visitor, local and government, so that coral reef conservation and tourism development can be blended into one effort. The major decision is whether to protect Paradise Reef for future generations or to further develop the coast for today's cruiser. A return to basics, perhaps focusing more on the slower and simpler times, such as the quaint Casa Denis restaurant, may serve to attract the less frenetic tourist. Continuing in the fast-paced and commercial mode of present-day Cozumel, the island's future is questionable.

References

Burkett, E.W. (1998) Quantification of community structure of Paraiso near Shore Fringe Reef. *University of Wisconsin: Caribbean Coral Reef Studies.* Available at: http://www2.uwsuper.edu/ccrs/Projects/Reefkeeper/Reefkeeper_Report.htm

Casado, M.A. (1997) Mexico's 1989–94 tourism plan: implications of internal political and economic instability. *Journal of Travel Research* 36(1), 44–51.

CEC (Commission for Environmental Cooperation) (1997) *Final Factual Record of the Cruise Ship Pier Project in Cozumel, Quintana Roo.* Communications and Public Outreach Department of the CEC Secretariat, Montreal. Available at: http://www.cec.org

Cousteau, J.-M. (1996) Cousteau watch: paradise reef test traders' Ecological scruples. *Planet ENN.* Available at: http://www.enn.com:80/planet enn/090296/feature1.htm

CTO Research Department (2004) Stay over and cruise arrivals in 2003. *Tourism Statistics and Publications.* Caribbean Tourism Organization. Available at: http://www.onecaribbean.org/information/documentview

Davies, H. (1969) Yucatan peninsula. In: Howell, D. (ed.) *The South American Handbook,* 45th edn. Rand McNally, Chicago, Illinois, pp. 807–813.

Greenberg, J.B. and Park, T.K. (1994) Political ecology. *Journal of Political Ecology* 1, 1–8.

Lawton, L.J. and Butler, R.W. (1987) Cruise ship industry – patterns in the Caribbean 1880–1986. *Tourism Management* 8(4), 329–343.

Marx, A. (1997) Cozumel Pier controversy. *Trade and Environmental Database Case Studies: An Online Journal* 7(2). Available at: http://www.american.edu/projects/mandala/TED/cozumel.htm

Merino, M. (1987) The coastal zone of Mexico. *Coastal Management* 15, 27–42.

MGTO (Mexican Government Tourism Office) (2000) Cruise arrivals 1989–1998. *Mexican Government Tourism Office (MGTO)*. Available at: http://www.quicklink.com/mexico/tourism/cruise.htm

Semarnap (Secretariat of Environment, Natural Resources and Fisheries) (1996) *The Cruise Ship Pier in Cozumel*. Secretaria de Medio Ambiente Recursos Naturales y Pesca, Tlalpan, DF (Semarnap).

Part V

Industry Issues

_____

Introduction

In Part IV the industry's interactions with the economic, social and natural environments were explored. Part V investigates a selection of a number of industry issues. They include an examination of the industry in relation to its economic contribution to ports, social issues and problems and theme park reflection. This is followed by two contributions on the globalization and supranationalism of cruise tourism. Finally the book is brought to a close with a brief discussion of the future of the industry.

In Chapter 33, Derek Robbins (England) explores the criteria used for port selection and benefits of cruise tourism for transit ports. He argues that cruise shipping is a valuable source of supplementary income for ports in the UK and this will continue to grow in the future. However, he warns that because of the seasonal nature of the cruise industry together with the increase in its fly–cruise character, cruise shipping cannot become the major economic driver of ports and therefore its potential should not be overstated.

In Chapter 34, Ross Klein (Canada) examines environmental and social issues associated with the cruise industry. He notes that while there are an increasing number of social activists, non-governmental organizations (NGOs) and local initiatives that confront the industry, it appears to be relatively effective in managing the media and influencing legislative processes. Therefore, he argues that in order to keep a sustainability focus on the cruise industry, NGOs and other interest groups will need to be more proactive in their future efforts.

In Chapter 35, Adam Weaver (New Zealand) explores the concept of 'Disneyization' on board certain mega-cruise ships. Weaver outlines the characteristics of such ships as being oriented around specified themes in which service employees are treated as 'emotional labour' where they are expected to shape their own emotions so as to evoke specified emotional responses in customers. Such themes and employee attitudes are purpose-built in order to foster 'dedifferentiated' and merchandized consumption.

Chapters 36 and 37 are contributions by two US authors. In Chapter 36, Robert Wood (New Jersey) suggests that no other industry is more deeply rooted in, and dependent on, globalization processes. He adds that it is almost completely controlled by transnational corporations and that as passengers and crew are global in scope, the ships themselves have become global microcosms. With their potential for being repositioned at any time, they have also become 'deterritorialized', to the extent that the ships are gradually becoming distanced from the sea itself. Following this theme

Dallen Timothy (Arizona) investigates the links between cruises, supranationalism and border complexities in Chapter 37. He describes several geopolitical aspects of the cruise sector, including its political complexities, its comparison to the growth of tourism at international boundaries and the role of cross-border regional cooperation in cruise tourism.

Completing the book is a brief review of the industry and what its future holds.

Silversea Cruises' *Silver Cloud* departing Picton, South Island, New Zealand, January 2005.

33 Cruise Ships in the UK and North European Market: Development Opportunity or Illusion for UK Ports?

Derek Robbins

Bournemouth University, School of Services Management, Fern Barrow, Poole, Dorset BH12 5BB, UK

Introduction

The UK has emerged as a cruise destination for a niche market. Wild and Dearing (2000) suggest that the market is divided evenly between British Isles cruises where the majority of calls are located in Great Britain and other cruises where the principle destination is Northern Europe. Over the last decade cruise capacity in Northern Europe has risen well in excess of global growth rates, and cruise ships are increasingly seen as an opportunity for economic growth. New ports are constantly entering or seeking to enter the market.

- Milford Haven marketed itself from 2001 with the objective of attracting its first calls in 2003 and achieved four cruise ship calls bringing 1900 cruise passengers.
- The Cumbria Tourist Board commissioned cruise a feasibility study in January 2002 using principally Barrow in Furness and Whitehaven. Barrow attracted two cruise ship calls carrying 700 passengers in 2003.
- Poole is the latest port to embark on a feasibility study for cruise ships, linked to an independent project to dredge to 7.5 m.

There has been a long-standing UK cruise industry with departures from turnaround ports such as Southampton and Tilbury for cruises to the Western Mediterranean or to the Norwegian Fjords, which is also a growing market. However, the new entrants are seeking to act as ports of call (also called transit ports and destination ports by some marketing initiatives) either as part of a UK/Western European itinerary or for ships on route further north. The industry is very competitive with many destinations seeking to attract cruise ships, and following initial success year on year growth has proved elusive for many ports in this growing market. This chapter explores the benefits of cruise tourism for transit ports, the competitive pressures and potential barriers to growth.

The World Cruise Market

Growth in passenger numbers

The world cruise market continues to grow (Table 33.1) with the dominant North American market (67% market share) growing at the rate of 8.4% per annum between 1980 and 2003 (CLIA, 2005). The market share of European cruise passengers is now rising with an 11% share of the global market of which the UK accounts for 7.3%.

British tour operators (initially Air tours in 1995 but quickly followed by others) entered the

Table 33.1. Total cruise passenger market ('000).

Year	North America	UK	Rest of Europe	Rest of world	Total
1990	3,640	179	330	345	4,495
1991	3,979	187	354	414	4,980
1992	4,136	219	407	490	5,460
1993	4,480	254	420	467	5,940
1994	4,448	270	502	1,196	6,280
1995	4,378	340	694	1,481	6,440
1996	4,656	416	785	NA	6,850
1997	5,051	522	928	NA	7,580
1998	5,428	663	902	850	8,210
1999	5,894	746	994	1,160	9,067
2000	6,882	754	1,096	NA	10,138
2001	6,906	776	1,205	1,380	10,267
2002	7,640	820	1,296	1,442	11,198
2003	8,195	964	1,709	1,500	12,268

Source: CLIA (2004), PSA (2004), Travel & Tourism Analyst No. 5 (2000), Scottish Tourist Board (1996, unpublished data), Peisley (2003).

cruise market in the mid-1990s. The impact of their entry was to widen the social, economic and age-base of cruise passengers from the UK with a lower cost product. By 1999 the tour operator segment had grown to 275,000 cruise passengers, which was around 35% of the total UK market.

Size and Market Share of Europe as a Destination Market

The European cruise market has seen a decade of steady growth to become the world's second largest destination after the Caribbean. This growth is well above the global average. Europe has attracted cruise capacity from North American operators (Table 33.2) who see Europe as an attractive alternative destination to the overcrowded and heavily discounted Caribbean.

With few exceptions (such as the Atlantic Islands) Europe is very seasonal and operates predominantly from April through to October. An analysis of cruise calls to Dover and to Falmouth demonstrates the strength of the seasonality with 44% of cruise calls in July and August.

The impact of a growing European market is clearly felt in the Caribbean where 64% of the annual capacity is offered between October and the following March and only 36% is available between April and September. This also establishes a small market of transatlantic cruises as

ships are repositioned (although some operators such as Cunard still offer a transatlantic itinerary not linked to positional requirements).

Table 33.2 clearly demonstrates the operational decisions made by cruise lines in the wake of 11 September. The Caribbean region which had shown below industry average growth rates since 1989 saw a dramatic 22% increase in capacity in 2002 as US lines redesigned their itineraries, a trend which has since continued. Many of the vessels repositioned in the Caribbean were removed from the Mediterranean that saw a 14% fall in capacity in 2002, although it has now recovered. Interestingly, the same phenomenon did not affect the rest of Europe where capacity continued to grow. This supports findings from primary data indicating that North Europe and certainly the UK was seen as a 'safe' destination by the US market.

This is not the first time that political or security decisions have affected the growth of the industry in the Mediterranean. In 1991 capacity was depressed in the wake of the Kuwait crisis and historically Mediterranean capacity was even more depressed following the highjacking of the Italian cruise ship, *Achille Lauro*, in 1985 by Palestinian terrorists. By 1987 the Mediterranean accounted for a mere 841,051 bednights or 4.1% of global capacity placing it behind Alaska, Mexico and Bermuda amongst others, and recovery was not fully achieved until the 1990s. These variations clearly demonstrate the volatility of the fly–

Table 33.2. Cruise capacity for selected destinations (CLIA members) bednights.

Destination	1989 Nights ('000)	%	1995 Nights ('000)	%	2001 Nights ('000)	%	2002 Nights ('000)	%	2004 Nights ('000)	%
Caribbean	10,982	44.5	15,245	42.8	21,833	36.6	26,741	42.1	32,210	45.1
Alaska	1,598	6.5	3,008	8.4	4,698	7.9	5053	8.0	5,913	7.7
Mediterranean	1,879	7.6	3,447	9.7	7546	12.7	6,497	10.2	8,704	12.6
North Europe	774	3.1	1,582	4.4	4,837	8.1	6,932	10.9	7,580	9.8
Transatlantic	407	1.6	658	1.8	1,129	1.9	1,006	1.6	1,425	1.8

Source: CLIA (2005).

cruise American market to parts of Europe, most particularly the Mediterranean.

Cruise itineraries from the UK to the western Mediterranean inevitably involve a longer cruise of 10–14 days and therefore cruise passengers to the Mediterranean from the UK are dominated by fly–cruises. Nevertheless, the ex UK market to the Mediterranean has shown strong growth and represents an opportunity for turnaround ports (Table 33.3). The UK's largest port of embarkation is Southampton (480,000 passengers in 2003) followed by Dover (over 130,000 cruise passengers) and Harwich (nearly 100,000).

Northern Europe

The generic description of North Europe as a destination incorporates a number of different markets. These can broadly be defined as: (i) the Baltic; (ii) Norway (including the Fjords), Northern Europe (the Faroe Islands and Iceland); and (iii) UK/Western Europe including round UK cruises. There is no accurate data to estimate the number of cruises in Northern Europe. Table 33.3 shows a UK market of approximately 140,000 cruise passengers in 2003 (including fly–cruises to Scandinavia/Baltic) but accurate figures do not exist for all source markets. The

Table 33.3. British cruise passengers.

	1996	1997	1998	1999	2000	2001	2002	2003
UK port cruises								
Mediterranean	40,512	42,600	60,338	37,854	45,290	52,253	70,061	75,158
Atlantic Islands	25,354	23,483	21,561	28,229	36,996	43,257	35,945	43,878
Norway	16,317	19,595	21,146	22,376	26,652	31,307	29,932	37,634
UK–Western Europe	6,704	9,242	20,009	12,877	25,246	27,226	29,659	53,157
Baltic	7,797	14,779	15,997	23,348	18,813	24,650	25,733	36,380
Caribbean (positioning)	5,473	4,082	6,324	5,688	9,156	6,506	9,250	8,549
Other	10,594	7,953	8,221	10,346	11,195	960	2,963	2,609
Charter	10,594	7,953	8,221	10,346	11,195	15,755	8,884	13,564
Total UK cruise	117,923	126,259	166,187	143,901	177,167	201,914	212,967	270,929
Fly–cruises (selected)								
Caribbean/ Bahamas	90,568	115,914	160,204	143,401	141,163	138,957	162,362	179,380
Mediterranean	132,904	200,212	225,687	332,644	288,800	318,000	320,000	334,475
Atlantic Islands	NA	NA	18,606	38,913	26,370	33,824	37,192	41,203
Scandinavia/ Baltic	11,889	8,748	8,432	9,467	14,450	14,598	15,042	15,989
Total fly–cruise	283,795	381,090	483,651	589,668	561,494	558,872	597,637	683,470
Total	416,106	521,559	663,210	746,243	754,416	776,173	822,770	963,580

Source: PSA (2004).

North American market was estimated at 300,000 cruises in 2000 (Wild, 2001a).

UK ports can be included on itineraries for Norway or the Baltic for cruises from UK or Western Europe as well as the relatively small, round UK and Ireland cruises or Western Europe itineraries. Incomplete data for 40 UK ports collected by the Passenger Shipping Association (PSA) showed a total of 227,000 passengers calling at UK ports (PSA, 2004).

Prospects for Continued Growth

Cruise companies and commentators forecast continued growth despite recent difficult trading conditions. Admittedly forecasters have downsized their forecasts in the aftermath of 11 September with Peisley (2003) now forecasting 17 million cruise passengers globally by 2010, replacing the initial forecast of 20 million.

Market penetration of cruise holidays

The starting point for the bullish and optimistic forecasts remains the large untapped market of customers who desire to undertake a cruise, can potentially afford to take a cruise but who currently have not done so. CLIA data show that 15% of US citizens have ever taken a cruise (CLIA, 2004).

Market penetration in the USA appears to cover a wide social and economic spectrum (Fig. 33.1). Cruises between 2- and 5-day duration are the fastest growing segment (Table 33.4), which has attracted some lower income households to cruising.

CLIA undertakes a large-scale market profile survey of the target population within the US population to measure the future potential for cruise growth. It shows that 50% of the target audience are interested in cruising in the next 5 years, of which 31% say they 'will definitely/probably cruise', which indicates a strong pool of untapped demand (CLIA, 2004). The CLIA clearly asks hypothetical questions and to that extent the data should be treated with some caution.

Similar arguments apply to the European market where 13% of UK residents have taken a cruise (Mintel, 2003). There was a similar trend

towards shorter cruises, which peaked at 18% of all cruises until the dramatic fall from 2001 (Table 33.5).

Increases in cruise ship capacity

Whilst increases in capacity of the cruise fleet have slowed with 5 of the 37 new vessels on order in 2002 delayed or deferred (Mintel, 2003) and only one order for a new vessel has been placed as a result of 11 September (Peisley, 2003), nevertheless around 38 vessels are scheduled for delivery between 2003 and 2008. Interestingly the rate of capacity growth between 1980 and 2003 was 8.3% per annum (CLIA, 2004), virtually in line with passenger growth so occupancy figures of cruise ships have remained virtually unchanged at an impressive 98%. The potential untapped market is the prime basis on which these vessels are being ordered and built.

Potential Barriers to Future Growth

Price discounting

Additional capacity must be filled by cruise lines and where necessary lines will discount prices rather than leave capacity empty. North American cruise passengers shop around to achieve discounts on brochure prices and yet cruise lines observe when actually on a cruise they are less careful with their spending. Cruise lines have found that they can increase revenue by increasing volume output where lower prices are offset by the potential 'on-board' spend. Currently, some 75% of US cruise passengers and 45% of UK cruise passengers are on discounted cruises, indicating recent growth may be more 'supply led' fuelled by discounts, rather than demand led. Continuous discounting appears to have affected cruise line profitability (Peisley, 2000).

Overcrowding in main destinations

Caribbean governments have been showing increasing concern at the rate of growth of the number of cruise passengers calling at Caribbean ports and fear market saturation

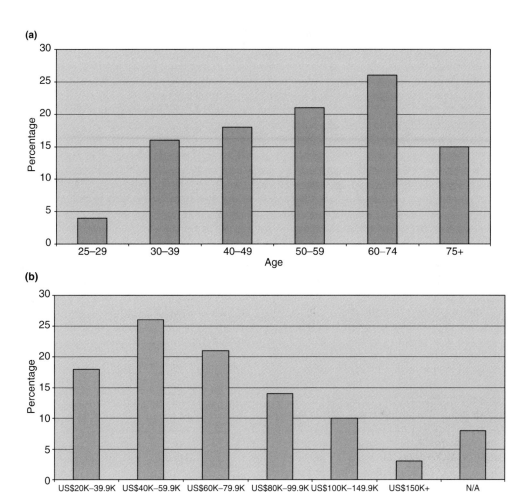

Fig. 33.1. Demographics of US cruise passengers: (a) age; (b) salary.

(Wood, 2004). Whilst this may offer some opportunity for future growth in Europe, Caribbean capacity falls during the European season and if the Caribbean is unable to accommodate much of the planned new ship capacity, particularly between October and March, then the continued growth and profitability of cruising in Europe will also come under increased threat.

Impact of Industry Trends on European Market

Length of cruise

Table 33.4. Market share of North American market by length of cruise 2003.

Length of cruise	%	% Growth 1980–2003
2–5 days	32.0	677.5
6–8 days	56.3	445.1
9–17 days	10.4	286.8
18+days	0.4	76.4
	100	472.6
Average growth 1980–2003: 8.4% per annum		

Source: CLIA (2005).

The average length of a cruise is decreasing (Tables 33.4 and 33.5). The total market size for longer cruises continues to grow but its market share has fallen. The sharp decline in short cruises taken by UK residents since 2001 reflects in part the collapse of the short-cruise market from Cyprus, due to perceived political instability, but the industry believes there is an underlying

Table 33.5. Duration of cruise for UK passengers.

Year	Under 5 days %	5–7 days %	8–14 %	15–21 %	22+ %	Total
1996	6	43	43	7	5	429,201
1997	13	45	34	6	2	521,559
1998	13	45	34	6	2	663,210
1999	16	52	26	4	2	746,243
2000	18	36	37	7	2	754,416
2001	14	46	34	5	2	776,173
2002	11	48	33	7	1	823,590
2003	7	51	33	7	2	963,580

Source: PSA (2004).

trend for growth and new short-cruise products are being developed from Majorca and Malta.

The average length of cruises in Europe is:

* Mediterranean – 7.5 days
* North Europe – 11.5 days

As cruise lines seek to increase penetration of the European markets, short cruises will become the most rapid growth area of European cruising over the next 10 years. North Europe will miss out on this opportunity unless the region also develops a new itinerary of shorter cruises to supplement its traditional market as is happening in the Mediterranean. There is some scope for 4-and 5-day itineraries in the English Channel, and in the Irish Sea, using Liverpool or Dublin as the homeport.

Size of vessel

Cruise vessels are getting larger.

* 1999 – *Voyager of the Seas*, The Royal Caribbean Lines, 137,300 gross registered tonnage (GRT), 3900 passengers.
* 2004 – *Queen Mary 2*, Cunard, 150,000 GRT, 2620 passengers.

The larger vessels bring economies of scale and hence lower unit operating costs, although they also change the very nature of the product with the ship itself becoming the key visitor attraction (Lester and Weeden, 2004; Wood, 2004). The very high crew to passenger ratio on the smallest vessels contributes to high operating costs.

As new large vessels are introduced to the Caribbean, those vessels repositioned in Europe for the summer are also larger as are ships purpose-built for the European market. In 1998 P&O Princess Cruises introduced the first 100,000-t ship to sail in the Mediterranean.

Traditionally, Northern Europe has been dominated by the smaller cruise vessels of under 800-passenger capacity, but this is also changing. Capacity for 2000 included seven vessels carrying between 1500 and 2000 passengers which accounted for:

* 9.5% of cruises (47 cruises);
* 28% of both passengers and bednights;
* 31% of capacity (Wild, 2001a).

The increased share for larger vessels holds a number of threats for European ports. It will concentrate on the number of ports that, from the rapid growth of cruise passengers, bring logistical problems to some ports. Most ports can cope with the draught, usually less than 8 m, but many have a limitation on the length of their berths. An additional logistical problem is the rapid movement of an increased number of cruise passengers away from the quay, especially if motorized transport is required. Furthermore, there is the whole issue of the socio-economic impact of the arrival of a large number of visitors in a rural area of low population density.

Age of cruise passengers

The average age of cruise passengers is falling. However, UK transit ports continue to attract the stereotypical older passengers due to smaller vessels, longer cruises and higher prices.

Seasonality

The relative prosperity of Europe as a cruise destination is inevitably linked to the health of the industry worldwide as cruise lines will have to operate their vessels outside Europe during the winter months.

Performance of UK Ports

Within the context of a growing cruise industry the operating environment for UK ports appear good. Cruise Europe collates data on cruise passenger numbers calling at 72 member ports predominantly based in North European waters. This primary data show that passenger visits to member ports rose by over 200% between 1996 and 2003 (Table 33.6) (Cruise Europe, 2004). The growth of ship visits is lower demonstrating the trend to larger vessels.

Cruise Europe includes data on 17 UK ports (excluding Southampton for which data are partial). Overall growth was 45% between 1996 and 2003. However, the key turnaround ports of Southampton, Dover, Harwich and Tilbury accounted for 50% of ship calls and a staggering 80% of passengers in 2003 (Fig. 33.2), mainly on large ships as the average number of passengers per ship was nearly 2000 (Cruise Europe, 2004). Many of these passengers are destined

for destinations outside North Europe. Analysis of the remaining 14 ports therefore creates a clearer picture of the performance of UK day call ports. This shows a respectable growth in passenger calls of nearly 90%.

Table 33.6 confirms that ships using UK ports as a destination are at the smaller end of the range. There did not appear the same pressure to use larger ships as elsewhere, although this trend does appear to be emerging now. Data from the PSA (2004) showed an average of 261 passengers per call in 2003 up from around 219 in 2000. The market did not show a significant downturn as a result of 11 September (although the number of ship calls was down in 2002) but has been largely static until impressive growth in 2003.

The US market is important, but not dominant. Most ports do not record passenger nationality, but data from nine UK, Channel and Irish Sea ports indicate a US market share of 30%. Other key markets are the UK (45%) and Germany (18%). The market is therefore susceptible to a downturn in US cruisers for security/ political reasons, but not entirely dependent on it. The much larger Baltic market for instance is more dependent on US visitors and saw a decline in 2002.

Figure 33.3 shows the performance of these 14 UK ports in more detail. Although over the whole period nine of the ports have shown an increase, four more than doubling their passenger calls, four ports have decreased. Furthermore, barely any port has achieved year on year growth with most having disappointing

Table 33.6. Cruise passengers at European ports.

	1996	1997	1998	1999	2000	2001	2002	2003	% change 1996–2003
Cruise Europe Total 72 ports									
Pass ('000)	1367	1456	2108	2409	2410	3103	3136	4284	213
Ships	2403	2348	3168	2930	3504	4238	4006	4900	91
Average per ship	569	620	631	719	688	732	783	874	
14 UK ports (excluding main turnaround ports)									
Pass ('000)	88	93	108	103	98	111	115	166	89
Ships	247	249	274	263	274	315	277	340	38
Average per ship	356	375	394	392	356	352	417	489	

Source: Analysis by the author of primary data collected by 72 member ports and collated by Cruise Europe. Data supplied by Agust Agustsson of Cruise Europe. Recent years are published in *Cruise Europe News* (2004).

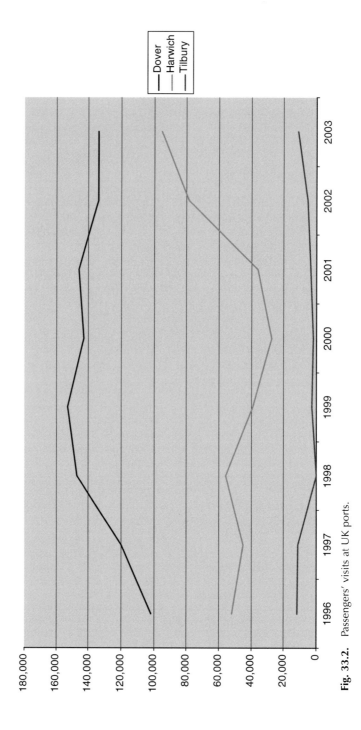

Fig. 33.2. Passengers' visits at UK ports.

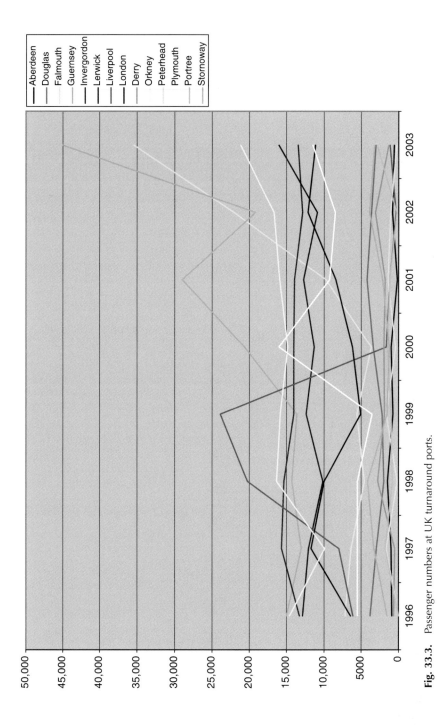

Fig. 33.3. Passenger numbers at UK turnaround ports.

years during the period. Some, such as Liverpool, which fell from 19 cruise calls in 1999 to 1 in 2000, demonstrate the volatility of the market. Liverpool's downturn was caused by over dependence on a single cruise line, 'Direct Holidays' which used Liverpool for turnaround cruises. The takeover of 'Direct Holidays' resulted in the relocation of this business to Southampton. Liverpool has since recovered business and attracted nine turnaround calls in 2004.

The lead time for cruise lines itinerary planning is long (over 12 months) so that a line will make its bookings for 2005 before it has undertaken its 2004 schedule. Therefore, if a destination port attracts repeat business from a new cruise line, it often does so only 2 years after the initial call. This particularly impacts on new port destinations, which tend to find a decline in the number of calls in their second year of operation.

Effective marketing can play an important role as shown by the dramatic success of the 'Cruise South-West' marketing programme, with Falmouth as a main beneficiary.

The cruise line industry is becoming increasingly concentrated with mergers and takeovers. Following Carnival's acquisition of P&O Cruises in April 2003, three companies now account for 70% of global capacity (Mintel, 2003; Peisley, 2003), so ports are increasingly marketing to a smaller number of supply-side players (Wood, 2004).

Port Selection Criteria

Given the volatility of the cruise market outlined in the previous section, primary data were collected through semi-structured interviews with two agencies responsible for regional development, six ports and two cruise lines.

The primary data set out to understand the most important port selection criteria. There are distinctions between the requirements for ports servicing 'transit calls' and those servicing 'turnaround calls'. Technical factors became more critical for the latter.

Two categories emerged:

- the relative merits of the port or its surrounding area as a tourist attraction;
- the facilities at the port.

Cruise lines placed the greatest emphasis for transit calls on tourist attractions. As one interviewee put it:

> it's not exactly rocket science, there must be something for our passengers to see or do.

There was a wide-ranging consensus that the maximum travelling time for a full-day excursion is 2 h in each direction. Portland, for instance, sited poor road connections as a major constraint in its development because it limited the potential of excursions. However, there was some friction between cruise lines and destinations. Excursions are a significant revenue earner for the cruise line but may take the visitors outside the direct economic hinterland of the port. Furthermore, visitors cannot spend while in transit.

When questioned about the port facilities, both ports and cruise lines felt it was important for vessels to tie up along the quayside. However, there was variation in the level of importance placed on this. One port described the need for:

> passengers to step straight off the ship.

Ideally, there will be sufficient covered areas or walkways to enable passengers to board excursion coaches without getting wet. Furthermore, reference was made to the average age of cruise passengers at UK ports and *the broken hip syndrome* when elderly passengers have to transfer to a tender. It was felt that this is more important in the UK than in the markets that attract a younger clientele. A visitor centre with tourist information and telephone facilities is desirable.

On the other hand one cruise line replied:

> we will put up with a lot such as tendering if the destination is right for us.

Guernsey has continued to show significant growth despite the requirement for anchorage (Fig. 33.2). One port argued that some cruise lines dropped ports in favour of anchorage alternatives on cost grounds alone. This was contradicted by both cruise line interviewees who argued that tendering was unpopular with crew and passengers alike, and pointed out that their high levels of repeat cruisers are achieved by offering the customers what they want.

The port needs to be in the right geographical location. For main turnaround ports this includes good access to an airport to service the fly–cruise market. Some fly–cruise passengers may use charter air services creating the potential for some ports to operate turnaround services in conjunction with a local regional airport. Portland developed turnaround capacity in conjunction with a regional airport (Bournemouth) copying a model developed by Dover using Kent International Airport at Manston. The main cruise operators prefer to focus on a limited number of turnaround ports and so turnaround activity for smaller ports will be limited. The development of drive to markets has enabled turnaround business to be developed at Liverpool, Falmouth and Portland.

The geographical-location requirement for day calls means it needs to be suitably located between two other ports of call to allow the traditional pattern of sailing at night followed by a port visit each day.

Cruise operators constantly develop new itineraries (Wood, 2000), especially at the small vessel luxury end of the market where this is important for the generation of repeat business. Passenger loyalty appears to be with the cruise line or even the ship, so constantly changing itineraries is both an opportunity to the ports to attract new ships and a major barrier to retaining existing business, helping create a volatile market.

Price was considered important by both ports and cruise lines. Port dues are between 9% and 10% of operating costs (Peisley, 2003); and although cruise lines do not opt for the cheapest, there is scope for ports to price themselves out of the market. The ports considered it to be a 'buyers' market', a phenomenon also noted in other regions of the world (Wood, 2004).

Financial Impacts from Cruising

Financial impact on the port

Cruise operations are not particularly profitable for ports. The Annual Report and Accounts for Dover shows a revenue of £3.1 million from cruising in 1999 from 122 vessels and 153,000 passengers. The average vessel size was 1250 so revenue equates to around £2500 per vessel or £20 per passenger. The annual port turnover was £47.8 million and whilst £3.1 million is useful, it places the relative importance of the

cruise market in context. Furthermore, turnaround port charges are higher than for day calls and large turnaround ports require significant investment. The second terminal building opened in 1999 represented an investment of £10.2 million. Ports publish their tariffs, which have the following elements:

1. Operational charges for the ship: anchorage or berthing; bunkering; and conservancy.
2. Passenger tax (charged per head).
3. Additional charges where appropriate: pilotage; tugs; security; and baggage handling (turnaround).

However, the primary research revealed that all of the ports interviewed were open to negotiation over rates and some ports quoted a single figure to cover both the ship charges and passenger tax to remain competitive. Port charges for transit calls are variable in this competitive market and depend also on the level of provision but average out at around £10 per passenger. Ports that offer anchorage rather than berthing tended to be cheaper. An exception is Liverpool, which despite offering anchorage is expensive at around £15 per passenger (CVC, 2000, unpublished data) due to the strong tidal nature of the Mersey creating the need to ferry passengers from the ship to shore using Mersey ferries (and not the ships' tenders).

There are three principal reasons why cruise activity is not profitable for most ports:

- The seasonal nature of the demand makes it difficult for many transit ports to reach viable numbers of calls. Staffs have to be hired in as required or substituted from other activities. Equipment also has to be hired.
- Cruise operations are an infrequent and yet complex activity and port operators described them as a disproportionately heavy on management time.
- Marketing in this highly competitive industry is continuous process where contacts need to be maintained.

The cruise industry is, we learned, a small community where everyone knows everyone else.

New entrants have to work hard to become known, and ports that attract relatively small numbers of calls have to retain their profile.

There was significant dispute amongst inter-viewees as to whether attendance at the main trade events (Miami and Genoa) is the best way to achieve this. Some small ports felt like the out-siders who make limited contact. Others argue:

you must attend in order to show you are serious.

Why do ports engage in cruising for such limited returns? The responses were varied but two ports, which were under some form of pub-lic sector or charitable trust ownership, argued that the port was a point of economic genera-tion for their region and hinterland for which they had a particular responsibility:

we have never made much money from cruise calls but the economic benefit the visitor spend brings to the area is of much greater value.

Commercial ports reiterated this point adding that:

as long as we are not losing money from cruising we will seek the business.

It was also argued that cruise calls were beneficial to the port's overall image raising the profile of the port worldwide. Furthermore, if the cruise activity occurs in historical dock areas close to the town centre when commercial port activity has long moved to deeper water downstream, it will give the image of maritime activity where previously there had been little evidence of such activity.

The financial performance of the cruise market makes it impossible for all but the largest turnaround ports to fund investment on purely economic grounds. The cruise facility project in Liverpool led by the City Council to develop a berthing area for transit visits is costed at £11.5 million (L&R Consulting, 2002, unpublished data). This can only be sustained by public-sector investment (including Objective 1 funding from the European Union (EU)), and is justified by the wider economic benefit of cruise passenger spend and is now strengthened by Liverpool's successful bid for European city of culture in 2008.

Economic impact on the region

In addition to the direct port dues discussed above there is wider economic benefit which takes the form of passenger spend onshore. None of the ports we interviewed had collected their own primary data on cruise spend.

ICCL (2003) stated that the average spend per US cruise passenger in a US port of call is US$82.00 (approximately €47). Can this figure extend to US visitors in Europe? Market research in Bergen in 2002 suggests 123,000 passengers spent €9 million or €74 per person (approximately £52). The BTA study used an average figure of £50 per passenger call 'if crew spending is included in the figure' (G.P. Wild, 2001b, unpublished data). The study of Liverpool estimated spending at £80 per call (CVC, 2000, unpublished data), Waterford at between £70 and £100 and Cork at a figure in excess of £100 (industry sources).

The evidence from primary sources also sug-gests that spend is very variable between ports and between types of passengers. It was indicated that on average around 65% of passengers who go on shore undertake an organized excursion, whereas 35% explore independently. The excursion has a number of impacts on the economic benefit the destination gains from cruise passenger spend:

- Some of the excursion spend is retained as profit by the cruise line (excursions are one of the three main on-board revenue earn-ers for cruise lines).
- A whole-day excursion can involve up to 2-h drive time in each direction during which there is no opportunity to spend.
- The nature of the excursion will determine the level of shopping opportunity. For visits to historical buildings, stately homes, etc. it is limited in comparison to a city centre location.
- The distance travelled may remove spend-ing from what is considered 'the local econ-omy'.

Surprisingly, given the nature of the product with overnight steaming and most days spent at a port of call, many passengers did not dis-embark. Neither the ports nor the cruise lines had undertaken formal surveys but one port offered an anecdotal observation that up to 30% of passengers would be on board during the middle of the day. This appears to be con-firmed by PSA data, which show 73% of pas-sengers calling at port take a shore excursion (PSA, 2004). Others observed that as all food was prepaid, some passengers went onshore for part of the day only so as to have lunch on board and:

gain maximum value for their cruise spend.

The percentage of passengers who do remain on board is directly influenced by:

- whether the ship is alongside or on anchorage;
- the weather (which itself has greater deterrent effect for vessels on anchorage).

Given the critical importance of passenger spend in the economic case for developing cruising, there is clearly a need for further research. Economic benefit surveys tend to estimate spend by multiplying the average spend (usually using a figure between £40 and £80) by the total number of passengers. This will overestimate spend in cases where significant numbers do not go ashore and is rather crude in terms of taking into account the variation created by the location (urban or rural), the range and opportunities for retail spend, the mix of passenger activity (independent or excursion) and the length of the excursion.

CREW SPEND ONSHORE. Crew spend is a significant additional benefit from cruise ship calls. The ICCL (2003) reported it at US$17.00 (around £9.65) per crew member per call in the USA and a survey in Cork in 2002 calculated crew spend at €1.4 million (compared to total passenger spend at €6.2 million) suggesting passenger spend is around 4.5 times greater. There is some discrepancy between the two because the ICCL data also suggest that passenger spending per head exceeds crew spend by just over 4.5 times whereas the Cork figure is total spend, and as there are fewer crew than passengers it shows spend per head is just under half the passenger spend.

Again crew spend is variable between ports and the primary data show that anchorage has a disproportionate impact. The increase in time required to go ashore by tender significantly reduces crew opportunity to do so.

VESSEL SPEND. The BTA study (G.P. Wild, 2001b, unpublished data) estimated a total figure for the UK of £10 million of which the vast majority was spent in the turnaround port. For transit calls 'it would be unwise to estimate a high average figure' for spending on stores and proposes an average of £500 per visit. None of the transit ports interviewed achieved any spend and indeed for vessels on anchorage it was at best very difficult if not impossible for the port to deliver stores, fresh water, deal with waste disposal or offer bunkerage. There is little scope for economic benefit from this source for transit ports.

Conclusion

The world cruise industry continues to grow despite the initial impact of 11 September and there is scope for UK ports to benefit. However, there are many cruise ports competing for a finite (if growing) number of cruise ship calls, and this oversupply creates a 'buyers' market'. The port authorities interviewed regarded prices as low and cruise business as not particularly profitable. Furthermore, they did not expect to see prices rise in real terms in the foreseeable future. The seasonal nature of North Europe as a destination makes investment in cruise facilities impossible to justify on purely economic grounds in all but the largest turnaround ports, and so significant investment requires some form of public-sector support. Small cruise ports will largely attract day call visits, as cruise lines like to concentrate turnaround calls at a few hub ports, but there is scope to attract some turnaround visits to other UK ports as cruise lines seek to maximize 'drive to' potential. The fly–cruise market from the USA is significant and therefore adds volatility.

The wider economic benefits accruing to a destination from cruising are crudely measured and surveys of cruise passenger spending patterns at ports are earmarked for further research. Cruise shipping is a valuable source of supplementary income for ports but is not the core business and cannot become the major economic driver of a port. It is a development opportunity, but its potential should not be overstated.

Acknowledgements

The author would like to acknowledge all members of the industry who kindly agreed to be interviewed; Julian Younger of the BTA for access and permission to use the BTA report (BTA Study: Economic Benefits of Cruise) commissioned from G.P. Wild (International, 2001, unpublished report); Pam Wilsher, Head of Tourism at Merseyside Partnership for access to Consultants reports on the development of a cruise facility in Liverpool; John Kelly of Liverpool City Council; Ted Sangster of Milford Haven Port Authority; Agust Agustsson of Cruise Europe for supplying data on ship calls and passenger numbers at 72 member ports; and Bryony Coulson of the Passenger Shipping Association (PSA) for access to the Census of UK Residents Undertaking Ocean Cruising and the Annual Cruise Holiday Market Digest of Statistics.

References

CLIA (Cruise Line International Association) (2004) *2003 Fall Overview*. New York.

CLIA (Cruise Line International Association) (2005) *2004 Fall Overview*. New York.

Cruise Europe (2004) *Cruise Europe News*, Vol. 11, No. 4. Port of Reykjavik, Iceland.

ICCL (2003) The cruise industry – 2002 economic summary. Arlington, Virginia.

Lester, J. and Weeden, C. (2004) Stakeholders, the natural environment and the future of Caribbean cruise tourism. *International Journal of Tourism Research* 6, 39–50.

Mintel (2003) Cruises. *Leisure Intelligence*, April. London.

Peisley, T. (2000) Cruising in crisis? *Travel & Tourism Analyst* 5, 4–25.

Peisley, T. (2003) *Global Changes in the Cruise Industry 2003–2010*. Seatrade Communications, Colchester, UK.

PSA (Passenger Shipping Association) (2004) *Annual Cruise Holiday Market Digest UK (Europe)*. IRN Research, London.

Wild, G.P. and Dearing, J. (2000) Development of and prospects for cruising in Europe. *Maritime Policy and Management* 27(4), 315–333.

Wild, P. (2001a) 2000: a year of consolidation. *Cruise Europe Handbook 2001/2*. Seatrade Communications, Colchester, UK.

Wood, R. (2000) Caribbean cruise tourism: globalization at sea. *Annals of Tourism Research* 27(2), 345–370.

Wood, R. (2004) Cruise ships: deterritorialized destinations. In: Lumsdon, L. and Page, S. (eds) *Tourism and Transport*. Elsevier, Oxford, 133–146.

34 Troubled Seas: Social Activism and the Cruise Industry

Ross A. Klein
Memorial University of Newfoundland, School of Social Work, St John's,
Canada NL A1C 5S7

The cruise industry's environmental record and practices in recent years have been challenged by non-governmental and grass-roots organizations. Oceana had a very public campaign to get Royal Caribbean Cruises to commit to installing advanced wastewater treatment systems on all its ships. Other efforts, such as Bluewater Network's lawsuits to force the US Environmental Protection Agency (EPA) to enforce clean water standards and its lobbying Carnival Corporation for a commitment to install advanced wastewater treatment systems on its ships were less public. There are many other social issues and problems associated with cruise tourism.

Social activism directed towards the cruise industry was limited through the 1990s. Activists tried to influence the outcome on select issues before the US Congress or the judicial system. On other issues activists remained passive. The question of whether foreign-flagged cruise ships are required to comply with the Americans with Disabilities Act is an issue where there have been both periods of activity and inactivity. Consumers and organizations representing the disabled have to varying degrees been involved in the last 15 years with cases that have wound their way through the courts and have made their way to the US Supreme Court. But this is just one issue. There are many others.

Labour Practices

Labour practices on cruise ships were one of the first issues to reach public awareness. It was 1989 and William Clay, Chair of the Labour Management Subcommittee of the Education and Labour Committee in House of Representatives, introduced HR 3238 which would extend collective bargaining rights and protection under labour standards (including payment of minimum wage) to seafarers on most foreign-flagged cruise ships operating from US ports (House of Representatives, 1994). He was supported by, among others, clergy associated with seafarer missions and seafarer labour associations. In hearings, his committee heard of seafarers working 100 h a week with no days off, many without an employment contract and some earning as little as 53 cents per hour. Though the subcommittee approved the bill in the summer of 1990, it went no further.

Clay reintroduced the legislation in 1991 as HR 1126. Claiborne Pell introduced a similar bill in the Senate. The House Education and Labour Subcommittee heard testimony of seafarers 'being required to work 18–20 h a day for less than US$1 per hour; of living conditions so unsanitary as to threaten life; of sailors being forced to provide kickbacks to labour contractors; [and] of sailors being abandoned in foreign ports and blackmailed from the industry for seeking to improve intolerable and inhuman conditions' (Glass, 1992). Despite the grave conditions, the act stalled in committee. It lacked support from the Bush Administration and was actively opposed by the cruise industry.

Representative Clay tried again after Bush left office. He introduced HR 1517 in 1993. Hearings yielded no new information, but the International Council of Cruise Lines (ICCL) threatened to relocate to non-US ports if legislation passed (House of Representatives, 1993). The legislation made its way to the floor of the House but failed to be heard. Some attribute the industry's threat as a factor in it becoming stalled; others suggest its demise was a result of the measure's lack of sponsorship in the Senate – Senator Pell had not reintroduced his bill – and the Clinton Administration had not extended its support for the legislation. Despite all of the attention given to the conditions of workers on cruise ships in the 1990s and early 2000s, including a Sweatships campaign launched in 2001 by UK-based War on Want and the International Transportworkers Federation (ITF), the matter has remained legislatively dormant since 1993.

Shipbuilding Subsidies

Most of the ships built in the 1990s were significantly subsidized. None, however, were built in the USA where commercial shipbuilding virtually collapsed after subsidies to shipbuilding yards were terminated in 1981. Shipyards in Europe, on the other hand, used subsidies to capture the burgeoning cruise ship business. The Italian government deliberately and effectively used subsidies to capture construction contracts for state-owned Fancantieri, which had not built a single cruise ship in 22 years. It secured a contract with Princess Cruises in 1988, and between 1990 and 2000 turned out more than two dozen ships. Other European shipyards – Chantiers de l'Atlantique in France, Kvaener in Norway and Meyer Werft in Germany – also benefited from government subsidies.

Subsidies made it difficult for some shipyards to compete. Wartsila in Finland had been the world's premier builder of cruise ships in the 1980s; however, the government did not provide subsidies sufficient for it to compete effectively.

Its bankruptcy in the late 1980s is in part the result of pressure to underprice ships it had contracted to build for Carnival Cruise Line. The degree of underpricing is apparent. Three ships originally contracted for US$200 million were renegotiated at costs of US$225 million, US$275 million and US$300 million, respectively (Mott, 1991). Carnival invested in Wartsila to keep it afloat long enough for delivery of the three ships.

The European Community put an end to shipbuilding subsidies for new ships in late 2000; subsidies continued for ships already under contract. Royal Caribbean International's *Jewel of the Seas*, for example, was delivered in June 2004 and had received German government aid worth 7% of the shipbuilder's contract, about US$25 million.

This subsidy is small in the context of ships built in the 1990s. While companies bragged about huge, new ships costing $300 million or more, they did not thank the taxpayers in the country where the ship was built who had contributed as much as 58% of construction costs. Ships also frequently received government-financing subsidies estimated to be worth another US$10 to US$20 million.

Shipbuilders in the USA complained about the unfair advantage given to European shipyards but were unsuccessful in persuading European governments to voluntarily stop subsidies. The Shipbuilding Trade Reform Act which was passed in the House of Representatives in May 1992 took a different approach. It removed the competitive advantage by requiring the owner of a cruise ship built or repaired at subsidized foreign shipyards to repay the subsidy, either to their own government or to the US Treasury, if the ship called at US ports (Adler, 1992). Despite strong lobbying by shipbuilding interests in the USA, the legislation was strongly opposed by the cruise industry and died in the Senate Finance Committee.

The Question of Liability

Cruise line liability was addressed by Congress in a tort reform measure attached to the Coast Guard Reauthorization Bill passed on 9 May 1995. The amendment, for the most part written by the ICCL, was introduced by Representative Don

Young. He referred to it as a 'non-controversial manager's amendment' (Glass, 1996). It passed the House by a vote of 406 to 12. Only afterwards did people read the final print.

For one thing, the amendment limited the rights of foreign seafarers to sue in US courts for grievances against foreign cruise lines (Gugliotta, 1996). This went against the stream of court cases taken up by the US government several years earlier. In 1991, the US Equal Employment Opportunity Commission (EEOC) won two cases against foreign-flag cruise vessels. In one, the court enjoined a foreign cruise line from discriminating on the basis of sex against any actual or potential job applicant. In the other, Norwegian Cruise Line (NCL) was charged with sex discrimination by an assistant cruise director who alleged she lost her job after becoming pregnant, and with discrimination by race and national origin by a bar manager who says he was forced to resign. NCL disregarded two subpoenas, claiming the EEOC lacked jurisdiction. It won in the US District Court in Miami but the decision was reversed by the US Court of Appeals in Atlanta which affirmed the EEOC's jurisdiction (Glass, 1991). This was a dangerous precedent for the cruise industry and Young's amendment gave them an out.

There were two other provisions in the amendment. One was designed to protect shipowners from unlimited liability in suits brought by passengers or crew members who were harmed by medical malpractice at a shoreside facility. It limited liability to that set by the laws of the state in which the medical provider is located. Currently, cruise line liability for shoreside treatment was unlimited.

The other provision, directed at mounting claims from injuries and sexual assaults, limited liability to passengers and crew for 'infliction of emotional distress, mental suffering or psychological injury', unless negligence or an intentional act can be proven. The American Trial Lawyers Association characterized the amendments as 'dangerous legislation' that 'jeopardized the safety of women on cruise ships'. Opposition also came from the Women's Defence Fund, the National Organization for Women's Legal Defence Fund, the Maritime Committee of the AFL-CIO and rape treatment centres (Fox and Fox, 1995).

The amendment languished for more than a year waiting to go to a House–Senate conference where lawmakers would resolve the House and Senate versions of the Coast Guard Reauthorization Bill. Lobbying by the industry continued, including a delegation of cruise line executives led by Carnival Corporation's CEO Micky Arison in March 1996. He and Celebrity Cruise's President Richard Sasso met with Senator Larry Pressler and separately with other members of the Senate Committee on Commerce, Science and Transportation. Pressler chaired the committee and would serve on the conference committee charged with reconciling the House and Senate versions (Rowe, 1996).

By 1 October, a compromise had been negotiated. Senator Ernest Hollings from the Senate's Commerce, Science and Transportation Committee observed before the Conference Committee that no one knows if the cruise ship people had enough votes to push the amendments through, but the cruise industry figures they have got 50% there and do not have much to lose (Rowe, 1996). When the Conference Committee convened, Hollings threatened to kill the entire reauthorization bill if ICCL's amendments remained. But in the end he capitulated after amended language was adopted for two of the provisions.

In the final version, shipowners were prohibited from limiting their liability in cases involving sexual harassment, sexual misbehaviour, assault or rape in cases where the victim is physically injured – limitations were allowed in all other situations; a cruise line sued by one of its workers in regard of treatment at a US health facility or doctor's office can invoke an award cap allowed medical practitioners under the laws of the state in which the care is provided; and the provision limiting seafarer's use of US courts was scuttled. It was replaced with a provision that seafarer employment contracts can block the worker from seeking legal remedies in US courts (Glass, 1996).

This last issue is the one that remains cloudy. The families of crew members who lost their life when Windjammer Barefoot Cruises' *Fantome* sank off Honduras during hurricane Mitch in October 1998 were initially denied the right to sue the cruise line in US courts by the District Court in Miami. But that decision was overturned by the 11th Circuit Court of Appeals in January 2003. The court justified the decision by citing the extent of the company's operations in the USA (Quigley, 2003).

Families of survivors of a May 2003 boiler blast on NCL's *Norway* in which eight crew members died and about 20 others were seriously burned were similarly denied the right to appeal to US courts even though the accident occurred while the ship was docked at Miami. The US District Court in Miami ruled workers' claims must be resolved in the Philippines in order to comply with the terms of contracts that workers and recruiters for the cruise ship in Manila signed with the Philippine government. The most they can expect to receive in the Philippines is US$50,000 (see Schwartz, 2003). The case was appealed and lost.

Another issue on which there is debate regarding US jurisdiction is medical malpractice on board a cruise ship. Cruise lines have traditionally argued that physicians and other medical personnel are independent contractors for whom they are not liable. The argument has generally been accepted, but in August 2003 was rejected by the 3rd District Court of Appeals in a case involving malpractice on a Carnival ship. The court ruled that ship doctors are legal agents of cruise companies and the cruise line is liable (Wilson, 2003b). A week earlier, the same court ruled in a case involving medical malpractice on a Royal Caribbean ship that a doctor may not use a ship's foreign registry as a shield against claims of malpractice in the death of a passenger's newborn (Wilson, 2003a). The case involving Carnival was appealed to the Florida Supreme Court. So was a case in which the Appeals Court ruled it had jurisdiction based on the Florida constitution which sets the state boundary to the edge of the Gulf Stream or 3 miles (5 km) out – whichever is the greater distance. In that case NCL's ship was 14 miles (20 km) off the Florida coast but had not reached the Gulf Stream.

Cases involving liability will continue in the courts. The issue is likely to surface also in Congress and in state legislatures. What the industry is unable to achieve in the courts it often accomplishes through legislation on the federal or the state level. And as in the past, social activists are likely to be more reactive than proactive.

Environmental Violations at the Core of New Activism

The USA began stricter enforcement for pollution offences in 1993 following a number of unsuccessful attempts to have the problem addressed by the state where offending ships were registered. The government was forced to take direct action and between 1993 and 1998 it charged 104 ships with offences involving illegal discharges of oil, garbage and/or hazardous wastes (General Accounting Office, 2000).

In April 1993, Princess Cruises was fined US$500,000 for dumping more than 20 plastic bags full of garbage off the Florida Keys. Videotape made by a couple on the cruise was used to indict Princess Cruises for unlawful dumping of plastics at sea and was the basis for a plea bargain. Because it is allowed by statute, and as an incentive aimed at encouraging cruise ship passengers to report illegal waste dumping, the court awarded the couple half of the fine. They received US$250,000 (Glass, 1993).

A year later, Palm Beach Cruises was fined US$1 million after Coast Guard surveillance aircraft videotaped the Viking Princess' intentional dumping of waste oil, leaving a 2.5 mile (4 km) slick 3.5 (6 km) miles from the port of Palm Beach. This was the first successful criminal prosecution of strict new federal oil dumping laws enacted after the Exxon Valdez spill. The fine was for both dumping and failing to report the incident (Booth, 1994).

In the months that followed, an investigation was undertaken of Royal Caribbean International for release of oil into the sea from one of its ships. The investigation soon expanded to include two ships in separate incidents. As well, Regency Cruises agreed to pay a fine of US$250,000 after admitting that two of its ships dumped garbage-filled plastic bags in Florida waters, and a US$500,000 fine was paid by Ulysses Cruises for two incidents of plastic-wrapped garbage being thrown from the *Seabreeze* off Miami and two cases of dumping oily bilge water. One incident involving garbage was observed by a musician, the other case by a passenger. Both incidents involving oily bilge water were detected by Coast Guard surveillance.

The issue of pollution from cruise ships hit headlines when Royal Caribbean International pleaded guilty in July 1999 to 21 counts of dumping oil and hazardous chemicals and lying to the US Coast Guard (USCG). With plea agreements in Miami, New York City, Los Angeles, Anchorage, Puerto Rico and the US Virgin Islands, the company agreed to pay US$18 million in fines. Just 1 year earlier it paid US$9 million in fines to settle cases initiated 4 years before in San Juan and Miami. Also in 1998 Holland America Line paid a US$1 million fine and US$1 million in restitution for a 1995 incident in which it pumped overboard oily bilge water in Alaska's Inside Passage. The assistant engineer reported the incident. He received a reward of US$500,000 – one-half of the company's fine.

Following Royal Caribbean's 1999 plea bargain, US Attorney General Janet Reno commented:

> Royal Caribbean used our nation's waters as its dumping ground, even as it promoted itself as an environmentally 'green' company . . . [and] to make matters worse, the company routinely falsified the ships' logs – so much so that its own employees referred to the logs with a Norwegian term meaning fairy tale book . . . [T]his case will sound like a foghorn throughout the maritime industry.
>
> (Vicini, 1999)

But environmental violations continued. In 2002, Carnival Corporation pleaded guilty to six counts of falsifying records in relation to oil discharges between 1998 and 2001 from five ships operated by Carnival Cruise Line and paid US$18 million in fines and restitution (McDowell, 2002); and NCL pleaded guilty to the discharge of oily bilge and falsifying its discharge logs between 1997 and 2000; it paid US$1.5 million in fines and restitution, an amount described by Federal prosecutors as lenient. Agents with the EPA say NCL's *Norway* 'also dumped raw sewage mixed with hazardous, even cancer causing, chemicals from dry cleaning and photo development into the waters near Miami for many years' (Adams, 2002).

It does not stop there. Carnival Corporation was summoned to federal court in July 2003 after a probation officer reported that the company failed to 'develop, implement and enforce' the terms of an environmental compliance programme stemming from its 2002 plea agreement; in particular that Holland America

employees submitted 12 audits that contained false, misleading and inaccurate information. Holland America is one of Carnival's 12 brands. In its reply to the court, Carnival Corporation said that three environmental compliance employees had been fired for the reports, but the company did not admit violating their probation. In a settlement signed on 25 August 2003, Carnival agreed to hire four additional auditors and to provide additional training for staff (Perez, 2003). The company was again under investigation in March 2004 for illegal discharges and in July 2004 a former vice president for environmental compliance pleaded guilty to certifying environmental compliance audits that had never been done (Klein, 2005). And there have been violations by other companies, including discharges of raw sewage in Juneau Harbour, in Puget Sound and in the Monterey Bay Marine Sanctuary.

The Backlash

The first concerted reaction to the cruise industry's environmental violations occurred in Alaska. Royal Caribbean settled all cases in the US federal court but was still vulnerable to charges by state and local jurisdictions. The state in August 1999 charged Royal Caribbean with seven counts of violating laws governing oil and hazardous waste disposal. In January of the following year, the company paid a fine of US$3.5 million for dumping toxic chemicals and oil-contaminated water into the state's waters, and it agreed not to discharge wastewater within 3 miles (5 km) of Alaska's coastline.

In the face of the suit by the state of Alaska, and an increasingly hostile attitude towards the cruise industry among many Alaskans in port cities, Royal Caribbean's President visited Alaska's main ports. He apologized for the company's past actions and made promises for the future. In most places the reception was cool to hostile.

His visits did not sway voters in Juneau against a proposed US$5 per passenger tax on cruise ship visitors. Approved with 70% voter support, the measure had failed 3 years before but was successful this time in large part because of negative feelings about Royal Caribbean.

Blue engine smoke rising over Juneau's harbour, throngs packing Juneau's pavements and streets and incessant noise from sightseeing flights ferrying cruise passengers to glaciers were among residents' complaints about cruise ships, said Joe Geldhof, an attorney for a labour union that organized the campaign. [The thing with Royal Caribbean] . . . just put people over the edge.

(Lloyd's List, 1999)

The tax was the first time any intermediate port in a US state had imposed such a fee. While other ports discussed adopting similar fees, the North-West Cruiseship Association (NWCA) – an association of cruise lines serving the Alaskan market – questioned its legality. It called for the US$3 million raised to be used to benefit the ships and their passengers directly. But the city did not bend. In response, Holland America announced it would withdraw much of its support to local charities. Al Parrish, a company vice president, reportedly said: 'If the community doesn't really want us there, if that's really truly what they're telling us, then we need to reassess what we're doing' (Rosen, 2000). Royal Caribbean withdrew its support in the spring of 2002 saying that 2001 had been a bad year (Chandonnet, 2002).

Voters in Haines, Alaska followed Juneau's lead by endorsing a 4% sales tax on shore excursions and onshore purchases. Many media suggested that the effort backfired when Royal Caribbean cancelled future stops at the port. However, the reason for the cancellations was purely economic. Its plea agreement with the US government debarred Royal Caribbean, meaning it could not enter into contracts with the Federal Government for 5 years. As such, it was effectively banned from Glacier Bay and went to Hubbard Bay instead, which required travelling further. To visit Skagway (which is a financially lucrative stop), Hubbard Bay and Haines, ships would have to travel at higher speed, which means higher fuel costs. The income generated by stopping at Haines would not offset this additional expense. Those ships that did stop in Haines dealt with the tax by reducing the amount paid to local tour vendors equal to the amount of the tax – the cost of shore excursions did not change for the cruise line, but the profit margin to the supplier was significantly reduced. The tax was eventually repealed after several failed attempts.

The town of Skagway considered in 2001 imposing a higher sales tax during the summer months, but the initiative was defeated in City Council. There was also an effort by a citizen group called Responsible Cruising in Alaska to have placed on the 2002 statewide ballot an initiative to charge a statewide head tax of between US$50 and US$75 on cruise companies, along with a corporate income tax and a 33% tax on on-board gambling. The initiative was put on hold late in 2001. However, it resurfaced in 2004 and a successful petition campaign placed a proposed US$50 head tax on the 2006 ballot. The cruise industry actively opposes the fee. Organizers say industry representatives interfered with collection of signatures during the petition campaign. After the petition was certified by the state's lieutenant governor and recertified by the state's director of elections, NWCA hired a former Secret Service agent to search for forgery among the more than 23,000 signatures submitted and several days later launched a lawsuit to challenge the tax (see Dobbyn, 2005; Volz, 2005).

You are not entirely welcome here

Another reaction to environmental violations was that some Alaskan communities chose to limit cruise ship visits. For example, voters in Sitka overwhelmingly voted down a proposal for construction of a wharf that would allow ships to offload passengers directly into downtown. The town of 8800 people believed that the need to tender passengers would keep a lid on its more than 225,000 cruise passenger visits per year.

The town of Tenakee Springs was more aggressive by proclaiming that cruise ship tourism is incompatible with the community's lifestyle, facilities and services. It vowed to take whatever steps necessary to prevent this type of tourism in the town. When the first cruise ship came to visit in August 1998, a small ship with only 120 passengers, the city tried to persuade the ship to cancel the visit. Failing that, cruise passengers were handed leaflets as they disembarked and were told that they were not welcome as part of a large organized tour, but they were welcome to return on their own. Most businesses had closed during the visit (Zucker-man, 1999).

Public support for monitoring and enforcement

The third major effect of the Holland America and Royal Caribbean cases is that they spurred an increased interest in monitoring cruise ships; not just oil pollution but sewage and air pollution. The State Department of Environmental Conservation (DEC), with the USCG, launched a cruise ship initiative in December 1999.

The initiative began with meetings between the State, USCG, EPA, cruise industry and environmental groups. The goal was to discuss cruise ship activities and operations with a view towards assessment of possible environmental issues. When the workgroups realized there was little technical data to support industry claims, a scheme was developed for sampling wastewater from cruise ships and for monitoring air emissions. Participation was voluntary and only 11 of 24 agreed to participate; others went beyond 12 miles (20 km) to dump raw sewage without monitoring and without limitations.

The results of monitoring during the summer of 2000 were, in the words of Alaska's governor, 'disgusting and disgraceful'. Seventy-nine of 80 ships' effluent had levels of faecal coliform or total suspended solids that would be illegal on land – up to 100,000 times the federal standard. This was true of both black water and grey water (see Knowles, 2000). As well, all samples indicated 'conventional pollutants' were part of the wastewater. According to the Juneau port commander for the Coast Guard, the results were so extreme that it might be necessary to consider possible design flaws and capacity issues with the Coast Guard–approved treatment systems (McAllister, 2000).

Monitoring of air emissions also gave reason for concern. The EPA had cited six cruise ship companies (involving 13 ships) for air pollution violations in the 1999 season. The situation had not improved. In August 2000, state investigators charged seven companies for 11 violations of state smoke-opacity standards when their ships were docked in Juneau between mid-July and mid-August.

The Alaska cruise ship initiative

Based on results of monitoring in 2000, Alaska Governor Tony Knowles introduced in March 2001 a legislation designed to strengthen state monitoring of the cruise industry's waste disposal practices and to enforce state clean air and water standards for cruise ships. The legislation imposed a US$1.00 fee per passenger to pay for pollution-monitoring programmes, inspections and enforcement by state officials.

The Act passed Alaska's House of Representatives but got held up in the state Senate's Transportation Committee where the chairman blocked its passage. The legislature adjourned without passing the Act; Governor Knowles responded by calling a special session for the expressed purpose of passing the Act. It passed and took effect on 1 July 2001. Though no more stringent than current US law regarding the disposal of sewage or pollution from smokestack emissions, the Act provided three things:

- a verified programme of sampling, testing and reporting of wastewater and air discharges;
- enforceable standards for what cruise ships may discharge in Alaska waters; and
- payment by the cruise ship industry of the costs of the programme.

Alaska significantly was the first state with authority to inspect ships, prosecute violators and regulate air pollution, trash disposal and hazardous waste handling as well as sewage. In this regard, Alaska's Environmental Compliance Programme reflects a basic lack of trust that the industry respects environmental regulations.

This lack of trust was reinforced while the bill was under consideration. In the first 5 weeks of the 2001 Alaska cruise season, four ships were cited for violations: the *Norwegian Sky* discharged treated sewage in the Alexander Archipelago – tests indicated that the effluent had faecal coliform counts 3500 times the allowable federal standard and suspended solids 180 times the standard (Rosen, 2001); Holland America Line's *Westerdam* accidentally discharged 100 gal. (378.5 l) of grey wastewater while docked in Juneau; Celebrity Cruises' *Mercury* was charged with discharging treated wastewater in Juneau without required certification of its systems – the wastewater was more acidic than permitted for discharging within a mile from shore (McAllister, 2001); and Royal Caribbean's *Rhapsody of the Seas* illegally discharged 200 gal. (757 l) of grey water into Juneau's harbour – according to Nancy Wheatley, a senior vice president for Royal Caribbean, 'they were using too many pumps, pumping it too fast, and they didn't shut the pumps off quite fast enough' (Dye, 2001).

Non-governmental Organizations Weigh In

Response by the environmental community to cruise industry practices and offences was slow in developing. Many groups well known for environmental concern remained silent about the cruise industry, but others spoke up. Some of these were organizations whose name suggests a focus on environmental protection, but in many cases are industry greenwashers (see Las Vegas Mercury, 2003; Klein, 2005). Let us look at groups that have taken a confrontational stance to force greater environmental responsibility.

Bluewater Network, based in San Francisco, is on the forefront of environmental activism related to the cruise industry. The organization began in 1996 as a project within Earth Island Institute. In 6 years it grew into a national organization with membership in four countries and had led the successful effort to ban two-stroke marine engines, rid almost all US National Parks from snowmobiles and jet skis, convinced the EPA to regulate air pollution from ships, helped ban MTBE (a gasoline additive) in California, and led the environmental community in a historic fight to reduce global warming pollution from cars and light trucks. In 2002, Bluewater Network became an independent, non-profit organization and in 2005 merged with Friends of the Earth.

Bluewater Network uses a mix of strategies. In regard to the cruise industry, it used the courts to pressure the EPA to promulgate regulations to control vessel emissions, to force cruise lines to stop their habitual violation of laws prohibiting the discharge of ballast water in California waters, and in 2003/04 to challenge EPA standards for air emissions from ships.

Bluewater Network also engages in political lobbying – it was successful in 2003 in having enacted two of three bills it sponsored in the California legislature; it sponsored three bills that were enacted in 2004. And it was involved in ensuring sufficient environmental protections around construction of a new cruise terminal in San Francisco. It teamed up with San Franciscans for a Clean Waterfront in some of these efforts.

Bluewater Network also supports efforts of organizations in other jurisdictions. It participated in a lawsuit in Washington State following discharge of raw sewage in Puget Sound by NCL, brought to light cruise line violations of emission standards set by the Port of Seattle, and has engaged in public education and social action campaigns in San Francisco and Seattle.

Campaign to Safeguard America's Waters (C-SAW) also began as a project of Earth Island Institute. It is dedicated to closing loopholes in federal and state water pollution regulations that allow millions of gallons of polluted wastes to be dumped into public waters, and is actively engaged in the debate about the use of mixing zones to circumvent water quality standards. The cruise industry has adopted a view that advocates the use of mixing zones, in effect saying 'dilution is the solution' to discharge of its wastes.

C-SAW's efforts around water quality standards and the EPA are national in scope; however, the campaign is also intimately involved in Alaska's efforts to contain and control pollution produced by cruise ships. The organization's founding is related to discharge of hazardous chemicals in the Inside Passage of Alaska, including waters around Haines on which the Campaign's founder had depended for salmon – the salmons are no longer there. C-SAW has also been a key player in referendum efforts that would tax cruise ships using Alaska's waters (Cockerham, 2004).

Oceans Blue Foundation (OBF) was established in 1996 through a cooperative effort involving the Vancouver Port Authority, Tourism Vancouver, Tourism British Columbia, the Canadian Tourism Commission, private foundations and business leaders in British Columbia. Its 'Cruise Ship Stewardship Initiative' was a key project. The Initiative focused on the cruise industry voluntarily adopting standards of environmentally responsible tourism. OBF's goal was

an eco-certification programme that would identify and reward cruise lines that took meaningful
and positive steps.

OBF held a series of meetings, including a
2002 roundtable involving representatives of
the cruise industry and environmental organizations, and sincerely hoped that industry practices would be changed. However, increasing
dialogue led the organization to believe that the
cruise industry was insincere in its talks of
changing practices and instead was using the
cooperative process to undermine OBF's efforts.
As the organization learned more about the
industry's practices and political gamesman-
ship, its strategies became more confrontational
culminating in *Blowing the Whistle and the Case
for Cruise Ship Certification*, an October 2002
report that directly confronts contradictions
between industry claims and practices. In retri-
bution for the report, OBF lost most of its funding. Tourism Vancouver criticized the report and
said '[t]here are better ways of being able to
encourage that kind of discussion and debate',
that the matter would be raised with the
Canadian Tourism Commission (CTC), and that
Tourism Vancouver would consider ending support for OBF. An official with the CTC was also
critical, suggesting that 'the CTC supports a
balanced approach between environmental
protection and economic development' (Tjaden,
2002). OBF closed its doors a year later. A follow-
up to the October 2002 report, completed in
September 2003, has not been published.

The Ocean Conservancy (TOC), formerly
known as the Centre for Marine Conservation,
became directly involved with cruise industry
issues with release in May 2002 of *Cruise
Control: A Report on How Cruise Ships Affect the
Marine Environment*. Royal Caribbean, which
had provided a grant of US$450,000
(US$150,000 per year for 3 years) through its
Ocean Fund, criticized the report and apparently
withdrew funding from TOC's projects. In contrast to the publicity given when the grant was
awarded, no publicity or press release was issued
when funding was withdrawn.

TOC engages in both national and local
activities. Through field offices in Monterey Bay
(California) and Key West (Florida), TOC has
been a key player in local initiatives to contain
and prevent cruise ship pollution in adjacent
National Marine Sanctuaries. In Monterey Bay

specifically, TOC has been a critical force in helping to coordinate efforts of a range of organizations, including public education, and in
applying pressure on local government. On a
national level, TOC (along with Bluewater
Network) was a key proponent for the Clean
Cruise Ship Act of 2004; however, resources
devoted to cruise ship issues are relatively small
in comparison to its other activities. The Clean
Cruise Ship Act was introduced in the US
Congress April 2004, but died in committee. It is
sure to be reintroduced.

Oceana is the newest player on the scene.
Established in 2001 with funding largely from
the Pew Charitable Trusts, Oceana (based in
Washington, DC) merged with the American
Oceans Campaign in 2002. It identified cruise
ship pollution as one of its key areas of interest
and undertook a cruise ship campaign in early
2003. Similar to Oceans Blue Foundation,
Oceana began collaborating with the cruise
industry – in its case engaging in discussions
with Royal Caribbean to secure a commitment
to upgrade wastewater treatment systems. At
the same time, Oceana engaged in public education and mild forms of social and political
action.

Discussions between Oceana and Royal
Caribbean broke down in July 2003. In Oceana's
words the two had been negotiating; Royal
Caribbean said the meetings were part of its routine outreach to interest groups, environmental
organizations, academic institutions and others
(Londner, 2003). With discussions ended,
Oceana launched a media campaign on 21 July
2003, and held rallies and media events in several cities across North America. In October
2003, it escalated its campaign with a call for a
national boycott of Royal Caribbean, and in
February 2004 placed advertisements for its
cruise ship campaign on google.com. After 2 days
the advertisements, which did not mention
Royal Caribbean by name, were banned; Google
claimed the advertisements violated its editorial
policy which prohibits advertisements criticizing
other groups or companies. The advertisements
reappeared two weeks later on Yahoo.

Oceana is a partner with Bluewater
Network and TOC in advocating for the Clean
Cruise Ship Act of 2004. These efforts can be
distinguished from those of Bluewater Network
more generally and Oceans Blue Foundation in

that the latter are more comprehensive. TOC's and Oceana's efforts focus largely on wastewater and bilge water. Bluewater Network and Oceans Blue Foundation include in their campaign ballast water, air emissions and toxic waste. None of the groups has focused directly on the 3.5 kg of solid waste produced per passenger per day on a cruise ship: 7 metric tonnes of garbage and solid waste per day on today's largest ships.

Local Initiatives

There are many local groups also working for protection of the coastal environment from cruise ship wastes. Friends of Casco Bay in Portland, Maine, was instrumental in securing state legislation to regulate wastewater discharges in state waters; Ocean Advocates has worked in concert with Bluewater Network in efforts to control and manage cruise ship wastes in Washington state waters and the Port of Seattle; and KAHEA – The Hawaiian Environmental Alliance has worked with Sierra Club to secure legislated standards for cruise ship emissions rather than reliance on a Memorandum of Understanding which is largely voluntary and lacks provisions for monitoring and enforcement.

The Santa Cruz office of TOC, in cooperation with Save Our Shores, Friends of the Sea Otter and others took a proactive approach to protecting the waters of the Monterey Bay National Marine Sanctuary – the largest marine sanctuary in the world. In advance of ships visiting Monterey in 2002, local officials asked and received from each cruise line a written commitment that there would be absolutely no discharges of waste while the ship is in the sanctuary.

Everything appeared to have worked fine until it was discovered in February 2003 that contrary to its written promise, Crystal Cruises' *Crystal Harmony* had in fact discharged 36,000 gal. (136,260 l) of sewage, grey water and oily bilge the previous October while in the sanctuary. When asked why they had not reported the discharge when it occurred, Crystal Cruises' vice president, Joseph Valenti, defended the silence by saying that the company had only broken its promise; it had not violated any laws (Laidman, 2003a). ICCL President, Michael Crye, also dismissed the violation telling a news

reporter that the ship's discharge occurred 14 miles (15 km) from the coast so it was not illegal (Fletcher, 2003).

The people of Monterey showed their displeasure. They barred Crystal Cruises from entering the port of Monterey for 15 years; the *Crystal Harmony* is barred forever (Laidman, 2003b; Madigan, 2003).

Not all activism is focused on the environment. Two groups in Key West, Florida, Livable Oldtown and Last Stand are equally as concerned about cruise tourism's impact on residents' quality of life – the influence of overcongestion at tourist attractions, kitschy shops that have sprung up around the port and disruptions caused by Conch Trains running cruise passengers around the town. In addition, there is great concern, particularly among restaurant and hotel owners, that cruise tourism displaces the traditional tourist market. People who stay at a hotel for a week spend money in restaurants and bars and shop in the stores are being driven away by changes in the city. The president of the Lodging Association of the Florida Keys and Key West says cruise passengers change the nature of a destination.

> Our whole advertising and marketing program is around Key West being an easy-going, laid-back, relaxed destination with interesting shops and stores and great cultural and historical resources. . . . Put yourself in the position of a visitor who comes for the first time, checks into one of our fine hotels, and then decides to take a stroll down this town's main drag – Duval Street – and encounters crowds more reminiscent of Times Square.
>
> (Babson, 2003)

The problem of people pollution hit its peak in March 2004. Local residents were already sensitive to the number of cruise passengers arriving in Key West, but then it was learned that the city had been violating a 1993 resolution placing a limit of seven cruise ships visits per week at Pier B – a privately owned dock adjacent to the Hilton Hotel. At about the same time *National Geographic Traveler* dubbed the city as a victim of crowding, poor planning and greed. 'Key West was heavily criticized for its influx of cruise daytrippers, coral reef die-offs, spring-break-like atmosphere and an overriding sense that the city's character was lost' (Buckley, 2004).

In response, and to focus attention to the severity of the problem, Livable Oldtown called for a protest by Key West residents on 11 March 2004 when there would be five ships visiting the city. They encouraged residents to drive up and down Duval Street between 11 AM and 12 noon. Though cruise passengers barely noticed the added congestion, the point was well made with city residents and city councilors by the 100 or so protestors (O'Hara, 2004). The issue so polarized segments of the community that the event's organizer received a bomb threat (from a downtown merchant) the day of the action. A flurry of newspaper editorials and guest columns followed.

The issues confronted in Key West are not unique. The problem is not cruise tourism, it is the question of how many cruise passengers a town or an island can comfortably accommodate. At what point does the number of cruise tourists change the attraction such that it is no longer what it was that made it an attraction?

The future of social activism and the cruise industry

We have seen examples of social activists confronting the cruise industry. While there is every reason to expect confrontations to continue, they admittedly are relatively few. Cruise industry practices, or report of major environmental or other impacts, can easily reignite large-scale responses from organizations and individuals. However, the industry appears to be relatively effective in managing the media and in influencing legislative processes (see Klein, 2005), and will continue to succeed in undermining efforts to ensure environmental, social and economic sustainability unless activists shift from a reactive to proactive mode.

References

Adams, M. (2002) US cracks down on cruise ship pollution. *USA Today*, 8 November. Available at: www.usatoday.com

Adler, J. (1992) US shipbuilders fighting back. *Los Angeles Times*, 31 May, L-6.

Babson, J. (2003) As the industry booms, key west considers limiting some cruises. *Miami Herald*, 5 January. Available at: www.maimi.com/mld/miamiherald/4876455.htm

Booth, W. (1994) Cruise ship owners plead guilty to dumping bilge oil in atlantic. *Washington Post*, 4 June, A-2.

Buckley, C. (2004) Key West dubbed victim of crowding, poor planning, greed. *Miami Herald*, 12 March. Available at: www.miami.com

Chandonnet, A. (2002) Cruise line to halt gifts of cash. *Juneau Empire*, 11 March. Available at: www.juneauempire.com

Cockerham, S. (2004) Voters to settle ship tax. *Anchorage Daily News*, 18 December. Available at: www.adn.com/front/v-printer/story/5924969p-5832072c.html

Dobbyn, P. (2005) Cruise ship association questions signatures. *Anchorage Daily News*, 7 January. Available at: www.adn.com/ front/v-printer/story/5989323p-5888669c.html

Dye, K. (2001) Ship pumps laundry water into city harbor. *Juneau Empire*, 19 June. Available at: www.juneauempire.com

Fletcher, E. (2003) Cruise ships are in the cross hairs. *The Sacramento Bee*, 23 June.

Fox, L. and Fox, B.R. (1995) Anchored in the docks. *Washington Post*, 8 October, E4.

General Accounting Office (2000) *Marine Pollution: Progress Made to Reduce Marine Pollution by Cruise Ships, but Important Issues Remain.* Washington, DC, GAO (Document # GAO/RCED-00-48).

Glass, J. (1991) US wins its employment case against cruise lines. *Lloyd's List*, 30 August, 3.

Glass, J. (1992) The sensitive subject of extending the reach of US labour laws to foreign-flag seafarers is again in the Capitol Hill spotlight. *Lloyd's List*, 10 October 4.

Glass, J. (1993) $250,000 award for reporting at-sea plastics dumping. *Lloyd's List*, 12 July, 1.

Glass, J. (1996) Compromise on US cruise tort. *Lloyd's List*, 1 October, 1.

Gugliotta, G. (1996) Coast guard bill cruises into trouble. *Washington Post*, 11 June, A15.

House of Representatives (1993) Hearings before the subcommittee on labor standards, occupational health, and safety of the Committee on Education and Labor of the House of Representatives, 13 May 1993. Washington, DC, GPO (Document # Y4 ED8/1 103-9).

House of Representatives (1994) *Coverage of Certain Federal Labour Laws to Foreign Documented Vessels.* Washington, DC, GPO, p. 1 (House Report # 103-818).

Klein, R.A. (2005) *Cruise Ship Squeeze: The New Pirates of the Seven Seas.* New Society, Gabriola Island, British Columbia.

Knowles, T. (2000) Knowles steps up pressure on congress for action on cruise ship discharges, Press Release # 00252, Office of the Governor, 6 October.

Laidman, D. (2003a) Cruise line says rookie mistake led to ship's waste dumping. *Monterey Herald*, 6 March. Available at: www.montereyherald.com

Laidman, D. (2003b) Crystal ships banned from Monterey for 15 years. *Monterey Herald*, 18 March. Available at: www.montereyherald.com

Las Vegas Mercury (2003) Quick and dirty: a notebook of news and politics. *Las Vegas Mercury*, 30 October. Available at: www.lasvegasmercury.com/2003/MERC-Oct-30-Thu-2003/22428503.html

Lloyd's List (1999) Lines may fight legality of juneau passenger levy. *Lloyd's List*, 8 October, 5.

Londner, R. (2003) Oceana, royal caribbean argue over sewage. *The South Florida Business Journal*, 21 July. Available at: southflorida.bizjournals.com/southflorida/stories/2003/07/21/daily8.html

Madigan, N. (2003) Monterey bans a cruise ship over dumping. *New York Times*, 6 March. Available at: www.nytimes.com

McAllister, B. (2000) A big violation on wastewater: some ship readings 100,000 times allowed amount. *The Juneau Empire*, 27 August. Available at: www.juneauempire.com

McAllister, B. (2001) Celebrity illegally dumping in port. *The Juneau Empire*, 5 June. Available at: www.juneauempire.com

McDowell, E. (2002) For cruise ships, a history of pollution. *New York Times*, 16 June. Available at: www.nytimes.com

Mott, D. (1991) Cruise ship price jumps. *Lloyd's List*, 19 April, 1.

O'Hara, T. (2004) Protesters cruise lower duval. *Key West Citizen*, 12 March. Available at: keysnews.com/280021664867615.bsp.htm

Perez, E. (2003) Carnival fires pollution auditors over false compliance reports. *Wall Street Journal*, 28 August, D1.

Quigley, J. (2003) Families allowed to sue cruise line. *Miami Herald*, 30 January. Available at: www.miami.com/mld/miamiherald/business/5060961.htm

Rosen, Y. (2000) Alaska officials plan crackdown on cruise ships. *Reuters News Service*, 22 February.

Rosen, Y. (2001) Alaskans see drawbacks to booming cruise business. *Reuters News Service*, 29 June.

Rowe, S. (1996) There oughta be a law. *Miami New Times*, 21 March. Available at: www.miaminewtimes.com/issues/1996-03-21/metro.html

Schwartz, N. (2003) Judge: suits in fatal Norway blast must be settled in Philippines. *Sun-Sentinel*, 15 October. Available at: www.sun-sentinel.com/news/local/Miami/sfl-dcruise15oct15,0,4527975.story?coll=sfla-news-miami

Tjaden, T. (2002) Cruise lines blasted: tourism-industry funded oceans blue in hot water following critical report on industry. *Business in Vancouver*, 12–28 November.

Vicini, J. (1999) Focus: Royal Caribbean to plead guilty to pollution. *Reuters News Service*, 21 July.

Volz, M. (2005) Suit filed to stop tax on ships. *Anchorage Daily News*, 19 January. Available at: www.adn.com/business/v-printer/story/6038748p-5928014c.html

Wilson, C. (2003a) Ship doctor said not sheltered from suit. *Associated Press*, 20 August. Available at: news/yahoo.com/

Wilson, C. (2003b) Court revives suit against cruise line. *Associated Press*, 28 August. Available at: news.yahoo.com/

Zuckerman, S. (1999) Come again, but leave your tour at home. *Tidepool Archives*, 6 October. Available at: www.tidepool.org

35   The Disneyization of Cruise Travel

Adam Weaver

*Victoria University of Wellington, Victoria Management School, PO Box 600,
Wellington, New Zealand*

Introduction

This chapter explores the extent to which vacations on board certain cruise ships exhibit qualities that exemplify Disneyization. For Bryman
(1999, p. 26), Disneyization is a process whereby
the principles that shape the way in which Disney
theme parks operate have come to dominate
many sectors across American society and other
parts of the world. These principles, in essence,
influence the character of many different institutions and built environments – in particular,
restaurants, casinos, zoos, theme parks and cruise
ships (Bryman, 1999, 2003; Beardsworth and
Bryman, 2001). The influence of Disneyization,
in Bryman's view, has become widespread.

There are four main principles that are
said to underpin Disneyization: (i) Disneyized
realms are themed; they are, in other words,
oriented around (often visual) motifs; (ii) clear
distinctions between different types of consumption within themed environments have,
in some instances, disappeared. Many authors
contend that when this disappearance of clear
distinctions occurs, consumption becomes
'dedifferentiated' (Sharpley, 1996; Bryman,
1999, 2003; Urry, 2002). Pleasure, profit and
customer service are interconnnected; (iii)
themed environments are used by the companies that own and operate them to promote the
sale of merchandise; and (iv) many service
employees within Disneyized environments
undertake a type of work that has been
described as 'emotional labour', a term conceived by Hochschild (1983).

Within the cruise industry, Disneyization
appears to manifest itself most visibly on board
'supersized' cruise ships. These ships can accommodate over 2000 tourists and are elaborate holiday enclaves; they contain casinos, discotheques,
performance halls, boutiques, restaurants and
bars. Many of these shipboard environments are
themed. Within certain themed environments,
different consumption-related activities have
become deeply intertwined. These activities,
which may defy easy classification and have perhaps become hybridized in nature, are usually
tied to the sale of various products and services.
Enormous cruise ships are 'powered' by sales (and
not sails). Tourists on board supersized cruise
ships are served by and have considerable contact
with service employees (e.g. restaurant waiters,
bar waiters and cabin stewards) who perform
emotional labour.

That many supersized cruise ships exemplify the principles that underpin Disneyization
cannot simply be attributed to the debut of
Disney-owned cruise ships in the 1990s. One
could make the case that Disneyization probably
started to influence cruise travel soon after the
establishment of Carnival Cruise Lines in the
early 1970s. The 'Fun Ship' concept developed
by Carnival ushered in an era of mass-market
cruise travel in which ships became holiday destinations (Dickinson and Vladimir, 1997; Wood,
2004). At present, Disney Cruise Line is one of
the several cruise ship companies that own ships
that possess features consistent with the four
core principles that drive the Disneyization
process.

The Disneyization process, for Bryman (1999, 2003), often operates in tandem with McDonaldization. Ritzer and Liska (1997) have used the term 'McDisneyization' to describe the way in which McDonaldization and rationalization have shaped many tourism-oriented environments – e.g. the Mall of America in Minneapolis, Minnesota, the West Edmonton Mall in Alberta, Canada and Disney-owned theme parks around the world. While Ritzer and Liska describe the core principles (efficiency, calculability, predictability and control) that are responsible for McDonaldization, they do not identify principles that underpin Disneyization. Bryman (1999, p. 27) has noted that Ritzer and Liska only emphasize 'the "Mc" part of the process' when they describe McDisneyization.

The McDisneyized environments described by Ritzer and Liska (1997) are composed of simulations. These simulations often consist of decorated surfaces and facades that serve as venues for consumption; they are spaces that are intended to both dazzle and reassure consumers (Hannigan, 1998). However, Ritzer and Liska do not explore the notion that simulated environments may have certain constituent elements. The concept of Disneyization, as it is articulated by Bryman, captures the important ways in which the consumption that occurs within these simulated environments (which are often themed) has become dedifferentiated, involves commercial transactions, and is made possible by workers who provide friendly customer service.

Themed Environments

Bryman (1999, 2003) states that Disneyized environments are usually oriented around certain themes. These themes are often borrowed from sports, history and popular entertainment. Themed environments are also sometimes shorthand stylizations of places; these environments may be crafted so that they bear some resemblance to a particular city or popular travel destination. There are some themed environments that do not make clear reference to a certain place or time. These environments are usually said to have a 'fun' or 'fantasy' theme. A number of scholars have noted that themed environments oriented around consumption

have become prevalent within many countries (Gottdiener, 1997; Hannigan, 1998; Chang, 2000; Frenkel and Walton, 2000; Wanhill, 2002; Paradis, 2004).

The themes that are used within entertainment- and tourism-oriented environments are intended to be easily understood and widely appreciated by consumers. Themed environments are rarely meant to provoke controversy. Themes provide a particular ambience to a space (a restaurant, a bar or a casino). This ambience is supposed to create a more memorable experience for consumers and, as a result, stimulate consumption.

Themed environments, for Gottdiener (1997), facilitate the production of profit. They are developed by corporations for the purposes of market differentiation. For example, they enable cruise ship companies to differentiate their ships from the ships of their competitors. Business owners use themed environments in order to make their products and services more noteworthy and distinctive.

One cruise ship architect who has created themed environments for several cruise ship companies refers to his work as 'entertainment architecture' (Slater and Basch, 2001, p. L23). This type of architecture is visible on board ships owned by Carnival Cruise Lines. Themed environments on-board *Carnival Triumph* are meant to evoke certain cities and travel destinations around the world. The main indoor promenade on board the ship is named World's Way and contains numerous abstract murals that depict different continents. This ship also has a number of consumption-oriented spaces that are named after prominent places around the world: the Oxford Bar, the Monte Carlo Casino, the New York Deli and the Hollywood Dance Club.

A ship that is nearly identical to *Carnival Triumph* in terms of size and exterior appearance is *Carnival Victory*. However, interior spaces on board *Carnival Victory* have a nautical theme. The shipboard casino is named the South China Sea Club Casino. One of the main bars on board the ship is named the Seventh Sea Bar. The main indoor promenade on board the *Carnival Victory* is named Neptune's Way.

There are many cruise ships that do not have a shipwide theme. These ships are a patchwork of different themes. For example, *Grand Princess*, a cruise ship owned by Princess

Cruises, has a number of elaborately adorned environments: an Italian restaurant (Sabatini's Trattoria), a restaurant that serves south-western-style cuisine (The Painted Desert) and a bar that has an exploration theme (the Explorer's Club). These themes are created with murals, sculptures and certain types of furniture (Fig. 35.1). Themed environments on board cruise ships vary in terms of their ability to evoke particular places. Many place-oriented themed environments simply possess colourful decor and scarcely resemble the places after which they are named.

Themed environments are not only a product of architecture and decoration. In the Explorer's Club, the costumes of employees support the bar's exploration theme. Bar waiters and bartenders wear pith helmets and tan-coloured safari clothes. The drinks that are served in the bar also support the theme. Tourists can order mixed cocktails named after Marco Polo, Christopher Columbus and several other renowned explorers.

A number of cruise ship companies own or rent private islands and beaches in the Caribbean and the Bahamas (Showalter, 1994; Wilkinson, 1999). These islands and beaches could be considered themed environments. In some instances, private islands and beaches are constructed out of sand that is imported from other places. This sand is sometimes raked between cruise ship visits in order to obliterate the footprints of previous visitors (Corbett, 1992). Private islands and beaches, then, have a carefully maintained appearance. They are essentially made to resemble archetypal secluded islands or beach environments. Themed environments (whether they are situated on board cruise ships or are private islands and beaches) are typically sites where many different types of consumption take place. The relationships that exist between different types of consumption are, at times, complex.

The Dedifferentiation of Consumption

Within Disneyized realms, consumption has become dedifferentiated. The distinctions that are typically believed to exist between different types of consumption are not necessarily very clear. Many consumption-oriented realms (e.g. cruise ships, theme parks, casinos and holiday resorts) are popular with tourists for a variety of reasons; they provide visitors with entertainment, contain shops where visitors can purchase merchandise, and serve as tourist attractions. The consumption-related activities

Fig. 35.1. Sabatini's Trattoria.

that take place within these environments are quite often interconnected.

Tourism and the purchase of various products and services can be deeply intertwined (Coles, 2004; Goss, 2004). On board *Explorer of the Seas*, there is an indoor pedestrian boulevard named the Royal Promenade (Fig. 35.2). There are shops, cafés and bars on both sides of this boulevard. Once a week, this boulevard is even the site of a parade. This parade features a variety of entertainers and costumed performers. The Royal Promenade has become both a retail-oriented site and a tourist attraction.

On board ships owned by Disney Cruise Line, tourists can attend theatrical performances that feature characters from animated films produced by the Walt Disney Company. The actors who portray the animated characters wear elaborate costumes. Various products sold within shipboard shops are emblazoned with representations of these characters. Tourists who attend the theatrical performances on board these ships are viewed by Disney Cruise Line as potential consumers of Disney-branded merchandise (plush toys and clothes). The ships and the merchandise promote each other; tourists may be inspired to travel on board a Disney-owned cruise ship because they are fans of the characters that have appeared in Disney films. These ships, at the same time, provide a venue for the Walt Disney Company to sell more of its branded merchandise. A self-referential system of product promotion has therefore been established.

The two ships that are owned by Disney Cruise Line have on-board restaurants that combine food consumption with entertainment. Both ships feature a restaurant named the Animator's Palate. The walls of these restaurants, when diners are initially seated, are adorned with black and white sketches of various Disney cartoon characters. Over the course of dinner, colour infuses the black and white sketches. This restaurant exemplifies the notion of 'eatertainment' whereby the distinction between entertainment and food consumption collapses (Hannigan, 1998; Josiam *et al.*, 2004). The decor of the restaurant provides entertainment as tourists dine. Restaurant waiters who work in the Animator's Palate on board both ships must synchronize their dress with the transformations that occur within these restaurants. At the start of dinner, restaurant waiters wear black and white vests. These waiters then don more colourful vests as the walls become 'animated'.

Within Disneyized environments, efforts are made to dissolve the distinctions between 'play' and 'consumption'. Brochures practically implore tourists to have 'fun' on board cruise ships. Indeed, Carnival Cruise Lines even refers to its vessels as 'Fun Ships'. 'Play' does, however, often come at a price. Various activities on board cruise ships require the payment of extra fees – in particular, casino entertainment. Tourists also must often pay a fee in order to rent certain pieces of equipment (for instance, rollerblades) for certain shipboard activities. It has been

Fig. 35.2. The Royal Promenade.

noted by Eco (1986) that tourists consume as they play, and play as they consume. The widespread availability of beer, wine and mixed cocktails on board cruise ships often creates an environment conducive to 'play'. These drinks are typically sold as products that complement or should accompany other activities (food consumption and relaxation) and events (theatre performances and even the ship's departure from port).

The way in which tourists 'pay for play' on board cruise ships, to some extent, obscures the monetary nature of shipboard transactions. Purchases are mostly made with debit cards that are similar in size to credit cards. Tourists are issued debit cards when they provide the cruise ship company with their credit card details. The purchases that are made with a shipboard debit card are then billed directly to the credit card. A debit card makes 'playful' consumption seem distant and removed from the actual expenditure of money. Tourists tend to spend money more freely when the money that they spend does not immediately come out of their pockets (Dickinson and Vladimir, 1997).

Merchandise

The sale of merchandise is essential to Disneyization. This merchandise possesses value that is derived from the brands and emblems that it bears. Theme parks and cruise ships have become emporiums that offer a wide variety of products to tourists. It is often the case, too, that tourism-oriented environments serve as the source for many of the brands and emblems that are popular with tourists. A number of companies within the cruise industry have undertaken cross-promotional endeavours. For example, Carnival Cruise Lines and MasterCard have issued a 'co-branded' credit card (Perez, 2001). This card features a picture of a cruise ship owned by Carnival. It also bears the corporate emblems of both Carnival Cruise Lines and MasterCard. When purchases are made with this card, the card holder receives reward points that can be used towards the purchase of cruise vacations. This reward system may prompt some consumers to use a credit card more frequently so that they accumulate more reward points.

Boutiques on board cruise ships offer a wide variety of branded merchandise. T-shirts and other items (e.g. key chains and postcards) that are available in these boutiques feature pictures of cruise ships. There are even some souvenirs (e.g. die-cast models and toys) that are miniature facsimiles of cruise ships. In 1997, Carnival Cruise Lines and Mattel introduced a Barbie doll that wears 'a nautical themed sports ensemble' (Bleecker, 1997, p. L4). The doll's shorts and hat are emblazoned with Carnival's corporate emblem. A perfume named 'Cruise' is also sold exclusively by Carnival (Levin, 1996). The perfume bottle's spray nozzle resembles the 'whale-fin' exhaust funnel of a Carnival ship.

In the 1990s, Royal Caribbean International entered into a partnership with Johnny Rockets, an American restaurant chain. This restaurant chain currently operates restaurants in nearly 30 American states. Five ships owned by Royal Caribbean International have shipboard restaurants that are operated by Johnny Rockets. These restaurants have themed decor; they have been made to resemble 1950s-style American diners. Tourists do not have to pay an additional fee for food items when they dine at a shipboard Johnny Rockets. Only milkshakes are extra-fee items. It would seem that the purpose of the shipboard restaurants is not to earn immediate revenue from tourists. Rather, these restaurants promote the Johnny Rockets brand so that tourists will visit Johnny Rockets restaurants after they return home from the cruise.

On board ships owned by Disney Cruise Line, tourists can purchase drinks at an ESPN Skybox bar. ESPN is an American multimedia sports broadcaster that distributes sports-related content via television and the Internet. At present, 80% of ESPN is owned by the Walt Disney Company (Burt, 2004). The ESPN Skybox bars essentially promote a multimedia broadcaster that is owned by the same company that owns the cruise ships. These bars are a conspicuous display of corporate affiliations.

A number of cruise ships feature shops that are owned by other companies. On board *Queen Mary 2*, tourists can purchase food items and clothes from a shop owned by Harrods. This onboard shop, similar to the Harrods department store in London, has an Edwardian theme. Various attributes of this shop support the theme – in particular, its floor tiles, furniture and fixtures.

There are four ships owned by Celebrity Cruises – *Millennium, Infinity, Summit* and *Constellation* – that have DKNY boutiques on board. The acronym DKNY stands for Donna Karan New York. This fashion house produces popular women's clothes. The same four cruise ships owned by Celebrity Cruises also feature culinary shops that are named after renowned French chef Michel Roux (Sarna and Hannafin, 2003). Tourists on board cruise ships are 'captive consumers'. When a ship is at sea, tourists can make purchases only from shipboard venues and concessions. These venues and concessions are either controlled by the cruise ship company or by companies that have established partnerships with the cruise ship company.

Emotional Labour

There is an important human element to the Disneyization process. This human element has been described as emotional labour. Emotional labour involves the expression of employer-desired dispositions and attitudes by service employees (Hochschild, 1983; Leidner, 1999). The central emotional task for many service employees is to display emotions that are not necessarily their own. Emotional labour necessitates that service employees manipulate their own emotions so as to stimulate a particular emotional response in customers. In most service-oriented workplaces, there are standards or rules that dictate the way in which emotions should be expressed or displayed to customers (Leidner, 1993). It is usually the case that employees are required to express particular emotions and suppress others when at work. Emotions and dispositions serve a purpose in service-oriented companies; they become elements to be controlled by employers in the interests of profit.

While some employees are responsible for the safe operation of the ship, other employees are responsible for service provision and, as a result, perform emotional labour. Employees on board cruise ships who perform emotional labour include restaurant waiters, bar waiters, cabin stewards, cruise directors and assistant cruise directors. These employees do not simply perform rudimentary tasks. They are also required to interact with – and sometimes even memorize the names of – the tourists whom they serve. These social interactions are important to many tourists. One cruise ship company executive interviewed by the author noted that cruise ship tourists have a tendency to remember the name of the restaurant waiter who served them dinner each day rather than the cruise ship's name.

The control that is exercised over cruise ship employees extends to the words that these employees can utter in the presence of tourists. On board ships owned by Princess Cruises, service employees are not permitted to say the word 'no' when they speak with tourists (Lindberg, 1999). The word 'no' is forbidden because its use could potentially undermine the sense of freedom and uninhibitedness that Princess Cruises wants its customers to experience. In a short article that provides a 'behind the scenes' tour of *Grand Princess*, a travel writer describes his (ultimately unsuccessful) efforts to verbally outmanoeuvre cruise ship employees so that they would inadvertently use the word 'no' (Lindberg, 1999). Employees on board ships owned by Princess Cruises therefore practice self-censorship.

In the cruise ship workplace, the movements and activities of cruise ship employees are strictly controlled. Restaurant waiters, bar waiters and cabin stewards must retreat immediately to crew-only areas of the ship when off-duty (Mather, 2002). That these employees retreat to crew-only areas when off-duty ensures that contact between tourists and employees is minimized. Rules therefore determine when and where emotional labour can take place.

One mechanism that is used by cruise ship companies to monitor and evaluate their employees is the comment card. The comment card is essentially a questionnaire survey that tourists are asked to complete at the end of the cruise. It is used to measure customer satisfaction and typically includes questions about customer service. A comment card can become an instrument of workplace surveillance. The data that is obtained from comment cards may be used by cruise ship companies to either promote or dismiss employees (Chapman, 1992).

It is not uncommon for service employees to use their emotions in ways that will benefit them rather than their employers. At times, service employees structure their emotional displays in order to accommodate their own personal aims and interests. Many cruise ship employees, for instance, solicit positive comment card comments from tourists (Gerstel, 1991; Showker and Sehlinger, 1995; Porter and Prince, 1997). These solicitations have also been reported by tourists who have submitted written reviews about their cruise vacations to Internet sites such as http://www.cruisemates.com.

Many cruise ship employees realize that the surveillance system oriented around comment cards is often blind to their work-related activities at the very end of a cruise. These employees may choose to circumscribe their emotional displays when they are aware that their actions will not be evaluated. On the final day of a cruise, once tourists submit their comment cards and pay their tips, restaurant waiters and cabin stewards may perform their emotional labour with diminished enthusiasm (Reynolds, 1998). The tourists that they have served for the past several days are about to depart. Restaurant waiters who have politely chatted with tourists suddenly become more reticent. The customer service that these waiters provide often remains courteous, but it rarely meets the exceptional standards that were set over the course of the cruise. This decline in service quality, while often subtle, can be quite noticeable.

Efforts by cruise ship employees to exercise some control over their workplace practices do not undermine the notion that emotional labour is necessary for the success of Disneyization. For many cruise ship tourists, customer service is an important element of the vacation experience. Employees who perform emotional labour contribute to the ambience on board cruise ships. These individuals undertake activities that are meant to make consumption more pleasurable for tourists.

Conclusion

The notion that cruise ships possess attributes similar to Disney-owned theme parks was initially explored, in a scholarly work, by Ritzer and Liska (1997). They contend that many cruise ships could be described as McDisneyized holiday environments. These McDisneyized ships contain fantasy-oriented realms that exemplify the core principles that characterize McDonaldization: efficiency, predictability, calculability and control. While Ritzer and Liska (1997) meticulously describe the ways in which many theme parks, casinos, holiday resorts and cruise ships exhibit these core principles, their work does not try to identify a set of attributes that typify simulated environments.

Bryman (1999, 2003) addresses the character of simulation-infused spaces when he describes Disneyization. It is possible to view McDonaldization and Disneyization as complementary concepts. The McDonaldization thesis seeks to capture the way in which rationalization permeates many aspects of contemporary society. While supersized cruise ships may operate in accordance with McDonaldized principles, Disneyization speaks to consumerism and the surface appearance of commodities and commodified realms. It is apparent, too, that distinctions between different types of consumption break down within Disneyized environments. This hybridized consumption is facilitated by service employees who perform 'emotional labour'.

An important notion raised by Ritzer and Liska (1997) when they define and discuss McDisneyization is that the production of pleasure can be an incredibly profitable endeavour for corporations. This relationship between pleasure and profit is similarly applicable to Disneyization. The pleasant consumer-oriented ambience on board Disneyized cruise ships – created via themed environments, attractively presented merchandise and friendly customer service – is important to the operation of these seaborne 'money machines'. That these money machines are popular with many tourists deserves more study. There is a need for researchers to explore the relationship between tourists and Disneyized environments. At present, the way in which tourists view and use Disneyized environments is poorly understood.

References

Beardsworth, A. and Bryman, A. (2001) The wild animal in late modernity: the case of the Disneyization of zoos. *Tourist Studies* 1, 83–104.

Bleecker, A (1997) Barbie ready to ship out on carnival cruise. *Orlando Sentinel*, 7 December, L4.

Bryman, A. (1999) The Disneyization of society. *The Sociological Review* 47, 25–47.

Bryman, A. (2003) McDonald's as a Disneyized institution. *American Behavioral Scientist* 47, 154–167.

Burt, T. (2004) ESPN sets up a powerplay for expansion. *Financial Times*, 20 January, 11.

Chang, T.C. (2000) Theming cities, taming places: insights from Singapore. *Geografiska Annaler* 82 B, 34–54.

Chapman, P. (1992) *Trouble on Board: The Plight of International Seafarers*. Cornell University Press, Ithaca, New York.

Coles, T. (2004) Tourism, shopping, and retailing: an axiomatic relationship? In: Lew, A.A., Hall, C.M. and Williams, A.M. (eds) *A Companion to Tourism*. Blackwell, Oxford, pp. 360–373.

Corbett, C. (1992) Zip-a-dee-dah cruise. *The Seattle Times*, 9 August, J1.

Dickinson, R. and Vladimir, A. (1997) *Selling the Sea: An Inside Look at the Cruise Industry*. John Wiley & Sons, New York.

Eco, U. (1986) *Travels in Hyperrealtiy*. Harcourt Brace Jovanovich, San Diego, California.

Frenkel, S. and Walton, J. (2000) Bavarian leavenworth and the symbolic economy of a theme town. *Geographical Review* 90, 559–584.

Gerstel, J. (1991) Food, excellent; service excellent; cruise, disaster. *Los Angeles Daily News*, 24 February, T3.

Goss, J. (2004) The souvenir: conceptualizing the object(s) of tourist consumption. In: Lew, A.A., Hall, C.M. and Williams, A.M. (eds) *A Companion to Tourism*. Blackwell, Oxford, pp. 327–336.

Gottdiener, M. (1997) *The Theming of America: Dreams, Visions, and Commercial Spaces*. Westview Press, Boulder, Colorado.

Hannigan, J. (1998) *Fantasy City: Pleasure and Profit in the Postmodern Metropolis*. Routledge, London.

Hochschild, A. (1983) *The Managed Heart: Commercialization of Human Feeling*. University of California Press, Berkeley, California.

Josiam, B.M., Mattson, M. and Sullivan, P. (2004) The historaunt: heritage tourism at Mickey's dining car. *Tourism Management* 25, 453–461.

Leidner, R. (1993) *Fast Food, Fast Talk: Service Work and the Routinization of Everyday Life*. University of California Press, Berkeley, California.

Leidner, R. (1999) Emotional labour in service work. *The Annals of the American Academy of Political and Social Science* 561, 81–95.

Levin, M. (1996) Carnival: from comedy to quality. *The Washington Times*, 31 March, E3.

Lindberg, P.J. (1999) Under the bridge: belowdecks, backstage, and behind the scenes on the world's biggest cruise ship. *Travel and Leisure* 29, 98–105; 138–141.

Mather, C. (2002) *Sweatships: What It's Really Like to Work on Board Cruise Ships*. International Transport Workers' Federation, London.

Paradis, T.W. (2004) Theming, tourism, and fantasy city. In: Lew, A.A., Hall, C.M. and Williams, A.M. (eds) *A Companion to Tourism*. Blackwell, Oxford, pp. 195–209.

Perez, E. (2001) Cruising on credit: carnival introduces vacation financing to get more aboard. *The Wall Street Journal*, 12 April, B12.

Porter, D. and Prince, D. (1997) *Caribbean Cruises and Ports of Call*. Simon & Schuster, New York.

Reynolds, C. (1998) Tips on gratuities for crews on cruise ships service. *Los Angeles Times*, 11 October, L2.

Ritzer, G. and Liska, A. (1997) 'McDisneyization' and 'Post-tourism': complementary perspectives on contemporary tourism. In: Rojek, C. and Urry, J. (eds) *Touring Cultures: Transformations of Travel and Theory*. Routledge, London, pp. 96–109.

Sarna, H. and Hannafin, M. (2003) *Frommer's Caribbean Cruises & Ports of Call 2004*. John Wiley & Sons, Hoboken, New Jersey.

Sharpley, R. (1996) Tourism and consumer culture in postmodern society. In: Robinson, M., Evans, N. and Callaghan, P. (eds) *Tourism and Cultural Change*. The Center for Travel and Tourism, Sunderland, Massachusetts, pp. 203–215.

Showalter, G. (1994) Cruise ships and private islands in the Caribbean. *Journal of Travel & Tourism Marketing* 3, 107–118.

Showker, K. and Sehlinger, B. (1995) *The Unofficial Guide to Cruises*. Simon & Schuster, New York.

Slater, S. and Basch, H. (2001) Cruise views: carnival launches a new spirit. *Los Angeles Times*, 3 June, L23.

Urry, J. (2002) *The Tourist Gaze*, 2nd edn. Sage, London.

Wanhill, S. (2002) Creating themed entertainment attractions: a nordic perspective. *Scandinavian Journal of Hospitality and Tourism* 2, 123–144.

Wilkinson, P. (1999) Caribbean cruise tourism: delusion? illusion? *Tourism Geographies* 1, 261–282.

Wood, R. (2004) Cruise ships: deterritorialized destinations. In: Lumsdon, L. and Page, S. (eds) *Tourism and Transport: Issues and Agenda for the New Millennium*. Elsevier, Amsterdam, pp. 133–145.

36 Cruise Tourism: A Paradigmatic Case of Globalization?

Robert E. Wood

Rutgers University, Department of Sociology, Camden, NJ 08102-1521, USA

Introduction

The intimate and deep relationship between tourism and globalization has been widely noted in the literatures of both fields. No other form of tourism – or arguably just about any other industry – is more deeply rooted in globalization processes than cruise tourism. This chapter explores the distinctively global nature of the cruise industry and argues that this form of 'globalization at sea' offers a paradigmatic case of globalization processes and outcomes generally. Because of this, cruise tourism has a special interest not only for tourism researchers but also for social scientists generally.

While the Caribbean region continues to attract about half of the world's cruise business, the rapid growth of cruise tourism has meant its extension to more and more ports around the world. Around the world cruises, with the option to join the cruise for a given section, have become increasingly popular, and large numbers of new ports of call are announced each year. Cruise ships themselves have become global microcosms. A manifest of Princess Cruises' *Sea Princess* (Schwartzman, 2001) showed passengers from 32 countries on every continent except Antarctica, which itself has become a significant cruise destination. The crew on a large cruise ship like the *Sea Princess* will typically hail from even more countries, although generally in reverse proportions to the passengers. The cruise industry is clearly global in scope, but what this chapter will focus on is its global structural underpinnings.

Globalization as Process and Project

Definitions of globalization are legion and reflect the particular orientations and interests of researchers, as well as the complex and multidimensional nature of the phenomenon itself. As a starting point, it is useful to distinguish between globalization as a process and globalization as a project (McMichael, 2000; Lechner, 2001). As a process, globalization is seen as occurring largely on its own and 'behind the backs' of actors, e.g. through technological innovation and its shrinking of the world through 'time-space compression'. As a project, globalization is viewed as the outcome of groups of people consciously pursuing their interests and visions of how the world should be. While the distinction is sometimes framed as a debate, most theorists see globalization as the outcome of both processes and projects. In this spirit, this chapter will focus on one process and one project that is believed to most fully capture the meaning of globalization together with particular relevance for understanding the cruise industry. The process is deterritorialization and the project is neoliberalism.

We commonly think of globalization as being about more extensive and deeper interconnections between places. But equally important is how this process changes the nature of the place itself, such that the global is now in the local. This in turn changes the relationship between the place and the social, cultural and economic life that goes on there, disembedding the latter from its immediate geography. As Tomlinson (2003, p. 273) has put it: 'Modern culture is less determined by location because location is increasingly penetrated by "distance"'. While this need not mean the 'end of geography' as some have claimed, it does mean that culture, social life and economic activity become increasingly *deterritorialized*, no longer rooted primarily in the immediate physical geography of place. This chapter argues that this is especially true for the cruise industry. It is a uniquely deterritorialized industry and cruise ships constitute uniquely deterritorialized destinations (Wood, 2004a).

While the deterriterrorialization of social life has many sources and is arguably rooted in modernity itself (Giddens, 1990; Tomlinson, 1999), it has been intensified in recent decades partly as the result of deliberate efforts. The late 20th century, Bauman (1998, p. 9) has claimed, was the 'Great War of Independence from Space' waged successfully by capital. 'The mobility acquired by "people who invest" – those with capital, with money which the investment requires – means the new, indeed unprecedented in its radical unconditionality, disconnection of power from obligations' to place-bound workers and communities. While it is important to recognize that deterritorialization has involved positive consequences for communities as well and that it has often gone hand in hand with processes of *reterritorialization*, in which the meaning of community and place is redefined, Bauman's point suggests a reciprocal connection between deterritorialization as a *process* and the dominant *neoliberal project* of globalization. This neoliberal project is briefly addressed here.

Actually existing globalization has been in large part the result of a conscious and coordinated effort to create a global economy based on neoliberal principles. Neoliberalism has been the dominant elite ideology in the industrialized world since the Reagan and Thatcher regimes of the 1980s, and has been built around two core ideas. The first has been an abiding faith in the superiority of markets in the allocation of resources in a society. Over time the magic of the marketplace became the mantra of free trade as neoliberalism embraced a global vision, which insisted that there was no viable alternative to maximally free markets based on the elimina-

tion of barriers to trade and investment. The second core idea involved a deep suspicion of the intrusion of government into economic affairs. With the buzzwords of deregulation and privatization, neoliberal elites sought to shift fundamental power and decision making from the public to the private sphere. Epitomized for many in the World Trade Organization (WTO), globalization has been deeply shaped by this strikingly successful neoliberal project.

In reality, however, very little of the world conforms to this neoliberal vision in any pure way. Even the great neoliberal achievement of North American Free Trade Agreement (NAFTA) included thousands of pages of politically negotiated departures and exceptions to pure free trade. As Ó Tuathail (1998, p. 87) puts it:

> Actually existing globalization is not the globalization of neoliberal visions, the Utopia of friction-free global markets or Internet-driven virtual worlds, but the contingent and unsteady symbiosis of imperfectly transnational networks, institutions and firms, and the 'ramshackle diversity' of international bureaucracies, states, police, mafias and other sources of power struggling for territorial authority in the post-cold war world.

But there is one place where something quite close to a realization both of a deterritorialized world and of the neoliberal vision of globalization does exist: the global cruise industry. As such, it is a source of potential insights into the relationship between tourism and globalization and into the uncertainties of globalization at sea.

Deterritorialization and the Cruise Industry

Global outsourcing has revealed seemingly place-bound things like factories to be detachable from communities and even nations, but cruise ships represent a unique level of deterritorialization. Huge floating chunks of capital, they are intrinsically mobile and capable of being repositioned at a moment's notice. Unlike land resorts, cruise ships can change their locations to escape bad weather, political instability, or other things their owners may not like. Major events like 11 September can elicit massive redeployments of whole fleets.

It is a common refrain in the industry, one that goes back at least to the 1930s (Douglas and Douglas, 2004, pp. 72, 95), that the cruise ship is the real destination for most passengers, not the ports of call. None the less, as Dowling and Vasudavan (2000, p. 21) observe, the full changeover from cruise ships to floating resorts required sufficient size 'to accommodate the kind of leisure and entertainment facilities that are available in lavish hotels ashore'. As such, the contemporary large cruise ship is a uniquely deterritorialized destination in a number of senses. Apart from the importance of sun – 77% of the world's cruise capacity is positioned in warm and sunny areas (Cartwright and Baird, 1999, p. 127) – both ship décor and ship life show striking and increasing similarities regardless of cruising region. Popular new features quickly become universal on new ships, e.g. atriums, the prevalence of cabins with balconies and the creation of alternative dining spaces. While the pastiche of architectural styles associated with carnival designer Joe Farcus may represent an extreme, virtually all the newer large ships have standardized features and are built around a notion of what one might call postmodern glitz. Cruise ships as deterritorialized fantasyscapes are epitomized in Celebrity Cruise's arrangement with Cirque Du Soleil that transforms observation lounges into 'The Bar at the End of the Earth™', where guests are invited 'to cross the mirror to another universe' (Celebrity Cruises, 2004).

To the degree that real places may be reflected in the décor, it is likely to be entirely divorced from the cruising region, as in Holland America Lines' appropriation of Indonesian designs and motifs while sailing almost exclusively in Caribbean, North and South American and European waters. The mainly European mid-size exceptions to this have been rapidly going under in the first decade of the 21st century with the collapse of such companies as Renaissance, First European/Festival and Royal Olympia Cruises, and with the increasing prominence in European waters of the large North American–based companies such as Carnival and Royal Caribbean and their subsidiaries.

For ship buffs, the ultimate form of deterritorialization might be seen as the gradual distancing of the ship from the sea itself. To maximize passenger cabins in desirable areas,

ships have become boxier and taller (Cartwright and Baird, 1999, pp. 168–198; Dawson, 2000; Cudahy, 2001, pp. 21–26), prompting traditionalists to bemoan the loss of an era when ships were ships, not floating resorts. A variety of onboard design features have reinforced the shift from the sea to the ship interior as the centre of vision and activity: deck chairs facing the pool and bar area, dining rooms with curtains covering the windows, even staterooms facing inward to the promenade and mall area. Since 1996, the creation of 'post-panamax' ships too wide to go through the Panama Canal has limited the cruising range of the largest ships, since their high centres of gravity also limit their ability to reposition via rough waters like those of the Cape Horn. Since large ships also require special port facilities, 'as ships get bigger for company purposes, the places to which they can go become fewer' (Douglas and Douglas, 2004, p. 19).

The concept of deterritorialized destinations may also be applied to the private islands frequented by a number of the major cruise companies in the Caribbean. While these technically are part of Caribbean nations, no locals live or are allowed on the premises unless they work there. Royal Caribbean even markets as a 'private island', a heavily fortified piece of Haiti and the promotion of a generic 'island paradise' have, according to one account (Orenstein, 1997), resulted in visitors not even realizing what country they are in. But while separated from the grit and hustle and bustle of Caribbean life, place can occasionally intrude, as with the cancellation of visits to Royal Caribbean's Labadee for 3 months on account of Haiti's political instability in 2004.

Not only their ships but also the major companies that own and operate them are uniquely deterritorialized as well. The largest ones are incorporated in places around the world that may have little or nothing to do with where they operate, or with who owns and manages them. Despite the fact that the world headquarters for both are in Florida, Carnival is technically a Panamanian company and Royal Caribbean a Liberian one. Malaysian-based Star Cruises is incorporated in Bermuda. While offshore incorporations have become increasingly common in the contemporary global environment, these companies derive special tax benefits from long-standing tax agreements that exempt foreign-owned passenger transport companies from most taxation in the countries they operate. The laws were designed as a reciprocal courtesy between air and shipping lines of different countries to avoid double taxation (e.g. United Airways and British Airways, each paying taxes in their country of origin), but cruise companies registered in international tax havens largely avoid even single taxation (Frantz, 1999).

Cruise tourism is almost completely controlled by transnational corporations (McNulty and Wafer, 1990). The globalization of the cruise industry has brought about relentless consolidation. Carnival took over Holland America, Windstar, Seabourn, Costa, Cunard and Princess Cruise Lines; Royal Caribbean took over Celebrity and Star Cruises took over Norwegian Cruise Line (NCL) and Orient. Many other companies went out of business or were absorbed into larger entities. Together the top three cruise companies control about 80% of the cruise market worldwide, an exceptionally high level of industry oligopoly even by global standards. While these brands have continued to be marketed separately, there is no question that the territorial link to their original countries of origin (Netherlands, UK, Italy and Greece) has been significantly attenuated.

So where exactly is one when one is at sea on a cruise ship? As Alice B. Toklas is reputed to have said of Oakland, California: 'There is no there there'. In a technical sense, one is on a floating chunk of whatever country the ship is registered in. But the situation is complicated by a patchwork of local, national and international regulations, laws, regimes and practices – as well as loopholes and weaknesses in the enforcement of all of these. The deterritorialized environment of the cruise ship is being reterritorialized in various ways, but the process remains contested and uneven. On balance, however, neoliberal globalization has reinforced and extended the industry's freedom from place and significant regulation. It is to this issue that we now turn.

Neoliberal Globalization and the Cruise Industry

At the core of the neoliberal vision of globalization is a commitment to the unobstructed movement of capital, goods and services, subject only to the discipline of market forces. Neoliberals tend to be either silent or ambivalent about comparable mobility rights for labour (Seabrook, 1998). Sophisticated neoliberal elites and institutions understand that markets themselves require regulation, and that a global economy requires an institutional infrastructure to ensure the provision of necessary public goods and to set and enforce the rules of the market. As noted earlier, actually existing globalization is partly the product of other forces besides neoliberal ideology. But it is the thesis of this section that the regulatory framework of the cruise industry, whatever its origins, is one that conforms in particularly striking fashion to the neoliberal deference to markets and private actors and to limits on politically based regulation. Cruise industry spokesmen regularly stress the highly regulated nature of their industry, due to the many international and territorial jurisdictions that impinge upon cruise ship operations. However, the international regulatory environment of the cruise industry, consistent with the basic tenets of neoliberalism, serves more to limit meaningful regulation in the key areas of safety, pollution and labour practices than to promote it.

Two interrelated aspects of the regulatory regimes within which cruise tourism operates stand out: (i) the open registry or flag of convenience (FOC) system; and (ii) the weakness of global governance and the privatization of cruise industry regulation.

Flags of convenience

FOCs go back at least several centuries, and originally involved ships of lesser powers flying the flag of greater powers for political and military protection (Thuong, 1987). In the second half of the 20th century they took a very different form, with shipowners from the traditional maritime powers preferring to flag their fleets in relatively poor countries that charge only nominal fees and largely exempt shipowners from taxation and regulation. United Fruit reflagged some of its Great White Fleet cargo ships, which also carried cruise passengers, from the USA to Honduras in the 1920s (Weiner, 2004; Wood, 2004b). But as late as 1940, there were only two FOC states and only 1% of the world's tonnage sailed under FOCs (Toh and Phang, 1993, p. 33). Today over half of the world's ship tonnage sails under FOCs (Alderton and Winchester, 2002, p. 151), and the figure is substantially higher for the cruise industry. In 2000, cruise ships accounting for 61.6% of the total cruise passenger capacity flew the flags of just three FOC states: Bahamas, Liberia and Panama (ITF, 2001, Table 20). These registries have been actively promoted by the US government for a variety of economic (keeping US-owned ships competitive by lowering their costs) and political/military reasons (Carlisle, 1981). With respect to the latter, special agreements with these registries give the US government comparable rights the UK government had in requisitioning *Queen Elizabeth 2* at the time of the Falklands War in 1982.

International law specifies that all countries must fly the flag of an internationally recognized state that belongs to the International Maritime Organization (IMO). Ships acquire the nationality of the flag state that registers them and it is the responsibility of the flag state to certify them and to enforce applicable international regulations. The 1958 Geneva Convention on the High Seas asserts that there should be a 'genuine link' between the state and the ship, especially in terms of control (Li and Wonham, 1999, p. 137), but in fact this is largely honoured in the breach in the case of most FOCs.

The FOC regime has been criticized for many years for being little more than a mechanism to obscure ownership and to avoid tax, safety, environmental and labour regulations. More recently it has come under scrutiny for its potential usefulness to terrorist organizations. FOCs have been a prime target in several grassroots campaigns targeting cruise ships: the International Transport Workers' Sweatship Campaign, Bluewater Network's Cruise Ship Campaign, Ocean Blue Foundation's Cruise Ship Initiative Campaign, Oceana's cruise pollution campaign and others. But the system has been largely impervious to change because of the way the IMO is structured. Voting rights are vested on the basis of tonnage, and so FOC states basically control the organization not only to the detriment of the traditional maritime states but also to the most developing countries as well.

This form of global governance, vesting power in those whose position depends on minimal regulation, clearly functions mainly to constrain it, much as the WTO exists as much to prevent others from regulating trade as setting the rules for trade itself.

The economic health of the cruise ship industry – and its competitive position *vis-à-vis* land resorts – is crucially based on the FOC system. This is most obviously true in the case of labour costs. National ship registries have traditionally required that a substantial proportion of a ship's crew be nationals and be governed by national labour regulations. Under competitive pressure from the FOCs, some national registries have loosened the crewing nationality requirements in systems that have become known variously as second or captive registries. But not all such systems exempt workers from national labour regulations entirely, and so FOCs have retained their competitive edge, particularly for cruise companies. In *Ship Management*, John Spruyt (1994, p. 51) calculated that for a ship with a 24-member crew, the difference between an all-northern European crew and an all-Chinese crew came to US$698,400 a year. Considering the fact that the larger cruise ships have over 1000 crewmembers (about 70% of them on the hospitality side), the labour cost savings afforded by FOCs are enormous. But wage savings are not the only factor, just about no country's labour laws would allow a company to require a 7-day week of 12 or more hours per day for 4–6 months at a time without a single day off – and effectively ban unions as well. Nor would they likely to allow the kind of ethnic recruitment and discrimination that goes on with some cruise lines, where different ethnic groups are slotted into different positions on the job hierarchy.

It is true that a cruise ship job may seem preferable to the available alternatives in Eastern Europe or South-east Asia, but the fact remains that only a combination of deterritorialization and globalization makes the existence of such jobs possible, for better or for worse. The cruise industry is unique in having access to a truly global labour force (see also Wood 2000, 2002). In a study of the shipping industry in general that sees it as having 'gone furthest down the globalizing path,' Bloor *et al.* (2000, p. 332) observe:

It might be thought that poor and hazardous working conditions are concentrated in the declining and backward sectors of the industry. This is not the case. Although conditions do vary considerably between different sectors, some of the very worst conditions for crews are actually to be found in the booming cruise sector.

FOC states are universally also tax havens. The combination of tax regimes in registry states and in (the often separate) states of incorporation, along with the unique double taxation provisions for passenger transport companies in the countries where cruise companies have their operational headquarters, results in the leading cruise companies paying almost no corporate taxes in the countries where they are actually headquartered. Carnival President Dickinson correctly observes in *Selling the Sea* that these tax and labour advantages of FOCs are what 'makes it possible . . . to offer cruises at much lower cost' than would be otherwise (Dickinson and Vladimir, 1997, pp. 66–67). These advantages have led the land-based tourism industry, particularly in the Caribbean, to complain bitterly about the lack of a level playing field between territorially rooted hotels and resorts on the one hand, and deterritorialized cruise ships on the other. So central are FOC-based prerogatives that one highly critical analysis of the effects of the FOC regime on cruise industry environmental behaviour none the less rejects the idea of eliminating FOCs out of hand because such an action 'would be financially devastating to the cruise industry' (Schulkin, 2002, p. 125).

For many shipowners, an additional appeal of FOCs is minimal regulation and hence lesser costs for vessel maintenance. Roughly 150 ships sink each year. The rate of FOC ship loss is well over twice the rate for nationally registered ships. Indeed, the growth of new FOC registries, e.g. in landlocked states that allow ship registration over the Internet with no documentation requirements, reflects 'the market-based nature of these registers', in which new FOC countries see a niche in servicing the needs of shipowners whose ships can not even meet the minimal requirements of traditional FOC states (Alderton and Winchester, 2002, pp. 154–158).

In the cruise sector, both market and political forces act to deter such extremes. While there appear to be differing levels of passenger acceptance of FOC registry (Cartwright and Baird, 1999, p. 32), cruise ship and passenger safety is central to the industry's marketing and profitability. Those aspects of cruise ship design that have been criticized from a safety standpoint, e.g. atriums that can spread fires and the logistics of unloading 5000 or more people from high-sided vessels on the high seas do not depend on FOC registry. None the less, questions of the adequacy of FOC state safety oversight have been raised in some cases, e.g. the cruise ship sinkings of *Fantome* in 1998, *Sun Vista* in 1999 and *Sea Breeze* in 2000.

Under the rules of the IMO that currently govern ship registration, the country of registration is responsible for the enforcement of relevant laws and conventions. There are three major limitations to this, however. The first is that FOC states are less likely to sign these conventions, and hence not be subject to them even if they do come into force. Alderton and Winchester (2002, p. 158) find that whereas traditional maritime states have on average ratified 61% of IMO conventions, 'old FOCs' (which include the major cruise line FOCs) have ratified only 49%, and 'new FOCs' only 37%. More specifically, of 22 cruise ship-relevant international conventions cited in an Ocean Conservancy study, the three major cruise ship FOC states of Panama, Liberia and Bahamas had failed to ratify 11, 9 and 8 of these conventions, respectively (Ocean Conservancy, 2002, pp. 60–62). Second, FOC states have sufficient voting power to prevent conventions coming into effect, since voting is linked to registered tonnage. For example, the highly relevant Annex IV (covering sewage treatment and discharge) of the International Convention for the Prevention of Pollution from Ships (MARPOL) has never come into effect because of insufficient FOC state ratification. Third, the fact that it is the responsibility of the registry state to investigate and punish ships flying its flag that violate either international or port state laws results only very rarely in any action. In the USA, a General Accounting Office (GAO) study found that of 111 cases of illegal discharges by cruise ships in US waters referred to registry states, no penalties were imposed apart from two minor fines (GAO, 2000). The IMO has absolutely no power to enforce its conventions itself.

The weakness of global governance and the privatization of cruise industry regulation

While the FOC system limits enforcement of safety, environmental and labour conventions, existing international law in these areas is very weak, especially for environmental and labour issues. Many laboriously negotiated agreements have never come into force because they have failed to get the required level of ratification. Those that have come into force are mostly very weak. For example, it remains totally legal for cruise ships to dump anything but plastics and oil in most of the world's oceans. The restrictions that exist apply almost entirely to territorial waters, usually only for 3 miles (5 km) from shore but occasionally 12 miles (20 km). Even with such limited restrictions, the cruise industry has been embarrassed by a steady string of violations of international and national environmental laws within territorial waters in recent years – violations that have only declined when port states imposed severe penalties. Indeed, assertion of port controls has been the major source of changes in cruise ship environmental practices in the past decade. But even if there were no violations within territorial waters, massive dumping of sewage and toxic substances could remain the norm outside.

In this context the cruise industry has sought to privatize environmental governance by making it a voluntary activity of industrial organizations. This can be seen as conforming to neoliberalism's distrust of government, so that when market solutions are not available other private arrangements among market actors are preferred. Held and McGrew (2002, p. 10) see such trends as reflecting what

> is sometimes referred to as the privatization of global regulation, that is, a redrawing of the boundaries between public authority and private power. From technical standards to the disbursement of humanitarian assistance . . . private agencies have become increasingly influential in the formulation and implementation of global public policy . . . Contemporary global governance involves a relocation of authority from public to quasi-public, and to private, agencies.

Two such arrangements have emerged in respect to cruise ship pollution in the past several years, voluntary codes of conducts and memorandums of understandings (MOUs) between cruise industry organizations and local authorities.

In June 2001, the International Council of Cruise Lines (ICCL), an organization of most of the major cruise lines announced that their members had unanimously adopted mandatory environmental standards for all of their cruise ships. Compliance with these standards was to be a condition of membership in the ICCL. This was clearly a response to pollution scandals of the previous several years involving almost all of its members and also to the fear that state and federal environmental legislation to deal with environmentally destructive cruise ship practices in Alaska would be extended to other areas.

While the ICCL policy went beyond international requirements in committing cruise ships to refrain from dumping toxic wastes anywhere, whether in territorial waters or not, in most respects the ICCL policy simply said that its members would observe current international and national environmental regulations, which are extremely minimal, as noted above. By and large the policy is weaker than the legislative controls in Alaska and also Canada's (non-binding) guidelines for cruise ships (Klein, 2003, pp. 25–26). The ICCL policy allows for the discharge of both blackwater (sewage) and greywater (mainly sink and drain run-off) 4 miles (6 km) from shore, and is silent on such subjects as air emissions and ballast water. Perhaps most importantly, the ICCL policy contains absolutely no mechanism either for monitoring or enforcing compliance. Since its promulgation, several of its members have been convicted of criminal acts that violate the ICCL policy, but no ICCL action has been taken against them. Hence in the eyes of most environmental organizations, the policy, while a step in the right direction, is no substitute for governmental or international regulation (Nowlan and Kwan, 2001; Ocean Conservancy, 2002; Oceans Blue Foundation, 2002; Klein, 2003).

The cruise industry has also sought to prevent regulatory legislation by negotiating MOUs with local authorities. The Florida Department of Environmental Protection and the Florida Caribbean Cruise Association (FCCA) signed a MOU in March 2000, and the state of Hawaii signed a MOU with the North-West Cruise Ship Association (NWCA) in October 2002. In March 2004, the NWCA signed a MOU with the Port of Seattle and the State's Ecology Department. In each case there was little or no public input and strong opposition from the local environmental community. Monitoring and compliance are voluntary.

As a Bluewater Network and Ocean Advocates report (Klein, 2003) makes clear, the outcomes of the voluntary MOU approach and legislative regulation first in Alaska and then in California have been strikingly different. In Alaska and California, not only have violations of environmental regulations significantly declined after initial convictions and fines but cruise companies also have shifted their least-polluting ships to those areas, leaving their more-polluting ships to serve MOU areas. As another report (Schmidt, 2004) states, 'Cruise ship pollution incidents have continued to occur since the cruise industry heeded the "wake-up call" of the Royal Caribbean cases. More than 50 incidents have occurred, many in violation of voluntary policies or MOUs.'

While calls continue to be made to establish mechanisms to force FOC states to meet their legal obligation of ensuring that the ships they register meet international safety, security, crewing and environmental standards, e.g. by the US Commission on Ocean Policy (2004), the assertion of port state control has come to be seen by many as the most politically available means to redress the failings of the FOC regime. European countries reached their own MOU – the Paris Memorandum of Understanding on Port State Control – to target cruise ships for regular inspection starting in 2003 (Klein, 2002, p. 53). In the USA, federal and state courts have gradually extended port state controls, particularly in connection with passenger rights and safety, and, as noted above, several states have put in place their own regulatory framework. The federal government has shown an increased willingness to file charges directly against cruise companies that violate anti-pollution regulations, rather than referring them to registry states. In addition, grass-roots campaigns have begun to produce some signifi-

cant cruise company responses most notably in Royal Caribbean's promise in 2004, in response to Oceana's boycott campaign against it, that it would install advanced wastewater purification technology on all its ships, both new and existing ones.

The Future of Globalization and Cruise Tourism

The global scope of the cruise industry is likely to grow. The industry sees the potential for continued expansion, both in the numbers of people in its traditional markets who have never taken a cruise but say they would like to and in the strong growth in new regional markets, particularly in Asia (despite the temporary setback during the financial crisis in the late 1990s). Moreover, neoliberal globalization is increasing dependency on international tourism in many countries, as their agricultural or manufacturing industries get dismantled in the wake of the end of subsidies and preferences. Ports around the world look to the cruise industry as a potential source of economic development.

Concentration in the industry is likely to increase even further. Certainly in North America and Europe there seems to exist no challenger to the dominance of Carnival, Royal Caribbean and Star, and it is likely that apart from niche players, the surviving regional companies will have a hard time remaining independent. Star's growth in Asia has been slower than the company had hoped and expected, but if Star can position itself as the Carnival of Asia, it could alter the balance between itself and the two other top oligopolists. It would seem likely that Asia would also be the most likely breeding ground for any new large-scale contenders.

The cruise industry is deeply rooted in – and dependent upon – key globalization processes and projects. Not only does the cruise industry come as close as any industry to the neoliberal ideal of a maximally unfettered global market but it also encapsulates some of the excesses of neoliberalism that are producing movements to rein it in and to explore alternative models of globalization. It may well be that the industry's freedom from meaningful regulation has peaked, and that a combination of grass-roots pressure, port state control and a strengthening of global regulatory regimes may gradually enforce a 'meaningful link' between flag states and their ships, limit the freedom of offshore financial centres, strengthen the conventions not only of the IMO but also of the International Labour Organization (ILO) and force the industry to cooperate more meaningfully in regional development efforts. Some of these changes may be helped along by security concerns (*The Economist*, 2002, p. 65). How the cruise industry responds to the changes in the wind will shape not only the future of cruise tourism but will also say something about the future shape of globalization itself.

References

Alderton, T. and Winchester, N. (2002) Flag states and safety: 1997–1999. *Maritime Policy and Management* 29, 151–162.

Bauman, Z. (1998) *Globalization: The Human Consequences*. Columbia University Press, New York.

Bloor, M., Thomas, M. and Lane, T. (2000) Health risks in the global shipping industry: an overview. *Health, Risk and Society* 2, 329–340.

Carlisle, R. (1981) *Sovereignty for Sale: The Origins and Evolution of the Panamanian and Liberian Flags of Convenience*. Naval Institute Press, Annapolis, Maryland.

Cartwright, R. and Baird, C. (1999) *The Development and Growth of the Cruise Industry*. Butterworth-Heinemann, Oxford.

Celebrity Cruises (2004) Celebrity Cruises and Cirque du Soleil launch otherworldly experience at sea. Press release (June 24). Available at: http://www.celebrity.com/pressrelease.asp?s=9535187 ED2&xref=23909

Cudahy, B.J. (2001) *The Cruise Ship Phenomenon in North America*. Cornell Maritime Press, Centerville, Maryland.

Dawson, P. (2000) *Cruise Ships: An Evolution In Design*. Conway Maritime Press, London.

Dickinson, B. and Vladimir, A. (1997) *Selling the Sea: An Inside Look at the Cruise Industry*. John Wiley & Sons, New York.

Douglas, N. and Douglas, N. (2004) *The Cruise Experience*. Pearson Education Australia, French's Forest, New South Wales, Australia.

Dowling, R.K. and Vasudavan, T. (2000) Cruising in the new millennium. *Tourism Recreation Research* 25, 17–27.

Frantz, D. (1999) Cruise lines profit from friends in congress. *New York Times*, 19 February, A1.

GAO (General Accounting Office) (2000) *Marine Pollution: Progress Made to Reduce Marine Pollution by Cruise Ships, but Important Issues Remain*. Washington, DC.

Giddens, A. (1990) *The Consequences of Modernity*. Polity Press, Cambridge.

Held, D. and McGrew, A. (2002) Introduction. In: Held, D. and McGrew, A. (eds) *Governing Globalization: Power, Authority and Global Governance*. Polity Press, Cambridge, pp. 1–21.

ITF (International Transport Workers Federation) (2001) *Flags of Convenience Campaign Report 2000*. Available at: http://www.itf.org.uk/itfweb/seafarers/foc/report_2000/

Klein, R.A. (2002) *Cruise Ship Blues: The Underside of the Cruise Industry*. New Society Publishers, Gabriola Island, British Columbia.

Klein, R.A. (2003) *Charting a Course: The Cruise Industry, the Government of Canada, and Purposeful Development*. Canadian Centre for Policy Alternatives, Ottawa. Available at: http://www.kahea.org/ocean/pdf/charting-a-course.pdf

Lechner, F. (2001) *Globalization Debates*. Available at: http://www.emory.edu/SOC/globalization/debates.html

Li, K.X. and Wonham, J. (1999) Registration of vessels: new developments in ship registration. *International Journal of Maritime and Coastal Law* 14, 137–154.

McMichael, P. (2000) *Development and Social Change: A Global Perspective*, 2nd edn. Pine Forge Press, Thousand Oaks, California.

McNulty, R. and Wafer, P. (1990) Transnational corporations and tourism issues. *Tourism Management* 11, 291–295.

Nowlan, L. and Kwan, I. (2001) *Cruise Control – Regulating Cruise Ship Pollution on the Pacific Coast of Canada*. West Coast Environmental Law, Vancouver. Available at: http://www.wcel.org/wcelpub/2001/13536.pdf

Ó Tuathail, G. (1998) Political geography III: dealing with deterritorialization. *Progress in Human Geography* 22, 81–93.

Ocean Conservancy (2002) *Cruise Control: A Report On How Cruise Ships Affect the Marine Environment*. Washington, DC. Available at: http://www.ocean-conservancy.org/dynamic/aboutUs/publica tions/cruiseControl.pdf

Oceans Blue Foundation (2002) *Blowing the Whistle' and the Case for Cruise Certification: A Matter of Environmental and Social Justice under International Law*. Vancouver, British Columbia. Available at: http://www.oceansblue.org/bluetourism/charta course/cruiseship/2002/Report_Blow_the_Whist le_Oct2002.pdf

Orenstein, C. (1997) Fantasy island: Royal Caribbean parcels off a piece of Haiti. *The Progressive* 61, 28–31.

Schmidt, K. (2004) *What Works Best, Regulatory or Non-Regulatory Solutions to Cruise Ship Pollution Prevention? The Environmental Perspective*. Blue Water

Network, San Francisco, California. Available at: http://bluewaternetwork.org/reports/rep_ss_cruise _sandiego2.pdf

Schulkin, A. (2002) Safe harbors: crafting an international solution to cruise ship pollution. *Georgetown International Environmental Law Review* 15, 105–132.

Schwartzman, M.T. (2001) *Globalization of cruising: your next cruise may have a decidedly international flavor. Cruise Travel*, September. Available at: http://articles.findarticles.com/p/articles/mi_m0 FCP/is_3_23/ai_80159247

Seabrook, J. (1998) A global market for all: if capital can move freely, so should people. *New Statesman* 127, 25–27.

Spruyt, J. (1994) *Ship Management.* Lloyd's of London Press Ltd, London.

The Economist (2002) Brassed off: how the war on terrorism could change the shape of shipping. *The Economist* 363(8273), 65.

Thuong, L.T. (1987) From flags of convenience to captive ship registries. *Transportation Journal* 27, 22–34.

Toh, R.S. and Phang, S.Y. (1993) Quasi-flag of convenience shipping: the wave of the future. *Transportation Journal* 33, 31–39.

Tomlinson, J. (1999) *Globalization and Culture.* University of Chicago Press, Chicago, Illinois.

Tomlinson, J. (2003) Globalization and cultural identity. In: Held, D. and McGrew, A. (eds) *Global Transformations Reader*, 2nd edn. Polity Press, Malden, Massachusetts, pp. 269–277.

US Commission on Ocean Policy (2004) *Preliminary Report of the US Commission on Ocean Policy.* Washington, DC. Available at: http://www.ocean-commission.gov/

Weiner, T. (2004) U.S. law puts world ports on notice. *New York Times*, 24 March, A6.

Wood, R.E. (2000) Caribbean cruise tourism: globalization at sea. *Annals of Tourism Research* 27(2), 345–370.

Wood, R.E. (2002) Caribbean of the east? global interconnections and the Southeast Asian cruise industry. *Asian Journal of Social Science* 30, 420–440.

Wood, R.E. (2004a) Cruise ships: deterritorialized destinations. In: Lumsdon, L. and Page, S.J. (eds) *Tourism and Transport: Issues and Agenda for the New Millennium.* Elsevier, Oxford, pp. 133–146.

Wood, R.E. (2004b) Global currents: cruise ships in the Caribbean Sea. In: Duval, D.T. (ed.) *Tourism in the Caribbean: Trends, Development, Prospects.* Routledge, London/New York, pp. 152–171.

37 Cruises, Supranationalism and Border Complexities

Dallen J. Timothy

Arizona State University, School of Community Resources and Development, PO Box 874703, Tempe, AZ 85287-4703, USA

Introduction

There are few types of tourism that have as many global and cross-border implications as cruises. Like organized tours and some independent travel, but with the exception of cruises that take place strictly in a domestic setting, cruises cross many borders and spend most of their time sailing through international waters. For example, the Caribbean and Mediterranean, two of the world's most popular cruising regions comprise many small and geographically fragmented countries. In addition to on-land stopovers, the territorial waters of these countries are traversed almost on a daily basis by cruise ships full of passengers. Thus, in nearly all cases, different levels of authority and sovereignty are traversed and negotiated. Yet, little attention has been paid by tourism scholars to the geopolitical context of cruises and how this plays out in the operation and globalization of the cruise sector.

This chapter aims to begin filling this gap by describing several geopolitical aspects of the cruise sector, including its political complexities, its comparison to the growth of tourism at international boundaries and the role of cross-border regional cooperation in tourism, especially as it pertains to cruises.

The Geopolitical Complexity of Cruises

There is general confusion about sovereignty and territorial issues in relation to the cruise sector (Simons, 1990). Wood (2000, 2004a,b) highlights many of the global and deterritorializing issues surrounding the cruise industry. Foremost among these is the use of flags of convenience (FOCs) or the registering and licensing of cruise ships in developing countries (primarily) far from the places where corporate headquarters are located. For example, there are no US-based cruise lines in the Caribbean that fly the US flag (Wood, 2000). Most cruise ships plying the world's waterways use FOCs in an effort to evade strict environmental, labour and safety laws and to skirt homecountry tax regulations. The countries most commonly used to license and register the ships are Liberia, Panama and the Bahamas, although there are a few others scattered throughout the developing world. These countries all have looser environmental standards, and safety inspections can be done rather quickly and problems 'resolved' much faster than in the developed world where the ships typically sail from. Additionally, labour laws that protect the rights of workers are almost non-existent in most FOC countries, and those working on board are subject to the laws of the country in which the ship is registered (Wood, 2000). This contributes to a globalized labour force, wherein migrants from all over the world can work aboard cruise ships, free of national and international regulation. The savings realized through lower taxes, lower employee wages and lower safety and environmental standards by registering in FOC countries are passed on to passengers in the form of lower cruise costs (Aspinwall, 1988; Wood, 2004a,b).

Most jurisdictional problems relate to issues of sovereignty. According to international law, a nation's sovereign authority and territory end 12 nautical miles from shore. Areas beyond the 12-mile (20 km) limit are known as international waters. Because cruise ships are typically registered in FOC countries and spend most of their time in international waters, they are relatively free from the laws of any particular nation and only slightly affected by international regulations – a condition that Wood (2004a, p. 134) calls unique 'deterritorialized environment'.

Such geopolitical anomalies allow the cruise sector to go almost unregulated in terms of environmental impacts. Even today, cruise ships dump large amounts of effluent and kitchen waste in the oceans. Additionally, the ships emit high quantities of air and water pollutants and have negative impacts on the ocean floor whenever anchors and chains are used (Cloesen, 2003; Lester and Weeden, 2004). This knowledge has created considerable debate and outcries, but the fact that the ships pass through so many different countries in one trip and primarily travel through international waters means that anti-pollution laws are very difficult to enforce (Wood, 2004a). In most cases, today, enforcement of environmental protection laws is under the control of the cruise lines themselves and the FOC countries where their ships are registered.

Cruise Ships and Ports of Call as Border Towns

In many parts of the world, communities located adjacent to international boundaries have grown and thrived because of tourism (Arreola and Curtis, 1993; Timothy, 2001b). This is particularly the case in North America, Europe, Asia and parts of Latin America. What

all of these border towns have in common is an infrastructure that has developed to cater to the needs of foreign visitors and landscapes that reflect a series of competitive advantages over what is offered on the other side of the boundary, and they owe their existence in most cases to their location at the border. Border towns that rely on tourism as the mainstay of their economy are typically laden with souvenir shops, duty-free stores, liquor stores, bars and nightclubs, brothels and casinos. These types of establishments thrive when their associated activities are not permitted on the other side of the border. Likewise, shopping is a critical activity in many of these border towns, owing to cheaper but higher quality products, lower taxes and a different range of merchandise than that available at home (Timothy and Butler, 1995; Timothy, 2005).

Cruises, especially the short cruise phenomenon that has been popularized so much in the last 10 years or so (Dowling and Vasudavan, 2000; Testa, 2002), have taken on very similar characteristics to those of traditional border towns. The ships and their ports of call resemble traditional border towns in that activities that might not be permitted in the country where the company is headquartered are allowed to flourish on board ships, because of their extraterritorial status and that they pass through international waters on a regular basis, and are therefore rarely under the sovereign control of any one government. Passengers on cruise ships do typically cross international boundaries, and therefore the activities that are permitted in border towns around the world also tend to be permissible on cruise liners and in ports of call. For instance, the deterritorialized status of cruise ships allows them to sell alcohol openly and to establish gaming facilities. Likewise, plying international waters allows duty-free purchases to be made on board.

One common similarity with border towns and cruises is high levels of alcohol consumption. One of the earliest associations between cruises and border town-type tourism began to appear in the early 1900s in North America and the Caribbean with the prohibition era (1918–1933), when the US government outlawed the manufacture, distribution and sale of alcohol. Prohibition was one of the primary reasons Mexican border towns grew so rapidly as visitor destinations, and the development of some of the earliest cruises was fuelled by the same phenomenon. Cruises to destinations such as Mexico, the Caribbean and Canada became very popular during the prohibition era as Americans sailed abroad in large part to consume alcoholic beverages (Lawton and Butler, 1987; Timothy, 2001a).

Similarly, 'booze cruises' have long been popular in Europe as a result of cross-border advantages in terms of taxes, drinking ages and alcohol-consumption limitations. The so-called booze cruises between Great Britain and France were very popular during the 1970s, 1980s and 1990s (Peisley, 1987; Essex and Gibb, 1989; Hidalgo, 1993), although the situation has changed somewhat since the implementation of duty-free restrictions between European Union (EU) member states. This has lessened some of the competitive advantage France has to offer, but despite these changes the cross-channel booze cruises are still popular (Brogan and Lumsden, 2004). The ferry boats between Finland and Sweden, and between Finland and Estonia also provide some of the same appeal that exists across the English Channel. Peisley (1992) noted that the dividing line between ferry services for transportation and mini-cruises is becoming increasingly blurred. This is certainly the case in the Baltic Sea, where the sailings between Finland and Sweden are more than simple modes of transportation. According to Peisley's early 1990s study, some 60% of cross-Baltic passengers took the trip for the pleasures the ride itself offered rather than as a way of getting from point A to point B. The ships are lavishly furnished and offer many types of entertainment, gaming and opportunities to drink. Peisley (1992) calls these and the mini-cruises across the English Channel 24-h 'cruises to nowhere' because the main attraction for many passengers is the trip itself with its many opportunities to play and drink, and many of the passengers do not even get off the boat at the other end.

Another type of short cruise has developed as a result of border and sovereignty issues, namely gambling/casino cruises. These have become very popular in recent years. They last from a matter of hours to a day or two, and what they have in common is that they go just beyond the territorial waters of countries or states where casino gaming is not permitted. Once

they reach the 12-mile limit, the casinos and bars open for business. In the USA, this phenomenon has become quite popular in the south-east, where some states prohibit casino gaming on land; in some cases the boats do not even go the full 12 miles. A similar business venture began off the coast of Israel in the late 1990s (Felsenstein and Freeman, 1998). Riverboat gambling cruises have also become popular in the USA in recent years where gaming is not allowed on land in certain states but it is permitted on board river ferries that ply navigable rivers between states (e.g. the Ohio, Mississippi and Missouri rivers).

Shopping, one of the most common border town tourist activities is especially popular on cruises and in ports of call. One form of shopping in this context is souvenirs. Clearly, people who visit interesting seaports as part of a cruise itinerary have an interest in buying reminders of their stopovers. In the Caribbean region, wood carvings and wicker products are among the most popular. Another type of shopping, which is the most popular on board, is duty-free retailing. When ships sail between countries and through international waters, they are entitled to sell products at duty-free prices. Similarly, most cruise destination ports have established tax-free shopping as a way of boosting gains from ship-based day visitors. In some cases, such as the island of St Martin, the entire island has been designated a 'duty-free' zone so that tourists are not required to pay import tariffs on the products they purchase (Timothy, 2005). The most popular products available at shipboard and port duty-free shops include liquor, tobacco, watches and jewellery, chocolate, perfumes and toiletries, and clothing. Specialized shopping cruises have also gained popularity in recent years owing primarily to the spread of duty-free retailing (Peisley, 1987). Fairly often, Canadian cruises in the north-eastern region and the St Lawrence Seaway area stop in at Saint-Pierre-et-Miquelon, a French territory off the coast of Newfoundland, Canada, because this is one way Canadians and Americans can purchase French products in France at duty-free prices without having to leave North America (Timothy, 2001a).

Most people who visit border towns are in statistical terms counted as international excursionists, because they typically stay abroad less than 1 day. Cruise passengers have this in common as well. While they are an important part of tourism in most port countries, they are in effect only international day trippers (Bar-On, 1988). Many small island countries depend heavily on these excursionists for the foundations of their tourism industries, although there has been some debate in recent years about the real effects of cruise-based tourism. Some argue that the visitors come in for a few or several hours, leave their negative impacts behind but spend relatively little money and see little of the islands. In addition, there are concerns that the small amount of spending that does take place only goes to benefit the wealthy elites, because they are the ones who own the shops adjacent to the harbours. Relatively few people in island states derive any benefits from cruise passenger spending.

Finally, border towns are often the only exposure some people get to travelling abroad, and many people like to cross borders just so they can say they have been in a foreign country. Border communities play this important role in tourism (Timothy, 2001b). Similar situations exist with cruises. For some passengers, cruises provide chances to visit several islands or countries that they might not otherwise have opportunities to visit. Passengers can get a taste of different places, and if they seek them out, occasions to see diverse cultures (Bar-On, 1988; Singh, 1999). Similarly, visiting different ports of call on different cruises gives them opportunities to 'collect' countries, or extend the list of places they have visited (Timothy, 1998).

Cruises and Border Formalities

Globalization refers to the process by which the world becomes a smaller place, and part of this notion refers to the fact that it is in most cases becoming easier for people to travel abroad. The cruise sector is an important part of the process of globalization. On regional cruises in the Caribbean, Mediterranean, South Pacific and South-East Asia, many international boundaries are crossed, but the border formalities associated with cruises are typically somewhat different from those encountered on land or in airports. In the Caribbean, for example, customs and immigration formalities are in large part carried out by the cruise company itself in close cooperation with the island and the US government. Many different agencies in the USA, such as the Customs Service, Coast Guard, Immigration and Naturalization Service, Homeland Security, Department of Health and the Department of Agriculture, have an interest in the territorial issues and immigration issues associated with cruises (Testa, 2002). The cruise companies must work closely with these agencies to ensure that their mandates are being fulfilled.

In the Middle East, cruises in the Persian Gulf are becoming popular, but there have been some visa-related impediments to its smooth development. For example, according to Peisley (2000), a cruise stopping in Oman, Qatar, Bahrain, Iran and the United Arab Emirates would have to charge tourists US$250 in additional fees just for visa costs. In addition to the cost, complications in getting visas for certain nationalities are difficult in the region, and while Middle East cruises are of considerable interest to Australians, for example, visa complications prevent many Australians from purchasing and tour operators and travel agencies from selling cruises in the region (Peisley, 2000). Apparently the situation has started to change. The Emirates have taken the lead in reducing the bureaucracy by establishing a low-cost and fast-track transit visa system for cruise passengers because its view is that they should be exempt from regular formalities and visas if they are only going to be in port for a matter of hours. Dubai has worked out a deal wherein cruise lines can get a 96-h transit visa for the entire shipload of passengers directly based on the passenger manifest list, no longer requiring individual visa applications. There is talk in other Gulf countries to adopt a similar fast-track visa system for cruise passengers as a way of attracting more tourists (Peisley, 2000, p. 9).

Cross-border Alliances

Since the middle of the 20th century, countries have begun working together and forming cross-border alliances at a regional level. These alliances, sometimes also referred to as trade blocs, economic alliances, customs unions or free-trade areas, have become commonplace throughout the world in response to globalization processes and the realization by individual nations that in today's modernized and high-tech world, cooperation is essential for economic survival in terms of both supply and demand for products and services (Balassa, 1961; Jessop, 1995; Bhalla and Bhalla, 1997; Timothy, 2003).

Several of these supranationalist coalitions have begun to consider tourism as an important component of intraregional trade and commerce. The Association of South-East Asian Nations (ASEAN), for instance, has established its own tourism section to deal specifically with enhancing the global image of the region, attempting to bring in more visitors and work with various sectors in the industry (e.g. airlines and cruises) and individual governments to abolish many of the border-restricted policies that have traditionally characterized cross-boundary traffic and services. The North American Free Trade Agreement (NAFTA) does not address tourism directly, although its environmental, transportation, immigration and trade policies have clear implications for the industry in all member states. Likewise, the EU has enacted many regulations and policies regarding tourism development in peripheral regions, economic development and conservation through tourism and environmental policies that directly affect tourism. Finally, several associations in the Caribbean, such as the Association of Caribbean States (ACS, 2002), the Organization of Eastern Caribbean States (OECS) and the Caribbean Community (CARICOM), all have strong interests in tourism development (Timothy, 2004).

In the regions where cruising is an important part of tourism, the sector has received some attention by alliance members. Cruises are becoming more prominent in South-east Asia with Singapore being a major port owing largely to its position as the region's main airport hub. As a result, ASEAN has become more interested in issues related to cruises, and as recently as 2003, ASEAN and Japan signed a joint cooperative agreement to promote cruises in East and South-East Asia and to improve safety conditions on board (ASEAN, 2003).

Likewise, the Caribbean's regional alliances have a common interest in the cruise sector, and a great deal of dialogue has taken place to understand cruise-related issues, such as the

one described earlier in relation to the limited benefits of day trippers, who contribute to the negative effects of tourism but do little to improve economic conditions (Caribbean Media Exchange, 2004). The Caribbean Tourism Organization (CTO) typically includes cruise tourism in its marketing and promotional efforts and has tried to address issues of standardization in the region's cruise industry.

Other types of international alliances have developed over the years that specially deal with the business side of cruises. However, they do not have any kind of political autonomy or extragovernment authority, as the EU, NAFTA, ASEAN and CARICOM have in setting common pricing and transportation policies. Instead they see their role as threefold. First, they promote cruise holidays collectively through advertising campaigns, publications and market research. Second, they are heavily involved in training travel agents and employees of tour operators on how best to sell cruises and the unique issues associated with the cruise sector. Some of them even offer training certificates for travel professionals who complete their sponsored training courses. Finally, they often join forces to lobby governments and international organizations related to issues concerning the cruise sector (WTO, 2003).

MedCruise is a good example of these business alliances and comprises members throughout the Mediterranean region, the Red Sea area and the Arabian Gulf (Peisley, 2000). Cruise Lines International Association, the International Council of Cruise Lines (ICCL), the Passengers Shipping Association and the International Cruise Council Australasia are examples of international industry alliances whose jobs are to promote the cruise product and build positive global images (Hall and Braithwaite, 1990; WTO, 2003).

Supranational cooperation from the standpoint of sovereign nations working together has the potential to contribute to more sustainable forms of tourism (Timothy, 2001b). Environment, employment, economic development, education, safety and security standards and reduced entry formalities are all affected by supranationalist movements and clearly have an influence on the cruise sector. Cooperation on a less-formal level in terms of cruise companies, airlines, destination management companies and tour operators working together to solve regional management and marketing problems may also decrease the barrier effects of borders and contribute to more sustainable forms and degrees of tourism.

Conclusion

Owing to their special 'deterritorialized' status, cruises operate within a fairly complex and dynamic geopolitical context. Wood (2000) has argued that cruises are somewhat of a laboratory for globalization processes at work, particularly in terms of the issue of FOCs and the registration, labour, safety and environmental implications this issue has for the tourism industry.

Several border implications also exist in the cruise sector. One of the most notable is that of parallelisms between cruise ships, ports of call and international boundaries. Within this framework, the ships and the ports they call at resemble the forms and functions of traditional border towns found throughout the world, where tourists typically engage in activities that are either forbidden at home or encouraged abroad through looser laws and regulations, lower prices and heavy tax breaks. Alcohol consumption, gambling and shopping are perhaps the most vivid examples of activities in border communities and on cruise ships.

Also related to political boundaries is the notion of cross-border collaboration in regional tourism development. Many supranational alliances exist and have significant bearings for cruise operations. Such economic communities are prominent in areas that tend also to be popular cruise destinations, such as the Caribbean, Mediterranean and South-east Asia. These alliances most typically have the following issues in common, all of which relate either directly or indirectly to cruises: environmental conservation and regulation, flow of people between member states, increased intraregional trade, improved transportation and infrastructure, multination promotional efforts and education. In addition to political and economic alliances, several business alliances have been formed during the last 30 years whose primary responsibilities include promoting cruise tourism at an international level, regardless of the existence of political boundaries.

The world is changing at a rapid pace, as more countries open up to the prospect of tourism development. Cruises are an important component of tourism in many coastal countries, and if recent history is any indicator of the future, it is certain that more countries will begin to see the potential value of cruise-based tourism. The process of globalization and the changing role of sovereignty and borders in relation to supranationalism will stimulate additional cruise tourism and assist destinations in finding new ways to capitalize from this unique form of international travel.

References

ACS (Association of Caribbean States) (2002) Special committee on transport. Available at: www.acs-aec.org/transport.htm

Arreola, D.D. and Curtis, J. (1993) *The Mexican Border Cities: Landscape Anatomy and Place Personality*. University of Arizona Press, Tucson, Arizona.

ASEAN (Association of South-east Asian Nations) (2003) Joint media statement – first ASEAN and Japan transport ministers meeting. Available at: www.asean.sec.org

Aspinwall, M.D. (1988) Passenger ships in the coastwise trade: US public policy since 1789. *Marine Policy* 12(2), 161–164.

Balassa, B. (1961) *The Theory of Economic Integration*. Richard, D. Irwin, Homewood, Illinois.

Bar-On, R. (1988) International day trips, including cruise passenger excursions. *Tourist Review* 43(4), 12–16.

Bhalla, A.S. and Bhalla, P. (1997) *Regional Blocs: Building Blocks or Stumbling Blocks?* Macmillan, London.

Brogan, B. and Lumsden, D. (2004) Brown gets EU deadline over 'booze cruises'. *TravelTelegraph*, 18 October.

Caribbean Media Exchange (2004) Regional tourism officials call for regional cruise ship policy. Available at: www.caribbeanmediaexchange.com

Cloesen, U. (2003) Environmental impact management of ship based tourism to Antarctica. *Asia Pacific Journal of Tourism Research* 8(2), 32–37.

Dowling, R.K. and Vasudavan, T. (2000) Cruising in the new millennium. *Tourism Recreation Research* 25(3), 17–27.

Essex, S.J. and Gibb, R.A. (1989) Tourism in the Anglo-French frontier zone. *Geography* 74(3), 222–231.

Felsenstein, D. and Freeman, D. (1998) Simulating the impacts of gambling in a tourist location: some evidence from Israel. *Journal of Travel Research* 37(2), 145–155.

Hall, J.A. and Braithwaite, R. (1990) Caribbean cruise tourism: a business of transnational partnerships. *Tourism Management* 11(4), 339–347.

Hidalgo, L. (1993) British shops suffer as 'booze cruise' bargain hunters flock to France. *The Times*, 22 November, 5.

Jessop, B. (1995) Regional economic blocs, cross-border cooperation, and local economic strategies in postcolonialism. *American Behavioral Scientist* 38, 674–715.

Lawton, L.J. and Butler, R.W. (1987) Cruise ship industry: patterns in the Caribbean 1880–1986. *Tourism Management* 8(4), 329–343.

Lester, J.A. and Weeden, C. (2004) Stakeholders, the natural environment and the future of Caribbean cruise tourism. *International Journal of Tourism Research* 6(1), 39–50.

Peisley, T. (1987) Sea ferry travel and short cruises. stop*Travel and Tourism Analyst* 1, 19–29.

Peisley, T. (1992) Transport: ferries, short sea cruises and the Channel Tunnel. *Travel and Tourism Analyst* 4, 5–26.

Peisley, T. (2000) The cruise industry in the Arabian Gulf and Indian Ocean. *Travel and Tourism Analyst* 1, 3–17.

Simons, M.S. (1990) Legal implications for cruise ships, travelers and tour operators: an Australian experience. *International Journal of Hospitality Management* 9(2), 135–141.

Singh, A. (1999) Growth and development of the cruise line industry in South-east Asia. *Asia Pacific Journal of Tourism Research* 3(2), 24–31.

Testa, M.R. (2002) Shipboard vs shoreside cruise operations. *FIU Hospitality Review* 20(2), 29–40.

Timothy, D.J. (1998) Collecting places: geodetic lines in tourist space. *Journal of Travel and Tourism Marketing* 7(4), 123–129.

Timothy, D.J. (2001a) Benefits and costs of smallness and peripheral location in tourism: Saint-Pierre et Miquelon (France). *Tourism Recreation Research* 26(3), 61–70.

Timothy, D.J. (2001b) *Tourism and Political Boundaries.* Routledge, London.

Timothy, D.J. (2003) Supranationalist alliances and tourism: insights from ASEAN and SAARC. *Current Issues in Tourism* 6(3), 250–266.

Timothy, D.J. (2004) Tourism and supranationalism in the Caribbean. In: Duval, D.T. (ed.) *Tourism in the Caribbean: Trends, Development, Prospects.* Routledge, London, pp. 119–135.

Timothy, D.J. (2005) *Shopping Tourism, Retailing and Leisure.* Channel View, Clevedon, UK.

Timothy, D.J. and Butler, R.W. (1995) Cross-border shopping: a North American perspective. *Annals of Tourism Research* 22, 6–34.

Wood, R.E. (2000) Caribbean cruise tourism: globalization at sea. *Annals of Tourism Research* 27(2), 345–370.

Wood, R.E. (2004a) Cruise ships: deterritorialized destinations. In: Lumsdon, L. and Page, S.J. (eds) *Tourism and Transport: Issues and Agenda for the New Millennium.* Elsevier, Oxford, pp. 133–145.

Wood, R.E. (2004b) Global currents: cruise ships in the Caribbean Sea. In: Duval, D.T. (ed.) *Tourism in the Caribbean: Trends, Development, Prospects.* Routledge, London, pp. 152–171.

WTO (World Tourism Organization) (2003) *Worldwide Cruise Ship Activity.* Madrid.

38   Looking Ahead: The Future of Cruising

Ross K. Dowling

Edith Cowan University, Faculty of Business and Law, School of Marketing, Tourism and Leisure, Joondalup, WA 6027, Australia

Introduction

Cruise vacations have reached a level of popularity few industry observers believed was possible 30 years ago. In 2004, 10.6 million people cruised, the industry's highest-ever total, representing an annual increase of 11%. According to the Association, 2004 was a banner year for the cruise industry in terms of newbuilds and passenger growth. In the previous year, cruise lines capped a record-setting, 5-year building boom that introduced 62 new ships to the North American market.

In 2004 there were more cruise departures and itineraries than ever before with 68 vessels having debuted between 2000 and 2005. In addition Cruise Lines International Association's (CLIA) member line ships sailed at 104% occupancy rate. According to the CLIA 'guests can find tranquility in state of the art spas, revel in a host of cutting-edge onboard activities or gaze at the stars while watching a movie on a 300-ft^2 poolside screen. Always seeking new ways to address its guests' vacation desires, the cruise industry will continue to grow through continued fleet expansion throughout this year and beyond. The cruise industry is undergoing major fleet renovation, with the average size of the ships increasing. The largest ships have a capacity for up to 3500 passengers and 1500 crew making them 'cities at sea'. CLIA fleets will introduce 20 more cutting-edge ships between now and 2008' (CLIA, 2005a).

The Association suggests that leisure cruising will continue to ride a wave of unprecedented passenger growth and popularity in 2005, buoyed by strong customer demand, an emphasis on ship introductions and innovations, more US homeport availability, a renewed demand for exotic ports, plus strong brand marketing and attention to quality and service standards. Although in 2005 capacity growth will be reduced compared with previous years, in the long run cruising's building boom will continue, as several lines are planning new vessels for 2006 and beyond. The Council of Cruise Lines estimates the total economic impact of the cruise industry as AUS$23 billion a year. Further, recent research conducted by the industry indicates that 30 million Americans have expressed an intent to cruise over the next 3 years (CLIA, 2005b).

Ward (2005, p. 25) suggests that future ships will continue with the present trends of small-, medium- and large-scale ships. The small ships will be high quality, luxury vessels able to access a greater number of destinations and offer increased adventure or expedition style cruises in maximum comfort. Medium-sized ships will be made larger by 'stretching' their ships with the addition of new midsections. Large ships are based on 'economy of scale' and will measure over 100,000 t and accommodate over 3000 passengers. These ships will rival the shore-based (often coastal) luxury resorts and offer similar amenities and services.

Thus the future of cruising looks bright. Indeed it is one of the star growth industries of the early 21st century. In the last decade the industry has been driven by both increased demand as well as increased supply. More people have wanted to go cruising and more ships have been built. There are a host of potential cruisers in both the developed as well as the nearly developed countries, and within these markets there are a number of growing market segments. Traditional cruise destination regions are being added to by a host of new ones – new continents, countries, ports and islands. Entire new regions are now being accessed by ships, which do not touch the land, instead the passengers being ferried ashore by tenders, lifeboats or smaller landing craft. On some expedition ships passengers are being taken ashore by helicopters.

Cruise lines are being absorbed in the process of industry consolidation, and at the time of writing three large cruise corporations make up the majority of the world's cruise capacity. Globalization has brought with it an increased responsibility and accountability, both of which have been hastened by the activism of local communities and non-government organizations (NGOs). Governments are getting in on the act and the cruise companies now find themselves with increased environmental regulations.

The industry itself is changing and recent additions include the launch of an apartment ship and a low-cost cruise line. But underpinning all of the above advances as well as the growth of the industry is the shadow of 11 September 2001 and the spectre of a possible terrorist threat. Thus safety and security is the most important aspect facing the future of the industry and so with this will come a range of initiatives, protocols, procedures, regulations and products. This cannot be overlooked and is an essential part of securing the future of the cruise industry.

Cruise Ships

Ships have become larger and now resemble floating resorts. That cruising has changed is evident from the ships we sail on. 'Just go for a jog around the sports deck on any new vessel

and there are miniature golf courses, computerized golf simulators, swim-against-the-tide lap pools, sports courts for basketball, volleyball and paddleball and more' (Schwartzman, 2004, p. 40). These innovations do not stop aboard the ship but extend before, during and sometimes after the cruise. For example, Norwegian Cruise Line (NCL) America has created a comprehensive shoreside golf programme on its *Pride of Aloha*, based in the Hawaiian Islands. The programme offers passengers shore-based outings to championship courses on all four main islands. In addition, the ship has its complete first golf pro-shop at sea and features on-board clinics with local golf professionals in its three practice nets.

Companies have competed vigorously to try to 'outdo' their competition. Thus the newest ships being launched today include new entertainment and communication technologies, an array of sports facilities and greater space devoted to health and spa facilities. In addition they have focused on being less formal and more casual with more dining choices and increased entertainment. Cabins are now being replaced by suites, many having balconies and shopping arcades are the norm. The exteriors have indented or flowing decks and many ships are decorated with flowing murals on their sides. The interiors reflect luxury resort hotels with grand foyers and elegant architecture. Even their launches are becoming more upmarket with 'celebrity launches' and appointment as 'godmothers'. All-in-all the cruise ships of today are vastly different to the ones of just a decade ago, and future ships will no doubt be significantly different from those being built today.

The cruise industry continues to grow and in 2006 the largest cruise ship in the world will be launched, Royal Caribbean International's 158,000-t *Freedom of the Seas*. But small- and medium-sized ships are also being built. For example, the success of the *Queen Mary 2* has prompted Cunard to place an order for a new panamax vessel to be named *Queen Victoria*. The 85,000-t ship will accommodate 1850 passengers and will enter service in 2007. Its design will follow the grand ocean-liner style of its sister ships.

One of the most innovative cruise lines is NCL. Since its inception in 1966 it has set the pace for modern cruising (White, 2004).

Originally called Norwegian Caribbean Line, it pioneered cruising from Miami, a virtually unknown port at the time. Since then it has pioneered many firsts at sea including:

1. New cruise destinations – e.g. Caribbean and more recently the Hawaiian Islands;
2. All-inclusive pricing – it was the first cruise line to offer a nationwide air/sea programme combining cruise, hotel and transfers from more than 150 cities in North America;
3. Freestyle cruising;
4. Internet cafes – the first Internet café was introduced on the *Norwegian Sky*;
5. Shore options – NCL's 'Dive-In' snorkelling programme was the first of its kind in the industry.

NCL recently announced two new ships ordered for delivery in October 2007. The vessels currently referred to as hull *S.669* and *S.670* will have a capacity of 2384 lower berths, cost US$510 million and be sister ships to the *Norwegian Jewel* (Table 38.1). The new orders will be the tenth and eleventh big new ships to join the NCL fleet since the fleet modernization began in late 1999. Once these ships are delivered in 2007, over 75% of NCL's inventory of beds will be on ships less than 8 years old. Investment in the NCL fleet modernization is now close to US$4 billion since 2000.

Propulsion

One of the new innovations in cruise ships is the use of the gas turbine engine. This rotary-type engine is part of a hybrid power system that also includes traditional diesel-electric engines. This advance has primarily come from the result of the US Environmental Protection Agency citing 13 cruise ships in Alaska in recent years for exceeding federal limits on air pollution in Juneau, Seward and Glacier Bay (Schwartzman, 2004). Since then the ships have included the latest technology for treating on board wastes and reducing air pollutants. Thus gas turbines have now been introduced by Celebrity Cruises, Cunard, Holland America Line, Princess Cruises and Royal Caribbean International. In some of the ships their turbines capture exhausts to drive a secondary steam turbine, which generates power for shipboard lighting and air conditioning.

Other features of the gas turbines are that they are lighter and smaller than their diesel-electric counterparts, do not cause as much vibration, and do not have to be put in the hull. For example, Princess Cruises' *Coral Princess* houses its two engines on its funnel, giving the ship an 'aircraft-type' look. Another innovation is the inclusion of 'pods', which pull rather than push a ship through the water. These machines are like large outboard motors and they replace the typical inboard engine, shaft and rudders of conventional ships. The pod reduces vibration and the ship's turning circle.

Interior design

Both 'retro' and 'contemporary' designs are being introduced on cruise ships in order to recreate the luxurious, welcoming interiors

Table 38.1. Recent Norwegian Cruise Line ships newbuilds.

No.	Year	Ship	Size (tonnes)	Passengers
1	2001	*Norwegian Sun*	77,104	1,936
2	2001	*Norwegian Star*	91,740	2,240
3	2002	*Norwegian Dawn*	91,740	2,224
4	2004	*Norwegian Spirit*	77,104	1,966
5	2004	*Pride of Aloha*[a]	77,104	2,002
6	2005	*Pride of America*	81,000	2,144
7	2005	*Norwegian Jewel*	91,740	2,376
8	2006	*Pride of Hawaii*	91,740	2,384
9	2007	*S.669*	91,740	2,384
10	2007	*S.670*	91,740	2,384

[a]Built in 1997 as *Norwegian Sky*, it was refurbished and renamed in 2004.

reminiscent of Europe's grand hotels (Ward, 2005, p. 17). Large ships have interiors with multistorey atriums, large theatres with revolving stages, Internet cafes, incabin interactive television and works of art throughout. As megaships have proliferated, an everincreasing number of people has been needed to fill their berths. To attract the nouveau passengers, 'the industry has outfitted its ships with a growing array of facilities and introduced an increasingly diverse range of on-board programming, such as enrichment series, specialty dining and art auctions, to name a few' (Schwartzman, 2004, p. 41).

New technologies

Cruise ships have embraced new technologies and many cruise liners provide a whole variety of ways for passengers to keep themselves occupied. One example is video bars to entertain passengers with over 200 h of video images. Also available are playstations, allowing passengers to play table-top games in interactive booths. Interactive television allows passengers to shop, order meals, arrange port trips, play casino games and order movies directly from the television in their cabin. SeaVision has developed an interactive television system that not only improves passengers' services and the deliverance of more entertainment options but also creates the opportunity for cruise ships to generate incremental revenue and the rise of on-board productivity (Dowling and Vasudavan, 2000).

Another technological introduction to the cruise ship industry is the use of multipurpose magnetic stripe cards by passengers. These cards are used for payment of everything on the ship, such as gifts from the gift shop, chips for the casino, drinks from the bar, massages, hair cuts and generally whatever else that can be purchased on the ship. This card is backed up by a credit card at a pre-approved amount, which can be instantly extended if the limit is exceeded by the passenger.

Technological advances have made it easier to stay connected when away from home. Most ships offer satellite telephone services and Internet access 24 h a day. Some vessels have multistation computer centres while others provide in-stateroom Internet access for guests

who bring their own laptops. Some even have wireless connections so guests can use their laptops or one rented on board from remote locations, such as on deck. For example, the Internet Café on Princess Cruises' 116,000-tonne *Diamond Princess* has 29 workstations and a café. It also features wireless Internet access in its Grand Plaza atrium for those passengers who have their own notebooks (Fig. 38.1). Computers are only the beginning of the communication at sea.

Health and fitness

Health and fitness centres are becoming more embedded in ships as the baby boomers take to the seas. With an increased interest in, and ability to pay for, health and well-being products, more space on ships is becoming devoted to health facilities. According to Ward (2005, p. 19) the basic sauna, steamroom and massage facility have evolved into huge, specially designed spas that include the latest in high-tech muscle exercising, aerobic and weight-training machines and relaxation treatments, such as hydrotherapy and thalassotherapy baths, jet-blitz, rasul (graduated steam and all-over body mud cleansing), seaweed wraps and hot and cold stone massage.

Fig. 38.1. Internet Café on Princess Cruises' *Diamond Princess*. Photo: Princess Cruises.

Dining

The newer, larger resort ships all offer intimate restaurants which are à la carte and fee-for-service. Generally they are small and offer high-quality food and service. Most new ships have flexible dining and all-day casual cafes and restaurants (Fig. 38.2). Ward (2005, p. 20) notes that 'although the concept is good, the delivery often is not (it is typically self-service eating and not the *dining* experience most passengers envisage)'.

Issues

Ward (2005, p. 20) notes a number of issues, which are facing the cruise industry. Most revolve around the ships being recast as floating hotels with an increased emphasis on the ship as a destination rather than as a mode of travel. He states that the large floating resorts that travel by night and are in port during the day provide little connection to nature and the sea. He adds that 'almost everything is designed to keep you inside the ship to spend money, thus increasing on-board revenue and shareholder dividends'.

   Ward (2005, pp. 20–21) also has problems with:

1. Bland entertainment;
2. Aggressive young cruise directors;
3. Homogenous bland cabins;
4. Referring to passengers as 'guests';
5. The introduction of 'hotel-speak';
6. The overuse of public address systems;
7. The disappearance of streamers and free champagne at bon voyage parties when ships leave port;
8. The decline in food and service standards;
9. The disembarkation process is neither considerate nor caring for passengers.

Passengers

A recent survey has shown that existing and potential passengers are seeking active, more adventurous cruises (CLIA, 2004a). It shows that passengers are becoming more youthful and are demanding more active itineraries. The number of full-time retirees is declining and family cruisers are increasing. The study shows that there is a call for longer cruises plus rare, exotic and intriguing ports of call. The North American cruisers surveyed also indicated that they chose their cruise according to the places visited. Favoured destinations are the Caribbean, Alaska, the Bahamas and Hawaii.

   Although cruise lines are adapting their offerings both on board and ashore for the active baby boomers, ironically though, another emerging problem is the size of some passengers. With people in western nations becoming larger, obesity is now a major health problem. This has been

Fig. 38.2. Casual dining – a central part of the cruise experience. In Silversea Cruises' *Silver Cloud's* Terrace Café restaurant, Tasman Sea, January 2005. Photo: Ross K. Dowling.

illustrated recently by dozens of seats on the *Queen Mary 2* being broken by obese passengers. It has been reported that the French company that supplied the chairs is repairing and replacing them as fast as possible (*The West Australian*, 2004). The company claims that many of the passengers are heavier than imagined!

Family cruising

A number of niche markets will emerge in the years ahead. One of the largest will be family cruising. This is becoming increasingly popular and will become a major niche market in future (Table 38.2). A recent analysis of the cruise market shows that families are an important segment of the cruise market. While a spouse is the most likely cruise companion, 16% of cruisers bring children under age 18 along on a cruise (CLIA, 2004b). Although multigenerational and family cruising has always been popular, this travel segment is increasing as families place a stronger emphasis on spending quality time together. Cruise ships, which offer activities and amenities for every age group, are an ideal environment for multigenerational family vacations.

CLIA (2004b) estimates that more than one million children under the age of 18 years sailed on CLIA's member line ships in 2004. This trend is expected to accelerate in 2005 and beyond, as cruise lines continue to add amenities and activities for the whole family – from toddlers to grandparents. Virtually all lines feature extensive, highly supervised children's programmes where kids are placed in age-appropriate groups. Teen lounges, video arcades, computer learning centres, toddlers' play areas and even special shore excursions for children are all a part of the mix. Multigenerational travel and family reunions at sea are also seeing sizeable growth. While children are occupied with their own sets of activities, parents and grandparents can take advantage of a plethora of on-board activities.

Ward (2005) notes that cruise ships provide a very safe, crime-free and encapsulated environment, and give junior passengers a lot of freedom without parents having to be concerned about where their children are at all times. He states that some cruise lines with family cruise programmes dedicate complete teams of children's 'tween and teens' counsellors who

Table 38.2. Children-friendly cruise lines.

Aida Cruises
Carnival Cruise Line
Celebrity Cruises
Cunard
Disney Cruise Line
Norwegian Cruise Line
P&O Cruises
Princess Cruises
Royal Caribbean International
Star Cruises
Thomson Cruises

Source: After Ward (2005).

run special programmes that are off-limits to adults. In some ships babysitting services are available with trained nannies and nurses and even night nurseries. Some ships have separate swimming pools and play areas for children, as well as teen centres, discos and video rooms.

The Disney Corporation added to its global theme parks by entering the cruise market in 1998 with two ships, *Disney Magic* and *Disney Wonder*. Both ships carry around 2750 passengers of whom over 35% are children. Holland America Line recently announced the introduction of a new youth programme, which will come into effect in 2006. Called 'Club HAL', it is part of a US$225 million 'Signature of Excellence' initiative aimed at ensuring passengers of all ages enjoy cruising (www.holland america.com). The club caters for children aged 3 years and above by offering their own play area with art tables, slide, big-screen television, electronic games and Internet access. Children aged 8 to 12 years have a dedicated area offering arcade games, air hockey, karaoke, Internet access and Sony playstations. Teenagers have an area called 'The Loft', a lounge designed to resemble a New York artist's loft complete with its own private sundeck and waterfall.

However, one of the problems noted for family-based ships is that while they may have a full children's programme at sea, this service is usually limited while the ship is in port.

Destinations

It has already been noted throughout this book that there are a plethora of emerging cruise destinations. Whereas once the cruise ship had to tie up to a dock at a port to unload passengers, today's ships use their own tenders or inflatable watercraft to ferry passengers to shore. Thus the increase in destinations is now virtually limitless. The leading cruise destination is still the Caribbean. Whereas there used to be one Caribbean destination, today there are four – Eastern, Western, Southern and 'Exotic' (Schwartzman, 2004). However, in the long term the present rapid growth of Caribbean cruising is likely to slow due to its environmental, biophysical, economic and social limits to growth, particularly in such fragile marine and terrestrial ecosystems that exist in the region (Wilkinson, Chapter 16, this volume).

Alaska

Alaska is emerging as one of the most popular cruise destinations in the world. The cruise industry is the State's second biggest and it is estimated that the industry employs 12,000 full-time equivalent jobs and adds US$878 million to the economy (North West Cruise Ship Association, 2005). In addition it is a major economic industry for the ship's ports of embarkation, namely Vancouver, Canada and Seattle, USA.

In 2003, 742,000 people visited Alaska via a cruise ship, which number is more than the whole of Alaska people (Romano-Lax, 2004). The prime reason for its popularity as a destination is its proximity to the large North American cruise consumer base. After the 11 September 2001 terrorist attacks on New York, a number of cruise lines repositioned ships to Alaska as homeland cruising emerged in response to North Americans fear of travelling overseas.

Its popularity is such that in 2004 it was also the leading cruise destination of Australians (Armstrong, 2005). Conversely Australia has become Holland America Line's largest market outside of the USA (Cruise Passenger, 2004a).

Polar cruising

Polar cruising is becoming extremely popular according to the CLIA (CLIA, 2005c). Cruise ships are now transporting travellers to every continent – including the North and South poles. The Arctic region, north of the Arctic

Circle, and the Antarctic Peninsula in the south, are attracting adventurous passengers to see and experience the beauty and spectacle of the world's most remote and unspoiled destinations. Many cruise ships now cross the Arctic Circle during the summer months, sailing from Scandinavian and Northern European ports to the region's vast forests, dramatic fjords and waterfalls, bathed in almost 24 h of sunlight. Antarctic cruises are offered from December through March and sail from South America's southernmost ports. These cruises showcase the Antarctic Peninsulas' awe-inspiring icescapes and abundant wildlife (Chapter 18, this volume). On top of the usual continental landings via inflatable expedition boats or flight-seeing tours by helicopter, many cruises now offer passengers additional activities such as climbing, kayaking or scuba diving.

Types of Cruises

As there is an increase in destinations, there is a parallel increase in the different types of cruises. They include coastal, around the world and adventure cruises. Coastal cruising is on the increase and it primarily focuses on recreational fishing, diving and sailing (Chapter 21, this volume).

The round-the-world (RTW) cruise industry is a small and relatively unexplored segment although a great start has been made by McCalla and Charlier (Chapter 19, this volume). They note that climate is a key factor in the RTW itineraries, which in turn leads to what they call 'choke (or congestion) points'. They note that this element of the cruise market can be further subdivided into partial and full RTW segments, and that apart from the seasonality aspect RTW cruising is defined by both spatial and temporal elements. Its economic importance should not be overestimated, though, and we want to make it clear that this is a marginal segment and that the bulk of the demand and offer in the cruise industry is for much shorter cruises.

Adventure cruises

Adventure cruises usually comprise smaller ships that visit remote and/or unusual destinations. According to Smith (Chapter 22, this volume) adventure cruises may be divided into four different types: nostalgia cruises (sailing ships and paddlewheelers), long-haul ferries, yachts and expedition cruises, including ice-breakers.

Expedition or exploration cruises visit remote and often rugged places such as the Arctic or Antarctic. Their smaller ships can access more places than larger vessels and generally passengers access land by tender or rubber dinghies (zodiacs). There is an increasing number of purpose-built expedition ships coming into service and this niche is growing rapidly (Smith, Chapter 22, this volume). One example is Celebrity Cruise Line's *Celebrity Xpedition*, which typifies these small ships by being only 2329 t and carrying only 98 passengers. The ship has been designed to operate soft-adventure cruises and it offers year-round weekly cruises in the Galapagos Islands. The ship is Ecuadorian registered and most of the crew and naturalist guides are locals. While the cabins are well appointed they do not have satellite television or Internet access, something that appeals to the growing number of ecocruisers.

In the middle of this decade there has been a number of expedition ships purpose built for the Australian market. North Star Cruises has just launched its new luxury adventure cruise ship *True North*. The 50-m vessel built at a cost of AUS$12 million carries 36 passengers and 16 crewmen (Fig. 38.3). The ship cruises prima-

rily on the north-west coast of Australia around the vast, remote Kimberley region. It features state-of-the-art maritime systems, an Internet café, forward observation lounge, indoor/outdoor bar and fine dining. All cabins feature ensuite facilities, inhouse entertainment and satellite telephones. The ship also carries a seven-seater helicopter and six on-board tenders to allow guests freedom to access the wilderness regions that the ships sail in. The region also hosts two other cruise lines. Coral Princess Cruises has launched its new ship *Oceanic Princess* whilst the other, Pearl Sea Coastal Cruises has launched the *Kimberley Quest II*, a 25-m charter vessel featuring nine private cabins to cater for up to 16 passengers.

Other recently launched Australian adventure ships include the *Discovery* and *Orion*. World Heritage Cruises' *Discovery* is 33 m long, has 3 decks and 12 cabins, and cruises in the Tasmanian World Heritage Wilderness Region (Ellis and Kriwoken, Chapter 23, this volume). Orion Expedition Cruises has launched its new 4000-t ship *Orion*, which can carry 106 passengers on its 5 star luxury expedition voyages.

Allied to this increase in expedition cruises in future will be the demand for quality interpretation of the places visited (Walker and Moscardo, Chapter 10, this vulome). As these ships visit more and more pristine regions, by extension this will place an even greater

Fig. 38.3.   North Star Cruises' *True North*, a small purpose-built expedition ship sailing in the Kimberley Region of Western Australia. Source: North Star Cruises.

demand for quality on-board and shore-based expedition leaders and/or guides. This demand will be generated by both the more environmentally aware passengers (demand) and the need for greater conservation of environmentally sensitive areas (supply).

Sustainability

The cruise industry faces a number of key environmental challenges related to its activities and operations in the world's oceans, particularly in and around priority conservation areas. The International Maritime Organization (IMO) has recognized this by designating particularly sensitive sea areas (PSSAs). They are recognized as having significance for ecological, socioeconomic or scientific reasons, which may be vulnerable to damage by international shipping activities. There are currently seven designated PSSAs with a further four having provisional approval (AMSA, 2004; Table 38.3). The PSSA Guidelines place an obligation on all IMO Member Governments to ensure that ships flying their flag comply with the Associated Protective Measures adopted to protect the PSSAs.

Sweeting and Wayne (Chapter 30, this volume) argue that there is significant potential for widespread adverse environmental impacts from mishandled waste and pollutants or poorly planned and implemented management processes. Although the major cruise lines have made progress in addressing and mitigating these impacts, there is still work to be done to fully minimize the effect of cruising on the natural environment.

Nowhere has this been more highlighted than in Alaska. The Alaskan cruise season is from May to August and in 2005 there were 39 cruise ships positioned in Alaskan waters (North West Cruise Ship Association, 2005). The growth of cruise tourism presents both opportunities and challenges for destination communities in Alaska (Ringer, Chapter 25, this volume). Adverse environmental impacts include air pollution, illegal dumping of sewage and solid waste, inadequate treatment equipment, damage to coral reefs and sensitive marine environments.

After the cruise lines paid huge fines for regulatory infractions, the cruise lines began to attend to improving their physical environmental record in this destination. The socioeconomic and cultural costs are equally significant, particularly in the isolated coastal and island communities increasingly attractive to cruise visitors because of their rural lifestyles and local traditions.

Alaska is leading the way in establishing ways to minimize negative environmental impacts by becoming the first American state to regulate water pollution from ships. Today over half of the ships visiting this destination now comply with the 2001 wastewater law. However, Alaska's community is divided on whether or not cruise ship tourism is an overall benefit for their community. The congestion effect created when thousands of passengers descend on a small town or city or a wilderness area is a growing concern in Alaska (Munro and Gill, Chapter 14, this volume). In 1998, the town of Tenakee Springs shut its doors on a cruise ship that visited and residents handed out leaflets informing passengers that they were not welcome in their town, and in the town of Haines residents held anti-cruise demonstrations (Romano-Lax, 2004).

To encourage the Alaskan communities and the cruise industry to work together, a set of guidelines has been implemented to maximize the benefits of tourism for both the residents and visitors. The Agreement Regarding Cruise Ships includes guidelines on the reduction of public address announcements and signals, standards for stack-effluents emissions whilst in port and the minimization of vessels' speeds by tenders in harbours (North West Cruise Ship Association, 2005).

Overall the cruise industry has embraced environmental good practice, and efforts are now being made to clean up the environmental practices of the industry through the installation of cleaner ship engines and the reduction of waste being dumped into the sea. They conclude that the major cruise lines have begun to respond effectively to the environmental challenges of the past decades. However, much remains to be done to ensure that the rapidly growing demand for cruising does not overwhelm the very assets of a pristine environment that attract people to cruises and cruise destinations.

To this end Dobson and Gill (Chapter 31, this volume) examined industry self-regulation

Table 38.3. Designated particularly sensitive sea areas (PSSAs).

No.	Area	Associated protective measures	MEPC endorsement
Designated PSSAs			
1	Great Barrier Reef – Australia	Compulsory pilotage, IMO-recommended pilotage, mandatory reporting	MEPC 30, September 1990
2	Archipelago of Sabana Camaguey – Cuba	Traffic separation schemes, area to be avoided, discharge prohibitions	MEPC 40, September 1997
3	Malpelo Island – Columbia	Area to be avoided	MEPC 47, March 2002
4	Florida Keys – USA	4 areas to be avoided, 3 mandatory no anchoring areas	MEPC 47, March 2002
5	Wadden Sea – Netherlands, Denmark, Germany	(Existing protective measures – no new measures) Compulsory reporting and traffic surveillance, traffic separation schemes, deep-water route, recommended and compulsory pilotage, MARPOL special area	MEPC 48, October 2002
6	Paracas National Reserve – Peru	Area to be avoided (ships >200 gross registered tonnage (GRT) carrying hydrocarbons and hazardous liquids in bulk)	MEPC 49, July 2003
7	Western Europe – Belgium, France, Ireland, Portugal, Spain, United Kingdom	Reporting obligations for single-hull tankers carrying heavy grades of fuel oil	MEPC 52, October 2004
Provisional PSSAs			
8	Torres Strait – Australia and Papua New Guinea	Compulsory pilotage, recommended two-way route	MEPC 49, July 2003 (provisional approval only, MEPC referred to NAV and Maritime Safety Committee)
9	Canary Islands, Spain	Five areas to be avoided. Two recommended routes, mandatory ship reporting systems	MEPC 51, April 2004 (provisional approval only, measures to be submitted to NAV in 2005)
10	Baltic Sea Area – Denmark, Estonia, Finland, Germany, Latvia, Lithuania, Poland, Sweden	(Existing protective measures – no new measures.) Compulsory reporting and traffic surveillance, routing systems, compulsory pilotage, MARPOL special area, emission-control area	MEPC 51, April 2004 (provisional approval only, measures to be submitted to NAV in 2005)
11	Galapagos Islands – Ecuador	Ban on any discharges from tankers, ban on any discharge of most types of garbage, avoid ballast operations, area to be avoided, additional routing chart (in 2006)	MEPC 51, April 2004 (provisional approval only, measures to be submitted to NAV in 2005)

Source: Australian Maritime Safety Authority (2004).

and voluntary guidelines vs command and control regulation, and argue that a variety of policy instruments within the regulation continuum can be combined to more effectively accommodate place-specific characteristics in the environmental regulation of the cruise ship industry.

Developing sustainable tourism is one of the challenges in working towards an environmentally friendly, economically viable and socially aware future for previously deprived regions. The only way to ensure a positive future is if mass tourism – in its current form and at its current levels – meets the criteria for sustainability with increasing regularity.

The international cruise sector of the tourism industry has enjoyed above-average growth rates over the past few years, which has resulted in considerable debate regarding costs and the value of this type of mass tourism. With its close links with regional coast development, cruise tourism in particular is a good example of the challenges involved in integrated sustainable development.

Operating both as a piece of technology and as holiday destinations, it is not the modern cruise ships themselves which represent the potential for conflict. These ships are generally sound examples of modern technology, and there is more than the average number of regulations for supply and disposal procedures. However, the sheer volume and the way the ships are run create burdens, which can exceed the environment's capacity limits. The actual potential for conflict with the aims of sustainability stems from the impact of the cruise companies in the tourist destination areas. The economic value of cruise tourism remains under dispute, especially for Caribbean destinations, and the socio-cultural effects on these regions are largely judged to be negative by those affected.

New Innovations

Today, just three cruise corporations dominate the industry. They are Carnival, Royal Caribbean and Star Cruises. Together they form 72% of the berths. All three groups use multi-brand strategies and cover all market segments. All have very young and modern fleets of ships, with an average age of 9.9 years. However, this industry consolidation through globalization has been questioned by a number of industry observers including some contributors to this book. Underpinning consolidation and globalization is the drive to increase profitability. Whilst traditionally it is assumed that cruise tourism makes money for all involved – the cruise lines and destination ports, Braun and Tramell (Chapter 26, this volume) note that an issue facing port communities is whether the potential benefits from cruise activity can justify the costs of building, maintaining and operating the infrastructure. This is echoed by Robbins (Chapter 33, this volume) who states that cruise shipping is a valuable source of supplementary income for ports but is not its core business. He adds that it cannot become the major economic driver of a port and that while it is a development opportunity, its potential should not be overstated. In addition, it has been argued that Florida's Day Cruise Industry is probably not a significant contributor to Florida's economy (Pennington-Gray, Chapter 27, this volume).

Other innovations are occurring in the industry such as celebrity launches, low-cost cruising and apartment living.

Celebrity launches

Firmly linking itself to the entertainment industry, cruise ships are now being launched by 'celebrities' in place of regal representatives or the company chairman's wife. While the *Queen Mary 2* was launched by Queen Elizabeth II in Southampton, England on 8 January 2004, other ships are being launched by celebrities. In 2003 the Italian line Mediterranean Shipping Cruises' (MSC) *MSC Lirica* was christened by her godmother Sophia Loren. In 2004 the NCL's 92,250-t *Norwegian Dawn*, homeported in New York, was christened by Kim Cattrall, star of the television show *Sex and the City*. Also in 2004 P&O's Australian homeported *Pacific Sun* was christened by godmother Lisa Curry Kenny, an Australian Olympic and Commonwealth Games swimmer.

Low-cost cruising

Low-budget 'no-frills' style airlines have been a growth industry in the 2000s. Now, the founder of one of the low-cost airlines, EasyJet, has started a low-cost no-frills cruise line – EasyCruise (www.easycruise.com). In January 2005, its founder Stelios Haji-Ioannou, a Greek Cypriot based in London, is copying his successful low-cost airline model that has made EasyJet the highest revenue-making budget carrier in Europe (Pfanner, 2005). The EasyGroup includes accommodation (EasyHotel), fast food (EasyPizza), mobile phones (EasyMobile), credit cards and car insurance (EasyMoney).

In May 2005, the 2840-t company flagship *EasyCruiseOne* (formerly *Renaissance II*), painted in its company colour orange, set sail in the Mediterranean (Fig. 38.4). The ship has six decks, one restaurant, two bars, a gym and a hottub. It has accommodation for 170 people in 86 cabins which includes four suites, seven bunkrooms and a cabin suitable for disabled passengers. Cabins may cost as little as £50 per night with food, drinks and cabin cleaning, etc. On-board amenities will be limited to a café, sports bar, tapas bar and jacuzzi. Founder Haji-Ioannou wants to appeal to younger passengers than are usually found on cruise ships. Aimed at 20–40-year-olds, the average age of guests on the first weekend voyage from Nice to Cannes, St Tropez was 35.

EasyCruiseOne is registered in Cyprus and managed by V Ships (based in Monaco). It was originally built in Italy in 1990 but refurbished to EasyCruise standards in Singapore. It has a multinational crew and more than half the passengers to have booked so far are British, followed by Americans, Germans and the Swiss. However, whilst there will be a rapidly growing niche market for low-cost cruises, it must never be forgotten that one of the hallmarks of traditional, modern and future cruising is service, as noted by Miller and Grazer (Chapter 7, this volume).

Apartment living

An area of possible expansion in future is the rise of apartment ships. Already there is one privately owned residential cruise liner, *The World*. The ship is 195 m long and weighs 43,000 tonnes (Fig. 38.5). It houses 110 luxury apartments, which were originally offered for sale in 2002 at prices ranging from US$2.0 million to US$7.5 million. Eighty were already pre-sold before the ship was built and each includes a sea view, private terraces fitted with jacuzzis, fully

Fig. 38.4. easyCruise.com's *EasyCruiseOne* offers a low-cost no-frills cruise around the Mediterranean. Source: easyCruise.com.

Fig. 38.5. ResidenSea's apartment ship *The World* in Sydney Harbour, 2003. Source: James Morgan/Cruise Travel Professionals.

equipped kitchens and the usual 24-h room service. In addition to the apartments there are two swimming pools, four restaurants, a gourmet grocery store, tennis court, disco, bookstore, minigolf course and helicopter pad. *The World's* staff of 320 includes doctors, massage therapists, firefighters, security agents and entertainers. The residents come from Europe (50%), the USA (40%) and Asia and the Middle East (10%). However, because residents can live on board in their own apartments, it has been reported anecdotally to me that the ship does not have a community feel about it. This is not helped by some apartments being left empty like holiday homes for large parts of the year. Time will tell whether sea-based apartment living is a genuine new opportunity for cruise lines or whether it is just a short-term fad.

New Markets and Destinations

A number of new markets and destinations are rapidly emerging in the cruise sector. One such place is the Peoples' Republic of China. In the middle of 2005, a forum on developing cruise tourism in China was held as part of the 42nd Meeting of the World Tourism Organization for East Asia and the Pacific (WTO, 2005). The purpose of the Forum was to provide a platform for the extensive exchanges and in-depth discussions between decision makers and executors who are involved in developing China's cruise industry and cruise tourism. In addition, it was a chance for industry professionals to exchange information on the development of cruise

tourism products, to learn from international standards and experience in the field, and therefore to understand and explore the possibility to develop cruise tourism in China.

Another emerging cruise destination is the Indian Ocean. South Africa and the Eastern African ports have some established cruise trade, 0.2% of the world market. In order to expand the potential for the industry, the KZN Cruise Tourism Industry Forum has created a functional framework, namely, the East African Indian Ocean Regional Cruise Tourism Forum in order to market the routing of passengers via South Africa as part of a broader Indian Ocean Rim itinerary. Similarly, the west coast is also resuscitating a once defunct 'Cruise Industry Working Group'. The National Ports Authority (NPA) will be strategically involved in any development of the cruise industry in this region. The challenge to the NPA is to ensure that efficient, effective services and facilities are provided to cruise liner vessels that do populate the South African coastline (Lighthouse Foundation, 2005).

A third emerging cruise destination is in Atlantic Canada based on the ports of Halifax, Saint John, Sydney, St John's and Charlottetown (Chesworth, Chapter 15, this volume). Still in its infancy, the region's close proximity to the burgeoning US cruise market makes it a logical area for expansion of the cruise industry.

Research recently released by CLIA revealed a growing trend for cruise lines to visit more ports previously unheard of on mainstream itineraries, to meet an increasing demand for 'exotic' ports of call. One example is

Tripoli, Libya, which was added to a number of Mediterranean itineraries for 2005 (Cruise Passenger, 2004b). MSC Cruises became the first cruise line to visit Libya after the USA lifted trade embargoes in September 2004 and in 2006 *MSC Lirica* will spend a season being homeported at Kiel, Germany, for cruises to the Baltic and North Sea. Silversea Cruises recently made maiden visits to Lebanon and Syria and Crystal Cruises has scheduled inaugural visits to 14 ports in 2005 including Bulgaria and Ireland.

Greater Accountability

The call for increased social and environmental accountability of the cruise industry will be a major force shaping its future (Klein, 2002; Chapter 34, this volume). Local communities and NGOs will shine an intense torchlight on the industry generally, as well as cruise lines and ships specifically. NGOs such as the Bluewater Network, Campaign to Safeguard America's Waters, Ocean Blue Foundation, The Ocean Conservancy and Oceana will continue to undertake campaigns aimed at the cruise industry, although Klein (Chapter 34, this volume) suggests that they will need to be less reactive and more proactive in future. This is bound to happen as baby boomers begin to wind back their full-time employment and focus on (sometimes) more altruistic pursuits in the social, ethical and environmental spheres.

Timothy (Chapter 37, this volume) notes that most cruise ships plying the world's waterways use flags of convenience (FOCs) in an effort to evade strict environmental, labour and safety laws and to skirt homecountry tax regulations. But that situation cannot last because the cruise industry's future growth is inextricably linked with the process of globalization. And as Wood (Chapter 36, this volume) has noted, no other form of tourism is more deeply rooted in globalization processes than cruise tourism, which has brought this upon itself by relentless consolidation. Therefore, it can be argued that just as a number of other industries have been caught up in the backlash of activism against globalization so too could the cruise industry come under fire, as outlined by Klein (Chapter 34, this volume).

Probably one of the most telling statements in this book is Wood's suggestion: 'It may well be that the industry's freedom from meaningful regulation has peaked, and that a combination of grass-roots pressure, port state control and a strengthening of global regulatory regimes may gradually enforce a "meaningful link" between flag states and their ships, limit the freedom of offshore financial centres, strengthen the conventions not only of the IMO but also of the International Labour Organization (ILO) and force the industry to cooperate more meaningfully in regional development efforts' (pxx).

Safety and Security

Safety and security is a hallmark of cruising. However, there have always been risks associated with ocean travel, some natural and others human-made. This has been evident from the days of the *Titanic* and will continue for as long as we travel the seas. In April 2005 a seven-storey-high wave damaged the *Norwegian Dawn* as it was returning to the USA from the Bahamas (*The West Australian*, 2005). The freak wave damaged the hull of the ship and flooded 62 cabins with four passengers being hurt. The ship was diverted to Charleston, South Carolina before continuing on to New York arriving 1 day later than scheduled. This is not an isolated example and this is just a small example listed on the 'Events at Sea' Website by Ross Klein (www.cruisejunkie.com). This list contains details of illness, cruise cancellations, suicides, passenger overboard, propulsion problems, environmental incidents, health issues as well as many others, all of which have occurred in the first half of 2005 only.

Security issues facing cruise ships include piracy, terrorism, drug smuggling, sexual assault and stowaways, etc. (Anderson, 2005). Piracy is a form of terrorism that has been troubling the maritime industry for years, but is largely ignored by most forms of media due to the frequency of attacks. Pirates generally target cargo ships by hijacking a ship and stealing the boat and its cargo. However, pirates can still pose a threat, albeit a small one to the cruise industry. The main cruise ships routes and geographical locations of areas of piracy include the Straits of Malacca, the Red Sea/Horn of Africa and

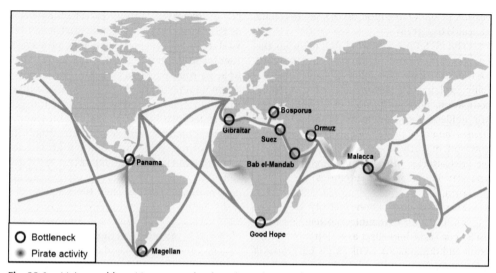

Fig. 38.6. Major world maritime routes, bottlenecks and areas of pirate activity. Source: OECD (2003).

Indonesian and Malaysian waters (Fig. 38.6). These continue to be areas of concern.

While piracy is also a problem in certain parts of the world, it is the single threat of terrorism that represents the gravest problem facing the cruise industry today. Terrorist incidents within the cruise ship industry have been very infrequent, with less than 2% of all terrorist attacks in the last 30 years having been carried out on maritime vessels. This may be due to difficult accessibility and the specialist skills and equipment required by terrorists to conduct seaborne attacks as opposed to those required to attack land-based targets (Chalk, 2002, p. 9). However, as the cruise ship industry grows so too does the potential for a terrorist attack.

The most infamous maritime terrorism incident involving a cruise ship occurred in October 1985, when the Italian cruise liner *Achille Lauro* was highjacked and a US citizen was killed. The terrorist group responsible was the Palestinian Liberation Organization (PLO), and the vessel was set on fire. Immediately afterwards, greater emphasis was placed on improving passenger safety and security by maritime agencies (Pine, 2002). In addition, in 2000 a Philippines ferry was blown up by a bomb placed on board by terrorists, killing 45 people (Chalk, 2002). In Hawaii during April 2003, the Royal Caribbean's *Legend of the Seas* arrived at Kailua-Kona, and was boarded by the FBI's Joint

Terrorism Task Force after written bomb threats were found aboard, but turned out to be hoaxes (Associated Press, 2003). At an Asia-Pacific Heads of Maritime Safety Agencies Forum held in Wellington, New Zealand, in April 2004, US Coast Guard (USCG) Admiral Tom Collins stated that cruise ships are favourable targets for terrorists, because of the high passenger numbers and the potential for using them as massive bombs (Kay, 2004).

After the 11 September 2001 terrorist attacks, governments and security agencies around the world suddenly realized how vulnerable the maritime industry was to an attack and hurriedly put together plans to improve security. In early 2002, IMO sent a proposal to all stakeholders in the maritime industry entitled *Review of Measures and Procedures to Prevent Acts of Terrorism, which Threaten the Security of Passengers and Crews and the Safety of Ships*. Nations around the world submitted their own recommendations and discussed the issues of terrorism at the Maritime Safety Conference held in London in 2002 (Petersen, 2002).

The IMO, in conjunction with the Maritime Security Council (MSC), maritime shipping companies, governments around the world and numerous security authorities proposed the International Ship and Port Safety (ISPS) Code, which were fully implemented as of 1 July 2004. The ISPS Code is essentially an updated version of the Convention on the Safety of Life at Sea (IMO, 2005).

The ISPS Code is a set of mandatory regulations that are now the international standard for the entire maritime industry. The code essentially explains the requirements for shipping companies, port authorities and governments and guidelines on how to reach the new standards. The code enables local port, security and government authorities to evaluate the risk of terrorist attacks, introduce preparedness levels and develop potential responses to threats (Petersen, 2003).

Port and destination security currently varies from country to country; however, once the ISPS Code came into effect as of 1 July 2004, all ports and destinations would meet the required international standards, while Australia and the USA would have even higher security measures in place, specifically designed to prevent terrorist attacks on maritime targets. The ISPS Code has three levels of security readiness with most ports being on 'level 1' and the USA and Australia being on 'level 2' (Maritime Security, 2005).

In Australia, the security level is set by the Department of Transport and Regional Services (DOTARS), in conjunction with intelligence agencies (DOTARS, 2005). In the USA, the new ISPS Code is used as well as the US Port and Maritime Security Act 2002, which was designed by the US Customs, FBI, the Department of Homeland Security and the USCG. Enhanced measures included in the US Maritime Security Act include the use of an automatic identification system (AIS) to track and identify ships, the ability of the USCG to board all vessels and allow the use of Sea Marshals. A 96-h 'advance notice of arrival' must also be submitted to the USCG, which will include a comprehensive list of all crew and passengers on board a cruise ship, which is then screened by the FBI counterterrorism branch, the US Department of Immigration and the US Customs Service (Petersen, 2003).

Other security precautions implemented by the USA have included USCG boats patrolling port entrances, surveillance equipment at sensitive areas and new command and control facilities (Zellen, 2003). USCG patrol boats also escort some cruise ships into port, and dive teams are often placed around cruise ships when anchored (McDowell, 2003). Armed police officers and private security firms also patrol US seaports, and the security of storage facilities that hold vital electronic and printed information such as training documents and ships manifests has been upgraded (Petersen, 2002). In terms of destinations, the Caribbean has been identified as a major security concern, and in the last 20 years efforts have been made by US authorities in cooperating with Caribbean authorities to improve port security and general law-enforcement operations in the region to reduce the threat of terrorism (Kelshall, 2002).

Australia has some of the most secure ports in the world, even more so than in the USA, with the recent establishment of a National Monitoring Centre in Melbourne. The Centre monitors a Closed Circuit Television System (CCTS), which provides 24-h digital quality remote viewing of 88 ports around Australia from 220 cameras (Carbone, 2003). Customs officers constantly patrol Australia's ports and use security measures such as detector dogs that can detect weapons and drugs, and trace particle detection systems that detect explosives (Carbone, 2003). It has also been publicly stated that the Queensland Police position dive teams to guard and check the hulls of any cruise ships that enter Queensland ports (OCH, 2003).

Passenger security

Before boarding a cruise ship, passengers undergo extensive background identification checks by numerous immigration departments and international intelligence agencies such as the Central Intelligence Agency (CIA), the FBI, and Australian Security and Intelligence Organization (ASIO). To help mitigate security problems, all major cruise lines have both security managers and officers on each ship, which also typically has a central station from which security activities, such as Closed Circuit Television (CCTV) monitoring and access control, are conducted (Anderson, 2005). All pasengers have their photo taken at the commencement of the journey (Fig. 38.7) and they are given an identification card with their photo on it. They must display this identification card when boarding or leaving the vessel (ICCL, 2005a; Fig. 38.8). All modern cruise ships carry all security equipment with them and this would

Fig. 38.7. A passenger has a digital photo taken to supplement his ship identification card. Source: ICCL (2005a).

Fig. 38.8. A US customs officer checks passenger passports and identification cards as they board their cruise ship. Source: ICCL (2005a).

usually consist of explosive detectors, X-ray machines and metal detectors.

A new US Visitor and Immigration Status Indication Technology (VISIT) programme has been developed to track foreign visitors who require a visa to the USA and was implemented as of 31 December 2003 (Zellen, 2003). In Australia, Customs and the Department of Immigration are slowly introducing a state-of-the-art biometric 'Smart Gate' face-to-passport navigation system, which will make it even harder for terrorists to falsify documents to gain entry to cruise ships or other maritime vessels (Carbone, 2003).

Maintaining ship security and controlling access to sensitive areas is a crucial aspect of counterterrorism measures. In 1996, the Automated Personnel Assisted Screening System (A-PASS) was introduced to all cruise ships. It is essentially an identification, tracking and access control system that monitors the movements of passengers and crew on board. Apart from the A-PASS, there are some other security measures put in place, such as the use of anti-piracy screens along lower decks, the use of lighting, radars to reveal small craft approaching the vessel and high-pressured water hoses. Under ISPS requirements, all ships must be fitted with a discrete emergency alarm that will alert maritime authorities in the event of a terrorist attack (Petersen, 2002).

Cruise ship crews are not specifically trained in anti-terrorism training, except for how to observe and detect suspicious behaviour of passengers and cargo. There are designated security officers on board who are usually highly trained ex-military or ex-law-enforcement officers and are trained in counterterrorism procedures (Petersen, 2002). Ship security personnel numbers are undisclosed and vary from ship to ship and depend on the route being travelled, passenger numbers and threat assessments made before departure. Ship Security officers are usually equipped with handcuffs, pepper spray and have access to firearms. However, in the event of a terrorist attack, they would offer very little resistance against a number of heavily armed terrorists. US Sea Marshals, who are undercover law-enforcement officers, are often placed aboard US-bound cruise ships (McDowell, 2003).

The elite operatives in military and law-enforcement counterterrorism units are often drawn from existing corps of the Navy, Air Force and Army and various law-enforcement agencies. They undergo an extremely strenuous and extensive selection and training process, and are taught in all aspects of warfare, particularly counterterrorism techniques such as hostage rescue. All units are trained in how to deal with maritime incidents including the boarding and capturing of cruise ships.

Some military units include the British Special Air Service (SAS), Delta Force, Australian SAS, New Zealand SAS, US Navy Sea Land and Air units (SEALS) to name a few. Law-enforcement units include Germany's GSG9, US Special Weapons and Tactics (SWAT) units, the FBI anti-terrorism unit and Australia and New Zealand Special Tactics Groups (STGs). Counterterrorism units would approach the ship via small rapid response craft under the cover of darkness and boarding the ship by climbing the hull using ladders or ropes. They may also approach the ship underwater, using minisubmarines and in scuba gear, or aerially via a helicopter landing or rappelling (USDOD, 2005).

Recommendations on the prevention of the possibility of a terrorist attack on the cruise industry are (after Petersen, 2002):

- Adopt a rigorous series of benchmark tests to ensure that a high consistency of security is reached on all ships, ports and destinations, and on a regular basis such as every 6–12 months (Fig. 38.9).
- Allow anti-terrorist units to practice drills of boarding hijacked cruise ships with a high number of hostages.
- Maritime authorities should make it compulsory that undercover Sea Marshals travel on cruise ships that travel along high-risk routes. This would thwart any offensive by terrorists whose initial plans could be to disable or kill security personnel.
- The major threat in the future is terrorists obtaining LTTE vessels and recruiting LTTE trained operatives to conduct operations against cruise ships. The other major threat is operatives masquerading as crew or passenger under false pretences. Therefore, it is crucial that intelligence agencies continue

Fig. 38.9. Divers with the KPLP (Indonesian Coast Guard) search the underwater hull of *Silver Shadow* before giving the ship clearance to depart Indonesian waters, February 2006. Source: Ross K. Dowling.

to conduct stringent background checks and accurate threat assessments.

- While the ISPS Code will dramatically improve the assessment of port security, there needs to be continual development of monitoring and screening port facilities and upgrading screening equipment.

- Greater emphasis needs to be placed on ensuring the security of computer systems on board ships through extra encryption. Guided tours on cruise ship bridges need to be curtailed, as they effectively present a golden opportunity to terrorists to capture the most important part of the ship.

- Another major issue is isolation, as at times, cruise ships are in the middle of nowhere making them enticing targets for terrorists. It would take a very long time for anti-terrorist units to reach a hijacked cruise ship, and in the event they had to forcefully board a vessel, the number of hostages would pose a major problem. Hence, an international Coast Guard could be formed that could effectively escort cruise ships through routes that may be deemed dangerous and the response time would be greatly reduced.

- Equipping cruise ships with discreet anti-air craft and ship weapons systems could also be investigated. This would provide protection against an airborne assault by terrorist groups who might use helicopters to board a cruise ship. An aerial assault by terrorists would bypass the current defences on cruise ship, which are designed specifically to deter seaborne assaults. Anti-ship missile systems would act as a defence to suicide craft or seaborne boarding attempts and these missile systems would only be used as a last resort.

While there is little the industry can do to prevent its occurrence, it can at least reduce the possibility through greater security both at sea as well as in port.

The pirate attack on the *Seabourn Spirit* on 5 November 2005 off the coast of Somalia highlights the readiness of modern cruisers to deal with such incidents. Since the 11 September 2001 terrorist attack in New York, world security has heightened and the cruise industry is certainly in on the act. Passengers on cruises in recent years will testify to the increased security in ports but it is also heartening to note that ship security at sea is also tight. In the case of the *Spirit*, the captain used a number of methods including the employment of a Long Range Acoustic Device, a directed high pitched sound beam that foiled the attackers, to ensure that the pirates were not successful in their attempts to board his vessel.

In late 2005 the German ship *Deutschland*, operated by Peter Deilmann Reederei cruise line, was tracked by the German navy as a 'routine measure' whilst cruising to Dubai via the Red Sea and Gulf of Aden (*World Wide Cruising News & Pictorial*, 2005). According to the line the navy continually monitored the ship throughout its passage in order to ensure maximum security.

The Final Word

Cruising is big business. A study found that in 2004 in North America alone, the cruise industry supported 135,000 jobs and had a total impact of US$30 billion on the US economy, an increase of more than 18% over the previous year (ICCL, 2005b).

The cruise industry is very exciting and has a bright future. If it can successfully address the issues outlined in this book, it will continue to grow and add value to many nations, cities, ports and communities. Along the way it will provide millions of people with an innovative vacation, one that they will never forget. Cruising can be a prosperous industry committed to economic, social and environmental well-being. Let us hope that it takes up the challenge responsibly and wholeheartedly, for if it does, then the promise of cruise ship tourism will be realized.

References

AMSA (2004) *Particularly Sensitive Sea Areas*. Australian Maritime Safety Authority, Fact Sheet, December 2004. Australian Government, Canberra, ACT.

Anderson, T. (2005) The cruise ship industry is adapting to evolving security demands. Available at: www.securitymanagement.com/library/000812

Armstrong, A. (2005) The cruise industry: Australian Broadcasting Corporation 'Background Briefing' radio documentary, Broadcast 8 May 2005.

Associated Press (2003) *Cruise Ship Released After Threat Scare*, 24 April. Available at: www.myrtle-beachonline

Carbone, A. (2003) Customs primary protector of border security. *Manifest – Journal of Australian Customs* 6(2), 3–21.

Chalk, P. (2002) *Threats to the Maritime Environment: Piracy and Terrorism*. Rand Stakeholder Consultation,

Ispra, Italy, 28 October. Available at: www.rand.org/randeurope/news/seacurity/piracyterrorism

CLIA (2004a) Cruising suits lifestyle, demands of today's new generation of retirees, says CLIA. *Cruise Lines International Association News Release*, 2 August 2004. Available at: www.cruising.org

CLIA (2004b) Married baby boomers heart of cruise market. *Cruise Lines International Association News Release*, 23 March 2004. Available at: www.cruising.org

CLIA (2005a) CLIA cruise lines ride the wave of unprecedented growth *Cruise Lines International Association News Release*, 16 March 2005. Available at: www.cruising.org

CLIA (2005b) CLIA celebrates 30 years of excellence with ambitious growth and marketing agenda. *Cruise Lines International Association News Release*. January 2005. Available at: www.cruising.org

CLIA (2005c) Explore polar opposites aboard ship: cruise vessels take travelers to the ends of the earth. *Cruise Lines International Association News Release*. April 2005. Available at: www.cruising.org

Cruise Passenger (2004a) Cruise news: oz market soars for HAL. *Cruise Passenger* 18, 26.

Cruise Passenger (2004b) Cruise news: next stop, Libya. *Cruise Passenger* 18, 28.

DOTARS (2005) Department of Transport and Regional Services. Available at: www.dotrs.gov.au/transsec/imo_isps_info.aspx

Dowling, R.K. and Vasudavan, T. (2000) Cruising in the new millennium. *Tourism Recreation Research* 25(3), 17–27.

ICCL (2005a) *The Safest Way to Travel: Cruise Ship Security*. International Council of Cruise Lines. Available at: www.iccl.org

ICCL (2005b) *The Cruise Industry: 2004 Economic Summary*. International Council of Cruise Lines. Available at: www.iccl.org.

IMO (2005) *Enhancing Maritime Security*. International Maritime Organisation Website, PDF document. Available at: www.imo.org/home.asp

Kay, M. (2004) Cruise ships may make NZ terrorist target. *Dominion-Post* newspaper, 15 April 2004.

Kelshall, R. (2002) Caribbean security focus, *INTERSEC*, 12(9), 262–263.

Klein, R.A. (2002) *Cruise Ship Blues: The Underside of the Cruise Industry*. New Society Publishers, Gagriola Island, British Columbia.

Lighthouse Foundation (2005) Cruise terminals are on the cards for South African ports. Press Release, February 2005.

Maritime Security Organisation (2005) Maritime security organisation. Available at: www.maritimesecurity.org

McDowell, E. (2003) Cruise lines' topic A: intensified security. *The New York Times* 2 Feb, p. 5.3.

North West Cruise Ship Association (2005) NWCA Alaska. Available at: www.nwcruiseship.org

OCH (2003) *Joint Standing Committee on Foreign Affairs, Defence and Trade Reference: Watching Brief on the War on Terrorism.* Official Committee Hansard, 7 November 2003, Brisbane. Available at: www.aph.gov.au/hansard/joint/commttee/J7131.pdf

Petersen, K.E. (2002) The maritime industry: the next terrorist target. *INTERSEC Journal* 12(3), 71–73.

Petersen, K.E. (2003) Protecting seaports and ships: industry and government respond to terrorism. *INTERSEC Journal* 13(2), 47–50.

Pfanner, E. (2005) Serial entrepreneur makes a splash. *International Herald Tribune,* Saturday–Sunday, 19–20 March 2005.

Pine, T. (2002) Maritime security and training. *INTERSEC Journal* 12(9), 264–267.

Romano-Lax, A. (2004) Rising tide. *Alaska Magazine* 70(4), 26–31.

Schwartzman, M.T. (2004) The modern cruiser. *Cruise Passenger* 18, 40.

The West Australian (2004) Heavy toll on *QM2* by cruisers. *The West Australian* newspaper, 9 December, p. 28.

The West Australian (2005) Giant wave lashes liner. *The West Australian* newspaper, 19 April 2005.

USDOD (2005) United States Department of Defence. Available at: http://www.defenselink.mil

White, K. (2004) Cruise line profile: Norwegian cruise line. *Cruise Passenger* 17, 86–88.

WTO (2005) Emerging cruise markets. *World Tourism Organization East Asia and Pacific News.* Available at: www.wto.org

Ward, D. (2005) *Berlitz Ocean Cruising & Cruise Ships 2005.* Berlitz Publishing, London.

World Wide Cruising News & Pictorial (2005) Cruise Ship Security. *World Wide Cruising News & Pictorial* 38, p. 11.

Zellen, B. (2003) Border technology & policy innovation at US Ports. *INTERSEC Journal* 13(7–8), 231–236.

Index